Perspectives on the Child's Theory of Mind

Edited by

George E. Butterworth
Department of Psychology
University of Stirling

Paul L. Harris
Department of Experimental Psychology
University of Oxford

Alan M. Leslie
Medical Research Council Cognitive Development Unit
London

Henry M. Wellman
Department of Psychology and Center for Human Growth
and Development
University of Michigan

BPS BOOKS (THE BRITISH PSYCHOLOGICAL SOCIETY)
OXFORD UNIVERSITY PRESS
1991

Published by the British Psychological Society and Oxford University Press.

Oxford University Press, Walton Street, Oxford OX2 6DP

Oxford   New York   Toronto
Delhi   Bombay   Calcutta   Madras   Karachi
Petaling   Jaya   Singapore   Hong Kong   Tokyo
Nairobi   Dar es Salaam   Cape Town
Melbourne   Auckland

and associated companies in
Berlin   Ibadan

Oxford is a trade mark of Oxford University Press

Published in the United States
by Oxford University Press, New York

A catalogue record for this book is available from the British Library.
Library of Congress Cataloging-in-Publication Data is available.

ISBN 0 19 852252 5

Printed and set in Great Britain by Latimer Trend & Company Ltd, Plymouth.

CONTENTS

Section 4: Theory of mind and understanding of emotion

Section 5: Theory of mind and communication

Section 6: Autism: Failure to acquire a theory of mind?

British Journal of Developmental Psychology (1991), **9**, 1–4 *Printed in Great Britain*

Editorial preface

Theory of mind

What is a 'theory of mind' and why all the recent interest in it? The larger topic, and an alternative terminology for it, is naive psychology—our everyday, lay notions about people as psychological beings. By using the phrase 'theory of mind' we emphasize that our everyday conception of people is mentalistic and coherent. Adults assume that people have minds: an interconnected network of mental states; a mental world of thoughts, ideas, imaginings; a private mental life beyond public, manifest action. Indeed, we assume that overt public actions stem from and are to be understood in terms of the mental states that lie behind and produce them—the actor's beliefs, desires and feelings. This everyday assumption of mind is powerful and constraining. It leads us to try to use the mind and increase its powers, to share inner experiences, to distinguish between purely imaginary and real events, and to interact with other persons by searching for and reaching out to their underlying mentalities.

Given the power of our everyday conception of mind, it is important to consider how we should best characterize children's achievements in this domain. Does their understanding of action and thought really cohere in a way that makes it appropriate to credit them with a naive theory or is this at best a catchy phrase or, worse yet, a seriously misleading misconstrual? The question is debated in this volume, particularly in the two theoretical introductory pieces. Indeed, these two papers illustrate that the debate about the status of a theory of mind helps to locate many of the major theoretical options within the field.

Regardless of whether children can be described as adopting a theory, and regardless of whether that theory is true, the mentalistic stance is a core feature of our everyday thinking and it is a stance whose origins psychology must explain. Piaget understood this. Children's understanding of the mind was one of the first topics he tackled (Piaget 1929). Research on theory of mind returns to this classic developmental topic, taking up again the question of how and when children come to adopt common-sense mentalism. That is one reason to be interested—the fundamental nature of the topic for any developmental account of cognition. However, the development of our common-sense theory of mind also provides an informative case study for cognitive science, understood in a broad multidisciplinary fashion. The assumption here is that our theory of mind constitutes a basic human knowledge system. Indeed, it seems likely that the human propensity for complex social collaboration and collusion is supported and constrained by an evolved neuropsychological mechanism for coding and manipulating information about mental states. That mechanism comes into operation in early childhood, and effectively sets the stage for its own elaboration and embellishment by enabling the young child actively to enter into the complex social life of the family and the surrounding culture.

Understanding development, cognition, biology, and culture in this necessarily interwoven fashion is a daunting enterprise, but it is an enterprise made tractable by converging interdisciplinary research. Of course, this case study is as yet incomplete. To date, research on theory of mind has concentrated on some strands but not others. By way of introduction we briefly review the history of the field, offer a thumbnail sketch of the core issues as they stand today, and point up some important but neglected issues.

Belief

An unfair caricature of much current research on theory of mind would be to say that it is the experimental study of Anglo-European preschoolers' understanding of the mental state of belief under laboratory conditions. This would be unfair because natural observational methods have an established and respected presence in the literature (e.g. Bretherton & Beeghly, 1982; Shatz, Wellman, & Silber,

1983); because understanding of desire (Wellman, 1990), intention (Shultz, 1988), appearance-perception (Flavell, 1988), and emotion (Harris, 1989) are solidly represented empirically; because research on atypical autistic children is vigorous and productive (Baron-Cohen, Leslie & Frith, 1985); and because there has also been recent attention to cross-cultural understanding (Avis & Harris, in press; Flavell, Zhang, Zou, Dong & Qi, 1983).

Nevertheless, there is some truth to the caricature. A brief historical note will show why belief was a key starting-point. Work on the child's theory of mind received an unexpected jolt from a paper by Premack & Woodruff (1978). Unexpected, because the work involved chimpanzees rather than children. Premack & Woodruff asked whether chimpanzees could predict what an actor would do next by observing the actor's efforts and inferring his or her underlying goal. A lively commentary on the results ensued; several authors converged on the suggestion that an acid test of psychological insight would involve not the attribution of goals but beliefs, and more specifically false beliefs. If the chimpanzee could grasp that an agent would act in accord with his or her belief even if that belief were false, it would show quite clearly that the chimpanzee could make genuinely psychological predictions, based on a reading of the agent's mental state. There are two important things to notice. First, a correct prediction would require the chimpanzee to realize that the agent would act not in accordance with the state of the world but rather in accordance with a mental representation of that world. Second, it would require the chimpanzee to set aside its own (accurate) representation of the world, and to take into account the other's mistaken representation. Thus, correct predictions could not be achieved by any simple process of reality assessment nor by analogy with the self, only through a genuine reading of the other's mental state.

That paper and the accompanying commentary set the scene for a flurry of research on children's understanding and misunderstanding of epistemic states, particularly false belief. Following the lead provided by Wimmer & Perner (1983), an emerging consensus now suggests that the years from 3 to 5 see notable advances in this critical conception. This consensus, however, continues to encompass several intriguing debates. For example, how is the child's understanding of belief translated into an ability to deceive—to deliberately engineer mistaken beliefs? What is the nature of representation and children's understanding of it? How do mental states such as dreams and imaginings (which deal with fiction) compare with epistemic mental states such as belief (which deal with fact)? These various concerns are all reflected in this volume.

Perception

A full understanding of epistemic states such as belief also involves an understanding of how beliefs arise. Many of our beliefs are grounded in empirical observation, either our own or that of others. For this reason, research on children's understanding of belief has joined hands with a somewhat older tradition of research on children's grasp of perception, notably visual perception. Some of the latest work on this topic also appears here.

Emotion

An understanding of belief, even adding in imagination and perception, is only part of everyday psychological theory. Much of our naive mentalistic psychology is essentially a belief–desire psychology. What the actor believes (George thinks it is raining) frames action, but what the actor desires (George wants to stay dry) motivates action. Beliefs and desires also play a crucial role in the causation of emotion. For example, whether George feels sad or happy about the rain depends on whether it corresponds to what he wanted. Whether he feels surprised depends on whether it corresponds to what he expected. Although the literature on social cognition has long indicated that young children are quite well informed about the type of situation that will elicit a particular emotion, it is not clear whether they adopt the mentalistic framework of belief–desire psychology.

Communication

Humans not only think, want, and feel, they speak. That is, they make public in speech, or attempt to do so, their private meanings, ideas, feelings, and desires. Searle (1983), Vendler (1972) and others loudly remind us of the intimate connection between speech acts and mental acts. Research on children's understanding of communication targets their understanding of this important aspect of mental and social functioning, and the relation between messages, meanings, and thoughts.

Autism

Is an understanding of the mind a foundational concept or is it tangential to children's cognitive and social development? One provocative way to address this question is to imagine what the cognition and life of a creature without a theory of mind might be like. This is more than an intriguing thought experiment; it is a viable neuropsychological possibility. If a theory of mind is biologically and neurologically prepared and specific, then there might be creatures that are human in all respects save this one. Research with autistic children suggests that they may suffer from just this sort of impairment.

Future directions

The research in this volume presents the latest findings and theorizing on children's understanding of a variety of mental states, notably beliefs, imaginings, perceptions, desires and emotions. It is worth noting, however, some important gaps. Most research on the child's theory of mind has concentrated on the post-infancy period. Indeed, so long as we think of mental states as ghostly operations hidden inside the machine it is tempting to conclude that infants could not divine their existence. If, on the other hand, we think of purposeful acts as having a characteristic form and motion, it would not be surprising to find that infants are well equipped to detect and interpret such acts (Premack, 1990). An interpretive device of this kind would provide relevant inputs for the simple desire-psychology that some see as the embryonic form of our more elaborate everyday conception of mind (Wellman, 1990). As yet, there is little experimental analysis of this issue. Still, observational research with infants points (teasingly) in the appropriate direction (Reddy 1991).

A second gap, both in this volume and in existing research, is the paucity of any computational analysis of the nature and underpinnings of a theory of mind. Although there have been some attempts to provide computational analyses of specific achievements (e.g. intention, cf. Shultz, 1988), more general analyses are needed. In particular, we want to know whether such analyses can identify logical properties that are peculiar to mental state attributions (Leslie, 1987). That would bolster the claim that the brain has evolved a dedicated machinery for such attributions.

The existence of these gaps is, in our view, a sign of health. A vigorous research programme brings into focus our ignorance as well as our knowledge. We are confident that this special issue does both.

References

Avis, J. & Harris, P. L. (in press). Belief–desire reasoning among Baka children: Evidence for a universal conception of mind. *Child Development*.

Baron-Cohen, S., Leslie, A. M. & Frith, U. (1985). Does the autistic child have a theory of mind? *Cognition*, **21**, 37–46.

Bretherton, I. & Beeghly, M. (1982). Talking about internal states: The acquisition of an explicit theory of mind. *Developmental Psychology*, **18**, 906–921.

Flavell, J. H. (1988). The development of children's knowledge about the mind: From cognitive connections to cognitive representations. In J. W. Astington, P. L. Harris, & D. R. Olson, (Eds), *Developing Theories of Mind*, pp. 244–270. New York: Cambridge University Press.

Flavell, J. H. Zhang, X-D., Zou, H., Dong, Q. & Qi, S. (1983). A comparison of the appearance–reality distinction in the People's Republic of China and the United States. *Cognitive Psychology*, **15**, 459–466.

Harris, P. L. (1989). *Children and Emotion: The Development of Psychological Understanding*. Oxford: Blackwell.

Leslie, A. M. (1987). Pretense and representation: The origins of 'theory of mind'. *Psychological Review*, **94**, 412–426.

Piaget, J. (1929). *The Child's Conception of the World*. London: Kegan Paul.

Premack, D. (1990). The infant's theory of self-propelled objects. *Cognition, 36*, 1–16.

Premack, D. & Woodruff, G. (1978). Does the chimpanzee have a theory of mind? *Behavioral and Brain Sciences, 1*, 515–526.

Reddy, V. (1991). Playing with other's expectations: Teasing and mucking about in the first year. In A. Whiten (ed.), *Natural Theories of Mind*, pp. 143–158. Oxford: Blackwells.

Searle, J. R. (1983). *Intentionality*. Cambridge: Cambridge University Press.

Shatz, M., Wellman, H. M. & Silber, S. (1983). The acquisition of mental verbs: A systematic investigation of the child's first reference to mental state. *Cognition, 14*, 301–321.

Shultz, T. R. (1988). Assessing intention: A computational model. In J. W. Astington, P. L. Harris & D. R. Olson (Eds), *Developing Theories of Mind*, pp. 326–340. New York: Cambridge University Press.

Vendler, Z. (1972). *Res Cogitans*. Ithaca, NY: Cornell University Press.

Wellman, H. M. (1990). *The Child's Theory of Mind*. Cambridge, MA: MIT Press.

Wimmer, H. & Perner, J. (1983). Beliefs about beliefs: Representations and constraining function of wrong beliefs in young children's understanding of deception. *Cognition, 13*, 103–128.

1
Theoretical overview

Preface

Several theoretical accounts underlie contemporary research on the child's understanding of mental life which, for convenience, can be divided into two fundamental sets of explanations. Both types of account agree that children come to appreciate the experiences of others as a result of cognitive development. However, the first set of explanations may be described as 'top down' theories. These theories attempt to explain strictly mental phenomena, such as 'false beliefs', by reference to the child's representational abilities; often without reference to their antecedents. Put starkly, it is argued that mental events are not publicly observable and that knowledge of various aspects of mental life is a matter of acquiring insight or theories about such hidden entities. The alternative, 'bottom up' view is that mental life is founded upon the publicly observable phenomena that support interpersonal behaviour. On this second account participation in social relations *reveals* properties of mind which provide the substrate for subsequent development of mentalistic concepts. Of course, the theoretical issues under debate are much more subtle but this dichotomy will serve to differentiate the field.

In the first review paper Astington & Gopnik distinguish six alternative theories of 'theory of mind'. The dominant 'theory theory' postulates that childrens' knowledge of psychological states arises by construction, analogous to a scientist testing hypotheses, with dramatic stage changes as one theory is falsified and replaced by another. A second possibility is that childrens' understanding of the mind is not based on a theory but reflects culturally influenced 'forms of life', especially as revealed in language and in cultural practices. A third, cognitive account is that understanding the mind is based on an innate 'module' for interpersonal behaviour. Dysfunction in such a module might explain why autistic children show profound deficits in understanding mental phenomena. A fourth approach is based on a computational metaphor which suggests that development may consist in elaborating new 'meta-representational' levels of computational mechanisms which are recursive upon existing structures, rather than in acquiring a theory *per se*. A fifth possibility is that childrens' understanding of mind depends upon the imaginative simulation of mental states on the basis of introspective evidence. A final possibility is that understanding the mind is like understanding a story; it entails entertaining various possible 'scenarios' rather than holding a specific, refutable 'theory'. These six theoretical possibilities are not mutually exclusive. They tend to be less concerned with the origins of knowledge of other minds than with its developmental elaboration.

Hobson's review takes the 'bottom up' approach by focusing our attention on those aspects of interpersonal relatedness which may underpin our knowledge of mental life. He insists that what is understood first in development are *persons* not disembodied *minds*. Hobson's account is based on the proposal that mental states are publicly observable, and grounded in adaptive relations with people and things in the world. In personal relations, the perception of emotions is primary and this does not require a step beyond experience into the realm of the purely mental. Emotions find bodily expression that can be observed and understood even by the naive infant. According to Hobson, innately constituted ways of feeling and acting provide a substrate within interpersonal relations to reveal aspects of mind in behaviour. He argues that reasoning about other minds by analogy to oneself presupposes a pre-existing capacity for interpersonal perception. Perceiving others as persons offers a basis in experience for observable mental states, it allows reasoning about other minds by analogy with one's own experience and the eventual understanding of covert mental states.

British Journal of Developmental Psychology (1991), **9**, 7–31   *Printed in Great Britain*   7

Theoretical explanations of children's understanding of the mind

Janet Wilde Astington*

Institute of Child Study, University of Toronto, 45 Walmer Road, Toronto, Ont. M5R 2X2, Canada

Alison Gopnik

University of California at Berkeley

This is a state-of-the-art review of children's understanding of the mind. It examines both empirical evidence and explanatory theories. Considering evidence, the key issue of children's understanding of false belief is first discussed. Then other evidence for children's folk psychological understanding is summarized, from late infancy to the end of the preschool period. Considering explanations, the dominant idea in the field, the 'theory theory', is discussed first. Then five other perspectives are considered: enculturation, nativism, folk psychology based on procedural knowledge, on experience, or on scripts. The positions, and the empirical predictions each would make, are compared. The paper concludes with a synthesis of the different views and a brief consideration of where the field is headed.

Children's understanding of the mind is currently a lively area of developmental research (e.g. Astington, Harris & Olson, 1988; Frye & Moore, 1991). This topic was first investigated by Piaget (e.g. 1926/1929) more than 50 years ago and it has been of interest to psychologists ever since. However, the past decade has seen a great expansion of research in the area, which has come to be known as *children's theories of mind*. A major question in the field is how to explain the remarkable and rapid development that occurs in children's understanding, especially during the preschool years. Much of this debate has been conducted within the field of children's theories of mind (Flavell, 1988; Forguson & Gopnik, 1988; Olson, 1988; Perner, 1988, 1991; Wellman, 1988, 1990). Other explanations of this development have been proposed by philosophers and psychologists working outside the immediate research area. This paper examines from a broad perspective the explanatory theories that are emerging of children's understanding of the mind.

There are two sorts of question to address: 1. What do children of different ages understand about the mind? What are the first signs of understanding, and how does this develop? 2. What kind of knowledge underlies this understanding? How can we explain the origin of, and the changes in, children's understanding? What sorts of explanation have different theorists put forward?

* Requests for reprints.

On the surface, these seem quite straightforward questions. The answer to the first set is a presentation of data, and the answer to the second is a presentation of various theories that have been proposed to explain these data. However, it is just not possible to make a neat separation between evidence and explanation. One cannot say: these are the data and this is the theory (or in this case, these are the theories people have proposed). Up to a point, what counts as data is determined by the theory in question. There can be no entirely theory-neutral laying out of the data. Nonetheless, these are different levels: a level of evidence and a level of theorizing. Thus, one can focus first on the evidence (the data) and then on the theories (the explanations) and that is the approach we take here.

At each of these levels a dominant issue has received considerable attention in the past decade. At the level of evidence this issue is children's understanding of belief and particularly false belief. At the level of explanation it is the idea that children's understanding of mind is dependent on the formation of implicit theories that develop and change over time, what is known as the 'theory theory'. In each section we will first discuss this key topic before going on to address our two sets of questions more broadly. The aim is to highlight the major issues for the general reader before examining other issues that have occupied those working in this field.

Children's understanding of the mind

The first question asks: What do children of different ages understand about the mind? What counts as evidence? We are not looking for explicit understanding of mind of the kind possessed by psychologists and philosophers, but for implicit understanding, such as can be inferred from what children say and do. This is the sort of understanding that is shown in our everyday interactions with each other, for example, in the ways we explain why we did something and the ways in which we predict what other people will do. In other words, it is common sense or folk psychology. Philosophers have often called this belief–desire psychology. It provides explanations of behaviour and makes predictions about people's actions by appealing to their beliefs and desires, to what people think, know, expect, want, intend, hope for and so on. What evidence is there that children have this sort of understanding of mind? What ought we to look for?

Children's understanding of false belief

Interestingly, this evidence was first sought not for children but for chimpanzees. Premack & Woodruff (1978) claimed that the chimpanzee's ability to predict what a human actor will do to achieve certain goals implies that the animal has a theory of mind; that is, the animal imputes mental states to the actor and predicts his behaviour based on these unseen states. In the debate generated by these claims a number of philosophers (Bennett, 1978; Dennett, 1978; Harman, 1978) suggested a basic experimental paradigm required to demonstrate indisputably that someone possesses a theory of mind. Both the paradigm and the term were taken up by Wimmer & Perner (1983) in a landmark paper. Parenthetically, the term was also independently adopted by other developmentalists (Bretherton, McNew & Beeghley-Smith, 1981;

Wellman, 1979), which helped identify the set of related concerns that now comprise the field of children's theories of mind.

The paradigm the philosophers described and the experiments Wimmer & Perner conducted require that an individual attribute a false belief to another. The reason for this is simple. In order to demonstrate conclusively that children (or chimpanzees) attribute beliefs to another, we must show that they are able to ascribe to the other beliefs that are different from their own, otherwise we would not know whether they were genuinely attributing beliefs to the other or simply assuming that the other shared their own beliefs. Suppose we arrange things so that the children's beliefs are true, that is they reflect the way the world is, and the other's beliefs are false. Then we can ask children what that other person will do in the situation. If the children can recognize that the other will act on the basis of his or her false beliefs, then we know they attribute beliefs to the other.

The original Wimmer & Perner (1983) false belief task was a story acted out for the child with dolls and toys. The essence of the story is this: A boy puts some chocolate in one place and goes away. In his absence, the chocolate is moved to another place. Then the boy comes back, hungry and wanting his chocolate. The child is asked where the boy will look for the chocolate. Most 3-year-olds predict that the boy will look in the new place, where the chocolate actually is. They do not seem to understand that the boy will look in the old place, where he thinks it is.

In its original form this task is quite hard even for 4-year-olds, but with a simplified task, that makes the salient features extremely clear 4-year-olds do quite well, but 3-year-olds do not (Perner, Leekam & Wimmer, 1987). Even if the story is made into a film (children are shown the actor looking in the old place, where he thinks the object is, not the real location where it now is, and the actor is shown looking surprised when he finds a different object in the old place), although 3-year-olds' performance is better than in the standard task, it is still not very good, i.e. no better than chance (Moses & Flavell, 1990).

Three-year-olds' difficulty with false belief can be seen in other ways too, not just involving unexpected locations but unexpected contents. If you show a 3-year-old a familiar candy box and let her find out it contains pencils, not candy, then put the pencils back and ask her what her friend, who has not seen inside the box, will think is inside it, most 3-year-olds will say the friend will think there are pencils in the box (Perner *et al.*, 1987).

Recently, Chandler, Fritz & Hala (1989) have suggested that predicting the statements or actions of a person who holds a false belief may be harder than actually creating false beliefs by deceiving another. Indeed, in their experiment 2- and 3-year-olds could use deceptive strategies in a hide-and-seek board game. This study was criticized for its lack of controls, especially since earlier research had shown that children could not deceive a competitor until 4 or 5 years of age (e.g. DeVries, 1970; LaFrenière, 1988; Shultz & Cloghesy, 1981). Chandler and his colleagues successfully replicated their study with the addition of appropriate controls (Hala, Chandler & Fritz, in press) but a very similar attempt failed to do so (Sodian, Taylor, Harris & Perner, in press). Moreover, in other recent new tasks the ability to deceive does not emerge until 4 or 5 years of age (Peskin, 1990; Sodian, 1991). Thus, 3-year-olds' ability to deceive others remains a matter of dispute.

It is not simply false belief in others that is hard for 3-year-olds to understand. They do not understand it in themselves either, that is, they do not recognize that their beliefs change when they find out they were wrong (Gopnik & Astington, 1988; Gopnik & Slaughter, in press). For example, consider the 3-year-old who thought there was candy in the box, and then she found out it had pencils in it; when the pencils are put back in the box again, if you ask her what she thought was in the box when she first saw it, she'll say 'pencils' not 'candy'. Although she may have said 'candy' when she first saw the box, she cannot remember this, even when prompted to do so (Wimmer & Hartl, 1991).

Three-year-olds seem not to understand how someone can believe something, different from what they know is really the case. In a similar way, they do not understand how something can look different from what it really is. In a series of very important experiments Flavell and his colleagues investigated children's understanding of this distinction between appearance and reality (Flavell, 1986; Flavell, Flavell & Green, 1983; Flavell, Green & Flavell, 1986). They showed the children objects that had a deceptive appearance, such as a joke store 'rock'—it looks like a rock but it is really a sponge. Children first saw it from a distance and presumably thought it was a rock, then they felt it and found out it was a sponge. After that they were asked what it looked like and what it really was. Four-year-olds could distinguish these two. However, 3-year-olds could not—once they found out it was really a sponge, they said it looked like a sponge. That is, they said it looked like what it really was. With other materials 3-year-olds made the opposite error, they said things really were the way they looked. For example, an orange crayon looks black when viewed through a blue plastic sheet; 3-year-olds said it looked black and it was really black. In both cases the younger children did not distinguish between the phenomenal appearance and the actual reality.

Flavell and his colleagues made numerous ingenious attempts to uncover the 3-year-olds' competence, without success. In one particularly convincing demonstration a white card was placed under a blue filter; 3-year-olds said it looked blue and it was really blue, even though they could see the white edge sticking out. Moreover, their difficulty was not merely with the language of the test questions. The experimenter took a piece out of the card while it was under the filter and then showed the child a white piece and a blue one: 3-year-olds chose the blue piece as the one the experimenter had just removed.

Thus, although 4-year-olds succeed on all the tasks so far discussed, 3-year-olds do not. What is most important to note about these different abilities is that they are not simply abilities that are acquired at about 4 years of age, but rather, individual children are likely to acquire them all at the same time. There are significant correlations between children's scores on false belief, belief change, and appearance–reality tasks (Gopnik & Astington, 1988; Moore, Pure & Furrow, 1990).

Indeed, false belief tasks have proved to have remarkable strength as indices of conceptual development. The test is simple, the results are reliable and have been replicated in more than 20 studies in Europe and North America and in at least one non-Western setting (Avis & Harris, in press). The replications have used a great variety of materials, involving false beliefs not just about an object's location and the contents of a box, but about identities of actual objects and of pictured objects, about perceptual properties such as colour and abstract properties such as number, and so on. In these tasks, the other to whom the false belief is ascribed has variously been a real other person, both child and adult, a doll, a puppet, or a character depicted in a story or on video. The tasks have used a variety of different linguistic forms of the question that asks what the other will think, and have also used various different questions, asking where the other will look, how the other will feel (Harris, Johnson, Hutton, Andrews & Cooke, 1989), and what the other will want (Astington & Gopnik, 1991).

Furthermore, considerable effort has been expended to ensure that younger children's competence is not masked by the experimental procedures used to test for the understanding of false belief. Where might 3-year-olds' difficulty lie? They might not remember the salient facts of the situation, but this is not the case, since they succeed on memory control questions (Perner *et al.*, 1987). They might be overwhelmed by perceptual reality at the moment of answering the test question, but this is not so. The transferred object is hidden in the new location, or the unexpected contents are put back into the box, before the question is asked. They might not understand the linguistic form of the test question, as has recently been claimed by Lewis & Osborne (1990). However, as we noted above, the question has been posed in a great variety of ways, including that used by Lewis & Osborne, without improving 3-year-olds' performance (Gopnik & Astington, 1988; Moses, 1990; Moses & Flavell, 1990). In general, a standard part of the methodology in the field has been to devise control tasks that require similar information processing capacity to the experimental tasks and use similar materials and questions (for particularly well-designed examples see, for example, Perner & Ogden, 1988; Perner & Leekam, 1990; Wimmer & Hartl, 1991). In sum, the extent and variety of task materials, manipulations, questions and controls, that investigators have used, lead us to the reasonable conclusion that 3-year-olds truly have a conceptual deficit.

Nonetheless, it seems not only possible but likely that precursors to a genuine understanding of false belief will be found in 3-year-olds. In tasks in which the true location of the sought-after object is unknown, or in which the object exists in two locations but the story character has seen only one of these, 3-year-olds are able to take account of the character's belief and correctly predict where he or she will look for the object (Wellman & Bartsch, 1988). However, in these cases the character's belief is not explicitly false and is not in conflict with a reality known to the child. More strikingly, if children are merely told the true location of the object but do not actually see it, 3-year-olds are able to predict that a story character who holds a false belief will look in the other location, where he thinks the object is (Zaitchik, in press). In this case children do report that the object's true location is where they were told it was; they have not, however, actually seen the object. Other cases in which there is no clear reality to conflict with the other's false belief involve beliefs about values and intentions, and 3-year-olds are able to attribute false beliefs concerning intentions (Moses, 1990) and values (Flavell, Flavell, Green & Moses, 1990), as opposed to matters of fact.

It might also be easier to explain actions premised on false beliefs than to predict them. For example, if the story character goes to look in the empty location, where he thinks the object is, and children are asked 'Why is he looking there?', some subjects will spontaneously say 'He thinks' it's in there' and others will say this when prompted with 'What does he think?'. Older 3-year-olds who could not predict action based on false belief could explain it in this way (Bartsch & Wellman, 1989; see also Wellman, 1990, p. 263). Somewhat similarly, Freeman, Lewis & Doherty (1991) have shown that 3-year-olds' performance may be improved by a hide-and-seek version of the change in location false belief task, that emphasizes the actor's 'need to know' the first location.

Much debate surrounds all of these tasks, focusing on whether the tasks assess a genuine understanding of false belief, whether the data show 3-year-olds have a concept of true belief but not false belief or whether they have no concept of belief at all (Perner, 1989; Wellman & Bartsch, 1989). This debate is likely to continue, as are the attempts to demonstrate false belief understanding in 3-year-olds. Before one pitches into this research it would be worth recalling that a particularly extensive and careful enterprise of this kind is already seen in Wellman's work (Bartsch & Wellman, 1989; Wellman, 1990; Wellman & Bartsch, 1988, 1989). It is instructive to note that Wellman eventually concluded that the difficulty 3-year-olds experience is essentially a cognitive one (Wellman, 1990, chapter 9).

Although, as this brief review shows, a great deal of experimental research in the past decade has focused on false belief, there is much more to ask about children's understanding of mind. For example, when do children first become aware of themselves and others as 'things which think' (Olson, Astington & Harris, 1988)? Are young children conscious of their own mental states, their beliefs, desires, intentions, emotions, and so on, and when do they show awareness of these states in others? What follows is a short summary of some of the available data, beginning in infancy.

Infancy

The focus of this paper is on the preschool years, between 2 and 5, but it is useful to keep in mind all the social interaction that infants engage in. They smile, make eye contact, coo, babble, ask (with gestures) to be picked up and to be given things, they offer things, they look where another person looks, and so on. Clearly infants distinguish between people and objects (Bates, 1976; Bruner, 1983; Stern, 1985; Trevarthen, 1980). However, at this stage it is hard to say how much they understand about people's minds, about people's beliefs, desires, and intentions. Obviously infants have beliefs, desires, and intentions, since they show surprise, frustration, and so on, but that is a different issue from their understanding of belief and intention, and their ability to attribute beliefs and intentions to other people. Nearly 10 years ago now Bretherton and her colleagues (Bretherton *et al.*, 1981) suggested that infants' ability to communicate with others shows that they have a theory of mind, but even these authors went on to say they were not suggesting that infants could impute mental states to others. Infants have an implicit theory of mind, they said, in the same way that 2-year-olds have an implicit theory of grammar.

Eighteen months to 3 years

A big change comes at the end of infancy, at about 18 months of age, with the development of symbolic abilities. This leads to two things that researchers in this field have particularly focused on: pretend play and language development.

(1) Very young children are able to pretend and to enter into pretend play with others (Leslie, 1988). This shows that they can reason about hypothetical situations. To use Leslie's example: a child picks up a banana and talks into it as if it were a telephone, that is, she sees it one way and she thinks about it in another. Even 2-year-olds can pretend like this.

(2) The interest in language development has focused especially on children's talk about internal states (Bretherton & Beeghly, 1982). You can talk about internal states without talking about the mind, for example, *hungry, sleepy, hot* and *cold*, whereas talk about perception and emotion seems closer to the mind, for example, *see, look, taste, happy, like, love, want*. These are all terms that children acquire around 2 years of age. Cognitive terms generally come later, but before they are 3 children also use words such as *know, think, remember*. It is important to look at more than simply the child's use of a mental term, since the use may be merely idiomatic or conversational, as in 'You know what?' to introduce a new topic. We need to look at the child's ability to use these words to refer to people's mental states, and to contrast mental states with reality; by 3 children can use mental verbs in this way (Shatz, Wellman & Silber, 1983).

(3) Two-year-olds also understand something about perception. They can produce perceptions in others by showing things to them, even difficult novel tasks, such as showing someone a picture in the bottom of a little box (Lempers, Flavell & Flavell, 1977). By 3 they can also deprive others of perception by hiding things. And by 3 they can judge another's perception or lack of it in other modalities too, such as hearing, smell, and touch (Yaniv & Shatz, 1988).

(4) Two-year-olds also understand something about how desires may determine actions (Wellman & Woolley, 1990). The children were told stories in which a character wanted to find something, such as his rabbit to take to school, and then he found it, or he found his dog, or he found nothing; older 2-year-olds could then say that in the first case he would go to school and in the other two cases he would carry on looking. That is, they could predict action based on desires but they could not predict actions based on beliefs, even in very similar tasks just as children talk about *wanting* before they talk about *thinking*).

(5) Older 2-year-olds can also make appropriate judgements of a person's emotion if they know the person's goal and the outcome (Wellman & Woolley, 1990).

Three-year-olds

Three- and 4-year-olds have been the focus of much of the research in this area. Children of this age show more explicit understanding of the mind.

(1) As noted in the section above on *Children's understanding of false belief*, 3-year-olds cannot distinguish between the apparent and real identity of deceptive objects. They can, however, distinguish between pretend and real identities, even when the

task employs the same materials as the apparent–real tasks (Flavell, Flavell & Green, 1987). Moreover, 3-year-olds can remember their own earlier pretences, even though they cannot remember their own earlier false beliefs (Gopnik & Slaughter, in press).

(2) Three-year-olds can also distinguish between real and mental entities (Wellman & Estes, 1986). For example, if they are told one boy has a cookie and another boy is thinking about a cookie, they can tell you which cookie can be eaten, shared, etc.

(3) As mentioned, 2-year-olds can show objects to others, and then they can hide objects from others. Three-year-olds have a more explicit understanding of the link between perception and knowledge and can recognize that if an object is hidden in a box someone who has looked in the box knows what is in there, and someone who has not looked does not know (Pillow, 1989; Pratt & Bryant, 1990).

(4) Similarly, 3-year-olds can infer that someone else might see an object not currently visible to themselves, what has been referred to as Level 1 perspective taking (Flavell, Everett, Croft & Flavell, 1981).

(5) As mentioned, 2-year-olds can predict a person's actions based on what the person wants; 3-year-olds can do more than this. They can predict a person's actions based on what the person thinks, so long as what the other thinks does not conflict with what the child actually knows to be the case (Wellman & Bartsch, 1988).

(6) Three-year-olds also understand something about intentions. In simple ways they can distinguish between intended and unintended action (Shultz, 1980). And they recognize that people are pleased when their intentions are fulfilled and sad when they are not (Yuill, 1984). They can also remember changes in their own intentions and desires (Gopnik & Slaughter, in press).

Four and 5-year-olds

However, despite all these achievements, there are many things that 3-year-olds cannot do that 4- and 5-year-olds can do. The best known of these abilities have already been discussed above in the section on *Children's understanding of false belief*. These are: children's understanding of false belief and their recognition of change in their own beliefs, children's ability to deceive others, and to distinguish between appearance and reality. However, a number of other important new developments occur at this age.

(1) Three-year-olds' difficulty understanding falsity is not limited to mental representation but is seen with photographic representation too. A photograph is taken of a puppet in a certain location, e.g. lying on a mat, and then another puppet is moved into that location. Then the children are asked who is lying on the mat in the photograph (which they do not see). Three-year-olds do not understand that it is the first puppet that is depicted in the photograph, and even 4-year-olds are only beginning to do so, but 5-year-olds do (Zaitchik, 1990). This study has recently been replicated with a control task demonstrating that the children's difficulty is with representation, and is not because they do not understand the camera (Perner & Leekam, 1990).

(2) As mentioned earlier, 3-year-olds understand that the one who has seen knows and the one who has not seen does not know, but they do not understand that people

may have different views of the same thing. Imagine a picture of a turtle lying flat on the table between the child and the experimenter. One person sees the turtle standing on its feet, but the person at the other side of the table sees it lying on its back. Four-year-olds can appreciate this, that is, they can perform such level 2 perspective taking but 3-year-olds cannot, or not very well (Masangkay *et al.*, 1974; Flavell *et al.*, 1981).

(3) Three-year-olds do not understand that people may acquire different information from the same perceptual experience depending on what they already know. Imagine a card with a little hole cut in it lying on top of a picture; a person who has seen the picture knows the few lines seen through the hole are part of a giraffe, but a person who has not previously seen the picture does not know that and sees only a few lines. Five-year-olds are beginning to understand such referential ambiguity (Taylor, 1988). Moreover, in a similar task, where the part seen through the hole could only be one of two alternatives and where the relevant perceptual information was made salient, 4-year-olds easily recognized that someone who had not seen the whole thing would not know which of the two it was (Ruffman, Olson & Astington, 1991).

(4) Three-year-olds can find out about things in different ways, for example, by sight or hearing or touch, and they remember what they have found out. But they do not remember the source of the information; 4-year-olds remember the source and know how they found out (Gopnik & Graf, 1988; O'Neill & Gopnik, in press).

(5) It is also not until 4 years of age that children understand that the acquisition of certain types of knowledge depends specifically on the modality of the sensory experience involved; for example, one has to see an object to know its colour, whereas one has to feel it to know its texture (O'Neill & Astington, 1990).

(6) As mentioned, 3-year-olds are able to distinguish between real and mental entities: 4-year-olds can do so even when the mental entities are imaginary creatures towards which they show some apprehension (Harris, Brown, Marriott, Whittall & Harmer, 1991).

(7) By 4 or 5 years of age children's understanding of intention becomes more sophisticated. Children are able to distinguish between intended and unintended action even in difficult cases where they have to infer information about actors' goals (Astington, 1990), and by this age they see intentions as means to ends (Astington, 1991).

(8) By 5 years of age children are beginning to recognize that people's emotional reactions to situations are determined by their beliefs (as well as by their desires which 2-year-olds understand). Five-year-olds recognize that someone will be surprised if he finds out his belief is not true (Hadwin & Perner, 1991), and that a person will be happy if she thinks she is getting what she wanted, even though they themselves know that in fact she is not getting it (Harris *et al.*, 1989).

(9) As mentioned, by 3 years of age children use terms such as *know* and *think* to refer to mental states. In a task where puppets made statements about the location of a hidden object, 4- and 5-year-olds recognized the relative certainty implied by the use of *know* over *think* or *guess* (Moore, Bryant & Furrow, 1989). Moreover, Moore *et al.* (1990) found correlations between scores on this task and on a similar one assessing understanding of the modal terms *must* and *might*, and on false belief, belief change, and appearance–reality tasks. Four-year-olds also recognize the presuppositions

created by the factive verbs *know*, *remember*, and *forget*, and understand that *think* is non-factive (Abbeduto & Rosenberg, 1985).

After 5 years

Thus, there is enormous development in children's understanding of the mind in the years between 2 and 5. Development after 5 is not reviewed here, but it is not claimed that 5-year-olds are exactly like ourselves. There is considerable development in their understanding of the mind during the school years. Developments come in many areas: in metacognition, in understanding personality traits, in knowledge about the mind and brain, in understanding embedded mental states such as beliefs about beliefs, and the social concepts that depend on this, such as responsibility, foreseeability, commitment, and reliance. There is also development in children's understanding of the expression of these concepts in speech acts, such as promising, lying, and irony. Nonetheless, by 5 years of age, children have acquired a remarkable understanding of the mind, in many ways quite like our own, and certainly very different from that of 2- or even 3-year-olds.

Theoretical explanations

It is time to turn to the second set of questions posed at the beginning of this paper: What kinds of knowledge underlie these abilities and how can we explain the origin of, and the changes in, children's understanding of the mind? What kinds of explanations are there and what specific explanations have different theorists put forward? One of the most prominent recent views sees the acquisition of folk psychology as the development of a kind of theory, and, as mentioned at the beginning of the paper, the general field has come to be known as *children's theories of mind*. However, many other views of this development are possible and have been advanced by both psychologists and philosophers. In the following sections we will consider both the theory theory and a number of possible alternatives by reviewing their answers to the following questions: What kind of knowledge underlies children's understanding of the mind? How and why does this knowledge change? What empirical predictions follow from different hypotheses about the nature and development of the child's folk psychology?

The theory theory

The general use of the phrase 'children's theories of mind' reflects the fact that the term 'theory' may be used as a kind of catch-all term for any organized body of knowledge. However, many investigators argue for a stronger, more highly structured notion of a theory, one that in particular draws close analogies between scientific theories and children's folk psychology (Forguson & Gopnik, 1988; Gopnik, 1990; Perner, 1991; Wellman, 1985, 1990; Wellman & Gelman, 1988). These arguments are part of a more general tendency to think of cognitive development in terms of theory formation (Carey, 1985, 1988; Gopnik, 1988; Karmiloff-Smith, 1988).

What would it mean for children's psychological knowledge to be theoretical in this stronger sense? Clearly, it does not mean that children could themselves explicitly formulate the account in theoretical terms. The 'theory' view would be better described as a way of characterizing a particular kind of implicit knowledge. Theories are abstract; they postulate theoretical entities that are far removed from immediate experience or evidence. They are coherent: there are complex law-like interrelationships between these theoretical entities. Theories allow one to generalize, to explain, and to predict. They have a complicated relation to evidence. On the one hand, a theory may serve to insulate knowers from counter-evidence, at least for a while, and may lead them to reinterpret or ignore it (see for example Carey, 1985; Gopnik, 1984; Karmiloff-Smith, 1988; Karmiloff-Smith & Inhelder, 1974/5). On the other hand, theories eventually change when faced with counter-examples to their predictions. Finally, while theories coherently organize many different types of evidence, they are still relatively domain specific: one may have a highly advanced theory in one area of knowledge and a relatively simple one in others.

Most importantly perhaps, the mechanism of development, on this view, is internal to the theory-formation process itself. Theory development is the result of both internal structural factors within the theory, a drive for simplicity, for example, and external factors such as the accumulation of confirming or disconfirming evidence. The theory itself influences the collection and interpretation of evidence, but new evidence also modifies aspects of the theory. This interaction between theory formation and theory testing drives the development of knowledge in children, just as it drives the historical development of knowledge in science.

Philosophically, this view has been advanced most ardently by 'eliminativists' such as Churchland (1984) and Stich (1983). The philosophical 'theory theory', as it has been known, is seen in particular as being in contrast to the classical introspectivist Cartesian view. The argument is that psychological knowledge has no special epistemological privileges; it is just a theory like our theory of the physical world. As a consequence our folk psychological concepts may be replaced by the concepts of cognitive science and, eventually, neurophysiology, just as earlier theoretical concepts such as *ether* and *phlogiston* have been replaced in physics.

The view of psychologists who advocate the theory theory may sound a very Piagetian one, and so it should—read 'schema' for 'theory' and 'assimilation and accommodation' for the 'reinterpretation of evidence and theory formation'. However, while the Piagetian underpinnings of the idea are clear (and historically, many of its advocates would consider themselves Piagetians in one way or another) both the specific accounts of the kinds of theories children hold and some of the more general features of the view are quite different from the classical Piagetian formulations. For example, Flavell's work definitively demonstrates that perspective taking of some kind is present very early on in development. More generally, notions like 'egocentrism' or 'preoperational thought' play little role in 'theory theory' accounts, and the domain specificity of the theory theory makes it quite different from stage theories.

What evidence might support the theory view? Wellman (1990) has marshalled much of it, but a few general points should be mentioned. Unlike more directly experience-based views (see below) this view would predict fairly general structural changes and reorganizations in the child's view of the mind, changes that might affect many areas of psychological knowledge simultaneously. In support of this we might note that 4-year-olds' new abilities, not just in understanding false belief, but belief change, appearance–reality, level 2 perspective taking, referential ambiguity, belief source, modality, and so on, can all be explained in terms of change in the theory they previously held (Gopnik, 1990; Perner, 1991; Wellman, 1990). Flavell (1988) also shows how simultaneous changes in children's understanding in many different domains can be explained in this way. Similarly, theoretical knowledge should be related to psychological experience in the ways we have described. Thus children who are in the grip of a theory might ignore even very strong counter-evidence to that theory. Consider the children in Moses & Flavell's (1990) study for example, who claimed that Cathy had thought there were rocks in the bag, even when they had just witnessed her evident great surprise at finding rocks there. Or consider the children in our own studies who claimed that they had said there were pencils in the box, when less than a minute before they had proclaimed that they were candy (Astington & Gopnik, 1988). On the other hand on a theory-formation view, unlike, for example, a maturational view, it should be possible to accelerate or alter the rate of children's development of a new theory by providing them with particularly salient evidence or counter-evidence. Such acceleration studies remain to be done.

The 'theory theorists' agree that there are moments in development when there are fundamental theory changes, almost paradigm shifts (Kuhn, 1962), and even identify similar shifts, although the exact interpretation of these shifts may vary. One such shift appears to take place at about 18 months, with the onset of the ability to pretend, to hypothesize, and to use language to refer to mental states (Forguson & Gopnik, 1988; Perner, 1988, 1991; Wellman, 1988, 1990). Another appears to take place at around 4 years of age and leads children to a new understanding of the causal links between the mind and the world, an understanding which, among other things, allows children to understand representation in a new way (Flavell, 1988; Forguson & Gopnik, 1988; Olson, 1989; Perner, 1988, 1991; Wellman, 1988, 1990; Wimmer, Hogrefe & Sodian, 1988).

However, within the general 'theory theory' camp there are many disagreements about how best to characterize children's theories and the ways in which those theories change. The question of when children begin to represent representations, to metarepresent in Pylyshyn's (1978) phrase, has been particularly fraught (Astington, 1991). Just about everyone agrees that, in infancy, children have representations of the real world, but that they do not represent those representations. At 18 months children begin to have and to talk about representations that do not refer to the real world. They begin to formulate pretences, hypotheses, and images and to differentiate these mental entities from real things. Do these abilities require metarepresentation?

Perner suggests that they do not. Rather, he suggests that children think of pretences or possibilities as being parallel to representations of reality, but making reference to possible or hypothetical worlds, rather than the real world. The child who pretends the banana is a telephone is not representing the representation 'this is a telephone' but instead is referring to the possible world in which the banana would be a telephone.

Others (Forguson & Gopnik, 1988; Leslie, 1988) argue that an understanding of pretence or imagination necessarily involves an ability to understand representations in some sense. On this view, while children may interpret veridical representations as simply referring to real things, they must recognize that non-veridical representations are merely psychological; they have no life outside the mind itself. Within this group too, however, there are arguments about the best ways of characterizing the shift from 3 to 4. For example, Wellman suggests that 3-year-olds already have a representational understanding of belief, and the shift from 3 to 4 involves a new conception of the mind as a complex information processor that enables children to understand one particular type of representation, namely misrepresentation (Wellman, 1988, 1990). Other authors have suggested that the shift may involve a new understanding of the causal relations between the mind and the world (Leslie, 1988), or a new appreciation of the sources of beliefs (Wimmer *et al.*, 1988). One can distinguish between 'a representation' as a mental entity and 'representation' as a process, and we have suggested that 3-year-olds may understand representation in the former but not the latter sense (Astington & Gopnik, 1991). The younger children may think of representation as a rather direct, almost Gibsonian, relation between events and knowledge, and only after 4 develop a truly representational view of representation.

As may be seen from this sketch, the arguments are subtle, and the concepts involved are intertwined in complex ways. It may be an inevitable problem with this approach that we must characterize children's theoretical structures using the vocabulary of our own adult theories, vocabulary that is itself somewhat unclear. However, despite this, the consensus is in many ways more striking than the disagreement. Different investigators share the same general view of the child's developing folk psychology: they identify the same two points of developmental shift, and characterize the 'before' and 'after' theories in strikingly similar ways. Moreover, they are in general agreement about the mechanisms of the change.

In the following sections we examine other theoretical explanations of children's acquisition of folk psychology that have been proposed as alternatives to the theory theory. Some of these suggestions have come directly from researchers working in the field of children's theory of mind (e.g. Harris, 1991), while others have come from beyond the immediate research area of theory of mind. We consider the ways in which children's knowledge of the mind is characterized from various different perspectives, and what predictions would follow from these different characterizations.

Folk psychology as a form of life

A radically different view might suggest that children's understanding of the mind is not really based on knowledge at all. The aim and nature of psychological understanding might not be to explain or predict experience or behaviour, but to regulate our interactions with others. On this view folk psychology is not a theory, is not indeed any kind of knowledge, but is instead what Wittgenstein would call a 'form of life', a set of social and cultural practices and conventions. The mechanism for development, on this view, would be socialization or enculturation—children would learn how to psychologize appropriately in the way that they learn how to dress properly or eat politely.

This view has been strongly argued in philosophy in a number of different ways. Davidson (1980) and Wilkes (1978) have argued that folk psychology serves functions other than explanation in everyday life. Dennett's (1987) notion of the intentional stance also has something of this quality: our decision about whether to attribute mental states to other beings has less to do with their behaviour than with our relationship to them. This view has, however, been rather surprisingly absent from the developmental debate. An exception is Bruner's (1989, 1990) view that children's developing understanding of mind is dependent on their growing up in a particular linguistic and cultural environment. Dunn (1988) provides detailed observations of young children's family life that illuminate this view.

This view and the theory formation view might make similar predictions about the behaviours in which children engage or the things they say. But their accounts of the mechanism of development would be very different. Theories always develop with reference to the outside world; put very simply, a theory former wants to get closer to the truth. Cultural practices on the other hand are, at least largely, self-constitutive: they make themselves the case. Theories are true or false, cultural practices are right or wrong.

Some aspects of folk psychology, particularly the understanding of emotions, and sophisticated aesthetic and moral states, seem to have this self-constitutive cultural quality. This is reflected in the historical and cross-cultural differences in such psychological constructs, differences that do not seem to reflect differing degrees of knowledge but rather reflect differences in the nature of the cultures themselves. La Rochefoucauld's aphorism that no one would fall in love if they hadn't read about it first has at least a grain or two of historical truth (see Stone, 1979). Certainly there is cultural variation in basic social psychological concepts in different societies, such as commitment and obligation (Rosaldo, 1982). And certainly there is variation in the way mental phenomena, such as dreams, are conceptualized in different cultures (Shweder & Levine, 1975).

If the enculturation hypothesis is correct we would expect to find variations in children's hypotheses about the mind, and, indeed, in children's minds, reflecting their particular cultural environment. Unfortunately, there is almost no information on children's understanding of mind in different cultures. All the evidence reported earlier has come from research in Western cultures. However, Avis & Harris (in press) have recently shown that Baka children of Cameroon develop the ability to predict action and emotion, based on a person's beliefs and desires, at roughly the same age that Western children do. On the other hand, McCormick's (1990) recent data show that 4- to 7-year-old Quechua children of Peru, whose language has a well-developed vocabulary for appearance and reality but not for belief, do well on appearance–reality tests but fail false belief tests using the same materials. In large part, the cross-cultural story remains to be told.

Even in our own culture we know rather little about how social interaction and socialization influence the development of theories of mind. Clearly, in our culture there is an enormous amount of psychological talk between parents and children (Bretherton, 1991; Dunn, 1988) and much of this talk has a normative quality;

parents tell children how they should feel and think as well as how they should behave. How this sort of interaction influences the final product is still unknown.

Folk psychology as an innate module

Yet another alternative to the 'theory theory' might suggest that children's understanding of the mind is innate, and that maturation is responsible for at least some of the changes in their behaviour and language. Several psychologists and at least one distinguished philosopher have made such arguments (Carey, 1985, p. 200; Fodor, 1987, p. 132; Leslie, 1987, 1988; Macnamara, 1989). Leslie has advanced this argument most fervently, suggesting that there is an innate *theory of mind* module. He has argued that the striking and specific absence of folk psychological abilities in autistic children (Baron-Cohen, 1989*a*, *b*; Baron-Cohen, Leslie & Frith, 1985), who presumably have an innate neurologically based deficit, is support for this view.

The most convincing evidence for such a claim would be a demonstration that folk psychological abilities were present in very young infants, and as we have seen there is as yet little evidence for such a view. However, there are apparently innate or at least very early abilities, that, while not themselves constituting a theory of mind, may be prerequisites or even precursors for the development of such knowledge. For example, very young infants' imitative abilities (Meltzoff, 1985), their ability to coordinate their emotions with those of others, and their ability to carry on 'proto-conversations', may imply the fundamental notion that other people are similar to the self, in a way that objects are not, as we mentioned above in the section on *Infancy*.

Indeed, Hobson (1989) has suggested that the specific autistic theory of mind deficit stems from a deficit in these more fundamental social abilities. Baron-Cohen (1991) suggests that other abilities in infancy, such as the ability to regulate joint attention, implied in 9-month-olds' pointing abilities, might serve as important prerequisites or precursors for an understanding of the mind, and has shown that these abilities are absent in at least some autistic children, although other social abilities are intact.

Of course, even if knowledge of the mind emerges later, the mechanism for its emergence might be maturational, and indeed Leslie (1987) has suggested, for example, that a 'metarepresentational capacity', what he calls 'decoupling', may mature at 18 months and so allow pretend play and other types of metarepresentation. The nativist viewpoint might also be partially supported by research with other primates, such as apes, demonstrating their abilities to attribute unseen states to other members of the species (Whiten, 1991). However, the primates might themselves be developing folk psychological abilities, on the basis of some more primitive social or cognitive skills.

An interesting theoretical issue about innateness that bears on these debates is whether we see innate conceptual structures as a set of constraints on later development, or as an initial state which is itself subject to later revision and reconstruction. The former view has been most popular among some of the most ardent nativists, namely linguists (or at least some of them). On this view, children could not develop a language that violated certain innate constraints; the form of this knowledge is fixed by the nature of the mental representations. But consider a different kind of innateness hypothesis: the suggestion of Bower (1982) and Meltzoff (1985) that at birth infants initially have an amodal system of representation, one that fails to differentiate between information from different senses. However, this initial amodal system of representation will be rapidly modified.

Similar distinctions might be made when we consider the innate bases for a theory of mind. Leslie's version is a variant of the 'constraints' hypothesis: the maturational mechanism sets limits on what a theory of mind might be like. The precursor view might be that the infant begins with something like a concept of the mind but that this view is deeply different from the adult view and will be radically revised as the infant learns more about the experience and behaviour of himself and others. This 'precursor' view might say that there is no point at which a 'theory of mind' emerges, instead there are many theories of mind from infancy onwards, and these theories change as the infant does. However, this might also suggest that the theory of mind we end up with may be strongly influenced by the one we start out with. People who start out without the infant apparatus, people with autism, for example, might never converge on the ordinary adult view.

At the moment the evidence, and particularly the evidence from autism, is compatible either with the view that some maturational timetable is unfolding, or that earlier abilities, some of which are innate themselves, are precursors for later, genuinely conceptual developments. For the maturational argument to go through in its strong form we would need to demonstrate that both the folk psychological developments themselves and their developmental timetable are universal, and that they are not attributable to differences in experience, or to other cognitive developments. However, without a fuller developmental picture, the innateness question is difficult to evaluate.

Folk psychology as procedural knowledge

Information processing models see the child's development of understanding of the mind as one part of a larger picture of development. They see general, formal patterns of development; for them, the developing understanding of desires, feelings, and beliefs provides an example of this pattern in one domain (Case, 1989). A consonant view sees the child's developing understanding of mind as part of the general development of recursive abilities, in thought and in language (Feldman, 1988). Leslie (1987) has proposed a detailed analysis of the representational mechanism underlying such abilities, and suggests that many later developments reflect elaborations of this system. Shultz (1988, 1991 *a*, *b*) has argued that little progress can be made in understanding the development of children's abilities to reason about mental phenomena, without models of how such reasoning is accomplished. He has proposed that a number of phenomena, such as distinguishing intentions from mistakes and predicting actions based on false beliefs, can be modelled by production systems in computer simulations. One virtue of this approach is that the attempt to implement these models demands that the proposed mechanisms be precisely specified.

Again the important point here is the nature of the mechanisms that propel development. On all of these views development is less a matter of acquiring knowledge or experience than of elaborating a computational mechanism, adding as it were more loops and levels, rather than adding more concepts or laws or propositions. Also implicit in these views is the idea that changes in children's general information-processing abilities, changes in memory or computational capacity, for example, are responsible for changes in their understanding of mind.

Because young children are not by and large highly articulate about their concepts of the mind (although see Wellman & Estes, 1986) we are almost always in the position of inferring their psychological concepts from their actions, or from isolated responses on particular tasks. The production of a particular response, or the failure to produce one, might indeed reflect information-processing capacities, rather than concepts or beliefs. How can we distinguish between these two alternatives? An implicit test comes in the methodology of many theory of mind research programmes. Investigators may try to vary the information-processing demands of various theory of mind tasks while holding their conceptual content the same, or vice versa to vary conceptual content and make the information-processing demands similar (for elegant examples of this strategy see Flavell *et al.*, 1986; Perner *et al.*, 1987; Wellman, 1990). If children are able to solve even difficult tasks with one type of conceptual content and yet fail simpler tasks with another kind, it is unlikely that information-processing demands *per se* are responsible for development.

Folk psychology as experience

Other investigators may say that children genuinely learn psychological concepts but still say that the child does not develop a theory of mind at all. They agree with the 'theory theorists' that the child comes to understand human behaviour through experience, and not through socialization, maturation or changes in information-processing capacities. But they argue that this understanding is not theory-like.

Some in this group say that children's early understanding is intuitive, rather than theoretical (e.g. Johnson, 1988). What the child understands is her own phenomenal experience. Through introspection, she becomes aware of her own desires, beliefs, and feelings, and can then use this awareness in understanding others. Harris (1991) develops this idea in some detail. He argues that the child who, for example, successfully tells you where the other person will look in a false belief task, is not making any theoretical prediction, but is engaging in mental simulation. She can imagine having the desires and beliefs the other has, and she can simulate what would follow, that is, what she would do, and how she would feel. This social use of one's first-person intuitions is also seen in role taking where one puts oneself 'in the other fellow's shoes', and thus one knows how he feels and what he will do (Chandler, 1989; Chandler & Helm, 1984; Flavell, Botkin, Fry, Wright & Jarvis, 1968). Such a view also appears to underlie some of Piaget's claims about childhood egocentrism.

The simulation account is spelt out in the philosophical literature by Goldman (1989) and Gordon (1986). These positions are also more generally embodied in a strong philosophical tradition about the nature of psychological knowledge. On this view, which conventionally has been identified with Descartes, introspective, first-person psychological knowledge has a specially privileged status. It is direct, and not the result of inference or construction. Indeed, for Descartes such knowledge was the foundation of all other kinds of knowledge, both physical and psychological. We need not take the strong Cartesian view that first-person psychological knowledge is incorrigible, to believe that it has special qualities, at least in the context of psychological claims.

What predictions would we make on this view? It seems to us (although see Harris, 1991) that a central prediction of such a view would be that children's understanding of their own minds, of their own beliefs, desires, and so on, would consistently precede their understanding of the minds of others. There is some evidence from the classical literature on perspective taking and egocentrism that supports this (Piaget, 1926/1929). However, there is some rather surprising evidence in the adult literature that people are often profoundly inaccurate in reporting their own motivations and desires (Nisbett & Wilson, 1977; Nisbett & Ross, 1980). Similarly, recent research suggests that children are no better at reporting their own immediately past mental states than they are at attributing similar mental states to others (Astington & Gopnik, 1991; Gopnik & Astington, 1988; Gopnik & Graf, 1988; Gopnik & Slaughter, in press; Wimmer & Hartl, in press). This evidence suggests, that, at least in part, even our own first-person experience is itself constructed.

Folk psychology as story

The introspectivist view sees the child's psychological knowledge not as an abstract construction, but rather as something closely related to the child's immediate psychological experience, particularly first-person experience. Another way in which an 'experience-based' view might differ from a theory construction view concerns the degree of coherence of psychological knowledge, and the nature of its organization.

Psychological knowledge, for example, might be organized in terms of scripts. Scripts organize knowledge, and they allow predictions, but they are more particular and less coherent than theories, and they lack theories' explanatory power. They are closer to being rough empirical generalizations, like the medical generalization that taking aspirin leads to a reduction in pain. On this view, children acquire expectations about the structure of common events (Nelson, 1981); these scripts map into more general schemata, or plans, and then in order to interpret a person's action one searches for a general plan to fit the situation. Thus one might know that a person will be likely to do x, given psychological circumstance y, without having any very clear theory of why this is so. Bruner's (1986, 1990) idea that psychological knowledge is organized in terms of narratives also might be relevant here. In philosophy, De Sousa (1987) has suggested that our emotional understanding may be organized in terms of 'paradigm scenarios', little dramas or perhaps melodramas, that we invoke in emotionally charged situations, an idea implicit also in the psychoanalytic tradition.

Again what empirical predictions might we make about the development of the mind, on this view? If children's knowledge of the mind is not a coherent and highly organized whole, then we might expect that there would be massive 'horizontal décalage', that children might be advanced in their understanding of some particular highly familiar domain (a script) and yet fail to apply this knowledge more generally to other domains, particularly novel or unusual ones. Moreover, we might expect that children's explanations of mental phenomena would be more like stories than theories.

Conclusion

When we attempt to separate the various theoretical positions in this way we always risk oversimplification. Many particular theorists' views combine different aspects of the accounts we have described here, and at the risk of sounding like wishy-washy liberals, there is some level at which they must all be true. However, even speaking as wishy-washy liberals, it appears that so far the theory formation view has been most productive, both in generating interesting empirical predictions, and in explaining the phenomena that have already been described. There seems in particular to be an elegant fit between this, the most prevalent theoretical framework, and the most closely investigated empirical phenomenon in the area, the shift in the understanding of belief and representation between 3 and 4 years. This may remind us of our earlier observations about the interactions of theory and data.

However, even if we accept a theory formation account, other processes must also play significant roles. Theory formation never takes place in a cultural vacuum, either for children or scientists; almost everything we know comes to us through a process of cultural transmission. Innate structures or abilities may indeed provide constraints on the kinds of theories we might build or provide a 'starting state' which will later be transformed by additional experience. Information-processing abilities also provide constraints; without calculus or the zero or modern computers, certain kinds of scientific theories would be impossible, and similarly without certain information-processing abilities certain theories of mind might be impossible. There could be no theoretical explanations without experience to explain, and that experience will almost certainly include introspective evidence and 'script-like' generalizations.

Moreover, while the field has focused on questions of belief and representation, folk psychology includes many varied kinds of knowledge, and different kinds of explanation might be appropriate for different kinds of development. For example, there might be a split in children's conceptions of the mind analogous to some of the deep splits in contemporary psychology itself. Children's 'folk cognitive science', their accounts of knowledge, representation and belief might be largely theoretical, while their 'folk social psychology', their accounts of affect, motivation, and social relations might develop through a process of enculturation, or be structured in terms of stories or scripts. Children's understanding of perception might depend very largely on introspective experience, their accounts of desire might be based more on behaviour and action, their understanding of affect might be based on innate interactional abilities, and so on.

To date, the empirical examination of children's understanding of false belief and the theory theory explanation of these data have dominated the field. In the next few years we see the field growing to include more extensive examination of the development of children's understanding in the many other areas that we have mentioned: desire, intention, perception, affect, and so on. We also see this work going beyond a focus on just the preschool period, to investigate the links between very young children's interactional abilities and their later developing more explicit understanding, and also to investigate more fully further development occurring in the school age years. As the field expands in this way and we begin to consider more kinds of development at more times, the alternative theoretical views that we have described are likely to play an increasingly important role in explanation. As we have noted at various points in the paper, numerous questions remain unanswered, indeed unaddressed, that bear on this theoretical debate. For example, we do not know whether or not development in all these different areas is similar across different social and cultural groups. Nor do we know whether it is possible to accelerate children's development at particular crucial times, for example around 3 to 4 years, by providing them with salient evidence and counter-evidence to the theories we suppose them currently to hold; the work that is already underway, investigating the precursors to a full understanding of false belief, is relevant here. Further, we do not know whether the mechanisms underlying development in all these different areas and at different age periods are similar or not. It seems likely that questions such as these will acquire increasing importance in the years to come. The one thing that seems absolutely indisputable is that there is plenty of work to be done.

Acknowledgements

Preparation of this paper was supported by grants from the Natural Sciences and Engineering Research Council of Canada and the Social Sciences and Humanities Research Council of Canada to J.W.A. An earlier version of the paper was presented at the Biennial Meeting of the Society for Research in Child Development, Kansas City, MO, April 1989.

References

Abbeduto, L. & Rosenberg, S. (1985). Children's knowledge of the presuppositions of *know* and other cognitive verbs. *Journal of Child Language*, **12**, 621–641.

Astington, J. W. (1990). Wishes and plans: Children's understanding of intentional causation. Paper presented at the Annual Meeting of the Jean Piaget Society, Philadelphia, PA, May.

Astington, J. W. (1991). Intention in the child's theory of mind. In D. Frye & C. Moore (Eds), *Children's Theories of Mind*, pp. 157–172. Hillsdale, NJ: Erlbaum.

Astington, J. W. & Gopnik, A. (1988). Knowing you've changed your mind: Children's understanding of representational change. In J. W. Astington, P. L. Harris & D. R. Olson (Eds), *Developing Theories of Mind*, pp. 193–206. New York: Cambridge University Press.

Astington, J. W. & Gopnik, A. (1991). Developing understanding of desire and intention. In A. Whiten (Ed.), *Natural Theories of Mind: Evolution, Development and Simulation of Everyday Mindreading*, pp. 39–50. Oxford: Basil Blackwell.

Astington, J. W., Harris, P. L. & Olson, D. R. (Eds) (1988). *Developing Theories of Mind*. New York: Cambridge University Press.

Avis, J. & Harris, P. L. (in press). Belief–desire reasoning among Baka children: Evidence for a universal conception of mind.

Baron-Cohen, S. (1989*a*). Are autistic children 'behaviourists'? An examination of their mental–physical and appearance–reality distinctions. *Journal of Autism and Developmental Disorders*, **19**, 579–600.

Baron-Cohen, S. (1989*b*). The autistic child's theory of mind: A case of specific developmental delay. *Journal of Child Psychology and Psychiatry*, **30**, 285–297.

Baron-Cohen, S. (1991). Precursors to a theory of mind: Understanding attention in others. In A. Whiten (Ed.), *Natural Theories of Mind: Evolution, Development and Simulation of Everyday Mindreading*, pp. 233–251. Oxford: Basil Blackwell.

Baron-Cohen, S., Leslie, A. M. & Frith, U. (1985). Does the autistic child have a 'theory of mind'? *Cognition*, **21**, 37–46.

Bartsch, K. & Wellman, H. M. (1989). Young children's attribution of action to beliefs and desires. *Child Development*, **60**, 946–964.

Bates, E. (1976). *Language and Context: The Acquisition of Pragmatics.* New York: Academic Press.

Bennett, J. (1978). Some remarks about concepts. *The Behavioral and Brain Sciences*, **1**, 557–560.

Bower, T. G. R. (1982). *Development in Infancy*, 2nd ed. San Francisco, CA: Freeman.

Bretherton, I. (1991). Intentional communication and the development of an understanding of mind. In D. Frye & C. Moore (Eds), *Children's Theories of Mind*, pp 49–75. Hillsdale, NJ: Erlbaum.

Bretherton, I. & Beeghly, M. (1982). Talking about internal states: The acquisition of an explicit theory of mind. *Developmental Psychology*, **6**, 906–921.

Bretherton, I., McNew, S. & Beeghly-Smith, M. (1981). Early person knowledge as expressed in gestural and verbal communication: When do infants acquire a 'theory of mind'? In M. E. Lamb & L. R. Sherod (Eds), *Infant Social Cognition*, pp. 333–373. Hillsdale, NJ: Erlbaum.

Bruner, J. (1983). *Child's Talk.* Oxford: Oxford University Press.

Bruner, J. (1986). *Actual Minds, Possible Worlds.* Cambridge, MA: Harvard University Press.

Bruner, J. (1989). The state of developmental psychology. Invited address presented at the Biennial Meeting of the Society for Research in Child Development, Kansas City, MO, April.

Bruner, J. (1990). *Acts of Meaning.* Cambridge, MA: Harvard University Press.

Carey, S. (1985). *Conceptual Change in Childhood.* Cambridge, MA: Bradford/MIT Press.

Carey, S. (1988). Conceptual differences between children and adults. *Mind and Language*, **3**, 167–183.

Case, R. (1989). A neo-Piagetian analysis of the child's understanding of other people, and the internal conditions which motivate their behaviour. Paper presented at the Biennial Meeting of the Society for Research in Child Development, Kansas City, MO, April.

Chandler, M. (1989). Fledgling theories of mind: Social cognitive development from infancy to adolescence. Paper presented at the Biennial Meeting of the Society for Research in Child Development, Kansas City, MO, April.

Chandler, M. J., Fritz, A. S. & Hala, S. M. (1989). Small scale deceit: Deception as a marker of 2-, 3- and 4-year-olds' early theories of mind. *Child Development*, **60**, 1263–1277.

Chandler, M. J. & Helm, D. (1984). Developmental changes in the contribution of shared experience to social role-taking competence. *International Journal of Behavioural Development*, **7**, 145–156.

Churchland, P. M. (1984). *Matter and Consciousness.* Cambridge, MA: Bradford/MIT Press.

Davidson, D. (1980). *Essays on Action and Events.* Oxford: Oxford University Press.

Dennett, D. C. (1978). Beliefs about beliefs. *The Behavioral and Brain Sciences*, **1**, 568–570.

Dennett, D. C. (1987). *The Intentional Stance.* Cambridge, MA: Bradford/MIT Press.

de Sousa, R. (1987). *The Rationality of Emotion.* Cambridge, MA: MIT Press.

DeVries, R. (1970). The development of role-taking as reflected by behavior of bright, average, and retarded children in a social guessing game. *Child Development*, **41**, 759–770.

Dunn, J. (1988). *The Beginnings of Social Understanding.* Cambridge, MA: Harvard University Press.

Feldman, C. F. (1988). Early forms of thought about thoughts: Some simple linguistic expressions of mental state. In J. W. Astington, P. L. Harris & D. R. Olson (Eds), *Developing Theories of Mind*, pp. 126–137. New York: Cambridge University Press.

Flavell, J. H. (1986). The development of children's knowledge about the appearance–reality distinction. *American Psychologist*, **41**, 418–425.

Flavell, J. H. (1988). The development of children's knowledge about the mind: From cognitive connections to mental representations. In J. W. Astington, P. L. Harris & D. R. Olson (Eds), *Developing Theories of Mind*, pp. 244–267. New York: Cambridge University Press.

Flavell, J. H., Botkin, P. T., Fry, C. L., Wright, J. W. & Jarvis, P. E. (1968). *The Development of Role-taking and Communication Skills in Children.* New York: Wiley.

Flavell, J. H., Everett, B. A., Croft, K. & Flavell, E. R. (1981). Young children's knowledge about visual perception: Further evidence for the Level 1–Level 2 distinction. *Developmental Psychology*, **17**, 99–103.

Flavell, J. H., Flavell, E. R. & Green, F. L. (1983). Development of the appearance–reality distinction. *Cognitive Psychology*, **15**, 95–120.

Flavell, J. H., Flavell, E. R. & Green, F. L. (1987). Young children's knowledge about the apparent–real and pretend–real distinctions. *Developmental Psychology*, **23**, 816–822.

Flavell, J. H., Flavell, E. R. & Green, F. L. & Moses, L. J. (1990). Young children's understanding of fact beliefs versus value beliefs. *Child Development*, **61**, 915–928.

Flavell, J. H., Green, F. L. & Flavell, E. R. (1986). Development of knowledge about the appearance–reality distinction. *Monographs of the Society for Research in Child Development*, **51** (1, Serial No. 212).

Fodor, J. A. (1987). *Psychosemantics: The Problem of Meaning in the Philosophy of Mind*. Cambridge, MA: Bradford/MIT Press.

Forguson, L. & Gopnik, A. (1988). The ontogeny of common sense. In J. W. Astington, P. L. Harris & D. R. Olson (Eds), *Developing Theories of Mind*, pp. 226–243. New York: Cambridge University Press.

Freeman. N. H., Lewis, C. & Doherty, M. J. (1991). Preschoolers' grasp of a desire for knowledge in false-belief prediction: Practical intelligence and verbal report. *British Journal of Developmental Psychology*, **9**, 139–158.

Frye, D. & Moore, C. (in press). *Children's Theories of Mind*. Hillsdale, NJ: Erlbaum.

Goldman, A. I. (1989). Interpretation psychologized. *Mind and Language*, **4**, 161–185.

Gopnik, A. (1984). Conceptual and semantic change in scientists and children: Why there are no semantic universals. *Linguistics*, **20**, 163–179.

Gopnik, A. (1988). Conceptual and semantic development as theory change: The case of object permanence. *Mind and Language*, **3**, 197–216.

Gopnik, A. (1990). Developing the idea of intentionality: Children's theories of mind. *Canadian Journal of Philosophy*, **20**, 89–114.

Gopnik, A. & Astington, J. W. (1988). Children's understanding of representational change and its relation to the understanding of false belief and the appearance–reality distinction. *Child Development*, **58**, 26–37.

Gopnik, A. & Graf, P. (1988). Knowing how you know: Young children's ability to identify and remember the sources of their beliefs. *Child Development*, **59**, 1366–1371.

Gopnik, A. & Slaughter, V. (in press). Young children's understanding of changes in their mental states. *Child Development*.

Gordon, R. M. (1986). Folk psychology as simulation. *Mind and Language*, **1**, 156–171.

Hadwin, J. & Perner, J. (1991). Pleased and surprised: Children's cognitive theory of emotion. *British Journal of Developmental Psychology*, **9**(2).

Hala, S., Chandler, M. & Fritz, A. S. (in press). Fledgling theories of mind: Deception as a marker of 3-year-olds' understanding of false belief. *Child Development*.

Harris, P. L., Brown, E., Marriott, C., Whittall, S. & Harmer, S. (1991). Monsters, ghosts and witches: Testing the limits of the fantasy–reality distinction in young children. *British Journal of Developmental Psychology*, **9**, 105–124.

Harris, P. L., Johnson, C. N., Hutton, D., Andrews, G. & Cooke, T. (1989). Young children's theory of mind and emotion. *Cognition and Emotion*, **3**, 379–400.

Harman, G. (1978). Studying the chimpanzee's theory of mind. *The Behavioral and Brain Sciences*, **1**, 591.

Harris, P. L. (1991). The work of the imagination. In A. Whiten (Ed.), *Natural Theories of Mind: Evolution, Development and Simulation of Everyday Mindreading*, pp. 283–304. Oxford: Basil Blackwell.

Hobson, R. P. (1989). Beyond cognition: A theory of autism. In G. Dawson (Ed.), *Autism: Nature, Diagnosis, and Treatment*. New York: Guilford Press.

Johnson, C. N. (1988). Theory of mind and the structure of conscious experience. In J. W. Astington, P. L. Harris & D. R. Olson (Eds), *Developing Theories of Mind*, pp. 47–63. New York: Cambridge University Press.

Karmiloff-Smith, A. (1988). The child is a theoretician not an inductivist. *Mind and Language*, **3**, 183–197.

Karmiloff-Smith, A. & Inhelder, B. (1974/5). If you want to get ahead get a theory. *Cognition*, **3**, 195–212.

Kuhn, T. S. (1962). *The Structure of Scientific Revolutions*. Chicago: Chicago University Press.

LaFrenière, P. J. (1988). The ontogeny of tactical deception in humans. In R. W. Byrne & A. Whiten (Eds), *Machiavellian Intelligence: Social Expertise and the Evolution of Intellect in Monkeys, Apes and Humans*, pp. 238–252. Oxford: Oxford University Press.

Leslie, A. M. (1987). Pretense and representation: The origins of 'theory of mind'. *Psychological Review*, **94**, 412–426.

Leslie, A. M. (1988). Some implications of pretense for mechanisms underlying the child's theory of mind. In J. W. Astington, P. L. Harris & D. R. Olson (Eds), *Developing Theories of Mind*, pp. 19–46. New York: Cambridge University Press.

Lempers, J. D., Flavell, E. R. & Flavell, J. H. (1977). The development in very young children of tacit knowledge concerning visual perception. *Genetic Psychology Monographs*, **95**, 3–53.

Lewis, C. & Osborne, A. (1990). Three-year-olds' problems with false belief: Conceptual deficit or linguistic artifact? *Child Development*, **61**, 1514–1519.

Macnamara, J. (1989). Children as common sense psychologists. *Canadian Journal of Psychology*, **43**, 426–429.

Masangkay, Z. S., McCluskey, K. A., McIntyre, C. W., Sims-Knight, J., Vaughn, B. E. & Flavell, J. H. (1974). The early development of inferences about the visual percepts of others. *Child Development*, **45**, 357–366.

McCormick, P. (1990). Quechua children's theory of mind. Paper presented at the Sixth University of Waterloo Conference on Child Development, Waterloo, Ontario, May.

Meltzoff, A. N. (1985). The roots of social and cognitive development: Models of man's original nature. In T. Field & N. Fox (Eds), *Social Perception in Infants*, pp. 1–30. Norwood, NJ: Ablex.

Moore, C., Bryant, D. & Furrow, D. (1989). Mental terms and the development of certainty. *Child Development*, **60**, 167–171.

Moore, C., Pure, K. & Furrow, D. (1990). Children's understanding of the modal expression of speaker certainty and uncertainty and its relation to the development of a representational theory of mind. *Child Development*, **61**, 722–730.

Moses, L. J. (1990). Young children's understanding of intention and belief. Unpublished doctoral dissertation, Stanford University, CA.

Moses, L. J. & Flavell, J. H. (1990). Inferring false beliefs from actions and reactions. *Child Development*, **61**, 929–945.

Nelson, K. (1981). Social cognition in a script framework. In J. H. Flavell & L. Ross (Eds), *Social Cognitive Development*, pp. 97–118. New York: Cambridge University Press.

Nisbett, R. E. & Ross, L. (1980). *Human Inference: Strategies and Shortcomings of Social Judgment*. Englewood Cliffs, NJ: Prentice-Hall.

Nisbett, R. E. & Wilson, T. D. (1977). Telling more than we can know: Verbal reports on mental processes. *Psychological Review*, **84**, 231–259.

Olson, D. R. (1988). On the origins of beliefs and other intentional states in children. In J. W. Astington, P. L. Harris & D. R. Olson (Eds), *Developing Theories of Mind*, pp. 414–426. New York: Cambridge University Press.

Olson, D. R. (1989). Making up your mind. *Canadian Psychology*, **30**, 617–627.

Olson, D. R., Astington, J. W. & Harris, P. L. (1988). Introduction. In J. W. Astington, P. L. Harris & D. R. Olson (Eds), *Developing Theories of Mind*, pp. 1–15. New York: Cambridge University Press.

O'Neill, D. K. & Astington, J. W. (1990). Preschoolers' developing understanding of the role sensory experiences play in knowledge acquisition. Paper presented at the Annual Meeting of the American Educational Research Association, Boston, MA, April.

O'Neill, D. K. & Gopnik, A. (in press). Young children's ability to identify the sources of their beliefs. *Developmental Psychology*.

Perner, J. (1988). Developing semantics for theories of mind: From propositional attitudes to mental representation. In J. W. Astington, P. L. Harris & D. R. Olson (Eds), *Developing Theories of Mind*, pp. 141–172. New York: Cambridge University Press.

Perner, J. (1989). Is 'thinking' belief? A reply to Wellman and Bartsch. *Cognition*, **33**, 315–319.

Perner, J. (1991). *Understanding the Representational Mind*. Cambridge, MA: MIT Press.

Perner, J. & Leekam, S. (1990). Children's difficulty with photography versus colour transmission: Zooming in on representation. Unpublished manuscript, University of Sussex, under review for *Child Development*.

Perner, J., Leekam, S. & Wimmer, H. (1987). Three-year-olds' difficulty with false belief: The case for a conceptual deficit. *British Journal of Developmental Psychology*, **5**, 125–137.

Perner, J. & Ogden, J. (1988). Knowledge for hunger: Children's problem with representation in imputing mental states. *Cognition*, **29**, 47–61.

Peskin, J. (1990). Ruse and representations: On children's ability to conceal information. Paper presented at the 98th Annual Convention of the American Psychological Association, Boston, MA, August.

Piaget, J. (1929). *The Child's Conception of the World*. London: Kegan Paul. (Originally published in French in 1926.)

Pillow, B. H. (1989). Early understanding of perception as a source of knowledge. *Journal of Experimental Child Psychology*, **47**, 116–129.

Pratt, C. & Bryant, P. E. (1990). Young children understand that looking leads to knowing (so long as they are looking into a single barrel). *Child Development*, **61**, 973–982.

Premack, D. & Woodruff, G. (1978). Does the chimpanzee have a theory of mind? *The Behavioral and Brain Sciences*, **1**, 515–526.

Pylyshyn, Z. W. (1978). When is attribution of beliefs justified? *The Behavioral and Brain Sciences*, **1**, 592–593.

Rosaldo, M. Z. (1982). The things we do with words: Ilongot speech acts and speech act theory in philosophy. *Language in Society*, **11**, 203–237.

Ruffman, T. K., Olson, D. R. & Astington, J. W. (1991). Children's understanding of visual ambiguity. *British Journal of Developmental Psychology*, **9**, 89–102.

Shatz, M., Wellman, H. M. & Silber, S. (1983). The acquisition of mental verbs: A systematic investigation of the first reference to mental state. *Cognition*, **14**, 301–321.

Shultz, T. R. (1980). Development of the concept of intention. In W. A. Collins (Ed.), *Development of Cognition, Affect and Social Relations. The Minnesota Symposium on Child Psychology*, Vol. 13, pp. 131–164. Hillsdale, NJ: Erlbaum.

Shultz, T. R. (1988). Assessing intention: A computational model. In J. W. Astington, P. L. Harris & D. R. Olson (Eds), *Developing Theories of Mind*, pp. 341–367. New York: Cambridge University Press.

Shultz, T. R. (1991 *a*). From agency to intention: A rule-based, computational approach. In A. Whiten (Ed.), *Natural Theories of Mind: Evolution, Development and Simulation of Everyday Mindreading*, pp. 79–95. Oxford: Basil Blackwell.

Shultz, T. R. (1991 *b*). Modeling embedded intention. In D. Frye & C. Moore (Eds), *Children's Theories of Mind*, 195–218. Hillsdale, NJ: Erlbaum.

Shultz, T. R. & Cloghesy, K. (1981). Development of recursive awareness of intention. *Developmental Psychology*, **17**, 465–471.

Shweder, R. & Levine, R. A. (1975). Dream concepts of Hausa children. *Ethos*, **3**, 209–230.

Sodian, B. (1991). The development of deception in young children. *British Journal of Developmental Psychology*, **9**, 173–188.

Sodian, B., Taylor, C., Harris, P. L. & Perner, J. (in press). Early deception and the child's theory of mind: False trails and genuine markers. *Child Development*.

Stern, D. (1985). *The Interpersonal World of the Infant*. New York: Basic Books.

Stich, S. (1983). *From Folk Psychology to Cognitive Science*. Cambridge, MA: Bradford Books/MIT Press.

Stone, L. (1979). *The Family, Sex and Marriage in England, 1500–1800*. Harmondsworth, Middx: Penguin.

Taylor, M. (1988). The development of children's understanding of the seeing–knowing distinction. In J. W. Astington, P. L. Harris & D. R. Olson (Eds), *Developing Theories of Mind*, pp. 207–225. New York: Cambridge University Press.

Trevarthen, C. (1980). The foundations of intersubjectivity: Development of interpersonal and cooperative understanding. In D. R. Olson (Ed.), *The Social Foundations of Language and Thought*, pp. 316–342. New York: Norton.

Wellman, H. M. (1979). A child's theory of mind. Paper presented at the conference The Growth of Insight in the Child, Madison, WI. (Published as Wellman, 1985.)

Wellman, H. M. (1985). The child's theory of mind: The development of conceptions of cognition. In S. R. Yussen (Ed.), *The Growth of Reflection in Children*, pp. 169–206. San Diego, CA: Academic Press.

Wellman, H. M. (1988). First steps in the child's theorizing about the mind. In J. W. Astington, P. L. Harris & D. R. Olson (Eds), *Developing Theories of Mind*, pp. 64–92. New York: Cambridge University Press.

Wellman, H. M. (1990). *The Child's Theory of Mind*. Cambridge MA: Bradford/MIT Press.

Wellman, H. M. & Bartsch, K. (1988). Young children's reasoning about beliefs. *Cognition*, **30**, 239–277.

Wellman, H. M. & Bartsch, K. (1989). Three-year-olds understand belief: A reply to Perner. *Cognition*, **33**, 321–326.

Wellman, H. M. & Estes, D. (1986). Early understanding of mental entities: A reexamination of childhood realism. *Child Development*, **57**, 910–923.

Wellman, H. M. & Gelman, S. A. (1988). Children's understanding of the non-obvious. In R. Sternberg (Ed.), *Advances in the Psychology of Intelligence*, pp. 99–135. Hillsdale, NJ: Erlbaum.

Wellman, H. & Woolley, J. (1990). From simple desires to ordinary beliefs: The early development of everyday psychology. *Cognition*, **35**, 245–275.

Whiten, A. (Ed.). (in press). *Natural Theories of Mind: Evolution, Development and Simulation of Everyday Mindreading*. Oxford: Basil Blackwell.

Wilkes, K. V. (1978). *Physicalism*. London: Routledge & Kegan Paul.

Wimmer, H. & Hartl, M. (1991). The Cartesian view and the theory view of mind: Developmental evidence from understanding false belief in self and other. *British Journal of Developmental Psychology*, **9**, 125–138.

Wimmer, H., Hogrefe, J. & Sodian, B. (1988). A second stage in children's conception of mental life: Understanding informational accesses as origins of knowledge and belief. In J. W. Astington, P. L. Harris & D. R. Olson (Eds), *Developing Theories of Mind*, pp. 173–192. New York: Cambridge University Press.

Wimmer, H. & Perner, J. (1983). Beliefs about beliefs: Representation and constraining function of wrong beliefs in young children's understanding of deception. *Cognition*, **13**, 103–128.

Yaniv, I. & Shatz, M. (1988). Children's understanding of perceptibility. In J. W. Astington, P. L. Harris & D. R. Olson (Eds), *Developing Theories of Mind*, pp. 93–108. New York: Cambridge University Press.

Yuill, N. (1984). Young children's coordination of motive and outcome in judgements of satisfaction and morality. *British Journal of Developmental Psychology*, **2**, 73–81.

Zaitchik, D. (1990). When representations conflict with reality: The preschooler's problem with false beliefs and 'false' photographs. *Cognition*, **35**, 41–68.

Zaitchik, D. (in press). Is only seeing really believing? Sources of true belief in the false belief task. *Cognitive Development*.

Received 1 March 1990; revised version received 7 December 1990

British Journal of Developmental Psychology (1991), **9**, 33–51   *Printed in Great Britain*

Against the theory of 'Theory of Mind'

R. Peter Hobson*

Department of Child and Adolescent Psychiatry, Institute of Psychiatry, London SE5 8AF, UK

The purpose of this paper is to argue against the view that young children develop a 'theory' *that* people have minds, and to suggest reasons why children's concepts of the mind and of mental states are not adequately characterized as 'theoretical' in nature. I propose that what children acquire is knowledge of persons with minds, and that they do so through experience of interpersonal relations. I emphasize that infants' capacity for personal relatedness, the psychological bedrock for their understanding of persons, is partly constituted by innately determined percep-tual–affective sensibilities towards the bodily appearances and behaviour of others. It is likely that children come to make inferences in the course of enriching and systematizing their concepts of mind, but this does not justify the view that 'mental states' are hypothetical constructs.

It has become fashionable for developmentalists to refer to young children's 'theory of mind', to offer suggestions as to how this theory arises, and to describe how it becomes increasingly sophisticated through the early years of life (e.g. Astington, Harris & Olson, 1988; Perner, 1990; Wellman, 1990*a*). I wish to argue that there is something—indeed, a number of things—seriously wrong with the use of these terms to refer to children's developing knowledge of people with their own mental life. Nor is this a mere terminological wrangle, for the terminology here not only embodies a theoretical and philosophical attitude to the subject matter in question, but it also suggests the kinds of developmental achievement we need to explain and which kind of explanation we should be seeking. It follows that any critic of the 'theory of mind' formulation needs to propose and defend an alternative way of framing the problem domain, one that reflects an arguably more adequate intellectual orientation. I suggest that it is more appropriate for psychologists to think in terms of children coming to acquire an understanding of the nature of persons, and acquiring a concept or set of concepts about people's minds. The grounds for my critique are that such understanding of minds amounts to something quite unlike a 'theory', not only in the kind of commitment that children and adults have to a way of conceptualizing the nature of people, but also because of the processes through which children come to acquire and sustain knowledge about their own and others' subjective experiences. Although there are certain respects in which children's concepts of mind are 'theory-like', it is more misleading than helpful to view such understanding as essentially 'theoretical' in nature.

* Requests for reprints.

I shall begin by illustrating the style of thinking that seems to have lain behind and/or to have come to characterize the theory of 'theory of mind', and I hope thereby to clarify what it may mean for psychologists to adopt or support such a theory. My illustrations will be selective, not least because many of those who employ the phrase 'theory of mind' seem to do so with little awareness of the conceptual baggage they may be taking on board. On the other hand, not every writer who adopts this 'theory theory' (Morton, 1980) would espouse each and all of the views I shall be criticizing. In order to avoid caricature, I shall give special attention to the form of the theory that is most compatible with my own contrasting approach, namely the version persuasively advocated by Wellman (1990a). Henceforth I shall employ capital letters in referring to children's supposed Theory of Mind, in order to distinguish this from the theory that such a Theory exists.

It was Premack & Woodruff (1978) who popularized the expression 'theory of mind'. These authors were explicit in justifying their choice of terms, as follows:

> In saying that an individual has a theory of mind, we mean that the individual imputes mental states to himself and to others (either to conspecifics or to other species as well). A system of inferences of this kind is properly viewed as a theory, first, because such states are not directly observable, and second, because the system can be used to make predictions, specifically about the behavior of other organisms (p. 515).

I shall focus on two points from this passage. The first is that the Theory under consideration is one that is supposed to explain or at least to encompass the fact that an individual 'imputes' mental states to himself, to other people and to animals. One might paraphrase this point by saying that individuals have a Theory about the nature of people and animals, namely *that* such creatures have minds. A principal concern of this paper is to examine the claim that the ascription of mental content to organisms entails something like the application of a theory.

The second point has to do with the nature of 'theory', and involves a claim about the epistemological status of the individual's awareness of the existence and nature of minds. Premack & Woodruff suggest that we are dealing with a 'system of inferences'. It is supposed that the individual is not in a position to observe mental states directly, so that the very existence of such states, not merely the identification of particular states in given circumstances, has to be 'inferred'. If this were correct, it would constitute adequate grounds for believing that people entertain a Theory about the existence of such states. The reasoning here may be illustrated by Hempel's (1958) reference to the distinction between two levels of scientific discourse: the level of empirical generalization concerning connections among the directly observable aspects of the subject matter under study, and the level of theory formation on which hypothetical entities account for the uniformities established on the first level and serve the purposes of systematization. As Braithwaite (1960) summarized the position, 'most philosophers of science would wish to ascribe a status to theoretical concepts different from that of directly observable things and qualities. They would maintain that the status of theoretical concepts is given by the role which these play in scientific systems' (p. 987). So it is that Premack & Woodruff take 'mental states' to be systematized theoretical constructs which are posited in order to explain and predict observable behaviour.

The theoretical position articulated by Premack & Woodruff (1978) is one that is widely shared. For example, Wellman (1990*b*) offers this pithy formulation of the common-sense view: 'Mental entities are internal, subjective, nonreal, and hypothetical whereas physical entities are real, external, substantial, and objective' (p. 2, pre-published manuscript). Or again, Olson, Astington & Harris (1988) not only stress how the 'theoretical concepts' of belief, desire, intention and feeling serve to explain and predict action, but they also state that if the Theory of Mind 'provides the best explanation and prediction of the events in the referential domain, the entities specified by the theoretical terms may be treated as real entities' (p. 3). The epistemological implications are clear: mental states are to be 'treated as real' only if the Theory of Mind works.

Concerning theory

If children are said to have a Theory of Mind, we need to press the question—a Theory, as opposed to what? This is tantamount to asking what a theory is. The question is difficult to answer in the abstract, for the reason that there are different kinds of theory which are entertained with varying degrees of conviction on a variety of grounds. I shall focus on selected contrasts between theory and perception on the one hand, and theory and knowledge on the other.

The distinction between a person having a theory about something, and a person perceiving something, is usually clear. The way in which one holds to a particular theory of evolution is obviously different from the way in which one perceives an apple. The picture becomes more complicated once one appreciates that much of perception is concept dependent (e.g. Hamlyn, 1981). In order to perceive an apple *as* an apple, for example, one needs both to understand what it is for something to be an apple, and to be correct in applying this concept to this particular object. A variety of experiences and indeed a range of concepts will have contributed to one's concept of apples, so that one might wish to claim that we only have a 'theory' about the existence and nature of apples(!). Aside from this issue, there arises the problem of circularity in accounting for the origins of concepts and percepts. If percepts are concept dependent, then how can concepts arise through perceptual experience? A way through the impasse may be to recognize, firstly, that even if certain forms of perception presuppose concepts, this is not to say that the requisite concepts arise *prior* to the percepts—they might both develop together—and secondly, that knowledge admits of degrees (Hamlyn, 1978). Thus a very young child might have either a minimal concept of what an apple is (e.g. that it is solid and edible), and/or a primitive *form* of sensorimotor 'concept-in-action', or what might be called a protoconcept (Woodfield, 1987). As Murphy & Medin (1985, pp. 310–311) observe: 'One might argue that children form their first concepts through perceptual similarity; then, as they learn more about the world, they incorporate knowledge into their concepts, where it has increasing importance . . . these biases and preconceptions may be biologically determined to some extent through perceptual and cognitive structures'. This being so, we need an account of what protoconcepts amount to, and of how they are anchored in early forms of perception.

The work of J. J. Gibson (1979) has given fresh impetus to theoretical perspectives positing the existence of basic 'meaning-sensitive' perceptual faculties.

According to Gibson, meanings in the form of 'affordances' are what the infant begins by noticing. For instance, 'the other animals of the environment afford, above all, a rich and complex set of interactions, sexual, predatory, nurturing, fighting, play, cooperating, and communicating' (Gibson, 1977, p. 68). It is clear that the organism might need to have sexual inclinations in order to perceive others *as* 'sexual', propensities to flee and to feel threatened in order to perceive others *as* 'predatory', and so on. I believe that two points are critical here. Firstly, organisms have innately constituted propensities to perceive the world in such a way as to engage their own tendencies to action and feeling. This is hardly surprising, given that perception has evolved in order to promote survival. Most animals' capacities to 'predict' each other's behaviour draw heavily upon such mechanisms. Secondly, we as observers may define a sense in which an organism perceives an object or event 'as' a this or a that (e.g. *as* a predator), even if the organism itself is merely reacting in an instinctive–mechanistic way. To offer such a definition is simply to indicate what kind of organism–environment relation this kind of 'perception' entails; it is *not* to suggest the organism recognizes itself to be 'seeing-as'. Werner (1948) tried to distil something of all this in his concept of physiognomic perception, pointing out how an infant's affective and conative attitudes are critical in shaping early modes of perception; or in the terms of Murphy & Medin (1985), biologically determined 'biases and preconceptions' may determine the earliest modes of categorization. The crux is that perceptual capacities need to be understood with reference to action and feeling tendencies that establish the relations between organism and environment. Perception is relational. All this may, indeed must, apply at a pre-theoretical level amongst most animals and during human infancy.

If we now come to consider how and when children acquire 'theoretical' concepts, a preliminary task is to establish the conditions that must apply if people are to hold a theory. When theorists derive hypothetical terms and 'entertain' a theory, they critically review how far the available evidence supports or refutes their position, and anticipate that in the light of new evidence they may have to modify or abandon the theory in favour of an alternative view of the way things are. It would seem that an individual theorist needs to formulate possibilities *as* possibilities in order to entertain and appraise alternative constructions of reality in this way. It is relevant to note that theory is 'used' by a person rather than operated by mechanisms at a subpersonal level. This implies that in order to have and apply a theory, an individual must know what it is to theorize, and for this he or she must *already* have a concept of his or her own theory-holding mind. In order to avoid an infinite regress, therefore, we should have to acknowledge that a person needs to begin by acquiring a concept of mind on some 'non-theoretical' basis.

The contrasting position would be to claim that *we* might ascribe to an organism a theory on one occasion and perception or indeed knowledge on another occasion, even if the organism itself could not differentiate amongst these conditions. The issue is whether this seriously distorts the meaning of 'theory', and especially whether it does so in psychologically relevant respects. For example, Wellman (1990*a*) argues the case that there is a level of theory—what he calls 'global theory', akin to Kuhn's (1962) notion of a paradigm—that can exist as an 'entity' but that is not generated by 'theorizing' nor amenable to empirical test, that may or may not involve an attempt to establish what is 'real', and that provides a framework both for more specific theories and for knowledge. He further suggests that Theory of Mind is a 'global theory' of this kind. But is it really appropriate to maintain that we are dealing with a 'theory' level and mode of conceptual organization, when this precludes so much of what is normally involved in 'theorizing'? There is an obvious danger that we might confound a special sense of 'theory' with the everyday meaning of 'theory'. Wellman (1988, 1990a) emphasizes that 'global theories' manifest coherence, they rest upon specific ontological distinctions or commitments (they specify the things and processes to which they refer), and they provide a causal–explanatory framework. But suppose a particular 'global theory' drew upon non-theory-like sources of conceptual coherence and ontological distinctions entailed an individual in conceptual commitment that were more like those entailed by perception or knowledge than theory, and reflected non-theoretical modes of perceptual and/or conceptual understanding—would *this* kind of framework for 'specific theories' and/or for knowledge still count as a theory? In such a situation, there would seem to be good reason to reject the notion of 'theory' and instead to analyse the system of understanding in terms of appropriate kinds of perception and/or knowledge.

What, then, of the contrast between theory and knowledge? Like others who have emphasized the role of theory in providing the background to a person's concept of the mind (or indeed to concepts of other kinds), Wellman has not been overly concerned with the distinction between theory and knowledge. It appears that, quite appropriately, Wellman is more interested in developing the kind of proposal made by Murphy & Medin (1985), whereby 'concepts are coherent to the extent that they fit people's background knowledge *or* naive theories about the world' (Murphy & Medin, 1985, p. 289, my italics). Theory and knowledge are alike insofar as they provide underlying principles for conceptual organization. On the other hand, our firm commitment to that which we know entails an attitude that is fitting for the acknowledgement of what is true (Hamlyn, 1990). We do not insist that a theory is 'true'. If we take an instrumentalist stance toward theory construction, we do not even have to suppose that the terms of the theory actually refer to real things and processes—all we require is that the theory is successful in making predictions. This is the spirit in which Dennett (1981) adopts the intentional stance towards psychological explanation. Philosophers such as Churchland (1984) and Stich (1983) would go even further: not only are our everyday concepts of mind inadequate as a starting-point for cognitive science, but they might be viewed as theoretical precisely by virtue of being candidates for radical revision—and thus emphatically not knowledge.

I shall make one final point about the relations among perception, theory and knowledge. Premack & Woodruff (1978) suggest that our concepts of mind are 'theoretical' because they are inferred (also Olson *et al.*, 1988). It is possible to adopt the position that *all* knowledge of the 'outside world' is reducible to theory by supposing that a mind-independent reality is only 'inferred' to exist on the basis of potentially misleading evidence provided through our senses. To select one recent example, Strawson (1988) has taken Ayer (1976) to task for offering just such an account. More precisely, Strawson has criticized Ayer for suggesting that the common-sense view of a really existing external world has the status of a theory with respect to a type of sensible experience which provides data for the theory.

Experience is said to be the source of evidence from which the common-sense view of a really existing external world is 'inferred'. Thus our ordinary perceptual judgements might be said to have the character of interpretations, in the light of theory, of what sensible experience actually presents us with. Strawson has taken issue with all this, and particularly with Ayer's view that our perceptual judgements 'go beyond' sensible experience in embodying or reflecting a certain view of the world, namely that there exists a mind-independent physical reality. The thrust of Strawson's argument is that in order for some belief or set of beliefs to be correctly described as a theory in respect of certain data, it must be possible to describe the data on the basis of which the theory is held in terms which do not presuppose the acceptance of the theory on the part of the observer. The problem is that the character of our sensible experience as we actually enjoy it *is* experience of objects as really existing—our sensible experience itself is thoroughly permeated with concepts of such objects. Thus 'our sensible experience could not have the character it does have unless—at least before philosophical reflection sets in—we unquestioningly *took* that general view of the world to be true' (Strawson, 1988, p. 96). It is not so much that we take a step beyond our sensible experience in making our perceptual judgements, but rather (as Strawson puts it) that we take a step back from our perceptual judgements in framing accounts of our sensible experience. It is because mature sensible experience presents itself as an immediate (not necessarily infallible) consciousness of the existence of things outside us, that the common realist conception of the world does not have the character of a 'theory' in relation to the 'data of sense'. These arguments are relevant for considering what young children's person-related sensible experiences are 'of'. More specifically, they introduce doubt as to whether young children ascribe mental states to others by employing a Theory of Mind to arrive at interpretations of 'non-mental' behavioural data.

Theory of Mind?

I shall now examine how the above considerations find application in the case of an individual's awareness that other people have minds.

The first question is as follows: would we be any more willing to give up our conviction that other people have minds, than we would be to give up our conviction that there exists a world of physically constituted objects? What kind of *evidence* would persuade us, one way or the other, on either of these issues? The answer is, no kind of evidence. Neither adults nor young children have a Theory of Mind, in the sense of a theory that people have minds, any more than they have a Theory of the Existence of Physical Reality. The point is not that it is impossible to introduce doubt, but rather that only a certain, rather forced kind of doubting is involved in either case. As Wittgenstein helpfully insisted: 'Doubting has an end' (Wittgenstein, 1958, p. 180). The attitude embodied in this statement is justified and necessary towards that which we take to be knowledge, but unjustified toward that which we construct as theory. Or to put this another way: '. . . theory is risky. It depends on a delicate balance of conjecture and fact . . .' (Morton, 1980, p. 29). I am suggesting it is a fact *that* people have minds—as much a fact as any fact—and at this basic level 'conjecture' does not enter the picture.

The next question concerns the status of 'mental states'. Are we mistaken in supposing not only that we know that people have minds, but also that we know that we ourselves have beliefs, wishes, feelings and so on? Are mental states to be understood solely in terms of the roles they fulfil in the overall workings of the mind, by their place in the 'system' of mental functioning? A difficulty with this kind of functionalist position has been that it fails to take account of a major factor that contributes to our knowledge of minds, namely the fact that we are conscious and are able to savour the phenomenal qualities of subjective experience ('qualia'), not only 'raw feels' but also secondary qualities such as colour and taste (McGinn, 1983). As Johnson (1988) emphasizes and Wellman (1990*a*) acknowledges, the structure of first-person phenomenological experience provides a 'non-theoretical' aspect to our awareness of the nature of mental life. Is there not something very odd about the suggestion that the concept of a person's feelings is a 'theoretical construct' (Olson *et al.*, 1988; Perner, 1990), or to put this even more strongly, that a person's feelings are 'hypothetical'? Both Olson *et al.* (1988) and Perner (1990) illustrate what a 'theoretical concept' is, by reference to the concept of 'gravity'—and this seems to provide a telling contrast with many mental state concepts. At most, our understanding of minds is only very partially Theoretical in nature (see, e.g., Otto & Tuedio, 1988).

The third question is whether the theory of Theory of Mind stands up to detailed examination. Once again, I start from Premack & Woodruff (1978). These authors stipulate that the Theory of Mind amounts to a 'system of inferences'. Two issues are critical here. The first is whether the role of children's inferences concerning the mind is such as to yield Theoretical understanding. We can acquire knowledge or pursue speculation by making inferences, so it is not the case that any instance of 'inferring' amounts to 'theorizing'. The second issue concerns which *aspects* of mind are supposed to be understood in a Theoretical manner. I shall consider how these issues arise in relation to differing approaches to Theory of Mind.

The first approach is that some form of 'inference' is required if an individual is to ascribe any subjective mental states to others. The most common argument involves an appeal to analogy. One begins with direct experience of one's own feelings, perceptions, and so on; one notes similarities between one's own physical attributes and those of the bodies of others; and by a process of analogy, one infers that the property of having mental states applies to the bodies-as-observed, just as it applies to oneself. For example, Perner (1990) writes: 'The argument is that empathy is based on identifying (an)other's inner state as an emotion they are familiar with from their *own inner experience* of being distressed. Empathic reactions are possible because infants project that familiar state as a *theoretical construct* onto the other person for understanding what goes on in the other . . .' (p. 19 of chapter 5, pre-published manuscript: author's italics). Or again, when Harris (1989) discusses an infant's capacity to 'see other people as creatures who have the potential to adopt an emotional stance—of curiosity, interest or anxiety—towards an object, just as they themselves do', he writes: 'I have argued that this insight does not depend upon a perceptual mechanism but on an ability to simulate or imagine the emotional state of another person by analogy with the state of the self' (p. 214).

The point at issue is whether a mechanism that involves the projecting of a 'theoretical construct' or the drawing of analogy could be the original source of 'understanding what goes on in the other' (Perner), or be the basis for seeing others as having 'the potential to adopt an emotional stance' (Harris). It is *not* in dispute (*a*) that imaginative role taking is important for young children's interpersonal understanding and more sophisticated forms of 'empathy' (e.g. Hoffman, 1984), (*b*) that a child's own subjective experiences contribute to that child's understanding of mental states, and especially the child's awareness of what it is like to have mental states, or (*c*) that some form of 'projection' might be possible even before a child has acquired much understanding of minds, say in infancy (along with many other psychoanalysts, I believe such processes do occur). Rather, the contentious claim is that the primary, 'basic' mode of awareness of others' subjective experiences originates in imaginative leaps from conceptualizations of one's 'own inner experience' to the ascription of similar states in others.

There are a number of problems with this view (e.g. Hobson, 1990*a*; Malcolm, 1962), and I shall merely cite those that are most pertinent for the present discussion. To begin with, the process as described presupposes that one has a 'self' capable of reflecting on one's own experiences, prior to and as a precondition for awareness of other minds. Such a developed sense of self may in fact presuppose awareness of other minds (Hobson, 1990*b*). Whatever the case in this regard, the putative bases for analogy are totally inadequate to account for the conviction with which we (and young children) hold that other people have minds. What I perceive and experience of my own body is almost totally unlike what I perceive and experience of other people's bodies, *if* it is supposed that my experience of my own body is suffused with subjectivity and the bodies of others are initially perceived in a cool, detached, non-personal way. How am I supposed to compare my facial expressions of emotion with the contortions I observe on the faces of other bodies; how do I apprehend such forceful similarity between my actions and what would appear only as movements of other bodies? The 'observed' similarities would have to be forceful indeed to persuade us to 'infer' subjectivity in others, for as Wittgenstein (1958) wrote: 'If one has to imagine someone else's pain on the model of one's own, this is none too easy a thing to do: for I have to imagine the pain which I *do not feel* on the model of pain which I *do feel*' (para 302). The point is that 'my feeling it' would be *the* essential criterion for what a pain is, and whether a pain exists—anywhere.

Then there is the issue of the basis or mechanism for 'ascribing' mental states to others. Insofar as behaviour (whether of the child or others) is supposed merely to provide 'cues' or prompts for such analogical reasoning, the account misrepresents the relation between experience and behaviour. There must be some form of necessary relation between the outward expressions and 'internal' experiences of at least certain mental states, and under at least certain conditions, for the business of identifying and ascribing mental states to get off the ground. Not only this, but such expressions of mental life must be perceived *as* expressive in a more or less 'direct' way. For example, it is mistaken to suppose that one can identify the same mental states or events as they recur in one's own private experiences, without recourse to some form of external confirmation or correction by others (Wittgenstein, 1958). The reason is that one needs to identify particular states, rather than merely treat different states as the same. In order for external confirmation to be possible, there must be public criteria according to which mental states can be judged. Or to put this another way, there must be sufficient regularity amongst people's observable expressions and behaviour and their experiences, for there to occur the agreement amongst judges which is necessary for interpersonal understanding of and communication about mental states to be possible.

A second approach is much less problematic, and probably correct. Cognitive processes akin to those of inference are likely to play a role not in providing the foundations for awareness *that* there are minds, but rather in promoting subsequent development towards a more sophisticated understanding of the representational mind. The significance of understanding 'representational' states such as beliefs and desires is that only through such understanding can someone comprehend how a person (*a*) mentally represents certain aspects of objects or events and, one might say, subsumes them under particular descriptions 'for' the person, (*b*) may have mental states that are directed toward non-existing entities and states of affairs, and (*c*) may misrepresent something as something else (e.g. Perner, 1990). There is no doubt that the 3- or 4-year-old's new-found ability to understand these aspects of people's mental attitudes is a major accomplishment that significantly alters and enriches their concepts of mind. Why, then, should we not suppose that children acquire a Theory that the mind is 'representational'? After all, it is questionable whether a child's (or adult's) notions of belief amount to knowledge, since some features of those notions—for instance, that beliefs are discrete and 'atomistic'—are simply false. And does not such a Theory amount to a 'system of inferences'?

My response here is to acknowledge that one might choose to emphasize those aspects of this understanding that are Theory-like, and Wellman (1990*a*) does so to good effect. On the other hand, the notion of Theory brings with it meanings that are distinctly *in*appropriate for characterizing the way a child understands and interprets the minds of others. In particular, we might easily be led to underestimate the degree to which a child *perceives* and *knows about* 'other minds'. Thus Wellman (1990*a*) writes: 'In part mental states cannot be simple empirical generalizations because there are no set of observable activities that consistently correlates with inferred mental states, no actions inevitably connected to having a belief or being possessed by a desire' (p. 3 of chapter 4 pre-published manuscript). This is perfectly true. In part, mental states may need to be 'inferred'. This means more than that, on certain occasions, inferences of various kinds (including those involved in role taking) will be necessary to evaluate others' mental states. Rather, the very nature of certain (relatively) unobservable mental states, most obviously but not exclusively those akin to beliefs, probably have to be deduced from prior understandings of those mental states that do have sufficiently regular observable expressions. It is not the case that mental states *per se* are unobservable— just that some are more observable than others. For example, Perner (1990) may be incorrect in stating that a person's state of distress or sadness 'is not directly observable' (p. 11 of chapter 6, pre-published manuscript). In my view, moreover, it is both arbitrary and unjustified to suppose that as children cross the threshold from 'observation' and begin to apply inferences, earlier forms of understanding the mind are superceded or transcended in such a way as to render the new mode of understanding essentially Theoretical in nature. Indeed, Wellman not only offers important suggestions about the way in which a 3-year-old's understanding of beliefs might be constructed out of (and partly inferred from) the 2-year-old's understanding of desires as internal causal states, but he also considers how desire psychology might in its turn come from an understanding of others as agents (also Poulin-Dubois & Shultz, 1988). Why might not 'inference' play a role in this earlier transition, too? I see no reason why inference-like reasoning about minds should not begin even before a child's first birthday, given that already by this age an infant recognizes other persons *as* persons with whom experiences of objects and events can be shared (Bretherton, McNew & Beeghly-Smith, 1981; Hubley & Trevarthen, 1978). Where, then, should one draw the line between what is Theoretical and what is pre-Theoretical? How far back should one go?

Perner (1990) appears to circumvent the problem by going back almost the whole way. He supposes that around 4 years of age, children simply exchange one Theory for another as they move from a Theory of Behaviour to a (representational) Theory of Mind. However, this manoeuvre leaves Perner open to the criticism that he is calling a very great deal of very young children's understanding Theoretical—and indeed he seems to view knowledge about the permanence of objects as a theory on the grounds that such a property is inferred (p. 18 of chapter 5). This surely detracts from the argument that we should view belief–desire psychology as a Theory because of the way in which it contrasts with basic knowledge of the physical world—and if it does not so contrast, why not call it knowledge?

The next problem is that too restrictive a concern with beliefs, desires, intentions and so on might lead us to formulate our understanding of what constitutes the mental according to the characteristics of these propositional mental states. For example, Wellman (1990*b*) sometimes refers to 'mental states' *en bloc* as 'hypothetical'. Olson *et al.* (1988) group 'feelings' along with beliefs, desires and intentions as the 'theoretical concepts' that comprise Theory of Mind, and Perner (1990) refers to the child 'imputing a state of distress as a hypothetical construct to the other person' (p. 11 of chapter 6). Thus the danger is that all mental state concepts, and/or all aspects of mental states, may be treated as equally Theoretical in nature, when in fact there is considerable diversity both in the nature of mental states and in the ways in which such states come to be understood. Mental states vary widely in their phenomenological attributes, for example. In addition, one might be led to suppose that an understanding of intentionality begins with and originates in an understanding of mental states such as beliefs and desires. I shall argue that this latter view is mistaken.

The implications of introducing radical developmental disjunctions between children's perception of bodies and their Theory of Mind, and between their understanding of non-propositional *vis-à-vis* propositional mental states, may be highlighted through the following quotation from Wellman (1990*a*): 'If no neutral observational data dictate the inferences of mental states, where do these inferences come from? Some intervening conceptual filter stands between observation of behavior and inference of mind, a theoretical lens that organizes the latter out of, or imposes it onto, the former' (p. 3 of chapter 4). Wellman's prime concern is again with beliefs and desires—but if there are other aspects of mind that are observable, then neither the existence of 'mind' *per se*, nor the 'imposition' of mind on to behavior, need operate via Theory. The critical mistake is to begin by positing or overemphasizing essentially non-observable and hypothetical entities, and to suppose that people perceive 'behaviour' and then ascribe mental states (in fact Wellman's view is not clear-cut in this regard). An alternative approach is to consider how very young children perceive certain mental states *in* behaviour, and subsequently (partly by inference) abstract out particular qualities of 'observed' mental attitudes to arrive at knowledge about the nature of subjective experience and about propositional states of mind. Shortly I shall complement the account of these earliest developments proposed by Wellman (1990*a*) and Poulin-Dubois & Shultz (1988), by examining additional sources of an infant's understanding of the subjectivity and intentionality inherent in people's minds.

A further problem with (some would say, advantage of) the theory of Theory of Mind is that it lends itself to a certain style of thinking about human beings and human development. The child-Theorist is often portrayed as an essentially isolated and almost exclusively 'cognitive' being, one in relation to whom it seems natural to adopt the approach of 'methodological solipsism' (Fodor, 1980) and to apply the 'computational metaphor'. This brings me to a further version of the Theory of Mind, Leslie's (1987) 'cognitivist' model for the 'specific innate basis of our commonsense "theory of mind"' (p. 412). Leslie's account pivots around the idea that mental state expressions are akin to pretence in that they depend on a child's capacity to 'decouple' veridical primary representations of the world, and so create representations of those representations which have novel properties. For instance, an individual might pretend that a block of wood 'can' make noises like a car just as one might believe something that is untrue, where neither pretending nor believing entails that the states of affairs pretended or believed actually hold true. Thus Leslie suggests that young children's abilities to pretend and to recognize the nature of mental states in themselves and others depend on an innately derived, cognitive 'metarepresentational' capacity.

I take it that according to such an account, one might not need to 'infer' the existence or nature of other people's minds, for the simple reason that certain critical aspects of one's Theory of Mind are innate (Fodor, 1987). The problem is, how does a child recognize that a species of metarepresented 'representations' amount to mental states, moreover mental states which belong to subjects of experience? Leslie (1987) finds it 'hard to see how perceptual evidence could ever force an adult, let alone a young child, to invent the idea of unobservable mental states' (p. 422). One of several difficulties for Leslie's theory (see also Hobson, 1990*c*) is how to account for those aspects of mental states that are *observable*—how does a child recognize the relation between other people's representations and their actions and expressions? Or to turn this around and place it in a developmental context, how does a child come to individuate its own and others' mental states, if it is not the case that at least some mental states are anchored in observables? In addition, many mental states not only have representational characteristics, they are also subjectively experienced. How do children become aware that others' representations are often (not always) associated with a phenomenology, and come to appreciate that it is appropriate and necessary to consider 'what it is like' to be another person (Nagel, 1979)? If one posits a primary, non-derived and essentially 'cognitive' representational (or in this case, meta-representational) capacity, then one faces thorny problems in trying to link up the representations not only with subjective aspects of mental life, but also with an outside world which includes bodies and the behaviour of bodily endowed persons — or more generally, to render meaningful whatever is supposed to pass 'in and out of the black box' of the computational mind (Hamlyn, 1990).

An alternative approach

I shall provide only a skeletal outline of an alternative to the theory of Theory of Mind (see also de Gelder, 1990; Reddy, 1990; Russell, 1984, for discussions of complementary issues). The central thesis is that children arrive at knowledge about the nature of persons, i.e. people with bodies and minds, through experience of affectively charged interpersonal relations. There are biological foundations for such relations in innate propensities to 'perceive' and relate towards the bodies of others with coordinated patterns of action and feeling. Insofar as such innate influences find expression in 'representational' capacities, the most important of these for the present context are those concerned with interpersonal relations *per se*, rather than any that are exclusively cognitive in form or content (Hobson, 1990*d*; Stern, 1985).

Although it is somewhat archaic to speak in terms of a child's concept or knowledge of 'persons', there are important reasons and precedents for doing so. A principal reason is that a child's understanding of persons arises in the context of interpersonal relations. The significant precedents are to be found in the works of a variety of philosophers (e.g. Strawson's 'Persons,' 1962, Macmurray's *Persons in Relation*, 1961, and Hamlyn's 'Person-perception and our understanding others', 1974). I shall begin by considering such philosophical perspectives on our understanding of persons.

Strawson expresses the nub of the matter thus: 'What we have to acknowledge . . . is the *primitiveness* of the concept of a person. What I mean by the concept of a person is the concept of a type of entity such that *both* predicates ascribing states of consciousness *and* predicates ascribing corporeal characteristics, a physical situation, etc. are equally applicable to a single individual of that single type. . . . The concept of a person is logically prior to that of an individual consciousness. The concept of a person is not to be analysed as that of an animated body or of an embodied anima' (Strawson, 1962, pp. 135–137). How, then, does a child arrive at such a concept? How does one individual apprehend another as a person who has both bodily and mental characteristics? Two quotations from Wittgenstein provide the answer. Firstly: '"We *see* emotion". —As opposed to what?—We do not see facial contortions and *make the inference* that he is feeling joy, grief, boredom. We describe a face immediately as sad, radiant, bored, even when we are unable to give any other description of the features' (Wittgenstein, 1980, para 570). This quotation echoes the point that Strawson (1988) made about our way of perceiving the external physical world: the perception of a person's emotion is primary, and does not involve us in taking a step beyond our sensible experience. This is important not only for our view of how children acquire concepts of mind, but also for appreciating how it is that children apply those concepts to appropriate kinds of 'thing' (especially but not exclusively, persons). Secondly: 'My attitude towards him is an attitude towards a soul. I am not of the *opinion* that he has a soul. . . . The human body is the best picture of the human soul' (Wittgenstein, 1958, p. 178). The nature of our perception of bodies, the attitudes and feelings and tendencies to action that contribute to its being perception of *this* kind, are essential to our understanding of persons with subjective mental life. We do not first perceive non-personal bodies, and impute mental states only at a relatively late stage of development: *a fortiori*, we do not 'infer' that others have mental states (also Johnson, 1988). Certain body–mental states *are* observable, and certain 'personal meanings' are apprehended directly (also Merleau-Ponty, 1964; Scheler, 1954). It is as true that persons have (intentional, experiencing) minds as that they have bodies, and the preconditions for coming to know that this is the case include innate capacities for perceptually anchored personal relatedness.

This is not the end of the matter, of course. A child's concepts of mental states, along with his or her concepts of persons who have such states, undergo development. What the present perspective introduces is the idea that we should begin by recognizing innate person-related (and often affect-related) meaning-sensitive faculties, and primitive forms of interpersonal sharing (Hobson, 1989*a*), and from this starting-point trace how 'self' and 'other' are increasingly differentiated from the primary interpersonal matrix (Werner & Kaplan, 1963). There is indeed growing evidence that even in the early months of life, infants may respond with coordinated feelings to expressions of feeling in others (e.g. Cohn & Tronick, 1983; Haviland & Lelwica, 1987), and that they can soon recognize the correspondence in meaning across facial and vocal expressions of given affects (Walker, 1982). According to the present account, it is unproblematic to recognize that there are public, behavioural criteria for at least some supposedly (but in fact, only potentially) 'private' experiences, in that such body–mind connectedness is posited as a prerequisite for further development in interpersonal understanding. For example, it is only because of such criteria that adults can play their role in enabling young children to conceptualize those mental states (e.g. certain emotions) that are recognized early in life. There are two reasons why this is so. Firstly, in order for adults to teach children what psychological concepts mean, they need to be able to identify mental states, perhaps especially the children's own mental states, according to behavioural–expressive criteria. Secondly, the children need to be able to learn from adults. It is at first through infants' perception of other people's bodily expressiveness, and through accompanying reciprocal interpersonal engagement with others, that they come to discern that other people are sources of mental attitudes, including attitudes towards themselves. Moreover, the nature of person perception is such that the children are naturally involved in having certain attitudes towards the attitudes of others (*vide* the final quote from Wittgenstein, above). In this way the preconditions for children having 'respect' for correction and truth, and specifically for acquiring knowledge of their own and others' minds, are satisfied (Hamlyn, 1982). Such knowledge entails agreement among judges about what is truly the case.

Crudely expressed, therefore, my suggestion is that direct perception of bodily anchored 'personal life', and with this the experience of personal relatedness, is the source of an infant's developing awareness of persons and the grounding for the young child's socially endorsed knowledge of minds. The crux is that it is only through the experience of personal relations, that children can come to acquire a concept of persons with minds. In this context, the biologically determined 'biases and preconceptions' (Murphy & Medin, 1985) are those that promote and reflect personal relatedness, and it is through such relatedness that an infant establishes the basic ontological distinction between persons and things. At no point during these early developments does anything like the use of a 'theory' enter the picture. When in an otherwise excellent account, Bretherton *et al.* (1981) refer to very young children's 'implicit' theory of mind (p. 356), it seems they are allowing the tail to wag the dog. True, the knowledge of minds that 3- or 4-year-olds acquire is, like all knowledge, somewhat theory-like, but this in no way justifies the ambiguous suggestion that a theory is implicit in the communication of non-language-using 9–12-month-olds, nor that by the end of their second year children have progressed to 'an *explicit, verbally expressible* theory of mind' (p. 356, authors' italics). What they actually have is an early and largely non-theory-like understanding of the nature of persons with their own subjective orientations towards the world.

I shall now be more specific in my treatment of certain issues that were raised earlier. I suggest that far from reflective self-awareness preceding the ascription of mental states, it is rather that some form of awareness of other minds is a precondition for acquiring reflective self-awareness. The reason is that in order to adopt a psychological orientation towards one's own mental states, one needs to appreciate that there *are* alternative vantage points that one can assume towards a mind-endowed self, and for this the experience of psychological 'co-orientation' with others may be necessary (Hobson, 1990*b*). This thesis has affinity with the views of Mead (1934) and Vygotsky (1962). The importance for the present discussion is that the acquisition of a concept of self will have implications for a child's developing concepts of mind. Only now can imaginative role taking begin. Far from the individual applying analogy in order to infer that others have minds, it is only once the child has already become aware that people have minds, that he or she can apply analogy. In order to conceptualize and explore its own mind and to recognize the appropriateness of putting itself 'in others' shoes', the child needs to have reached a position to reflect on itself as a 'self' who has a status in common with other persons conceived to be 'selves'. It is probably from some time around the beginning of the second year of life that a child can and does apply analogy 'from its own case' in order to infer or understand the experiences of others, and to empathize in *this* way—but only people (or animals) already conceived to have minds are so like oneself that they become fitting recipients for analogy (Hamlyn, 1974).

It remains to explain how children come to appreciate what has been called the intentional quality of mental states, that is, to recognize that at least in some senses, mental states are 'about' objects that have formal rather than physical existence; a 'something' that is loved or believed may not even exist (Brentano, 1874/1973). Then there is the matter of explaining how a child derives the idea of unobservable mental states, given that mental states are often covert. These facts about the mind do not preclude the possibility that children first become aware of those mental states in others that (*a*) are observable, and (*b*) find bodily expression in physical actions that are perceived to have directedness to the outside world. That is, the observable directedness of behaviour might complement the observed 'expressiveness' of bodies in providing a child with pointers towards the directed quality of mental states, and at the same time towards the mind's meaning-conferring rather than reality-reflecting characteristics. Perner (1990) emphasizes that 'what gives the mind *intentionality* is not its being directed at objects or scenes in the outer world but its ability to make "intentional inexistence" of objects possible' (p. 12 of chapter 6). Surely, both these aspects of the intentionality of mind are important—and it might very well be the case that children's understanding of 'the representational mind' is acquired by way of earlier understanding that people have differing subjective orientations and attitudes towards given objects and events perceived to be 'out there' in a world that is both fixed and shared.

Consider the situation involved when a 1-year-old engages in 'social referencing' (Feinman, 1982; Klinnert, Campos, Sorce, Emde & Svejda, 1983). A child who encounters a visual cliff finds it mildly anxiety provoking, and looks to its mother's face; on finding mother watching the scene happily, the child appears to become less anxious and proceeds across the cliff (Sorce, Emde, Campos & Klinnert, 1985). The directedness of the mother's gaze can make a critical difference in such contexts. As Sorce & Emde (1981) have illustrated, mother's presence is not enough: her emotional orientation, as perceived through her expressions and physical orientation, can have a decisive influence on her infant's behaviour in settings of this kind. If facial expressions are recognized to be 'expressive' even at this early age, therefore, and if the attitudes so expressed are perceived to have directedness, then situations involving social referencing afford an infant the possibility of discovering that a given, commonly perceived situation has meaning-for-self and meaning-for-other (I am not arguing that this necessarily happens as soon as social referencing begins, not least because the child also requires an adequate concept of self). A given object or event may be understood to have different 'descriptions' for different people, albeit (and this is important) descriptions which at first refer to the object or event 'as' the very same object or event (also Flavell, 1988).

I believe that this discovery is intimately linked with the infant's dawning awareness of the fact that people can 'see-as', even though at this early stage the kind of 'seeing' in question reflects people's affective-conative attitudes, e.g. 'I am seeing this as a frightening situation, she sees it as OK' (see also Reddy, 1990, for a delightful account of teasing by infants). To cut a long story very short, more sophisticated understanding of the varieties of 'seeing-as', 'construing-as', 'believing-that' and so on can follow as and when a child achieves a more differentiated grasp of mind-to-world mental relations (see, for example, Flavell, 1988; Forguson & Gopnik, 1988). Once a child has acquired a grasp of body-anchored and 'outer-directed' subjectively experienced mental states on a largely if not exclusively non-inferential basis, then the child *can* employ inferences or other intellectual strategies to learn more about its own and others' minds *vis-à-vis* reality 'as represented' (once again, compare the acquisition of knowledge in other domains). The mind is increasingly recognized to have its own 'objects' which may fall under mind-specific descriptions, or may not exist: the mind is intentional. This is part of what 'subjectivity' means. The developmental transition is from an infant's apprehension of the 'propositionally styled' actions and expressions of others (Hamlyn, 1978), to a more sophisticated grasp of the nature of selves with propositional attitudes *per se*. According to this account, the notion of 'belief' entails a kind of sophisticated distillate of what is already perceived as the 'intentional aspect' of psychologically expressive bodily states and actions. Developmentally, beliefs might be viewed as mental states relatively abstracted from physical expression (they are much else besides, of course, especially in having reference to what is taken to be true). Correspondingly, a condition such as autism which involves a relative inability to understand the notion of belief (e.g. Baron-Cohen, Leslie & Frith, 1985; Baron-Cohen, 1989) might arise through impairment in the perception and understanding of bodily expressed and intersubjectively experienced mental states—especially feelings—through which an understanding of the qualities of intentionality essential to beliefs, and an understanding of 'selves' who hold beliefs, is ultimately acquired (Hobson, 1989*a, b,* 1990*e*).

I wish to conclude by mentioning a final complication to my account. There are aspects of our (and children's) concepts of the mind which take the form neither of Theory nor of knowledge. I have already referred to the (mistaken) notion that beliefs are atomistic, and a further example treated by psychoanalysts and philosophers (see Wollheim, 1969) and apparent to common sense, is that the mind is often conceptualized in terms of spatial metaphors—beliefs are thought of as entities 'in' the mind, one can 'release' feelings, and so on. It is clear that a full account of the development of *conceptions* of the mind will need to reach beneath the surface of belief–desire psychology. Here a quotation from Gilbert Ryle serves to bring us full circle:

> The combination of the two assumptions that theorizing is the primary activity of minds and that theorizing is intrinsically a private, silent, or internal operation remains one of the main supports of the dogma of the ghost in the machine. People tend to identify their minds with the 'place' where they conduct their secret thoughts. They even come to suppose that there is a special mystery about how we publish our thoughts instead of realizing that we employ a special artifice to keep them to ourselves (Ryle, 1949, p. 28).

Theorizing is not the primary source of children's knowledge about minds, nor are minds first understood by children as especially private, 'theorizing' minds—they are the minds of people who are perceived and felt to act and feel, as well as turning out to be the minds of people who think and believe. As Ryle's comments might suggest, the developmental progression is from an infant's perception and growing understanding of the public, psychologically expressive behaviour and attitudes of persons, to a young child's more sophisticated knowledge of the nature of persons and their potentially but only partially undisclosed minds.

Conclusion

I have presented arguments to suggest that young children do not acquire a Theory that other people have minds. I have also suggested why it is important to clarify which forms of understanding of persons with minds they do acquire, not least in order that we might properly discern the processes through which they achieve such understanding. I have suggested that children come to know that people have minds, and that such a knowledge is acquired through experience of personal relations. I have also indicated something of the way that personal relations are rooted in biologically based capacities for 'personal relatedness', and especially in innate perceptual–affective propensities and other determinants of patterned interpersonal and intersubjective coordination. To return to Hempel's (1958) formulation on the nature of theory, the *non*-theoretical level of empirical generalizations that concern 'connections among the directly observable aspects of the subject matter under study' (p. 41) and which *also* 'lend themselves . . . to explanatory, predictive, and postdictive use' (p. 42) is far more important for a child's understanding of mental states, even propositional mental states, than the theory of Theory of Mind would allow. A child's concepts of the mind develop, but even to the extent that one might restrict the focus to belief–desire psychology as a partial conceptual framework for characterizing the nature of people's subjectively experienced, intentionally directed mental states, concepts of mind are only a little Theory-like and a lot un-Theory-like, especially in their developmental origins.

Acknowledgements

This paper was written while I was supported by an MRC Project Grant. My indebtedness to David Hamlyn's writings will be evident from the text; I should also like to thank Professor Hamlyn for his personal help and criticism. I am grateful to James Russell for his detailed criticisms, and to Henry Wellman and Josef Perner for allowing me to read their pre-published writings.

References

Astington, J. W., Harris, P. L. & Olson, D. R. (1988). *Developing Theories of Mind*. Cambridge: Cambridge University Press.

Ayer, A. J. (1976). *The Central Questions of Philosophy*. Harmondsworth, Middlesex: Penguin.

Baron-Cohen, S. (1989). The autistic child's theory of mind: A case of specific developmental delay. *Journal of Child Psychology and Psychiatry*, **30**, 285–297.

Baron-Cohen, S., Leslie, A. M. & Frith, U. (1985). Does the autistic child have a "theory of mind"? *Cognition*, **21**, 37–46.

Braithwaite, R. B. (1960). Explanation. *Encyclopaedia Britannica*, vol. 8, pp. 987–989. Chicago: Encyclopaedia Britannica.

Brentano, F. (1973, originally 1874). *Psychology from an Empirical Standpoint*. (Translated by A. C. Rancurello, D. B. Terrell & L. L. McAlister). London: Routledge & Kegan Paul.

Bretherton, I., McNew, S. & Beeghly-Smith, M. (1981). Early person knowledge as expressed in gestural and verbal communication: When do infants acquire a "Theory of mind?". In M. E. Lamb & L. R. Sherrod (Eds), *Infant Social Cognition: Empirical and Theoretical Considerations*, pp. 333–373. Hillsdale, NJ: Erlbaum.

Churchland, P. M. (1984). *Matter and Consciousness*. Cambridge, MA: MIT/Bradford.

Cohn, J. F. & Tronick, E. Z. (1983). Three-month-old infants' reaction to simulated maternal depression. *Child Development*, **54**, 185–193.

de Gelder, B. (1990). Intentional ascription, autism and troubles with content. In J. Verschueren (Ed.), *Pragmatics at Issue*. Amsterdam/Philadelphia: Benjamins.

Dennett, D. C. (1981). *Brainstorms: Philosophical Essays on Mind and Psychology*. Brighton: Harvester.

Feinman, S. (1982). Social referencing in infancy. *Merrill-Palmer Quarterly*, **28**, 445–470.

Flavell, J. H. (1988). The development of children's knowledge about the mind: From cognitive connections to mental representations. In J. W. Astington, P. Harris & D. R. Olson (Eds), *Developing Theories of Mind*, pp. 244–267. Cambridge: Cambridge University Press.

Fodor, J. A. (1980). Methodological solipsism considered as a research strategy in cognitive psychology. *Behavioral and Brain Sciences*, **3**, 63–73.

Fodor, J. A. (1987). *Psychosemantics*. Cambridge, MA: MIT/Bradford.

Forguson, L. & Gopnik, A. (1988). The ontogeny of common sense. In J. W. Astington, P. L. Harris & D. R. Olson (Eds), *Developing Theories of Mind*, pp. 226–243. Cambridge: Cambridge University Press.

Gibson, J. J. (1977). The theory of affordances. In R. Shaw & J. Bransford (Eds), *Perceiving, Acting and Knowing*, pp. 67–82. Hillsdale, NJ: Erlbaum.

Gibson, J. J. (1979). *The Ecological Approach to Visual Perception*. Boston: Houghton-Mifflin.

Hamlyn, D. W. (1974). Person-perception and our understanding of others. In T. Mischel (Ed.), *Understanding Other Persons*, pp. 1–36. Oxford: Basil Blackwell.

Hamlyn, D. W. (1978). *Experience and Growth of Understanding*. London: Routledge & Kegan Paul.

Hamlyn, D. W. (1981). Cognitive systems, 'folk psychology', and knowledge. *Cognition*, **10**, 115–118.

Hamlyn, D. W. (1982). What exactly is social about the origins of understanding? In G. Butterworth & P. Lights (Eds), *Social Cognition*, pp. 17–31. Brighton: Harvester.

Hamlyn, D. W. (1990). *In and Out of the Black Box*. Oxford: Blackwell.

Harris, P. L. (1989). *Children and Emotion*. Oxford: Blackwell.

Haviland, J. M. & Lelwica, M. (1987). The induced affect response: Ten-week-old infants' responses to three emotion expressions. *Developmental Psychology*, **23**, 97–104.

Hempel, C. G. (1958). The theoretician's dilemma: A study in the logic of theory construction. In H. Feigl, M. Scriven & G. Maxwell (Eds), *Minnesota Studies in the Philosophy of Science*, vol. II: *Concepts, Theories, and the Mind–Body Problem*, pp. 37–98. Minneapolis: University of Minnesota Press.

Hobson, R. P. (1989*a*). On sharing experiences. *Development and Psychopathology*, **1**, 197–203.

Hobson, R. P. (1989*b*). Beyond cognition: A theory of autism. In G. Dawson (Ed.), *Autism: Nature, Diagnosis, and Treatment*, pp. 22–48. New York: Guilford.

Hobson, R. P. (1990*a*). Concerning knowledge of mental states. *British Journal of Medical Psychology*, **63**, 199–213.

Hobson, R. P. (1990*b*). On the origins of self, and the case of autism. *Development and Psychopathology*, **2**, 163–181.

Hobson, R. P. (1990*c*). On acquiring knowledge about people, and the capacity to pretend: Response to Leslie. *Psychological Review*, **97**, 114–121.

Hobson, R. P. (1990*d*). On psychoanalytic approaches to autism. *American Journal of Orthopsychiatry*, **60**, 324–336.

Hobson, R. P. (1990*e*). Social perception in high-level autism. In E. Schopler & G. Mesibov (Eds), *High-functioning Autism*. New York: Plenum.

Hoffman, M. L. (1984). Interaction of affect and cognition in empathy. In C. E. Izard, J. Kagan & R. B. Zajonc (Eds), *Emotions, Cognition, and Behavior*, pp. 103–131. Cambridge: Cambridge University Press.

Johnson, C. N. (1988). Theory of mind and the structure of conscious experience. In J. W. Astington, P. L. Harris & D. R. Olson (Eds), *Developing Theories of Mind*, pp. 47–63. Cambridge: Cambridge University Press.

Klinnert, M. D., Campos, J. J., Sorce, J. F., Emde, R. N. & Svejda, M. (1983). Emotions as behavior regulators: Social referencing in infancy. In R. Plutchik & H. Kellerman (Eds), *Emotion: Theory, Research and Experience.*, vol. 2: *Emotions in Early Development*, pp. 57–86. New York: Academic Press.

Kuhn, T. (1962). *The Structure of Scientific Revolutions*. Chicago: University of Chicago Press.

Leslie, A. M. (1987). Pretense and representation: The origins of "theory of mind". *Psychological Review*, **94**, 412–426.

Macmurray, J. (1961). *Persons in Relation*. London: Faber & Faber.

McGinn, C. (1983). *The Subjective View*. Oxford: Clarendon Press.

Malcolm, N. (1962, originally 1958). Knowledge of other minds. In V. C. Chappell (Ed.), *The Philosophy of Mind*, pp. 151–159. Englewood Cliffs, NJ: Prentice-Hall.

Mead, G. H. (1934). *Mind, Self and Society* (edited by C. W. Morris). Chicago: University of Chicago Press.

Merleau-Ponty, M. (1964). The child's relations with others (translated by W. Cobb). In M. Merleau-Ponty (Ed.), *The Primacy of Perception*, pp. 96–155. USA: Northwestern University Press.

Morton, A. (1980). *Frames of Mind*. Oxford: Clarendon.

Murphy, G. L. & Medin, D. L. (1985). The role of theories in conceptual coherence. *Psychological Review*, **92**, 289–316.

Nagel, T. (1979, originally 1974). What is it like to be a bat? In *Mortal Questions,* pp. 165–180. Cambridge: Cambridge University Press.

Olson, D. R., Astington, J. W. & Harris, P. L. (1988). Introduction. In. J. W. Astington, P. L. Harris & D. R. Olson (Eds), *Developing Theories of Mind,* pp. 1–15. Cambridge: Cambridge University Press.

Otto, H. R. & Tuedio, J. A. (1988). *Perspectives on Mind.* Dordrecht: Reidel.

Perner, J. (1990). Pre-publication manuscript edition of *Understanding the Representational Mind.* Cambridge, MA: MIT/Bradford.

Poulin-Dubois, D. & Shultz, T. R. (1988). The development of the understanding of human behavior: From agency to intentionality. In J. W. Astington, P. L. Harris & D. R. Olson (Eds), *Developing Theories of Mind,* pp. 109–125. Cambridge: Cambridge University Press.

Premack, D. & Woodruff, G. (1978). Does the chimpanzee have a theory of mind? *The Behavioral and Brain Sciences,* **4**, 515–526.

Reddy, V. (1990). Playing with others' expectations: Teasing and mucking about in the first year. In A. Whiten (Ed.), *The Emergence of Mindreading: Evolution, Development and Simulation of Second Order Representations.* Oxford: Basil Blackwell.

Russell, J. (1984). *Explaining Mental Life.* London: Macmillan.

Ryle, G. (1949). *The Concept of Mind.* Harmondsworth, Middx: Penguin.

Scheler, M. (1954). *The Nature of Sympathy.* (Translated by P. Heath). London: Routledge & Kegan Paul.

Sorce, J. F. & Emde, R. N. (1981). Mother's presence is not enough. *Developmental Psychology,* **17**, 737–745.

Sorce, J. F., Emde, R. N., Campos, J. & Klinnert, M. D. (1985). Maternal emotional signaling: Its effect on the visual cliff behavior of 1-year-olds. *Developmental Psychology,* **21**, 195–200.

Stern, D. N. (1985). *The Interpersonal World of the Infant.* New York: Basic Books.

Stich, S. (1983). *From Folk Psychology to Cognitive Science.* Cambridge, MA: Bradford Books.

Strawson, P. F. (1962, originally 1958). Persons. In V. C. Chappell (Ed.), *The Philosophy of Mind,* pp. 127–146. Englewood Cliffs, NJ: Prentice-Hall.

Strawson, P. F. (1988, originally 1979). Perception and its objects. In J. Dancy (Ed.), *Perceptual Knowledge,* pp. 92–112. Oxford: Oxford University Press.

Trevarthen, C. & Hubley, P. (1978). Secondary intersubjectivity: Confidence, confiding and acts of meaning in the first year. In A. Lock (Ed.), *Action, Gesture and Symbol: The Emergence of Language,* pp. 183–229. London: Academic Press.

Vygotsky, L. S. (1962). *Thought and Language.* (Translated by E. Hanfmann & G. Vakar). Cambridge, MA: MIT Press.

Walker, A. S. (1982). Intermodal perception of expressive behaviors by human infants. *Journal of Experimental Child Psychology,* **33**, 514–535.

Wellman, H. M. (1988). First steps in the child's theorizing about the mind. In J. W. Astington, P. L. Harris & D. R. Olson (Eds), *Developing Theories of Mind,* pp. 64–92. Cambridge: Cambridge University Press.

Wellman, H. M. (1990*a*). Early pre-publication manuscript edition of *The Child's Theory of Mind.* Cambridge, MA: MIT/Bradford.

Wellman, H. M. (1990*b*). From desires to beliefs: Acquisition of a theory of mind. In A. Whiten (Ed.), Pre-publication manuscript edition of *The Emergence of Mindreading: Evolution, Development and Simulation of Second Order Representations.* Oxford: Basil Blackwell.

Werner, H. (1948). *Comparative Psychology of Mental Development.* Chicago: Follett.

Werner, H. & Kaplan, B. (1963). *Symbol Formation.* New York: Wiley.

Wittgenstein, L. (1958). *Philosophical Investigations.* (Translated by G. E. M. Anscombe). Oxford: Basil Blackwell.

Wittgenstein, L. (1980). *Remarks on the Philosophy of Psychology,* vol. 2. G. H. von Wright & H. Nyman (Eds). (Translated by C. G. Luckhardt & M. A. E. Aue). Oxford: Basil Blackwell.

Wollheim, R. (1969). The mind and the mind's image of itself. *International Journal of Psycho-Analysis,* **50**, 209–220.

Woodfield, A. (1987). On the very idea of acquiring a concept. In J. Russell (Ed.), *Philosophical Perspectives on Developmental Psychology,* pp. 17–30. London: Routledge & Kegan Paul.

Received 1 March 1990; revised version received 17 October 1990

2
Theory of mind
and perception

Preface

The child's developing knowledge of visual perception is the main theme of this section. How do children understand perception? How do they understand the relation between attending, seeing and knowing? One of the classical questions in developmental psychology, ever since the earliest work by Piaget (1926) on childhood egocentrism, concerns perspective taking or understanding that people can see the world from different points of view. Stated colloquially perspective taking requires one 'to put oneself in another's shoes'. We may distinguish between perceptual perspective taking, which concerns the conditions that allow perception and conceptual perspective taking which requires taking into account another person's state of knowledge. Conceptual perspective taking can include knowledge about perception, although it is not restricted to that domain and both perceptual and conceptual perspective taking may interact (Yaniv & Shatz, 1988).

The first paper by Butterworth & Jarrett is concerned with perceptual perspective taking in babies. How does a baby redirect her own attention in order to look where an adult is looking? It might be supposed that babies would be incapable of joint visual attention, given traditional views on infant egocentrism (see Butterworth, 1987), yet they will redirect their own line of sight to seek out an interesting object, contingent upon a change in the mother's direction of gaze. The authors argue that there is no need to suppose that babies are imputing mental states to others in 'looking where someone else is looking'. Joint visual attention depends on the infant perceiving the adult's expressive movements as signalling a possible object for the infant's attention, located within visual space. This innate mechanism, and its elaboration through developmental changes in space perception, is sufficient to ensure a 'meeting of minds' in the objects of visual experience.

Flavell, Green, Herrera & Flavell report on 3–5-year-old children's knowledge of the conditions that allow visual perception. Babies from approximately one year locate the object of another person's attention by 'geometrically' extrapolating a straight line from the adult to the object but this need not mean that they know that lines of sight are necessarily straight. Flavell *et al.* suggest that it is not until around 5 years of age that children acquire sufficient metacognitive awareness of the conditions for visual experience to be able to reason that visual perception is not possible along curved looking paths.

The third paper illustrates the interaction between conceptual and perceptual perspective taking. Ruffman, Olson & Astington suggest that understanding that visual information can be ambiguous requires the child to make use of the same 'theory of mind' as is demonstrated in 'false belief' tasks. The child must differentiate between her own up-to-date knowledge and another person's incomplete knowledge to be aware when the other is entertaining a false belief. In the case of perceptual ambiguity two different toys of the same or different colour are both partially hidden, so that only identically shaped portions of each toy remain visible. When the salience of the colours is stressed, 4-year-old children (but not 3-year-olds) understand that another observer would only be able to identify a differently coloured pair of animals from the visible information available. The similarity to understanding false belief arises because both tasks require the child to understand what could not be known by another person.

References

Butterworth, G. E. (1987). Some benefits of egocentrism. In J. S. Bruner & H. Haste (Eds), *Making Sense: The Child's Construction of the World,* pp. 62–80. London: Methuen.

Piaget, J. (1926). *The Language and Thought of the Child.* New York: Routledge & Kegan Paul.

Yaniv, I. & Shatz, M. (1988). Children's understanding of perceptibility. In J. Astington, P. L. Harris & D. Olson (Eds), *Developing Theories of Mind,* pp. 93–108. Cambridge: Cambridge University Press.

British Journal of Developmental Psychology (1991), **9**, 55–72 *Printed in Great Britain*

What minds have in common is space: Spatial mechanisms serving joint visual attention in infancy

George Butterworth

Department of Psychology, University of Stirling, Stirling, Scotland FK9 4LA

Nicholas Jarrett

Psychology in Education Service, Borough of Hammersmith and Fulham

A series of experiments is reported which show that three successive mechanisms are involved in the first 18 months of life in 'looking where someone else is looking'. The earliest 'ecological' mechanism enables the infant to detect the direction of the adult's visual gaze within the baby's visual field but the mother's signal alone does not allow the precise localization of the target. Joint attention to the same physical object also depends on the intrinsic, attention-capturing properties of the object in the environment. By about 12 months, we have evidence for presence of a new 'geometric' mechanism. The infant extrapolates from the orientation of the mother's head and eyes, the intersection of the mother's line of sight within a relatively precise zone of the infant's own visual space. A third 'representational' mechanism emerges between 12 and 18 months, with an extension of joint reference to places outside the infant's visual field.

None of these mechanisms require the infant to have a theory that others have minds; rather the perceptual systems of different observers 'meet' in encountering the same objects and events in the world. Such a 'realist' basis for interpersonal knowledge may offer an alternative starting point for development of intrapersonal knowledge, rather than the view that mental events can only be known by construction of a theory.

Developmental theories make different presuppositions about the ability of young children to comprehend their relatedness to people and things. Piagetian theory, for example is premised on the assumption that the infant begins life totally egocentric, and is therefore unable to comprehend the possibility of any viewpoint save his or her own. Yet in the last 25 years our evidence on the perceptual and social competence of very young infants has radically altered the presuppositions we may be entitled to make about the origins of development, especially in their interpersonal aspects.

Adults monitor very closely the focus of the infant's attention and adjust their own

---

* Requests for reprints.

gaze to maintain shared experience. Schaffer (1984) reviewed a number of studies which show that the majority of episodes of joint attention arise as a result of the mother monitoring the infant's line of gaze. Nevertheless, infants are able to adjust their own attention contingent on a change in the adult's line of gaze. Scaife & Bruner (1975) were the first to show that infants as young as 2 months would readjust their gaze contingent on a change in the focus of visual attention of an adult. The capacity for joint attention is a reciprocal phenomenon; the baby may be aware of a spatial objective of the mother's change of gaze. Detailed information on the signalling functions of gaze for human infants may therefore be useful in helping to establish how social experience in the physical world may underpin communication and shared aspects of mental life.

Butterworth & Cochran (1980) confirmed Scaife & Bruner's observations. They found that babies aged between 6 and 18 months adjust their own line of gaze on the basis of changes in the mother's focus of attention. An important discovery was that babies' capacity for joint attention is limited by the boundaries of the visual field. When the mother looked at locations behind the infant, the infant would scan in front, within the infant's own visual field. It is as if the infant experiences its own visual space as held in common with others but fails to comprehend the possibility of a space outside the range of immediate visual experience. If this is the case, then there are important implications for concepts of childhood egocentrism (see Butterworth, 1987). It is noteworthy that a similar inability to search at locations out of view of the infant has recently been demonstrated in a manual search task involving rotation of the infant relative to objects that were first hidden in the field of view (Landau & Spelke, 1988). Thus, the same spatial constraints may be manifest both in social and physical cognition.

This paper reports a series of experiments which aim to establish in greater detail how joint visual attention may operate between infant and adult, i.e. how a baby may know where someone else is looking. The results have implications for the origins of referential communication and may help us to understand how even infants may share the experiences of others.

General methodology of the studies

The studies were carried out under strictly controlled conditions in an undistracting laboratory lined with white linen covered screens measuring 3.95 metres long × 2.6 metres wide by 2.1 metres high. The conditions of the experiments, the apparatus and the physical dimensions of the room were very similar to those reported in Butterworth & Cochran (1980) so the experiments may be taken as an extension of that series. Mother and infant were seated in the centre of the room, facing each other, about 40 centimetres apart with their eyes at approximately the same level. Identical square yellow cardboard targets (20 × 20 cms) mounted on stands at eye level (1.2 metres), were placed at fixed positions relative to the mother and infant. The positions of targets varied depending on the particular experiment. These conditions allow relatively unambiguous conclusions to be drawn concerning how the baby is able to single out the referent of the mother's gaze since distractions and other possible artifacts are eliminated. The mother was instructed to obtain eye contact, to interact naturally with the infant and then, on a signal to turn, in silence and without pointing manually, to inspect for approximately six seconds, a designated member of a set of targets. The particular target was specified by a series of lights on a small box placed beneath the infant's seat, each corresponding to a particular target position. Once the trial was over, the interaction was resumed and a new trial began when the mother had recaptured the infant's attention. Although the laboratory setting and the baby's interaction with the mother is somewhat unnatural, these conditions enable us to gain a high degree of control over the social and environmental factors involved in allowing joint attention. It is unlikely that the results are due to the infant being inexperienced with this type of task. The general developmental sequence is replicated under widely varying conditions in which not only visual coorientation but also comprehension and production of manual pointing by the baby has been studied (see e.g. Grover, 1988 and Butterworth & Franco, 1991). Babies were between 6 and 18 months; the interaction was video-recorded using a split screen system (Sony AV 3670ACE), which yielded a close-up view of the infant's face and a wide angle view of infant and adult. The videotapes were subsequently scored by two independent observers who noted the direction and accuracy of the infant's response relative to the target at the focus of the mother's line of gaze.

Experiment 1

Subjects. Subjects were 54 babies in three age groups comprising: 18 infants whose mean age was 6 months 10 days (SD 5.7 days) range 6 months 3 days to 6 months 20 days; 18 infants mean age 12 months 9 days (SD 7.7 days) range 12 months 0 days to 12 months 27 days; 18 infants mean age 18 months 9 days (SD 6.2 days) range 18 months 1 day to 18 months 20 days. Within each age group equal numbers of males and females were tested. A further 21 infants were excluded because they failed to cooperate (7 at 6 months, 8 at 12 months and 6 at 18 months).

Procedure. The layout of the laboratory is shown in Fig. 1. The targets were presented four at a time, two on each side of the room, each pair separated by 60 degrees of visual angle relative to the infant. That is targets at 150 degrees relative to the infant were paired with targets at 90 degrees (positions 1 and 2 paired with 5 and 6 in the diagram); targets at 120 degrees relative to the infant were paired with targets at 60 degrees (positions 3 and 4 paired with 7 and 8) and targets at 90 degrees were paired with targets at 30 degrees (positions 5 and 6 paired with 9 and 10). The groups of four targets were presented in random order. Within groups, individual targets were designated randomly until the mother had completed one trial at each location. Occasionally, where the mother failed to gain the cooperation of the infant, the experimenter substituted in order to obtain the data. There is no reason to suppose that this influenced the results.

Data scoring. The videotapes were scored by two independent observers. A transparent template was fixed on the television screen on which was drawn lines extending in the direction of the 'virtual' positions of the offscreen targets. The infant's response was scored according to the zone of space that was fixated: correct C; wrong W; no response O. A correct response was defined as looking in the zone of space + or − 30 degrees around the target being fixated by the mother. An incorrect response was defined as looking in the zone of space + or − 30 degrees horizontally in the plane of the target not being fixated by the mother, on the same side of the room.

Generally speaking, infants' responses terminated on the target. However, a number of other infant response categories were also scored: When the wrong target was fixated and then the response was corrected by the infant; infant turning before the mother fixated target; infant looking down; when the infant's scan terminated after target; or the infant's scan terminated before the target; when the infant's scan was to the opposite side of the room. The latency of the response relative to the mother fixating the target was measured and whether the infant made an eye movement only; a head movement only, or made a coupled eye and head movement.

Results

Table 1 summarizes the data for correct and incorrect target fixation and also shows the number of occasions when no response occurred. Of a total of 648 trials, 366 responses were to the correct side of the room, 50 were to the wrong side of the room and 185 trials produced no response or looking down. Inter-rater agreement on scoring of response categories was 93.1 per cent. Since there was little evidence that infants confused the two sides of the room, the data is summarized across sides for targets pairs. Figures 2a, b and c summarize the results graphically in a form that may be easier to follow than Table 1.

The results replicate Butterworth & Cochran (1980); infants tend to pick out a target in front of them when the mother looks at a target behind them. The table shows that infants across all three age groups seldom located the targets at positions outside their own visual field (150 and 120 degree positions). At 6 months the baby was significantly more likely to locate a target on the same side of the room within the visual field than to locate a target behind them. At 12 and 18 months performance was at chance level for locations behind the infant.

The spatial accuracy of responses was assessed by comparing the proportion of correct to correct plus incorrect target fixations. For targets within the infant's visual field (90, 60 and 30 degrees) babies in all three age groups were accurate in locating the target when it was the first one they encountered along the scan path from the

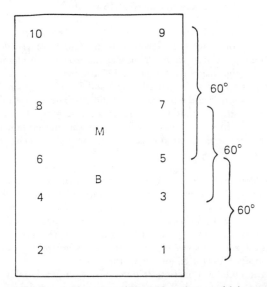

Figure 1. Replication study—visual angles constant. Target locations and laboratory layout; 6, 12 and 18-month infants. Targets were presented in pairs on either side of the infant so that each pair was separated by 60° of visual angle relative to the infant.

Table 1. Infant's first eye/head movement following the visual fixation of the target by the adult.

	Target position														
	visual field (Mother's)						Baby's field			visual field					
	1 and 2 150° 2nd			3 and 4 120° 2nd			5 and 6 90° 1st or 2nd			7 and 8 60° 1st			9 and 10 30° 1st		
Age	6	12	18m	6	12	18m	6	12	18m	6	12	18m	6	12	18m
C	1	6	8				9*	21**	25**	18**	29**	27**	22**	26**	30**
W	8*	15*	17*				2	3	5	1	0	0	1	0	0
N	22	11	9				21	11	5	11	4	8	9	9	6
							(1st on scan path)								
C				2	12	10	7	16*	22**						
W				11**	14	19	9	8	2						
N				19	7	5	12	9	7						
							(2nd on scan path)								

Key. C = eye movement to correct quadrant of the visual field.
W = eye movement to wrong quadrant, correct side of the visual field.
N = no codeable response.
1st = 1st target on infant's scan path from adult.
2nd = 2nd target on infant's scan path from adult.
Proportion of responses C:W *$p < .05$, **$p < .01$ binomial test (tests were independently administered for targets on same side of the room).

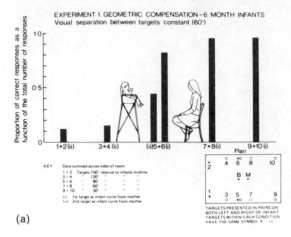

(a)

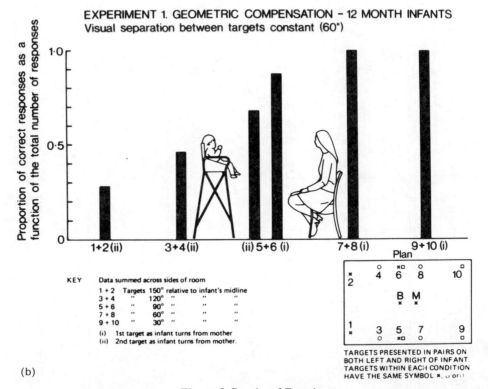

(b)

Figure 2. Results of Expt 1.

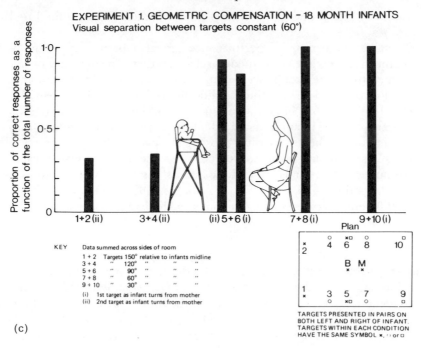

EXPERIMENT 1. GEOMETRIC COMPENSATION – 18 MONTH INFANTS
Visual separation between targets constant (60°)

Proportion of correct responses as a function of the total number of responses

1+2 (ii)　3+4 (ii)　(ii) 5+6 (i)　7+8 (i)　9+10 (i)

Plan

KEY　Data summed across sides of room

1 + 2　Targets 150° relative to infants midline
3 + 4　　"　　120°　"　　"　　"
5 + 6　　"　　90°　"　　"　　"
7 + 8　　"　　60°　"　　"　　"
9 + 10　"　　30°　"　　"　　"

(i)　1st target as infant turns from mother
(ii)　2nd target as infant turns from mother

(c)

```
        o    xo    o         o
   x              4    6    8        10
   2
                      B    M
                      x    x
   1
   x              3    5    7         9
        o    xo    o         o
```

TARGETS PRESENTED IN PAIRS ON
BOTH LEFT AND RIGHT OF INFANT.
TARGETS WITHIN EACH CONDITION
HAVE THE SAME SYMBOL x, ○ or □

mother. However, a critical test of the ability accurately to localize the target occurs at locations 5 and 6 (90 degrees). In one condition these targets were the first to be encountered (when paired with 1 and 2 at 150 degrees). In another condition, targets 5 and 6 were the second to be encountered (when paired with 9 and 10 at 30 degrees). As Table 1 and Figs 2a,b and c show, all three age groups were accurate in locating the target at 5 and 6 when it was the first encountered. However, only the 18-month group reliably localized 5 and 6 when it was second along the scan path. The results for the 12-month group approached significance. The 6-month group was at chance level, i.e. although they accurately perceived the correct *direction* (left or right) in which to look, they could not tell which of the two possible *locations* on the same side of the room the mother was inspecting.

An analysis of variance was performed to establish whether there was a differential probability of a response with age, (this analysis was of infant responses in the correct direction regardless of the accuracy of subsequent target fixation). A significant main effect of age $(F2, 48) = 24.10$, $p < .01$) and of conditions $(F(11, 528) = 2.76)$ and a significant interaction between age and sex $(F(2, 48) = 5.72)$ were found. Scheffé comparisons showed the 18-month infants to be significantly more likely to respond than 6-month babies $(F(1, 48) = 12.67, p < .05)$; females were significantly more likely to respond than males at 12 months $(F(2, 48) = 12.34$ (males p .56, females p .82) but not at 6 or 18 months (average p .42 and .76 respectively). There was an overall effect of conditions, $(F(1, 528) = 5.3, p < .05)$. Planned comparisons showed that infants were significantly more accurate for the positions within the infant's visual field (positions 5 to 10 Fig. 1) than for positions behind the infant (positions 1 to 4) ($F(11$, $528) = 2.76$, $p < .05$).

Other, qualitative aspects of performance are also of interest. Infants fixated intently on the mother while she turned to select a target. The majority of the infants' responses in all three age groups were conjoint movements of the head and eyes, in the correct direction and terminating on a target: (6 months 79 per cent, 12 months 67 per cent, 18 months 69 per cent conjoint eye and head movements). That is, the mother's signal leads the infant to make a definite reorienting movement, they are not simply tracking her as she turns or just moving the eyes in the appropriate direction. The infant's response invariably occurred after the mother was stationary and fixating the target. The mean latency of the infants' responses were: (6 months 1.99 s, SD 1.74; 12 months 1.47 s, SD 1.50; 18 months 1.80 s, SD 1.90). There was no significant difference between the age groups in the latency of response.

Discussion

At 6 months, babies looked to the correct side of the room, as if to see what the mother is looking at, but they could not tell *on the basis of the mother's action alone* which of the two identical targets on the same side of the room the mother was attending to, even with angular separations as large as 60 degrees between the targets. The babies were accurate in locating the object referred to by the mother's change of gaze, when the correct target was first along their path of scanning from the mother to the target, as were the two older groups. However, the 6-month infants were at chance level when the correct target was second along the scan path. Furthermore, infants at all three ages localized targets within their own visual field and hardly ever located targets which the mother looked at in the region behind the baby, out of view.

If the mother looked at a target behind the baby, the infant either fixated a target in front and within the visual field or did not respond. This phenomenon is not caused by any inability of babies to turn; indeed they often would turn behind them on first being seated in the laboratory or in response to some inadvertant noise. In another study we showed that when the visual field is emptied of targets and the mother looked behind the baby, 12-month infants turned through about 40 degrees in the appropriate direction, in their visual field, then they gave up searching (Butterworth & Cochran, 1980). They did not search behind them, even though there was no distraction from targets within the field of view. The most likely explanation is that there is a basic inability to attribute the mother's signal to the space outside the immediate visual field.

Babies had no difficulty in locating the target if it was the first on their scan path from the mother. This suggests that the *direction* in which to look (i.e. to left or to right) was accurately perceived from the mother's signal. Accurate performance at the first target among 6-month infants could therefore be a result of turning in the correct direction with no specification of the spatial location of the target. By 12 months, however, the infants were beginning to localize both the targets correctly, whether first or second along the scan path. Correct search at the second target implies that not only the direction (left or right) but also the location of the target within that visual hemi-field is specified by the mother's signal. It is interesting to note that the infant fixated intently on the mother while she was turning, then when the mother was still, the infant made a rapid eye and head movement to the target. The brief interval after the mother stopped moving may be sufficient for the baby to register information about the angular orientation of the mother's head. This new ability to isolate the referent of the mother's gaze, as plotted from the infant's position, is revealed in a rudimentary way at 12 months and is definitely present by 18 months. This age-related change in the accuracy of joint visual attention led us to carry out further experiments with 6- and 18-month infants.

Experiment 2: Limits of accurate spatial localization at 18 months

This experiment was designed to extend our knowledge of the capabilities of the older infants. Mother and infant were seated in the middle of the room as in Expt 1, except that targets were behind the baby and the part of the room in the baby's visual field was empty, (see Fig. 2). This study is an extension of one reported in Butterworth & Cochran (1980) which showed that 12-month infants failed to search behind them when the visual field was emptied of targets.

Subjects. A new group of 24 infants comprising equal numbers of boys and girls was tested. Their average age was 18 months 11 days (SD 7.8 days, range 18 months 0 days–18 months 24 days).

Apparatus and procedure. The general details of the procedure were as for Expt 1 except that targets were presented only behind the baby, with the visual field in front being completely devoid of targets. Targets were presented in random order of pairs at 120, 150 and 165 degrees relative to the infant. (These positions are shown as locations 3 and 4; 1 and 2; A and B′ in Fig. 3.) Mothers were instructed to fixate the designated targets either by making an eye movement, or by making a combined eye and head movement. The order of trials (eyes only vs. head and eyes) was counterbalanced across subjects, with all trials of one type being completed before trials of the other type. Inter-rater agreement on the scoring of responses was 93.3 per cent.

Results

Table 2 shows that the babies of 18 months could search behind them when the visual field was emptied of targets. The mother's eye movement was sufficient to lead the infant to turn and fixate the target, although a combined head and eye movement was more effective (49 vs. 66 correct responses). Analysis of variance was carried out with main effects of target position, sex and signal type on correct responses. This showed a significant effect of signal type ($F(1, 253) = 4.74, p < .05$ eyes vs. head and eyes). The difference between types of signal might be partially accounted for by an increase in the number of infants turning in the wrong direction following an eye movement alone (13 eyes + head vs. 24 eyes only: responses to the wrong side of the room). A further analysis of variance was carried out on the probability of response (C + W vs. N) to establish whether there was any difference between types of signal. The difference in total responding between E only and H + E did not reach significance ($F(1, 242) = 2.87$, n.s. $p < .10$) which suggests that the difference in performance between signal types is best accounted for in terms of the accuracy of the resulting response rather than in its likelihood of occurrence. That is, infants found it easier to turn and locate the correct target behind them when the adult made a head and eye

Table 2. Limits of accurate spatial localization: 18-month infants with targets behind them and an empty visual field.

Target positions	120°		150°		165°		Total	
Signal type	E	E+H	E	E+H	E	E+H	E	E+H
Correct	16	24	19	22	14	20	49	66
Wrong	3	1	5	5	6	5	14	11
No response	20	22	14	17	21	15	55	54

Notes. Excludes 37 responses to the wrong side and 5 spoiled trials.
E = mother signals with eye movement only
E + H = mother signals with eye and head movement.

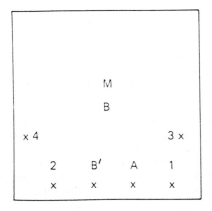

Figure 3. Experiment 2: Eye vs. head and eye movements in 18-month-old infants. Targets were presented in pairs one either side of the infant. Each target position inspected by M with eye movement only and with head and eye movements (*N* = 24).

movement than when the signal comprised an eye movement alone. There was no significant difference between the three pairs of target positions.

Discussion

Butterworth & Cochran (1980) found that babies at 12 months failed to search behind them, even when the visual field was emptied of targets. That is, infants at 12 months do not seem to be able to access a space outside their own field of view in joint attention tasks. By 18 months however, as Expt 2 showed, infants of 18 months were able to interpret the adult's visual attention as referring outside their own visual field. However, this ability became apparent only when competition from targets within the field of view was eliminated. That is, infants of 18 months could access a *represented* space when there was no competition from within their *perceived* space. As Expt 1 showed, when there is a target in the visual field at 90 or at 60 degrees, they select the incorrect target if the correct target is behind them (at 150 or at 120 degrees). The fact that an eye movement alone is sufficient to redirect the infant's attention shows that when 18-month babies fail to search behind in Expt 1 it cannot be due simply to the fact that the mother only made a small movement to indicate targets behind the baby. A head and eye movement is more effective in eliciting a correct response. Perhaps this is because the combined movements signal more clearly a change in the adult's focus of attention than eye movements alone. An incidental aspect of the results is that infants, like adults, are able to make use of information from eye and head movements to determine whether or not they are being looked at (Gibson & Pick 1963).

In summary, infants at 18 months identified both the direction and the location to which the adult was attending. This ability to interpret the adult's referential looking with respect to a represented space only became apparent under the conditions of this experiment, where there is no conflict with targets in the field of view.

Experiments 3*a,b,c*: Limits of accurate spatial localization at 6 months

It appeared from the results of Expt 1 that babies aged 6 months were restricted to targets within their field of view in their response to the mother's change of attention. The next series of experiments was designed to obtain further information about the limits of spatial localization in 6-month infants. Butterworth & Cochran (1980) suggested that joint visual attention might require the infant to 'bridge the spatial gap' between the mother and a possible target by holding the mother in the extreme periphery of vision on one side, while turning until a target is encountered in the periphery of vision in the direction indicated by the mother's signal. This series of experiments enabled a test of this hypothesis to be made by systematically varying the spatial separation between mother and a possible referent.

Subjects. A new group of 24 babies, comprising equal numbers of boys and girls, was tested. Their mean age was 6 months 12 days (SD 8.6 days, range 6 months 0 days to 6 months 27 days).

Apparatus and procedure. The general apparatus and procedure was as for Expt 1, except that mother and infant were seated in a corner of the laboratory, facing forward, separated at a distance of 40 cm and the targets were presented in a random order of pairs around the edge of the room (similar to Fig. 4). The pairs were at 0 and 60 degrees; 10 and 70 degrees; 20 and 80 degrees 30 and 90, 0 and 45 degrees and 45 and 90 degrees with respect to the infant's mid-line. Thus, some of the pairs of targets straddled the corner of the room, other pairs were along the long wall of the room. The maximum visual angle between the mother at about 45 degrees in the left periphery of vision of the infant and the spatially most distant target was 135 degrees within the infant's field of view (i.e. 45 degrees to the left plus 90 degrees to the right).

Results

Table 3*a* summarizes the data. As the table shows, infants invariably located the correct target when it was first along their scan path from the mother (total 1st target 45 correct vs. 4 incorrect; $Z = 5.13$, $p < .001$) and just as regularly, they located the incorrect target when the mother was looking at a more peripheral target (total 2nd target 4 correct vs. 45 incorrect, $Z = 5.71$, $p < .001$). This is true whether the

Table 3a. Limits of accurate spatial localization at 6 months. Two targets at a time, mother and baby in corner of room

Target location:	0&60		10&70		20&80		30&90		0&45		45&90°		Total
Correct target	8*	1	7	0	8*	0	10*	1	5	2	7*	0	49
Wrong target	0	10*	2	10*	1	6*	0	6	3	9*	1	5*	53
No response	16	12	11	13	14	16	13	16	14	13	16	17	171

Ratio of C:W *$p < .05$ or $p < .01$, binomial test.
Fifteen responses to the wrong side of the room excluded.

separation between the targets was 60 degrees (1st target: total 33 correct vs. 3 incorrect, second target: total 2 correct vs. 32 incorrect) or 45 degrees (1st target total: 12 correct vs. 2 incorrect; second target 4 correct vs. 14 incorrect fixations). Inter-observer agreement was 93 per cent. That is, the greater spatial separation between targets, and whether targets straddled the corner of the room or were along the long wall made no difference to the accuracy of response. (This indirectly shows that possible influences of the topology of the room have little effect on accuracy of the infant's response at this age). At 6 month infants did indeed comprehend the *direction* of the mother's signal but this did not carry information for object location. The maximum visual separation accurately bridged between mother and target was 90 degreees (in the 45 paired with 90 degree condition). A further test of the limits of accurate spatial localization was carried out by presenting the targets one at a time around the periphery of the room.

*Experiment 3*b

Apparatus and procedure. The apparatus and procedure were identical to Expt 3a except that targets were presented one at a time at 10 degree intervals around the end and side wall of the room. Mother and infant were seated in the corner of the room as before. Under these circumstances the infants did not have to make a choice between targets, they merely had to single out the target, contingent upon the mother's signal (Fig. 4).

Subjects. A new group of 18 infants, equally divided between males and females, whose mean age was 6 months 10 days (SD 5.2 days, range 6 months 3 days to 6 months 18 days) were subjects. Five infants who failed to cooperate were excluded.

Results

The results are presented in Table 3*b*. The video-recordings were analysed to determine whether the infant terminated the scan directly on target, in which case the response was classified as correct, or whether the scan was terminated before or after the target in which case it was classified as incorrect (or in a very few cases when the infant scanned the opposite side of the room). Inter-rater agreement was 95 per cent.

The results show that when infants responded, they predominantly turned to fixate the appropriate zone of space. Relatively few fixations terminated in the wrong zone. Furthermore, infants would locate targets up to 90 degrees from their mid-line,

Table 3*b*. Limits of accurate spatial localization at 6 months. One target at a time, mother and baby in corner of room.

	0	10	20	30	40	50	60	70	80	90°	Total
Correct target	8	6	7	6	7	11	10	7	7	6	75
Wrong zone	1	1	3	1	4	1	0	2	3	4	19
No response	9	7	7	11	7	6	8	7	7	6	75

Note. Six spoiled trials and four on wrong side excluded.

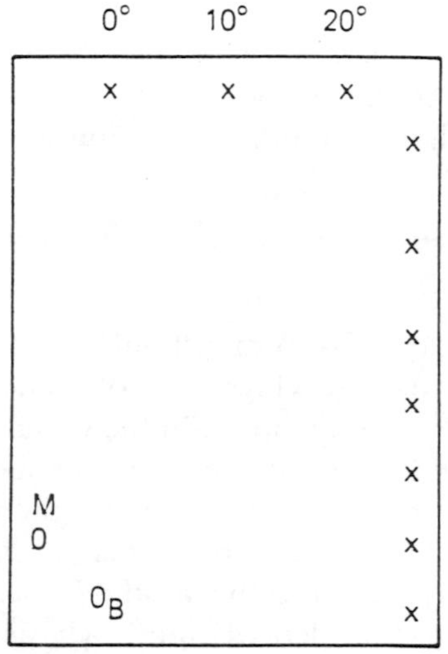

Figure 4. Experiment 3: Limits of accurate spatial localization at 6 months. Targets presented one at a time at each of the 10 locations.

which is roughly equivalent to 135 degrees between the mother in the periphery on one side and the most extreme target on the other. An analysis of variance was carried out which showed there was no significant difference between locations in successful localization; females were significantly more accurate than males ($F(1, 16) = 4.90$, $p < .05$) and females were also significantly more likely to respond than males ($F(1, 16) = 10.92$, $p < .01$). As a check whether presenting targets one at a time may have influenced the results a further group of 6-month infants was tested in the original spatial configuration of Expt 1 but now with targets presented singly (see Fig. 1).

Experiment 3c

Subjects. A new group of 12 babies was tested. Their mean age was 6 months 8 days (SD 5.4 days range 6 months 1 day to 6 months 19 days). A further four subjects were excluded because they failed to cooperate.

Apparatus and procedure.   The general details were the same as in Expt 1. The mother and infant were seated in the centre of the laboratory and the procedure was identical except that targets were presented one at a time, in a random order until trials had been completed at all 12 locations shown in Fig. 1. Inter-observer agreement was 95 per cent.

Results

Table 3*c* summarizes the data across left and right sides of the room since there was no difference in the probability of response to either side (L 24 R 22). The table shows that babies never fixated the wrong target for spatial positions within the visual field up to 90 degrees from the mid-line. Targets at 120 and 150 degrees elicited some wrong fixations of the empty visual field in front of the baby and an increase in the number of zero responses.

Analysis of variance showed there to be an overall significant difference between conditions in the number of correct responses ($F(9, 90) = 1.98$, $p < .05$) but Scheffé comparisons did not yield a significant difference between any target positions owing to the low numbers of cases.

Discussion

This series of experiments reveals that 6-month infants took the mother's change of attention to specify the direction in which to look. They were able accurately to localize the target when it was the only object in the visual field. However, they were unable to identify the correct location if they had to choose between two identical targets and they were also restricted to targets within their visual field. Butterworth & Cochran (1980) suggested a mechanism which might explain this pattern of performance. The infant may perceive the mother's head and eye movement as signalling the appropriate direction (left or right). The infant may then turn in the correct direction with the mother in the periphery of vision on one side until a potential target enters the periphery on the other side. At one moment, mother and target would be connected in the infant's visual field. With mother and infant in the corner of the room, 6-month infants could bridge a very wide gap of 135 degrees between mother and target, yet when both are seated 'en face' in the middle of the room, accuracy drops off at targets located between 90 and 120 degrees from the infant. While the mechanism linking mother, infant and target proposed by

Table 3*c*. Limits of accurate spatial localization at 6 months. One target at a time, mother and baby in centre of room.

	150	120	90	60	30°	Total
Correct target fixated	2	7	14	12	11	46
Wrong zone fixated	5	2	0	0	0	7
No response	13	10	7	9	9	48

Notes. Fourteen trials to wrong side, five spoiled trials excluded.
Target locations are in degrees relative to the baby's mid-line.

Butterworth & Cochran (1980) is still just possible, it seems more likely that the mother's change of visual attention triggers a search within the infant's field of vision, which terminates as a salient target is encountered in the periphery. The implication for the 6-month infants is that the mother's signal does not carry information about the *location* at which to look, only the *direction* is specified.

Such a mechanism might still enable joint attention in reality because once the infant looks in the direction given by the mother's signal, objects may single themselves out. This earliest mechanism of joint attention may operate by virtue of the intrinsic attention-capturing properties of objects. What attracts the mother's attention and leads her to turn may then capture the infant's attention. Grover (1988) obtained some evidence for the effects of such an 'ecological' mechanism by adding movement to the targets. Infants at 9, 12 and 15 months showed almost 100 per cent likelihood of attending to the first target along the scan path, when it was set in motion, contingent upon the mother's signal.

General discussion and conclusion

Our results demonstrate that even very young babies may enter into a communication network with others through comprehension of an adult's direction of gaze; communication is not solely dependent upon the greater cognitive sophistication of the adult. We propose that three mechanisms underlie joint visual attention in the first 18 months of life (for a fuller justification see Butterworth, 1990, 1991; Butterworth & Grover, 1988, 1990 and Grover, 1988). At 6 months, the signal value of the mother's head and eye movement will indicate the general direction (left or right) in which to look; the easily distractible baby will attend to the same attention-compelling features of the objects in the environment as the mother. Such an ecological foundation for agreement on the objects of shared experience might reasonably be considered a prerequisite for communication. When seen in social context, the earliest 'ecological' mechanism allows communication in relation to publicly shared objects, through their common effects on the intrinsic attention mechanisms of mother and baby. This basic mechanism depends on the fact that attentional mechanisms in infant and adult operate in much the same way.

It is a common-sense notion that unrelated minds may nevertheless experience the same object, either sequentially or simultaneously. As William James (1947, p. 82) noted long ago, such a proposition stands or falls with the general possibility of things existing with other things, including people with other people. 'But if my reader will only allow that the same "now" both ends his past and begins his future; ... or that when I pay him a dollar the same dollar goes into his pocket as came out of mine; he will also in consistency have to allow that the same object may conceivably play a part in, as being related to the rest of, any number of otherwise *entirely different minds*' James goes on to argue that joint visual attention depends on expressive movements which lead unrelated minds to share the same perceptual object; 'your mind and mine may terminate *in* the same percept, not merely against it . . .' (p. 83), objects are *conterminous*, *mutual* aspects of experience. Indeed, he argues that other minds are known only by virtue of the body's expressive movements and their effects on one's own perception (p. 77).

From James' perspective of 'natural realism', other minds are postulated by analogy with one's own experience but we do not need to attribute any knowledge of mental life to the pre-reflective infant. It is more parsimonious to suppose that changes in another person's visual orientation signal to the infant the *possibility* of an object (see Quinton, 1973), just as changes in emotional expression may refer 'transparently' to the feeling states that accompany them (see Coulter, 1979). James argues that what minds have in common is *space as a receptacle for experience*. The experiences themselves may or may not be held in common. 'The next thing beyond my percept is not your mind but more percepts of my own, into which my first percept develops' (p. 83). As William James might predict and as Hamlyn (1978) pointed out, perception *necessarily* involves a point of view but this need not involve an initial solipsism or privacy of experience (see also Butterworth, 1987).

Thus we do not need to postulate knowledge of other minds, or 'mindreading', to explain how the young baby can attend to the same object as the adult. We do need to explain how the baby recognizes the signal value of the adult's visual reorientation and we need to explain why the baby behaves as if infant and adult hold visual space in common. A 'realist' theory of direct perception, such as that of J. J. Gibson (1966) enables us to understand that perception of an object must originate at a particular viewpoint, yet the same object may be common to diverse viewpoints. The phenomenon of joint visual attention presupposes a world of objects, albeit seen from different points of view, which exist in a common space. The mother's signal is informative because it specifies the *possibility* of an object, *somewhere* in visual space. Whether mother and infant actually engage in joint attention, depends upon whether they attend to the same object and for the youngest babies, this in turn depends on the object singling itself out.

With cognitive development a 'geometric' localization of the referent of the mother's gaze is superimposed on the basic ecological mechanism. By this we mean that the infant from his/her position becomes able to extrapolate a relatively accurate trajectory from the adult to specify the location of a target in visual space. Such a mechanism might correspond to Piaget's (1954) description of 'invisible displacements', whereby the infant from about 12 months can infer unseen trajectories between different positions in space. Now, targets that are identical in all respects except position can be singled out by the infant. On our theory this supplements the earlier ecological mechanism, it does not supplant it. The geometric mechanism offers, on spatial criteria alone, the possibility of agreement on an object of common experience. Once again, 'mindreading' is not involved and need not be postulated.

For the infant to engage in joint visual attention with respect to a space that extends beyond the boundaries of immediate visual perception it would seem that there develops a representation of space as a *container* of infant, adult and potentially shared objects (see Piaget, 1954). There is evidence that such a representation of space is available to 18-month infants, so long as they are released from the primacy of perceived space. Again, we do not consider representation to be a necessary condition for joint reference; our evidence shows that the ecological and geometric mechanisms precede representation and each allows definite reference within the limits of immediate perception. By the same token, representation of space as a container does not amount to mindreading. It merely extends the domain within which interpersonal relations may be understood to take place and where properties of mind may be revealed.

Joint visual attention is one of the most elementary of cognitive processes but it illustrates the important sense in which the experiences of others may be transparent to the baby. If development does not start from the strictly private world presupposed by theories of absolute egocentrism then even naive minds may 'meet' other minds in a world of objects. There is no need to suppose that the developing child eventually comes to understand mental events, beliefs, emotions or desires by constructing a 'theory' about unobservables. On the contrary, a taxonomy of the varieties of shared experience, as revealed in the social relations of babies, would show that both perception and emotion have their perceptible objects. From such objective foundations, in direct experience, beliefs about other minds may eventually develop.

Acknowledgements

This research was carried out under a grant from the Economic and Social Research Council of Great Britain. Some of the implications of the experiments reported here have been discussed at conferences whose proceedings were subsequently published. Issues discussed include theories of egocentrism (Butterworth, 1987), the relation of visual coorientation with pointing and the origins of language (Butterworth & Grover 1988, 1990) and the phylogenetic significance of joint visual attention (Butterworth 1991).

Paul Harris acted as editor for this submission.

References

Butterworth, G. E. (1987). Some benefits of egocentrism. In J. S. Bruner & H. Haste. *Making Sense: The Child's Construction of the World*, pp. 62–80. London: Methuen.

Butterworth, G. E. (1990). The geometry of pre-verbal communication. Final report to the ESRC: British Library.

Butterworth, G. E. (1991). The ontogeny and phylogeny of joint visual attention. In A. Whiten (Ed.), *Natural Theories of Mind*, pp. 223–232. Oxford: Basil Blackwell.

Butterworth, G. E. & Cochran, E. (1980). Towards a mechanism of joint visual attention in human infancy. *International Journal of Behavioural Development*, 3(3), 253–272.

Butterworth, G. E. & Franco, F. (1991). Motor development: Communication and cognition. In L. Kalverboer, B. Hopkins & R. H. Gueze (Eds), *A Longitudinal Approach to the Study of Motor Development in Early and Later Childhood*. Cambridge: Cambridge University Press (in press).

Butterworth, G. E. & Grover, L. (1988). The origins of referential communication in human infancy. In L. Weiskrantz (Ed.), *Thought Without Language*, pp. 5–25. Oxford: Oxford University Press.

Butterworth, G. E. & Grover, L. (1990). Joint visual attention, manual pointing and preverbal communication in human infancy. In M. Jeannerod (Ed.), *Attention and Performance XIII*, pp. 605–624. Hillsdale, NJ: Erlbaum.

Coulter, J. (1979). Transparency of mind: The availability of subjective phenomena. In J. Coulter (Ed.), *The Social Construction of Mind*. London: Macmillan.

Gibson, J. J. & Pick, A. D. (1963). Perception of another person's looking behaviour. *American Journal of Psychology*, **76**, 386–394.

Grover, L. (1988). Comprehension of the manual pointing gesture in human infants. Unpublished PhD thesis, University of Southampton.

Hamlyn, M. (1978). *Experience and the Growth of Understanding*. London: Routledge & Kegan Paul.

James, W. (1947). *Radical Empiricism*. New York: Longman (first published 1912).

Landau, B. & Spelke, E. (1988). Geometric complexity and object search in infancy. *Developmental Psychology*, **24**, 512–521.

Piaget, J. (1954). *The Construction of Reality in the Child*. New York: Basic Books.

Quinton, A. (1973). *The Nature of Things*. London: Routledge & Kegan Paul.

Scaife, M. & Bruner, J. S. (1975). The capacity for joint visual attention in the infant. *Nature*, **253**, 265–266.

Schaffer, R. (1984). *The Child's Entry into a Social World*. New York: Academic Press.

Received 23 October 1990; revised version received 30 January 1991

British Journal of Developmental Psychology (1991), **9**, 73–87   *Printed in Great Britain*   73

Young children's knowledge about visual perception: Lines of sight must be straight

John H. Flavell*, **Frances L. Green, Carla Herrera**
and **Eleanor R. Flavell**
Department of Psychology, Jordan Hall, Stanford University, Stanford, CA 94305-2099, USA

Four studies were done to test the hypothesis that, although knowledgeable about some important facts concerning visual perception, 3-year-olds have not yet learned that lines of sight must always be straight. Subjects of 3 to 5 years of age were asked whether they (Study 1) or toy observers (Studies 2–4) would be able to see objects via looking paths that were curved rather than straight: for example, by looking through a bow-shaped hollow tube or along the curve of its outside wall. Consistent with the hypothesis, 3-year-olds gave no evidence of possessing this straight-line-of-sight rule. In contrast, 5-year-olds showed at least some command of it.

There is now considerable evidence (e.g. Astington, Harris & Olson, 1988; Wellman, 1990) that children acquire some basic knowledge about the mind during the preschool years. Part of that knowledge concerns visual perception. Research suggests that by 3 years of age children already know something about the conditions governing the visibility of objects (Flavell, 1978; Flavell, Shipstead & Croft, 1978; Hughes & Donaldson, 1979; Lempers, Flavell & Flavell, 1977; Yaniv & Shatz, 1988, 1990). They seem to realize that, in order to see an object, the observer's eye or eyes have to be (*a*) open and (*b*) facing in the general direction of the object; they also realize that (*c*) there cannot be any large vision-blocking object or screen interposed between observer and object (Flavell, 1978). A study by Hughes & Donaldson (1979) nicely illustrates this knowledge. Subjects of 3 and 4 years looked down at a table containing a small boy doll, two small walls, and two policeman dolls. The walls intersected at right angles to form a cross shape as viewed from above. The policemen were stationed at the outer ends of two adjacent walls, facing inward towards their intersection. The subjects' task was to position the boy such that he could not be seen by either policeman. Even the 3-year-olds succeeded in correctly placing the boy in the quadrant furthest from the policeman—the only location not visible to either of them.

Do young children also know that lines of sight are always straight? That is, do they understand that the visual path from an observer to a target cannot be curved but must always be straight? One would at first assume that they must understand it. Even as infants children seem able to determine approximately where another person

---

*Requests for reprints.

is looking from looking at the person's eyes (e.g. Butterworth & Cochran, 1980). They can even do this when there is no visual target present, i.e. when the person is just staring in a certain direction (Churcher & Scaife, 1982). Infants probably do this by projecting a roughly straight line of sight outward from the person's eyes, with its direction computed from the eyes' spatial orientation. This suggests that when reading people's gazes they may operate under the tacit assumption that the looking-paths of these gazes are straight. Such understanding is also suggested by young children's sensitivity to conditions *b* and *c* above, as shown by their good performance on Hughes & Donaldson's (1979) and other Flavell (1978) visual perspective-taking tasks. Finally, they certainly could have learned from countless visual experiences in everyday life that they cannot 'bend' their looking paths over, under, or around visual barriers. For example, one would think that they must have learned from experience that they cannot see around corners without moving their heads.

However, it is still possible that 3-year-olds might possess the foregoing skills and knowledge and yet not command any explicit, general, or rule-like understanding that lines of sight are necessarily straight. For example, they may tacitly assume that lines of sight are *normally* straight without yet explicitly recognizing that they are *always* and *necessarily* straight. That is, they might tacitly expect them to be straight without yet knowing that they cannot be curved. Likewise, they may conclude that an observer's view of an object is blocked only when, as they themselves glance from observer to object, they see interposed between the two an object that is easily recognizable as a visual barrier; examples would be a wall set perpendicular to the observer's line of sight or the sharply angled corner of a building with the object located around the corner from the observer. The 3-year-olds in Hughes & Donaldson's (1979) study could have used such a procedure to solve the boy-and-policemen problem: namely, place the boy such that when you look from each policeman to the boy you see an interposed wall. On the other hand, if task conditions were such that subjects saw nothing that looked like a vision-occluding object when glancing from observer to target, they might assume that the observer could in fact see the target, even when seeing it would clearly require the observer to look along a curved rather than a straight line of sight. They might do this even while consciously aware of its curved nature, providing only that they did not construe anything they saw as being a visual barrier between observer and target.

We report four studies designed to test the hypothesis that young children lack a general rule that lines of sight must be straight and, therefore, would believe that it is possible for observers to see objects via curved looking paths, provided that there are no conspicuous interposed objects in the task display that would trigger a correct negative judgement.

Study 1

In Study 1 we asked 3-year-old and 5-year-old children to predict whether they would be able to see through a hollow tube that was progressively bent to greater degrees of curvature, as shown at the top of Fig. 1: 180° (straight), followed in succession by 140°, 90°, and 0° (candy-cane shaped). We predicted that at least the

3-year-olds would think they could see through it, except perhaps when the degree of curvature became too extreme. We then provided the children with explicit feedback that even a slightly curved tube (140°) did not afford visibility of the target and subsequently retested them for learning and transfer on the same items used in the first part of the study.

Method

Subjects.   The subjects were 14 female and five male 3-year-olds (mean age = 3:5; range = 3:2 to 3:10) and 15 female and 4 male 5-year-olds (mean age = 5:2; range = 4:7 to 5:7). The children were drawn from a university laboratory preschool and were largely from upper-middle-class backgrounds. All subjects were individually tested in a single session by the same female experimenter. No subject failed to complete the procedure.

Procedure.   The stimuli were three silver-coloured flexible pieces of hollow tubing, 60.3 cm in length and 6.4 cm in diameter, sufficiently stiff that they would stay in any shape until bent by the experimenter. A small object (flower, toy bear, or toy soldier) was suspended just inside one of the ends of each tube.

The three tubes were introduced in straight-line viewing position (180°) to the subjects in the following fashion. The experimenter randomly selected one of the tubes and let the subject see that a small object was present at one of the ends. She then held the tube horizontally above the child's head, perpendicular to his/her line of vision, and asked: 'Do you think if you looked through here (she tapped the viewing end of the tube with her finger), that you'd be able to see this (object name)?' (She tapped the end with the suspended, but not currently visible, object.) Following the subject's prediction, he or she was allowed to look through the tube and was asked whether the object was seen. The experimenter then gave each subject a chance to look through the other two tubes. The purpose of this part of the procedure was to make sure the children understood the meaning of our prediction-of-seeing questions and knew that all three tubes were hollow. Three blocks of trials were then given in the following order.

Pre-feedback trials.   The experimenter randomly selected one of the tubes and asked four prediction questions, in fixed order, about the visibility of the small object when the tube was held above her head, first straight (180°), then somewhat curved (140°), then more curved (90°), then bent double (0°), and finally straight (180°) again. (The degree indicated for each tube is that of the angle formed by the intersection of lines drawn perpendicular to, and into, each mouth of the tube. See Fig. 1 for the actual appearance of the successive curvatures shown to the child.) Prior to each question she called the subject's attention to the alteration of the tube by saying: 'Now I'm going to make this tube (or it) like this. Watch.' The tube was held in horizontal position above the child's head, with the ends slightly tilted upward, such that the angle of curvature, but not the suspended object, was perceptible to the child. The test question was the same throughout this block of trials: 'If you look through here (the experimenter tapped the viewing end of the tube), will you be able to see the————?' (tapping the other end). Following the fourth question only (prediction for 180°), the child was allowed to look through the tube to show that the previous alterations in the shape of the tube had not made it impossible to see through when straight.

Feedback trials.   The subject was allowed to choose one of the remaining two tubes for this block of six questions. As in the previous block of trials, the experimenter began by holding the tube above the child's head in the 180° position and calling the child's attention to the alteration of the tube as she bent it to 140°. The subject was then asked to predict his/her view for 140° ('If you look through here, will you be able to see the————?'), and following this to test whether the object was visible for 140° when he or she actually looked ('Do you see the————?'). If the subject erred on the second question (i.e. said he or she could see the object), the experimenter looked through the tube herself, gave the correct answer, and repeated the question until a correct response was obtained. The same prediction followed by feedback questions was next asked when the tube was straightened to 180°, and then once again when bent to 140°. Thus, the sequence was prediction followed by feedback, first for 140°, then for 180°, and then for 140° again. This meant that subjects predicted for 140° once before and once after

STUDY 1 TUBE POSITIONS

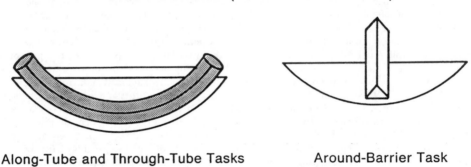

180°

140°

90°

0°

STUDY 2 STIMULI (from child's aerial view)

Along-Tube and Through-Tube Tasks   **Around-Barrier Task**

Figure 1. *Stimulus displays used in Studies 1 and 2.*

experiencing an inability to see the object at that degree of curvature, and had a total of two such feedback experiences before making predictions on the post-feedback trials.

Post-feedback trials. The experimenter said: 'Let's try it again with a different toy' (the third tube), and repeated the order of questioning and viewing positions given in the first block of trials, i.e. 140°, 90°, 0°, and 180°. Feedback was not given following these final four prediction trials.

Results and discussion

As would be expected, subjects in both age groups usually predicted correctly that they would be able to see the object through straight (180°) tubes. Of more interest was the accuracy of their predictions when the tubes were not straight. Percentages of subjects in each age group correctly predicting that they could not see the object on these trials are shown in Table 1. A 2 (age) × 3 (degree of curvature) analysis of variance carried out on the three pre-feedback prediction trials revealed significant

Table 1. Percentage of subjects in each age group correctly predicting non-visibility through tubes of various curvatures in Study 1

	Trials							
	Pre-feedback			Feedback		Post-feedback		
Age				Before	After			
	140°	90°	0°	140°	140°	140°	90°	0°
3	16	26	32	16	26	21	32	32
5	47	47	68	26	79	84	84	89

main effects for age (F (1,36) = 5.06, $p < .05$) and degree of curvature (F (2,72) = 4.20, $p < .05$) with no significant interaction. *Post hoc* Tukey tests indicated ($p < .05$) that the 0° task was easier than both the 140° and 90° tasks. On the feedback trials, t tests showed that the 5-year-olds performed significantly better on the second, subsequent-to-feedback 140° trial than the 3-year-olds did. They also performed significantly better on this second trial than they themselves had done on the first, prior-to-feedback 140° trial, whereas the 3-year-olds showed no such improvement. On the post-feedback trials, the same 2 × 3 ANOVA yielded a significant effect for age only (F (1,36) = 23.91, $p < .001$). Related t tests indicated that the 5-year-olds also performed significantly better on the post-feedback trials than on the pre-feedback trials of the 140° and 90° tasks, but not the 0° task; the 3-year-olds showed no such significant pre-to-post improvement on any of these three tasks.

These results suggest the following picture of each group's performance across this series of eight trials. Most 3-year-olds initially assumed that they could see through the tube no matter how extreme its curvature. For example, 13 of the 19 predicted that they could see the object even when the tube was bent double on the pre-feedback (0°) task. Seventeen subjects erred on at least one of the three pre-feedback trials. Moreover, they did not appear to learn anything from two subsequent experiences, during the feedback trials, of not being able to see the object even when the degree of tube curvature was slight (140°): again, 13 of them were incorrect on the post-feedback 0° task. Although the 5-year-olds performed better than the 3-year-olds prior to feedback, their level of performance was not very high in absolute terms (26–68 per cent correct). Eleven of these older subjects erred on at least one of the three pre-feedback trials. However, a single feedback trial sufficed to teach most of them that they could not see through curved tubes: percentages correct following that first feedback trial ranged from 79 to 89 per cent. Taken all together, the results of this study clearly provide strong preliminary support for the hypothesis that young children do not understand that lines of sight must be straight.

Study 2

The data from Study 1 suggested that, prior to explicit training to the contrary, even young 5-year-olds may accept the possibility of seeing along curvilinear looking paths, and that 3-year-olds accept it even after training. However, it is possible that the experimental procedures and materials used in that study may have masked underlying competencies in any or all of the following ways: (*a*) the subjects probably had had little prior experience looking through tubes (especially bent ones); (*b*) a hollow tube 'affords' (à la Gibson) and invites looking and seeing through; (*c*) when presented with the first non-straight tube the subjects had just had the experience of being able to see through three straight tubes, thereby perhaps engendering a tendency to say 'yes' to subsequent questions; (*d*) questions about their own seeing abilities may stimulate overly optimistic 'I can do it' responses; and (*e*) the conditional format of the question '*If* you look through here, *will* you be able to see the X?' may have been problematical for some of the younger children.

Study 2 was intended to be a better assessment of 3-year-olds' and 5-year-olds' explicit untutored understanding that one cannot see along curvilinear visual trajectories. Several changes were made. We used a 90° curve in three different tasks. While looking directly down at the appropriate stimulus display (similar to the reader's view of Fig. 1), the children were asked whether one doll character (O) could see another doll character (X): (*a*) 'by looking through a curvy tube'; (*b*) 'by looking along a curvy line' (along the outside wall or perimeter of the tube); and (*c*) 'by looking along a curvy line' (around a barrier set midway between O and X and at right angles to a line between O and X). We added a question at the end about looking along a right-angle, L-shaped path (around the sharp corner formed by two sides of a box) that we predicted even the youngest children would answer correctly. We also predicted that the around-barrier task would prove easier than the other two curved trajectories, despite its having the same 90° curvature, because of the salience of the barrier as a visual obstacle. The stimulus displays for tasks *a–c* are depicted at the bottom of Fig. 1. Curved and straight lines highlighting the curvature were drawn in on the stimulus displays, as shown.

We began the session by calling the subjects' attention to the different visual appearances of a curved vs. straight line. Next we introduced the toy figure O who could look at things but not move from a 'chair', and made sure the subjects knew that the O could see, but not touch, an object held at a distance. The experimental task was then defined by introducing a second toy figure, X, who liked to play hiding games, and by asking the subject to decide whether or not O could see X from various hiding positions. Prior to each of the three critical test trials (*a–c* above) we gave the subjects two experiences in ascertaining whether or not O could see X, one involving a clearly impossible looking path (correct answer = no), and the other involving a straight-line looking path (correct answer = yes). For example, on one 'no' warm-up trial the looking path traced by the experimenter went up, over, and behind the O's head to the X situated behind a wall to the rear of O. On the 'yes' warm-up trial paired with this experience, a straight-line looking path was traced from the O to the X who was only partially obscured by a small flower. We confirmed the correctness of the subjects' responses on these warm-up trials and corrected any mistakes before proceeding to the test questions. A major purpose of these warm-up trials was to show the children that observers cannot always see things along suggested looking paths—that it is all right to say 'no' to some 'Can O see X?' questions. Thus, there were six warm-up trials, two preceding each test trial; three curvilinear test trials (through tube, along tube, and around barrier), administered in counterbalanced order; and one right-angle test trial given at the end. Children failing two or more warm-up trials (six 3-year-olds) were not retained as subjects in the study. Thus, all subjects had experience saying both 'yes' and 'no' to proffered looking paths prior to the test questions. Passing the warm-up trials ensured that just prior to the test questions subjects were neither attributing magical visual powers to the O nor confusing physical locomotion with vision along the proffered paths. A few probes, to be subsequently described, concluded the session.

Method

Subjects. The subjects were 10 female and eight male 3-year-olds (mean age = 3:7; range = 3:3 to 3:11) and nine female and nine male 5-year-olds (mean age = 5:1, range 4:10 to 5:7). The subjects were drawn from the same preschool described in Study 1, but tested by a different female experimenter. None of the subjects had participated in the first study. All subjects were tested individually in a single session.

Procedure.   *Pretraining and task introduction.* First the experimenter demonstrated the difference between a 'curvy' line and a 'straight' line. Two Playmobil toy figures served as the O and the X in the hiding game. The O was presented to the child in a sitting position and attached by two rubber bands to a cardboard 'chair' to emphasize a lack of physical mobility throughout the study. Seated, the O was 4 cm tall. The experimenter said 'Our game today is about how we can see things. Here is a little doll named Jack. Let's pretend he is a real little child and that he can see with his eyes just the way we can. Jack is a very little boy and is too young to walk around. His mother has fastened him down in a child's seat so he won't fall out. But he likes to look at things'. The experimenter then positioned Jack in front of the subject such that they shared the same line of vision and held a small block approximately 51 cm in front of them. She asked 'Can Jack see this block right now? That's right (or actually), he *can* see it. We are pretending he can see with his eyes just the way we do. Can Jack touch this block right now? That's right (or actually), he *can't* touch the block because he is fastened to his child's seat. He can't move from his seat in this game. He can only look at things with his eyes'. (Two subjects erred on the see question, and three subjects erred on the touch question.) Next, the X, never affixed to a chair, was introduced: 'Here is Suzy, Jack's sister. These children like to play a hiding game. Suzy thinks it is a whole lot of fun to try to hide so her brother can't see her. In our game today I'll show you some places where Suzy is trying to hide and you decide whether or not Jack can see her'.

Materials.   The display for the through-tube and along-tube tasks was affixed to a large sheet of white cardboard placed on the floor of the testing room. This display consisted of one of the tubes from Study 1 taped permanently to the cardboard in an approximately 90° curvature (see bottom of Fig. 1). Along the middle of the top of the tube a piece of blue yarn was taped to indicate the curvature of the looking path within the tube. A pen-drawn straight purple line connected the ends of the tube. On test trials, the tube looked like a shallow U from the seated subject's aerial viewing position mid-way between O and X. For use in the along-tube task, this same display had a curved green line drawn along the outer wall of the tube, the one nearest the child. This curve's end points were connected by a straight orange line that was partially interrupted by the placement of the tube, as shown in Fig. 1. The stimulus display for the around-barrier task was another large piece of white cardboard with a curved green line drawn on it that was identical to the curved path through the tube. Its end points were joined by a straight orange line. A cardboard wall (6 cm thick at its base, 8 cm tall, and 36 cm long) bisected the straight line but did not interrupt the curve (see Fig. 1). For both the around-barrier and along-tube tasks the subjects could see that the eye lines and body positions of both dolls were oriented toward the curved rather than the straight-line paths. On the through-tube task, however, the O and X were placed just inside the ends of the tube and were therefore not visible to the subject.

Warm-up trials. The ordering of the test trials was counterbalanced across subjects, with each trial preceded by a particular pair of warm-up trials, one involving a clearly possible looking path, the other a clearly impossible looking path. The two warm-up trials were given in randomized order. The question for each warm-up trial was as follows: 'Suzy is trying to hide from Jack right here. Can Jack see Suzy by looking along this way?' (The experimenter traced with her finger along the looking path from O to X.) Following the subject's response, the experimenter said, 'That's right (or actually), Jack *can (can't)* see Suzy'. The clearly impossible looking paths traced were always curvilinear and barrier related. The clearly possible ones included inadequate barriers behind which X was clearly visible. An example of each was given in the introduction to this study. The two figures remained visible to the subjects on both kinds of trials. To be correct on an impossible trial, therefore, subjects had to assert that Jack could not see Suzy even though they themselves could see her.

Test trials. On each test trial, the O and the X were placed on the stimulus display and the subject was asked: 'Suzy is trying to hide from Jack here. Can Jack see Suzy by looking along a curvy line (through a curvy tube) like this?' (The experimenter traced the curve with her finger.) Unlike in the warm-up trials, the looking paths were explicitly identified as 'curvy' and no feedback was given following a test question.

Following a subject's third test trial, he or she was asked whether the X could be seen along a right-angle visual path. The O was positioned at the end of one of the long sides of a flat rectangular box 26 cm wide, 38 cm long, and 6 cm tall, and the X placed at the end of the far short side, diagonally opposite. The experimenter asked: 'Can Jack see Suzy by looking along this way?' and traced a right-angle path from O to X.

Probe and feedback. Following the fourth test question, the experimenter repositioned O and X for the along-tube task and said: 'I think you said that Jack could (could not) see Suzy by looking along this curvy line like this. Why can (can't) Jack see Suzy by looking along a curvy line like this?' Next, the subject was positioned behind the O at approximately the same eye-level and asked whether he or she could see Suzy by looking along the curved line. Some of the subjects tried to look through the tube as well at this time. The child was returned to his or her mid-line aerial viewing position and the along-tube and through-tube tasks were readministered, in that order. The purpose of readminstering the through-tube task was to test for the ability to generalize from the recent experience of inability to see along a curved line in the along-tube task. However, given that some of the subjects had also just experienced an inability to see through the tube, the data we report may overestimate subjects' capabilities.

Results and discussion

Table 2 shows the percentages of subjects in each age group correctly judging that O could not see X in each viewing condition. A 2 (age) × 4 (viewing condition) analysis of variance performed on these data showed significant main effects for age (F $(1,34) = 5.73$, $p < .02$) and viewing condition (F $(3,102) = 12.20$, $p < .001$) with no significant interaction. Of the 18 subjects at each age level, 15 3-year-olds and eight 5-year-olds erred on at least one of these four tasks. In contrast, eight 3-year-olds and 14 5-year olds responded correctly to at least three of them; when they missed only one, it was almost always the through-tube task. *Post-hoc* Tukey tests showed the following significant effects ($p < .01$) between viewing conditions: right-angle task easier than through-tube and along-tube tasks, and around-barrier task easier than through-tube task. We also did an additional 2 × 2 ANOVA combining the two conditions we had predicted would be easier (right-angle and around-barrier) and the two we had predicted would be harder (through-tube and along-tube). This analysis yielded significant main effects for age (F $(1,34) = 5.73$, $p < .02$) and viewing condition (F $(1,34) = 31.12$, $p < .001$) and a significant age by condition interaction, (F $(1,34) = 4.77$, $p < .04$). *Post hoc* Tukey tests showed that the 5-year-olds performed significantly better than the 3-year-olds in the harder (tube) conditions only, and that the 3-year-olds performed significantly better in the easier conditions than in the harder ones.

Table 2. Percentage of subjects in each age group correctly predicting non-visibility in different viewing conditions in Study 2

	Viewing condition			
Age	Through tube	Along tube	Around barrier	Right angle
3	28	39	67	89
5	61	78	83	94

Of the seven 3-year-olds who had correctly indicated that O could not see X on the along-tube task, only three (43 per cent) alluded to the impossibility of seeing along curved lines or to the necessity of seeing along straight ones when asked to say why during the subsequent probe and feedback period. The comparable figures for the 5-year-olds were 14 and 11 (79 per cent). Also, during that probe and feedback period, 78 and 100 per cent of the 3- and 5-year-olds, respectively, judged correctly that O could not see X along the tube after having just experienced their own inability to do so a moment before ($t(34) = 2.20, p < .05$). A moment later, 44 per cent of the 3-year-olds vs. 77 per cent of the 5-year-olds judged correctly that O could not see X through the tube either, when the through-tube task was readministered ($t(34) = 1.71, p < .10$). Both groups performed significantly ($p < .05$, by t tests) worse on this readministered through-tube task than on the readministered along-tube task immediately preceding it.

The results of Study 2 seem largely consistent with those of Study 1. Consider first the performance of the younger children. As in Study 1, most 3-year-old subjects showed no evidence of understanding that lines of sight have to be straight. They showed some recognition that O would be unable to see X only when there was a prominent barrier set squarely between O and X as in the around-barrier task, or when O's looking path had to make an abrupt 90° turn around a corner as in the right-angle task. Without these salient and prototypical obstructions, which they may have learned to recognize as specific obstacles to seeing from numerous visual experiences in everyday life, they freely accepted curved lines of sight. Indeed, more than half of the 3-year-olds continued to accept curved lines of sight (through the tube) even after having just experienced their own inability to see along them (along the tube), just as in Study 1. One could reasonably have concluded from Study 1 alone that children of this age would only accept curved looking paths that strongly tempt acceptance, such as the passage through a curved hollow tube. This conclusion is contradicted by the results of Study 2, however, because in that study 3-year-old subjects did not perform significantly better on an along-tube task than on a through-tube task involving a looking path of identical curvature; the same was true of 5-year-olds. We conclude that, if through-tube tasks do underestimate young children's understanding of this fact about vision, they do not underestimate it by much. The pretraining, the warm-up trials, the presence of drawn-in straight and curved lines in the task displays, the instructions, and the feedback trial at the end—all of these task features should have made it easy for subjects possessing even the most implicit straight-line-of-sight rule to use it in Study 2. The finding that 3-year-olds did not use it suggests that they did not possess it.

In contrast, the majority of the 5-year-olds did show evidence of possessing something akin to this rule, at some level of accessibility. Under the favourable task conditions of Study 2, many responded correctly on the critical through-tube and along-tube tasks. They also frequently referred explicitly to the curvature of O's looking path as an obstacle to O's seeing X when justifying correct responses to the along-tube task. Examples are: 'Because people can't see in curvy lines unless their eyes can stick out and around'; 'Because his eyes can only see straight'; 'Because, see, eyes don't curve along things, they are looking straight'.

Studies 3 and 4

The data from Studies 1 and 2 strongly suggest that most 3-year-olds have not yet acquired an explicit rule that lines of sight must be straight. However, it is possible that the methods used in these studies underestimated children's knowledge of that rule. For example, in Study 2 the experimenter explicitly identified each proposed looking route as 'curvy' and asked the subjects whether it was possible to see along that route. Her purpose in doing so was to help the children by calling explicit attention to its curved nature. It is conceivable, however, that this procedure may instead have had the opposite effect of suggesting that it was indeed possible to see along at least some curved paths. Although it obviously did not very often lead them to accept the curved route presented in the around-barrier task, it may have done so on the harder along-tube and through-tube tasks.

Studies 3 and 4 were carried out both to check this possibility and to provide additional evidence regarding young children's understanding of the straight-line rule. Three considerations led us to use looking paths that went through tubes. First, tubes visually define the looking path for the child, thereby making it easy for the experimenter to communicate the task without manually tracing the path or verbally describing its straight or curved shape. Second, in Study 2 looking paths through tubes did not prove to be significantly harder than looking paths along the outside of tubes. Third, we wanted a task that the subject could not solve merely by seeing an obvious visual obstacle interposed between toy perceiver and target. Rather, we wanted one that would require the knowledge that perceivers cannot see along curved looking paths.

In Study 3, after brief pretraining, 3- and 4-year-old-subjects were presented with a stimulus display of four hollow tubes. Three of the tubes were placed such that open ends were equidistant from and aimed directly at a small toy zebra: one tube was straight, one was bent to approximately 90° of curvature as in Study 2, and one was bent into a circular coil with the two open ends extending past each other. The open end of the fourth tube (a straight tube) was aimed away from the target toward the other straight tube. Thus, only the first-mentioned of the four tubes afforded visibility of the target. Playmobil toy figures, strapped to chairs, were placed in the opposite ends of each of the four tubes and subjects were asked which figures could see the zebra and which could not. Tubes not spontaneously categorized by the subjects were queried individually. We expected the subjects to be largely correct on the two straight-line tubes and the circular tube. We expected it would be possible for subjects to succeed on the circular tube task through mere visual inspection of the stimulus display rather than explicit rule knowledge. Given the severity of the curve and the proximity of the bend to the eyes of the toy observer, the tube wall of the display presents a barrier-like obstacle to seeing. However, if subjects failed to possess the explicit rule that line-of-sight cannot be curved they might say vision was possible through the 90° tube, as in the previous studies. Although we were basically interested in the performance of the 3-year-olds we also tested 4-year-olds, reasoning that if we found similar results with older children better able to deal with the complexities of the task, we would have greater confidence in the 3-year-old data. Finally, a fourth study was conducted with 4-year-old subjects using much of the same procedure but only asking yes-no questions about the visibility afforded by each of the four tubes.

Method

Subjects. Study 3 subjects were six female and 12 male 3-year-olds (mean age = 4:7, range 3:5 to 3:11) and nine female and nine male 4-year-olds (mean age = 4:5, range 4:0 to 4:10). The subjects were drawn from the same preschool described in Study 1. Four additional subjects (three 3-year-olds and one 4-year-old) were excluded from the experiment. Three of these subjects denied that any of the toy perceivers could see the target, and a fourth child refused to answer the questions. All subjects were tested individually in a single session by the same female experimenter in Study 2. A second experimenter recorded responses.

Procedure. *Pretraining and task introduction.* As in Study 2, the subjects were first acquainted with two different lines, one of which was curved and the other straight. The hollow tubes, placed elsewhere in the room on the floor in a preset display, were described as before as hollow and empty and then the experimenter introduced the game: 'The game today is about how we see things with our eyes. Here are four children (Playmobil figures strapped to seats via rubber bands) who like to look at things. They are fastened down to chairs so they can't walk around in our game. But in our game they can look at things with their eyes, just like we can. Can they walk around in this game? That's right/actually, they *can't* walk around in this game. Can they look at things with their eyes in this game? That's right/actually, in our game they *can* see things with their eyes just the way we do'. Using three different toy animals, the experimenter then selected one of the toy perceivers and gave in randomized order three control trials with an animal positioned directly in front of the observer, behind his head, and directly behind a cardboard barrier. The questions to the subject were 'Can he see the X right now or not?' Feedback was given after each trial and in those instances where an error was made (four 3-year-olds and two 4-year-olds made at least one error) the question was re-asked. All subjects initially incorrect were correct when the questions were posed a second time and no subject had to be excluded from the study. The reason for giving these control trials was to give the subjects experience of saying both yes and no to different viewing conditions and to ensure that they entered into the spirit of the game, allowing the possibility for the toy perceiver to 'see' under normal viewing conditions. The control trials were concluded by the experimenter saying 'Sometimes these children *can* see things from where they are sitting and sometimes they *can not*'. The experimenter and the subject then moved to the preset display of tubes where the subject was seated and, as in Study 2, given an aerial view of the display.

Materials. The four tubes previously described were displayed in two different spatial arrangements, with half of the subjects in each group receiving one arrangement and half the other. These different arrangements turned out to have no discernible effect on performance. The 'correct' straight tube (the one through which a toy perceiver could see the target), the circular tube, and the 90° tube were all directed toward a small toy zebra (5 cm tall and 6 cm long) approximately 10 cm away from the end of each tube. The 'wrong' straight tube was placed perpendicular to the side of the correct straight tube with its open end 5 cm away from it. The circular tube was bent such that when a toy perceiver was placed inside one end of the tube, he faced in the direction of the zebra.

Test trial. Each subject was presented with one of the stimulus displays. For half the 3-year-old subjects and all the 4-year-old subjects, probe questions were asked at the end of the task about each of their responses to the four tubes. The experimenter positioned the zebra in the display and asked the subject to watch as she placed a toy observer in the opposite end of each tube such that each observer was no longer visible to the child. The experimenter then reminded the subject a second time where each observer was sitting and said 'From where they are sitting, some of them *can* see the zebra and some of them *can not* see the zebra'. Next, in fixed order, the experimenter asked 'Which ones *can* see the zebra from where they are sitting?' 'Which ones *can not* see the zebra from where they are sitting?' 'If a child did not spontaneously categorize a viewing position, the experimenter asked: 'How about this one (points)? From where he is sitting, can he see the zebra or not?' Thirty-three per cent of the 72 responses to tubes had to be individually queried in this way for 3-year-olds and 14 per cent for 4-year-olds. Across all subjects, the correct straight tube had to be queried five times, the wrong straight tube 10 times, the circular tube six times, and the 90° tube 10 times. In the probe period, subjects were first asked about their response to the 90° tube, then the tubes identified as not affording visibility, and then the tubes identified as affording visibility. The probe question was 'How come this one *can* (*can not*) see the zebra from where he is sitting?' No child in the study claimed that all tubes afforded visibility and no child was inconsistent in identifying the same tube as one that did and did not afford visibility. As previously noted, three subjects claiming no observer could see the zebra were excluded from the study.

Study 4, conducted with 12 4-year-olds (mean age = 4:5), was very similar to the above procedure. However, the subjects were not told that some of the viewers could see the target and some could not. Instead, these subjects were simply asked about each viewing position in turn: 'From where he is sitting (points) can he see the zebra or not?' These subjects were given two tasks, one with each spatial arrangement of the tube positions. Their responses were queried at the end of the procedure. Four additional subjects were excluded from Study 4: three denied that anyone could see the target and one failed the control tasks. The reasons for conducting Study 4 were twofold: (1) we wished to make the task as easy as possible for subjects by questioning them about only one tube at a time; (2) we wanted to ensure that the wording of the question in Study 3 ('which ones *can* see the zebra . . . ?') had not strongly suggested that more than one of the four tubes afforded visibility. Had subjects performed considerably better in Study 4 than Study 3, then one might argue that either the Study 3 procedures were flawed or the task was too complex even for 4-year-old subjects.

Results and discussion

Table 3 shows the percentages of 3- and 4-year-olds correctly predicting visibility or non-visibility through each tube in the two studies. Table 3 shows the percentages for predictions made either spontaneously or following the experimenter's follow-up query; the percentages are very similar if only the spontaneous predictions are included. A 2 (age) × 4 (tube) analysis of variance performed on the Study 3 data showed a significant main effect for tube (F (3,102) = 18.51, $p < .001$) a near-significant main effect for age (F (1,34) = 3.83, $p < .06$) and no significant interaction. *Post hoc* Tukey tests showed that the children predicted significantly ($p < .01$) less accurately on the 90° tube than on each of the other three. The results of Study 4 were very similar. A simple analysis of variance performed on the Study 4 data also yielded a significant effect for tube (F (3,33) = 5.47, $p < .004$) with *post hoc* tests again showing significantly ($p < .05$) more incorrect predictions on the 90° tube.

Table 3. Percentage of subjects in each age group correctly predicting visibility–non-visibility through different tubes in Studies 3 and 4

Study	Age	Tube			
		Correct straight	Wrong straight	Coil	90°
3	3	78	83	83	22
	4	100	94	78	39
4	4	92	96	75	50

Note. The target could be seen through the correct straight tube (visibility) but not through the other three tubes (non-visibility).

Some of the responses to the probe questions suggested that the children making them did explicitly believe that curved looking paths are possible. The following examples are justifications by 4-year-olds for their judgement that the observer could see the target through the 90° tube: (1) 'Because the tube goes curved and he can see all the way through to the zebra'; (2) 'Because it goes from there and it's curvy'; (3) ' 'Cause this (tube) is turned around this way'. As in Study 2, there were also justifications of correct responses that testified to the opposite belief, e.g. 'It can't see bended', 'He can only see to here, until the curvy part', and 'No, because it's curvy'. Thus, the results of Studies 3 and 4 are consistent with those of Studies 1 and 2 in suggesting that young preschoolers tend to be unaware of the fact that one cannot see along a curved looking path.

General discussion

We conclude by briefly discussing the questions of what develops in this area, when, and how. As to what and when, these and previous studies suggest that by the age of 3 years or so children are normally aware that to see something an observer's eye(s) must be (*a*) open and (*b*) aimed in the general direction of the visual target. For example, in the Studies 2–4 warm-up trials, 3-year-old subjects realized that an observer could not see something located behind him or her while facing straight ahead. They also will usually infer that (*c*) an observer cannot see the target if they detect a conspicuous and familiar visual barrier interposed between observer and target, such as the walls used in the Hughes & Donaldson (1979) task, and those employed in our around-barrier and right-angle tasks in Study 2 and in our warm-up or control tasks in Studies 2–4. However, children of this age do not yet seem to have acquired what might be considered a refinement or elaboration of knowledge *b* and *c*, namely, that (*d*) an observer not only normally, but always and necessarily, sees targets via straight-line looking paths. Because they lack knowledge *d*, they will tend to accept curved looking paths—sometimes even very curved ones—whenever they do not detect a visual barrier.

It may seem surprising that even 3-year-olds would lack such an obvious generalization about the visual process, but there may be good reasons for the lack. One possible reason is that information about eyes open, direction of gaze, and visual obstacles is more perceptually and cognitively salient for young children than information about eye line. For example, when young children fail to see object A because object B is in the way, it seems much more likely that they would be consciously aware that B is a visual obstacle than that their looking path could not bend around it. Awareness of obstacles requires only attending to *what* is seen, an earlier, Level 1 type of cognition in Flavell's analysis of the development of percept knowledge (e.g. Flavell, 1978). In contrast, awareness of eye line would seem to require attending to *how* the seeing is accomplished, a presumably later-developing, more Level-2-like type of cognition that focuses on perceptual process rather than perceptual product. Another factor that might retard children's awareness that one *cannot* bend one's looking path is their awareness that one *can* change its direction. That is, perhaps young children may confuse looking around a curve that bends right or left with simply looking to the right or left. Similarly, they may also confuse it with seeing things to the right or left without changing fixation, i.e. in peripheral vision.

Our data suggest that by about 5 years of age children seem to have acquired some command of a straight-line looking path rule, and can access and use it, at least under facilitative task conditions. Further research would be needed to uncover any subsequent development that may occur here. One would think that the people who understand the rule best would be those who understand why it is valid: namely, because seeing an object occurs when light travelling on a straight-line path from the object enters the eye. However, it is uncertain whether even most adults possess this model of the visual process; surely most children do not (Guesne, 1985, p. 29).

How might this rule be acquired? We can think of two developments that might contribute to its acquisition. The first is a general increase with age in children's awareness of perceptual processes and experiences. The growth of a Level 2 understanding of perception beginning around 4 or 5 years of age is part of this development. This increased awareness should make it more possible for children to notice what they can and cannot do visually. The second might be the development of a more explicit concept of a straight line (Piaget, 1956). Perhaps it is only after children acquire such a concept, bringing with it the ability spontaneously to notice and reflect on the straightness vs. non-straightness of lines, that they become able to induce the rule from the visual evidence. Prior to that, they may only be able to use their visual experience to form generalizations of a more global sort, such as knowledge *a*, *b*, and *c*. Consistent with this possibility is evidence by Piaget (1956) and others (Estes, 1956; Lovell, 1959) that children acquire several abilities involving straight lines during the preschool and early elementary school years. An early one is the ability to discriminate straight and curved lines when copying geometric figures, e.g. to include only straight lines when drawing a square or a rectangle. A later one is the ability to imagine and construct a straight line, as when asked to align a set of objects so that they form one. It is possible, therefore, that an increasing sensitivity to perceptual phenomena coupled with an increasing sensitivity to straightness vs. non-straightness of lines helps children acquire an explicit understanding that lines of sight must always be straight.

Further research is needed to find out when children acquire explicit knowledge of other basic facts and phenomena concerning vision. For example, when do they become consciously aware that we sometimes see things poorly rather than well, and aware of some of the conditions under which vision is indistinct or blurred (e.g. objects seen only in peripheral vision, at a great distance, in poor illumination, etc.)? There is some evidence on this question (Flavell, Flavell, Green & Wilcox, 1980; Yaniv & Shatz, 1988) but not much. Similarly, when do they understand explicitly that we sometimes do not immediately detect visual targets that are 'right in plain sight' because they require visual search, e.g. embedded figures or objects that otherwise blend with their backgrounds? The child has to realize in these cases that conditions *a*, *b*, and *c* are necessary but not sufficient for good seeing, i.e. that there can be obstacles to good visibility other than closed or wrongly oriented eyes and interposed objects.

Acknowledgements

This research was supported by NIMH grant 40687. We are grateful to the children, teachers and parents of Bing School of Stanford whose cooperation made these studies possible.

References

Astington, J. W., Harris, P. L. & Olson, D. R. (Eds). (1988). *Developing Theories of Mind*. New York: Cambridge University Press.

Butterworth, G. & Cochran, E. (1980). Towards a mechanism of joint visual attention in human infancy. *International Journal of Behavioural Development*, **3**, 253–270.

Churcher, J. & Scaife, M. (1982). How infants see the point. In G. Butterworth & P. Light (Eds), *Social Cognition*, pp. 110–136. Chicago, IL: University of Chicago Press.

Estes, B. W. (1956). Some mathematical and logical concepts in children. *Journal of Genetic Psychology*, **88**, 219–222.

Flavell, J. H. (1978). The development of knowledge about visual perception. In C. B. Keasey (Ed.), *Nebraska Symposium on Motivation*, vol. 25, pp. 43–76. Lincoln, NE: University of Nebraska Press.

Flavell, J. H., Flavell, E. R., Green, F. L. & Wilcox, S. A. (1980). Young children's knowledge about visual perception: Effect of observer's distance from target on perceptual clarity of target. *Developmental Psychology*, **16**, 10–12.

Flavell, J. H., Shipstead, S. G. & Croft, K. (1978). Young children's knowledge about visual perception: Hiding objects from others. *Child Development*, **49**, 1208–1211.

Guesne, E. (1985). Light. In R. Driver, E. Guesne & A. Tiberghien (Eds), *Children's Ideas in Science*, pp. 11–32. Philadelphia, PA: Open University Press.

Hughes, M. & Donaldson, M. (1979). The use of hiding games for studying the coordination of viewpoints. *Educational Review*, **31**, 133–140.

Lempers, J. D., Flavell, E. R. & Flavell, J. H. (1977). The development in very young children of tacit knowledge concerning visual perception. *Genetic Psychology Monographs*, **95**, 3–53.

Lovell, K. (1959). A follow-up study of some aspects of the work of Piaget and Inhelder on the child's conception of space. *British Journal of Educational Psychology*, **29**, 104–117.

Piaget, J. (1956). *The Child's Conception of Space*. London: Routledge & Kegan Paul.

Wellman, H. M. (1990). *The Child's Theory of Mind*. Cambridge, MA: Bradford Books/MIT Press.

Yaniv, I. & Shatz, M. (1988). Children's understanding of perceptibility. In J. W. Astington, P. L. Harris & D. R. Olson (Eds), *Developing Theories of Mind*, pp. 93–108. New York: Cambridge University Press.

Yaniv, I. & Shatz, M. (1990). Heuristics of reasoning and analogy in children's visual perspective taking. *Child Development*, **61**, 1491–1501.

Received 17 August 1989; revised version received 19 September 1990

British Journal of Developmental Psychology (1991), **9**, 89–102   *Printed in Great Britain*   89

Children's understanding of visual ambiguity

Ted Ruffman*, **David R. Olson** and **Janet W. Astington**
*Ontario Institute for Studies in Education, Centre for Applied Cognitive Science, 252 Bloor Street West,
Toronto, Ontario, Canada M5S 1V6*

Two stages have been suggested in children's understanding of the mind between
ages 4 and 8. The first stage is signalled by success on false belief tasks around age 4
and is thought to indicate an understanding of the mind as 'representational'. The
second stage is signalled by success on ambiguity tasks around age 6–8 and is
thought to indicate a new understanding that people 'interpret' or 'process'
perceptual information. The study reported here was carried out with 108 subjects
aged 3–6 to determine whether children begin to understand that ambiguous visual
cues are an insufficient source of knowledge around age 6 as previous research
suggests (e.g. Taylor, 1988), or whether this development occurs around age 4
when they begin to understand related tasks such as false belief. Two differently
coloured (unambiguous) and two same coloured (ambiguous) stuffed animals were
introduced to a subject and another character. The animals from one pair were then
secretly placed in two separate boxes which had a small hole in the centre enabling a
viewer to see each animal's colour but not the shape. Almost no 3-year-olds, but
about half the 4-year-olds and most 5- and 6-year-olds, recognized that the other
could identify the unambiguous pair, but not the ambiguous pair. It is argued that
an understanding of ambiguity develops around age 4 because it requires an
understanding that beliefs may be false, and that there is one stage (at least with
respect to these abilities) rather than two.

In their investigations of children's developing 'theory of mind' researchers have
focused on when children come to realize that an other may hold a false or mistaken
belief. In a typical false belief task a protagonist sees an object placed at a first
location. This object is then moved to a second location in the protagonist's absence
and when the protagonist returns children are asked where she or he will think the
object is. Research has shown that, whereas 3-year-olds tend to claim incorrectly that
the protagonist will think the object is in the second location (where it really is),
5-year-olds tend to claim correctly that the protagonist will hold a false belief,
namely, that the object is in the first location (Hogrefe, Wimmer & Perner, 1986;
Moses & Flavell, 1990; Perner, Leekam & Wimmer, 1987; Wimmer & Perner, 1983).
Similarly, research has shown that most children also begin to be able to recognize
their own previous false beliefs at about 4 years of age (Gopnik & Astington, 1988).

*Requests for reprints.

A second topic of interest for theory of mind researchers is children's understanding of ambiguous perceptual information. For instance, Taylor (1988) gave children between the ages of 3 and 8 years a task in which they were asked to assess how visually ambiguous information would affect a viewer's knowledge. A subject but not an 'other' (a puppet) was shown a picture of an animal (e.g. a giraffe). Then the experimenter covered most of the animal leaving visible either: (*a*) an informative portion which would allow the other to identify the animal, (*b*) a small uninformative portion which would not allow identification, or (*c*) no portion of the animal at all which obviously would not allow identification. The other was then shown one of these views and children were asked whether the other knew there was a giraffe in the picture. Results indicated that it was not until 6–8 years of age that children recognized that the other would know which animal was in the picture when an informative, identifiable portion was visible, and that the other would *not* know which animal was in the picture when either no portion was visible or when an unidentifiable portion was visible.

A number of researchers have obtained similar results both for children's understanding of visual ambiguity (Chandler & Helm, 1984; Olson & Astington, 1987) and for their understanding of verbal ambiguity (an ambiguous message) (Beal & Flavell, 1984; Bonitatibus, 1988; Olson & Hildyard, 1983; Robinson, Goelman & Olson, 1983; Robinson & Robinson, 1983; Robinson & Whitaker, 1986; Singer & Flavell, 1981; Sodian, 1988).

On the basis of these findings two broad stages have been proposed in children's understanding of the mind between the ages of about 4 and 8 (Chandler, 1988; Flavell, 1988; Forguson & Gopnik, 1988; Taylor, 1988). In the first stage, which begins around age 4 and is signalled by success on false belief tasks, children recognize beliefs as representations of the real world (Perner, 1988). By 5 years of age most children recognize that an other's beliefs may be false and, consequently, not represent the true state of affairs in the world. In this stage, however, the mind is still thought to be essentially passive. It is claimed that children have no understanding that people 'interpret' or 'process' information. Thus, even if the information to which the other has access is ambiguous, he or she will still be thought to know. In other words, it is said that children believe seeing leads to knowing and not seeing leads to not knowing (Taylor, 1988). Chandler & Boyes (1982) refer to young children as having a 'copy' theory of knowledge, Wellman (1988) describes them as having an 'encounter' theory of knowledge, and Olson & Astington (1987) claimed children did not realize that seeing could be non-epistemic. Then, in the second stage, which takes place between 6 and 8 years and is signalled by success on ambiguity tasks, it is thought that children come to recognize that another interprets the available perceptual information, realizing that seeing does not lead to knowing if what is seen is ambiguous.

However, the results of past research into children's understanding of ambiguity are somewhat puzzling in that ambiguity tasks would seem to be false belief tasks at heart. In order to understand why this is so it is necessary to consider what is involved in children's recognition that ambiguous information prevents another from knowing. It could be argued that in such tasks children must recognize what people could falsely *think* in order to recognize that they will not *know*: that is, children must recognize (*a*) that an ambiguous stimulus can be represented or interpreted in more than one way, (*b*) that as a result a person could think the stimulus is something other than what it really is, and (*c*) that as a consequence the other will not know what it is. Further, when children themselves know what is true (e.g. what the animal in question really is), this second step, in which children recognize that a person could think something *different,* would amount to an understanding that a person could think something false. In this way ambiguity tasks are in essence false belief tasks.

Given the similarity one might expect that children would come to understand false belief and visual ambiguity at about the same time, and that between 4 and 8 years there would be one stage in children's understanding of the mind rather than two. Hence, we are left with the question of why past research has indicated that an understanding of ambiguity is acquired around age 6–7, whereas an understanding of false belief is acquired around age 4.

One possibility is that the perceptual cues, which include the key information upon which subjects' judgements of the other's knowledge rests, are much more salient in false belief tasks than in ambiguity tasks: that is, in the typical false belief task the other's not seeing the object moved from the original location to a new location is a clear cue that the other has not had access to key information. On the other hand, in ambiguity tasks perceptual cues are typically much less salient. Part of the problem lies in the nature of ambiguity where, unlike false belief, perceptual information is not presented in an all-or-nothing format. Consider, for instance, Olson & Astington's (1987) visual ambiguity task. A child and a viewer were introduced to two same coloured animals (a blue pig and a blue dog). The viewer then went away and the child watched while the animals were placed behind two windows such that the colour but not the shape of the animals was visible. Because the animals were the same colour they would be ambiguous to the viewer. Children were then asked whether the viewer would know which animal was which.

As in a false belief task, children were required to realize that the viewer's not seeing an object placed behind a window limits her knowledge. However, unlike false belief, the viewer is then given access to perceptual information—she is shown a portion, albeit an ambiguous portion, of the animal in question. This second source of information could understandably confuse children when judging the viewer's knowledge unless all relevant information is made very clear to them (e.g. that the animals behind the windows are the same colour). Recognizing that the viewer will not know which animal is which without such clarification is, consequently, more difficult than arriving at the same recognition in a false belief task.

In the present study we made perceptual cues more salient by including prompts and reminder questions to help children keep track of relevant details. The purpose, therefore, was to determine whether children begin to understand ambiguity around age 4 as our argument suggests, or around 6–8 as previous research suggests.

Method

Subjects

A total of 108 subjects (57 boys, 51 girls) drawn from lower middle-class and middle-class homes, and divided into four age groups (3, 4, 5 and 6 years), participated in this study. There were 24 3-year-olds (mean age 3:6; range 3:0–3:11; 9 boys, 15 girls), 24 4-year-olds (mean age 4:6; range 4:0–4:11; 13 boys, 11 girls), 24 5-year-olds (mean age 5:7; range 5:1–5:11; 12 boys, 12 girls), and 36 6-year-olds (mean age 6:5; range 6:0–6:11; 23 boys, 13 girls). The 3- and 4-year-olds attended metropolitan day care centres, the 5- and 6-year-olds, elementary school.

Materials

Materials consisted of two differently coloured stuffed animals (a green turtle and a brown chicken) and two same coloured stuffed animals (a grey elephant and a grey rabbit). The animals fitted into identical cardboard boxes (14 cm long × 14 cm wide × by 5 cm deep). There was a 2 × 3 cm hole in the centre of each box which enabled a viewer to see an animal's colour but not its shape. Children were asked to judge the knowledge of a doll named 'Katy' (38 cm tall). This doll is subsequently referred to as 'the other'. When the animals were placed in boxes Katy was covered with a blanket (43 cm × 25 cm) and she was said to be 'sleeping'. This sometimes took place behind a cardboard screen which was 195 cm long × 85 cm high.

Procedure

Children were taken individually to a quiet room. The subject and experimenter sat next to each other at a table. The doll, screen and objects were placed on the centre of the table and the doll was introduced to the subject as 'another person, just like you and me'.

There were three conditions: a condition in which the animals were unambiguous to both subject and the other (control), a condition in which the animals were ambiguous to the other but not to the subject (opposite perspective), and a condition in which the animals were ambiguous to both subject and other (same perspective).*

Unambiguous (control) and opposite perspective ambiguous conditions. The procedure for the opposite perspective ambiguous condition and the unambiguous control condition was identical except that the same coloured elephant and rabbit were used in the former, and the differently coloured turtle and chicken were used in the latter. In both conditions the experimenter showed the pair of animals to the subject who was then asked what the doll would say each animal was, and whether the doll would say the animals were the *same* colour or *different* colours. The experimenter then named the colour of each animal and emphasized that the doll knew the colour of each animal and that they were either the same colour or different colours. If subjects answered the *same–different* question incorrectly, they were corrected.

The doll then lay down, a blanket was pulled over her head, and she went for a 'nap'. The subject was instructed that, when 'sleeping', the doll could not hear or see anything. The subject then watched as the

---

* A fourth condition involving objects with a misleading appearance (e.g. a candle which looked like an apple) and designed to measure children's understanding of false belief was also given to the 4-, 5- and 6-year-olds. The misleading objects were placed in boxes, each of which had a small hole in the centre and subjects were asked what a viewer, who had not been shown that the objects had a misleading appearance, would think was in a particular box. Unfortunately, performance on this condition was very poor. While previous research has shown that most 4-year-olds typically understand that another will hold a false belief, only 67 per cent of the 5-year-olds showed a similar recognition in this condition. Children's difficulty was apparently due to the extra demands of the task. In a standard false belief task (e.g. using a familiar candy box filled with pencils) children's understanding that a viewer will hold a false belief depends on their recognizing that the appearance is misleading and that the other has not been shown this. In contrast, in the present study, because the misleading objects were placed in boxes in which there was a small hole in the centre, children were required to recognize that the object in question was misleading, that the other had not been shown this and, in addition, that even though the other could see a small part of the object and could therefore identify it as one object rather than the other (because the two misleading objects were different colours), this identity was still incorrect (due to the fact that the appearance was misleading). Not surprisingly, this latter requirement increased the complexity of the task so that children's performance was not comparable to their performance on previous false belief or appearance–reality tasks. Consequently, the results for this task are not discussed further.

experimenter placed each animal in a box. The boxes were placed upright on opposite sides of the table so that the colour (but not the shape) of each animal was clearly visible through the hole in the centre. Consequently, the same coloured animals would have been ambiguous to the doll who had not seen which animal was placed in which box but would have been unambiguous to the subject who had seen this. On the other hand, the differently coloured animals would have been unambiguous to both subject and other (by virtue of their different colours).

At this point, the doll 'woke up', went to the place where each box was located, and looked through the box holes at each animal. The child, likewise, was instructed to look through the box holes at each animal. As a reminder, the experimenter then asked the children two questions: (1) 'Now remember, did Katy see which animal was put in which box, or was she asleep then?', and (2) 'Will Katy say these animals are the same colour or different colours?' The experimenter then repeated that the doll knew the colour of each animal (i.e. 'that the turtle is green and the chicken is brown') and that they were either the same or different colours. Subjects were corrected if they answered either of these reminder questions incorrectly. The experimenter then pointed to one of the boxes and asked the subject a number of experimental questions. In the unambiguous condition the experimenter always pointed to the box containing the chicken and in the ambiguous condition the experimenter always pointed to the box containing the elephant.

The unambiguous condition served as a control. In order for their responses on the ambiguous conditions to be meaningful, children had to recognize that both they and the other would know which animal was in which box when confronted with the differently coloured animals. In the opposite perspective condition, because children (but not the other) saw which of the same coloured animals was placed in which box, they always knew the identity of the animals. It was for this reason that we were particularly interested in children's performance in this condition. Recall that we suggested when children themselves know what is true, their ascriptions of ignorance to another (in an ambiguity task) may amount to a recognition that the viewer could think something false.

Same perspective ambiguous condition.　The same coloured animals were also used in the same perspective condition. The procedure for this condition was similar to that of the opposite perspective condition except that the animals were made ambiguous to the subject as well as to the other. They were ambiguous to the subject because, unlike the opposite perspective condition, in the same perspective condition the animals were taken behind the screen before they were placed in boxes. Consequently, the subject, like the doll, did not see which animal was placed in which box and when subsequently shown the boxes could see only an ambiguous grey segment of each animal. Table 1 summarizes the main features of the three conditions.

Experimental questions.　The experimental questions were as follows:
1. 'Did you [Katy] *look* at the animal that's in this box, yes or no?'
2. 'When you [Katy] looked, did you [she] *see* the animal that's in this box, yes or no?'
3. 'Do[es] you [Katy] *know* it's the chicken [elephant], yes or no?'
4. 'What do[es] you [Katy] *think* is in this box, the chicken [elephant] or the turtle [rabbit]?'
5. (*a*) 'How do[es] you [Katy] know what's in this box?' or (*b*) '*Why* do[es]n't you [Katy] know what's in this box?'

There were two series of questions—one pertaining to self, one pertaining to the other (the doll). The order in which each series was given was counterbalanced. The 'look' and 'see' questions were intended to highlight the significance of the doll's exposure to the animals in the boxes. In the unambiguous control condition the subject was asked five questions for self and five for other. In the same perspective ambiguous condition neither the subject nor the other had grounds for knowing which animal was in which box. Consequently, the think question would have been misleading and was excluded, leaving four questions for self and four for other. In the opposite perspective ambiguous condition the other again had no grounds for knowing which animal was in which box. Consequently, the think question was excluded for other, leaving five questions for self and four for other. When the think question was included, the order of the know and think questions was counterbalanced. Apart from this arrangement, questions in each series were given in the order shown above.

Table 1. Summary of experimental method

Unambiguous (control) condition
  Animals are different colours
  Subject but not other sees which animal is placed in which box
  Subject and other look at animals through box holes
  Animals unambiguous to both subject and other because are different colours

Ambiguous opposite perspective condition
  Animals are same colour
  Subject but not other sees which animal is placed in which box
  Subject and other look at animals through box holes
  Animals unambiguous to subject because saw animals placed in boxes, ambiguous to
  other because are same colour

Ambiguous same perspective condition
  Animals are same colour
  Neither subject nor other sees which animal is placed in which box
  Subject and other look at animals through box holes
  Animals ambiguous to both subject and other because are same colour

---

If a subject incorrectly answered 'No' to question 1 this question was rephrased: 'Did you [Katy] look at *a part of* the animal that's in this box?' Likewise, if a subject incorrectly answered 'No', to question 2, this question was rephrased: 'When you [Katy] looked, did you [she] see *a part of* the animal that's in this box?' These questions were intended to highlight the fact that there was information available to the other when she looked through the box holes.

Design

The counterbalancing of condition order, the order of self and other questions, and the order of know and think questions was carried out as follows. There were four different condition orders, and in each age group a quarter of the children received a form with a given condition order. Within each of the condition orders the order in which self and other questions were asked was then counterbalanced, and within each of the self and other question sets, the order of the know and think questions was counterbalanced (when a think question was asked). Thus, while each of the individual variables was counterbalanced across subjects at each age level, any possible interaction effects were randomized.

Results

Order effects

Order effects for each variable were analysed as main effects. There were no significant effects (as measured by chi-square) for condition order, the order of self and other questions, or the order of know and think questions. Nor were there any significant sex differences.

Reminder questions

While all 5- and 6-year-olds answered the reminder and perception questions correctly, some 3- and 4-year-olds were not as successful. The reminder question in which children were asked if the animals were the same or different colours was answered incorrectly on at least one of three trials by six 3-year-olds (25 per cent), and on at least one of four trials by one 4-year-old (4 per cent). These children did not appear to have learned the meaning of 'same' and 'different'. The reminder question in which subjects were asked if the doll had seen which object was placed in which box was answered incorrectly on at least one of three trials by three 3-year-olds (13 per cent). The *see* perception question was answered incorrectly on at least one of six trials by three 3-year-olds (13 per cent), and on at least one of eight trials by two 4-year-olds (8 per cent). All other children answered the perception questions (or their modified form) correctly. The modified version, which asked whether they had seen *a part of* the animal, was needed more often for older children than for younger children. While failures on the reminder and perception questions may have reduced the likelihood of correct responding on the know and think questions, children who failed in this manner were not excluded from the following analysis on the basis that excluding their data might have overestimated children's understanding of ambiguity.

Control condition

Fourteen children failed the control condition by incorrectly claiming the other would not know which animal was in the box when the cues were unambiguous, or by claiming that the other would think the animal in question (a chicken) was a turtle. One 3-year-old (4 per cent), five 4-year-olds (21 per cent), three 5-year-olds (13 per cent) and five 6-year-olds (14 per cent) responded in this manner. At first glance, this result seems rather odd; it appears that the youngest subjects understood better than the older ones that another could infer what an animal was by virtue of seeing an unambiguous patch of colour. However, most 3-year-olds always claimed that the other would know which animal was in which box even when the perceptual cues were ambiguous (as the results to be presented in more detail later will show). Thus, they failed to distinguish between ambiguous and unambiguous perceptual information and seemed to base their claims that the other would know which animal was which on the fact that she could see a portion of the animal (a seeing = knowing strategy). This strategy led to correct responding in the unambiguous condition but incorrect performance in the ambiguous conditions. On the other hand, the older children did usually differentiate between ambiguous and unambiguous perceptual information (as described below). When the older children failed the control condition, they almost always did so by claiming that the other would not know because she had been absent when the animals were placed in the boxes. Thus, these children failed because they let a perceptual cue which most 3-year-olds did not even consider (the other's absence) override the significance of a second cue (what the other could see upon her return).

The data for children who failed the control condition were excluded from further analysis. This precaution was taken even if these children passed the ambiguous conditions because it would not be clear whether they understood ambiguity, or were simply following a strategy which equated not seeing the animals placed in boxes with not knowing. In contrast, children who passed the control claimed that the other would know which animal was which despite the fact that the other had been absent when the animals were placed in the boxes. Therefore, these children clearly understood that the other's absence, by itself, was not enough to induce ignorance unless in addition the perceptual cues were ambiguous. Children who passed the control and who passed the ambiguous conditions must have based their attributions of ignorance to the other in the ambiguous conditions on the fact that the perceptual cues were ambiguous. After eliminating the data of those who failed the control condition the remaining sample consisted of 23 3-year-olds (mean 3:6; range 3:0–3:11; 8 boys, 15 girls), 19 4-year-olds (mean 4:6; range 4:0–4:11; 11 boys, 8 girls), 21 5-year-olds (mean 5:7; range 5:1–5:11; 11 boys, 10 girls) and 31 6-year-olds (mean 6:5; range 6:0–6:11; 20 boys, 11 girls).

Ambiguous conditions

In order to compare our results with those of past research (e.g. Taylor, 1988) we examined the percentage of children who, having passed the control condition, correctly stated that the other would not be able to identify the animals in the two conditions (same and opposite perspective) in which the visual cues were ambiguous. This information is presented in Fig. 1.

While Taylor's (1988) results (and the results of all previous research) suggested that the transitional age in children's understanding that ambiguity restricts knowledge is 6 years, our results indicate that the transitional age is 4. In the present study, there were very few 3-year-olds who recognized that ambiguity restricts knowledge, but about half the 4-year-olds and almost all 5- and 6-year-olds had attained this understanding. This pattern held for both the same and opposite perspective conditions*.

Table 2 provides a more detailed breakdown of the data. It lists the percentage of children who responded correctly on knowledge questions for the self and for the other on the same and opposite perspective conditions. Table 2 shows that in the opposite perspective condition all children were perfect when judging their own knowledge. In addition, in the opposite perspective condition every child but one 3-year-old answered the self 'think' question correctly: that is, they correctly named the elephant when asked what they thought was in the box. Children clearly demonstrated, therefore, that they knew what the true state of affairs was in the opposite perspective condition (which animal was in which box). Because children knew what was true, their correct claims that the other would not know appear to signify an understanding that the other could think something false: that is, they appeared to recognize that the other would not know because she could falsely think the elephant was the rabbit.

---

* It might be thought that if children were given the control condition first (when the other knew the identity of the animals) they would assume that the other would again know the identity of the animals in the subsequent ambiguous conditions (having been biased by the control condition). If so, this might explain the poor performance of 3-year-olds. However, 3-year-olds actually performed slightly better in the opposite perspective condition when given the control question first (four of 11 were correct in attributing ignorance to the other in the opposite perspective condition when given the control question first, while only two of 12 were correct when given the opposite perspective condition first). Likewise, there was a similar pattern for 3-year-olds' performance in the same perspective condition. Clearly, therefore, 3-year-olds did not fail the ambiguous conditions because they were misled by the other's knowing in the control condition.

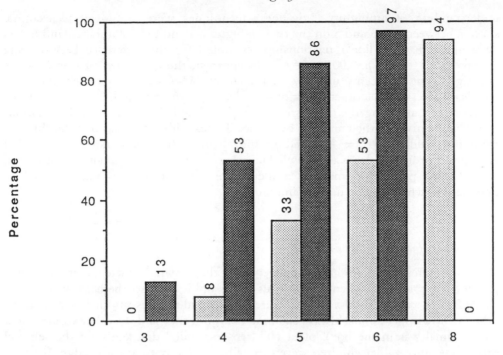

Figure 1. Percentage of children counted as understanding the implications of ambiguity. ■, present study; ⊡, Taylor (1988).

In sum, Fig. 1 and Table 2 show that there was a sharp developmental shift between the ages of 3 and 5 on judgements of the other's knowledge over the control and two ambiguous conditions, indicating an impressive development in children's

Table 2. Percentage of subjects correctly assessing their own and the other's knowledge in the two ambiguous conditions

| | Age | | | | | | | |
| | 3 | | 4 | | 5 | | 6 | |
Condition	S	O	S	O	S	O	S	O
Ambiguous opposite persp. *know*	100	26	100	58	100	95	100	97
Ambiguous same persp. *know*	17	17	42	74	71	86	90	100
Passing both	17	13	42	53	71	86	90	97

Note. S represents subjects' ascriptions of knowledge to self, O to other. In the opposite perspective ambiguous condition cues are unambiguous to subject and ambiguous to other. In the same perspective ambiguous condition cues are ambiguous to both subject and other. 'Passing both' refers to children passing both control and ambiguous conditions.

understanding of ambiguity. Log-linear techniques were employed to examine success between age 3 and 5 on the two ambiguous conditions combined and it was determined that the linear relationship accounted for the difference between age groups ($\chi^2(2) = 25.9$, $p < .001$, $N = 63$). In contrast, the quadratic relationship was non-significant. It seems unlikely that children who were correct in this way (correctly assessing the other's lack of knowledge on the two ambiguous conditions and correctly assessing the other's knowledge and beliefs in the control condition) could have arrived at their answers by chance. Instead, it seems clear that the children from our study who are included in Fig. 1 must have understood, first, that perception ordinarily leads to knowledge (when visual cues are unambiguous) and, second, that perception may be non-epistemic and sometimes fails to lead to knowledge (when visual cues are ambiguous).

Assessments of own vs. other's knowledge

Also of interest is children's assessments of their own knowledge in the same perspective condition when the animals were ambiguous to them as well. While Table 2 shows that most 3-year-olds were equally bad at assessing their own and the other's knowledge (almost always claiming that both they and the other would know what animal was in the box), older children responded differently on the self and other questions. Older children were generally less likely to acknowledge that they did not know which animal was in the box than they were to acknowledge that the other did not know this. There were nine 4-year-olds, four 5-year-olds and three 6-year-olds who incorrectly attributed knowledge to themselves but correctly attributed ignorance to the other. On the other hand, there were no children in these age groups who showed the opposite pattern. This pattern was significant for the 4-year-old group (McNemar's $\chi^2(1) = 7.11$, $p < .01$, $N = 24$). In contrast, all but one child (a 3-year-old) correctly assessed their own knowledge and beliefs in the control and opposite perspective conditions when the cues were unambiguous to them.

While it could be argued that children's relatively poor performance on self knowledge questions when visual cues were ambiguous indicates that they do not understand ambiguity, this argument does not account for their good performance on questions about the other's knowledge. If children did not understand that ambiguity restricts knowledge, then they would not have correctly attributed knowledge to the other when the visual cues were unambiguous, and correctly attributed ignorance to the other in the two conditions when visual cues were ambiguous. Perhaps a more plausible explanation for the poor performance on the self questions of the same perspective condition is either that children are reluctant to admit that they do not know something, or that they treat the knowledge question for themselves as an invitation to guess. Indeed, there is now a wide body of research which indicates that when children err they almost always do so by incorrectly attributing knowledge to themselves rather than by incorrectly attributing ignorance to themselves. Results of this nature have been obtained with tasks measuring children's understanding of ambiguity (Astington & Gopnik, 1988; Olson & Astington, 1987; Sodian, 1988), inference (Sodian & Wimmer, 1987) and their understanding of informational access as a source of knowledge (Marvin, Greenberg & Mossler, 1976; Ruffman & Olson, 1989; Wimmer, Hogrefe & Perner, 1988).

Discussion

Possible explanations for results

There are a number of reasons why children may have done better on our tasks than they have on tasks used in past studies. Consider, for example, our study in relation to that of Taylor (1988). First, there are differences between the design and experimental questions of the two studies. Subjects in Taylor's study were given one control condition and four experimental conditions for each of three pictures (for a total of three control conditions and 12 experimental conditions). However, the knowledge questions asked in the different conditions varied in level of difficulty. In the experimental conditions there were 12 knowledge questions asked about animals in which no part was visible, and three asked about animals where only a tiny edge was visible. These questions would almost certainly be easier to answer than the remaining nine knowledge questions (of the experimental conditions) where a larger portion of the animals was visible. Most importantly, the latter nine knowledge questions of Taylor's study represent more stringent tests of children's understanding of ambiguity and are comparable to the two ambiguous conditions and knowledge questions of the present study. Likewise, in the study by Chandler & Helm (1984), children had to make six judgements of the other's knowledge. Consequently, one might argue that because children received more conditions and had to answer correctly a larger number of knowledge questions in these studies they performed more poorly overall. On the other hand, in the study by Olson & Astington (1987), children received only one condition and two questions about the other's knowledge when stimuli were ambiguous. Yet these children still performed markedly worse than children in the present study. This result suggests that some factor other than the number of questions is responsible for the discrepancy in results.

A second possibility is that we measured a different type of visual ambiguity than that measured by Taylor (1988) or Chandler & Helm (1984). While the ambiguity in the tasks of these researchers rested on the form of the stimuli and the potential possibilities of what it could be were almost endless, in our task the ambiguity rested on colour (a perceptual quality) and presented children with two stimuli such that each could realistically be interpreted in only one of two ways. However, the results of Olson & Astington (1987) suggest that this is not the correct explanation either because they used similar stimuli but obtained very different results.

Perhaps the most likely explanation is related to the salience of the perceptual cues. We reminded children several times that the other knew the ambiguous animals were the *same* colour and that the unambiguous animals were *different* colours. By bringing this information to children's attention it is likely that we enabled them to demonstrate their understanding of how it would affect an other's knowledge.

Furthermore, while in a second experiment Taylor (1988) found that training significantly improved the performance of 4-year-olds, suggesting that the emphasis on perceptual cues in the present study may have served a similar function to that provided by training, the results of our study show that such an understanding is attained without training.

Salience of cues

It could be argued that when the cues are made as salient as they were in this study children have essentially been given the answers to the questions and that this is, therefore, not a true test of their understanding of ambiguity. However, we would argue that there are two reasons for thinking otherwise. First, while the task employed in the present study did undoubtedly make things easier for children by highlighting and clarifying relevant information, they still could not provide the correct answers to the knowledge questions without an understanding (*a*) that this information was, in fact, ambiguous, and (*b*) of how ambiguous information leads to a lack of knowledge. In effect, we reduced the ambiguity (that is, the implicitness) of the procedure itself, yet still required children to recognize ambiguous information as ambiguous information and to understand its relation to knowledge. As suggested earlier, such procedural changes merely make this study more comparable with false belief tasks where relevant cues are more salient. For instance, in a false belief task one must recognize the *significance* of the other's absence during the critical event (e.g. the hiding of the object) before one can correctly recognize the other's false belief; research has shown that an awareness of the other's absence is insufficient by itself (Hogrefe *et al.*, 1986). Similarly, being reminded that two animals are the same colour is without benefit unless children recognize the way in which such information will be construed by the other; because they are the same colour and only a small ambiguous portion is visible, each animal could be represented in two different ways.

Secondly, if the cues we provided children with were overinformative, leading them to the correct answer without their having to recognize the implications of the cues, then should not more or even all subjects have correctly assessed the other's knowledge? Perhaps it is equally significant not only that many 4-year-olds do seem to understand ambiguity, but that 3-year-olds cannot solve these tasks despite efforts to make them as easy as possible. This result is consistent with that obtained by Moses & Flavell (1990) who made similar efforts to simplify a false belief task yet found that 3-year-olds still were not able to understand an other's false belief. It seems clear that these children, like those in our own study, were simply incapable of taking advantage of the relevant perceptual information when judging an other's mental state. We would argue that they are unable to do so because they are incapable of meta-representation.

Summary and implications

In summary, we believe our results show that an understanding of visual ambiguity begins around age 4 and is firmly in place by age 5. This result is contrary to the results reported by Chandler & Helm (1984), Olson & Astington (1987) and Taylor (1988). We have argued that the most likely reason for the improved performance of children in our study is that we made perceptual cues more salient, which probably made things easier for children but still required them to recognize ambiguous information as ambiguous information and to understand the way it would lead to the other's not knowing. Further, we argued that these changes merely made our task more comparable to false belief tasks in which the perceptual information is more salient. Finally, we suggested that the reason ambiguity tasks are solved around age 4 is that they are false belief tasks at heart—in recognizing that the other would not know, children were required to recognize that the other could hold a false belief. Further research is needed to establish the precise nature of the relationship between false belief and ambiguity tasks.

Our results have important implications for theoretical accounts offered to describe children's developing theory of mind. At the outset we mentioned the two-stage model that has been proposed to describe children's understanding of the mind between the ages of 4 and 8. It has been argued that in the first stage, around age 4, children begin to separate beliefs from the real world, and then in the second stage, around age 6, begin to recognize that the mind is not passive, but that it processes or interprets information. Our results suggest the possibility that there is only one stage and that ambiguity and false belief tasks tap the same underlying development—an understanding that beliefs may be false. If true, then a reworking of Chandler & Boyes (1982) 'copy' theory of knowledge seems in order. While these descriptions possibly do reflect 3-year-olds' theory of knowledge, our results suggest that this rudimentary theory is in the process of being replaced by a more sophisticated, adult-like theory by as early as age 4.

Acknowledgements

This study was carried out as part of the first author's PhD thesis at the Ontario Institute for Studies in Education under the supervision of the second author. The authors would like to thank the children and staff at the York Regional Board of Education and the various day cares for their participation in this study, the reviewers for their helpful comments, Bill Postl for statistical assistance, Lola Ruffman for technical assistance, the Social Sciences and Humanities Research Council of Canada for financial support to Ted Ruffman (Award #452-89-0699) and to David R. Olson and Janet Astington, the Natural Sciences and Engineering Council of Canada for support to David R. Olson and Janet W. Astington, and the Ontario Ministry of Education through its Block Transfer Grant to David R. Olson through OISE.

References

Astington, J. W. & Gopnik, A. (1988). Knowing you've changed your mind: Children's understanding of representational change. In J. W. Astington, P. L. Harris & D. R. Olson (Eds), *Developing Theories of Mind,* pp. 193–206. Cambridge: Cambridge University Press.

Beal, C. R. & Flavell, J. H. (1984). Development of the ability to distinguish intention and literal message meaning. *Child Development,* 55, 920–928.

Bonitatibus, G. (1988). Comprehension monitoring and the apprehension of literal meaning. *Child Development,* 59, 60–70.

Chandler, M. (1988). Doubt and developing theories of mind. In J. W. Astington, P. L. Harris & D. R. Olson (Eds), *Developing Theories of Mind,* pp. 387–413. Cambridge: Cambridge University Press.

Chandler, M. & Boyes, M. (1982). Social–cognitive development. In B. B. Wolman (Ed.), *Handbook of Developmental Psychology,* pp. 387–402. Englewood Cliffs, NJ: Prentice-Hall.

Chandler, M. J. & Helm, D. (1984). Developmental changes in the contribution of shared experience to social role-taking competence. *International Journal of Behavioural Development,* 7, 145–156.

Flavell, J. H. (1988). The development of children's knowledge about the mind: From cognitive connections to mental representations. In J. W. Astington, P. L. Harris & D. R. Olson (Eds), *Developing Theories of Mind,* pp. 244–267. Cambridge: Cambridge University Press.

Forguson, L. & Gopnik, A. (1988). The ontogeny of common sense. In J. W. Astington, P. L. Harris & D. R. Olson (Eds), *Developing Theories of Mind,* pp. 226–243. Cambridge: Cambridge University Press.

Gopnik, A. & Astington, J. W. (1988). Children's understanding of representational change and its relation to the understanding of false belief and the appearance–reality distinction. *Child Development,* **59**, 26–37.

Hogrefe, G. J., Wimmer, H. & Perner, J. (1986). Ignorance versus false belief: A developmental lag in attribution of epistemic states. *Child Development,* **57**, 567–582.

Marvin, R. S., Greenberg, M. T. & Mossler, D. G. (1976). The early development of conceptual perspective taking: Distinguishing among multiple perspectives. *Child Development,* **47**, 511–514.

Moses, L. J. & Flavell, J. H. (1990). Inferring false beliefs from actions and reactions. *Child Development,* **61**, 929–945.

Olson, D. R. & Astington, J. W. (1987). Seeing and knowing: On the ascription of mental states to young children. *Canadian Journal of Psychology,* **41**, 399–411.

Olson, D. R. & Hildyard, A. (1983). Psychology of written language: A developmental and educational perspective. In M. Martlew (Ed.), *Writing and Literal Meaning,* pp. 41–65. New York: Wiley.

Perner, J. (1988). Developing semantics for theories of mind: From propositional attitudes to mental representation. In J. W. Astington, P. L. Harris & D. R. Olson (Eds), *Developing Theories of Mind,* pp. 141–172. Cambridge: Cambridge University Press.

Perner, J., Leekam, S. R. & Wimmer, H. (1987). Three-year-olds' difficulty with false belief: The case for a conceptual deficit. *British Journal of Developmental Psychology,* **5**, 125–137.

Robinson, E., Goelman, H. & Olson, D. R. (1983). Children's understanding of the relations between expressions (what was said) and intentions (what was meant). *British Journal of Developmental Psychology,* **1**, 75–86.

Robinson, E. J. & Robinson, W. P. (1983). Children's uncertainty about the interpretation of ambiguous messages. *Journal of Experimental Child Psychology,* **36**, 81–96.

Robinson, E. J. & Whitaker, S. J. (1986). Children's conceptions of meaning–message relationships. *Cognition,* **22**, 41–60.

Ruffman, T. K. & Olson, D. R. (1989). Children's ascriptions of knowledge to others. *Developmental Psychology,* **25**, 601–606.

Singer, J. B. & Flavell, J. H. (1981). Development of knowledge about communication: Children's evaluations of explicitly ambiguous messages. *Child Development,* **52**, 1211–1215.

Sodian, B. (1988). Children's attributions of knowledge to a listener in a referential communication task. *Child Development,* **59**, 324–335.

Sodian, B. & Wimmer, H. (1987). Children's understanding of inference as a source of knowledge. *Child Development,* **58**, 424–433.

Taylor, M. (1988). The development of children's ability to distinguish what they know from what they see. *Child Development,* **59**(3), 703–718.

Wellman, H. M. (1988). First steps in the child's theorizing about the mind. In J. W. Astington, P. L. Harris & D. R. Olson (Eds), *Developing Theories of Mind,* pp. 64–92. Cambridge: Cambridge University Press.

Wimmer, H. & Perner, J. (1983). Beliefs about beliefs: Representation and constraining function of wrong beliefs in young children's understanding of deception. *Cognition,* **13**, 103–128.

Wimmer, H., Hogrefe, J. & Perner, J. (1988). Children's understanding of informational origins as a source of knowledge. *Child Development,* **59**, 386–396.

Received 6 October 1989; revised version received 9 August 1990

3
Theory of mind, imagination, belief and deception

Preface

This section spans some central topics in current research on theory of mind. Perhaps what is distinctive about folk psychological explanations is that they relate actual behaviour to imaginary circumstances. This observation links the child's understanding of pretence with his ability to understand false belief. The challenge is to spell out more exactly what this link is and how the different ways of thinking about imaginary situations in relation to behaviour develop. These themes are represented in the following papers.

In the first paper, Harris, Marriott, Whittall & Harmer confirm previous demonstrations that preschoolers sharply distinguish between real and pretend objects. They then go on, however, to show that under some circumstances about half the children, even in the 6-year-old group, behave in a way which indicates that they may not be entirely sure that an imaginary creature is not real. Here is an intriguing phenomenon concerning the role of imagination in our mental life. How many of us will have found ourselves alone late at night, idly imagining what it would be like if an intruder were to creep up silently behind us ... and feeling rather foolish as we quickly look round! The boundary between imagination and reality is perhaps not so straightforward after all.

The second of our papers takes up false belief. Wimmer & Hartl return to the 'Smarties' task, one of the now standard false belief tasks. Their concern is with the relationship between the child's understanding of own previous false belief and the prediction of a friend's belief under similar circumstances. Previous studies have found somewhat confusing results. Perner, Leekam & Wimmer (1987)'s findings indicated that Self was slightly easier than Other, while Gopnik & Astington (1988) found the reverse. Wimmer & Hartl find that the difficulty is about equal, with most 3-year-olds failing and most 4-year-olds passing. They argue from this that the mind's contents are not transparent to itself but require the application of theory.

Freeman, Lewis & Doherty undertake an examination of the task demands of a standard false belief task. Rather than link the child's understanding of false belief in an all-or-none fashion to success on standard tasks, Freeman *et al.* ask under what conditions might a young child attribute belief. Their guiding idea is that young children will compute someone else's belief more readily if the other person has some obvious reason for forming a belief about some aspect of a situation. They suggest that needing to know something for carrying out a plan of action is a case in point. This leads them to study a hide-and-seek variant of the standard Sally/Anne task. Two things emerge. First, the children's performance is enhanced in the need-to-know circumstances of hide-and-seek. Second, the children do better when allowed to act out the protagonists search behaviour than when required to answer verbally.

The next paper also examines conditions under which young children perform better on false belief tasks. Sullivan & Winner find that children under 4 years do better after explanation highlights the possibility that people can be wrong about the contents of a box. This increases the numbers who subsequently pass a Smarties type task. But this only works for older 3-year-olds. Younger 3-year-olds are not helped by this nor by a condition in which the trickery of the Smarties task is made explicit. Sullivan & Winner suggest that older 3-year-olds are on the point of grasping belief and ignorance and that 'highlighting' triggers them into bringing their knowledge to bear where otherwise they would fail.

Our final paper in this section moves on to the topic of deception. Sodian takes up the false belief controversy by asking when preschoolers are able to deceive a competitor. She finds, consistent with results from standard false belief tasks, that it is not until around $4\frac{1}{2}$ years that children are able reliably to find means to induce a false belief in a competitor though they know perfectly well how to block the competitor from his goal behaviourally. Sodian argues for the strong conceptual deficit position that, although they are not behaviourists, children less than 4-years-old suffer a serious cognitive impairment in being unable to conceive of beliefs.

Understanding belief not only requires relating actual behaviour to imaginary circumstances, it is also one of the twin pillars of our adult belief–desire reasoning system. Thus, much of the controversy in the field at the moment centres on the question of preschooler's understanding of belief and deception. The present section reflects, then, the importance of this question in the field at large.

British Journal of Developmental Psychology (1991), **9**, 105–123 *Printed in Great Britain* 105
© 1991 The British Psychological Society

Monsters, ghosts and witches: Testing the limits of the fantasy–reality distinction in young children

Paul L. Harris*, Emma Brown, Crispin Marriott, Semantha Whittall
and **Sarah Harmer**

Department of Experimental Psychology, South Parks Road, University of Oxford, Oxford OX1 3UD, UK

Estes, Wellman & Woolley (1989) have shown that children as young as 3 years of age can distinguish between mental entities such as an image or dream of an object and a real object. Nevertheless, children often show persistent fear of imaginary creatures, particularly monsters (Jersild, 1943). To find out what conception children have of such imaginary creatures, 4- and 6-year-olds were questioned about three types of item: real items (e.g. a cup), ordinary imagined items (e.g. an image of a cup) and supernatural imagined items (e.g. an image of a monster). In two experiments, both age groups sharply differentiated the real items from both types of imagined item. Despite this apparently firm grasp of the distinction between fantasy and reality, two further experiments showed that 4- and 6-year-olds are not always certain that a creature that they have imagined cannot become real. Having imagined a creature inside a box, they show apprehension or curiosity about what is inside the box, and often admit to wondering whether the creature is actually inside. The experiments suggest that children systematically distinguish fantasy from reality, but are tempted to believe in the existence of what they have merely imagined.

It has often been claimed that young children fail to distinguish systematically between mental phenomena and real phenomena. For example, Piaget (1929) claimed that young children cannot distinguish a real entity from a dream or image of that entity. Recent research has led to a re-evaluation of this traditional claim. Wellman & Estes (1986) found that even 3-year-olds can use behavioural–sensory criteria to distinguish between real objects (e.g. a balloon) and mental objects (e.g. an imagined balloon). They correctly judge that real objects can be seen and touched; that other people can perceive such objects; and that objects exist in a stable fashion over time. They appreciate that mental entities, by contrast, cannot be seen or touched; cannot be perceived by other people; and may have only a fleeting existence. Young children also appreciate some of the special qualities of mental entities, for example that they may be non-existent, impossible entities (e.g. pigs that fly).

---

* Requests for reprints.
† Portions of this paper were presented at the European Conference of Developmental Psychology, Budapest, Hungary, June, 1988, and the Society for Research in Child Development meeting, Kansas, USA, April, 1989.

Estes *et al.* (1990) went on to assess the scope of children's ability to distinguish mental from real entities by presenting 'close impostors' of mental entities, for example shadows or smoke. Although these items are as impalpable as dreams or images, 3-year-olds distinguished among them appropriately. They often produced responses such as 'He's thinking about it in his head', or 'He's just dreaming', for mental entities but rarely for close impostors. Thus, preschoolers appear to have a firm grasp of the distinction between imagined entities and real entities, even when behavioural–sensory criteria might be misleading.

The present study was inspired by a phenomenon that is not easy to reconcile with that conclusion. Young children are often scared of creatures such as monsters or ghosts that they have presumably only dreamed about or imagined. On the basis of parents' reports, Jersild (1943) found that children's fear of imaginary creatures increases between 2 and 6 years of age. Similarly, when children aged 5 to 12 years were asked to report on their own fears, fears of imaginary or supernatural creatures constituted one of the most frequently cited categories.

Although these fears may sometimes be triggered by encountering frightening creatures in a story or film, children's own imagination can also serve as the trigger. For example, one of the authors observed two preschool children pretending that there was a monster behind a closed door. When one of them went to open the door, the other retreated from it apprehensively. Similarly, DiLalla & Watson (1988) report the case of a young child who was pretending to be a monster in order to frighten other children but, having burst into tears himself, explained that he was frightened of the monster.

These observations raise the possibility that young children have a firm understanding of the fantasy–reality distinction, but only with respect to common, everyday objects. Children might be less sure of the imaginary status of more supernatural, exotic creatures, such as monsters. This would provide a plausible explanation of their fear of such creatures. Experiment 1 was designed to test this possibility.

Experiment 1

Four- and 6-year-old children were asked to make judgements about three different types of item: real items (e.g. a cup); ordinary imagined items that were counterparts of the real items (e.g. a mental image of a cup); and supernatural imagined items for which no real counterpart exists (e.g. a mental image of a witch that flies in the sky). With respect to items of all three types, children were asked two questions: whether or not the experimenter could see the item, and whether or not it was real. In line with Estes *et al.*, (1989), it was predicted that children in each age group would make a clear distinction between the real items and the ordinary imagined items (e.g. the cup versus the imagined cup). The experimental question was how children would judge the supernatural imagined items (e.g. the imagined witch). On the one hand, they might judge them to be like the real items, publicly visible and real. Alternatively, they might judge them to be similar to the ordinary imagined entities, neither publicly visible nor real. Comparisons between the pattern of judgement for the three types of items were planned to assess these two possibilities.

Method

Subjects. The subjects were 14 younger children, ranging from 3 years 9 months to 5 years 2 months (mean age: 4 years 5 months) and 14 older children, ranging from 6 years 1 month to 7 years 3 months (mean age: 6 years 7 months). The younger age group were recruited from a preschool playgroup, and the older age group from a primary school, both in Oxford. Children in each age group came from a broad range of socio-economic backgrounds.

Procedure. Each child was tested on two pre-test items before being given nine test items. The test items were equally divided among three different types: there were three real, three ordinary imagined and three supernatural imagined items. For each of these 11 items (i.e. pretest + test items), the child was asked two questions in the following fixed order: (1) 'That (item), can I see it?' and (2) 'That (item), is it a real one?'

The (male) experimenter was familiar with all the subjects, having been at the school/playgroup previously on several occasions. The children were tested individually in a quiet area, seated opposite the experimenter with a low table in between. On the table were a balloon, a cup, and a pair of scissors, which children were invited to handle, to put them at ease. While they were handling the objects, the experimenter recorded the child's name, age, sex and date of testing on a standard scoresheet. The experimenter then said: 'I'm going to ask you about these things on the table, but I'm also going to ask you to close your eyes and make a picture inside your head as well, OK?'

Pre-test items. Following this preamble, the table was cleared of the balloon, cup and scissors, and the first pre-test item, a pencil, was brought out and placed upon the table. The experimenter said, 'OK. Now, that pencil on the table can I see it?' If the child gave the right answer (yes), the experimenter said, 'Yes, that's right and you can see it too'. If the child gave the wrong answer, the experimenter said, 'Well, you can see it and I can see it too', and the question was repeated. The experimenter then went on to the next pre-test question by saying, 'OK. That pencil on the table—is it a real one?' If the child gave the right answer (yes), the experimenter said, 'Yes, that's right, it's a real pencil'. If the child gave the wrong answer, the experimenter said, 'Yes it is, it's a real pencil', and the question was repeated. For the second pre-test item, the experimenter said, 'Now, I want you to close your eyes up tight and make a picture in your head of a pencil. Have you done that? Have you made a picture inside your head of a pencil? OK. That pencil in your head can I see it?' If the child gave the right answer (no), the experimenter said, 'That's right, I can't see it, only you can see it inside your head'. If the child gave the wrong answer, the experimenter said, 'Well, I can't see it; only you can see it inside your head', and the question was repeated. For the final pre-test question, the experimenter said, 'That pencil in your head—is it a real one?' If the child gave the right answer (no), the experimenter said, 'That's right, the pencil in your head is not a real pencil'. If the child gave the wrong answer, the experimenter said, 'No, it isn't a real pencil, it's just inside your head', and the question was repeated.

This systematic feedback was given to encourage children to distinguish carefully between real and imagined entities. Note that children received no pre-test feedback on supernatural items.

Test items. The child was then given the nine test items in random order without feedback. For each of the three real items, the item was placed on the table and the experimenter pointed to it, asking, 'That (item) on the table can I see it?' and, 'That (item) on the table is it a real one?' Each item was removed from the table before going on to the next. For the three ordinary imagined items and the three supernatural imagined items, the experimenter said, 'Now close your eyes up tight and make a picture in your head of a (item). Have you done that? Is it inside your head?' Then, he said, 'That (item) in your head. Can I see it?' and 'That (item) in your head. Is it a real one?' All answers were recorded as Yes or No.

The real entities were a balloon, a cup and a pair of scissors. The ordinary imagined entities were an image of a balloon, an image of a cup and an image of a pair of scissors. The supernatural imagined entities were an image of a monster that wags its tail, an image of a witch that flies in the sky, and an image of a ghost that comes through the window.

Results

Performance during the pre-test was fairly accurate even prior to corrective feedback (71.4 per cent correct for younger children; 92.9 per cent correct for older children).

Preliminary inspection of children's replies on test items showed little variation across the three items falling within a given type (e.g. cup as compared with balloon and scissors). In addition, the overall proportion of correct replies was similar for the visibility question (89.7 per cent) and the reality status question (90.1 per cent). Accuracy was somewhat lower for the supernatural items but occurred at similar levels for each question (86.9 per cent for visibility question; 85.7 per cent for reality question).

Accordingly, responses were collapsed across items (within each item type) and across the two questions: children were scored for the number of realist responses (i.e. affirmative responses) that they gave (out of a total of six) for each of the three types of item. Mean scores are presented in Table 1 as a function of age and item type.

Inspection of Table 1 shows that children in both age groups distinguished sharply between real items on the one hand and ordinary and supernatural imagined items on the other.

Table 1. Mean number of affirmative replies (out of six) as a function of age and item type (Expt 1)

	Item type		
Age	Real	Ordinary imagined	Supernatural imagined
Younger	5.57	1.21	1.57
Older	6.00	0.36	0.07

To check these conclusions, an analysis of age (2) × item type (3) was carried out. This analysis produced the expected main effect of item type ($F(2,52) = 192.83$, $p < .0001$) and also an interaction of age × item type ($F(2,52) = 5.62$, $p < .006$). Planned t tests confirmed that for each age group real items received more realist responses than ordinary imagined items (4-year-olds: $t(52) = 10.89$, $p < .0001$; 6-year-olds: $t(52) = 13.63$, $p < .0001$). In addition, real entities received more realist responses than supernatural imagined items (4-year-olds: $t(52) = 9.66$, $p < .0001$; 6-year-olds: $t(52) = 14.09$, $p < .0001$). By contrast, the two types of imagined items— ordinary and supernatural—were judged similarly (4-year-olds: $t(52) = 1.23$, n.s.; 6-year-olds: $t(52) = 0.46$, n.s.).

Despite this overall similarity in the pattern of judgement across the two age groups, tests of the simple effect of age for each item type showed that 4-year-olds produced more realist judgements than 6-year-olds; this age difference was absent for real items ($F(1,78) = 0.75$, n.s.) but was marginally significant for ordinary imagined items ($F(1,78) = 3.01$, $p < .10$) and significant for supernatural imagined items ($F(1,78) = 9.21$, $p < .01$).

Since the data in Table 1 were subject to ceiling and floor effects, individual response patterns were also examined non-parametrically. Table 2 shows the number of children making 0, 1–3, or more than 3 errors (out of a possible total of 18). The *a priori* probability of answering all 18 test questions without error is very low (0.5^{18}).

Hence, the likelihood of one or more children performing without error is < .0001 for each age group. Yet inspection of Table 2 reveals that most 6-year-olds and almost half the 4-year-olds performed without error.

Table 2. Number of children making 0, 1–3, or more than 3 errors as a function of age (Expt 1)

Age	Number of errors			
	0	1–3	>3	N
Younger	6	4	4	14
Older	12	1	1	14

Discussion

The results of Expt 1 were very clear. Four- and 6-year-olds alike made a sharp differentiation between real and imagined items. They typically judged that items such as a cup, a balloon or a pair of scissors were visible to the experimenter and were real, whereas they judged that imagined instances of those items were not visible to the experimenter and were not real. In addition, they made correct judgements about supernatural entities such as imagined ghosts, monsters and witches. They mostly denied that those entities were publicly visible or real. There was some tendency for 4-year-olds to produce more realist replies for imagined items, but almost half the 4-year-olds avoided making a single error; among 6-year-olds, this error-free pattern was exhibited by almost all subjects.

Although Expt 1 produced clear results, it throws no further light on children's persistent fears of imaginary creatures. If children appreciate that when they can conjure up such creatures in their imagination, they are neither real nor publicly visible, the persistence of their fear—sometimes into middle childhood—remains unexplained. It is possible to argue, however, that certain types of imagined creature arouse fear, and it is precisely because they arouse fear, that children start to regard them as real. For example, a child might fantasize about a monster attacking him or her. If such images elicit some of the standard physiological or subjective changes associated with fear of real creatures, children might be tempted to conclude that such emotional cues could only be precipitated by a real creature. Experiment 2 was designed to explore this possibility.

Experiment 2

Experiment 2 was modelled after Expt 1 in that children made the same two types of judgement about real, ordinary imagined, and supernatural imagined items. However, the presentation of the supernatural imagined items was altered. After having 'made a picture' in their head of, for example, a witch that flies in the sky, children were told, 'Now make a picture of a witch that flies in the sky and comes chasing after you'. It was judged that this extra step in the fantasy would be mildly frightening, albeit no more so than the content of a typical fairy story involving a witch, giant or dragon. Following questions about the visibility and reality status of the supernatural imagined items, children were asked whether they were scared of the item, and why they were scared or not scared.

Method

Subjects.   Subjects again fell into two age groups. The younger group, from a selection of local playgroups and preschools in Oxford, consisted of 14 children ranging from 3 years 6 months to 5 years 0 months (mean age: 4 years 1 month). The older group, from an infants' class at an Oxford primary school, consisted of 14 children ranging from 5 years 7 months to 7 years 6 months (mean age: 6 years 7 months).

Procedure.   Children were tested individually in a relatively quiet area. They sat on a chair facing the experimenter across a small table. In order to put children at ease, the experimenter spent a few minutes asking general questions (e.g. 'What is your favourite kind of icecream?'), and then asked the child's name and birthday. The name, sex, age and date of testing were recorded on a standard scoresheet.

The general procedure, including the pre-test, the items and the questions posed, was similar to that used in Expt 1. However, the procedure for supernatural imagined items (an image of a monster that wags its tail; an image of a witch that flies in the sky; and an image of a ghost that comes through the window) was supplemented. The experimenter introduced each item by saying, 'Now close your eyes and make a picture in your head of a (item). Have you done that? Is it inside your head?' When the child said yes, the experimenter said, 'Now make a picture of (item) as it comes chasing after you'. The experimenter then asked, 'That (item, e.g. monster that wags its tail and comes chasing after you) in your head. Can I see it . . . Is it a real one?' Finally, children were asked, 'That (item) in your head—were you really scared when it came chasing after you, or just pretend scared?' This form of words was chosen in order to encourage children to distinguish between being really scared and imagining themselves feeling scared as they conjured up an image of the monster chasing after them. Depending on whether or not they claimed to have felt really scared, they were asked, 'Why were you scared/not scared?' Answers were recorded without feedback.

Results

Performance during the pre-test was again quite accurate even prior to corrective feedback (82.1 per cent correct for younger children; 85.7 per cent correct for older children). On test items, there was no obvious variation among items falling within a given type. Moreover, the proportion of correct replies was high for both questions (98.8 per cent for the visibility question; 91.3 per cent for the reality question). Even when questioned about supernatural items, replies remained quite accurate (97.6 per cent for the visibility question; 83.3 per cent for the reality question).

Table 3. Mean number of affirmative replies (out of six) as a function of age and item type (Expt 2)

| Age | Item type | | |
	Real	Ordinary imagined	Supernatural imagined
Younger	6.00	0.50	0.93
Older	6.00	0.07	0.21

To analyse these findings, children were again scored for the number of realist responses (out of a total of six) they gave for each item type. Mean scores are presented in Table 3 as a function of age and item type.

Inspection of Table 3 shows that children in both the older and younger groups distinguished sharply between real items on the one hand and both types of imagined item on the other. To check these conclusions, an analysis of age (2) × item type (3) was carried out. The only significant result was the main effect item type($F(2,52) = 677.33$, $p < .0001$). t tests confirmed that children offered more realist responses for real items as compared with both ordinary imagined ($t(52) = 32.65$, $p < .0001$) and supernatural imagined items ($t(52) = 31.02$, $p < .0001$). The two types of imagined item were judged similarly ($t(52) = 1.63$, n.s.).

As in Expt 1, children's individual response patterns were also examined. Table 4 shows the number of children making 0, 1–3, or more than 3 errors (out of a possible total of 18). Inspection of Table 4 shows that most 6-year-olds and more than half the 4-year-olds performed without error.

Table 4. Number of children making 0, 1–3 or more than 3 errors as a function of age (Expt 2)

	Number of errors			
Age	0	1–3	>3	*N*
Younger	9	2	3	14
Older	11	3	0	14

With respect to supernatural imagined items, children were asked whether or not they felt afraid. Five younger children and nine older children acknowledged real fear for one or more of the supernatural imagined items. Children were scored (out of 3) for the number of items where they acknowledged such fear. The younger group admitted to fear for a mean of 0.79 items, whereas the older group did so for a mean of 1.36 items ($t(26) = 1.19$, n.s.). Thus, if the children's self-reports are accepted as valid, the attempt to elicit a mildly frightening fantasy was partially successful.

As a further check on the impact of this manipulation on children's visibility and reality judgements, attention was focused on that subset of supernatural imagined items for which fear was acknowledged. Even for these items, younger ($N = 5$) and older ($N = 9$) children usually made non-realist judgements (68.2 per cent and 94.7 per cent correct, respectively). These proportions were only slightly lower than those obtained by the same younger and older children for the comparable set of ordinary imagined items (77 per cent and 100 per cent correct, respectively) for which these children presumably felt no fear.

The responses given by subjects to the probe question 'Why were you/were you not afraid?' were also analysed. Responses were assigned by two independent judges to five different categories: *not real* (e.g. 'It's not real!'); *item properties* (e.g. 'It's got big teeth' or 'It might eat me'); *subject's powers* (e.g. 'I can run faster'); *positive view of item* (e.g. 'I like witches'); and *other* (e.g. 'I thought it was a polar bear'). Interjudge agreement was 91 per cent (62 agreements out of 68 judgements). Disagreements were resolved by discussion. The replies were distributed among the five different categories as shown in Table 5.

Table 5. Number of replies falling in each of five categories (number of subjects giving those replies in parentheses)

			Category		
Age	Not real	Item properties	Subject powers	Positive	Other
Younger	11 (6)	11 (5)	13 (6)	1 (1)	3 (3)
Older	7 (3)	18 (9)	0 (0)	3 (2)	1 (0)

A t test confirmed that the age difference for *subject powers* was significant ($t(26) = 2.88$, $p < .01$). In sum, some children in each age group acknowledged fear of the supernatural imagined items. Several younger children claimed to be able to overpower or escape from the creature, a response that none of the older group made.

Discussion

As in Expt 1, children in both age groups distinguished sharply between real items on the one hand and both types of imagined items on the other. Despite the supplement to the supernatural imagined items designed to make them mildly frightening, both age groups continued to treat those items as quite different from the real items but as similar to the ordinary imagined items. It could be argued that the manipulation was too mild, and that a stronger manipulation would have resulted in more realist responses on the supernatural items. However, acknowledgement of fear was not uncommon particularly among the older children, and yet there was no indication of any increment in the number of realist responses in consequence. If anything, fewer realist responses were given by children in Expt 2 as compared with Expt 1, and the age difference in the frequency of realist responses observed in Expt 1 was not replicated. Finally, scrutiny of those supernatural imagined items for which children acknowledged fear revealed no clear increment in realist judgements relative to ordinary imagined terms.

Experiments 1 and 2 provide solid support for the conclusions reached by Wellman and his colleagues (Estes *et al.*, 1990; Wellman & Estes, 1986). Young children have a firm grasp of the distinction between real items and imagined items. So firm is the distinction, that many children were systematically correct across the entire set of 18 questions. Thus combining data from the two experiments, 54 per cent of the 4-year-olds and 83 per cent of the 6-year-olds made no errors; a further 21 and 14 per cent respectively made a small number of errors (1–3). Admittedly, children were given corrective feedback during the pre-test warm-up. On the other hand, performance on pre-test items was also quite accurate. Moreover, Wellman & Estes (1986) obtained comparable levels of performance even though they did not include any pre-test warm-up.

Experiment 3

In Expt 3, we explored children's behaviour toward imaginary creatures more directly. As in Expts 1 and 2, children were asked to imagine a creature such as a monster. However, two related changes in procedure were introduced. First, children were not asked to imagine a creature 'in their head' but to pretend that there was a creature in each of two large black boxes located in the room (a monster in one box and a puppy in the other). Second, they were asked how they would behave toward the boxes, and in due course their actual behaviour was observed.

If children assume that such imaginary creatures have no genuine existence, then they should behave indifferently toward the two boxes. If, on the other hand, children wonder, however fleetingly, whether what they have imagined is actually present inside each box, then this should be reflected in selective behaviour toward the 'monster' box as compared with the 'puppy' box.

Method

Subjects.   There were 20 younger subjects ranging from 3 years 4 months to 5 years 1 month (mean 4 years 6 months) and 20 older subjects ranging from 5 years 1 month to 6 years 10 months (mean 5 years 11 months). The children were recruited from preschools and primary schools in Oxford.

Procedure.   Children were tested individually in a quiet room in their school. When they came into the room two black cardboard boxes (measuring approximately 1 m along each side) were positioned close to one of the walls. A small hole (diameter = 1.5 cm), large enough to admit a child's finger, was visible in the upper front face of each box. Each box had a flap door at the back. A 30 cm wooden stick, slightly smaller in diameter than the hole in each box, was also available.

During the *introduction*, all children were asked to pretend that there was a monster in one of the two boxes (designated randomly) and a puppy in the other. They were then questioned about the two pretend creatures. Questioning fell into five successive stages: *memory check, hypothetical choice of box, reality check, actual choice of box*, and *debriefing*. Order of mention of the two creatures was systematically varied across subjects, but remained constant throughout the entire procedure for any given subject.

Introduction.   The experimenter introduced the task as follows, 'We're going to play a game of pretend, OK. I expect that you're good at pretend games. First of all, I want you to pretend that there's a monster in this box, OK? Can you do that? Now pretend that the monster is a big, scary monster, and if you put your finger in this big hole here (point), he'll bite your finger right off! And, pretend that there's a puppy in this box, OK? Can you do that? Now pretend that the puppy is a little, friendly puppy, and if you put your finger in this hole here (point), he'll lick your finger'.

This wording illustrates the order: monster, puppy; half the subjects heard this introduction and half heard the same introduction with the order of mention reversed. In describing the two creatures, the experimenter introduced an appropriate intonation into her voice—dramatic for the monster, warm and friendly for the puppy.

Memory check.   Children's memory for the location and characteristics of the two creatures was then checked. They were asked which box each creature was in and whether he would bite or lick their finger if they put it in the hole.

Hypothetical choice of box.   Next, subjects were asked which of the two boxes they wanted to put their finger in, 'the one with the monster in or the one with the puppy in'. Having made their choice, they were asked whether they would prefer to put their finger in the hole or poke a stick into it instead (their attention was drawn to the stick placed nearby).

They were also asked about the other box, 'Now, what if I ask you to put your finger in the other box as well—the box with the monster/puppy inside. You can choose though—you can either put your finger right inside the hole or you can put this stick in the hole instead'.

Reality check.   Children were asked with respect to each creature whether there really was such a creature that would bite or lick their finger or whether they were just pretending.

Actual choice of box.   Children were then asked to act, as follows, 'OK you show me now. You put your finger right inside one of the boxes or poke this stick into the hole'. The child's choice of box and use of the finger versus the stick was noted.

After the child withdrew the stick or finger from the box, the experimenter counted silently to 10, and recorded whether or not the child approached the second box. If the child had not approached the second box at the end of the count, the experimenter prompted the child as follows, 'What about the other box with the monster/puppy inside?' If the child hesitated for a further count of 10, the experimenter stopped the experiment. If the child approached the second box, the choice of box, and the manner of approach (i.e. finger versus stick) was again recorded.

Debriefing.   Before the child left, he or she was asked, 'You look behind the boxes. They've got a door in the back, so you can look to see what's inside'. When the child had looked at each box and found them both to be empty, the experimenter reinforced this conclusion by saying, 'See there's nothing in the boxes. But you were very good at playing this pretend game with me'.

Results

Memory check.   All 20 older children and 18 younger children correctly answered all four memory questions, indicating that they remembered which pretend creature was in which box and what each creature would do. Two younger children made a single error, claiming that the monster would not bite them. (Both on being corrected said that they knew that they had been told that the monster would bite, but they did not think this was correct.)

Hypothetical choice of box.   The majority of subjects in each age group opted to approach the puppy box first. In the older group, 18 out of 20 subjects chose the puppy box first (χ^2 (1, $N = 20$) $= 12.80$, $p < .001$), and in the younger group, 13 out of 16 subjects (four subjects remained silent) chose the puppy box first (χ^2 (1, $N = 16$) $= 6.25$, $p < .02$). Preference for the puppy box was highly significant when both groups were combined (χ^2 (1, $N = 36$) $= 18.78$, $p < .001$).

Children were also more willing to use their finger rather than the stick for the puppy box as compared with the monster box. In the older group, 12 subjects opted to use the stick for both boxes, and two subjects to use their finger for both boxes. The remaining six subjects, who switched their choice, all chose to use their finger for the puppy box and the stick for the monster box. A similar pattern emerged for the younger group. Of the 14 subjects who made a clear choice with respect to each box (six subjects failed to make a clear choice for one or both boxes), 11 opted to use the stick for both boxes; the remaining three subjects, who switched their choice, all opted to use their finger for the puppy box and the stick for the monster box. Combining data from the older and younger group, a sign test confirmed that subjects who shifted in their choice switched from using their finger for the puppy box to using the stick for the monster box, rather than the reverse ($p < .004$).

Reality check.   Among the older children, 16 subjects claimed both with respect to the puppy and the monster that they were just pretending, whereas the remaining four subjects claimed in each case that there really was both a puppy and a monster.

Selection of the pretend option as opposed to the real option was greater than would be expected by chance for both creatures (χ^2 (1, $N = 20$) = 7.20, $p < .01$), in each case.

Among the younger children, 11 subjects claimed that they were only pretending there was a puppy, seven claimed that there really was a puppy, and two failed to make a clear reply (χ^2 (1, $N = 18$) = 0.89, n.s.). With respect to the monster, 13 claimed that they were only pretending, three claimed that there really was a monster, and four failed to make a clear reply (χ^2 (1, $N = 16$) = 6.25, $p < .02$).

In summary, the majority of children maintained that neither creature was real although this conclusion was less secure among the younger children, especially for the puppy.

Actual choice of box. Among older subjects, 14 approached the puppy box and six the monster box (χ^2 (1, $N = 20$) = 3.2, $p < .1$). Among the younger subjects, 12 approached the puppy box, seven the monster box, and one failed to make a clear choice (χ^2 (1, $N = 19$) = 1.32, n.s.). Preference for the puppy box was significant when the two age groups were combined (χ^2 (1, $N = 39$) = 4.33, $p < .05$).

Turning to the question of how subjects approached the box, 10 older children used a stick for both boxes, one used a finger for both, and seven shifted in their choice, using a finger for the puppy box, and a stick for the monster box (the remaining two subjects approached only one box). Among the younger children, 12 used a stick for both boxes, but none used a finger for both. Four younger children shifted in their choice: three used a finger for the puppy box and a stick for the monster box, and one shifted in the reverse direction (the remaining four children failed to approach one or both boxes). Combining the two age groups, 10 subjects were more cautious in approaching the puppy box than the monster box; only one child showed the reverse pattern. A sign test confirmed that this difference was significant ($p < .006$).

Discussion

Children easily remembered the location and attributes of the two creatures. In the case of the monster, the majority of children in each age group also insisted that it was just a pretend creature. Nevertheless, they were wary of the monster box. Asked which of the two boxes they would approach, a majority opted for the puppy box. Those children who said that they would approach the two boxes differently, proposed being more cautious (i.e. using the stick) in approaching the monster box. Asked to actually approach the boxes, the majority initially approached the puppy box and then the monster box, and when greater caution was shown to one of the two boxes, it was almost always to the monster box and not the puppy box.

These results suggest that, despite their understanding of the distinction between reality and fantasy, children may not be convinced of the non-existence of a creature that they have imagined. Although children usually asserted that there really was no monster in the box—that they were just pretending—they were more hesitant in approaching the monster box. Their choices suggested that they wondered whether the boxes contained a puppy and a monster. Had they been certain that the boxes were empty, they should have been indifferent in choosing between them, both hypothetically and in actuality.

However, a plausible objection to this interpretation is that children were simply colluding with the experimenter. The experimenter's questions and instructions may have led children to assume that they were being invited to play an elaborate game of make-believe with the experimenter, in which their role was to talk and act as if there were a puppy in one box and a monster in the other box.

Various incidental observations cast doubt on this alternative interpretation. After the experiment, nine children spontaneously suggested where the monster had gone (e.g. 'It's gone to that University place where they put skeletons'). Even when they stated earlier that the monster was pretend, children now implied that it had disappeared before they had a chance to see it. However, a final experiment was designed to rule out the likelihood of demand effects.

Experiment 4

Experiment 4 was similar to Expt 3 but several important changes were made. First, to eliminate the demand characteristics of the experimenter's presence, children's behaviour toward the imaginary creatures was filmed in her absence. Second, at the outset of the experiment, children were asked to look inside the two boxes to check that each box was empty (the boxes also remained in full view throughout the experiment so that children could be sure that nothing was physically inserted into them). Once they had established that the boxes were empty, children were asked to imagine that either a friendly creature (a rabbit), or a frightening creature (a monster) was inside one of the two boxes. Their understanding of this instruction was checked, and their appreciation that the creature was a pretence rather than real was also checked. The experimenter then claimed to have forgotten something and left children alone for two minutes; their behaviour was recorded by a hidden camera during her absence. After the experimenter returned, she asked further questions about their behaviour in her absence and their beliefs about the imagined creature. In particular, children were asked whether they had wondered if there was a creature inside one of the two boxes.

Method

Subjects.   Forty-eight children were used as subjects from three schools in Oxford. Twenty-four younger children ranging from 3 years 10 months to 4 years 11 months (mean = 4 years 6 months), amd 24 older children ranging from 5 years 11 months to 6 years 10 months, (mean = 6 years 3 months) were tested. Each age group included 12 girls and 12 boys.

Procedure.   Testing took place in a small school room. The two boxes (used in Expt 3) were placed on the floor in the middle of the room about one yard apart facing a chair. Both boxes were free standing and readily visible to the child seated in the chair. A video camera was placed inconspicuously on the floor, in a box covered with a cloth, in a position from which it could record the child sitting on the chair, the two boxes, and any movement of the child toward the boxes.

Half the children in each age group were assigned to the pretend monster condition and half to the pretend rabbit condition. Each child was brought into the room individually and the experimenter sat down (at some distance from the boxes) next to the child. The experimenter asked the child to look in the back of the boxes to see if there was anything inside. When the child had agreed that both boxes were empty, the experimenter said, 'It doesn't matter that the boxes are empty because we are going to play a game of pretend. I expect you're good at pretend games, aren't you? Do you like bunny rabbits (monsters)? I want you to pretend there's a bunny rabbit (monster) in that box', (pointing to one of the two boxes at random). She continued, 'Now pretend that the rabbit (monster) in the box is a nice, white, friendly rabbit (a horrible, mean, black monster). Pretend that he's sitting in the box and he wants to come out so that you can stroke him (come out and chase you)'.

The experimenter then asked five questions to check whether the child had both understood and remembered the instructions. Questions (1)–(4) concerned the colour, friendliness, desires and location of the pretend creature. In question (5), children were asked about the reality status of the creature: 'Now is there really a nice, friendly, white bunny that wants to be stroked (a horrible, mean, black monster that wants to come out and chase you), or are you just pretending?'

If the child gave the wrong answer to any of the questions, she/he was not corrected. The experimenter then left the room under the pretext of going to fetch some sweets which she had forgotten. On leaving the room she asked the child to wait for her and added that although it was not necessary to stay sitting down, the child should wait in the room to answer some more questions on her return. Before finally leaving, the experimenter asked children whether that was OK and did not leave the room if they said they did not want her to leave.

The experimenter was absent for two minutes, during which time the child was filmed by the video camera. When the experimenter re-entered the room, she gave the child a sweet as a reward for helping and asked the child the following questions: (6) 'What did you do while I was gone? Did you stay sitting or did you stand up?' (7) 'And did you look inside one of the boxes?' (8) 'And which box did you look inside?' If the child acknowledged opening one of the boxes, the experimenter asked which one and continued (9), 'And what did you think when you went to open the box? Did you think there was nothing inside or did you think to yourself: "I wonder if there's a nice, white, bunny rabbit (horrible, mean, black monster) inside"?' If the child denied looking inside the boxes, the experimenter asked why not and asked, 'Were you sure there was nothing inside the box or did you wonder whether there was a bunny (monster) inside?' Finally, pointing to the unused box, the experimenter asked (10), 'What about that box there? What if you pretended very, very hard that there was a monster (rabbit) inside, what would happen? Would there suddenly be a monster (rabbit) inside the box if you pretended very hard? ... Why? (Why not?)'

Results

Questions 1–4. Questions 1–4 were simple memory questions designed to check whether children had retained the experimental instructions. Table 6 shows the mean number of correct replies (out of four) as a function of age and creature.

Table 6. Mean number of correct replies (out of four) by age and creature

	Creature	
Age	Rabbit	Monster
Younger	3.50	2.42
Older	3.17	3.50

A two-way ANOVA of age × creature revealed an interaction of age × creature $(F)1,44 = 4.235$, $p < .05$). As compared with older children, younger children were less accurate concerning the monster but just as accurate concerning the rabbit.

Question 5. Almost all children asserted that the creature was not real. Among the younger children, 22 (out of 24) said that they were only pretending ($\chi^2 (1) = 16.67$,

$p < .001$) and among the older children, 21 (out of 24) answered in the same way ($\chi^2 (1) = 13.5$, $p < .001$).

Departure of the experimenter.   Four of the younger children said that they did not want the experimenter to leave because they were scared. All four were in the monster condition. Only one of the four had answered question (5) incorrectly. Thus, three of the children were afraid to be left alone, despite having said a few seconds earlier that they were only pretending there was a monster. In each of these four cases, the experimenter looked inside the boxes again with the child to prove that they were empty and then tried to leave the room again, but all four children said once more that they did not want to be left alone because they were scared. The experimenter stayed with these children and concentrated on reassuring them.

Behaviour in the absence of the experimenter.   Ten (out of 20) younger and 10 (out of 24) older children either touched or opened one or both boxes. Each child was scored for the number of seconds that elapsed before they touched either the pretend box or the neutral box. These scores are shown in Table 7 as a function of age, creature, and box. In cases where subjects failed to touch one or both of the boxes, they were given a score of 120 seconds (equivalent to the entire period during which the experimenter was absent).

Table 7. Mean number of seconds before touching box, as a function of age, creature and type of box.

		Type of box	
Age	Creature	Pretend	Neutral
Younger	Rabbit	88.8	105.0
	Monster	74.9	101.3
Older	Rabbit	78.4	91.7
	Monster	86.8	107.8

A three-way ANOVA of age × creature × box produced no effects of age or creature but a main effect of box ($F(1,14) = 9.80$, $p < .003$). Children approached the pretend box more quickly than the neutral box.

Of the 20 children who touched at least one of the boxes, 12 children touched only one box, or touched one box more often than the other. In 10 of these 12 cases, the pretend box was touched more ($\chi^2 (1) = 5.33$, $p < .05$).

Nine children opened only one box, or opened one box more often than the other box. In all of these cases, the pretend box was opened more ($p < .004$ by two-tailed binomial test).

In summary, children's behaviour was not affected by the identity of the pretend creature, but they approached the pretend box more quickly and touched and opened it more often than the neutral box.

Interview after experimenter's return. When the experimenter returned, she asked the children about their activity during her absence. The majority of children truthfully said whether they had remained seated or not, whether they had looked inside one of the boxes, and if so which.

Question (9) asked whether children wondered about the existence of the pretend creature. Replies were obtained from 20 younger and 24 older children. Surprisingly, 11 of the younger children and 11 of the older children admitted that they did wonder whether the imagined creature was inside the box as opposed to thinking there was nothing inside.

Children's replies to question (5) (i.e. whether the creature was pretend or real) were compared to those for question (9) by means of a sign test for each age group. This showed that children either gave equally credulous or sceptical replies to both questions, or shifted from a sceptical reply to question (5) (i.e. insisting that the creature was not real) to a credulous reply to question (9) (i.e. admitting that they wondered about the creature's existence). In the younger group, 10 offered the same reply to each question, but 10 were more credulous in their reply to question (9) ($p < .002$, by two-tailed sign test). In the older group, 16 offered the same reply to each question but eight were more credulous in their reply to question (9) ($p < .008$, by two-tailed sign test).

Finally, in reply to question (10), the majority of children in the younger group (14 out of 20) and in the older group (19 out of 24) denied that pretending could generate a real creature ($\chi^2 (1) = 3.2, p < .1$ and $\chi^2 (1) = 8.17, p < .01$, respectively). Despite this sceptical orientation, six younger children and five older children did think they could generate a real creature through pretence. Even among those who denied they could do so, five younger and five older children added that they lacked the appropriate magical skills, implying that such transformations were possible, even if they themselves were incapable of producing them.

In summary, children's replies on the return of the experimenter uncovered some magical or non-realist thinking. Almost all children had insisted prior to her departure that the creature was only a pretence, but almost a half admitted wondering in her absence whether the box contained a creature; a minority said that they could generate a creature through pretence, or that even if they could not, it could be achieved by magic.

Discussion

The results of Expt 4 form four distinct but connected parts: children's memory for details of the imaginary creature, their initial claims about the status of the imagined creature, their behaviour during the experimenter's absence and their responses in the final interview.

Children were quite accurate in remembering the properties and location of the imagined creature. Nevertheless, some errors did occur especially among younger children. They were likely to forget the properties of the monster. Such forgetting may have been deliberate distortion rather than genuine forgetting. Recall that children in Expt 3 had admitted to such distortion.

Prior to the experimenter's departure, almost all the children maintained that they were only pretending there was a creature in one of the boxes, making a clear verbal distinction between reality and fantasy. However, their subsequent behaviour and their replies in the final interview revealed a more complex picture. Four of the younger children in the monster condition said they were scared to be left alone even after checking a second time that the boxes were empty. Of those children who were left alone, almost half got up to touch or open one or both boxes. Such behaviour was unlikely to have been idle curiosity about what might be inside the box or boxes. First, children had seen (at the outset) that both boxes were empty. Second, they were more likely to investigate the pretend box than the neutral box. Third, children often acknowledged in the final interview that they wondered whether there was a creature in the box. Finally, although most children denied that they could generate a real creature by pretending, some insisted that they could, or implied that others could by the use of magic.

General discussion

The results of the four experiments confirm the paradox described in the introduction. Young children appear to have a firm grasp of the distinction between fantasy and reality. They understand that the products of their imagination are not publicly visible or real. On the other hand, they sometimes respond as if such imaginary creatures could actually exist. How should these findings be reconciled? We will consider three different explanations.

At first glance, it is tempting to argue that the paradox turns on the difference between what children say and what they do. They say that fantasy creatures are not real, but that verbal assertion does not regulate their behaviour. This interpretation certainly covers many of the differences between the results of Expts 1 and 2 on the one hand and Expts 3 and 4, on the other. However, it falls short of a full explanation. Recall that in the final interview of Expt 4, half the children questioned admitted to wondering about the existence of the pretend creature and a smaller group insisted that they could create real creatures by exercising their imagination. Hence, even at the verbal level, children do not always maintain a firm barrier between fantasy and reality.

A second explanation can be based on the intriguing hypothesis of Subbotskii (1985). He argues that children have two inconsistent philosophies: everyday scepticism that entails a sharp distinction between fantasy and reality and a residual set of beliefs that allows for magical transformations. In the presence of adults, children are constrained to express everyday realism but left to their own devices, their latent belief in magic comes to the surface. Subbotskii (1985) reports experimental support for this hypothesis. It is also consistent with fieldwork among children: quasi-magical beliefs and practices abound in their games and rituals and have remained stable for generations (Opie & Opie, 1959, chapter 11). Again, this hypothesis explains some of our findings but not all of them. Although children expressed scepticism quite consistently in Expts 1 and 2, they expressed both fear and credulity to the experimenter during Expt 4 and (in informal remarks) following

Expt 3. These findings cast doubt on the suggestion that children hold two inconsistent sets of beliefs, one of which they suppress in the presence of adults.

We favour a third explanation of our results. Our general explanation is that when children imagine a creature such as a monster or rabbit in a box they start to wonder whether there is such a creature in the box, and they cannot completely discount that possibility. Thus, children's imagination increases the subjective likelihood that certain fantasy creatures might be encountered. These shifts in subjective likelihood can occur for harmless creatures as well as frightening creatures. Accordingly, in Expts 3 and 4, children's behaviour toward the boxes was influenced by what they thought the boxes might contain. In Expt 3, they approached a box containing a friendly creature more readily than an unfriendly creature. In Expt 4, a box containing a friendly or an unfriendly creature was approached more than a neutral, and presumably empty box. Recall that despite their ability to allocate pretend creatures to the realm of pretence, children often admitted that they wondered if a creature might be inside the box when they went to look inside it (c.f. questions (5) and (9) of Expt 4).

Granted the general claim that children's imagination leads to a shift in the subjective likelihood of an encounter, we need to specify in more detail how that shift comes about. Two different possibilities may be considered. We will refer to these two possibilities as the 'availability' and 'transmigration' hypotheses, respectively. According to the 'availability' hypothesis, imagining a possibility makes it easy to bring to mind, and that mental 'availability' alters its subjective likelihood (see Acknowledgement). Tversky & Kahneman (1973) have shown that when adults judge the likelihood of an event, they are influenced by its 'availability' (i.e. the ease with which an example of the event can be brought to mind). Thus, objectively rare events may be judged as quite common if appropriate examples of the event can be readily brought to mind.

Assuming that our instructions in Expts 3 and 4 led children to imagine a creature being in the box, it seems likely that such a possibility would be readily 'available', i.e. easily brought to mind during the experimenter's absence. The resultant increase in the subjective likelihood of there being a creature in the box would tempt children to investigate the box. According to this interpretation, the decline of children's fear of imaginary creatures in later childhood (Jersild, 1943) would be explicable in terms of an increasing resistance to such 'availability' effects. Thus, children might forestall such effects by deliberately refraining from conjuring up frightening images. Alternatively, they might recruit other pieces of knowledge to offset shifts in subjective likelihood. For example, they could remind themselves that there really are no monsters in the world. Six-year-olds are able to attenuate the intensity of their sadness at a fictional event by reminding themselves that the event is not real (Meerum Terwogt, Schene & Harris, 1986). They might learn to extend such strategies to the products of their own imagination.

The 'transmigration' hypothesis explains shifts in subjective likelihood differently. In particular, it implies a much sharper discontinuity between children and adults. Despite their ability to distinguish sharply between fantasy and reality, young children might still remain unsure of the rules that govern transformations between those two realms. This cognitive stance need not involve any inconsistency. Knowledge of the properties that distinguish between two categories may be insufficient for determining the conditions under which mutation from one category to the other may occur. For example, a child might know what properties are normally associated with boys versus girls, or with skunks versus raccoons, but require further biological knowledge in order to be quite sure that a member of one category cannot be transformed into a member of the other (Bem, 1989; Keil, 1986). Similarly, although children can distinguish between mental items and real items as documented by Wellman and his colleagues (Estes *et al.*, 1989; Wellman & Estes, 1986), and replicated in Expts 1 and 2, they might not know enough about the causal links between mind and reality to be sure that an imagined creature cannot change into a real creature. According to this second interpretation, the decline in children's fear of imaginary creatures would be explicable in terms of their changing conception of the causal links between mind and reality. Recent evidence shows that there are important changes in young children's understanding of epistemic, reality-oriented mental states, notably perception and belief (Olson, Astington & Harris, 1988; Perner, 1991; Wellman, 1990). It is likely that there are related changes in their understanding of imagination and fantasy. Thus, just as children increasingly realize that beliefs may be causally disconnected from current reality—they may be outdated or distorted representations rather than faithful copies—so children may also realize that the imagination can entertain fantasies that are causally disconnected from reality. In each case, the mind is increasingly seen as an autonomous domain, with its own internal causal regularities. Beliefs are not directly caused by current reality, and reality is not directly influenced by fantasy.

Further research will obviously be required to distinguish between the 'availability' and 'transmigration' hypotheses. For the moment, we may underline one important difference between them. The 'availability' hypothesis implies that acts of fantasy increase the subjective likelihood of *pre-existing* possibilities. Thus, if young children think there is a remote possibility of there being a monster in a box, fantasy will make it appear more likely. By contrast, the 'transmigration' hypothesis implies that acts of fantasy can generate *ex nihilo* entities that have no pre-existing likelihood and project them into the outside world. Thus according to the 'transmigration' hypothesis (but not the 'availability' hypothesis) young children should sometimes credit their imagination with the power to bring about violations of the known laws of object permanence and displacement. We plan further experiments to check this possibility.

Acknowledgement

The authors are very grateful to Carl Johnson for suggesting the 'availability' hypothesis.

References

Bem, S. L. (1989). Genital knowledge and gender constancy in preschool children. *Child Development*, **60**, 649–662.

DiLalla, L. F. & Watson, M. W. (1988). Differentiation of fantasy and reality: Preschoolers' reactions to interruptions in their play. *Developmental Psychology*, **24**, 286–291.

Estes, D., Wellman, H. M. & Woolley, J. D. (1989). Children's understanding of mental phenomena. In H. W. Reese (Ed.), *Advances in Child Development and Behaviour*. San Diego, CA: Academic Press.

Jersild, A. T. (1943). Studies of children's fears. In R. G. Barker, J. S. Kounin & H. F. Wright (Eds), *Child Behavior and Development*. New York: McGraw-Hill.

Keil, F. C. (1986). The acquisition of natural kinds and artifact terms. In W. Demopoulos & A. Mirras (Eds), *Language Learning and Concept Acquisition*. Northwood, NJ: Ablex.

Meerum Terwogt, M., Schene, J. & Harris, P. L. (1986). Self-control of emotional reactions by young children. *Journal of Child Psychology and Psychiatry*, **27**, 357–366.

Olson, D. R., Astington, J. W. & Harris, P. L. (1988). Introduction. In J. W. Astington, P. L. Harris & D. R. Olson (Eds), *Developing Theories of Mind*. New York: Cambridge University Press.

Opie, I. & Opie, P. (1959). *The Lore and Language of Schoolchildren*. Oxford: Oxford University Press.

Perner, J. (1991). *Understanding the Representational Mind*. Cambridge: Bradford Books/MIT Press.

Piaget, J. (1929). *The Child's Conception of the World*. London: Routledge & Kegan Paul.

Subbotskii, E. V. (1985). Preschool children's perception of unusual phenomena. *Soviet Psychology*, **23**, 91–114.

Tversky, A. & Kahneman, D. (1973). Availability: A heuristic for judging frequency and probability. *Cognitive Psychology*, **5**, 207–232.

Wellman, H. M. (1990). *The Child's Theory of Mind*. Cambridge: Bradford Books/MIT Press.

Wellman, H. M. & Estes, D. (1986). Early understanding of mental entities: A reexamination of childhood realism. *Child Development*, **57**, 910–923.

Received 18 October 1989; revised version received 23 May 1990

British Journal of Developmental Psychology (1991), **9**, 125–138   *Printed in Great Britain*

Against the Cartesian view on mind: Young children's difficulty with own false beliefs

Heinz Wimmer* and **Michael Hartl**

Institute of Psychology, University of Salzburg, Hellbrunner Strasse 34, A-5020 Salzburg, Austria

The present study was concerned with children's ability to identify a prior expectation of their own as false belief. In Expt 1 a sharp improvement was found between 3 years and 5 years not only in the ability to identify own beliefs but also in the explanation of what caused that belief and in the ability to infer another person's belief from exposure to misleading information. Experiment 2 ruled out that 3-year-olds' failure with belief identification was due to a memory problem or to a misunderstanding of the test question. Experiment 3 excluded the further possibility that 3-year-olds simply failed belief identification because of embarrassment about having said something false. The younger children's difficulty with the identification of own beliefs contradicts Wimmer, Hogrefe & Sodian's (1988) proposal that young children's difficulty in understanding another person's false belief is solely due to a failure to understand informational origins of beliefs. The present finding also speaks against the Cartesian assumption that the mind is transparent to itself, an assumption which underlies the perspective taking tradition.

In the study of children's developing conception of mind, the mental state of false belief plays a prototypical role (Astington, Harris & Olson, 1988; Perner, 1991; Wellman, 1990). This concern with false belief is quite justified since the ability to understand a mental state as a false belief is a convincing demonstration that the mind not only functions but is also seen as a representational medium that may misrepresent reality. However, most of the developmental studies on belief understanding were concerned with children's understanding of the false belief of another person and not with children's understanding of own false beliefs. This reliance on another's false belief in the study of children's conception of mind is somewhat inappropriate since understanding the other person's belief may require more than just the understanding of a mental state as false belief.

For example, in the well-known tradition originating from Piaget (1932), which conceives social–cognitive development as a movement from egocentrism to perspective taking, the understanding of another person's false belief has nothing to do with an understanding of mental states but is seen as a problem of perspective taking, 'to put oneself in the other person's shoes'. If the other's position can be taken, then

*Requests for reprints.

introspection of one's own mind, which is seen as posing no difficulty, guarantees that the other's mental state is understood. Thus, the perspective taking tradition shares the Cartesian assumption (see the Discussion section) that the mind is transparent to itself via introspection.

An alternative analysis of what is involved in understanding another person's false belief was recently proposed by Wimmer, Hogrefe & Sodian (1988). These authors proposed that another's false belief does not constitute a problem of perspective taking but depends on the child's general 'theoretical' understanding of the causal relationship between informational conditions on the one hand and resulting epistemic states on the other. For example, when in the Wimmer & Perner (1983) false belief task the typical 3-year-old fails to attribute a false belief to the other person, then according to Wimmer *et al.* (1988) the child does not appreciate that the other person's exposure to misleading information is of critical importance since this exposure causes the other person's belief. Wimmer *et al.* explicitly deny that 3-year-olds may have a problem in understanding the representational nature of belief. According to the stage conception of these authors, the representational nature of thought is already understood with the emergence of pretence in the second year as argued by Leslie (1987, 1988). Wimmer *et al.* added as a second major stage that around the age of 4 years children gain awareness of the 'silent' informational causation of thought.

A quite different theoretical explanation of children's understanding of the other person's false belief was proposed by Perner (1988) and similarly by Forguson & Gopnik (1988) and Flavell (1988). Perner claimed that the typical 3-year-old fails the Wimmer & Perner (1983) false belief task because this child cannot understand that the other person considers as true fact a particular thought (e.g. 'the chocolate is in the green cupboard') which from the child's point of view is simply false. The more general developmental claim is that up to the age of about 4 years the child does not understand the representational nature of thought.

Astington & Gopnik (1988, p. 202 ff) argued that the child's understanding of own false belief adjudicates between these two differing theoretical conceptions since in the case of own false belief no understanding of informational origins but only an understanding of the representational relationships between belief and fact seems necessary. Their finding (Gopnik & Astington, 1988) that children find their own beliefs even more difficult to understand than other persons' beliefs, led Astington & Gopnik to decide against Wimmer *et al.*'s (1988) stage conception and in favour of the alternative view that not before the age of 4 years will children understand the representational nature of thought.

However, we note that Astington & Gopnik's argument about the decisive role of own false belief understanding only holds under one particular condition, namely that the content of what has to be identified as false belief is still in mind. If this is not the case and if therefore the own belief has to be inferred or reconstructed from prior informational conditions then understanding of own false belief may well be more difficult than understanding of other's belief. To make this point more concrete, we analyse Gopnik & Astington's (1988) experimental paradigm to see whether the critical condition for belief identification was fulfilled. Gopnik & Astington modified an experimental paradigm which was introduced by Hogrefe, Wimmer & Perner (1986, Expts 2 and 3). The basic idea of this paradigm was that the subject should experience the same situation that would then be imagined for the other person. In the original Hogrefe *et al.* procedure the child was shown a typical container (e.g. a matchbox) and was asked about its content. When the child had answered appropriately, e.g. with 'matches', the actual content, e.g. a piece of chocolate, was revealed. After the box was closed again the child was asked about the actual content and about his or her belief, e.g. 'Now, what is really in this matchbox? And what did you think was in there?'. Children who did not answer the latter question correctly were reminded of their original answer and then the experimenter proceeded with the test questions about what another child (waiting outside) will think when shown the closed box and asked about its content.

For the present analysis, two aspects of this procedure are important. First, by asking the child in the beginning about the content of the box it was ascertained that a definite expectation was built up that afterwards could be identified as false belief. Second, the time lag between inducement of the expectation and belief question referring to this expectation is rather short: just revealing the actual content and closing the box. Thus, we may conclude that in the original version of the Hogrefe *et al.* paradigm there is a good chance that the initial expectation is still in mind and thus can be simply identified as false belief when such a concept is present. When Perner, Leekam & Wimmer (1987, Expt 2) used exactly this paradigm they found that 72 per cent of their 3-year-olds responded correctly to the own belief question and 45 per cent were correct on other's belief.

Gopnik & Astington (1988) modified the Hogrefe *et al.* (1986) procedure in such a way that the critical condition for belief identification (i.e. initial expectation still in mind) no longer seems to hold. The most critical modification was that Gopnik & Astington did not ask for the child's initial expectation. Without such a question children may not have formed any expectation since each child was confronted with more than one misleading object. If, however, no such initial expectation is present, then the question about own belief requires difficult hypothetical reasoning of the sort, 'If I did not know what's in this matchbox then I would think . . ".

The goal of the present study was to provide reliable evidence on children's developing competence with the identification of a prior expectation as false belief. In particular, we were concerned about the quite discrepant findings for 3-year-olds' ability with belief identification which ranged from 72 per cent (Perner *et al.*, 1987) to about 30 per cent (Gopnik & Astington, 1988). In the following three experiments several methodological attempts will be described which were introduced to rule out false negative but also false positive characterizations of children's ability with own belief identification.

Experiment 1

In this first experiment it was ascertained that children had built up a definite interpretation of the critical fact before the belief question was asked. The misleading container task was used and children were asked in the beginning about the expected content of the container. A further goal of the present experiment was to contrast children's ability to identify a false belief of their own with the ability to infer that another person has a false belief.

Method

Subjects. Subjects were 85 children from local kindergartens. Seven children (three 3-year-olds, three 4-year-olds and one 5-year-old) had to be excluded because of various reasons which are mentioned in the Procedure section. The final sample of 78 children was divided into 32 3-year-olds (median: 3:5, range 3:2 to 3:11, 17 boys, 15 girls), 31 4-year-olds (median: 4:8, range: 4:0 to 4:11, 19 boys, 12 girls), and 15 5-year-olds (median: 5:3, range: 5:1 to 5:10, five boys, 10 girls).

Procedure. Each child was confronted with just one misleading container problem. To familiarize children with the situation they were first told a story (taken from Wimmer & Perner, 1983) which was centred around a protagonist's false belief. If a child was completely silent to questions about this story then he or she did not participate further. Three children were excluded for this reason.

In the first step of the following experimental task the child was presented with either a matchbox or a familiar chocolate box and was asked about the expected content (*expectation question*). With the exception of four children who were excluded, all children responded with the expected content at least after a second question. Then the expectation was disconfirmed. The experimenter opened the box and said: 'No, look, what is really in here?' The child's answer (all children responded correctly) was confirmed: 'Yes, a [sweet (in matchbox)/little man (in chocolate box)] is in here.'

Now the box was closed and the child was asked the *belief identification question*: 'Listen, when in the beginning I took the box out of my bag and showed it to you, what did you think is in here?'* A correct answer was followed by a *justification question*: 'Why did you think there is (expected content) in here?' If the child answered the belief identification question with the actual content, he or she was reminded of his or her original answer: 'But in the beginning you thought there is (expected content) in here, didn't you?' If necessary, this reminder was asked a second time. When the child agreed, the justification question followed.

In the second part of the task the child was asked what another person will think about the content of the very same box the child was asked about before. The experimenter questioned the child about who is his or her best friend in the kindergarten and then said: 'Now imagine (name of friend) comes in and I ask her/him: '(name of friend), look what I've got here. What do you think is in here?' After this prologue the *belief inference question* followed: 'What will (name of friend) say is in the box?'†

Results

Belief identification. With the exception of one child all subjects responded either correctly with the initially expected content (e.g. matches) or incorrectly with the actual content (e.g. sweet) to this question. One child's answer had no relationship to the expected or the actual content and was considered wrong.

A stepwise logistic regression analysis was carried out for between-subject factors on the proportion of correct responses to the belief identification question using the BMDP statistical software package (Dixon, 1981). For the factors age and kind of box (matchbox vs. chocolate box), main effects and the interaction were

---

*All the experiments of the present study were performed in the German language. The essential part of the belief question in German was '. . . Was hast du geglaubt, was da drinnen ist?'; the word-by-word translation would be '. . . What have you believed what is in here?' Notice that the subordinate clause 'what is in here' is formulated in present tense indicative. Thus, without the main clause the subordinate clause would refer to the actual content. This feature of the German belief question is retained in the present English translation of the belief identification question '. . . What did you think is in here?' In Expt 2 the potentially misleading formulation of the subordinate clause of the German belief question was tested against a grammatically somewhat incorrect, but less misleading formulation and no negative effect was found.

† This formulation of the belief inference question seemed to be more concrete than the formulation using 'think'. However, an experimental comparison of the two formulations (Perner *et al.*, 1987, Expt 1) gave identical results.

considered in a hierarchical model (considering higher order effects after all component lower order effects had been introduced). Factor sex was included as main effect only.

In this analysis the main effect of age (χ^2 (1, $N = 78$) = 27.2; $p < .001$) contributed to the prediction of proportions correct. Table 1 shows that only about 30 per cent of the 3-year-olds but about 70 per cent of the 4-year-olds and all 5-year-olds correctly identified their belief.

Justifications. A child's answer to the justification question ['Why did you think there is (expected content) in the box?'] was scored correct if a child referred to the misleading character of the box (typical answers: 'because it is a matchbox' or 'because there are always matches in it') or to his or her ignorance of the actual content (typical answers: 'because I didn't know what's in it', 'because I didn't look into the box'). The majority of correct answers (i.e. 41 out of 47) was of the first category.

The failures to respond correctly to the justification question fell into various types. Interestingly, two children (one 3-year-old and one 5-year-old), after repeating their initial expectation in response to the belief identification question, denied their false belief in response to the justification question (e.g. 'I didn't think matches are in the box'). Eight children (four 3-year-olds and four 4-year-olds) gave no answer or responded with 'I don't know'. Another nine answers (seven 3-year-olds and two 4-year-olds) were uninformative (e.g. 'I just thought so'; 'a sweet was in it'). However, the most remarkable finding was that 12 children (10 3-year-olds and two 4-year-olds) could not be asked the justification question at all. After responding with the actual content to the belief identification question any attempt to remind them of their initial expectation failed. They responded consistently with 'no' to the repeated reminder (e.g. 'But in the beginning, you thought there are matches in here, didn't you?').

A substantial association was found between children's correct or incorrect response to the belief identification question and the correct or incorrect response to the justification question. For the total sample the association was $C_{corr} = .72$ ($\chi^2(1, N = 78) = 27.1, p < .001$).

We note that 83 per cent of 49 correct responses to the belief identification question were justified correctly, while only 21 per cent of 29 incorrect responses to the belief identification question were followed eventually (after an affirmative response to the reminder, e.g. 'But didn't you think there are matches in the box?') by

Table 1. Percentage of children with correct answer on belief identification and belief inference tasks

Task	Age		
	3($N = 32$)	4($N = 31$)	5($N = 15$)
Belief identification (self)	34	73	100
Belief inference (other)	25	78	87

a correct justification of the initial expectation. The high percentage of correctly justified responses to the belief identification question rules out the possibility that children in response to this question simply repeated their response to the former expectation question.

Belief inference.   All children responded either with the initially expected content (e.g. matches) or with the actual content (e.g. sweet) to the question about the other person's belief and could therefore definitely be judged as correct or incorrect.

The effects of age, kind of box, and sex on proportions correct were tested by stepwise logistic regression analysis in the same way as in the case of the belief identification question. Again, age was found to be highly significant (χ^2 (1, $N = 78) = 24.8$, $p < .001$) and more correct responses were given to the chocolate box (64 per cent) than to the matchbox (53 per cent) (χ^2 (1, $N = 78) = 4.6$, $p < .05$). Table 1 shows that only a minority of 3-year-olds but most 4- and 5-year-olds correctly inferred the other's belief.

Inference of other's false belief did not prove more difficult than identification of their own false belief, as Table 1 shows. The existing small differences were tested with McNemar's tests and not found reliable either for each age group separately or the total sample: all p values $> .30$.

The main finding of this first experiment was that the identification of a prior expectation as false belief was not possible for many 3-year-olds and even some 4-year-olds despite the fact that the present procedure ascertained that the children had built up an initial expectation that then turned out to be wrong. Belief identification was as difficult as belief inference.

Experiment 2

This experiment examined the possibility that the young children in Expt 1 responded with the actual content of the box to the question about their prior belief because they misunderstood the belief identification question ('. . . what did you think is in the box?') as a fact question ('. . . what is in the box?'). To examine this possibility, children's answers to the belief identification question in the original change-of-mind problem were contrasted with their answers to the identical question in a change-of-state problem. The change-of-state problem was designed in such a way that its surface characteristics were quite similar to the change-of-mind problem. As in the change-of-mind problem the child was induced to form an expectation about the content of a critical box (e.g. a matchbox). However, in contrast to the change-of-mind problem this expectation was confirmed when the critical box was opened: e.g. the matchbox actually contained matches. Then the child observed a change in situation. The expected content was replaced by an atypical one (e.g. the matches were replaced by a sweet). So when the box was closed again, the situation was identical to the one in the change-of-mind task, that is, the appearance of the box was misleading with respect to its content. The experimenter then asked the same belief identification question as in the change-of-mind task: 'When I first took the bag out of my box and showed it to you, what did you think is in here?' If children misunderstand this question as a fact question (i.e. as '. . . what is in here?') then they should respond in the same way as in the change-of-mind problem, namely with the present actual content of the box, e.g. with 'sweet'. If, however, children understand that the question 'What did you think is in here?', refers to the prior episode where the child was asked about the content of the box, then the question should be answered correctly, i.e. with 'matches'. This is to be expected because in this condition the child's initial interpretation of the critical fact must not be identified as a false belief. The child's answer to the expectation question is just the expression of a correctly apprehended prior state of affairs.

A further variation of the present experiment was that the present tense required in German (see the footnote in Expt 1) for the subordinate clause of the test question 'What did you think *is* in this box?' was contrasted with a grammatically incorrect past tense formulation: 'What did you think *was* in the box?' This variation was motivated by the hypothesis that children may completely ignore the 'did you think' phrase of the test question. In this case the present tense formulation of the test question will lead to wrong, actual state responses even in the change-of-state condition while the past tense formulation in this condition should lead to correct answers.

Method

Subjects. Twenty-nine children (median age: 4:1, range: 3:1 to 4:6, 17 boys, 12 girls) participated. Of the original sample seven children had to be excluded. In four cases children did not respond to the initial question about the content of the matchbox, two further children were excluded, because after a correct response to the test question they could not answer the question about the actual content, and one child had to be excluded because of an error by the experimenter.

Design. Each child participated both in a change-of-mind and in a change-of-state task. Order of task as well as assignment of container (matchbox and chocolate box) to task were counterbalanced. In the two tasks for each child different boxes were used. To half the children both test questions were given in the original and grammatically correct present tense formulation of the subordinate clause; the other half was confronted with the subordinate clause in past tense formulation.

Results and discussion

Separate stepwise logistic regression analyses were performed for proportions of correct answers in the change-of-mind task and in the change-of-state task. The specified model was complete (including interaction effects) for the factors test question (present vs. past tense of subordinate clause) and position of task (first vs. second). Type of box and sex were included as main effects only. There were no significant effects in either of the two analyses: all p values $> .10$.

Interestingly, in both tasks the proportion of children with correct response was somewhat higher when the grammatically correct but possibly misleading present tense formulation of the subordinate clause was used (43 vs. 30 per cent in change-of-mind, 87 vs. 84 per cent in change-of-state task).

Table 2 shows the contingency between responses to the two tasks. From the third column (Total) it is evident that again a majority of children was unable to identify a former expectation as a false belief. However, of these 18 children, 15 (first column) correctly identified and remembered their expectation of a prior state of affairs in the

Table 2. Contingency between change-of-state and change-of-mind understanding

	Change-of-state		
Change-of-mind	Correct	Incorrect	Total
Correct	10	1	11
Incorrect	15	3	18
Total	25	4	29

change-of-state task. Only one child showed the opposite combination of responses (McNemar's test: χ^2 (1, $N = 29$) = 10.5, $p < .001$).

The finding that the change-of-state condition posed no problem shows that children's wrong answers to the test question in the change-of-mind condition cannot be due to a misunderstanding of the test question or to a memory problem. The latter explanation is excluded since the time lag between the expectation question and the test question was of about the same length in both conditions.

Experiment 3

A rather obvious explanation of 3-year-olds' failure with belief identification is that these children were embarrassed about having said something wrong initially and were reluctant to repeat this false statement in response to the belief identification question. The present experiment examined this possibility by contrasting the *own belief* task with an *own/other* belief task where both the subject and another person were simultaneously tricked. This new task was designed in such a way that not the child but *another* person is depicted as being the victim of a trick. In this own/other belief task the child witnessed how a typical container (e.g. a matchbox) is presented to another person and how the other person responded to the question about the content according to the appearance of the box (e.g. with 'matches'). After that the child witnessed how the actual content (e.g. a sweet) was revealed to the other person. Then the child was asked the test question about what the other person had originally thought the content of the box was. The important feature of the task is that in the beginning the child was as ignorant as the other person about the box's actual content. Thus, the other's expressed expectation also was the child's own expectation. According to the Cartesian view, the child's expectation self-transparently turned into a false belief when the actual content was revealed. Therefore, in the own/other belief task there was an identical change of mind as in the own belief task, but the test question could now be asked about the other's prior belief instead of the embarrassing reference to the subject's own false belief. Furthermore, the other person in the own/other belief task was 'Kasperl' the main figure of the traditional Austrian-German puppet play (comparable to the Punch and Judy show) who is well known among children for his proverbial silliness.

Method

Subjects.   Twenty-four children from local kindergartens participated. Their age was between 3:1 and 4:2 (median: 3:8, 14 boys and 10 girls). Nine children had to be replaced because they did not respond to any questions in the warming-up conversation.

Procedure and design. The assessment of the child's identification of his or her own prior false belief (own belief task) was done exactly as in Expt 1. Understanding of another's prior false belief (own/other belief task) was tested in the following way. The experimenter first introduced Kasperl. Then the following dialogue between the experimenter and Kasperl about the content of a matchbox or a chocolate box took place: 'Kasperl, look what I've got here (experimenter points to the box). What do you think is in here?' Kasperl responds (experimenter's voice): 'I know exactly what's in here. Matches (in the matchbox version) are in here.' Experimenter: 'No, look, there are no matches in here. We have already used all the matches and have put a sweet in here.' (Content of box is shown to Kasperl and the child.) The box was then closed and the experimenter asked the child: 'Listen, when in the beginning I showed the box to Kasperl, what did Kasperl think *is** in here?'

After a correct answer to this other's belief question the child was asked the justification question 'Why did Kasperl think there are matches in the box?' In the case of a wrong answer the child was reminded of Kasperl's initial answer ('Didn't Kasperl say there are matches in the box?') and in the case of an affirmative response the justification question was asked.

Each child participated both in an own and an own/other task. The order of the two tasks as well as the kind of container used in each task (chocolate box, matchbox) were counterbalanced. Half of the children were asked both questions in the *think version* (one for self, one for other), the other half were asked the two questions in the *say version* (e.g. 'Listen, when in the beginning I showed the box to Kasperl, what did Kasperl *say* is in here?').

Results

Two separate stepwise logistic regression analyses for own and own/other tasks were performed. In both analyses the predictors were kind of question (think vs. say), position (first vs. second), and the interaction of these factors. Kind of box (chocolate vs. matches) and sex were used as main effects only. Both analyses showed no factor was significant: all p values $> .10$. There was also no reliable difference between own and own/other tasks either in the case of the think version or in the case of the say version (McNemar's tests: $p > .70$). Table 3 shows the percentage of children with the correct response to the think and say questions in self and other tasks.

Children's responses to the justification question were evaluated in the same way as in Expt 1. Again an association was found between correct response to test question and correct justification ($C_{corr} = .68$, χ^2 (1, $N = 24$) $= 7.17$, $p < .01$ for self and $C_{corr} = .58$, χ^2 (1, $N = 24$) $= 4.8$, $p < .05$ for other). As in Expt 1, children quite often could not be reminded of their own initial expectation. When children had responded

Table 3. Percentage of children with correct answer to think and say version of the test question in own belief and own/other belief task

Task	Question		
	Think	Say	Total
Own belief	33	42	38
Own/other belief	33	50	42
Total	33	46	

*See previous footnote in Expt 1, p 128.

with the actual content to the test question then quite often they denied their own (66 per cent) or the other's (57 per cent) initial expectation in response to the reminder and, therefore, could not be asked the justification question.

The findings of the present experiment definitely rule out the hypothesis that in Expts 1 and 2, 3-year-olds failed to answer correctly the question about their own mistaken belief because they were embarrassed to admit it. This explanation can be discounted as these children had the same difficulty answering the question about a character who is renowned for saying silly and wrong things.

General discussion

Relationship to other studies

The findings of the present series of experiments are in agreement with Gopnik & Astington's (1988) original finding on the development of own belief understanding. A clear cut developmental trend in the understanding of own false belief was found. A majority of 3-year-olds showed no such understanding, while about 80 per cent of the 4-year-olds, and all 5-year-olds were correct. The difficulty of the 3-year-olds with belief understanding in the present task apparently cannot be explained by superficial task factors and thus seems to be caused by an underlying conceptual deficit. In support of this conclusion it was found that the identical test question (i.e. 'What did you think is in the box?') did not pose a problem for 3-year-olds when it referred to a prior statement of the child that turned out to be correct. On the other hand it was found that various attempts to make the own false belief task easier for 3-year-olds had little or no success. Embarrassment about having been wrong could not be the problem in the own/other condition of Expt 3 but still the majority of 3-year-olds failed. In Expt 3 it was also found that asking the test question in more concrete terms ('What did you *say* . . .?' instead of 'What did you *think* . . .?') was not helpful.

The theoretically important finding is that 3-year-olds' difficulty with own false belief understanding persisted despite our attempts to make sure that the initial critical expectation was still in the child's mind when the belief identification question was asked. The child was asked an expectation question in the beginning, the interval between expectation question and belief identification question was short and each child was tricked only once. By these procedural characteristics it was excluded that the child in response to the belief identification question had to go through a process of counterfactual reasoning: 'If I did not know what is really in the box then I would think matches are in the box since normally matches are in matchboxes.' Such counterfactual reasoning was identified above (see the introduction to this study) as a possible problem of the procedure used in the Gopnik & Astington (1988) study.

While the present findings are in agreement with Gopnik & Astington they are certainly discrepant from Perner *et al.* (1987) where it was found that about 70 per cent of the 3-year-olds responded correctly to the question about a prior own belief. Gopnik & Astington had already pointed out that Perner *et al.* had asked the belief question in such a way that it was suggested to the child that the correct answer must be different from the answer to the immediately preceding reality question ('Look, what is really in the box?' was followed by 'But what did you think is in the box?').

This kind of questioning may have led to an overestimation of 3-year-olds in the Perner *et al.* study. Further support for younger children's difficulty with own false belief is provided by an unpublished study by Moses & Flavell (1987) where a group of older 3-year-olds and of 4-year-olds (3:6 to 4:9) was found to respond correctly in only about 60 per cent of the trials (50 per cent correct due to guessing).

False belief understanding: Understanding representation or informational causation?

The present finding of 3-year-olds' difficulty with own belief contradicts Wimmer *et al.*'s (1988) explanation that the typical 3-year-old child fails other person's false belief task only because of one specific conceptual deficit, namely, that this child in general does not understand how informational conditions cause thoughts and thus cannot infer the other person's specific false belief from the misleading informational conditions to which the other person was exposed. Obviously this explanation cannot be the whole story since in the present case of own belief the specific expectation of the box's content simply was there (as a result of exposure to misleading information conditions) and still 3-year-olds were most often unable to identify this expectation as a false thought. This finding supports Perner's (1988) alternative proposal that the 3-year-old child has not yet acquired an understanding that thoughts may function as representations of states of the world, as represent-ations that may be considered true (by oneself in the past or by another person at present) despite the fact that they are false.

However, several aspects of the present findings suggest that understanding of informational causation plays a role in the understanding of false belief although not the exclusive one proposed by Wimmer *et al.* (1988). One relevant finding was that most children who were able to identify their prior expectation as false belief were also able to respond correctly to the more demanding justification question, that is, they could explain how they got their false belief. This finding suggests that informational causation is entailed in the child's concept of belief. The specific proposal is that the 4-year-old child possesses a concept of false belief that is not just 'a false thought about x which is/was believed to be true' but which includes an additional component '. . . since it was caused by normally reliable information'. This entailment about causation corresponds to a similar causational component in the concept of knowledge which allows children from about 4 years onwards to distinguish between 'know' and 'guess' (Sodian & Wimmer, 1988; see also Perner, 1991, Chapter 4, for a detailed account of the acquisition of the concept of knowledge). That the mentioned entailment about causation is important for the concept of belief can be seen from the emotions of fun (e.g. in Commedia dell' Arte) or tragedy (e.g. Oedipus' belief about Jocasta) which on occasion arise together with the understanding of false belief.

Evidence against the Cartesian view and for the theory view of mind

An obviously difficult but interesting question is how the present findings stand in relation to the two main philosophical positions on mind. In his lucid exposition P. Churchland (1984) refers to these positions as 'traditional view' and 'theory view'. In the traditional view most prominently presented by René Descartes (1639/1981) concepts of mental states are acquired by introspection:

> the soul acquires all its information by the reflexion which it makes either on itself (in the case of intellectual matters) or (in the case of corporeal matters) on the various dispositions of the brain to which it is joined which may result from the action of the senses or from other causes (p. 66).

Furthermore, as stated by Thomas Hobbes (1651/1968), understanding of one's own mind is considered a precondition for understanding other minds:

> Whosoever looketh into himself, and consedereth what he doth, and when he does think, opine, reason, hope, feare, &c, and upon what grounds; he shall thereby read and know, what are the thoughts, and Passions of all other men, upon the like occasions (p. 82).

This relationship between understanding own mental states and mental states of the other person is still the underlying assumption of the perspective taking tradition in the study of social cognitive development.

The present findings speak against this precondition relationship between own and other's mental states since understanding of own belief was found to emerge at about the same age that was found critical for children's understanding of other persons' belief (Hogrefe *et al.*, 1986; Perner *et al.*, 1987; Wimmer & Perner, 1983). Of course, the Cartesian position is not committed to the conclusion that all past mental states of the self must be accessible. Therefore, the present findings of own belief difficulty can only speak against the Cartesian assumption if the prior expectation was still in mind, when the surprising state of affairs was revealed. As argued above, the present procedure was carefully designed to fulfil this requirement. Furthermore, Expt 2 showed that the time lag between expectation question and test question posed no problem when the test question referred to a prior state of affairs and not to a belief.

The present findings of own belief difficulty seem to concur with the basic assumption of the 'theory view', which states that introspection of own mental states is a form of conceptual identification. Accordingly, introspection depends on an already given system of mental concepts and cannot be the source of these concepts. A further postulate is that the acquisition of this system of concepts shares the general characteristics of 'theory' acquisition:

> According to his general view, the mind/brain is a furiously active theorizer from the word go . . . its (the newborn infant's) mind/brain sets about immediately to formulate a conceptual framework with which to apprehend, to explain, and to anticipate that world. Thus ensues a sequence of conceptual inventions, modifications, and revolutions that finally produce something approximating our common-sense conception of the world . . . At life's opening the mind/brain finds itself as confusing and unintelligible as it finds the external world . . . With time, it does learn about itself, but through a process of conceptual development that parallels exactly the process by which it apprehends the world outside of it (Churchland, 1984, p. 80).

An important domain in which to apply any conceptual acquisitions about mind is the child's own mental functioning. Therefore, one's own mind may provide interesting opportunities for new conceptual developments. One might speculate that the experience of misled expectations and misguided actions as in the present study may help children to reinvent and/or adopt the folk-psychological conception of mind which among other things claims that what a person thinks to be the case about a certain situation is the product of his or her perceptions and inferences. Without such conception there must be confusion when as in the present task one and the same fact is apprehended in two different ways (e.g. first as 'there are matches in this box' and then as 'there is a sweet in this box'). The folk-psychological conception of mind provides a solution to such contradictions since it makes allowance for identifying and retaining the first interpretation as a false belief that is seen as having been caused by misleading information. In fact this theory may not be just a useful invention but a true discovery. As happens with other theories too, the truth of the folk-psychological theory of mind becomes so self-evident that it is difficult to see it as a theory at all. The child reminds us that it may in fact be a theory.

Acknowledgements

The helpful suggestions and critical comments of Paul Harris, Josef Perner and Beate Sodian are gratefully acknowledged.

References

Astington, J. W. & Gopnik, A. (1988). Knowing you've changed your mind: Children's understanding of representational change. In J. W. Astington, P. L. Olson & D. R. Harris (Eds), *Developing Theories of Mind,* pp. 193–206. Cambridge, MA: Cambridge University Press.

Astington, J. W., Harris, P. L. & Olson, D. R. (Eds) (1988). *Developing Theories of Mind.* Cambridge, MA: Cambridge University Press.

Churchland, P. M. (1984). *Matter and Consciousness.* Cambridge: MIT Press.

Descartes, R. (1981). *Philosophical Letters* (Translated and edited by A. Kenny.) London: Blackwell. (Original work published 1639.)

Dixon, W. J. (Ed.) (1981). *BMDP Statistical Software.* Berkeley, CA: University of California Press.

Flavell, J. H. (1988). The development of children's knowledge about the mind: From cognitive connections to mental representations. In J. W. Astington, P. L. Harris & D. R. Olson (Eds), *Developing Theories of Mind,* pp. 244–267. Cambridge, MA: Cambridge University Press.

Forguson, L. & Gopnik, A. (1988). The ontogeny of common sense. In J. W. Astington, P. L. Harris & D. R. Olson (Eds), *Developing Theories of Mind,* pp. 226–243. Cambridge, MA: Cambridge University Press.

Gopnik, A. & Astington, J. W. (1988). Children's understanding of representational change and its relation to the understanding of false-belief and the appearance–reality distinction. *Child Development,* **59**, 26–37.

Hobbes, Th. (1968). *Leviathan or the Matter, Forme & Power of a Commonwealth Ecclesiastical and Civill* (C. B. McPherson, Ed.). London: Penguin. (Original work published 1651.)

Hogrefe, J., Wimmer, H. & Perner, J. (1986). Ignorance versus false belief: A developmental lag in attribution of epistemic states. *Child Development,* **57**, 567–582.

Leslie, A. M. (1987). Pretense and representation: The origins of 'theory of mind'. *Psychological Review,* **94**, 412–426.

Leslie, A. M. (1988). Some implications of pretense for mechanisms underlying the child's theory of mind. In J. W. Astingon, P. L. Harris & D. R. Olson (Eds), *Developing Theories of Mind,* pp. 19–46. New York: Cambridge University Press.

Moses, L. & Flavell, J. (1987). Attributing past or future false beliefs to self and other. Unpublished manuscript, Stanford University, Stanford, CA.

Perner, J. (1988). Developing semantics for theories of mind: From propositional attitudes to mental representation. In J. W. Astington, P. L. Harris & D. R. Olson (Eds), *Developing Theories of Mind,* pp. 141–172. New York: Cambridge University Press.

Perner, J. (1991). *Towards Understanding Representation and Mind*. Cambridge, MA: MIT Press.

Perner, J., Leekam, S. R. & Wimmer, H. (1987). Three-year-olds' difficulty understanding false belief: Representational limitation, lack of knowledge or pragmatic misunderstanding. *British Journal of Developmental Psychology*, **5**, 125–137.

Piaget, J. (1932). *The Moral Judgment of the Child*. London: Kegan Paul.

Sodian, B. & Wimmer, H. (1988). Children's understanding of inference as a source of knowledge. *Child Development*, **58**, 424–433.

Wellman, H. M. (1990). *The Child's Theory of Mind*. Cambridge, MA: MIT Press.

Wimmer, H., Hogrefe, J. & Sodian, B. (1988). A second stage in children's conception of mental life: Understanding informational accesses as origins of knowledge and belief. In J. W. Astington, P. L. Harris & D. R. Olson (Eds), *Developing Theories of Mind*, pp. 173–192. New York: Cambridge University Press.

Wimmer, H. & Perner, J. (1983). Beliefs about beliefs: Representation and constraining function of wrong beliefs in young children's understanding of deception. *Cognition*, **13**, 103–128.

Received 11 October 1989; revised version received 9 March 1990

British Journal of Developmental Psychology (1991), **9**, 139–157 *Printed in Great Britain* 139

Preschoolers' grasp of a desire for knowledge in false-belief prediction: Practical intelligence and verbal report

N. H. Freeman,* C. Lewis† and M. J. Doherty

Department of Psychology, University of Bristol, 8–10 Berkeley Square, Bristol BS8 1HH, UK

Preschoolers often fail a false-belief test. Competing explanations have been offered from two perspectives: the theory of mind and the theory of reasons for action. A concept which unifies the two has been overlooked—the concept of a 'need to know', whereby someone has a reason for directing actions to the goal of forming a mental representation. Current tests that present the actor as a passive information user rather than an active information collector might underestimate preschoolers' conception of psychology.

In Expt 1, a theory of mind test presented a false belief as the outcome of an actor's plan of action involving her need to know something. Preschoolers showed 85 per cent success when the test took the form of hide-and-seek, whilst success in a standard false-belief test was 48 per cent. In Expts 2 and 4 it was found that success was not due to a low level heuristic: in the former, asking children to act out the plan of action gave 94 per cent success compared with 66 per cent from a modified standard task. Success from conventional verbal questioning was reliably lower. Further probes revealed flexibility; in a true-belief test children recognized that the actor's plan would succeed, and in an ignorance test (Expt 3) they showed understanding that the seeker would not know where to search.

We suggest that traditional tests underestimate preschoolers in two ways. One is in neglecting practical intelligence in favour of verbal questioning. The other is in challenging them with tests which pose an inferential problem about the intentionality of the actor and thus disturb children's 'intentional stance'. Traditional tests reveal an important limitation on preschoolers' use of a theory of mind but not an organizational gap in their construction of psychology.

Contributors to Astington, Harris & Olson (1988) have presented various explanatory frameworks accounting for preschoolers' successes and failures in coordinating (*a*) inferences about how mental states such as beliefs affect behaviour with (*b*) inferences about how events cause an agent to hold one belief rather than another. There are indeed reciprocal links between what people think and what they do. As Miller & Aloise (1989, p. 269) put it, '. . . the causal link between mental states and behavior is bidirectional'. What is at stake is the child's 'construction of psychology'.

---

* Requests for reprints.
† C. Lewis is at the Department of Psychology, University of Lancaster.

We discuss here preschoolers' use of a simple chain of inferences about how someone's mental state (one of uncertainty) can cause an action that gives her reason to form a new mental state (a belief) which in turn forms her reason for a future action.

Uncertainty about a state of affairs can be characterized as a mental state that can be resolved by acquiring a representation of the state of affairs. An act of perceptual investigation of a state of affairs is impelled by a special desire, a desire for knowledge, that has the formation of a belief as its goal. The terms mentioned—perception, action, belief and desire—form the basic level of Searle's (1983) characterization of intentionality and here appear in one 'bidirectional loop' of activity. Berlyne (1960) was the first psychologist to formulate relations amongst the four factors and to show that investigation is self-motivating ('epistemic desire') thus making a step in a 'Newtonian revolution' in the study of motivation (Bhaskar, 1989). Do preschoolers understand what goes on when an actor is seen to investigate? If they do, then one can infer that preschoolers have an important insight into how actors use their minds to plan action and use the outcome to 'make up their minds'. In the experiments below we tested whether preschoolers understand that when an investigator has a reason for being committed to act on the outcome of the investigation and when the outcome is a *false belief* she will make an honest mistake, but when the outcome is a *true belief* she will not err. A baseline is that, when no investigation has occurred, the actor will be *ignorant* of the state of affairs so will not necessarily succeed in a future action. To anticipate the data, adding the privileged case of a 'need to know' to false-belief tests enabled *many* 3-year-olds to succeed, and allowing the children to join in the game by acting out their prediction enabled *most* 3-year-olds to succeed.

False beliefs and hedonic desires

There is ample evidence that preschoolers find it difficult to grasp that an actor will act on the basis of a false belief (Perner, 1988a). Johnson & Maratsos (1977) presented a scenario in which Sally hid John's toy duck at A and misinformed him that the duck was at B. If John intends to get his duck, he should act on the misinformation, even though the target of his desire is elsewhere. The mean success of 3-year-olds was only 42 per cent, compared with 4-year-olds' 80 per cent. Subsequent work inspired by Wimmer & Perner (1983) showed the effect in different test-settings. But the effect is not easy to explain.

John's false belief (that the duck is at B) is at variance both with the *facts* (the duck is at A) and with the *condition of satisfaction of his desire* (only going to A will fulfil his desire). Current accounts deal with both mismatches but in different ways. Perner (1988a) focused initially on the former mismatch, between the falsity of the belief and the true state of affairs. The argument is that preschoolers find it difficult to grasp that as long as John himself deems his false belief to be true he will act on it. That formulation stems from the traditional problem of mind in which 'the puzzle of false belief' is that if a seeker aims at 'an outcome in the *real world*, why should a match for her goal specification be sought in the *counterfactual situation* described by her belief? (Perner, 1988a, p. 157, italics in original; see also Leslie, 1990). What is at stake is the preschooler's understanding of the representational status of John's false belief: it is his mental model of the situation.

Bartsch & Wellman (1989, p. 963) concentrated on the desire component: preschoolers might well understand the representational status of the false belief, but faced with 'conflict between reasoning about what would satisfy the actor's desire . . . and reasoning in terms of the actor's beliefs . . . 3-year-olds predict according to what would satisfy the actor's desire . . . Young children are disinclined to suppose that an actor would act in a manner to thwart his or her own desire'. Children have a problem in belief–desire reasoning. The formulation is traceable to the traditional problem of reason in which the 'puzzle of an honest mistake' is to account for how a belief can 'attach' to a desire (see Locke, 1974) in such a way that *the reason why* something happens to John (failing to find his duck at B) is not *his reason for* action.

In both accounts young children 'recapitulate' encounters with philosophical dilemmas, and there are precedents for such approaches (Matthews, 1980). But it follows that a good false-belief test for probing the very early stages of a theory of mind would do well to side-step such dilemmas. That means finding a design in which there is a natural belief–desire link and the actor has his or her own reason for being committed to his or her *false belief* as a representation. If preschoolers should still fail such a test, the inference would be that they indeed lacked insight into psychology. If preschoolers were to find the test easier than the standard versions, it might then become possible to reconcile analyses based on the problem of mind and the problem of reason. In order to design such a test, we now consider the unified position adopted by some philosophers in reaction against the mass of arguments which the traditional dilemmas engendered.

Detection of the actor's unified intentionality

Dennett (1987) argued that human beings are characterized by their 'intentional stance'. One example of the stance is an observer watching a scenario and trying to make sense of what occurs by puzzling out the actor's most basic intention. As Bennett (1976) pointed out, there is a level in any analysis at which intention is irreducible (see also Bhaskar, 1989): we suggest that children try to detect that level in false-belief tests. In John's duck scenario, John *explicitly* intends to get his duck (satisfying hedonic desire) and can be *inferred* as intending to act on the information received (using a belief). A unified test would make his intention to act on belief more explicit; and to devise the design let us consider Searle's (1983) analysis of intentionality. He argues that beliefs and desires are 'secondary forms' based on the 'biologically primary' perception and action (p. 36). The intentionality of perception and action is given by the fact that both are directed to the external world, but they are directed in different ways. Perception has 'world-to-mind direction of causation' and 'mind-to-world fit' (p. 53): that is, the world provides the input for triggering a representation and the 'responsibility' of the actor is to get the representation to map on to the state of affairs. Action usually has the reverse character in being designed to alter the world to fit what is in the mind. But in the privileged case of investigation the intention is to alter or make up one's own mind. Bennett (1976) treated 'inquisitiveness' as an instance of irreducible intentionality. We therefore suggest that if preschoolers can see John collaborating in losing his duck in a game of hide-and-seek, and then actively exploring to find out where the duck has gone, John's irreducible intentionality should be clear. John can acquire a false belief if he picks up a *miscue* about where the duck is—the duck could unexpectedly change location between the time John sees it and the time he decides to fetch it. The design corresponds with the 'unexpected change' paradigm introduced by Wimmer & Perner (1983) that baffles so many preschoolers, but with the addition of epistemic desire.

Would such a scenario be easy or difficult for preschoolers to understand? A direct application of the Bartsch–Wellman formulation suggests that it would be difficult, for John would have thwarted his epistemic desire to attain a true belief and thwarted his hedonic desire to get his duck—a double perversity. A direct application of the Perner formulation also suggests that such a test would be difficult since John's false belief is at variance with the true state of affairs to which it is supposed to be directed. It has been found that preschoolers were not aided either by a scenario where the actor herself asks for information about the target's location (Perner, Leekam & Wimmer, 1987) or by the protagonist extracting a promise which subsequently becomes broken (Perner & Wimmer, 1988). However, those studies were not based on a unified intentional design in which the protagonist *misinforms herself*.

To summarize, the proposed paradigm involves false belief in which hedonic desire is thwarted via a mismatch between truth and falsity, but there is no belief–desire split in a desire to acquire a belief, nor is there an action–perception split in an act designed to acquire perceptual information. We assume with Poulin-Dubois & Shultz (1988) that an understanding of self-generated plans is built up over the first three years of life and we expected preschoolers to show understanding of John's plan and its determinants. To understand a plan, in the present context, involved understanding that agents can plan *ahead* what to do before they actually do it. In the formulation of Anderson (1984, p. 612), human beings are characterized by 'the ability to use the mind as a mental laboratory, where plans and actions can be contemplated without the expenditure of physical effort'. In our proposed design, John's active exploration should be a cue to the children that he has set his mental laboratory to work. Versions of hide-and-seek have been canvassed as settings which readily make 'human sense' to preschoolers (Hughes & Donaldson, 1979). It is difficult to formulate the pragmatics of 'human sense' (and at least one suggestion of Donaldson, 1978, about an inferential test turned out to be empirically wrong: Freeman, 1985; Freeman & Schreiner, 1988). In the present context the issue can be focused on whether the new test induced false positives in the data by enabling children to regard the hide-and-seek either as a sort of ritual drama play in which actors play allotted roles or a sort of chasing game like follow-my-leader, which has rather mechanical rules. Some experiments in the series reported below probe these possibilities.

Experiment 1

The false-belief test used by Baron-Cohen, Leslie & Frith (1985) was of an 'unexpected change' design. The child witnessed Sally leaving her marble at A and going away, and the marble was then moved to B in Sally's absence; the question is then where Sally will look if she comes back wanting to get her marble. That can be adapted for a hide-and-seek game by replacing the marble with another doll with whom Sally is playing hide-and-seek. Instead of Sally's exit from the room, Sally hides her eyes and starts to count to 10 but she cheats, seeing the hider go to A. Then whilst Sally completes her count, the hider unexpectedly moves to B. Sally will have actively acquired the false belief that A is the place to search in her self-generated plan. In a pilot test on 40 children of mean age 3:10 (SD 5 months), 16 children passed both hide-and-seek and the standard test, 13 failed both, nine passed only on hide-and-seek and two passed only on the standard test (the 9–2 split is significant at $p < .05$, binomial). The design therefore seemed worth pursuing.

The standard test has been criticized as 'unnecessarily clumsy' (Chandler, 1988), and adding a hide-and-seek story-line with the seeker cheating adds yet more complexity. Some of that can be smoothed out by making places A and B share a partition so that the hider can, in effect, continue her act of hiding by pushing under the partition. This change also needs another test which is intermediate between hide-and-seek and the standard test, where the actor has no prior uncertainty about the location of what she seeks, and the target pushes under the partition. The design is that Debbie puts her pet into place A and whilst she is away the pet pushes under a partition into B. That procedure provides continuity between places A and B in terms of the action of leaving and entering by the pet, but Debbie has no prior uncertainty.

The design of the first experiment thus necessitates three tests: hide-and-seek, Debbie losing her pet, and Sally hiding her marble. In line with the position described in the introduction, we predicted that only hide-and-seek would prove easier than the standard test. Note that though the different conditions are comparable in certain respects, many differences remain. Experiment 1 thus served to see *whether* an effect would be obtained but was of limited value in discerning *why* any effect obtains.

Method

Subjects.   There were 80 subjects, 36 girls and 44 boys, from four urban nursery schools. Forty formed the younger group, mean age 3:10 (SD 3 months) and 40 formed the older group, mean age 4:6 (SD 2 months).

Apparatus and procedure.   (1) *Hide-and-seek test.* The apparatus shown in Fig. 1 consisted of two open-topped boxes, one red and one green, with a corresponding coloured path leading to an open side of each. The apparatus was made of cardboard, so whilst the two boxes looked quite separate, it was possible for a Playpeople doll (7.5 cm high) to be pushed unexpectedly under the partition from one box to the other. The blue doll was introduced by a girl's name and a larger orange doll (9.5 cm high) was introduced as her father:

> This is [Sarah] and this is her daddy. Sarah and her daddy are going to play a game. They are going to play hide-and-seek. Sarah is going to run off and hide, and daddy is going to shut his eyes like this [experimenter covers his eyes]. Then he is going to look for Sarah. So Sarah runs off down the green path [experimenter moves Sarah halfway down the green/red path]. But what is happening here? Daddy's not covering his eyes at all, he's looking [experimenter angles daddy to look at Sarah]. So daddy can see Sarah go into the green shed [Sarah enters shed]. Then daddy goes, '1, 2,

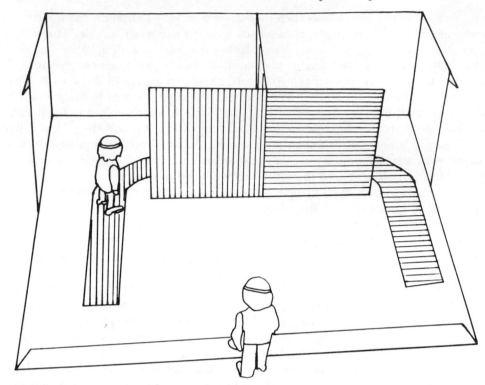

Figure 1. Apparatus used in the hide-and-seek test, with protagonists at the 'cheating stage'.

3, 4, 5'. But look, Sarah crawls into the red shed [Sarah pushed under partition and stood in red/green shed], '6, 7, 8, 9, 10'. Then daddy says, 'Coming!'

The child was then asked the critical belief question, 'Where do you think daddy will look for Sarah?' Then a reality control question was asked, 'Where is Sarah?' followed by a memory control question, 'Where did Sarah hide in the beginning?'

(2) *Debbie's pet test.* Debbie was as above, as was the apparatus, except that it was reduced in size by half and the open side of the boxes closed. A grey mouse was included, 1 cm high × 3 cm long. The protocol, with appropriate acting out, was:

This is [Debbie]. This is a red box. This is a green box. This is Debbie's pet mouse. She takes her pet mouse and puts it into the green (red) box so it won't run away. Then she goes out to play [experimenter removes Debbie from the scene altogether]. But while she is away, what is happening here? The mouse crawls into the red (green) box. A bit later, Debbie comes back [Debbie placed at fork in path]. Where do you think Debbie will look for her mouse?

The reality and memory control questions were then asked.

(3) *Sally standard test.* The apparatus was as above, except that a marble was used instead of a mouse and a second doll was included. The procedure was taken from Baron-Cohen *et al.* (1985) in which Sally places her marble in box A, exits, and Anna removes it to box B. The questioning was as before, covering where Sally will look for her marble, where it is now, and where it was before.

Forty children had hide-and-seek as their first test, and then 20 of those went on to the Debbie test and 20 on to the Sally test. The remaining 40 children were age-matched to those with reverse order of test administration.

Results and discussion

All the children passed the reality control questions; 13 who failed on any of the remaining control questions were dropped, with replacement, to make up the sample as described. Each child had thus grasped the facts of each episode.

We now consider success at predicting search at A on the first test encountered by each child (as well as verbal replies, non-verbal responses were accepted, e.g. picking up the seeker and making it go to a box). Hide-and-seek proved easy, with 85 per cent of the total sample succeeding. The two age groups were very similar with 90 per cent success in the older group and 80 per cent in the younger (no significant difference by Zubin's t; Marsh, 1967). Overall success for both other tests combined was 48 per cent, well below the hide-and-seek level ($\chi^2(1) = 8.3$, $p < .01$). Detailed scrutiny revealed no difference between the Debbie's pet and Sally's marble tests, with Debbie's pet yielding 50 per cent passes (60 and 40 per cent passes for the older and younger children, respectively) and the corresponding figures with Sally's marble were 45 per cent (40 and 50 per cent). We have amalgamated the two tests within each age group under the heading standard test in reporting the raw data. Section (1) of Table 1 shows the results of just the first test given.

Table 1. Performance on different false-belief tests by two age groups

Test order	Older		Younger		Total	
	Pass	Fail	Pass	Fail	Pass	Fail
(1) First test						
Hide-and-seek	18	2	16	4	34	6
Standard	10	10	9	11	19	21
(2) Second test						
Hide-and-seek	20	0	11	9	31	9
Standard	15	5	12	8	27	13
(3) Both tests: hide-and-seek then Standard						
Pass both		14		12		26
Pass hide-and-seek only		4		4		8
Pass standard only		1		0		1
Pass neither		1		4		5
(4) Both tests: standard then hide-and-seek						
Pass both		10		8		18
Pass hide-and-seek only		10		3		13
Pass standard only		0		1		1
Pass neither		0		8		8

Note. The two versions of the standard test described in the Method section (Debbie's pet and Sally's marble) have been amalgamated as explained in the text.

Section (2) of Table 1 contains data from the second test given to each child. The older group who had previously achieved 50 per cent success with the standard test here achieved 100 per cent with hide-and-seek, and even the subgroup now given the standard test achieved 75 per cent success (better than the 50 per cent level at $p = .02$, binomial). Turning now to the younger children it can be seen that there was very little difference between hide-and-seek and the standard test, with success levels lying intermediate between—and not significantly different from—those set out in section (1) (Zubin's t; Marsh, 1967).

To summarize, the only occasion on which the older sample did not perform better than chance was when the standard test was the first one they met; and the only occasion on which the younger sample did perform better than chance was when hide-and-seek was the first one they met ($p < .01$, binomial). It seems likely that transfer effects were operative, and in different directions in the two age groups.

Sections (3) and (4) of Table 1 set out the repeated measures component of sections (1) and (2). Overall, in the older group 14 succeeded only with hide-and-seek and failed with the standard test, with one counter-example ($p < .001$, binomial). The effect occurred at half the level in the younger group, with the corresponding figures being 7–1 ($p = .035$, binomial). Over both groups, therefore, hide-and-seek led to an upwards assessment of the ability of 21 children, with two counter-examples.

It seems possible that preschoolers' readiness to infer commitment to a false belief is greater than has been supposed. But how, precisely, did the new test bring this out?

The most important consideration is that hide-and-seek may not even engage the child in reasoning about the seeker's mind, and thus might generate false positives in those children who said daddy would go to A. Josef Perner (in a personal communication) suggested that children might be led to behave ritualistically and make daddy fail to find Sarah because that is the sort of role play that a good game of hide-and-seek involves, without reference to what the protagonists might or might not know. Paul Harris (in a personal communication) suggested that children might pick up on Sarah's movement down the path and think of daddy as mechanically following in an automatic 'follow-my-leader' fashion.

Experiment 2

One test for ritual drama play is a true-belief control in which daddy sees Sarah go to A during hide-and-seek and Sarah stays there. Daddy now knows where to find Sarah, but if children regard daddy's mental state as irrelevant, daddy should be sent off to B because that is 'how the game should be played'. Accordingly, a significant drop from a high success level as found in Expt 1 would be evidence for ritualization. The strongest evidence would be a reversal of the results to a high failure rate, but a chance level would be enough to challenge the rationale for the particular design used so far. That is the control used in the following experiment (a second way of testing ritualization is included in Expt 3).

The present experiment incorporates a second variable, that of allowing the child to demonstrate insight by joining in and acting out the seeker's search pattern. Traditional false-belief tests merely rely on verbal questioning, and that may be unsafe in the light of Lewis & Osborne's (1990) demonstration of how easily preschoolers may misunderstand the question. We can supplement that by case examples from the pilot phase of the present investigation. Three 4-year-olds failed a standard false-belief test by predicting that the actor would search where the toy really was and not where his false belief represented it as being. One child spontaneously explained that that was because the actor would already have looked in the empty place and then gone on, and two children offered that explanation when questioned. Some false negatives may occur by children reporting on the end-state of the actor's search without realizing that the experimenter only wanted an initial stage report. They had grasped the actors' plan and mentally run through it. Such false negatives can be blocked by asking children to act out the plan, within hide-and-seek and standard tests.

The third modification made in the next experiment was to take a closer look at the proposed role of epistemic desire by replacing the standard test with a test which resembles hide-and-seek more closely, except that the seeker does not manifest initial uncertainty about place. Anna and daddy are out for a walk, daddy sees Anna go to place A, and walks on. In his absence, Anna moves into place B. Since daddy had not actively been seeking Anna at the time he saw her at place A, we predicted that the test would be harder than hide-and-seek, even though it also embodied a joint activity which should readily make human sense to the child.

But it is still possible that success on hide-and-seek could be achieved by a follow-my-leader chase. This can be tested for by having another version of both hide-and-seek and Anna's walk in which Sarah/Anna locks the partition door behind her after moving into B, whilst the experimenter comments that now no-one can get through. The child should grasp that it is now impossible for daddy to follow his daughter's track. That condition should therefore block some false positives, leaving a grasp of daddy's commitment to his false belief as the reason why daddy would be predicted to go to the wrong place and thwart his own desire by coming up against an impassable barrier.

Finally, we expected acting out to give evidence on the competence of a number of children who would be classed as failing just on the basis of their verbal report; and it then becomes an open question whether the hide-and-seek facilitation effect would be abolished. If that occurred, then it would be plausible that hide-and-seek removes a temporal indeterminacy by establishing the actor's state of mind as a referent. If acting out raised absolute success levels but still maintained hide-and-seek facilitation, then that would strengthen the possibility that establishing a need to know has an intrinsic cue value in helping the child determine precisely *what* it is about daddy's state of mind which needs computing.

Method

Subjects. There were 98 subjects, 43 boys and 55 girls, from two nursery schools and four playgroups. Mean age was 3:11 (SD 4 months). They were assigned to subgroups with as close age matching as possible as described below.

Apparatus and procedure. The apparatus was as for hide-and-seek in Expt 1: two joined boxes and a branching path, except that (*a*) the apparatus was professionally made of plywood, (*b*) a door replaced the partition between the boxes which were painted yellow and red, and (*c*) a door at the side was provided as the entrance to each box. Each child was given one of four tests as next described, or the control described later.

(1) *Sarah's hide-and-seek.*
   Episode 1. This is Sarah and this is her daddy. Sarah and her daddy are going to play. They are going to play hide-and-seek. Sarah is going to run off and hide and daddy is going to shut his eyes like this. Then he is going to look for Sarah. So Sarah runs down the red (yellow) path [the experimenter makes her stop at door of red (yellow) shed]. But what is happening here? Daddy's not covering his eyes, he's looking. Now daddy goes, '1, 2, 3, 4, 5' [Experimenter covers daddy's eyes, and makes Sarah go into red (yellow) shed]. Oh look! Sarah finds a little door.

   Episode 2. Open access alternative: Sarah goes into the yellow (red) shed. That was easy wasn't it. Daddy goes, '6, 7, 8, 9, 10'. Then daddy says, 'Coming'.

   Locked door alternative: Sarah goes into the yellow (red) shed and locks herself in. Now no one can get through that door! Daddy goes, '6, 7, 8, 9, 10'. Then daddy says, 'Coming'.

(2) *Anna's walk.*
   Episode 1. This is Anna and this is her daddy. Anna and her daddy are going out for a walk [dolls enter left (right) at right-angle to path]. They have walked a long way, and Anna is a bit tired. [Experimenter makes Anna and daddy stop at red (yellow) shed door]. Daddy leaves Anna at the red (yellow) shed and walks a little bit further. He will come and fetch Anna in a few minutes. [Experimenter makes daddy walk to where the paths join, the starting-point of the hide-and-seek game above, and stand with his back to Anna. Experimenter makes Anna go into red (yellow) shed]. Oh look! Anna finds a little door.

   Episode 2. Open access alternative: Anna goes into the yellow (red) shed. That was easy wasn't it! Daddy comes back from his walk. He is going to fetch Anna.

   Locked door alternative: Anna goes into the yellow (red) shed and locks herself in. Now no one can get through that door. Daddy comes back from his walk. He is going to fetch Anna.

Finally, the child was asked the critical false-belief question, 'Where will daddy look for Sarah/Anna?' followed, in the counterbalanced order, by the reality control question, 'Where is Sarah/Anna?' and the memory control question, 'Where did Sarah hide/Anna go in the beginning?' Then the child was asked to act out the search: 'You take daddy to find Sarah/Anna'.

(3) *True-belief control.* The procedure was as for the hide-and-seek locked door condition except that (*a*) Sarah stopped in A and locked the door she was facing, and (*b*) half the children saw the game begin with Sarah placed directly at the entrance to A instead of moving down the path (that was designed to minimize a cue mechanically to make the seeker chase Sarah, and is examined further in Expt 3). The control questions do not apply to this condition so were omitted.

Results and discussion

The total sample was reduced to 86 by children failing the memory control question, leaving unequally sized subgroups; and administrative error led to one subgroup receiving too many of the sample, resulting in Ns = 17, 18, 16 and 24, in the four conditions hide-and-seek, hide-and-seek plus lock, Anna's walk, Anna's walk plus lock, respectively, and 11 in the true-belief control. The respective mean ages of the subgroups were 3:11 (SD 4 months), 3:11 (SD 4 months), 3:11 (SD 3 months), 3:11 (SD 4 months) and 3:11 (SD 6 months). Given the unequal numbers, data are reported as percentages.

We begin by considering the children's success at acting out the seeker's path in the four main tests. The overall success level was high, at 79 per cent, and a hide-and-seek advantage is apparent from the first two rows of Table 2, with 94 per cent success on hide-and-seek and 66 per cent on the walk. Logistic regression (GLIM) was carried out to determine the relative influences of age (the 41 children below age 4:0 vs. the 34 above that age), type of activity (hide-and-seek vs. walk) and door condition (free access vs. locked) on the proportion of scores correct. The procedure examines the contribution of all three variables and discards those which do not contribute significantly to the regression. The only significant effect was for hide-and-seek vs. walk ($\chi^2(1) = 10.2$, $p < .01$); scaled deviance $= 4.57$ with 4 residual d.f.

We had expected the results of the reply to the false-belief question to be somewhat below the acting-out levels of success, but they turned out to be even lower than anticipated: overall success was only 31 per cent (this is considered later). Even so, the data set out in Table 2 reveal something of a hide-and-seek advantage. Logistic analysis revealed that, again, age and door condition contributed little to the regression. The contrast between hide-and-seek and walk did contribute but just fell short of being significant ($\chi^2(1) = 2.70$; critical value for $p = .05$, $1 - T = 2.71$; scaled deviance $= 3.5$ with 6 residual d.f.).

Table 2. Percentage of children showing success at identifying the path of a seeker with a false belief under conditions in which the seeking is part of a game or a walk, and a door remains openable or becomes locked

Scenario	Response	Door	
		Openable	Locked
Hide-and-seek	Acting out	88.2	100
Walk	Acting out	68.8	62.5
Hide-and-seek	Verbal	29.4	50.0
Walk	Verbal	25.0	20.8

In sum, acting out was clearly more successful than verbal reply. There were 38 children who gave a wrong verbal reply yet successfully acted out daddy's honest mistake, with two counter-examples ($p < .001$, binomial).

Whilst collecting the data, it was possible to do some opportunistic testing of 18 children aged between 2:10 and 3:4. Pooling data across conditions, over which the sample was thinly spread, only 2/13 who passed the control questions gave a correct verbal reply (of whom one gave a correct acting out and one gave a wrong acting out), and 10 gave a wrong verbal reply and a correct acting out. It will be necessary to conduct a full investigation, but a total of 11/13 giving correct acting out is higher than chance ($p = .011$, binomial) and suggests that the general technique may come to reveal expertise below the age of 3:6 which would flatly contradict the Bartsch–Wellman formulation of 3-year-olds' inability to resolve 'belief–desire conflict'.

Finally, in the true-belief control only two children said that the seeker would go to the empty box B. One of them was from the direct placement condition, and he followed his error by acting out the seeker going to B. The other child began acting out in the same way but spontaneously self-corrected just as the seeker had been made to reach B. Counting both children as erring, the uneven split, 9–2, in favour of judging that the seeker would act on his belief, rather than ritualizing to make a good game, is significant at $p = .033$ (binomial). Of the two erring children, one was the third oldest (4:5) and the self-corrector was the fourth youngest (3:7).

The evidence points to hide-and-seek allowing many children to register the consequences of the seeker's commitment to his reason for acting even though that will bring him up against a locked door. Whilst the effect of locking the door was non-significant, it was the experimenter's impression that the locked door enabled children to enjoy the joke of the actor digging a pitfall for himself. Some children acted out the seeker's surprise at meeting an unexpected obstacle:

David (3:6) Gave wrong verbal reply in Sarah locked door condition. Then acted out daddy going into empty shed: 'He can't get in . . . [shouts] . . . Sarah! Let me in!' [David makes Sarah unlock the door].
Carina (3:10) Gave correct verbal reply. On making daddy go into empty shed and meeting locked door shouted 'No!'

The locked door was designed to block follow-my-leader but the variable would only work if the child is alerted to the adverse consequence of making the seeker chase the hider. A technique of directly placing the hider at the entrance to A at the onset would remove a modelling of how to chase, and that technique was used in the next experiment which was designed to probe for false positives in two ways.

Experiment 3

Despite the failure of the true-belief control to reveal ritual role play, it is still possible that the false-belief test evokes a ritualized response in children because they see the hider apparently 'trying to be hard to find'. The locked door might help build that impression, and it did exert a non-significant facilitation on verbal predictions (though we interpret the effect as the children's grasp of the joke). But it could be the case that the acting-out advantage occurred because direct placement was not used in the main hide-and-seek tests of Expt 2 and copying the hider's actions may have been more tempting in acting out than in verbal report. This cannot explain the acting-out advantage in Anna's walk because the protagonists there approached the boxes at right angles to the path (a variable embodied in hide-and-seek in Expt 4). Nonetheless, the possibility has to be controlled for in hide-and-seek. The following test was designed to check for ritualization and for copying movement.

The proposed design is an *ignorance test*. If cheating is removed, the seeker cannot know where the hider has gone. He would thus have to choose his path at random. Any outcome significantly different from chance would challenge the proposal that hide-and-seek is a theory of mind test. A bias towards the empty box irrespective of the hider's movements would favour a ritualization account. A bias towards (*a*) the empty box when the hider moves from A to B, and (*b*) the box containing the hider where the hider stops in A, would favour a mechanical chase account. To make the test more comparable with the traditional unexpected change paradigm, the seeker was 'out of the room' whilst the hider hid so that ignorance was guaranteed.

Method

Subjects. There were 48 children, 18 girls and 30 boys, of mean age 3:10 (SD 5 months).

Apparatus and procedure. The apparatus was as in Expt 2. The procedure was an adaptation of the hide-and-seek locked door condition, with the minimum changes necessary to convert the test into an ignorance test. Each child was given one of the following tests which were distinguished by whether the hider moved from A to B in an equivalent of the false-belief paradigm, or stopped in A in an equivalent of the true-belief control. Both tests began in the same way. A doll was taken from the experimenter's pocket and the child told, 'Here is David. He is going to play hide-and-seek with his mummy. Mummy will come along later [doll shown to be still in experimenter's pocket]. David goes here'. At this point, half the children saw David move down a path to box A and half saw him placed directly into A. The door was then locked, and mummy was handed to the child whose hand was then guided to the fork in the paths, with the comments 'Mummy's coming up to play. You show me where she goes'.

To summarize, the four tests were (*a*) David moved down path and went through A to B, (*b*) David moved down path and stopped in A, (*c*) David directly placed in A and went through to B, and (*d*) David directly placed in A and stopped there.

Results and discussion

Six children moved David at the same time as, or just before, moving mummy, thus making their responses impossible to score unambiguously: perhaps that is evidence that they wanted to show 'how a game could go', and the ritualization possibility is worth taking seriously. By replacement as testing proceeded it was feasible to maintain almost equal-sized groups: data from those 42 are set out in Table 3.

It is apparent that there was no difference between the conditions: in none of them did choice of box differ from chance (total choice of empty box was 57 per cent). There was no discernible effect of age: the mean age of children choosing the empty box was 3:11 (SD 5 months), and that of children making the seeker find the hider at first attempt was 3:9 (SD 5 months). It is possible that the data reveal that some

Table 3. Number of children choosing empty box or full box in a hide-and-seek ignorance test, under four conditions of target movement

	Condition			
	Hider shifts from A to B		Hider stops at A	
Choice	Direct placement	Path movement	Direct placement	Path movement
Empty box	5	7	6	6
Full box	5	4	4	5

children are ritualizers and some not, so a second test was opportunistically run in which each child was switched between hider stopping in A/hider moving from A to B (maintaining path movement or direct placement). The proportion of children who switched between choice of full box and choice of empty box (or vice versa) was 38 per cent. That shows some lability as is congruent with the seeker's ignorance.

The variable of moving the hider down the path did not encourage chasing. The results did not support the prediction of a higher than chance bias towards the seeker ritually seeking in the empty box. That is somewhat surprising, since there are many current anecdotes about ritualized hide-and-seek. Indeed, one of the authors witnessed a 3-year-old throwing a tantrum when a visiting child took his favourite hiding-place. Perhaps there is an age lag in the tendency to internalize the ritual role of a seeker. In a pilot study of six children aged between 4:10 and 5:3, with path movement plus stay in A, all six made the seeker look in the empty box ($p = .016$, binomial). We do not know of any experimental evidence on younger children's ritualization of seeking, though it conceivably occurs in contexts where the game is often repeated in real life. It seems safe to presume that the hide-and-seek advantage found in the first two experiments was not a ritual role play happening to coincide with the correct answer based on using a theory of mind.

Experiment 4

The studies so far have shown the following. Hide-and-seek revealed false-belief competence more than did tests based on or developed from the traditional passive protagonist paradigm. It may be that hide-and-seek makes salient the way in which the seeker forms a belief to which he is committed, whether the belief is true or false. Asking children to act out the seeking also enhanced performance, even with a traditional format (Anna's walk). It remains to make hide-and-seek more comparable with Anna's walk by having the hider approach the boxes from the side: a cleaned up replication of the locked door test of Expt 2.

This final test almost uses up the available subjects in the particular catchment areas used so far, so tests which can probe further predictions have to be postponed. However, it became possible to assign some children to a probe test designed to look ahead, as follows. The logic of the experimentation so far has been to focus on hide-and-seek as a paradigm of unified intentionality, under conditions of false belief, ignorance and true belief. One component of the next round of experiments could well turn back to Anna's walk and probe that in depth. Here we add epistemic desire to Anna's walk: Daddy leaves Anna at A, turns and looks back to check her location, and then walks on. The value of adding that probe test is in checking for the possibility of extremes of success and failure. An extreme of failure would immediately disconfirm the present account since we could not explain what is occurring if the addition of epistemic desire were to depress performance on Anna's walk. By the same token, the seeker's uncertainty is only presented as happening to occur during the walk, so if success were raised above hide-and-seek in which uncertainty is an integral aspect of the seeker's unified intentionality, that would be inexplicable in the terms used so far. A useful result would be a rank ordering of success with Anna's walk at the bottom then Anna's walk plus epistemic desire then hide-and-seek, with a significant difference between each pair of conditions. But we cannot claim to have enough evidence on the salient task demands to warrant the confident prediction of that ordering.

Method

Subjects. There were 44 subjects from one nursery and one playgroup, assigned to three subgroups with as close age matching as possible as described below.

Apparatus and procedure. The apparatus was as in Expt 2. Each child was given one of three tests. Two tests were based upon the protocol for Anna's walk described in Expt 2. The procedure was altered slightly to provide two variations one of which gave daddy a reason for remembering where Anna was. In both conditions, when the child was told that 'Anna is a bit tired', the experimenter continued, 'Daddy will come and fetch Anna in a few minutes'. In the standard Anna condition the experimenter said, 'Daddy says "Goodbye Anna, see you later"' as he made daddy walk away. In the condition where daddy manifests epistemic desire the experimenter continues, 'Daddy says, "Where is Anna? (turning daddy to look at Anna). *There* she is at the red (yellow) shed"'. The third test was as the hide-and-seek game in Expt 2 except that Sarah and daddy approached the boxes from the side (as they did in Anna's walk) and daddy walked along the floor away from the boxes and round the edge of the board to stand at the fork where he performed his cheating.

Results and discussion

Five children failed a control question, leaving 15 in Anna's walk (age $M = 4:0$, SD 5 months), 12 in Anna's walk plus epistemic desire ($M = 4:0$, SD 5 months) and 12 in hide-and-seek ($M = 3:11$, SD 6 months). Overall, there was again an acting-out advantage with 18 children who had failed the verbal questioning then correctly showing the seeker's trajectory and no counter-instances ($p < .001$, binomial). Given that 14 children failed both verbal questioning and acting out, the use of acting out has led to an upwards assessment of competence, compared with the traditional reliance on verbal report, by 18/32, i.e. 56 per cent. The results for each test are shown in Table 4.

Table 4. Number of children succeeding in reply to verbal question and request to act out their prediction under three conditions

Pass/fail	Anna's walk	Anna's walk plus epistemic desire	Hide-and-seek
		Condition	
Pass action and verbal	3	1	3
Pass action, fail verbal	5	6	7
Fail action and verbal	7	5	2
Fail action, pass verbal	0	0	0

The replication prediction that hide-and-seek would yield better performance than Anna's walk was upheld, in that hide-and-seek acting out saved a higher proportion of those who failed the verbal questioning than did Anna's walk: 9/11 and 5/15, respectively ($p = .05$, Zubin's t, $1 - T$). Presumably that was due to an overall higher level of acting-out success in hide-and-seek than in Anna's walk (10/12 and 8/15, respectively, $p = .05$, Zubin's t, $1 - T$). Anna's walk plus epistemic desire fell between the other two tests, but did not significantly differ from either. Thus the results certainly confirm the value of asking for acting out, and ordering of data can be deemed congruent with the proposed role of epistemic desire. We leave it as an open question whether use of younger children would reduce the absolute level of success at the unmodified Anna's walk enough to reveal a significant effect of the addition of epistemic desire in relation to Anna's walk and/or hide-and-seek.

General discussion

There were two interesting findings. One was that hide-and-seek revealed that preschoolers would send the seeker off to the *empty place* in accordance with a *false belief*, to the *hiding place* in accordance with a *true belief*, and indifferently to *either place* in accordance with seeker's *ignorance*. Flexibility in response was put forward as an essential criterion for evidence of a theory of mind by Perner (1988*b*; pp. 290–291). It remains to be seen how many children would show all three insights: the carry-over effects suspected to be operative on the second trial of Expt 1 led us to rely on between-subjects designs for this first round of research.

The second interesting finding was that acting out raised the level of successful false-belief predictions significantly compared with verbal questioning (without completely abolishing the hide-and-seek advantage). There are several ways of accounting for that. One is that verbal questioning induces false negatives in the data, as suggested in the introduction to Expt 2: a problem of temporal indeterminacy as to which point in the actor's foreseeable path of search the answer should be narrowed. When asked to execute the actor's plan of action, there is no temporal indeterminacy because the child takes up the story exactly where the actor would, at his starting-point. Only if children err in acting out can one be confident that they have not grasped the actor's plan. There were few such errors in the false-belief tests used here with hide-and-seek. The studies which formed the bedrock evidence for the Perner and Bartsch–Wellman formulations may have underestimated competence. It was noticeable that verbal success fluctuated saliently between the experiments reported here, as they have in the past (Wimmer, Hogrefe & Sodian, 1988). In one of the tasks reported by Wimmer & Perner (1983) half the 5-year-olds in the sample apparently did not grasp the referent of 'What will Maxi do?' (after his chocolate had inadvertently been displaced). It would be interesting to know whether researchers who have replicated traditional tests have sometimes come across unexpectedly low absolute levels of verbal success, and have withheld publication on the grounds that experiments occasionally do not work.

One way of accounting for the acting-out/verbal disparity is to question whether acting out led to false positives. One possibility is that children unreflectingly copied a path of acting that had been modelled; but we found no modelling effect in the data.

Another possibility is that the children fell into a familiar ritual when invited to join in, by acting out a drama of failure to find followed by finding. The data from the true-belief and ignorance tests did not support that interpretation either. We fully agree that real-life hide-and-seek is full of both ritual and fairly routinized actions, but we see no reason for thinking that these experiments triggered either to a significant extent. Finally, it is possible that acting out truly did tap competence but at a lower level than that required for asserting that children have a conception of mind which is theory-like in any interesting sense. Whilst we agree that most 4-year-olds know something about the mind that most 3-year-olds do not, there is no consensus about whether that indicates a step from a lack of theory to a grasp of theory (see Wellman, 1988).

We suspect that delineating a sharp criterion for the acquisition of a theory of mind can lead to writing off the early steps in children's implementation of a theory as 'only' practical. There is now a tradition of constructing models of how reflective awareness emerges gradually from the implicit practical intelligence organizations which are its necessary precursors (e.g. Bickhard, 1978; Karmiloff-Smith, 1988). We suggest the following critical tests of whether the practical intelligence manifest in those children who successfully acted out *any* of the tests reported above is theory-like, in the way in which proponents of verbal questioning propose. The criterion is that the child should be able successfully to act out on the basis of information about the actor's intentionality and ignore (*a*) the actual state of affairs if the actor has no knowledge or a false belief and (*b*) information about the intentionality of others in the scenario.

Finally, let us return to the wider issues raised in the introduction. The child's conception of psychology is a complex topic in which some synthesis has to be achieved between the problem of mind and the problem of reason. Current accounts in this fast developing area tend to emphasize one or the other. The Bartsch–Wellman formulation of desire taking precedence over belief in the child's conception of reasons for action seems to be defective in its particulars, since 85 per cent of the children here passed hide-and-seek 'thwarting of own desire' on their first test in Expt 1 and 94 per cent passed in the acting-out probe of Expt 2. Yet an appeal to the child's conception of reasons for action seems right. The Bartsch–Wellman formulation overlooked the privileged case of epistemic desire which has an epistemic state (belief) as its goal. The concept of an epistemic state is squarely within the problem of other minds. The accounts of Leslie (1988) and Perner (1988*a*) specified modellings of epistemic states but became steadily less precise where conative questions begin to be implied, and the traditional dilemma of the problem of reason remained acute. The present tests were intended as a step towards a unified intentionality approach by putting together instantiations of epistemic desire and of planning an action. As with all experiments there is need for adversarial tests of models and hypotheses. But, in the long run, the task is to synthesize the split approaches. From the problem of mind perspective it is an essential consideration that seekers had grounds for deeming their belief to be true. From the problem of reason perspective it is an essential consideration that they had a reason both for informing themselves and acting out of conviction. What one does not know is the relative weights of those in children's judgement.

It has often been pointed out that formulations of what children of different ages understand about the mind need not map directly on to formulations of how development occurs (e.g. Astington, 1989). The present experiments were aimed at the former—to answer the question of whether a standard false-belief test was likely to underestimate children. But our general intentionality approach does indicate a possible developmental course which is, in principle, testable. Briefly, children in the fourth year of life have a conception of people (reasons for action, self-generated plans) and of epistemic states (pretending, thinking, belief–uncertainty link) but they also have little conception of how people's intentions lead them sometimes to undertake investigatory reality monitoring (Foley, Johnson & Raye, 1983; Johnson & Raye, 1981) and sometimes to act self-motivatedly (impulsively jumping to conclusions/sedately doing armchair reasoning). Perhaps the bottom line of why we were able to demonstrate a high degree of practical intelligence is that the children were able to read the plan of action of the seeker (deciding which path to choose) straight out into an action response (choosing a path). The role of epistemic desire might be to alert children to the inference that the seeker is engaged in forward planning.

Acknowledgements

We are grateful to Peter Bryant, Paul Harris and Josef Perner for incisive comments on earlier drafts, and to Peter Diggle and Mich Green for statistical help with Expt 2.

We should like to thank the staff and children at Barton Hill, Greaves Park, Willow Lane, Birley, Hillsborough and Ringlow Road Nursery Schools, Brookhouse, Hala, Scotforth and University playgroups, and the University Preschool Centre, Lancaster.

References

Anderson, R. E. (1984). Did I do it or did I only imagine doing it? *Journal of Experimental Psychology (General)*, **113**, 594–613.

Astington, J. W. (1989). Developing theories of mind: What develops and how do we go about explaining it? Paper presented at the Biennial Meeting of the Society for Research in Child Development, Kansas City, April 1989.

Astington, J. W., Harris, P. L. & Olson, D. R. (1988). *Developing Theories of Mind.* Cambridge: Cambridge University Press.

Baron-Cohen, S., Leslie, A. M. & Frith, U. (1985). Does the autistic child have a 'theory of mind'? *Cognition*, **21**, 37–46.

Bartsch, K. & Wellman, H. M. (1989). Young children's attribution of action to beliefs and desires. *Child Development*, **60**, 946–964.

Bennett, J. (1976). *Linguistic Behaviour.* Cambridge: Cambridge University Press.

Berlyne, D. E. (1960). *Conflict, Arousal and Curiosity.* New York: McGraw-Hill.

Bhaskar, R. (1989). *The Possibility of Naturalism*, 2nd ed. Brighton: Harvester.

Bickhard, M. H. (1978). The nature of developmental stages. *Human Development*, **21**, 217–233.

Chandler, M. (1988). Doubt and developing theories of mind. In J. W. Astington *et al.* (Eds) (1988), pp. 387–413.

Dennett, D. C. (1987). *The Intentional Stance.* Cambridge, MA: Bradford/MIT Press.

Donaldson, M. (1978). *Children's Minds.* London: Fontana.

Foley, M. A., Johnson, M. K. & Raye, C. C. (1983). Age-related changes in confusion between memories for thought and memories for speech. *Child Development*, **54**, 51–60.

Freeman, N. H. (1985). Reasonable errors in basic reasoning. *Educational Psychology*, **5**, 239–250.

Freeman, N. H. & Schreiner, K. (1988). Complementary error patterns in collective and individuating judgements: Their semantic basis in 6-year-olds. *British Journal of Developmental Psychology*, **6**, 341–350.

Hughes, M. & Donaldson, M. (1979). The use of hiding games for studying coordination of viewpoints. *Educational Review*, **31**, 133–140.

Johnson, C. N. & Maratsos, M. P. (1977). The early comprehension of mental verbs: Think and know. *Child Development*, **48**, 1743–1747.

Johnson, M. K. & Raye, C. L. (1981). Reality monitoring. *Psychological Review*, **88**, 67–85.

Karmiloff-Smith, A. (1988). The child is a theorist not an inductivist. *Mind and Language*, **3**, 183–196.

Leslie, A. M. (1988). Some implications of pretence for mechanisms underlying the child's theory of mind. In J. W. Astington *et al.* (Eds) (1988), pp. 19–46.

Leslie, A. M. (1990). Pretence, autism and the basis of 'theory of mind'. *The Psychologist*, **3**, 120–123.

Lewis, C. & Osborne, A. (1990). Three-year-olds' problems with false beliefs: Conceptual deficit or linguistic artefact? *Child Development*, **61**, 975–983.

Locke, D. (1974). Reasons, wants and causes. *American Philosophical Quarterly*, **11**, 169–179.

Marsh, R. W. (1967). Tables for testing the significance of difference between proportions. *Australian Journal of Psychology*, **19**, 223–229.

Matthews, G. B. (1980). *Philosophy and the Young Child*. Cambridge, MA: Harvard University Press.

Miller, P. H. & Aloise, P. A. (1989). Young children's understanding of the psychological causes of behavior: A review. *Child Development*, **60**, 257–285.

Perner, J. (1988*a*). Developing semantics for theories of mind: From propositional attitudes to mental representation. In J. W. Astington *et al.* (Eds) (1988), pp. 141–172.

Perner, J. (1988*b*). Higher-order beliefs and intentions in children's understanding of social interaction. In J. W. Astington *et al.* (Eds) (1988), pp. 271–294.

Perner, J., Leekam, S. R. & Wimmer, H. (1987). Three-year-olds' difficulty with false belief: The case for a conceptual deficit. *British Journal of Developmental Psychology*, **5**, 125–138.

Perner, J. & Wimmer, H. (1988). Misinformation and unexpected change: Testing the development of epistemic-state attribution. *Psychological Research*, **50**, 191–197.

Poulin-Dubois, D. & Shultz, T. R. (1988). The development of the understanding of human behaviour: From agency to intentionality. In J. W. Astington *et al.* (Eds) (1988), pp. 109–125.

Searle, J. R. (1983). *Intentionality*. Cambridge: Cambridge University Press.

Wellman, H. M. (1988). First steps in the child's theorising about the mind. In J. W. Astington *et al.* (Eds) (1988), pp. 64–92.

Wimmer, H., Hogrefe, J. & Sodian, B. (1988). A second stage in children's conception of mental life: Understanding informational accesses as origins of knowledge and belief. In J. W. Astington *et al.* (Eds) (1988), pp. 173–192.

Wimmer, H. & Perner, J. (1983). Beliefs about beliefs: Representation and constraining function of wrong beliefs in young children's understanding of deception. *Cognition*, **13**, 103–128.

Received 22 November 1989; revised version received 21 August 1990

British Journal of Developmental Psychology (1991), **9**, 159–171   *Printed in Great Britain*   159
© 1991 The British Psychological Society

When 3-year-olds understand ignorance, false belief and representational change

Kate Sullivan*

Boston College and University of Massachusetts, Downtown Campus, Boston, MA 02125–3393, USA

Ellen Winner

Boston College and Harvard Project Zero

This study examined conditions under which 3-year-olds can conceptualize ignorance, false belief, and representational change, and assessed the order of emergence of these three abilities. One hundred and twenty children between 2:11 and 4:1 were randomly assigned to one of three conditions: standard, explanation, and trick. In the standard condition, children were administered a standard false belief task. In both experimental conditions, the discrepancy between children's false expectation and reality was highlighted. In the explanation condition, children were also given an explanation of the source of a false belief. In the trick condition, the questions were placed in the context of a deceptive game. None of the experimental manipulations affected the younger subjects (2:11–3:7). However, for the older subjects (3:8–4:1), performance on the ignorance question was significantly elevated by both the highlight alone and a combination of the highlight with either explanation or trick; performance on the false belief question was significantly elevated by the highlight alone; and performance on the representational change question was significantly elevated by a combination of the highlight plus explanation. Thus, only children over 3:7 can be helped to pass the standard ignorance and false belief questions. Finally, contrary to previous findings, all three kinds of understandings emerged simultaneously, suggesting that all require a similar level of representational ability.

The understanding of the representational nature of beliefs, and of their role in determining behaviour, is central to what has come to be called holding a 'theory of mind' (Premack & Woodruff, 1978). Numerous studies have demonstrated that children under the age of four lack such understanding (Gopnik & Astington, 1988; Hogrefe, Wimmer & Perner, 1986; Perner, Leekam & Wimmer, 1987; Wimmer & Perner, 1983). Specifically, these studies have shown that children under the age of 4 are unable to conceptualize a state of ignorance or false belief in another person, or a false belief previously held by themselves.

The claim that children under 4 lack such seemingly commonplace abilities is a surprising and counter-intuitive one. The claim is surprising given findings that

* Requests for reprints

2-year-olds use mental state terms in a causal way (Bretherton & Beeghly, 1982), 3-year-olds distinguish between real and mental events (Wellman & Estes, 1986), and 2- and 3-year-olds occasionally talk about ignorance and false belief in their spontaneous speech. For example, the 2-year-old son of the second author was told by his grandmother not to touch the dials on the radio. When she went out of the room, he played with the dials. Upon her return, he looked at her mischievously and said, 'You didn't know this, but I was fixing it'. And another 2-year-old we know pretended to cry when his aunt said that she could not come over to play with him. When she then said that she would come, the child turned to his mother and said triumphantly, 'I tricked her. I made her think I was sad so she would come'.

Taken together, these findings led us to question the claim that 3-year-olds cannot under any circumstances grasp ignorance and false belief. The primary purpose of this study was to determine whether children under 4 can demonstrate such understanding if the experimental situation is made either (*a*) more clear, by explaining how false beliefs arise, or (*b*) more true to life, by placing the test question within the context of a deceptive game. The study was also designed to answer a second question: do the abilities to conceptualize ignorance, false belief in another and representational change (false belief in self) emerge simultaneously, or is one or more of these concepts more difficult and hence later to emerge? We discuss both questions in more depth below.

Evidence that 3-year-olds lack false belief understanding

There is now ample evidence that 3-year-olds fail false belief tasks (e.g. Gopnik & Astington, 1988; Hogrefe *et al.*, 1986; Moses & Flavell, in press). In a classic series of experiments, Wimmer & Perner (1983) presented children with stories in which an actor places an object in location X, which is then moved in his absence. Children were asked to predict where the actor would think the object was when he returned. Children under 4 were unable to attribute to the actor a false belief about the location of the object.

Perner *et al.* (1987) developed a simplified 'Smarties' paradigm designed to make the notion of false belief clearer to children. The task was set up so that subjects themselves would at first entertain a belief (that there were Smarties in a Smarties box) which they would then recognize to be false (there were actually pencils in the box). Subjects were then asked a question assessing their ability to attribute the same false belief to another. Despite the fact that children correctly reported their *own* false belief, most 3-year-olds proved unable to attribute a false belief to another.

Various explanations have been put forth for the 3-year-olds' lack of false belief understanding. It has been argued that children under 4 are unable to assign conflicting truth values to a single proposition (Perner *et al.*, 1987), do not understand the representational nature of beliefs (Forguson & Gopnik, 1988; Moses & Flavell, in press), do not grasp the causal relation between mental states and the world (Leslie, 1988); or fail to understand the causal role of informational access in belief formation (Wimmer, Hogrefe & Sodian, 1988). All such explanations attribute children's failure to an *underlying conceptual deficit*.

Evidence that 3-year-olds have some awareness of false belief

Chandler, Fritz & Hala (1989) and Wellman (1990) have questioned the conclusion that 3-year-olds fail false belief tasks because of an underlying inability to conceptualize another's false belief. Bartsch & Wellman (1989) have found that despite failure to predict another's false belief, 3-year-olds are able to *explain* actions in terms of false belief. They argue that 3-year-olds subscribe to a rudimentary belief–desire reasoning scheme and understand that mental states (desires and beliefs) are the *causes* of overt actions. Bartsch & Wellman suggest that 3-year-olds consistently fail false belief prediction tasks because they weight desire satisfaction over belief satisfaction, and thus tend to credit an actor with the belief that will satisfy his or her desires. For example, the child would reason as follows: Maxi wants the chocolate which is in the cupboard. Therefore, Maxi will look for it in the cupboard, where the *child* knows it is. Thus, Wellman (1990) concludes that the 3-year-old's failure to solve false belief prediction tasks is not indicative of a deficit in understanding false belief, but rather is the result of an 'interesting complication' in belief–desire reasoning. Bartsch & Wellman's explanation has been criticized, however, for not being able to account for cases in which children are asked to state the *contents* of a protagonist's belief, rather than predict a particular action; and for not being able to account for failures where desire plays no role, as in the 'Smarties' task (Moses & Flavell, in press; see also Perner, 1989; and Wellman, 1990).

Chandler and his colleagues (Chandler, Fritz & Hala, 1989; Wellman & Bartsch, 1989) claim that even 2-year-olds can be shown to understand false belief if an entirely different paradigm is used. Instead of asking children to predict or explain a false belief, they show that children can act to create a false belief in another. In their studies, children as young as 2:5 years acted to deceive another person about the location of a hidden treasure by removing tell-tale footprints, creating false footprints, and lying. The same children who acted to instill a false belief in another, failed the standard measure of false belief (Where will she look for the treasure?).

Chandler's studies have, in our view, successfully withstood potentially serious criticisms. Sodian (1989), and Sodian, Taylor, Harris & Perner (in preparation) argued that Chandler's subjects may have laid down false tracks merely to alter the *behavioural choices* of the competitor rather than to influence their opponent's *beliefs*. They also argued that children may have laid false tracks not with the intent to deceive, but simply for the indiscriminate fun of making footprints. In support of this claim, Sodian *et al.* (in preparation) report that children laid 'false' tracks even in a cooperative condition in which children were asked to inform a collaborator.

However, Hala, Chandler & Fritz (in preparation) report just the opposite. They found that children behaved selectively in a deceptive vs. cooperative condition: in the deceptive condition, children laid false tracks while in the cooperative condition, they laid helpful tracks. Hala *et al.* conclude that these results clearly show that children understand the implications of their deceptive action, and thus, that it is unreasonable to withhold from 3-year-olds the ability to conceptualize false belief.

The research by Wellman, Chandler, and their colleagues suggests an earlier ability to understand ignorance and false belief than is suggested by the research of Perner and his colleagues. Thus, the present study was designed to determine whether, under certain conditions (described above), children under 4 can pass the standard ignorance and false belief questions.

Understanding of ignorance, false belief, and representational change: Order of emergence

The second goal of this study was to clarify the relationship among ignorance, false belief, and representational change.

Ignorance vs. false belief

Hogrefe *et al.* (1986) found that children succeeded on an ignorance question (Will he know what is in the box?) about one year before they succeeded on a false belief question (What will he think is in the box?). Hogrefe *et al.* account for this lag by arguing that only false belief questions require the assignment of conflicting truth values to the same proposition, while the ignorance question can be answered correctly simply by representing the actual contents of the box and remembering that the other person did not see inside.

False belief vs. representational change

With respect to understanding false belief vs. representational change, the evidence is conflicting. According to the findings of Hogrefe *et al.* (1986) and Perner *et al.* (1987), children can recognize a false belief in themselves (representational change) before recognizing a false belief in another. However, Gopnik & Astington (1988) found just the opposite, and argue that children learn to appreciate changes in their own beliefs by appreciating differences between their own and others' beliefs. They reason that it is easier to overlook internal contradiction (I used to believe X which I now know to be false) than a contradiction between one's own and another's beliefs (I believe X but he believes Not-X). To complicate the picture further, Wimmer & Hartl (1989) found no lag between the ability to identify one's own previous false belief and the ability to infer another's false belief. This finding suggests that it is no easier for the child to understand his/her own mind than that of another.

The present study was thus also designed to try to replicate the finding that ignorance emerges before false belief, and to clarify the disputed relation between false belief and representational change.

Method

Subjects

Subjects were 119 children recruited from local day-care centres. There were 33 'young' 3-year-olds (range 2:11 to 3:3, mean 3:1), 44 'middle' 3-year-olds (range 3:4 to 3:7, mean 3:5), and 42 'old' 3-year-olds (range 3:8 to 4:0, mean 3:9). Age groups consisted of approximately equal numbers of boys and girls.

Materials and procedure

Children received variants of the Perner *et al.* (1987) Smarties task, adapted from Expt 2, Hogrefe *et al.* (1986). This task was chosen because it is simple and does not rely on a narrated story, but rather places subjects directly in a situation involving a false belief. Three sets of materials were used. Children were shown an 'M&Ms' bag which when opened revealed two small pencils; a box of animal crackers which when opened revealed two white tissues; and a small Crayola crayon box which when opened revealed red string.

Children were tested individually in quiet areas of their day-care centres by one or two experimenters, for one 15-minute session. Children were randomly assigned to one of three conditions. In the standard condition, children received a standard version of the Perner *et al.* (1987) Smarties task. Two experimental conditions were designed to make the tasks clearer (explanation condition), and more engaging and true to life (trick condition). Each subject received three trials per condition.

Standard condition.   The standard condition began with the experimenter saying, 'We are going to play a game together. I will show you some things and then we will play a game with them'. Children were then shown the first set of materials. The order of presentation of the three sets of materials was counterbalanced across all conditions, so that each set of materials was administered first, second, and third an equal number of times. (In what follows, we always use the M&M item for an example.) The experimenter continued with 'Look what I've got. What do you think is in here?' After the child answered with the stereotypical contents (M&Ms), the experimenter continued, 'So you think there are M&Ms in there? Let's look and see. Here, you open it'. The experimenter then gave the M&M bag to the child for him/her to open and examine. After the child had opened the bag the experimenter said, 'Oh my goodness, there are pencils in there!' The experimenter than took the bag from the child, closed it up and asked, 'Now, what is really in this bag?' This control question was repeated up to two times until each subject answered with the correct contents, pencils. This ensured that the subject understood the actual state of affairs, i.e. that the 'trick' contents (pencils) were in the bag, and not the expected contents (M&Ms). The actual contents were always less desirable than the 'expected' contents (e.g. pencils rather than M&Ms) to insure that children did not pass simply by choosing the more interesting objects. The bag was then closed, and the actual contents were removed from the child's sight to guard against 'perceptual seduction' (Bryant, 1974).

Children were then asked three forced-choice test questions designed to tap their understanding of representational change, ignorance, and false belief. Forced-choice questions were used because they have been found to be easier for younger children than open-ended questions (Brandt, 1978). The three questions were always asked in the above order because this is the most logical sequence. In addition, Hogrefe *et al.* (1986) found that young children are biased towards an incorrect response when ignorance questions are asked after false belief questions. Thus, the experimenter first asked, 'What did you think was in the bag before we looked in it, pencils or M&Ms?' (representational change question). The order of the two response choices was counterbalanced across stimulus sets, trials, and questions. After answering this question, children were given feedback. Children answering correctly were told, 'That's right, before we opened the bag you thought there were M&Ms in there'. Children answering incorrectly were reminded, 'Remember, before we opened the bag, you thought there were M&Ms in there'.

The experimenter then continued with, 'Next, I'll play this game with [name of the child's favorite playmate], but let me ask you some questions first. When [name] sees this bag all closed up, will he know what's really in the bag, yes or no?' (ignorance question). After the child responded, the experimenter continued with 'What will [name] think is in the bag, M&Ms or pencils?' (false belief question). The experimenter then said, 'That was fun. I know, let's play again'. The entire procedure was then repeated two more times for a total of three trials.

Explanation condition.   The explanation condition began exactly as the standard condition. The first stimulus item was shown and children were asked what they thought was in the container. After the child answered with the stereotypical contents, the experimenter continued, 'So you think there are M&Ms in there? Let's look and see. Here, you open it'. The experimenter then gave the M&M bag to the child for her to open and examine. After the child opened the bag the highlight statement was introduced. The experimenter said, 'Oh my goodness, there are pencils in there! You thought there were M&Ms in there, but there were really pencils. I guess sometimes people can be wrong about what's in a bag'. The highlight underscored the discrepancy between the child's expectation [M&Ms] and reality [pencils], and the experimenter explicitly stated that people can be wrong about the contents of a bag. We hypothesized that if children were on the verge of the ability to conceive of ignorance, false belief, and representational change, this slight change in presentation might be enough to trigger comprehension. In addition, we reasoned that this form of presentation would make it clear to the child that it is permissible to state a belief that she knows to be false. The procedure then continued with the control question, 'Now, what is really in this bag?', followed by the representational change, ignorance and false belief questions, each of which was administered exactly as in the standard condition.

After Trial 1, the explanation component was introduced. The experimenter *explained* that false beliefs can occur when people do not have sufficient informational access. For those subjects who answered the false belief question correctly, the explanation of false belief was as follows, 'That's right, [name of playmate] couldn't know that there are pencils in the bag. You know that there are pencils in the bag because we opened it and looked inside. But [name] can't *see* inside the bag, can he? Remember, if you didn't see the pencils inside the bag, you would think there are M&Ms in there. So, if [name] sees the bag all closed up, he will think that there are M&Ms in the bag. Remember, people can be wrong about what's in a bag'. For subjects who answered the false belief question incorrectly, the explanation of false belief was identical except for the first sentence, which was, 'But wait, how can [name of playmate] know that there are pencils in the bag?'

This entire procedure, including the explanation of the source of false beliefs, continued for a second trial. On the third trial, no explanation was provided after the final false belief question. Thus, over a total of three trials, subjects were given the explanation a total of twice, following trials one and two, respectively.

Trick condition.   The first trial of the trick condition was identical to the explanation condition up to the false belief question. The experimenter then continued, in a conspiratorial tone, 'This is so funny! I've played a trick on you. You thought there were M&Ms in the bag, and I tricked you with pencils. I know, let's play a trick on [name of playmate], just like the one I played on you'. The experimenter then gave the second set of materials [e.g. a crayon box] to the subject and said 'Let's take out the crayons from this box and put in string instead. This is so much fun. You are so tricky. Isn't it fun to trick someone?' The experimenter then encouraged children to replace the original contents of the box [crayons] with the 'trick' contents [string]. All complied.

After the trick contents were placed in the box [e.g. string in the crayon box], the experimenter removed the original contents [crayons] from the subject's sight and asked, 'Now, what is really in this box?' After the subject responded to the control question, the experimenter continued with the ignorance question: 'Remember our trick. When [name of playmate] sees this box all closed up, will he know what's really in the box, yes or no?' This was followed by the false belief question: 'Remember our trick. What will [name] think is in the box, crayons or string?' The representational change question was not asked on Trials 2 and 3 of the trick condition, since subjects in this condition did not make an initial guess about the contents of the stimulus items, and thus did not need to revise their beliefs.

At the conclusion of Trial 2, the experimenter said, 'That was so much fun. Let's play another trick on [name]'. The experimenter then produced the third set of materials [e.g. an animal cracker box] and said, 'Let's take out the crackers from this box and put in tissues instead. This is so much fun. You are so tricky. Isn't it fun to trick someone?' Again, the experimenter encouraged the subjects to replace the contents of the box with the trick materials by themselves. The same procedure continued for Trial 3.

Results

Preliminary analyses for each question showed no differences in the performance of the youngest (age 2:11–3:3) and the middle groups (age 3:4–3:7). These two groups were thus collapsed (hereafter referred to as the young group), and compared to the oldest group (age 3:8–4:1). In addition, preliminary analyses showed no differences between the explanation and trick conditions. These two conditions were thus collapsed and compared to the standard condition. This could not be done for all trials of the representational change question, since this question was not asked in the trick condition on Trials 2 and 3. When collapsed, the two conditions are hereafter to here as the explanation/trick condition.

Two kinds of analyses were then carried out. First, the effects of the between-subjects factors (age and condition) were examined. For each of the test questions, a logistic regression was performed on the proportion of subjects passing Trial 1 (to examine the effects of the highlight alone), and Trials 2 and 3 (to examine the combined effect of the highlight plus either the explanation or trick manipulation). For factors age and condition, a saturated model including all main and interactions effects was considered. Each trial consisted of one question. Thus, to pass Trial 1, subjects needed to respond correctly only once. Since Trials 2 and 3 were identical except for the stimulus items, a more conservative criterion was adopted: subjects needed to respond correctly on *both* trials.

The within-subject factor of question type was then analysed. Two logistic regressions with factors age and question type were performed, once for the proportion of subjects passing Trial 1, and once for the proportion of subjects passing Trials 2 and 3. For Trial 1, the scores on the explanation and trick conditions were collapsed. For Trials 2 and 3, however, only performance in the explanation condition was considered, since the representational change question was not asked in the trick condition on these trials.

Between-subjects analysis

Representational change question. Table 1 shows the number and per cent of subjects who passed the representational change question. Only among the older subjects in the explanation condition did a majority of subjects pass (76 per cent on Trial 1, and 92 per cent on Trials 2 and 3). This pattern held for both Trial 1 and Trials 2 and 3.

Table 1. Number and per cent of subjects giving correct responses to representational change question

| | Trial 1 | | Trial 2 and 3 | |
Condition	Standard	Explan/Trick	Standard	Explanation
Age Young	10 (37)	14 (28)	8 (30)	4 (16)
Old	9 (53)	19 (76)	8 (47)	11 (92)

Note. Percentages in parentheses.

For the representational change question, a main effect of age significantly contributed to the prediction of proportion of subjects passing Trial 1 ($\chi^2 (1) = 14.14$, $p < .01$), and Trials 2 and 3 ($\chi^2 (1) = 14.58$, $p < .01$). There was no main effect of condition. On Trial 1, the improvement in prediction resulting from the introduction of the interaction of age and condition approached significance at $\chi^2 (1) = 2.97$,

$p < .08$. For Trials 2 and 3, however, the introduction of the interaction of age and condition was highly significant ($\chi^2 (1) = 7.87$, $p < .005$). Thus, the older group's performance was significantly boosted by the combination of the highlight plus explanation.

In addition, once they had heard the explanation of false belief, almost all subjects in the older group answered the representational change question correctly on *both* Trials 2 and 3. Only one subject in the explanation condition responded correctly on only one trial, while in the standard condition, 25 per cent of the older subjects did so. This suggests that the explanation triggered comprehension for those who were on the verge of understanding.

Ignorance question. Table 2 shows the number and per cent of subjects who passed the ignorance question. As with the representational change question, only among the older children on the explanation/trick condition did a majority of subjects pass (80 per cent on Trial 1, and 84 per cent on Trials 2 and 3). This pattern held for both Trial 1 and Trials 2 and 3.

Table 2. Number of subjects giving correct responses to ignorance question

Condition	Trial 1		Trial 2 and 3	
	Standard	Explan/Trick	Standard	Explan/Trick
Age Young	12 (44)	19 (38)	10 (37)	22 (44)
Old	6 (35)	20 (80)	7 (41)	21 (84)

Note. Percentages in parentheses.

For the ignorance question, a main effect of age significantly contributed to the prediction of proportion of subjects passing Trial 1 ($\chi^2 (1) = 5.21$, $p < .05$), and Trials 2 and 3 ($\chi^2 (1) = 7.86$, $p < .01$). There was no main effect of condition. On Trial 1, and Trials 2 and 3, the improvement in prediction resulting from the introduction of the interaction of age and condition was significant for Trial 1 ($\chi^2 (1) = 7.04$, $p < .008$, and Trials 2 and 3 ($\chi^2(1) = 7.86$, $p < .01$). These results again demonstrate the facilitating effect, for the older subjects, of the highlight, and of the highlight plus explanation and trick.

Table 3. Number and per cent of subjects giving correct responses to false belief question

Condition	Trial 1		Trial 2 and 3	
	Standard	Explan/Trick	Standard	Explan/Trick
Age Young	10 (37)	12 (26)	8 (29)	11 (22)
Old	6 (35)	16 (64)	8 (47)	9 (76)

Note. Percentages in parentheses.

False belief question. Table 3 shows the number and per cent of subjects who passed the false belief question. Again, only among the older children did a majority pass, and this pattern held for both Trial 1 (64 per cent) and Trials 2 and 3 (76 per cent).

A main effect of age significantly contributed to the prediction of proportion of subjects passing the false belief question for both Trial 1 (χ^2 (1) = 5.89, $p < .02$), and Trials 2 and 3 (χ^2 (1) = 13.96, $p < .01$). There was no main effect of condition. On Trial 1, the interaction of age and condition significantly improved the prediction of proportion correct (χ^2 (1) = 4.23, $p < .04$), which again demonstrates the facilitating effect of the highlight for the older subjects. On Trials 2 and 3, however, the improvement in prediction resulting from the introduction of the interaction of age and condition was only marginal (χ^2 (1) = 2.51, $p < .11$).

Taken together, these results yield a clear picture. Consistent with previous findings, most children in *both* age groups failed all three questions in the standard condition. The experimental manipulations were of no benefit to the younger children. However, the manipulations significantly elevated performance for the older children on all three test questions.

Within-subjects analysis

As can be seen from Table 4, most (83 per cent) of the older subjects passed all three test questions on Trials 2 and 3. Recall that a score of passing meant that the subject answered the question correctly on both trials. Thus, contrary to previous findings, all three questions were of equal difficulty for the older group. About half (52 per cent) of the younger subjects failed all three test questions. For the remaining younger subjects who passed only one or two of the test questions, there was no clear pattern (see Table 4). Thus, no question emerged as consistently easier than any other, for either age group.

Table 4. Contingency among questions: Number and per cent of subjects achieving correct scores on Trials 2 and 3 of the explanation condition

Age	Young	Old
Response pattern		
All 3	1 (4)	10 (83)
FB + IG	4 (16)	0
IG + RC	1 (4)	1 (8)
FB + RC	1 (4)	0
IG	4 (16)	0
FB	0	0
RC	1 (4)	0
All 3 incorrect	13 (52)	1 (8)

Note. Percentages in parentheses.

The logistic regression showed no effects of test questions, or test question by age.

Discussion

The primary question of this study was whether 3-year-olds understand ignorance, false belief, and representational change. The results were mixed. First, we replicated previous research showing that, in the standard procedure, young 3-year-olds' have considerable difficulty with these types of questions. Second, children in the younger group (2:11–3:7) continued to perform poorly, despite our efforts to make the origin of false beliefs more clear (explanation condition), and to make the attribution of false beliefs more plausible (trick condition). These findings demonstrate that young 3-year-olds are unable to conceptualize ignorance and false belief states. Despite the fact that we (*a*) underscored the discrepancy between expectation and reality, (*b*) explained the source of false beliefs, and (*c*) embedded the standard questions in a deceptive game, most young 3-year-olds continued to fail.

The performance of the older group in the standard condition hovered around chance on all three questions, again replicating findings that 3-year-olds cannot conceptualize ignorance and false belief states. In contrast, for the older group, performance was dramatically helped by the highlight statement (Trial 1), and by a combination of highlight plus either an explanation of the source of false belief, or a trick context (Trials 2 and 3).

The middle-age group (3:4–3:7) performed identically to the youngest group, rather than in between the youngest and oldest groups. There was no evidence of a gradual increase in performance with age. Thus, it appears that at the age of 3:8, and not before, the ability to represent ignorance and false belief states emerges 'full blown'.

Taken together, these findings suggest that older 3-year-olds are on the verge of conceptualizing ignorance, false belief, and representational change. The introduction of a small amount of information (highlight), the description of the see–know relationship (explanation), and the embedding of the questions within a deceptive game (trick) are enough to trigger incipient understanding.

Why did our explanation condition facilitate performance, and why did it do so *only* for the older 3-year-olds? We suggest that the explanation helped because it laid bare the causal relationship between lack of informational access and a false belief state. In effect, the children were told: if you don't see inside a bag, you will be wrong about what is inside it. Once alerted to the causal relationship between seeing and knowing, older 3-year-olds can use this knowledge in a new situation (Trials 2 and 3), and thus succeed on the questions. Younger children apparently cannot make use of this see–know relationship in new situations.

Why did our trick condition facilitate performance for the older 3-year-olds? We suggest that the trick context helped because it embedded the questions in the kind of false belief-engendering situation in which children spontaneously engage: hiding and trickery. In this condition, children were given the explicit goal of tricking another person. They were encouraged to put in the trick contents themselves, and to think about the pleasure of tricking someone. In this situation, children *wanted* another to be ignorant or wrong. This may have rendered the ignorance or false belief state of the tricked party more salient then in the standard condition.

Even more surprising than the facilitating effect of both the explanation and trick conditions, was that of the highlight statement alone for the older group. This highlight statement consisted simply of stating the discrepancy between the subject's false expectation and reality (you thought there were M&Ms, but there were really pencils), and stating that people can be wrong about the contents of a container. The highlight was thus relatively brief and merely accented the subject's own false belief. Yet, the highlight by itself proved sufficient to trigger comprehension in the older group. This statement may have made it clear that the task was *about* false belief.

It is of course possible that the statement, 'People can be wrong about what's in a box'. (Occurring in both the highlight and explanation condition) can be accounted for by the use of a low level heuristic. Children may have reasoned that the correct answer was to pick the *wrong* contents. However, the fact that this statement helped *only* the older children argues against this possibility. If this statement triggered such a low level strategy, one would expect the younger children to also benefit from it.

Although the younger group was not helped by the experimental manipulations, their spontaneous comments during the testing procedure suggest that even our 'easier' procedure may lead us to underrepresent what children actually know. For example, while replacing the standard with the 'tricky' contents required in the trick condition, several younger children gleefully voiced comments such as, 'He's never going to know what's in here', or 'No one will know that we put pencils in here!' These comments suggest that children were not only delighted by their participation in the trick, but were aware that the other person would be in the dark as to the contents of the box. Surprisingly, the very same children who, in the trick condition, spontaneously commented on another's ignorance went on to *fail* the ignorance question. Thus, these children clearly understood another's ignorance, but the ignorance *test question* did not reveal this understanding. Similarly, one child who responded correctly to the ignorance question (Will he know what's really in the bag) by saying, 'No, he'll say M&Ms and I'll say no', failed the subsequent false belief question. The discrepancy between children's spontaneous comments and their performance in experimental situations strongly suggests the need for tests better able to assess what children know.

The second question motivating this study was the order of emergence of the three forms of understanding investigated. Our results showed that, contrary to previous claims, understanding of ignorance and false belief emerge simultaneously, as do understanding of false belief and representational change. These results suggest that comprehension of all three test questions requires a similar level of representational ability. We suggest that children may be able to pass the false belief question without assigning conflicting truth values to a proposition. A simpler way to arrive at the correct answer, and one that seems to us more plausible, is to represent two different propositions which happen to conflict. One proposition is about the actual state of affairs (There are pencils in the box), and the other is about another's mental state (He believes there are M&Ms in the bag). This seems almost identical to what is required for the ignorance question. Here one must also hold in mind a proposition about the actual contents and a proposition about another person's mental state (There are pencils in the box; he does not know what is in the bag). If this analysis is correct, it is not surprising that ignorance and false belief questions are answered correctly at the same age. In addition, the fact that false belief and representational change emerge simultaneously suggests that the mind is not transparent to itself, and that it is no easier to reflect on the contents of one's own than another's mind.

In conclusion, our findings demonstrate that the ability to represent ignorance, false belief, and representational change emerges the later part of the third year, somewhat earlier than has been previously shown. Our results show that children can achieve these understandings, but only under certain conditions, and only after the age of 3:7.

Whether younger children's failure on the test questions reflects a genuine conceptual deficit, or whether it merely reflects the difficulty of the standard questions, remains to be determined. On the one hand, there are findings (including those of the present study) showing that young 3-year-olds do not pass the standard questions in which they are asked to predict another's mental state, or to reflect on their own past mental states. On the other hand, Chandler *et al.* (1989) have shown that children as young as 2:5 years can act to instill a false belief in another, and Wellman (1990) has shown that young 3-year-olds can explain actions by referring to false belief. Similarly, the spontaneous comments of our young 3-year-olds showed an understanding of mental states not tapped by our questions. The underlying representational ability of young 3-year-olds remains in question.

Acknowledgements

This research was supported by a Boston College Faculty Research Expense Grant to the second author. We gratefully acknowledge the staff and children of the day-care centres we visited. We would also like to thank Liesbeth ter Schure for her help with the data analysis, and two anonymous reviewers for their helpful comments.

References

Bartsch, K. & Wellman, H. (1989). Young children's attribution of action to beliefs and desires. *Child Development*, **60**, 946–964.

Bretherton, I. & Beeghly, M. (1982). Talking about internal states: The acquisition of an explicit theory of mind. *Developmental Psychology*, **19**, 906–921.

Brandt, M. M. (1978). Relations between cognitive role-taking performance and age, task presentation and response requirements. *Developmental Psychology*, **14**, 206–213.

Bryant, P. (1974). *Perception and Understanding in Young Children*. London: Methuen.

Chandler, M., Fritz, A. & Hala, S. (1989). Small-scale deceit: Deception as a marker of two-, three-, and four-year-olds' early theories of mind. *Child Development*, **60**, 1263–1277.

Forguson, L. & Gopnik, A. (1988). The ontogeny of common sense. In J. Astington, P. L. Harris & D. R. Olson (Eds), *Developing Theories of Mind*. New York: Cambridge University Press.

Gopnik, A. & Astington, J. (1988). Children's understanding of representational change and its relation to the understanding of false belief and the appearance–reality distinction. *Child Development*, **59**, 26–37.

Hala, S., Chandler, M. & Fritz, A. (1990). Fledgling theories of mind: Deception as a marker of 3-year-old's understanding of false belief. *Child Development*, **62**, 83–97.

Hogrefe, G. J., Wimmer, H. & Perner, J. (1986). Ignorance versus false belief: A developmental lag in attribution of epistemic states. *Child Development,* **57**, 567–582.

Leslie, A. (1988). Some implications of pretense for mechanisms underlying the child's theory of mind. In J. Astington, P. L. Harris & D. R. Olson (Eds), *Developing Theories of Mind.* New York: Cambridge University Press.

Moses, I. J. & Flavell, J. H. (1990). Inferring false beliefs from actions and reactions. *Child Development,* **61**, 929–945.

Perner, J. (1989). Is 'thinking' belief? Reply to Wellman & Bartsch. *Cognition.* **33**, 315–319.

Perner, J., Leekam, S. & Wimmer, H. (1987). Three-year-olds' difficulty with false belief: The case for a conceptual deficit. *British Journal of Developmental Psychology,* **5**, 125–137.

Premack, D. & Woodruff, G. (1978). Does the chimpanzee have a theory of mind? *The Behavioral and Brain Sciences,* **1**, 516–526.

Sodian, B. (1989). The development of deception in young children. Paper presented at the Society for Research in Child Development, Kansas City, Mo, April.

Sodian, B., Taylor, C., Harris, P. & Perner, J. (in preparation). Early deception and the child's theory of mind: False trails and genuine markers.

Wellman, H. M. (1990). *The Child's Theory of Mind.* Cambridge, MA: Bradford Books/MIT Press.

Wellman, H. M. & Bartsch, K. (1989). Three-year-olds understand belief: A reply to Perner and more. *Cognition,* **33**, 321–326.

Wellman, H. M. & Estes, D. (1986). Early understanding of mental entities: A reexamination of childhood realism. *Child Development,* **57**, 910–923.

Wimmer, H. & Perner, J. (1983). Beliefs about beliefs: Representation and constraining function of wrong beliefs in children's understanding of deception. *Cognition,* **13**, 103–128.

Wimmer, H. & Hartl, M. (1989). The Cartesian view and the theory view of the mind: Developmental evidence from understanding false belief in self and other. Paper presented at the Society for Research in Child Development, Kansas City, Mo, April.

Wimmer, H., Hogrefe, G. J. & Sodian, B. (1988). A second stage in children's conception of mental life: Understanding informational access as origins of knowledge and belief. In J. Astington, P. L. Harris & D. R. Olson (Eds) *Developing Theories of Mind.* New York: Cambridge University Press.

Received 5 March 1990; revised version received 10 January 1991

British Journal of Developmental Psychology (1991), **9**, 173–188   *Printed in Great Britain*

The development of deception in young children

Beate Sodian*

University of Munich, Leopoldstr. 13, 8000 München 40, Germany

The ability of 3- to 5-year-old children to deceive a competitor in a hiding game was studied in three experiments in a paradigm similar to the one introduced by Woodruff & Premack (1979) for the study of deception in chimpanzees. The first two experiments showed a significant increase with age in the frequency of deceptive pointing, with children below the age of about $3\frac{1}{2}$ years consistently failing to deceive a competitor even under very conducive conditions. The third experiment showed that two deception tasks (deceptive pointing and telling a lie) were significantly more difficult for 3- to 4-year-old children than parallel 'sabotage' tasks (i.e. tasks testing the ability to physically prevent a competitor from gaining a reward). These findings are consistent with previous research on false belief representation in indicating a conceptual deficit in 3-year-old children. They are discussed with regard to recent controversies on the early acquisition of a theory of mind.

The concept of belief is central to the common-sense interpretive framework that we use in predicting and explaining human behaviour. How to characterize the young child's understanding of belief has recently been discussed controversially in research on the early acquisition of a 'theory of mind'. Wellman & Bartsch (1988) claim that by the age of 3 years children share the most important principles of our adult belief/desire framework in interpreting human action. In a series of experiments, they showed that 3-year-olds are able to make sensible predictions of a protagonist's action when told what this person wants and thinks. When told, for instance, that Jane wants a banana, that she thinks that there are only bananas in the cupboard and that she doesn't think there are bananas in the refrigerator, 3-year-olds correctly predicted that she will look for a banana in the cupboard.

However, 3-year-olds fail to make correct predictions of a protagonist's action when given information on her *false belief* (e.g. they said that Jane would look for her kitten in the playroom when told that Jane thought the kitten was in the kitchen but that it really was in the playroom). This result is consistent with numerous findings on the development of false belief representation (e.g. Flavell, Flavell, Green & Moses, 1990; Moses & Flavell, 1990; Perner, Leekam & Wimmer, 1987; Wimmer &

* Requests for reprints.

Perner, 1983) that demonstrate 3-year-olds' difficulty in understanding false belief even under very simple task conditions. Perner *et al.* (1987), who ruled out a series of alternative explanations for 3-year-olds' poor performance on false belief tasks, conclude that these results indicate a serious conceptual deficit in young children's understanding of the mental domain. Unlike Wellman & Bartsch (1988), these authors argue that false belief understanding is a critical test for belief understanding in general. Wimmer & Perner (1983) pointed out that if one wants to show that children are capable of belief-based reasoning it is necessary to rule out the possibility that they can arrive at correct answers (e.g. predictions of a protagonist's action) by alternative strategies, for instance by simply taking 'belief' and 'think' terms as cues to reality. Perner (1989) argues that young children could succeed on the tasks that Wellman & Bartsch (1988) used to demonstrate an understanding of belief by alternative strategies, one of which is to interpret 'think' terms as statements of preference or interest rather than belief (see Perner, in press, for a detailed discussion of the distinction between 'thinking of' and 'thinking that'). Thus, Perner (1989) concludes, the findings by Wellman & Bartsch (1988) do not prove an early understanding of belief but, on the contrary, demonstrate once again how difficult it is for 3-year-olds to understand belief.

If 3-year-olds do not understand belief they do not share one of the most important features of our adult folk-psychological theory. One might be reluctant to assume such serious cognitive impairments in 3-year-old children. One reason for this reluctance is that the evidence on false belief understanding that has been collected thus far is based on tasks that place relatively high demands on children's verbal understanding. Although children's understanding of the story information was of course controlled for in studies of false belief understanding and although 3-year-olds do not seem to have problems understanding similar stories that do not involve false belief representation (Wellman & Bartsch, 1988), one might still argue that an ability for false belief representation may be present from early on and may be displayed in children's everyday actions, but may not have been adequately assessed so far.

A good candidate for a 'naturalistic' context in which false belief representation may emerge in young children is deceptive action. While deception in non-human primates has been studied both observationally and experimentally (see Byrne & Whiten, 1988; Mitchell & Thompson, 1986; Premack & Woodruff, 1978; Whiten & Byrne, 1988; Woodruff & Premack, 1979), surprisingly little cognitive developmental research has addressed the development of deception in children. An early observational study of the development of children's lies was conducted by Clara and William Stern (Stern & Stern, 1909). They distinguished between 'true' lies, that is false utterances made with the intention to deceive, and various forms of mistakes, fantasies, and 'pseudo' lies. They did not observe any true lies in their own children below the age of 4 years; however, 'pseudo' lies such as 'no' responses when accused of a forbidden action were observed earlier. The reason for classifying these as pseudo lies was that Stern & Stern regarded them as affective responses rather than intentionally false statements of fact (the young child says 'no' when asked whether he committed a misdeed because he fears blame or wishes not to be remembered). This early form of deception that according to Stern & Stern does not fulfil the criteria for 'true' deception was recently studied systematically by Lewis, Stanger & Sullivan (1989) in a sample of 3-year-olds. Children were instructed not to peek at a toy while the experimenter left the room. The great majority of the children did peek. When asked, 38 per cent admitted the truth, another 38 per cent said 'no' and the rest gave no response. Thus, while a substantial proportion of 3-year-olds made a false utterance, the majority did not. In a similar study with 5-year-olds Nunner-Winkler & Sodian (1989) found that the great majority of the children who had peeked denied their transgression when asked. Thus, denying the truth after having committed a transgression does not seem to be as prevalent in 3-year-olds as in older children.

Young children who deny a transgression, who pretend to be hungry at bedtime or to be sick when they have to go to nursery school may be employing 'deceptive' action in a similar way to Ashley's dog, who behaved as though he wanted to be let out when he really wanted his master to get up from his (the dog's) favourite armchair. Dennett (1978) argues that these behaviours may be parsimoniously explained without attributing an ability to represent other persons' intentional states to the dog (or the child). Deceptive action is less easily explained as a routine manipulation of other persons' *behaviour* if it occurs in novel situations and is employed flexibly (see Mitchell, 1986, 'fourth-level deception'). Studies of children's performance in strategic hiding games that require the flexible use of deceptive strategies (DeVries, 1970; Gratch, 1964; Shultz & Cloghesy, 1981) indicate that only at the age of 4 to 5 years do children start to deliberately manipulate their opponents' intentional states in such situations. While success in these tasks requires a number of skills besides the ability to intentionally manipulate others' beliefs, two recent studies have employed simpler tasks explicitly designed for the study of deception. LaFreniere (1988) found that children below the age of 4 years were generally not successful at deceiving an adult competitor about the location of a hidden object. However, the primary aim of this study was to investigate whether or not children *succeeded* at fooling a competitor, the strategies they used, and the reasons why they did not succeed (i.e. verbal or non-verbal leakage).

The question of when children first begin to *attempt* to deceive another person was addressed in a recent study by Chandler, Fritz & Hala (1989). In their task, an adult could be deceived about the location of a hidden object by removing 'footprints' that a doll-hider had left, or by laying false trails. Chandler *et al.* (1989) found that even 2½-year-olds removed the tell-tale footprints and—after some modelling by the experimenter—laid false trails. The authors conclude from these findings that an ability to intentionally manipulate others' beliefs is present in children far earlier than was previously thought. Such a conclusion has far-reaching consequences for present accounts of the early acquisition of a theory of mind (see Astington, 1989, for a review). However, some caution seems to be warranted, as Chandler *et al.* did not rule out the possibility that young children may wipe out footprints and lay false trails regardless of instructional condition. This could be controlled for by introducing a cooperative interaction condition where the child's task is to help the partner find a hidden object. A theoretically more interesting question is whether young children who wipe out footprints and lay false trails understand the informational significance of footprints or whether they simply act on an understanding that the competitor will follow the footprints just as he would follow a railroad track. Thus, the significance of Chandler *et al.*'s results for the understanding of *belief* is not clear.

Like Chandler *et al.*'s study the present study investigates the age at which children begin to attempt to deceive a competitor in a hiding-game context.* The main purpose was to explore whether 3-year-olds' performance on deception tasks is as poor as one would expect from their performances on false belief attribution tasks, and whether their presumed difficulties are specific to deception. The experimental paradigm used in the present study was developed by Woodruff & Premack (1979) for the study of deception in chimpanzees. In this paradigm, the subject's task is to mislead an ill-intentioned competitor by indicating a location in which an attractive target is not hidden. Subjects' behaviour is compared with a cooperative control condition in which it is appropriate to indicate truthfully the place where the target is hidden to a benevolent partner.

Experiment 1

The aim of Expt 1 was to determine the age at which children begin to intentionally deceive a competitor in a playful context. Deception was functional in this game to win a reward. The competitor was introduced as a nasty character who would keep the reward for himself if he found it. He was contrasted with a nice character who gave the reward to the child if he found it. The competitor could be deceived by indicating the empty one of two hiding places. Care was taken to point out to the child that on each trial the partner had only one chance (i.e. he was not allowed to look in the other location if he did not find the target on the first try), and that the competitor's success was the child's loss, whereas the cooperator's success meant success for the child.

Method

Subjects.   Fifty-one children, 25 boys and 26 girls, participated in the experiment. Nineteen children were 3 years old (range 3:1 to 3:11, mean age 3:7), 20 were 4 years old (range 4:0 to 4:11, mean age 4:5), and 12 were 5 years old (range 5:1 to 5:11, mean age 5:5). All children attended kindergartens, play groups or day-care centres in Munich.

Materials.   Two hand-puppets, a king and a robber, served as interaction partners. Two $12 \times 8 \times 3$ cm cardboard boxes, a yellow and a blue one, were used as hiding places, and golden paper stars were used as rewards.

Procedure and design.   Children were tested individually in a quiet room in their kindergarten. First the child was introduced to the puppets. The king was described as a nice man who helped the children and the robber was introduced as a nasty one who teased the children. The experimenter then said that the child was going to play a game with the puppets in which he or she could win many golden stars. The game was introduced as a hiding game in which the puppets could not see (they had to go away) where the child hid a golden star. The puppets went off stage (were put under the table) and the child was encouraged to hide a golden star in one of the boxes.

---

* When the present experiments were designed and conducted, I did not know the then unpublished work by Chandler, Fritz & Hala (1989). Thus, the present study was not designed to allow a direct comparison with Chandler *et al.*'s results.

After the child had hidden the star the king was brought back. The experimenter pointed out to the child that the king did not know where the target was, because he had not been present when the child hid it, and that he wanted to find it. Then the king asked the child 'Where is the star?'. When the child indicated the hiding place the king opened the box and said 'I am glad that I found the star. Because you showed me where it is, I will give you the star.' The king then put the star into the child's 'winner's box' and the experimenter emphasized that the child had won a star. Then the procedure was repeated with the robber. When the child indicated the hiding place to him, he opened the box, took the star out and kept it for himself, gleefully. The experimenter pointed out that now the robber had won and the child had lost a star.

After the introductory procedure, the following questions were asked to control for the child's understanding of the puppets' behaviours: 'When the king finds a star, will he give it to you or will he keep it for himself?' 'When the robber finds a star will he give it to you or will he keep it for himself?' When the child had answered these questions correctly, the introductory phase was completed and the test phase started.

Each child received four test trials, two cooperative and two competitive ones in two different random orders. Half the children started with a cooperative trial while the other half started with a competitive one. The experimenter introduced the task by saying that now the child was going to play the game with the puppets 'seriously': 'Let's see how many stars you can win. First you'll play the game with the king/the robber. Do you want the king/the robber to find the star or don't you want him to find it?' If the child answered the question incorrectly (e.g. indicated that she wanted the robber to find the star), it was pointed out again that the robber would keep the star for himself and the child would not get it. Then the question was repeated. It was also pointed out again that the king/the robber had only one chance to find the star.

The hiding procedure was then performed in the same way as in the introductory phase. The child was instructed to hide a star and to call the king/the robber back when he or she had finished. The king/the robber reappeared and asked 'Where is the star?' (the question was asked with about the same intonation pattern for both puppets). After having asked the question for the puppet, the experimenter said to the child: 'The king/the robber asks you where the star is. Where do you want to point?' If the child did not react to this question or refused to give an answer (to the robber), the experimenter proceeded: 'Do you want to point to this box or to this box?' (indicating the boxes). Both puppets always searched in the location that the child indicated and reacted to finding or not finding the star in the way that was outlined in the introductory phase.

Results and discussion

All children correctly answered the control questions at the end of the introductory phase, indicating that they understood that the king would give them the reward if he found it and that the robber would keep it for himself. All children correctly said that they wanted the king to find the star in response to the question checking their intentions in the game. However, seven 3-year-olds, three 4-year-olds and one 5-year-old said that they also wanted the robber to find it. After the experimenter had explained once more that the robber would keep the star and the child would lose it, they all replied to the repeated question that they did not want him to find it.

In the cooperative condition, all children except for one 3-year-old and one 4-year-old correctly indicated the location where the star was hidden on both trials. The two children who pointed to the empty location on the first trial for the cooperative partner were excluded from further analysis.

Table 1 shows the percentage of children of each age group who pointed to the empty location twice, once or not at all in the competitive condition. Performance in this condition significantly improved with age (with 3, 4- and 5-year-olds defined as age groups and subjects with two or one correct answers compared with subjects with no correct answer) (χ^2 (2) = 6.15, $p < .05$). Thus, contrary to Chandler *et al.*'s (1989) results, there was a significant age trend in deceptive action between the ages of 3 and 5 years even when a liberal criterion was used to define success.

Table 1 shows that only one out of nine children who were younger than 3:6 indicated the empty location to the competitor. The majority of the children older than 3:6 indicated the empty location on at least one out of two trials (in all but one case, the children who pointed to the empty box only once did so on the second trial). However, only in the older 4-year-olds and the 5-year-olds did the majority of the children deceive the competitor consistently on both trials. As almost all instances of deceptive pointing in those children who were inconsistent occurred on the second trial, one might suspect that after having experienced failure to win the reward on the first trial, children simply tried the only other behavioural alternative they had on the second trial without necessarily understanding the effects of their action on the competitor's belief. On the other hand, observations by the experimenters indicated that some of the children did not dare to deceive the competitor on the first trial and only did so when they had fully grasped the competitive and 'immoral' nature of the game.

While it is debatable from these findings to what extent 4-year-old children are competent at deceptive action, the results clearly indicate that young 3-year-olds do not spontaneously attempt to deceive a competitor and do not learn to do so on a second trial. This is consistent with research on false belief attribution (Perner *et al.*, 1987). However, before the results can be interpreted as indicating a genuine inability to deceive, several other explanations have to be considered. A substantial number of the young 3-year-olds (5 out of 9 children) indicated by their response to the control question that they had not spontaneously formed an intention to prevent the competitor from getting the reward. Although these children changed their mind after renewed explanation, this may be attributable to their wish to comply rather than to a true task understanding. Young children's failure to deceive may thus be due to a more general failure to interpret the situation as a competitive one. This is in line with observations by Gratch (1964) and deVries (1970) who found that 2½- to 3½-year-old children tended to show the target spontaneously to their partner in a competitive hiding game, displaying joy instead of disappointment at the partner's

Table 1. Percentage of children of each age group who correctly indicated the empty location to the competitor twice, once or not at all in Expt 1

| | Number of correct indications | | |
Age	2	1	0
3:0–3:5 (*N* = 9)	11	0	89
3:6–3:11 (*N* = 9)	22	67	11
4:0–4:5 (*N* = 11)	45	27	27
4:6–4:11 (*N* = 8)	63	12	25
5:1–5:11 (*N* = 12)	67	25	8

success. Thus, the experimental situation may have been too confusing or not sufficiently motivating for them to form a competitive intention.

One way to avoid the problem that young children may fail to form a competitive intention in a playful context is to ask children to 'advise' another person whose intentions are made explicit to them on how she should act towards a competitor. If children are able to construct a deceitful utterance but do not do so because of lack of competitive motivation or moral considerations, they should display this competence when told that someone else (e.g. a doll) does not want a 'baddie' to find a target. Wimmer & Perner (1983) tested 4- and 5-year-olds in such a condition and found little evidence for an ability to construct a deceitful utterance in 4-year-olds. However, their task was rather complicated as it was designed to be parallel to a task in which children had to construct a deceitful utterance on the basis of a false belief representation. Whether 3- and 4-year-old children can communicate deceitfully under the simplest possible conditions has not been investigated.

Experiment 2

Experiment 2 was designed to investigate the age at which children begin to communicate deceitfully under conditions where a protagonist's intention to prevent a competitor from obtaining an attractive reward is made explicit. As in Expt 1, the competitor could be misled by deceptive pointing. Children were asked to tell a doll who did not want the competitor to find a hidden sweet which of two locations she would indicate for the competitor. As in Expt 1, children's responses in the competitive condition were compared with a cooperative control condition.

Method

Subjects. Fifty-five children, 30 boys and 25 girls, participated in the experiment. Twelve children were aged 2:8 to 3:6 (mean age 3:2), 18 were 3:7 to 4:0 years old (mean age 3:10), 16 were 4:1 to 4:6 (mean age 4:3), and 9 were 4:7 to 4:11 years old (mean age 4:8). None of these children had participated in Expt 1.

Materials. The same puppets and boxes were used as in Expt 1. A girl-doll named Susi was used as a protagonist.

Procedure and design. Each child received two stories, one about Susi and the king, and one about Susi and the robber. Half the children started with the cooperative and the other half with the competitive story. The experimenter first introduced the puppets in the same way as in Expt 1. Then the king and the robber went off-stage and Susi appeared. In the competitive condition, the experimenter told the child the following story: 'This is Susi. She has bought a sweet. She does not want to eat it right away but she will put it into one of these boxes. Where should she put it? When the child indicated a box, Susi put the sweet there and the experimenter proceeded: 'Make sure that you remember where she put it. Now who comes here? (Produces robber). This is the robber. He has not seen where Susi put her sweet. He does not know where it is. He asks Susi: "Did you buy a sweet today?" Susi says "yes". "Where did you put the sweet?" Susi thinks: "The robber is a nasty man. He always teases me. Now I want to tease him, too". Susi does *not* want the robber to find the sweet. What should she say?' If the child did not answer right away the experimenter proceeded: 'Should she point to this box or should she point to this box?' (indicating the boxes). After the child had answered, a memory control question was asked to make sure that the child remembered correctly where the sweet was.

In the cooperative condition, the procedure was the same except that the child was told: 'Susi thinks "The king is a nice guy who always helps me. Now I want to help him, too". Susi wants the king to find the sweet.'

Results and discussion

All children correctly answered the memory control questions and correctly instructed Susi to indicate the box where the sweet was hidden in the cooperative condition. Twenty-five per cent of the children under 3:6, 66 per cent of the $3\frac{1}{2}$- to 4-year-olds, 75 per cent of the 4- to $4\frac{1}{2}$-year-olds and 89 per cent of the $4\frac{1}{2}$- to 5-year-olds instructed the doll to indicate the empty box in the competitive condition. Performance in this condition improved significantly with age, $(\chi^2 \ (3) = 11.19, p < .05)$. While both the younger and older 3-year-olds' performance was not significantly different from chance level, the 4-year-olds performed significantly above chance level. These results are consistent with those of Expt 1 in indicating that deception is difficult for 3-year-old children. Moreover, Expt 2 shows that young 3-year-olds fail to communicate deceptively even under very conducive conditions and thus indicates that this age group's difficulty with deception is a deep-seated one.

Although this result is in line with the evidence on false belief representation, one might still argue that young children's failure on deception tasks can be attributed to a variety of reasons as long as it is not shown in a convincing control condition that their problem is specific to deception. Such a control task should be parallel to the deception task in every other relevant aspect except that it does not require the manipulation of *belief*. Everyday experience suggests that 3-year-olds are quite capable of preventing other persons from taking objects away from them. A common tactic is to try to physically block or sabotage* the other person's access to the critical object. Thus young children may be able to hinder competitors from attaining their goals by means of sabotage but not by means of deceit. A sabotage task that is constructed to be parallel to the deception task would thus appear to provide an adequate control condition.

Experiment 3

Experiment 3 was designed to investigate whether children who fail to deceive a competitor are able to prevent him from attaining his goals by means of sabotage. Two tasks, each including a deception and a sabotage condition, were constructed. In one task, the 'two boxes' task, the deception condition was similar to the one used in Expt 1, where the child could mislead a competitor by deceptive pointing. In the parallel sabotage condition, the child could prevent the competitor from getting the reward by locking the box which contained it. Parallel to the deception task, a cooperative control condition is also necessary in the sabotage task to make children's behaviours interpretable. Given a choice of which one of two boxes one wants to lock, the appropriate behaviour under cooperative conditions is to lock the

---

* I realize that the term 'sabotage' is not fully accurate here as it is usually applied to acts of destruction rather than obstruction. It is used as a convenient 'shorthand' label for the control tasks in Expt 3.

empty box so that the cooperative partner will open the box which contains the reward. Intuitively, this appears to be very difficult. Thus, success on this task should provide a conservative measure of children's ability to perform acts of sabotage.

The only form of deception that has been studied in Expts 1 and 2 is deceptive indication of location. In order to investigate the consistency of young children's deceptive actions across tasks, a second deception task was added in Expt 3 that required lying to the competitor about the accessibility of the hidden object. In this task, the 'one box' task, children could prevent the competitor from getting the reward by telling him that the box where the reward was hidden was locked, when in reality it was open. A parallel sabotage task is to let children decide whether to lock a box or to leave it open for a competitive vs. a cooperative partner. Intuitively, the distinction between locking and not locking a box should be easier to master than the distinction between locking a full box for a competitor and an empty one for a cooperator.

Thus, in Expt 3 children's performance on sabotage and deception tasks was compared where both deception and sabotage were assessed in two different tasks.

Method

Subjects.   Thirty-nine children, 21 boys and 18 girls aged 2:8 to 4:7 (mean age 3:8) participated in the experiment. Another five children between 2:6 and 2:11 were tested but did not cooperate.

Materials.   The same hand-puppets were used as in Expts 1 and 2. Two $14 \times 11 \times 6$ cm metal boxes (cashboxes), a red one and a green one, that could be locked with keys were used as hiding places. Additional materials were toy money and a small bag ('the king's treasure bag').

Design and procedure.   Except for four children who received only one task (two only the 'one box' and two only the 'two boxes' task), each child received two tasks, the 'one box' and the 'two boxes' task, each including a sabotage and a deceit condition. Half the children received the 'one box' task first, the other half started with 'two boxes' task. Within each group, half the children started with the sabotage and the other half with the deceit condition. The task was designed so that each child would receive two pairs of trials (a pair consisting of a cooperative and a competitive trial) in each condition. However, there were fourteen children who did not complete two pairs of trials in each condition (i.e. who received only one pair in at least one condition). Thus, consistency information is available only for a subgroup of the total sample. Half the children in each condition started with a cooperative trial which was followed by a competitive one, while the other half received the two trials in the opposite order. On the second pair of trials, the order of presenting the cooperative vs. the competitive trial was reversed.

In both the 'one box' and the 'two boxes' tasks, the experimenter introduced the task as a game in which the child could win a big treasure (showing the toy money). The introductory phase was similar in both tasks: the experimenter introduced the puppets in the same way as in Expts 1 and 2. She then demonstrated that when the king found a coin in a box he put another one out of his treasure bag into the box, and the child could keep them both, and that when the robber found a coin he stole it and kept it for himself. At the end of the introduction children's task understanding was assessed in the same way as in Expt 1, asking what the king and the robber did when they found a coin.

In the 'one box' task, the sabotage condition was introduced by demonstrating that the box could be locked with a key. Then the child was instructed to hide a coin in the box. The experimenter then produced the king/the robber from under the table and instructed the child: 'Now you make it easy for the king to get the coin. Help him find it.' 'Now you make it hard for the robber to get the coin. Don't let him get it.' Test question: 'What do you want to do? Do you want to lock the box or do you want to leave it open?'

In the deceit condition there was no key to lock the box. The hiding procedure was the same as in the sabotage condition. When the king/the robber reappeared, the experimenter held the puppet far off and the puppet said: 'I wonder whether this box is locked or open. I can't see it from here (the lock was always on the side that faced the child). If it's locked it's no use making the long walk.' The experimenter then instructed the child to make it easy or hard for the puppets in the same way as in the sabotage condition and asked the test question: 'What do you want to say? Do you want to say it's locked or do you want to say it's open?'

In the 'two boxes' task, the sabotage condition was introduced by showing that each of the two boxes could be locked with a key. Then the child was given the choice of in which box to hide the coin. The king/the robber was fetched and the child was instructed to make it easy or hard for them in the same way as in the 'one box' condition. The test question was: 'Which box do you want to lock? Do you want to lock this box or do you want to lock this box?' (indicating the boxes in counterbalanced order).

In the deceit condition, the procedure was the same except that there were no keys, and the king/the robber asked the child: 'Where is the coin?' Then the experimenter asked the test question: 'Where do you want to point? Do you want to point to this box or do you want to point to this box?'

Results and discussion

All children correctly answered the control questions assessing their understanding of the puppets' behaviours. Table 2 shows the frequencies of response patterns to the test questions on the two tasks, separately for the sabotage and the deceit conditions, for the first pair of trials (i.e. one cooperative and one competitive trial).

In the 'one box' task, 27 (73 per cent) of the subjects correctly locked the box for the competitor and left it open for the cooperator, whereas only 10 (27 per cent) lied to the competitor in the parallel deception condition (i.e. said the box was locked when in reality it was open). Within-subject contingencies showed that deception was significantly more difficult than sabotage in this task: seventeen children showed the correct response pattern in the sabotage condition and an incorrect one in the deception condition, whereas the reverse pattern did not occur (McNemar's test, χ^2 (1) = 15.05, $p < .001$). Nine children failed on both deception and sabotage and nine were correct on both. Two children's patterns on the deception task were uninterpretable because these children insisted on holding the box shut with their hands in the deception condition and (truthfully) said that it was 'shut tight' to the competitor.

In the 'two boxes' task, 22 (59 per cent) of the children showed the correct pattern on the sabotage task, whereas only 11 (29 per cent) were correct in the deceptive pointing condition (see Table 2). Another five children failed the sabotage task, locking the full box for both the competitor and the cooperator; however, when the king appeared, they handed him the key to the box where the treasure was hidden or reopened the box. In the deception condition, one child failed to deceive but refused to indicate a box for the competitor. Within-subject contingencies again showed a significant difference between deception and sabotage, with 13 children correct on sabotage and incorrect on deception, and two children showing the reverse pattern (McNemar's test, χ^2 (1) = 6.66, $p < .01$); nine children were correct in both deception and sabotage and 13 children failed both.

Although the 'one box' sabotage task proved to be slightly easier than the 'two boxes' sabotage task, the difference was not significant: eight children passed the 'one

Table 2. Frequencies of response patterns for the sabotage and deception conditions in Expt 3, separately for the 'one box' and the 'two boxes' tasks (first pair of trials)

Task	Sabotage Response pattern		Deception Response pattern	
One box	R: locked box K: opened box	27[a]	R: lied K: told truth	10
	R: opened box K: opened box	9	R: told truth K: told truth	21
	R: locked box K: locked box	1	R: lied K: lied	4
	R: opened box K: locked box	0	R: told truth K: lied	0
			Uninterpretable	2
Two boxes	R: locked full K: locked empty	22	R: pointed empty K: pointed full	11
	R: locked full K: locked full	14	R: pointed full K: pointed full	24
	R: locked empty K: locked empty	0	R: pointed empty K: pointed empty	1
	R: locked empty K: locked full	1	R: pointed full K: pointed empty	0
			Uninterpretable	1

Notes. R = Robber; K = King. First row shows correct response patterns.
[a] Four of these children initially locked the box for the cooperator, but unlocked it spontaneously when the cooperative puppet appeared.

box' and failed the 'two boxes' task, while four children showed the reverse pattern. There was also no significant difference between the 'one box' and the 'two boxes' deception tasks. The majority of the 35 children who received both tasks performed consistently on the 'one' and the 'two boxes' tasks (62 per cent for sabotage and 70 per cent for deception). The great majority of those children who failed both deception tasks mastered at least one sabotage task (17 out of 21 children = 81 per cent), eight of these children (38 per cent) passed both sabotage tasks. The reverse pattern (i.e. two or one deception tasks correct and both sabotage tasks incorrect) occurred only in one case (McNemar's test, χ^2 (1) = 12.5, $p < .001$). Note that of the 14 children younger than 3:6 who received both the 'one box' and the 'two boxes' tasks, 12 failed both deception tasks; nine of these children passed at least one sabotage task (i.e. were correct on both the cooperative and the competitive trial); the opposite pattern did not occur (McNemar's test) χ^2 (1) = 7.11, $p < .01$). Thus, even in the youngest age group the majority of those children who failed deception were at least partially successful at sabotage.

For those children who received two pairs of trials on both deception and sabotage, additional information on contingencies between these conditions was available.

Table 3 shows that in both tasks the great majority of the children (92 per cent) were correct on at least one pair of trials in the sabotage condition (60 per cent in the 'one box' and 64 per cent in the 'two boxes' task were correct on both pairs of trials). In contrast, only 28 per cent (one box) and 31 per cent (two boxes) consistently passed deception and 54 per cent (one box) and 42 per cent (two boxes) consistently failed on both trials. Sabotage was significantly easier than deception on both the 'one box' task (McNemar's test, χ^2 (1) = 10.08, $p < .01$) and the 'two boxes' task (McNemar's test, χ^2 (1) = 4.90, $p < .05$). Table 3 shows that only very few of those children who failed deception also failed sabotage.

As in Expts 1 and 2, deception proved to be difficult for 3- to 4-year-olds in Expt 3. This was shown for two forms of deception, deceptive pointing and telling an outright lie. Two 'sabotage' tasks which were constructed to be parallel to the deception tasks proved to be significantly easier for the children. Even the 'two boxes' sabotage task, which intuitively appeared to be difficult because it required the child to lock an empty box in the cooperative control condition, was mastered by the majority of the children. These children's failure on the deceptive pointing task cannot be attributed to a general reluctance to operate on the empty one of two locations. Even those children who failed the 'two boxes' sabotage task showed that they understood how they could prevent the competitor from gaining the reward: in

Table 3. Within-subject contingencies between deception and sabotage conditions separately for the 'one box' and the 'two boxes' tasks (only for those subjects who received two pairs of trials in each condition)

Task	Condition		
	Deception	Sabotage	
One box	1 or 2 correct	1 or 2 correct	12
	1 or 2 correct	0 correct	0
	0 correct	1 or 2 correct	12
	0 correct	0 correct	2
Two boxes	1 or 2 correct	1 or 2 correct	13
	1 or 2 correct	0 correct	1
	0 correct	1 or 2 correct	9
	0 correct	0 correct	1

Note. Number of times correct (2, 1 or 0) refers to pairs of trials (cooperative and competitive trial correct).

almost all cases they failed because they locked the full box for both the cooperator and the competitor, not because they left the full box open for the competitor. This result along with children's good performance on the 'one box' sabotage task indicates that their failure to deceive a competitor cannot be attributed to a general inability or reluctance to act competitively, to a lack of interest or basic problems in task understanding. Thus, it appears that young children's difficulty with deception is due to a specific problem with the manipulation of other persons' beliefs.

General discussion

The present study demonstrates once again 3-year-olds' difficulty with false belief representation. Inducing a false belief in another person proved to be a very difficult task for 3-year-olds, especially for children who were younger than $3\frac{1}{2}$ years. In contrast, most 3-year-olds were quite capable of preventing a competitor physically from attaining his goal in a parallel 'sabotage' task. Young children's failure to deceive was demonstrated in three experiments, employing two different deception tasks under several instructional conditions. Young 3-year-olds consistently told a competitive interaction partner the truth even when the necessity of preventing him from getting a reward was made very salient. These negative findings are consistent with the results of research on false belief *attribution* (e.g. Perner *et al.*, 1987) and with observational and experimental evidence on the development of deception that indicates that children start to deceive around the age of 4 years (e.g. LaFreniere, 1988; Shultz & Cloghesy, 1981; Stern & Stern, 1909). Premack (1988) proposed as a rule of thumb that 'capacities that do not appear in the $3\frac{1}{2}$-year-old child will not be found in the ape' (p. 173). The results of the present application of Woodruff & Premack's (1979) method to the study of deception in children fit remarkably well with this rule of thumb, suggesting that as far as metarepresentation is concerned, capacities that do not appear in the ape will not be found in children below the age of about $3\frac{1}{2}$ years. This supports the assumption of a serious conceptual deficit in children below this age.

The present results contrast sharply with the findings reported by Chandler *et al.* (1989) indicating that even $2\frac{1}{2}$-year-olds proficiently employ deceptive strategies in a hiding-game context and that there is no significant improvement in deception between the ages of $2\frac{1}{2}$ and 5 years. One might argue that Chandler *et al.*'s task was for some reason more motivating or more easily understandable for very young children and therefore better suited to reveal their true competence at deceptive action. However, Expt 3 showed that the majority of the 3-year-old children in the present study understood the relevant features of the task and were highly motivated to play the game and to win the reward in a condition where they could win by means of sabotage rather than deception. In fact, children's performance in the sabotage condition in Expt 3 was about as good as the performance reported by Chandler *et al.* for the children of the same age range. As was outlined in the introduction, one problem with the interpretation of Chandler *et al.*'s findings is that it is not clear whether young children understood the 'tell-tale footprints' in the same way as adults would. Children might have been successful without an understanding of the informational significance of footprints. Rather, they may have understood that a person is physically led to a location by the footprints just as by a ladder or a railroad track. Three-year-old owners of toy railways may well be aware that by removing a track they can prevent a younger sibling from pushing her/his carriage through the tunnel and that by setting up a new track at an intersection thay can lead her/him in the wrong direction. Thus, young children may have been successful on Chandler *et al.*'s task on the basis of an understanding of sabotage not of deception.

The present results, along with other research on false belief representation, indicate that it is very hard for 3-year-olds to understand that by giving false information one can influence other people's beliefs and consequently influence their actions. Observations in Expt 3 indicate that children who had received the sabotage condition first often asked for the key when faced with the deception task; when they were told that the key was lost, they tried other means of sabotage (e.g. holding the box in which the target was hidden shut tight, removing the box from the table or taking the target out of the box). When the experimenter repeated the test question, encouraging the child once more not to let the competitor find the target, and presented them with the alternative of indicating the full or the empty box, they nevertheless pointed to the full one. Although they were apparently highly motivated to influence the competitor's behaviour to produce a desirable result for themselves, they obviously did not understand that giving false information could help them to achieve the desired outcome.

The present account of 3-year-olds' difficulty with false belief understanding might be taken to suggest that 3-year-olds are pure behaviourists, unaware of mental states. Several recent studies have impressively demonstrated that this is not the case: children start to talk spontaneously about what they themselves and other people want and think in their third year of life (Shatz, Wellman & Silber, 1983), they predict people's actions from information on what they want and think (Wellman & Bartsch, 1988), they understand that people may think differently about matters of taste or preference (Flavell, Flavell, Green & Moses, 1990) and they prefer mentalistic to behaviouristic descriptions of human action (Lillard & Flavell, 1990). Thus, young children seem to understand that people 'think' and that their thinking is related to their actions. Perner (in press) has characterized this understanding of 'thinking' as an understanding of 'thinking of' rather than an understanding of 'thinking that', that is, children understand that people can think of objects and events in the world, that their thinking about these objects and events is related to their actions and also that what another person thinks of something can differ from what oneself thinks of it. However, what these young children do not seem to understand is that someone can think that something is true that oneself knows to be false. Yet this is exactly what makes our understanding of human thinking so powerful. The young child may well understand that people usually act on what they think; however, young children's poor performance on false belief tasks indicates that they do not understand that thinking something is the case constrains a person's actions in the sense that she will necessarily act on what she thinks to be true and not on what the child knows to be the case. Young children may also understand that what people think has something to do with what they are shown or told. However, they do not seem to understand that a person's access to information determines his or her knowledge and beliefs. Once they begin to understand that what you show or tell someone determines what this person will believe to be true, they can use communication as a powerful tool in strategic interaction. The present research indicates that although young children are capable of strategic interaction in the sense that they manipulate others' behaviour, they acquire the ability intentionally to manipulate others' beliefs only around the age of 4 years.

Acknowledgements

The present research was supported by a grant from the *Deutsche Forschungsgemeinschaft* (So 213/1–1). Parts of this paper were presented at the Biennial Meeting of the Society for Research in Child Development in Kansas City, April, 1989. I would like to thank Josef Perner and Heinz Wimmer for many discussions of the project and Merry Bullock, John Flavell, Frances Green, and Louis Moses for their comments on an earlier version of this paper and their suggestions for further research on deception. I am grateful to Krista Beureux, Daniela Brust, Aurelia Hölker, and Petra Schlarb for their assistance in data collection and to the staff and children of various kindergartens and day-care centres in Munich for their friendly cooperation.

References

Astington, J. W. (1989). Developing theories of mind: What develops and how do we go about explaining it? Paper presented at the Biennial Meeting of the Society for Research in Child Development, Kansas City, April.

Byrne, R. W. & Whiten, A. (Eds) (1988). *Machiavellian Intelligence: Social Expertise and the Evolution of Intellect in Monkeys, Apes, and Humans*. New York: Oxford University Press.

Chandler, M., Fritz, A. S. & Hala, S. (1989). Small scale deceit: Deception as a marker of 2-, 3-, and 4-year-olds' early theories of mind. *Child Development*, **60**, 1263–1277.

Dennett, D. C. (1978). *Brainstorms*. Brighton: Harvester.

DeVries, R. (1970). The development of role-taking as reflected by behavior of bright, average, and retarded children in a social guessing game. *Child Development*, **41**, 759–770.

Flavell, J. H., Flavell, E. R., Green, F. L. & Moses, L. J. (1990). Young children's understanding of fact beliefs versus value beliefs, *Child Development*, **61**, 915–928.

Gratch, G. (1964). Response alternation in children: A developmental study of orientations to uncertainty. *Vita Humana*, **7**, 49–60.

LaFreniere, P. J. (1988). The ontogeny of tactical deception in humans. In R. W. Byrne & A. Whiten (Eds), *Machiavellian Intelligence: Social Expertise and the Evolution of Intellect in Monkeys, Apes, and Humans*, pp. 238–252. New York: Oxford University Press.

Lewis, M., Stanger, C. & Sullivan, M. W. (1989). Deception in 3-year-olds. *Developmental Psychology*, **25**, 439–443.

Lillard, A. S. & Flavell, J. H. (1990). Young children's preference for mental state versus behavioural descriptions of human action. *Child Development*, **61**, 731–741.

Mitchell, R. W. (1986). A framework for discussing deception. In R. W. Mitchell & N. S. Thompson (Eds), *Deception: Perspectives on Human and Nonhuman Deceit*, pp. 3–40. New York: State University of New York Press.

Mitchell, R. W. & Thompson, N. S. (1986) (Eds), *Deception: Perspectives on Human and Nonhuman Deceit*. New York: State University of New York Press.

Moses, L. J. & Flavell, J. H. (1990). Inferring false beliefs from actions and reactions. *Child Development*, **61**, 929–945.

Nunner-Winkler, G. & Sodian, B. (1989). Moral behavior and emotions in a real life situation of temptation. In F. E. Weinert & W. Schneider (Eds), *The Munich Longitudinal Study on the Genesis of Individual Competencies (Report No. 5)*. Munich: Max Planck Institute for Psychological Research.

Perner, J. (1989). Is 'thinking' belief? Reply to Wellman and Bartsch. *Cognition*, **33**, 315–319.

Perner, J. (in press, *b*). On representing that: The asymmetry between belief and desire in children's theory of mind. In C. Moore & D. Frye (Eds), *Children's Theories of Mind*. Hillsdale, NJ: Erlbaum.

Perner, J., Leekam, S. R. & Wimmer, H. (1987). Three-year-olds' difficulty with false belief: The case for a conceptual deficit. *British Journal of Developmental Psychology*, **5**, 125–137.

Premack, D. (1988). 'Does the chimpanzee have a theory of mind?' revisited. In R. W. Byrne & A. Whiten (Eds), *Machiavellian Intelligence: Social Expertise and the Evolution of Intellect in Monkeys, Apes, and Humans*, pp. 160–179. New York: Oxford University Press.

Premack, D. & Woodruff, G. (1978). Does the chimpanzee have a theory of mind? *The Behavioral and Brain Sciences*, **1**, 515–526.

Shatz, M., Wellman, H. M. & Silber, S. (1983). The acquisition of mental verbs. *Cognition*, **14**, 301–321.

Shultz, T. R. & Cloghesy, K. (1981). Development of recursive awareness of intention. *Developmental Psychology*, **17**, 465–471.

Stern, C. & Stern, W. (1909). *Erinnerung, Aussage und Lüge in der ersten Kindheit*. Leipzig: Barth.

Wellman, H. M. & Bartsch, K. (1988). Young children's reasoning about beliefs. *Cognition*, **30**, 239–277.

Whiten, A. & Byrne, R. W. (1988). Tactical deception in primates. *The Behavioral and Brain Sciences*, **11**, 233–273.

Wimmer, H. & Perner, J. (1983). Beliefs about beliefs: Representation and constraining function of wrong beliefs in young children's understanding of deception. *Cognition*, **13**, 103–128.

Woodruff, G. & Premack, D. (1979). Intentional communication in the chimpanzee: The development of deception. *Cognition*, **7**, 333–362.

Received 28 July 1989; revised version received 25 January 1990

4

Theory of mind
and understanding of emotion

Preface

As adults, we know the emotional impact of a vast number of situations. We know what will make us feel proud or frightened, digusted or embarrassed. Children's understanding of emotion must depend, in part, on the acquisition of this situational knowledge. They might start by understanding the situations that elicit simple emotions such as happiness and sadness and move on to more complex emotions such as pride and guilt.

However, emotional understanding requires more than this catalogue. It depends on some conception of how the mind works and more specifically of how desires, beliefs and emotion interrelate (Harris, 1989). Exactly the same situation may cause happiness or sadness in different people depending on whether the situation corresponds to what they want. Similarly, exactly the same situation may elicit surprise in one person and indifference in another depending on what they expect. Thus, the emotion that a situation arouses depends on the desires and beliefs that are brought to it; situations do not arrive with an inherent quality that automatically guarantees the triggering of a specific emotion.

The results described by Hadwin & Perner take up this issue. They describe three stages in children's understanding of mind and emotion. In the initial stage—at about 3 years—children appreciate that people will feel pleased if an outcome corresponds to what they wanted, but not if it fails to correspond. Thus, 3-year-olds have an appreciation of the impact of desires on emotion. By 4 years of age, they have progressed further. They realize that someone may have a false belief about an outcome. Still, it is not until the third stage—around 5 years of age—that they systematically take such beliefs into account. For example, they realize that if someone is given a box and she thinks it contains her favourite sweets, she will be pleased, even if that belief is mistaken. They also realize that, given her mistaken belief, the person will be surprised when she opens the box and discovers its true contents.

Wellman & Banerjee also examine the role of desires and beliefs. They too conclude that children start by understanding the impact of desires, and are slower to grasp the relevance of beliefs. Still, their timetable does not correspond to Hadwin & Perner's. They claim that when children are asked to *explain* someone's surprise, 4-year-olds, and to some extent even 3-year-olds, appropriately refer to the protagonist's mistaken beliefs.

A possible explanation for these divergent findings is that children find it easier to work backwards than forwards. They can infer a belief from an emotion, but not the reverse. Notice that one's own mistaken beliefs only come into focus retrospectively, after the surprise has been experienced. Until the surprise is experienced, the belief giving rise to it may remain tacit. In one's own case, the emotion of surprise is rarely predicted. After all we mostly assume that our beliefs are not mistaken. Once experienced, however, surprise highlights the mistaken expectation that led to it.

Reference

Harris, P. L. (1989). *Children and Emotion: The Development of Psychological Understanding*. Oxford: Blackwells.

British Journal of Developmental Psychology (1991), **9**, 191–214   *Printed in Great Britain*   191

Mind and emotion: Children's understanding of the emotional consequences of beliefs and desires

Henry M. Wellman* and Mita Banerjee

Center for Human Growth and Development, University of Michigan, 300 North Ingalls Building (10th level), Ann Arbor, MI 48109, USA

We investigated preschool children's understanding of mind and emotion by examining their understanding that emotions such as happiness and surprise depend on the actor's desires and beliefs. We report four investigations: a study of 3-year-olds' ratings of actors' happiness and surprise, a natural language analysis of adults' use of the word *surprise* in conversation to a preschool child, and two studies of 3- and 4-year-olds' abilities to explain the causes of desire-dependent and belief-dependent emotional reactions, such as happiness and surprise respectively. We demonstrate that children as young as 3 years appropriately understand the relevant mental states underlying happiness, sadness, surprise and curiosity, although they misunderstand the usage of some related lexical terms, especially *surprise*. The findings are discussed with regard to the early development of children's understanding of emotion and their understanding of mind, including children's early understanding of the notion of belief and their ability to distinguish beliefs from desires.

Mind and emotion can be seen as related topics within everyday or common-sense psychology—our ordinary understanding of people. For example, in everyday psychology certain common emotional reactions (such as happiness and surprise) are construed as linked to and shaped by a variety of mental states (such as the actor's desires or beliefs). Therefore, understanding the nature and causes of emotions is part and parcel of acquiring a theory of mind and understanding internal states of mind is part and parcel of acquiring an understanding of emotion. This study aims to shed light on children's understanding of mind and emotion by investigating their understanding of such reactions as happiness and surprise. To set the context for our research we consider briefly prior research on children's understanding of mind and on their understanding of emotions.

To possess as theory of mind is to have at your disposal a network of mentalistic constructs—such as an actor's ideas, hopes, wishes, goals, doubts and confusions—with which to understand and explain people's actions and psyches. It is useful to consider such mental states as falling into two generic classes, the actor's beliefs and

---

* Requests for reprints.

desires (e.g. Davidson, 1963), and thus to construe our naïve reasoning about action as an everyday belief–desire psychology. These constructs allow us to reason about such things as, for example, why Bill went to the swimming pool. He *wanted* to swim and *thought* the pool was open. The fundamental idea is that people engage in actions because they believe those actions will achieve certain desires. Furthermore, one's actions lead to outcomes in the world, and these outcomes lead to reactions. At least two basic sorts of emotional reactions are encompassed by our everyday theory: reactions dependent on desires and reactions dependent on beliefs. That is, the outcome of an action can satisfy or fail to satisfy the actor's desires, leading, generically, to happiness reactions. You want something and get it and you are happy, or you fail to get it and you are sad or angry. Also, the outcome of an action can match or fail to match an actor's beliefs, generically termed surprise reactions. You think something will happen and it does not, so you are surprised or puzzled. This brief sketch does not do justice to our everyday theory of mind (for an extended discussion see Wellman, 1990, chapter 4), but it is sufficient to begin to consider when children understand beliefs, desires, and their impact on various emotional reactions.

Recently, researchers have begun to systematically study young children's understanding of belief–desire psychology using a variety of methods (Gopnik & Astington, 1988; Perner, Leekam & Wimmer, 1987; Shatz, Wellman & Silber, 1983; Wellman & Bartsch, 1988; Wimmer & Perner, 1983). Many (e.g. Flavell, 1988; Harris, 1989; Perner, 1988; Wellman, 1988) now agree that 4-year-olds do understand much of the belief–desire–action triad, that is, they construe people as possessing mental states of both belief and desire, and understand that such mental states cause external actions. Controversy surrounds younger children's understanding of beliefs. Some researchers contend that 3-year-olds understand belief and hence participate in naïve belief–desire psychology (e.g. Chandler, Fritz & Hala, 1989; Wellman & Bartsch, 1988); others maintain that such understanding is not evident until age 4 or so (Forguson & Gopnik, 1988; Perner, 1988).

What of children's understanding of emotion? Over the last ten years, researchers have been intensively studying this topic. They have found that 2-year-olds begin to talk about emotions in everyday conversation, using such terms as happy, sad and angry (Bretherton & Beeghly, 1982; Ridgeway, Waters & Kuczaj, 1985). By 3 or 4 years children can match many emotion terms to representative facial expressions (Borke, 1971; Bullock & Russell, 1984; Harter, 1983). At the same time children come to understand something of emotion display rules, for example, that the emotion displayed need not match the emotion that is felt. Early studies suggested that children did not understand how to display false emotions until the school years (Gnepp, 1983), but more recently, 4-year-olds have been shown to understand a distinction between real and apparent emotion (Harris, Donnelly, Guz & Pitt-Watson, 1986). Preschool children can also sensibly describe situations that typically elicit emotions such as happiness, sadness, fear and anger (Borke, 1971; Harter, 1983; Trabasso, Stein & Johnson, 1981).

With few exceptions, the research on children's understanding of emotion has proceeded without concern for everyday belief–desire psychology, and vice versa. But this has begun to change (see, e.g. Harris, 1989). One important point of overlap concerns children's understanding of the causes of various emotional states, for example, children's appreciation of the actors' goals, or their desires, as an important causal influence on emotion. Thus, Yuill (1984) studied children's judgements of story characters' satisfaction as based on the characters' desire. She presented 3-, 5-, and 7-year-old children with two sorts of stories depicting a desire, an action, and an outcome: match stories (outcome same as desire) and mismatch stories (outcome different from desire). After each story, children made judgements of the characters' satisfaction (happy or sad). Children as young as $3\frac{1}{2}$ years judged satisfaction as dependent on whether the outcome was desired or not.

More systematically, Stein & Levine (1987, 1989) have looked at children's understanding of the causal organization of emotional events. They point out that our understanding of how children make distinctions between emotion terms has often left out how this emotion knowledge is organized and used to predict people's actions. They suggest that emotional experiences centre around a person's goals and plans—happiness arises when a desired state is maintained or an undesired state is avoided and sadness/anger results when one fails to attain a desired state or fails to escape an undesired state. Stein & Levine (1989) presented preschool children, first grade children and college students with narratives encompassing the possible combinations of goals (wanting, not wanting) with outcomes (having, not having). After each story, the subject was asked if the character would be happy, sad, or angry, and why the character would feel that way. Both children and adults used the issue of goal failure and attainment to discriminate between emotions, and to provide explanations about them. Children as young as 3 referred to the protagonist's desire over 65 per cent of the time. Indeed, Wellman & Woolley (1990) have shown that even 2-year-olds understand this basic aspect of desire-dependent emotions— wanting and getting leads to happiness, wanting and not getting leads to sadness.

Much less research has focused on what we construe as belief-dependent emotions, emotions such as surprise. Trabasso *et al.* (1981) found that 3- and 4-year-olds cited generally appropriate causes for emotional reactions of happiness, sadness, excitement, anger, and surprise. But it is not clear whether they required mention of the actor's beliefs to be credited with an appropriate explanation of an actor's surprise. Wellman & Bartsch (1988) presented 4-year-olds with a variety of stories, about actors wanting or not wanting an occurrence, thinking or not thinking it would happen, and the occurrence happening or not happening. Children were asked to rate the actor's happiness by choosing a picture from an array of sad, happy and neutral faces, and to rate the actor's surprise by choosing a picture from an array of surprised and not surprised faces. Four-year-olds were essentially perfect at rating actors' happiness/sadness in accord with the actor's desires (and the relevant outcomes). They were less consistent, but still significantly accurate, at rating actors' surprise in accord with the actor's beliefs (and the relevant outcomes). Thus 4-year-olds appeared to have an important understanding not only of desire-dependent emotional reactions such as happiness, but also of belief-dependent emotional reactions such as surprise. These findings raise the question of whether younger children might not also understand that to be surprised requires a specific belief state on the part of the actor. If they did, then returning to a consideration of belief–desire understanding, this would imply that 3-year-olds do have some understanding of belief.

Hadwin & Perner (1991), however, used a task similar to that of Wellman & Bartsch (1988) and found no evidence for a belief-dependent understanding of surprise. Children were presented with stories where protagonists had specific beliefs and specific desires, and met with various outcomes. Hadwin & Perner found 3- and 4-year-olds were quite proficient in rating the character's happiness, but found no understanding of surprise until age 5. This raises the question whether 4-year-olds, as reported by Wellman & Bartsch (1988), let alone 3-year-olds, understand surprise.

In short, there is controversy as to whether 3-year-olds understand belief and a lack of clarity as to whether 3-year-olds, or indeed 4-year-olds, properly understand belief-dependent emotional reactions such as surprise. In the studies that follow we examine what, if anything, 3- and 4-year-olds know about belief-dependent emotions such as surprise, in comparison to their understanding of desire-dependent emotions such as happiness.

Study 1

Our first study represented a straightforward extension to younger children of the methods of Wellman & Bartsch (1988). Three-year-olds were presented stories about protagonists who had clearly stated beliefs and desires, and encountered specific outcomes. Children rated the actors' emotional reactions, specifically their happiness and surprise.

Method

Tasks.   Three types of brief stories about single protagonists were used. An example story is:

> Here's Lisa. Lisa *wants* it to be sunny today because she wants to play on her new swingset. But, Lisa *thinks* it's going to rain today. She thinks it's going to rain because she heard the weather man say it might rain. Look, it *rains*.

Each story included three sorts of information (in italics in the above example) about two possible outcomes (e.g. sun vs. rain): the character's desire, the character's belief, and the outcome itself. The three different story types represented different combinations of wanting, thinking and outcomes, as presented in Table 1. Table 1 also shows the hypothetical correct emotional reaction of the protagonist in regard to both happiness and surprise. This arrangement of stories includes several contrasting controls. For example, across the three story types wanting an outcome was paired with both thinking (stories 3 and 4) and not thinking (stories 1 and 2 and 5 and 6) that it would happen. Wanting an outcome was also paired with both having it occur (stories 5 and 6) or not (stories 1–4). Finally, thinking that something would happen was paired with having it occur (stories 1 and 2) and not occur (stories 3–6).

Subjects.   Thirteen 3-year-olds (3:0–3:9, $M = 3:5$) participated. There were eight boys and five girls, recruited from two racially mixed but predominantly white middle class preschools in a small midwestern US city.

Procedure.   The children were tested in two 15 min sessions by a single interviewer. In each session, they were first presented with a warm-up task designed to familiarize them with the terms and procedures for identifying characters' emotions. The procedures for identifying emotions used line drawings of pairs of faces showing someone who was happy vs. unhappy, or someone who was surprised vs. not surprised. In the warm-up task the child was told of a character and an emotion ('This is Jeff. It's his birthday and his father gives him a big present. He is very happy') and asked to pick out 'the picture that shows how Jeff feels' from the happy vs. unhappy faces. Similarly for surprise, the child was told of a character and

Table 1. An outline and comparison of the three story types used in Study 1

Story type	Want	Think	Outcome	Correct emotional reaction
1. Want *x*, think not *x*, not *x* occurs	(1) sunshine	rain	it rains	unhappy, not surprised
	(2) fire station	park	visit park	unhappy, not surprised
2. Want *x*, think *x*, not *x* occurs	(3) hot oatmeal	hot oatmeal	get cold spaghetti	unhappy, surprised
	(4) goldfish	goldfish	get a cow	unhappy, surprised
3. Want *x*, think not *x*, *x* occurs	(5) dinosaur book	kitten book	get dinosaur book	happy, surprised
	(6) grapejuice	milk	get grape juice	happy, surprised

emotion ('This is Billy. Billy goes into the bathroom to get a toothbrush and finds an elephant in the bathroom. He is very surprised') and asked to pick out 'the picture that shows how Billy feels' from the surprised and not-surprised pictures.

To illustrate the procedure, consider the story about Lisa (who wants sunshine) described above. The information about beliefs and desires was presented while the experimenter pointed to a line drawing of a child ('This is Lisa'). After presentation of this information the child's recognition of the pertinent beliefs and desires was checked by asking: 'What does Lisa want?' and 'What does Lisa think?'. Children were always correct at remembering the story information at this point. Next, the child was told the appropriate outcome; this was done by turning over the drawing of the character and revealing and describing a drawing of the outcome ('Look, it rains'). With this picture of the outcome visible (but no depiction of the story character visible), the child was asked to rate the character's reaction. For happiness, they were asked, 'How will (Lisa) feel; will she be happy or unhappy?'. For surprise, they were asked, 'How will (Lisa) feel; will she be surprised or not surprised?'. The appropriate pictures from the warm-up tasks were available to aid children in responding.

Each child was presented with all six of the different stories shown in Table 1, two each of the three different types, divided evenly into male and female characters. For each child, half the stories (one of each of the three story types) were presented and judgements for happiness were elicited in one session, and the remaining three stories were presented and judgements for surprise were elicited in a separate session. Order of presentation of each set of stories and the presentation of the happy or surprise session first were counterbalanced.

Results

The two left-hand graphs in Fig. 1 depict the ideal, correct responses as outlined in Table 1, once for happiness ratings and once for surprise. The right-hand graphs show 3-year-olds' observed ratings. As can be seen, children's ratings of happiness correspond to the ideal pattern, but their ratings of surprise do not. Indeed, children's ratings of surprise correspond to the ideal pattern for happiness. Statistical tests confirm these graphical analyses.

A 2 (sex) × 2 (rating type: happy vs. surprise) ANOVA was conducted on the

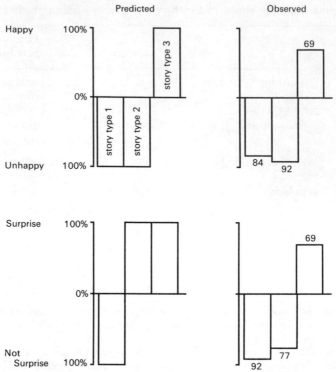

Figure 1. Ideal correct responses (on the left) and observed responses (on the right) for happiness (at the top) and surprise ratings (at the bottom) in Study 1.

number of correct responses. Only a significant main effect for rating type was found ($F(1,11) = 6.91$, $p < .05$). Children were more correct when rating the characters' happiness ($M = 2.46$ out of 3) than when rating their surprise ($M = 1.85$).

More importantly, notice in Fig. 1 that it is only for story type 2 that correct responding requires different ratings for happiness vs. surprise (i.e. *no* for happy, but *yes* for surprised). In an analysis of variance on children's judgements of these stories alone, no significant differences were found between the ratings for happy and for surprised. In short, across all three story types, children's judgements for happiness and surprise were parallel: when the characters were happy, children judged them also to be surprised; when not happy, children judged them as not surprised.

Discussion

While this study showed that 3-year-olds understand the desire-dependent emotion happiness, the data failed to show any understanding of surprise as a belief-dependent emotional reaction. Thus, the data fail to extend Wellman & Bartsch's (1988) findings on surprise to younger children, and instead replicate Hadwin & Perner's (1991) finding that 3-year-olds fail to understand surprise appropriately.

Note, however, that our initial studies (Study 1 above and Wellman & Bartsch,

1988) and Hadwin & Perner's studies all attempt to assess young children's understanding of belief-dependent emotional reactions via the rating of a character's surprise. Children's difficulty on such tasks could stem from a specific misunderstanding of the term *surprise*, rather than a general failure to understand that some emotional reactions depend on beliefs. Specifically, young children may think that surprise is intimately joined with happiness. Suppose, for example, that when parents talk to young children about 'surprises' or 'being surprised' they typically join surprise and happiness. Children might be told mostly about such things as a surprise for their birthday or for Christmas: surprises that are inevitably pleasant, albeit (perhaps) unexpected. Young children may almost never hear of a surprise that is horrible, painful or distinctly unpleasant.

To assess whether this speculation has any validity we looked at adults' use of the term *surprise* in natural language conversation to children. We used the transcripts collected by Kuczaj of speech to and from his son Abe (Kuczaj & Maratsos, 1975). These transcripts sample Abe's speech and adult speech to him for approximately $\frac{1}{2}$ to 1 hour every two to four weeks from the time Abe was $2\frac{1}{2}$ years until he was older than 5. We have used these records in prior work (Shatz, Wellman & Silber, 1983). For the present test we searched for all occurrences of the term *surprise* in speech to Abe; there were 44 such instances. We then examined these utterances and their surrounding context to rate them as one of three simple types. (1) The surprise being talked of was some obviously *positive* occurrence. Examples here are, 'You can't have any more surprises', said to tell the child he cannot have any more sweets as treats, or 'I have a surprise for you', said before giving the child a present of special new gloves. (2) The surprise was an obviously *negative* occurrence. An example here was 'I bet that was a surprise', said about the time the child unexpectedly fell in some cold dirty water. (3) The surprise referred to was an *unexpected* occurrence that seemed merely dramatic or striking but neither positive nor negative, or was an event where it was impossible to tell from context if the occurrence was positive or negative to the child. An example was 'What a surprise', said by the child's mother when she was tossing a pizza in the air and it landed on a cactus by mistake. Reliability in coding all 44 instances by two independent coders was 92 per cent.

In this sample 86.4 per cent of all uses of *surprise* referred to positive events; 6.8 per cent referred to negative events and 6.8 per cent referred to unexpected or indeterminate occurrences. From such exposure to *surprise* children could plausibly come to understand the term in a limited fashion, as something inevitably pleasant. In fact, when other researchers have asked young children to rate various emotional expressions (e.g. to pair emotion words, such as *surprise*, with various photographs of facial expressions) they have found that preschool children match the term *surprise* to happy expressions (Bullock & Russell, 1984; Russell & Bullock, 1986).

If young children understood *surprise* in this limited fashion, as inevitably linked with pleasantness, then they would perform poorly on our tasks and on similar ones such as those used by Hadwin & Perner. They might do so in two different fashions. First, a child asked to rate a character's *surprise* might, in essence, ask him- or herself if the character got something pleasant in the sense of getting what was wanted. If the character did, the child would then judge that the character was surprised (i.e. 'happy') and if not then not surprised (i.e. 'not happy'). Many 3-year-olds in Study 1 did just this. Second, in Wellman & Bartsch's (1988) stories, and in Hadwin & Perner's (1991) as well, when a character was described as getting something unexpected (e.g. Jill's dad reads a book about kittens when she was expecting he would read about dinosaurs), the outcome seems pleasant in some absolute sense. (After all her dad does read her a nice story.) In such situations (those of characters experiencing generally pleasant outcomes) a child who misunderstands *surprise* as inevitably joined to pleasantness might well judge that all the story characters are surprised. That is, all the characters should be mildly pleased even if not precisely happy (i.e. they get something pleasant even if it is not exactly what they wanted). In Wellman & Bartsch (1988) a substantial number of 4-year-olds evidenced this pattern of response, and this seems to be true of Hadwin & Perner's subjects too (see pp. 230–231).

In Study 2, therefore, we utilized a different method to address the question of whether young children, 3- and 4-year-olds, understand that some emotional reactions (such as surprise) depend on the characters' beliefs, beyond the characters' desires.

Study 2

In this study, we used an emotion explanation method rather than an emotion rating method. We presented children with characters who were said to experience a specific emotion (e.g. Jeff visited his grandma and when he got to her house he saw that it was purple; he was very surprised). Then we asked children to explain the character's reaction ('Why was Jeff so surprised?'). We have found in prior work that such explanation tasks can at times be more sensitive with young children than prediction or rating tasks (Bartsch & Wellman, 1989). More specific to the present case, we reasoned that if children understood that *surprise* was belief-dependent at all (albeit also denoting a pleasant experience) that they would be able to refer to characters' beliefs in order to explain their surprise. For example, they might say that 'Jeff didn't think the house would be purple'.

We tested each child on four different emotional reactions, two that depend on the relation between a person's desires and outcomes (happiness and sadness) and two that depend on the relation between a person's beliefs or knowledge and outcomes. One of the belief-dependent emotions was surprise. In an attempt to extend our consideration of belief-dependent emotional reactions beyond surprise, the second was curiosity. To be curious is to be lacking in knowledge or in a definite verified belief about an outcome.

The top portion of Fig. 2 outlines some hypothetical patterns of responding which help to explain our reasoning in designing this study. Consider first the top two left-hand graphs, titled the adult pattern. As we have explained it thus far, in our everyday belief–desire reasoning the appropriate explanation for a character's happiness concerns his desires (e.g. he got what he wanted) and for surprise concerns the actor's beliefs (e.g. he didn't think that would happen). Thus, the adult pattern depicts frequent desire explanations for happy and sad emotions but frequent belief explanations for surprise and curious. The important aspect of these graphs is their qualitative comparisons (e.g. that there would be more desire explanations for a character's reaction of happiness than for reactions of surprise), not precise quantitative predictions (e.g. some precise percentage of one sort of explanation or the other).

Suppose children's understanding of surprise simply confuses surprise with happiness as seemed to occur in Study 1. In this case, children should evidence something like the pattern in the top middle two graphs (titled desire only), providing essentially desire explanations for all the different emotions we present.

What if children confuse surprises with pleasant, desirable occurrences, but at the same time understand that surprises are unexpected as well? That is, what if children understand something of the belief-dependence of emotional reactions such as surprise in addition to seeing them as desire-dependent? In that case, results qualitatively like those depicted in the top two rightmost graphs might be obtained. The critical comparison is at the far right, specifically the depiction that belief explanations for surprise and curious should significantly exceed belief explanations for happy and sad. Substantively, this pattern would evidence an understanding that the character's prior beliefs cause, and hence explain, reactions of surprise, and thus this pattern is similar to the adult pattern. Methodologically, note that belief explanations for happy and sad constitute a measure of random or baseline belief responding which can be used to test the significance of belief responding to surprise and curious. Finally, according to this possibility, children might provide substantial numbers of desire explanations to surprise (and curious) emotional reactions, because they also see surprises as desirable and desired. Study 2 provides data about these sorts of patterns of responding when young children are asked to explain why characters are having various emotions.

Method

Subjects.   The participants were 23 3-year-olds (3:2–3:11, $M = 3:7$) and 20 4-year-olds (4:2–5:0, $M = 4:8$). There were 17 girls and 26 boys recruited from the same schools used in the first study.

Materials and procedure.   There were two stories of each of the four types. The *happy* stories described a character who got juice for a snack or received a visit from grandma (and was 'very happy'). The *sad* stories concerned a character who saw rain out of the window, or who went to a library that had no picture books (and was 'very sad'). The *surprise* stories concerned a character who saw giraffes on an ordinary farm or who visited grandma and found that her house was purple (and was 'very surprised'). The *curious* stories were about characters who found a closed box in a closet or who saw another child bring a closed bag to school for show and tell (and were 'very curious').

Each child was tested in a single 10- to 15-min session. Each child received all eight stories in one of two different orders. In both orders children heard a curious story first followed by a scrambled mix of the seven remaining stories. Half the stories were about a male child and half about a female child, counterbalanced across the four story types.

After each story was presented, the subject was asked to explain the character's emotion. First the child was asked an open-ended question: 'Why is the character so happy (sad, surprised or curious)?'. As a follow-up to this first question the child was also asked two more specific questions: 'What is the character wanting?' and 'What is the character thinking?'. For surprise and curious stories the thinking follow-up question was asked before the wanting question. For happy and sad stories this order was reversed.

Results

Response coding.   For responses to open-ended questions, appeal to the character's belief on the surprise and curious stories vs. appeal to the character's desires on the happy and sad stories would indicate some understanding that certain emotional reactions are belief-dependent in addition to the understanding that other emotional reactions are desire-dependent. However, consider the surprise stories further. Following our earlier discussion, children might understand *surprise* as meaning happy or pleased in addition to meaning something unexpected. If so, then it would be appropriate for them to answer the initial open-ended question ('Why is Jeff so surprised?') with a desire explanation (e.g. 'He likes purple'). The child could still evidence an understanding of the belief-dependent nature of surprise (i.e. that a surprising outcome is unexpected), however, by answering the follow-up thinking question appropriately; by saying, for example, 'He didn't think it would be purple' or 'He thought it would be white', when asked specifically about the character's thoughts. A child who had no understanding of the belief-dependent nature of surprise would instead fail to answer this thinking question appropriately. Thus, responses to either the open-ended or follow-up questions could reveal children's understanding of the belief-dependence of certain emotions such as surprise, in addition to the desire-dependence of emotions such as happiness.

Responses to the *open-ended* question were coded as either appeals to desires or appeals to beliefs. Appeals to desires included mention of the character's wants, preferences or values (e.g. 'She wants orange juice'; 'It's her favorite'). Appeals to beliefs included mention of the character's thoughts, knowledge, ignorance, or desire to know (e.g. 'She thought it would be white'; 'He doesn't know what is there'; 'He wants to know what's inside'). We included 'wanting to know' as a belief explanation because it mentions the character's knowledge or lack of knowledge explicitly, and because it represents perhaps the most appropriate possible belief explanation for a character's curiosity. (Most mentions of 'wanting to know' did occur for characters whose described reaction was curiosity, not surprise. Ten such explanations were given for curious characters, one for surprised characters, and none for happy or sad characters.)

To be coded as a desire or belief response to the open-ended question, the child's response had to include explicit mention of the appropriate mental terms (e.g. *wants, likes, thinks, knows*). It was possible for a child to mention both a desire ('he wants his grandma's house to be white') and a belief ('he didn't think it would be purple') for a single emotion. Therefore desire and belief explanations were not mutually exclusive. Other responses besides appeals to beliefs or desires also were produced, including mostly the simple mention of the objective situation (e.g. 'It's purple', 'It's raining'), but also uninterpretable answers, and 'don't knows'.

Children's responses to the *follow-up* thinking and wanting questions were coded as appeals to appropriate beliefs or appeals to appropriate desires.* For the surprise

* To be counted as a belief explanation to the follow-up thinking question for a surprise or curious story, children had to give an appropriate belief answer (e.g. 'he didn't think it would be purple'). To be counted as a belief explanation for a happy or sad story, children had only to give a brief answer that was related to the story content (e.g. 'she thought it was time for grandma to visit'). This asymmetry in our coding was necessary because happy and sad stories, by their nature, give no information about a specific appropriate belief. At the same time this asymmetry makes our methods *conservative*; to be significant children must give more belief explanations to surprise and curious stories than they do to happy and sad. Similarly, to be counted as a desire explanation of a happy or sad story, children had to cite the appropriate desire; but for surprise and curious, they had only to cite a desire generally related to the story content.

stories, appeals to appropriate beliefs included the character's relevant thoughts or ignorance (e.g. he thought that 'it would be white', or that 'there were no giraffes'). For curious stories, appeals to appropriate beliefs included the character's relevant thoughts or ignorance (e.g. 'He doesn't know what's in the box') and desiring to see or know the hidden contents (e.g. 'He wants to know'; 'He wants to find out what's in there'). For happy and sad stories, appeals to appropriate desires included mention of the character's wants, preferences, and values just as for the open-ended questions.

Twenty-five per cent of children's answers (more than 100 relevant responses) were coded by a second independent coder. Agreement between the two codings was 92.3 per cent.

Initially, analyses that included sex of subject and the two presentation orders as factors were conducted on the measures described above. Sex was never significant and there was only one uninterpretable higher order interaction of presentation order. Consequently, we ignored these factors in the analyses that follow.

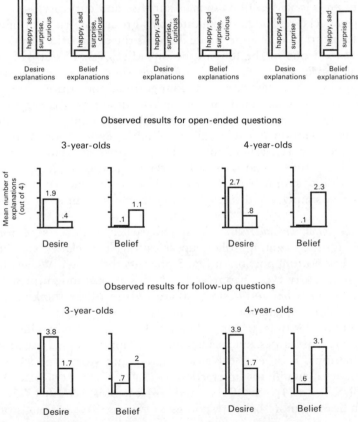

Figure 2. Hypothetical (at the top) and observed (middle and bottom) patterns of explanation to the happy and sad vs. surprised and curious stories.

Open-ended responses. Children's responses to the two desire-dependent story types (happy, sad) were very similar; and their responses to the two belief-dependent story types (surprise, curious) were very similar. Therefore, the middle portion of Fig. 2 presents the data for 3- and 4-year-olds collapsed into these two types of stories. We conducted two 2 (age) × 2 (story type: happy and sad vs. surprise and curious) analyses of variance, one for desire explanations to the stories and one for belief explanations. For desire explanations the effects of age ($F(1,41) = 5.02$, $p < .05$) and story type ($F(1,41) = 57.64$, $p < .001$) were significant but their interaction was not. Most importantly, both 3-year-olds ($t(22) = 5.27$, $p < .001$) and 4-year-olds ($t(19) = 5.40$, $p < .001$) gave more desire explanations for happy and sad emotions than for surprise and curious.

For open-ended belief explanations, age and story type were again significant but these effects were subsumed under a significant age × story type interaction ($F(1,41) = 8.40$, $p < .01$). Most importantly, both 3-year-olds ($t(22) = 3.75$, $p < .001$) and 4-year-olds ($t(19) = 6.85$, $p < .001$) gave more belief explanations for surprise and curious emotions than for happy and sad, although as the interaction shows, this difference also increased with age. This greater number of belief explanations to surprise and curious emotions, significantly more than the baseline level provided to happy and sad emotions, documents a significant understanding of the belief dependence of emotional reactions such as surprise and curiosity.

Individual subjects' responding replicated this group pattern. Out of a total of 20 4-year-olds, 19 mentioned an appropriate desire as the explanation for the character's emotion on at least one of the four happy or sad stories; 17 out of 20 4-year-olds mentioned an appropriate belief or knowledge state as the explanation for the character's emotion on at least one of the four surprise and curious stories. Eighteen out of 23 3-year-olds mentioned an appropriate desire as the explanation of the character's emotional reaction on at least one of the four happy or sad stories; 12 out of 23 3-year-olds mentioned a relevant belief as the explanation of the character's emotional reaction on at least one of the four surprise and curious stories. Thus, belief explanations from 3-year-olds were rarer than from 4-year-olds; still, 52 per cent of 3-year-olds spontaneously provided at least one such relevant belief explanation when simply asked to explain a character's surprise or curiosity.

Responses to the follow-up questions. As noted earlier, children's responses to the specific thinking and wanting follow-up questions can clarify their open-ended explanations. The bottom portion of Fig. 2 presents these data. We again conducted two 2 (age) × 2 (story type: happy and sad vs. curious and surprise) analyses of variance on relevant belief and desire responses given to the thinking and wanting questions. For desire explanations, only story type was significant ($F(1,41) = 156.30$, $p < .001$). Both 3-year-olds ($t(22) = 8.90$, $p < .001$) and 4-year-olds ($t(19) = 8.83$, $p < .001$) provided more desire explanations for happy and sad reactions than for surprise and curious. For belief explanations, age and story type were significant, subsumed under a significant interaction ($F(1,41) = 7.85$, $p < .01$). Again, both 3-year-olds ($t(22) = 4.71$, $p < .001$) and 4-year-olds ($t(19) = 7.61$, $p < .001$) provided significantly more belief responses to surprise and curious stories than to happy and sad.

Individuals' data support this pattern of findings. From a total of 20 4-year-olds and 23 3-year-olds, 19 in each group provided an appropriate belief response to at least one of the four surprise and curious stories.

Discussion

These findings demonstrate, in a preliminary fashion, three things. First, they show once again that young children understand that emotional reactions such as happiness and sadness are dependent on the character's prior desires. Beyond this now familiar result (see Hadwin & Perner, 1991; Stein & Levine, 1989; Wellman & Bartsch, 1988; Wellman & Woolley, 1990; Yuill, 1984), the data also indicate that children understand emotional reactions such as surprise and curiosity to be dependent on the character's belief states, although this understanding is also masked by young children's tendency to think that such emotions are intimately dependent on desires as well. Thirdly, these findings show considerable development in young children's understanding: 3-year-olds evidence significant understanding but, in the years from 3 to 5, children become increasingly accurate and consistent.

For several reasons, we wanted to replicate and extend these results. First, since these data constitute the first demonstration that 3-year-olds understand that reactions such as surprise rest on the actors' prior states of belief, they deserve replication. Furthermore, we wished to tackle two alternative explanations for our results. In Study 2 when asking follow-up questions we always asked first that question which seemed most appropriate to the emotion being discussed (e.g. about a character's surprise, our first follow-up question was 'What is he thinking?'). We did this to make our questioning as natural as possible, but note that this means our first follow-up for surprise was about belief, while for happy this was our second follow-up question. It could be argued that our results for follow-up questions (see Fig. 2) are simply products of this procedure. Children might give some reasonable response to the first follow-up question asked (a belief question for surprise, but a desire question for happy) and then provide fewer or uninterpretable answers to the second follow-up question, because of fatigue or boredom. This alternative explanation cannot account for our open-ended results, nonetheless, in Study 3 follow-up questions appeared in the same order for both surprise and happy emotions.

More substantively, a large literature exists on young children's understanding of the situations that elicit various emotions. Quite young children can cite appropriate eliciting situations for a variety of emotions (Barden *et al.*, 1980; Borke, 1971; Harris *et al.*, 1987; Trabasso *et al.*, 1981). Underlying this research is a conceptual possibility that younger children's understanding of the causes of emotions is confined to an understanding of the links between certain emotions and certain distinctive eliciting situations. We will call this the situationist hypothesis (see also Harris, 1989, pp. 65–70). It is conceivable that children's explanations of emotions in Study 2 could result from a simple linking of certain mental states with certain specific situations, rather than from a more general understanding of how belief and desire relate to emotional reactions. In particular, in Study 2 our description of characters' emotions included situational information (e.g. Bill was going to his uncle's farm; when he got there he saw giraffes; he was very surprised). Moreover, the situations described were different for the different emotions (e.g. seeing giraffes on a farm led to surprise, but getting grapejuice for a snack led to happiness). Conceivably, children's appeals to beliefs and desires in Study 2 could have been simply triggered by the specific situations we described rather than the emotions said to follow. Thus, when asked 'Why is the character so ——?' the child simply responds by reporting the most salient mental aspect of the situation described (e.g. in one case 'he didn't think there would be giraffes' but in the other 'she likes grapejuice'). In this possibility the child's knowledge of situations results in his or her selectively reporting beliefs at some times and desires at others. But we wish to show that children understand that emotions such as surprise generally depend on beliefs, and those such as happiness depend on desires. The best way to rule out this sort of situationist hypothesis is to present children with story characters who have divergent emotional reactions to the *same* situation (e.g. on one occasion Jill gets grapejuice for a snack and is happy; on another Jill gets grapejuice for a snack and is surprised). Differential explanations of Jill's emotion by appropriately referring to her desires in one case but her beliefs in the other would provide the needed data. In Study 3 we include descriptions of characters who experience the same situation but then are said to have different emotions.

Study 3

Method

Subjects.   The participants were 14 3-year-olds (3:0–3:11, $M = 3:6$) and 12 4-year-olds (4:1–4:9, $M = 4:4$). There were 19 girls and seven boys recruited from the same schools used in Studies 1 and 2.

Materials and procedures.   Materials and procedures were identical to those used in Study 2 with the following amendments. To keep things simple and to allow us more easily to construct comparable situations leading to different emotions, only the emotions happy and surprise were used. There were four stories describing a surprised character and four describing a happy one. Two of the four happiness stories were carefully paired with two of the surprise stories so as to depict identical situations leading to different emotions. For example, in one of these story pairs, Alice goes into the bathroom, opens a box of plasters and when she looks inside she sees that it is full of balloons. When Alice sees the balloons, then in one story she is very happy and in the other story she is very surprised. In the other pair, Greg goes to the library to get a book; when he gets there he finds the building has become a toy shop full of toys. When Greg sees the toy shop, then in one story he is very surprised, and in the other story he is very happy. The other two happy and surprised stories were the two used in Study 2, making four of each type.

Each child was tested in two 5 to 10 min sessions. In one session they received two happy and two surprise stories, then several days later they received the remaining stories in a second session. The happy and surprise versions of the critical story pairs were always presented in different sessions (to avoid confusing children with successive stories about the same character and same situation). Otherwise the stories were counterbalanced across the two sessions.

After each story was presented, the subject was asked to explain the character's emotion. First the child was asked an open-ended question: 'Why is the character so happy (surprised)?'. As a follow-up to this first question the child was also asked two more specific questions: 'What is the character thinking?' and 'What is the character wanting?', always in that order.

Results

Responses were coded exactly as in Study 2. Intercoder reliability was again assessed and agreement was 94.7 per cent. First the data were analysed for all the stories, thus replicating the analyses for Study 2. Subsequent analyses focused on the critical story pairs.

Open-ended responses for all stories. The top row of Fig. 3 presents the data in a fashion parallel to that used in Study 2. As in Study 2, two 2 (age) × 2 (story type) ANOVAs were conducted, one for desire explanations and one for belief explanations. For desire explanations, only the effect of story type was significant $(F(1,24) = 5.16$, $p < .05)$ indicating, as shown in the figure, that desire responses were given more often to happy emotions than to surprise, although (as expected from Study 1) desire responses to surprise were also numerous. Individually, 12 out of 14 3-year-olds provided at least one desire explanation of the four happy stories; 10 out of 12 4-year-olds did so.

For belief explanations, age $(F(1,24) = 4.82, p < .05)$ and story type $(F(1,24) = 4.71,$

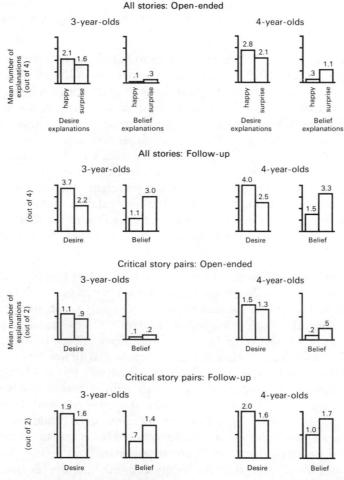

Figure 3. Patterns of explanations to all the stories (top two rows) and to just the critical story pairs (bottom two rows).

$p < .05$) were significant. Again, the story type effect shows that belief responses to surprise stories outweigh belief responses to happy stories (which constitute a baseline measure of responses expected by chance). As Fig. 3 shows, however, floor effects are obvious in these data on belief explanations, so non-parametric examination of individuals' responding becomes more important. For 3-year-olds, four out of 14 children provided at least one unprompted belief explanation to the surprise stories; for 4-year-olds, six out of 12 gave at least one unprompted belief explanation for surprise stories. The critical question is whether children were more likely to give belief responses for surprise emotions than for happy. Three 3-year-olds gave more belief explanations for their surprise stories than for their happy stories, none evidenced the reverse pattern, and 11 were tied giving equal numbers of belief explanations (typically none) to both sorts of stories. Five 4-year-olds gave more belief explanations for their surprise stories than for their happy stories, only one evidenced the reverse. Altogether eight children evidenced the correct pattern of response and only one reversed it ($p < .01$, sign test). However, these sparse findings place greater emphasis on children's responses to the follow-up questions.

Follow-up responses to all stories.   The second row of Fig. 3 presents these responses. A 2 (age) × 2 (story type) ANOVA on desire explanations indicated only an effect of story type ($F(1,24) = 68.08$, $p < .001$). Children gave more desire responses to happy than to surprise, albeit giving substantial desire responses to surprise as well. Both 3-year-olds and 4-year-olds evidenced this significant pattern of results ($ps < .001$). A 2 (age) × 2 (story type) ANOVA on belief explanations indicated only an effect of story type ($F(1,24) = 82.52$, $p < .001$). Both 3-year-olds and 4-year-olds gave significantly more belief explanations for surprise emotions than they did for happy ($ps < .001$). (Again, belief responses to happy represent the appropriate baseline comparison for belief responding to surprise.) Individual data confirm these analyses. All 3- and 4-year-olds gave at least three desire explanations to the four happy stories. All 3- and 4-year-olds gave at least two belief explanations to the four surprise stories.

Open-ended responses to the critical story pairs.   The third row of Fig. 3 presents the data from only the carefully contrasting story pairs, coded just as before. The scale here is from 0 to 2 (rather than 4) because each child received only two happy–surprise pairs describing an identical situation leading to a divergent emotional response. Two 2 (age) × 2 (story type) ANOVAs yielded no significant effects. In the case of desire explanations this was because children gave substantial desire responses to both happy and surprise stories. In the case of belief explanations this was because children gave few unprompted belief explanations even to surprise stories—only three out of 14 3-year-olds and five out of 12 4-year-olds ever gave unprompted belief responses. In this case, non-parametric consideration of individual children adds useful information. Two 3-year-olds gave more unprompted belief explanations for surprise stories than for their happy stories and none the reverse. Four 4-year-olds gave more belief explanations for surprise than for happy and only one the reverse. Altogether six children evidenced the correct pattern and only one the reverse ($p < .05$, sign test).

Again, however, these sparse findings shift the primary emphasis to children's responses to the follow-up questions.

Follow-up responses to the critical story pairs.   The bottom row of Fig. 3 presents these data. A 2 (age) × 2 (story type) ANOVA on desire explanations indicated only an effect of story type ($F(1,24) = 8.49$, $p < .01$). Both 3- and 4-year-olds gave significantly more desire explanations to happy stories ($ps < .05$), albeit giving considerable desire explanations to surprise as well. Because of the ceiling effects here a non-parametric test is again useful. Three 3-year-olds gave more desire explanations to their happy stories than to their surprise stories; none reversed this pattern and 11 were tied giving equal numbers to both. Four 4-year-olds gave more desire explanations to happy than to surprise; none reversed and eight were tied. Altogether seven children evidenced the correct pattern of response and none reversed it ($p < .01$, sign test).

A 2 (age) × 2 (story type) ANOVA on children's belief explanations yielded only a significant effect of story type ($F(1,24) = 14.87$, $p < .001$). Both 3- and 4-year-olds ($ps < .05$) gave belief explanations to the surprise stories more often than to the comparable happy stories (which described an identical situation). Here ceiling effects were not an issue but the non-parametric data are still of interest: 13 out of 14 3-year-olds gave at least one appropriate belief explanation to the two surprise stories; 11 out of the 12 4-year-olds did so. More importantly, eight 3-year-olds gave more belief explanations to surprise emotions than to happy ones; one reversed this pattern and the rest tied. Seven 4-year-olds gave more belief explanations to surprise than to happy, one reversed this pattern and the rest tied. Altogether 15 evidenced the proper asymmetry of response with only two reversals ($p < .01$, sign test).

These data for the follow-up responses confirm that children's knowledge of the belief dependence of surprise and the desire dependence of happiness goes beyond a situationist ability simply to cite appropriate specific mental states as linked with distinctly different situations. Even for characters described as experiencing the *same* situation, when they experienced *different* emotions (surprise vs. happiness) then children's explanations significantly and differentially appealed to beliefs vs. desires, as appropriate.

For these contrasting pairs it is possible to look closely at children's answers to the thinking and wanting follow-up questions. This is possible because these stories specifically present the child with two different outcomes, or contents, which the story character could want or think. Consider for example the story about Alice who looks into a box of plasters and finds balloons. Two possible options or contents are presented: plasters and balloons. When asked 'What is Alice wanting?' (or thinking), the child could randomly answer either plasters or balloons. However, if the child understands the character's stated emotion (happy or surprised) then he or she should answer non-randomly. Specifically, if told that Alice is happy, ordinary belief–desire reasoning leads to the conclusion that Alice got what she wanted, thus the answer to 'what was she wanting?' should be balloons. Similarly, if told that Alice is surprised, the conclusion should be that Alice was *not* expecting the outcome that did occur, thus the answer to 'what was she thinking?' should be plasters.

In this regard, when the character (e.g. Alice) was said to be happy, children tended to answer the wanting question correctly by saying that she wanted the outcome (balloons) not the other option (plasters). For all children, 15 cited the outcome more often than the other option, five reversed this pattern and six were tied ($p < .01$, sign test). Given children's generally good understanding of desires and happiness (in our own and others' research), the more important issue concerns surprise and belief. When the character was said to be surprised children tended to say correctly that she *thought* the other option was true (plasters) not the actual outcome (balloons). For 3-year-olds, 11 children more often cited the other option, none reversed this pattern, and three were tied. For 4-year-olds, 11 children more often cited the other option, and one child reversed the pattern. Altogether 22 children evidenced the appropriate pattern of understanding as against only one reversal ($p < .001$, sign test).

In these analyses it is also the case that children appropriately differentiated their responses to the same question (e.g. the thinking follow-up) across the stories. Thus children were more likely to say the character was thinking the other option (plasters) rather than the actual outcome (balloons), when asked what the surprised character was thinking than when asked what the happy character was thinking. Eight 3-year-olds gave the appropriate pattern of response (more often citing the other option for the thinking question asked of the surprised character than of the happy character), one gave the reverse, and five were tied. Seven 4-year-olds gave the appropriate pattern, none reversed and five were tied. Altogether 15 children evidenced the appropriate pattern of understanding as against only one reversal ($p < .001$, sign test).

Discussion

These data replicate those from Study 2 in all essential regards. First, 3- and 4-year-old children were once again shown to understand that happiness stems, at least in part, from receiving desired outcomes. Moreover, we replicated the critical pattern of results from Study 2 showing that young children understand that the reaction of surprise depends on the actor's prior beliefs. The critical data here are that children made reference to characters' beliefs significantly more often when explaining a character's surprise than when explaining a character's happiness. Children evidenced less mention of beliefs in their answers to the open-ended explanation questions in Study 3 than in Study 2, although still evidencing the appropriate pattern of response. But, we have contended all along that if children think that surprises represent desirable outcomes then it is appropriate to appeal, firstly, to the actor's desires. This simply makes the data from the follow-up questions all the more important. The follow-up data also replicate Study 2.

Since the follow-up thinking question explicitly asked 'What is she thinking', it could be argued that children's responses are only to be expected, reflecting *pro forma* mention of some conceivable belief content without true understanding that beliefs are implicated in surprise. Consider this hypothesis further. Imagine a hypothetical child who fails to understand that an emotional reaction such as surprise is dependent on a character's prior beliefs. Instead, this hypothetical child understands surprise only in desire terms. If such a child was told that a character was surprised (as they were told in our stories) it would mean something like if an adult or older child was told simply that the character was happy. Because such a description provides no information as to the character's belief state, such a child should be extremely unlikely to provide appropriate belief responses to the thinking question. Of course, a child like this might provide some apparently appropriate belief responses by chance, because the question asks 'What is she thinking?'. However, if belief responses are emitted in this unwitting fashion, then such a hypothetical child should be as likely to provide belief responses to the thinking question asked for the happy characters as to the thinking question asked for curious characters, because in neither case has the child any clue as to the character's thoughts.

On the other hand, what if children do understand surprise to be belief-dependent. In that case, to be told that a character is surprised is to be told something about the character's prior belief (namely that the character was not thinking that the specified event would happen). A child who understands something of the belief-dependence of surprise, therefore, should give significantly more belief responses to the thinking question for surprised characters than for happy ones. As shown in Fig. 2 for Study 2 and again in Fig. 3 for Study 3, this is what happens. Both 3- and 4-year-olds give cogent belief responses to the thinking follow-up question significantly more often when explaining a character's surprise than when explaining his or her happiness. Indeed, in Study 3 all 3- and 4-year-olds gave at least two appropriate belief explanations to the four surprise stories.

The methods used in Study 3 include several controls that strengthen and extend the findings, beyond just replicating the results of Study 2. The most important control involved the inclusion of carefully contrasting pairs of stories describing the same character experiencing the same situation but with divergent emotional reactions (in one instance being happy and in the other being surprised). For these contrasting story pairs the critical patterns of results were also obtained, most obviously and most importantly in children's responses to the follow-up questions (see Fig. 3). These data confirm that children's understanding of the causes of emotion extend beyond a facile situationist understanding of links between various situations and associated emotions or associated mental states. Young children evidence a more subjectivist understanding of emotion—understanding that the same situations can yield divergent emotions—and a more appropriate understanding of the link between beliefs and desires and emotions. Specifically, children's explanations evidence the understanding that if a character (confronting the same situation) experiences happiness this is because of her desires, whereas if she experiences surprise this is because of her beliefs. These findings thus show an impressive, albeit rudimentary, grasp of the core relation between mind and emotion assumed in everyday belief–desire psychology.

General discussion

Our results bear on three interrelated issues that will be discussed in turn: (1) methods, (2) the early development of children's understanding of emotion, and

(3) the early development of children's understanding of the mind, including the notion of belief.

The explanation methods of Studies 2 and 3 represent an advance over the rating methods used in previous studies such as Study 1. Most obviously, this second method circumvents young children's imperfect understanding of terms such as *surprise* and reveals their nascent understanding of the belief-dependence of these sorts of emotional reactions. But there is a further advance as well. In general our aim is to investigate children's understanding of various emotions, beyond their first-hand experience of those emotional states. Rating methods such as that used in Study 1, by Wellman & Bartsch (1988) and by Hadwin & Perner (1991) present children with a character's belief (or desire)—Jane thinks she'll get milk—and then the outcome—look, it's grapejuice—and ask them to rate Jane's surprise. Since the children themselves first hear information supporting a particular belief—'she'll get milk'—and then experience a story outcome—'look, it's grapejuice'—they could conceivably respond not from an understanding of emotional reactions but simply by reporting their own reaction (the children themselves become surprised or happy and say so). The explanation task avoids this problem. In Studies 2 and 3 an emotional reaction is stipulated (he's very surprised) and the child is queried for an explanation of that reaction. This requires children to go beyond a simple reporting of emotions. In order to provide the sorts of appropriate explanations elicited in these studies, children cannot just report their own emotions, nor is it acceptable to simply report those of the story character (e.g. reiterate the character's surprise). Instead children must be able to move beyond such reports and explain the reasons for those emotions, by making reference to the character's beliefs and desires.

Of course, in any given situation children experience their own beliefs and desires, too. Could they simply be reporting those? We think not, as our discussion of the situationist hypothesis illustrates. Consider a child asked to answer our Study 2 explanation questions: for example, asked why Jeff is so surprised that his grandma's house is purple. Presumably a child might experience a salient mental state in a situation like this, e.g. not expecting a purple house. If children simply report their own mental state, they might produce the results in Study 2. But in Study 3 children do more than this. They appropriately cite desires more often for characters said to be happy but cite beliefs more often for the *same* character experiencing the *same* situation but said to be surprised. In short, children's appropriate responding shows that they understand something about how emotional reactions differentially depend on prior mental states of desire or belief, beyond simply having emotions, beliefs, and desires themselves, and reporting them. Children's ability to put themselves imaginatively in the characters' shoes probably does play a role here (see Harris, 1989), but the data reveal a more organized understanding of mind and emotion too, beyond simply the experience of, or the imagination of, specific mental and emotional states.

With regard to children's developing understanding of emotions, the findings reveal an early emergence of an initial understanding of certain 'cognitive' emotions, such as surprise and curiosity. In past studies of emotion, either such emotional reactions have not been studied or no attention has been paid to their special link to beliefs as opposed to desires. Only recently (e.g. Wellman & Bartsch, 1988) have these sorts of emotional reactions received specific attention. Including such reactions paints a larger, more comprehensive, picture of children's understanding of the full variety of human emotional reaction. Similarly, investigating the cognitive emotions expands our knowledge of children's understanding of the causal organization of emotion. Our data reveal that young children understand, for certain emotions anyway, that an actor's prior belief states are causally important to emotional reactions, in addition to the desire or goal states which have been more typically considered and investigated (Stein & Levine, 1987).

Turning to the third issue—children's developing knowledge of the mind—our data show initial understanding in children as young as 3 years and important developments as well. For example, the current data on children's understanding of surprise and curiosity shed light on the controversy as to whether 3-year-olds understand that people have beliefs beyond desires, or whether such an understanding of belief is a later development apparent only in 4-year-olds. Our finding that 3-year-olds cite the character's beliefs for surprise and curious reactions provides evidence that they understand human action and reaction as dependent on people's beliefs as well as desires. Suppose such young children had no understanding of belief, why would they ever spontaneously cite relevant beliefs when asked why the character reacted as he did (why is he so surprised?). A child with no understanding of belief could simply cite desire. Even when asked the thinking follow-up question children could simply cite desire (e.g. 'He thinks he wants one'; 'He thinks he likes it best'). Children did occasionally respond in just this fashion, which underwrites the availability of such responses and the plausibility of such responding. In our coding scheme, however, such responses do not qualify as relevant belief responses; they were coded as desire responses instead. Much more frequently, young children, even 3-year-olds, consistently cited the character's relevant beliefs. In doing so, they showed evidence of an understanding that surprise reactions, for example, are peculiarly dependent on what a character thinks, not just on what he wants.

Part of the controversy surrounding 3-year-olds' understanding of beliefs centres on their understanding of false beliefs—for example, their knowledge that if an apple is really in the refrigerator someone could think falsely that it was in the cupboard. Some writers assert that unless young children can solve false belief tasks (e.g. predict the deceived character in the above example will search in the cupboard not the refrigerator), they cannot be credited with an understanding of beliefs (e.g. Perner, 1988, in press). We have contended that children can evidence understanding of beliefs and still fail false belief tasks (Wellman, 1990; Wellman & Bartsch, 1988). The current data support the claim that even 3-year-olds understand belief, indeed even something about false beliefs. Children's responses to the follow-up questions to the critical story pairs in Study 3 are most important here. Beyond just appropriately appealing to beliefs to explain surprise, in these critical story pairs children referred specifically to characters' false beliefs. For example, they said the character was surprised because she was thinking about plasters even though there really were balloons in the box. These data are consistent with other recently emerging studies indicating that 3-year-olds at times evidence genuine understanding of false belief (e.g. Bartsch & Wellman, 1989; Lewis & Osborne, 1990; Siegal & Beattie, in press). Such evidence adds to the conclusion that 3-year-olds understand a substantial amount about beliefs (see e.g. Wellman & Bartsch, 1988) and is consistent with the claim that 3-year-olds indeed understand the core notion behind surprise; namely that surprise results when characters experience something they do not believe will occur.

The data, while showing significant understanding in 3-year-olds, also show consistent developmental increases in understanding between 3 and 4 years contributing to an increasingly detailed account of early developments within children's thinking about the mind. Two developments are most obvious in our data, one concerning children's early understanding of beliefs and the other of desires. Children's understanding of the existence of false beliefs and how unfulfilled beliefs lead to surprise develops substantially in the years 3 to 4. Many of our analyses showed age × story type interactions depicting increasingly consistent and accurate understanding of the belief dependence of surprise in these early years. Note also that our explanation tasks diverge slightly from classic false belief tasks. In stating that a character was surprised because she thought there would be plasters, not balloons, young children are properly citing the character's beliefs and noting that surprise requires a discrepancy between prior belief and reality. But they need not acknowledge fully that one's *current* beliefs can be diametrically opposed to reality. This is what is required in tasks such as Wimmer & Perner's (1983) false belief task where children must predict the actor's current action by reference to his current false belief. Fully realizing that a character possesses, right now, a firm belief that is directly contrary to current reality seems a particularly difficult understanding for young children to achieve or maintain. But younger children, even 3-year-olds, do seem able to grasp at times the crucial discrepancy between beliefs and reality. In our task, for example, they evidence the understanding that people have beliefs and that prior beliefs can be discrepant from actual later happenings. Therefore, in Studies 2 and 3 they can understand that prior beliefs can be overruled by current facts and hence cause an actor to experience surprise (that is, that people's expectations are, as predictions, not always right). In short, the current data contribute to a growing picture that beginning at age 3 children understand much about beliefs, enough to participate sensibly in belief–desire reasoning of several impressive sorts, while at the same time acknowledging considerable rapid development in children's understanding of belief from age 3 to $4\frac{1}{2}$ or so.

The gradual emergence of an increasingly consistent understanding of belief in the years from 3 to 5 goes hand in hand, we believe, with another development evident in our data, a relative diminution in children's reliance on interpreting human behaviour solely with regard to desires. In other research (Wellman & Woolley, 1990), we have argued that at an early age, evident for 2-year-olds, children are ignorant of beliefs and only consider desires in understanding actions. If so, then it is reasonable that when children first begin to understand beliefs, at around the third birthday, their understanding of action still gravitates more to desire than belief. Our data do not directly test this hypothesis, but they do document a high reliance on citing the character's desire in 3-year-olds' explanation of emotion (coupled with a significant but lesser appeal to beliefs) which diminishes in part from ages 3 to 4. In Studies 2 and 3, 3-year-olds' unprompted explanation of emotions often relied predominantly on desire, with, for some children, only occasional glimpses of appeal to beliefs. By 4 years children's appeal to beliefs and desires was more consistent and their citation of belief as well as desire more robust, when appropriate (see, for example, Fig. 2). Consistent with this trend, while most 3-year-olds provided at least some appropriate belief explanations in our tasks, some never did, even when explicitly asked 'what is she thinking?'. Across Studies 2 and 3, four of the 37 3-year-olds never provided an appropriate belief response even to the follow-up questions while providing many cogent desire explanations; no child ever evidenced the reverse pattern. Young children's tendency to interpret surprises as desirable in Study 1 also fits this developmental pattern, albeit such a misinterpretation is also fuelled by parental usage.

In short, developmental trends in the current data are strong, and they are consistent with the following account. Children of 3 and 4 years have a well-established understanding of desires and such desire-dependent emotions as happiness and sadness. Children as young as 3 years have, as well, an initial sensible understanding of such cognitive emotions as surprise and curiosity, based on a beginning understanding that characters have beliefs as well as desires, and that reactions such as surprise depend on discrepancies between beliefs and outcomes. Such early understanding, however, exists at first in the shadow of a powerful residual tendency to understand mind and emotion largely in terms of characters' desires alone, ignoring beliefs. In the years from 3 to 5, children's initial understanding of belief develops in import and consistency as reflected in a more consistent and accurate understanding of surprises, beliefs and false beliefs.

Acknowledgements

This research was supported by grants to the first author from the US National Institutes of Health and the Vice President for Research at the University of Michigan, and by a Social Science and Humanities Research Council of Canada fellowship to the second author. We wish to thank the children, parents, teachers and staff of the University of Michigan Children's Centers. We also thank Paul Harris for his help and suggestions.

References

Barden, R. C., Zeko, F. A., Duncan, S. W. & Masters, J. C. (1980). Children's consensual knowledge about the experiential determinants of emotion. *Journal of Personality and Social Psychology, 39*, 968–976.

Bartsch, K. & Wellman, H. M. (1989). Young children's attribution of action to beliefs and desires. *Child Development, 60*, 946–964.

Borke, H. (1971). Interpersonal perception of young children: Egocentrism or empathy. *Developmental Psychology, 5*, 263–269.

Bretherton, I. & Beeghly, M. (1982). Talking about internal states: The acquisition of an explicit theory of mind. *Developmental Psychology, 18*, 906–921.

Bullock, M. & Russell, J. A. (1984). Preschool children's interpretation of facial expressions of emotion. *International Journal of Behavioral Development, 7*, 193–214.

Chandler, M., Fritz, A. S. & Hala, S. (1989). Small scale deceit: Deception as a marker of 2-, 3-, and 4-year-olds' early theories of mind. *Child Development, 60*, 1263–1277.

Davidson, D. (1963). Actions, reasons, and causes. *Journal of Philosophy, 60*, 685–700.

Flavell, J. H. (1988). The development of children's knowledge about the mind: From cognitive connections to mental representations. In J. Astington, P. Harris & D. Olson (Eds), *Developing Theories of Mind*. New York: Cambridge University Press.

Forguson, L. & Gopnik, A. (1988). The ontogeny of common sense. In J. Astington, P. Harris & D. Olson (Eds), *Developing Theories of Mind*, pp. 226–243. New York: Cambridge University Press.

Gnepp, J. (1983). Children's social sensitivity: Inferring emotions from conflicting cues. *Developmental Psychology,* **19**, 805–814.

Gopnik, A. & Astington, J. W. (1988). Children's understanding of representational change and its relation to the understanding of false belief and the appearance–reality distinction. *Child Development,* **59**, 26–37.

Hadwin, J. & Perner, J. (1991). Pleased and surprised: Children's cognitive theory of emotion. *British Journal of Developmental Psychology,* **9**, 215–234. Unpublished ms, University of Sussex.

Harris, P. L. (1989). *Children and Emotion.* Oxford: Basil Blackwell.

Harris, P. L., Donnelly, K., Guz, G. R. & Pitt-Watson, R. (1986). Children's understanding of the distinction between real and apparent emotion. *Child Development,* **57**, 895–909.

Harris, P. L., Olthof, T., Meerum Terwogt, M. & Hardman, C. E. (1987). Children's knowledge of situations that provoke emotion. *International Journal of Behavioral Development,* **10**, 319–344.

Harter, S. (1983). Children's understanding of multiple emotions: A cognitive–developmental approach. In W. Overton (Ed.), *The Relationship between Social and Cognitive Development,* pp. 147–194. Hillsdale, NJ: Erlbaum.

Kuczaj, S. A. & Moratsos, M. P. (1975). What children *can* say before they *will. Merrill–Palmer Quarterly,* **21**, 89–111.

Lewis, C. & Osborne, A. (1990). Three-year-olds' problems with false belief: Conceptual deficit or linguistic artifact? *Child Development,* **61**, 1514–1519.

Perner, J. (1988). Developing semantics for theories of mind: From propositional attitudes to mental representations. In J. Astington, P. Harris & D. Olson (Eds), *Developing Theories of Mind.* New York: Cambridge University Press.

Perner, J. (in press). *Understanding the Representational Mind.* Cambridge, MA: MIT Press/Bradford.

Perner, J., Leekam, S. R. & Wimmer, H. (1987). Three-year-olds' difficulty with false belief. *British Journal of Developmental Psychology,* **5**, 125–137.

Ridgeway, D., Waters, E. & Kuczaj, S. A. (1985). Acquisition of emotion-descriptive language: Receptive and productive vocabulary norms for ages 18 months to 6 years. *Developmental Psychology,* **21**, 901–908.

Russell, J. A. & Bullock, M. (1986). On the dimensions preschoolers use to interpret facial expressions of emotion. *Developmental Psychology,* **22**, 97–102.

Shatz, M., Wellman, H. M. & Silber, S. (1983). The acquisition of mental verbs: A systematic investigation of first references to mental state. *Cognition,* **14**, 301–321.

Siegal, M. & Beattie, K. (in press). Where to look first for children's knowledge of false beliefs. *Cognition.*

Stein, N. L. & Levine, L. J. (1987). Thinking about feelings: The development and organization of emotional knowledge. In R. Snow & M. Farr (Eds), *Aptitude, Learning and Instruction,* vol. 3, *Cognition, Conation and Affect,* pp. 165–198. Hillsdale, NJ: Erlbaum.

Stein, N. L. & Levine, L. J. (1989). The causal organization of emotional knowledge: A developmental study. *Cognition and Emotion,* **3**, 343–378.

Trabasso, T., Stein, N. L. & Johnson, L. R. (1981). Children's knowledge of events: A causal analysis of story structure. *The Psychology of Learning and Motivation,* **13**, 237–281.

Wellman, H. M. (1988). First steps in the child's theorizing about the mind. In J. Astington, P. Harris & D. Olson (Eds), *Developing Theories of Mind,* pp. 64–92. New York: Cambridge University Press.

Wellman, H. M. (1990). *The Child's Theory of Mind.* Cambridge, MA: MIT Press/Bradford.

Wellman, H. M. & Bartsch, K. (1988). Young children's reasoning about beliefs. *Cognition,* **30**, 239–277.

Wellman, H. M. & Woolley, J. D. (1990). From simple desires to ordinary beliefs: The early development of everyday psychology. *Cognition,* **35**, 245–275.

Wimmer, H. & Perner, J. (1983). Beliefs about beliefs: Representation and constraining function of wrong beliefs in young children's understanding of deception. *Cognition,* **13**, 103–128.

Yuill, N. (1984). Young children's coordination of motive and outcome in judgments of satisfaction and morality. *British Journal of Developmental Psychology,* **2**, 73–81.

Received 21 February 1990; revised version received 27 September 1990

British Journal of Developmental Psychology (1991), **9**, 215–234 *Printed in Great Britain*   215

Pleased and surprised: Children's cognitive theory of emotion

Julie Hadwin
University of Sussex

Josef Perner*
University of Sussex and *Max-Planck Institute for Psychological Research, Munich*

This study looks at two emotions that are determined by whether a person's mental state matches or mismatches the state of the world. Results show that children from 3 years understand that being 'pleased' is a function of the match or mismatch between desire and reality. That is between what a person wants and what a person gets. A structurally similar problem is presented by the emotion 'surprise'. 'Surprise' is a function of the match or mismatch between belief and reality. That is between what a person believes or expects to be the case and what actually is the case. It is shown that 'surprise' is not understood until children are 5 years old at the earliest. This developmental discrepancy can partly be explained by the fact that 'surprise' requires an understanding of belief as a misrepresentation. This is not typically understood before children reach 4 years of age. However, children younger than 4 years can understand 'pleased' as the result of reaching or not reaching a desired situation. Results also show that it is not until 5 years of age that children understand 'happiness' when 'happiness' is made dependent on belief about reality and not on reality itself. The fact that children understand 'surprise' and belief-based 'happiness' later than 4 years indicates a general lag between understanding belief and its role in determining emotion.

This paper investigates how young children come to understand the cognitively defining aspects of emotions. It is an investigation of children's acquisition of our common-sense theory of emotion and not of psychological theories of emotion. Controversies in psychology as to whether emotions are perceived physiological disturbances (James, 1884), of a reflexive nature (Zajonc, 1980, 1984), or whether they always have a cognitive–evaluative basis (Lazarus, 1982, 1984; Lyons, 1980; Schacter & Singer, 1962) are therefore avoided.

The common-sense theory of emotion is embedded in the way we use emotion terms like 'happy', 'sad', 'surprised', etc. Dating back to Aristotle (Calhoun & Solomon, 1984, pp. 3–5) philosophers in the tradition of 'natural language philosophy' (Bedford, 1986; Kenny, 1963) have pointed out that implicit constraints on

* Requests for reprints should be addressed to Dr J. Perner, Max-Planck Institute for Psychological Research, Leopoldstr. 24, D-8000 Munich, Germany.

the use of emotion terms show logically necessary connections with other mental states. That is, with emotion terms we do not describe some internal state but express different ways of being conscious or aware of the world.

Our common-sense theory about the mind is sometimes referred to as *belief–desire psychology* (Churchland, 1984; Dennett, 1978) because desire (how we *want* the world to be) and belief (how we *believe* the world is) are the two basic ways in which we mentally relate to the world.

From this viewpoint there are two simple emotions: 'pleased' (closely related to 'happy' and 'sad') and 'surprised'. 'Pleased' describes a relation between *desire* and *reality* (i.e. if you get what you want you are happy, if you do not you are sad). 'Surprise' describes a relation between *belief* and *reality* (if your belief is confirmed you are not surprised, if the world differs from what you believe you are surprised). In these cases the relationship between mental state (desire or belief) and the world are necessary, defining, characteristics of these emotions. This is shown by the fact that one cannot say (at least not without additional explanation): 'He was pleased (happy) about "X", but he didn't want "X" '; or, 'He was surprised that "X", but he knew "X" would happen'.

Previous studies of how children's understanding of these emotions develops have ignored the defining mental aspects of the emotions. On the whole, children's understanding of emotions has been reduced to their understanding of stereotypic situations that usually accompany certain emotions (Barden, Zelko, Duncan & Masters, 1980; Fabes, Eisenberg, McCormick & Wilson, 1988; Gnepp, McKee & Domanic, 1987; Green, 1977; Harris, 1983). For example, Michalson & Lewis (1985) have shown that children as young as 2 years were able to label a birthday party situation as eliciting a 'happy' emotional response. Birthdays, however, although stereotyped as happy situations, have no conceptual link to happiness. If one's birthday wishes have not been fulfilled it is possible to feel sad on one's birthday. Such studies inform us only about children's scripted knowledge of stereotypic events. They tell us little about the child's understanding of the essential mental criteria of emotions.

Other research has investigated children's production and understanding of facial expression (Cicchetti & Hesse, 1983; Ekman, 1980; Izard, 1971; Michalson & Lewis, 1985). The facial expressions 'smiling' and 'surprise' have both been identified as occurring within the first 3 months of life. The former in response to goal achievement and the latter in response to some novelty in the environment (Cicchetti & Hesse, 1983). Research into children's understanding of facial expression has shown that 'happiness' is the most easily recognized facial expression (Ekman, 1980; Izard, 1971), with recognition occurring at 2 years of age. It has also been shown that, in a similar recognition task, most children of 2 years and above were able to recognize a 'surprise' face correctly (Michalson & Lewis, 1985). The production of the facial expressions of emotion shows us the beginnings of infants' emotional life and the recognition of emotional expression is an important social skill. Neither, however, tell us about the deeper conceptual understanding of the mental–cognitive aspects of emotion.

This series of experiments focuses on children's appreciation of the mental aspects of the emotions 'pleased' and 'surprise'.

Experiment 1

Initial investigations are based on a study by Yuill (1984). Yuill gave children stories that depicted a protagonist wanting to throw a ball to one of two other characters. The protagonist's desire was depicted by a 'want-bubble' above his/her head. In one story outcome the intended recipient caught the ball, whereas in the other story the other character caught it. Children as young as 3 years understood that the story character who achieved what he/she wanted felt more pleased than the one who did not achieve it.

Performance by 3-year-olds on this task is unusually good. The task requires children to relate the description of a mental state (the 'want-bubble') to a description of reality (the final outcome). The ability of children to understand this relationship so early is surprising since there is an increasing amount of literature that shows at 3 years children find it difficult to relate a false belief to reality (Astington,1988; Leekam & Wimmer, 1987; Wimmer & Perner, 1983). There are two possible resolutions to this discrepancy. One possibility is that the explicit depiction of a mental state in the 'want-bubble' makes it easier for children to understand the relationship between mind and world. If this is the case, 3-year-olds should find an analogous problem where desire is replaced by belief and the emotion to be judged is 'surprise' equally easy. The second possibility is that belief is more difficult to understand than desire. (Astington, 1988; Perner, 1988; Perner, in press).

These two possibilities are tested in Expt 1. This was done by slightly modifying Yuill's stories. A high wall was introduced between the protagonist and the other two story characters. In this way the meaning of Yuill's 'want-bubble' could be changed to that of a 'think-bubble'. The 'think-bubble' depicts who the protagonist *thinks has the ball*. In one story the protagonist's belief is *matched* by reality behind the wall. Therefore, when the protagonist looks behind the wall he/she would *not* be *surprised* to find what he/she expected. In the other story there is a *mismatch* between reality and the protagonist's belief so that the protagonist would be *surprised* when looking behind the wall.

Method

Subjects. Sixty-four children from a local state nursery took part in the study. There were two age groups; 3 years (3.0–3.92, mean age = 3.54, 13 boys, 19 girls), and 4 years (4.0–4.92), mean age = 4.42, 11 boys, 21 girls).

Materials. Three coloured pictures for each story depicted the important story events. Schematic drawings of faces were used to help subjects indicate their choice of emotion. In the *surprise condition* one face showed a 'surprise' expression and the other a neutral expression. The surprised face was based on typical descriptions of the facial expression of the emotion surprise: eyebrows raised, rounded and open eyes, open and oval mouth (Darwin, 1904; Ekman, 1980; Izard, 1971). In the *pleased condition* the neutral face was used together with a 'pleased' face. The pleased face was based on the one used by Yuill (1984).

Design and procedure. Thirty-two 3- and 4-year-olds were randomly assigned to either the surprise or the pleased condition. For familiarization with the story procedure and materials each subject was told two practice stories. These were followed by two test stories. Different story contents were used for the practice and test stories.

At the beginning of each story the subjects were shown the appropriate pair of schematic faces and their attention was drawn to the difference between them. An emotion label was used when introducing the pictures ('surprised' and 'not surprised' or 'pleased' and 'not pleased'). The subjects were told that at the end of the story they would have to point to one of the pictures to show how the person in the story would look.

In the *pleased condition* the two practice stories involved a boy who wants something, e.g. icecream, and either gets it (match story; pleased) or does not get it (mismatch; not pleased). The desire of the character was depicted in a 'want-bubble' above his head. The use of the bubble was explained to subjects.

The structure and content of the test stories were the same as in Yuill (1984). For example, the *first picture* showed Debbie, a story protagonist, in front of a tall wall holding a ball. Two other characters, Anne and Peter, were behind the wall out of the protagonist's sight. A 'want-bubble' above Debbie's head showed whether she *wants* Anne or Peter to catch the ball. For example, Debbie wants Anne to catch the ball. The *second picture* showed the protagonist throwing the ball over the wall. The *third picture* showed that either Anne (match story) or Peter (mismatch story) caught the ball.

The subject's understanding of the protagonist's goal was checked by asking: 'Did Debbie want "X" to catch it?'. If a subject answered incorrectly they were asked a further question: 'Who did Debbie want to catch the ball?'. The subjects were then told that the protagonist was going to look behind the wall and find out who had caught the ball. This was followed by the *emotion question*: 'Do you think that Debbie will be *pleased or not pleased* that "X" has caught the ball?'. The subjects could either answer verbally or point to one of the two schematic faces.

In the *surprise condition* the practice stories consisted of an expected event and a truly surprising event. For example, a boy goes to collect eggs from his goose and either finds eggs or discovers that it has laid an apple. The protagonist's original expectation (that there would be an egg there) was shown in a 'think bubble'. Again the use of the bubble was explained to the subjects.

In the test stories similar pictures to those in the pleased condition were used. In the *first picture* the protagonist was at one side of the wall and the other two characters were at the other side. In this condition, however, the ball was lying behind the wall with the other two characters. A 'think-bubble' showed who the protagonist *thinks* will pick up the ball. In the *second picture* one of the two characters picks up the ball. In the *third picture* the protagonist looks behind the wall to find his/her expectation either confirmed (match story) or violated (mismatch story). The subject's understanding of the protagonist's expectation was checked by asking: 'Did he think "X" would be holding the ball?'. As in the pleased condition, if the answer to this question was negative then a further question was asked: 'Who did he think would be holding the ball?'. The subjects were then asked the *emotion question*: 'Do you think he will be *surprised* or *not surprised* that "X" is holding the ball?'.

Throughout each story the subjects were asked questions about important events. If a subject responded incorrectly to any of these questions prior to the emotion question then the story was repeated again from the beginning. If any of the questions were not answered correctly on the second hearing then the wrong answers were recorded. Incorrect answers on the second hearing only occurred in the surprise mismatch condition. Two 3-year-olds answered the memory question about what the protagonist had been thinking wrongly by answering in terms of the actual situation.

Results and discussion

The subjects' responses were scored as correct if their answers to both the emotion questions in the match and mismatch stories were correct. The proportion of children with correct attributions of emotion were analysed by stepwise logistic regression using the BMDP statistical package (Dixon *et al.*, 1981). For the factors age, sex, type of emotion (pleased or surprised), story order (match/mismatch or mismatch/match) a saturated model including all main and interaction effects was used. The introduction of effects into the model was constrained by a hierarchical rule where interactions are only considered if their component effects are already in the model. This method was used in all subsequent experiments.

Type of emotion was the only significant effect (χ^2 (1) $=25.42, p<.01, N=64$). Of the 3-year-olds 81.25 per cent and 93.75 per cent of the 4-year-olds correctly predicted that the story protagonist would be pleased if he/she achieved the desired outcome and not pleased otherwise. While only 12.5 per cent of 3- and 37.5 per cent of 4-year-olds predicted that the story protagonist would be surprised when his/her expectation differed from reality and would not be surprised otherwise. (For all other effects $p>.05$.)

A look at the frequency of response patterns for the match and mismatch stories may give a clearer picture of why the subjects found the surprise stories so difficult. This contingency is shown in Table 1. Results in the pleased condition confirm the early competence reported by Yuill (1984). The majority of the subjects in both ages accurately inferred the protagonist's satisfaction on the basis of his/her stated goal.

Table 1. Frequency of response patterns on match–mismatch stories in Expt 1

Answer pattern for match–mismatch stories	Age		
	3	4	Both ages
Pleased condition			
p + np+	13	15	28
p + p −	1	0	1
np − np+	1	1	2
np − p −	1	0	1
Surprised condition			
ns+ s +	2	6	8
ns+ ns −	6	0	6
s − s +	7	6	13
s − ns −	1	4	5

Note. p stands for a response indicating that the protagonist was pleased, np for not pleased, s for surprised, and ns for not surprised. Each response is marked with + if it is the correct one for the particular story condition or with − if incorrect.

In the surprise condition performance was quite different. Even 4-year-olds showed no reliable sign of understanding surprise. In order to get the most statistical power for detecting some trace of competence both age groups were combined (last column in Table 1). The proportion of subjects who gave correct responses on both surprise stories, however, was not significantly different from the proportion of children giving the exact opposite answers (McNemar's χ^2 (1) $=0.70$, $p>.30$, $N=13$).

The difficulty with the surprise condition cannot be explained by the familiarity of the emotion labels used. Bretherton, Fritz, Zahn-Waxler & Ridgeway (1986) reported that 13 per cent of 2-year-olds use the word 'surprise' whereas the use of 'pleased' was not even recorded. Also, the subjects' failure to make correct surprise attributions cannot be due to their forgetting what the protagonist thought. The subjects were explicitly asked about this just before they had to make an emotion judgement. Only two 3-year-olds were unable to remember the belief. This question, however, only ensured that the subjects were made aware of what the protagonist thought. Their correct answer may not reflect a deeper understanding of expectation or belief. If it did reflect a deeper understanding of belief then the 3-year-olds' answers would be surprisingly good. Children of this age are known to have difficulty understanding false belief (Harris, Johnson & Harris, personal communication; Perner *et al.*, 1987; Wellman & Bartsch, 1988; Wimmer & Perner, 1983).

The 3-year-olds' problem with surprise, therefore, could be due to their known difficulty with belief. This explanation, however, is implausible for 4-year-olds. Previous studies have reported a good understanding of belief in this age group (Perner *et al.*, 1987). There are at least two possible explanations for the 4-year-olds' unexpected difficulty. One problem may be that our stories did not really justify why the protagonist had a certain expectation. This is not a problem with stating a person's goal in the pleasedness condition. We are used to being told what a person wants. A person's belief, however, especially a deviant one, needs some justification (Dennett, 1987). This we attempted to achieve in the next experiment.

The second possibility that could explain the 4-year-olds' difficulties may have been the use of the word 'surprise' in the emotion question. Although children are quite familiar with the word, it may carry a different meaning for them. Studies have shown that for children 'surprise' is often used to denote something *nice* (like a wish fulfilled) rather than something *unexpected* (Michalson & Lewis, 1985; Bullock & Russell, 1984, 1986; Strayer, 1986). To obviate this potentially misleading feature we avoided the use of that word in Expt 2 and relied solely on pictures of the facial expression of surprise.

The omission of the term 'surprise' should not adversely affect children's understanding of the emotion. Research has shown that at approximately 2 to 3 years of age children have a good understanding of the facial expression 'surprise'. Michalson & Lewis (1985) have shown that the majority of children at 2 years old are able to discriminate a 'surprised' face from other emotion faces.

Experiment 2

This experiment concentrated only on attribution of surprise and was designed to overcome the potential shortcomings in procedure of Expt 1.

In this experiment the protagonist's expectations were better motivated than in the previous experiment. An object which the protagonist thought to be in one place was unexpectedly and unbeknown to him/her brought to a different place. This provided a reason for why he/she would not expect that object to be in the new place.

To avoid the potentially misleading connotation of 'surprise' as something 'nice' the subjects were not asked whether the protagonist was surprised or not surprised. Instead they were asked whether he/she looked like a person in a photograph with a surprised expression or like a person in a photograph with a neutral expression.

The impression in the previous experiment was that some subjects only appeared to understand the point of the surprise stories after they had seen the contrast between match (belief matches reality) and mismatch (belief differs from reality). Therefore, in this experiment subjects were told the experimental stories twice, a day apart. If our impression was correct then performance on the second set of stories should be much better than on the first set.

Method

Subjects.   Our initial strategy was to demonstrate good performance in 5-year-olds and then apply our improved method to younger age groups. The results, however, were such that older age groups had to be looked at instead.

Forty-eight children from a local primary school took part in the study, aged 5 years (5.0–5.75, mean age = 5.3, eight girls, eight boys), 6 years (6.0–6.75, mean age = 6.46, nine girls, seven boys) and 7 years (7.33–7.83, mean age = 7.53, five girls, 11 boys).

Materials.   Two black and white photographs were used for subjects to indicate their choice of emotion. One photograph showed 'surprise' and the other a neutral facial expression.

There were two stories; the 'flag' story and the 'rabbit' story. For each story there was a match and a mismatch version. Each version had four pictures.

In the mismatch version of the 'rabbit' story a boy and a girl are playing with a rabbit. The rabbit escapes and they both look for it. The boy has to go home for lunch while the girl keeps looking. She finds the rabbit and puts it back into its cage. She goes for lunch. After she has gone the boy returns and takes the rabbit to his home. At this point it was checked whether the subjects understood that the girl expected the rabbit to be still in the cage. A *belief question* was asked: 'Where does she think the rabbit is?'. Then the story continues with the girl going over to the boy's house. She sees him holding the rabbit. The subjects were asked the *emotion question*: 'When she sees that he has the rabbit, how will she look?'. The subjects were asked to respond by pointing to either the surprised or the neutral face.

In the match version of the story the girl gives the rabbit to the boy to take home. When she visits later she expects to find the rabbit there with him. The 'flag' story had the same story plot except that the rabbit in the cage was replaced by a flag on a sandcastle which gets blown off in the wind. As in Expt 1 the belief of the protagonist was depicted in a 'think-bubble' above his/her head.

Design and procedure.   The subjects were told one match story and one mismatch story. Assignment of story contents (flag or rabbit) to the match and mismatch stories were counterbalanced. Subjects were told the two stories twice. The first time was simply to familiarize the subjects with the experimental procedure and materials. Answers to these stories are not analysed in the results. One day later the subjects were told the stories again. For the second hearing the order between stories was reversed. Different story contents were used for the match and mismatch stories from one day to the next.

At the beginning of each story session the pictures with the emotion expressions were shown to the subjects. Attention was drawn to the difference between them. The subjects were told that they would hear two stories, at the end of which they would have to point to one of the photographs to show how the person in the story would look. After choosing a picture the subjects were asked to justify their choice of emotion.

Results and discussion

The subjects' responses were scored as correct if their answers to the emotion question was correct for both the match and mismatch stories on the second hearing. There was no discernible change in performance from the first to the second hearing.

Only responses for the second session were analysed. Table 2 shows the pattern of responding on the second match, mismatch pair. At the age of 5 years there were no more children with the correct pattern than with the opposite pattern. Only by 6 years did a convincing majority make correct attributions (McNemar's χ^2 (1) = 10, $p < .01$, $N = 10$).

Table 2. Frequency of response patterns on match–mismatch stories in Expt 2

Answer pattern for match–mismatch stories	Age		
	5	6	7
ns+ s +	3	10	14
ns+ ns −	2	2	0
s − s +	6	4	2
s − ns −	5	0	0

The 5-year-olds' failure to make correct surprise attributions cannot be accounted for by problems understanding belief. All but one of the subjects were able to infer the correct answer to the belief question in the mismatch story. Looking at the error patterns in Table 2 it appears that most errors occurred in the match story. That is, the subjects (wrongly) answered that the protagonist would feel surprised. A reason for this may be that the story is rather bland since everything develops as foreseen. We may get a better picture if we only look at children's response in the mismatch story and see whether their justifications indicate some understanding of surprise. Of the nine children who correctly pointed to the surprised face three gave no justification. Two clearly referred to the belief–reality discrepancy: 'She is thinking the bunny was in the cage but it wasn't'; 'she didn't know'. The remaining four gave answers which could be interpreted as indirect references to the belief–reality discrepancy: 'cause she's surprised he's got it'; 'because he's lost it'; 'because he founded the rabbit'; 'cause he took the rabbit away'. Although these justifications indicate that 5-year-olds may understand more about surprise than their answers to our control story indicated, it still seems that understanding that surprise depends on belief violation emerges somewhat later than the understanding of belief and its influence on action. This emerges at 4 years (Wimmer & Perner, 1983) or even slightly earlier (Perner *et al.*, 1987).

In view of our persistently negative results for 4- and 5-year-olds we were intrigued when we learned of data by Wellman & Bartsch (1988) showing that even 4-year-olds could make surprise judgements on the basis of the belief–reality discrepancy. Their experiment was very similar to Expt 1. The subjects were told, without any justification, what the story protagonist *thinks*: 'This is Lisa. Lisa thinks it will not rain today. Lisa likes it when it rains and she likes it when it doesn't rain, but she thinks it will not rain today.' The subjects were then asked: 'So, what does Lisa think?' and had their correct answer reinforced. Lisa's face was then turned away and a picture of either dry weather (match story) or rain (mismatch story) was shown. The subjects were asked: 'How does Lisa feel, surprised or not surprised?' and were then required to choose a surprised or neutral face.

Despite this similarity there were also potentially important differences that could account for the reported better performance. One difference was that Wellman & Bartsch gave the subjects 'warm-up' stories. These stories were structurally the same as the test stories but with different story contents. The important difference between these and our own warm-up stories was that Wellman & Bartsch gave subjects feedback on how the protagonist would feel. This could have *taught* the subjects that they were supposed to point to the surprised face when there was a discrepancy between the protagonist's thoughts and the story outcome leading to correct responding without real understanding.

Another difference in procedure was that in our experiments the subjects saw the story develop and, therefore, knew about the critical outcome before the protagonist found out about it. Consequently the outcome was not surprising to subjects. In Wellman & Bartsch's experiment the subjects were first told what the protagonist thought would happen. Then they found out, together with the protagonist, the story outcome. The subjects may well have formed the same expectation as the protagonist and have been surprised themselves. This opens the possibility that subjects simply labelled the event 'surprising' according to their own perception and therefore judged that the protagonist was 'surprised' because they themselves were seeing a 'surprising' event. In other words, the subjects could have given correct answers without understanding that surprise depends on a belief–reality discrepancy.*

A third difference in procedure with Expt 2 is that Wellman & Bartsch directly described the protagonist's belief and repeatedly emphasized what it was, as we did in Expt 1. In Expt 2 the subjects were able to infer it from the story events.

The next experiment tested whether these procedural differences could account for the differences in results between studies.

Experiment 3

To explore the potential reasons for subjects' better performance in Wellman & Bartsch's study we manipulated three factors. First of all we taught half the children what emotional response a person would show when that person's belief was violated and when it was not violated, as Wellman & Bartsch had done in their warm-up stories.

Secondly, we manipulated whether the subjects were *surprised themselves* by the story, as in Wellman & Bartsch's procedure or whether they had *advanced knowledge* and had to infer the protagonist's surprise purely on grounds of his/her belief.

The third manipulation concerned *presentation of belief*. On half the stories subjects were simply told what the protagonist believed (as in Wellman & Bartsch's stories and Expt 1) without further motivation as to why. On the other half the subjects had to infer the belief from story events, as in Expt 2. In this case the origin of the protagonist's belief was *motivated*. We originally thought that a background story showing the reasons for the protagonist's belief would improve surprise judgements. However, the data reported by Wellman & Bartsch compared to the performance of

---

*This possibility is reminiscent of a recent finding about children's understanding of knowledge (Wimmer, Hogrefe & Perner, 1988). Three-year-olds are perfectly able to judge whether they know or do not know the contents of a box with no apparent understanding of how they acquired that knowledge (i.e. that they know because they looked inside or were told).

our 5-year-olds in Expt 2, raises the possibility that our manipulation might have had the opposite effect.

Method

Subjects. Forty-eight children from a local primary school took part in the study. There were three age groups; 4 years (4.66–4.92, mean age = 4.79, 10 girls, 6 boys), 5 years (5.0–5.83, mean age = 5.32, 8 girls, 8 boys) and 6 years (6.0–6.83, mean age = 6.45, 8 girls, 8 boys).

Materials. For each story two or three coloured pictures were used depicting the important story events. There were four stories: 'rabbit', 'flag', 'rain' and 'chocolate' stories. The first two stories were adapted from Expt 2. The 'rain' version was adapted from one of Wellman & Bartsch's stories. For each story there was a match and a mismatch version.

As an illustration of our stories we give here a *teaching story* in which the protagonist's belief is *motivated* and subjects have *advanced knowledge* of the story outcome. *Picture one* (showing a girl throwing a ball for her puppy). Sophie is throwing a ball for her puppy in the garden. Now it is time for tea. Sophie puts her puppy in the pen and goes to fetch the ball. Sophie likes it when her puppy is in its pen outside and she likes it when her puppy is in the kitchen. She has put her puppy in the pen. *Picture two* (showing the puppy jumping out of the pen). While Sophie is fetching the ball the puppy jumps out of the pen and runs indoors. Sophie didn't see the puppy do that. Sophie thinks the puppy is in the pen outside. *Picture three* (showing Sophie in the kitchen and the puppy under the table). Sophie goes into the house for her tea. She thinks the puppy is in the pen. She walks into the kitchen and sees the puppy under the table. She didn't think it was there. Sophie will look like that (point to picture with surprised face) when she sees the puppy under the table.

In the corresponding *test story* the subjects were not told what the protagonist thought but had to infer his/her belief. Also the final information in the last two sentences was replaced by a *belief question*: 'Did she think it was there?', and an *emotion question*: 'How will Sophie look when she sees the puppy under the table?'.

To produce the *unmotivated belief* version the background story was omitted. The puppy's actual location and where the girl thought it was were directly stated. To create the stories where the subjects themselves were surprised the information given in picture two, about the puppy jumping out of the pen, was simply suppressed.

In all test stories the subjects were asked to indicate protagonist's emotion by pointing to one of the two pictures used in Expt 2.

Design and procedure. The experiment was a mixed within–between subjects design. The subjects were randomly assigned to one of the four experimental conditions produced by the two between-subject factors advanced knowledge and teaching surprise. The within-subject factor was presentation of belief (depicted, unmotivated belief vs. inferred, motivated belief).

In each condition subjects had four stories, two match stories and two mismatch stories. Stories were told in match-mismatch story pairs. One match and mismatch story pair were such that the belief was depicted and in the other pair the belief had to be inferred. For each of the four stories different story materials were used. The order of within-subject condition (depicted vs. inferred belief) and the order of match–mismatch stories within the story pairs were counterbalanced.

The subjects in the teach conditions were taught one match story and one mismatch story. The important feature of these stories was that the subjects were told what emotion the protagonist should have.

Results and discussion

The subjects were scored as correct in a particular condition if they made correct surprise attributions on both the match and the mismatch story pairs. Otherwise they were scored as incorrect.

The first analysis concerned the within-subjects factor. That is whether *presentation of belief* had an effect on performance. This contingency between motivated and unmotivated stories is shown in Table 3. Table 3 shows the pattern of correctness for the frequency for all the subjects. The first column shows there were nine subjects who found surprise attribution easier in the stories where they had to infer a well-motivated belief than in the stories where the belief was just described. Only four subjects showed the opposite pattern. This difference was not significant (McNemar's χ^2 (1) = 1.92, $p < .2$, $N = 13$).

Table 3. Frequency of correctness in belief presentation condition across between-subject conditions in Expt 3

Correct in the two belief presentation conditions	Total	Age			Advanced knowledge		Teaching	
		4	5	6	yes	no	yes	no
Perfect	24	2	10	12	15	9	15	9
Motivated only	9	3	4	2	1	8	3	6
Unmotivated only	4	3	1	0	2	2	0	4
Both incorrect	11	8	1	2	6	5	6	5

To keep the subsequent analysis of between-subjects factors concise we scored the subjects as correct if they made correct surprise attributions on all four stories, and as incorrect otherwise. Logistic regression on the proportion of 'correct' subjects with factors age, sex, teaching (two teaching stories vs. none) and advanced knowledge showed four significant effects, age (χ^2 (1) = 13.5, $p < .001$, $N = 48$), advance knowledge (χ^2 (1) = 4.2, $p < .03$, $N = 48$), teaching (χ^2 (1) = 4.6, $p < .04$, $N = 48$) and an interaction between teaching and age (χ^2 (1) = 4.8, $p < .03$, $N = 48$).

Looking at the first row in Table 3, there is a sharp rise in correct attributions between 4 and 5 years (χ^2 (1) = 8.5, $p < .01$, $N = 32$). Performance by the 4-year-olds was still very bad and there is not statistically significant indication that any of them understood the basis for surprise attribution.

The effect of *advance knowledge* was expected but in the opposite direction. We thought that if subjects had no advance knowledge of story outcome they would experience the same surprise as the protagonist which would help them understand his/her emotion. In fact, fewer subjects made correct surprise attributions to the protagonists in this condition than in the one where subjects did have advance knowledge of story events. This is shown in Table 3.

The third significant main effect was teaching. This effect was as expected. If one tells the subjects in the teaching trials what a protagonist feels then more are able to make the same attributions in the test stories than without such teaching. This factor also interacted significantly with age. This interaction is due to the fact that 4-year-olds showed no sign of correct surprise attribution whether they were taught or not. At 5 and 6 years, however, teaching had an effect. With teaching all 5- and 6-year-olds were perfect, whereas without teaching only half of them were perfect.

Regardless of condition, these results confirm that 4-year-olds find surprise attribution on the basis of belief violation close to impossible. The interesting aspect of this is, of course, not that they are 4 years old (Wellman & Bartsch's sample seemed a bit more advanced in this respect), but that these subjects were very proficient at understanding false belief.

The best test for understanding false belief was the mismatch story in which the belief had to be inferred. All but one 4-year-old were able to make this inference and remember what the protagonist's belief was to the end of the story. Clearly, there is a substantial lag between understanding belief, a good understanding at 4 years, and understanding its emotional consequences, surprise attributions are not perfect before 6 or even 7 years. In the next experiment we look at a possible reason for this large developmental gap.

Experiment 4

The previous experiments established a consistent and quite considerable developmental lag between children's ability to understand false belief or expectation and their ability to understand surprise as triggered by the observed mismatch between expectation and reality. In this experiment we explore the possibility that this particular lag is an instance of a more general problem, namely that there is a developmental lag between understanding belief and understanding that emotional reactions depend on belief.

To test this theoretical possibility we were interested in looking at other belief-dependent emotions, especially at those emotions that are understood early in life. Happiness and sadness, the first emotions that children talk about, in principle, also depend on belief. This dependency is usually ignored because a person's belief about reality coincides with reality. When a person is mistaken about reality, however, then his/her emotional reaction will depend on what he/she believes rather than on what is actually the case. For example, if a person is mistaken about the content of a coke can that is presented to him/her as a gift, then his/her emotional reaction will depend on what he/she believes is in the can and not on what actually is in it. If the person likes coke than he/she would be happy, at least until the can is opened and it is discovered that the contents are, e.g. milk, which the person dislikes.

Hogrefe, Wimmer & Perner (1986) and Perner *et al.* (1987) found that by 4 years children become very proficient in understanding that a naïve person looking at a typical container like a coke can will think that it contains coke, even though the child knows that it contains something different. Harris, Johnson, Hutton, Andrews & Cooke (1989) used this experimental paradigm to assess children's understanding of happiness and sadness based on false belief. These authors found that few children before the age of 5 years, but a majority after that age, understood the belief dependence of these emotions. Even some 6- and 7-year-olds had difficulty. Harris *et al.* attributed this difficulty to the possibility that their experimental procedure failed to make children understand the protagonist's false assumptions about the container's contents (Harris *et al.*, 1989, pp. 390–391).

For the present experiment we adopted this misleading container paradigm. Children's understanding of protagonists' happiness and sadness and also of protagonists' surprise when they find out about the container's real contents was tested. We anticipated a replication of the results by Hogrefe *et al.* (1986) and Perner *et al.* (1987) that 4-year-olds will understand that a protagonist will be misled by a container's appearance. If we then find that children who understand the protagonist's false expectation also understand the dependence of happiness and sadness on that false expectation, but do not understand surprise, then the general hypothesis that there is a gap between understanding false belief and understanding its impact on emotions can be rejected. If, however, there is a comparable gap between understanding belief and belief-based happiness as there is between understanding belief and belief-based happiness as there is between understanding belief and surprise then the more general hypothesis will be confirmed.

Method

Subjects. Seventy-two children from a local school took part in the study. There were three age groups: 4 years (4.16–4.83, mean age = 4.64, 10 girls, 14 boys), 5 years (5.0–5.75, mean age = 5.41, 14 girls, 10 boys) and 6 years (6.0–6.83, mean age = 6.4, 9 girls, 15 boys).

Materials. There were four different stories. A smarties box and a jelly-baby packet were used for the 'sweets' story, a milk carton and juice carton for the 'drinks' story, a cornflakes box and egg box for the 'food' story and a crisp packet and peanut packet for the 'snacks' story. For each story there was a match and a mismatch version. Cardboard figures represented the four different story protagonists and their mother.

As an illustration we present the mismatch 'sweets' story in which the protagonist feels happy: 'Tommy's mother is going to buy Tommy something to eat. Tommy likes smarties, but he doesn't like jelly-babies'.

Check question: 'What does he like?' 'What doesn't he like?' 'Tommy's mother tells Tommy that she is going to buy him smarties. She goes off to the shops, she sees the smarties and jelly-babies. She picks up the smarties for Tommy'.

Check question: 'What does Tommy like?' 'What doesn't he like?' 'Before Tommy sees the smarties we'll play a trick on him. We'll take the smarties out of the box and put some jelly-babies in there'.

Check question: 'Did Tommy see us do that?' ['no'] 'Tommy comes into the room, he sees the packet on the table. Tommy hasn't looked inside yet'.

Belief question: 'What does Tommy think is in the packet?'

Emotion question: 'How will Tommy look when he sees the packet on the table?' (choice between happy and neutral face). 'Why?'

The story ended by asking how Tommy will look (happy or not happy) when he discovers the real content. Practically all subjects were, however, correct on this question.

In the version where the protagonist, upon seeing the box, was *not happy*, mother by accident bought jelly-babies which were surreptitiously replaced by smarties. In the surprise versions of these stories it was initially emphasized that the protagonist liked both items equally much: 'Tommy likes smarties and Tommy likes jelly-babies, he likes them both the same'. After the belief question these stories continue with: 'Tommy goes over to the packet and has a look inside, he sees the jelly-babies in there'. This is followed by an *emotion question*: 'How will Tommy look when he sees the jelly-babies in the smarties box?' (choice between surprised and neutral looking face.)

In a match story the protagonist's belief matched reality. In the surprise version when the protagonist's belief is confirmed he will not be surprised. In the happy version a protagonist either likes or dislikes an item which he thinks is in a container. On seeing an item and discovering that his belief about its contents is true the protagonist will be happy or not happy.

In all stories children had to respond to the emotion question by pointing to one of two faces showing the relevantly different emotional expressions. The surprise pictures were the same as those used in Expts 2 and 3. For the happy stories a black and white photograph showing a happy face was used along with the same neutral face as in the surprise condition.

Design and procedure. Half the subjects in each age group were randomly assigned to surprise and happy conditions. In both conditions each subject heard four stories, two match stories and two mismatch stories. In the surprise condition this meant that the subjects heard two stories that resulted in surprise and two in no surprise. In the happy condition the subjects heard a match story and a mismatch story that resulted in the protagonist being happy and one that resulted in him/her not being happy. Match and mismatch stories were counterbalanced for each condition. In the happy condition the assignment on happiness and no happiness was also counterbalanced across the match and mismatch stories.

At the beginning of the first story the subjects were shown the pictures with the two different emotion expressions. Their attention was drawn to the difference between the two faces. The subjects were told that at the end of each story they would have to point to one of the pictures to show how the person in the story would look.

Results and discussion

Of the four stories that each subject was tested on we treated the first two as warm-up stories and based our analysis only on the second story pair. Inspection of the data showed no systematic difference between responses on the first and second story pair.

The proportion of subjects who made correct attributions of surprise or belief-based happiness in the second story pair was analysed by stepwise logistic regression. For the factors age, sex, emotion condition (happy or surprised), story order, age was the only significant effect (χ^2 (1) = 12.6, $p < .001$, $N = 72$).

Table 4 shows the number of subjects with a particular response pattern on the match and mismatch story for happy and surprise condition separately. In both conditions the proportion of 4-year-olds with a correct response pattern (first row in each panel) was not significantly different from guessing in the happy (McNemar's χ^2 (1) = 0.67, $p > .5$, $N = 4$) or in the surprise condition (McNemar's χ^2 (1) = 0.2, $p > .7$, $N = 3$). In both conditions a significant proportion of 5-year-olds gave correct

Table 4. Frequency of response patterns on second match–mismatch story pair in Expt 4

Answer pattern for match–mismatch stories	Age			All ages
	4	5	6	
Happy condition				
+ +	4	7	11	22
+ −	5	5	1	11
− +	2	0	0	2
− −	1	0	0	1
Surprised condition				
ns+ s +	3	6	7	16
ns+ ns −	2	1	0	3
s − s +	5	5	4	14
s − ns −	2	0	1	3

Note. In the happy condition a match or a mismatch story could lead to a 'happy' or a 'not-happy' outcome. Since there was no discernible effect as story outcomes, these response differences are not reported.

answers in the happy (McNemar's χ^2 (1) = 7.0, $p < .01$, $N = 7$) and in the surprise condition (χ^2 (1) = 6.0, $p < .02$, $N = 6$). For the surprise condition this result closely replicates results from the last experiment showing that surprise is understood as a function of belief violation at about the age of 5 years. The results from the happy condition closely replicate the finding by Harris *et al.* (1989) where only a significant proportion of children older than 5 years can make belief-based attributions of happiness. Furthermore, in both conditions there is a large and statistically reliable gap between understanding belief and making belief-based attributions of emotions. Only four subjects in the happy (two 4- and two 5-year-olds), and two subjects in the surprise condition (two 4-year-olds) failed to infer the protagonist's false belief correctly. Consequently there were 12 subjects in the happy condition who failed to make correct attributions of happiness despite correct belief inference while only two subjects showed the opposite pattern (NcNemar's χ^2 (1) = 4.6, $p < .05$, $N = 14$). In the surprise condition these two frequencies were 18 and nought (McNemar's χ^2 (1) = 18.0, $p < .001$, $N = 18$).

The similarity in performance and of the gap between understanding belief and belief-based attribution of emotions in the two conditions strongly suggests that children encounter a general problem of understanding that belief determines emotions. It is not understood before the age of 5 or 6 years, even though most 4-year-olds have a firm understanding of when people are mistaken about reality.

General discussion

Experiment 1 provided a clear replication of Yuill's (1984) results that children as young as 3 years are very proficient in understanding 'pleased' as a function of the match or mismatch between a mental state (desire) and reality (the actual outcome). We initially hoped that Yuill's method of explicitly depicting a mental state to infer emotional consequences from its correspondence with reality would enable us to demonstrate that 3-year-olds have some understanding of false belief, which other studies have reported as very difficult at this age (Perner *et al.*, 1987; Wellman & Bartsch, 1988; Wimmer & Perner, 1983). This was dispelled, however, when we found how difficult it is for children to understand surprise as a function of the match or mismatch between belief and reality.

This difficulty of surprise attribution for children can have two kinds of explanation. The difficulty can have a non-cognitive source in the emotion surprise. We will consider several possibilities but conclude that they cannot explain our results satisfactorily. Alternatively, it may be the cognitive basis for surprise which is difficult to understand.

Concerning non-cognitive sources of difficulty with surprise, one might look at different theories of emotion for an answer. Most theories distinguish between basic emotions and complex emotions. It would be reasonable to assume that basic emotions are easier to understand than complex emotions. This could explain why 'pleased' is understood so much earlier than 'surprised' if a theory classifies 'pleased' as a basic emotion while classifying 'surprise' as a complex emotion. Unfortunately, most theories of emotion do not provide an explanation for the developmental gap observed. For instance, Ekman, Friesen & Ellsworth (1972) classify emotions as basic if there is a physiologically determined facial expression of the emotion. Similarly Tomkins (1962) and Izard (1977) emphasize the importance of the role of facial response in the expression of emotion. All these authors consider 'surprise' and 'pleased' ('joy') to be basic emotions.

Other authors, however, have questioned surprise as a basic emotion (Izard, 1971) or even as an emotion at all (Ortony, Clore & Collins, 1988). They are in agreement with other theorists (Roseman, 1984, Stein & Levine, 1987), firstly in the acknowledgement that cognition plays a major role in determining an emotion, and also, in noting the transience of the emotion surprise. They propose that surprise will occur as the result of some unexpected event but will be quickly replaced by some negative or positive emotion that is directly related to an individual's goals or desires. So the desirability or undesirability of some event to a person will be the predominant force in the determination of his/her emotion.

The surprise stories in Expts 2 to 4 were presented to children so that the neutrality of the story outcome in terms of fulfilment or non-fulfilment of the protagonist's desires were stressed. It was hoped that this would emphasize the unexpectedness and expectedness of a situation and so make the emotions 'surprise' and 'not surprise' easier to attribute on the basis of that dimension.

But emphasis on neutrality of outcomes may not have completely eliminated the possibility that children overlook the surprise aspect of the stories in favour of an emotion that reflects the desires of the protagonist. Since this possibility only applies to the attribution of surprise, it can account for the fact that 'surprise' was much more difficult to attribute than 'pleased'. It could not, however, explain the late development of children's understanding of belief-based happiness. In this case the story outcome is directly related to the beliefs and desires of the protagonist, yet children show a developmental understanding that parallels an understanding of surprise.

Other non-cognitive reasons to explain why pleased is understood earlier than surprised can be excluded. One can dismiss the possibility that familiarity of emotion label accounts for the observed difference. As noted in Expt 1, Bretherton *et al.* (1986) reported that even before the age of 3, 13 per cent of children used the word 'surprised', while 'pleased' is not even mentioned in their frequency count.

Another possibility is that children were interpreting surprise in a way that other authors have mentioned (Wellman & Bartsch, in press), as being a 'pleasant surprise', and that our precaution of omitting the verbal label 'surprise' was ineffective. The experimental stories were written to emphasize the unexpectedness of the story outcome and its neutrality in terms of desirability to the protagonist. None of the story outcomes, however, could be considered to be undesirable to the protagonist. If children interpret every outcome as being a 'pleasant surprise' one would expect a high proportion of the children who made errors in their choice of emotion to have chosen a 'surprise' response for both a match and a mismatch story outcome.

To investigate this possibility we looked at the response patterns for all children younger than 6. Of the children who gave wrong response patterns in Expts 1 to 4, 54, 46, 43 and 66 per cent respectively, said that the protagonist would be 'surprised' regardless of story outcome. This indicates and gives further evidence that many children younger than 6 may indeed interpret surprise as being something pleasant rather than something unexpected.

However this explanation for why younger children made so many errors in attributing 'surprise' leaves one question unanswered: Why do children of 6 years and above switch to a different understanding of surprise?

This question can be answered by the finding of Expt 4 that children at that age acquire the ability to predict emotions on the basis of belief. So it is at this age that they can switch from interpreting 'surprise' as a 'pleasant event' to 'something unexpected' since the notion of 'unexpected' is based on 'violating one's belief'. We have to consider the reason why understanding of belief and prediction of emotion based on belief develops relatively late.

The observed developmental lag between attributing 'pleased' and 'surprised' is very surprising because the tasks are structurally almost identical. The only difference is that the bubble needs to be understood in one case as depicting a desire and in the other as depicting a belief. However, Perner (1988) argued that to understand false belief children need to understand what the belief *represents*. In the case of our story, the boy's belief (mis)represents the situation behind the wall. In contrast, desire need not be understood as representation but can be understood as a desirable situation. That is, the content of the 'want-bubble' depicts the situation (it need not depict the representation of a situation) which the protagonist desires, namely that the girl catches the ball. The last picture in the story shows that either this situation has become reality (and the protagonist is pleased given his desired situation has become real) or a different situation has materialized (and the protagonist won't be pleased). The important point of this analysis is that desire need not be interpreted as a 'mental representation' but only as a mental attitude towards a situation (the protagonist desires the situation shown in the bubble).

An obvious question is why the same analysis would not apply to belief. To make the necessary distinction clear Perner (in press) drew attention to two different uses of the word 'think'. When combined with the particle *'of'* it expresses a mere thought, not belief. For example, I can say: 'Sam *knows* that the boy has the ball but he *thinks of* the girl holding it'. In contrast, I cannot say: 'Sam *knows that* the boy has the ball but *thinks that* the girl has it'. This sentence is contradictory because when paired with 'that' the word 'think' expresses a belief, and a person cannot know something and believe in something different at the same time. Alternatively, one can know something and think of it as being different at the same time.

The important point of this analysis is that one could indeed interpret a 'think-bubble' like a 'want-bubble' as depicting some situation to which the protagonist is mentally linked. However, such an interpretation would amount only to a 'think-of-bubble', while what is needed to understand surprise is a 'think-that-bubble'. To see that 'that' is necessary, all we need to do is to rephrase the story by using 'thinks of': 'Sam *thinks of* the girl having the ball (which leaves open the possibility that he actually knows that the boy has it). So, when Sam looks behind the wall and sees that the boy has it will he be surprised?'. This question has no clear answer since the story information did not specify what Sam believed. He may have known that the boy had the ball and would, therefore, not have been terribly surprised to find that confirmed.

Perner (1988) has argued that to understand belief (as opposed to mere thought, i.e. 'thinking of') requires conceptualizing mental states as mental *representations*, rather than orientations towards situations. Since understanding the cognitive basis of surprise requires understanding belief ('thinking that') as mental representation it becomes clear why surprise is not understood before the age of 4 years (Wimmer & Perner, 1983; Perner, 1988).

The fact that belief is understood at about 4 years of age, however, leaves unexplained why surprise attributions do not become systematic until about 5 or 6 years. Our answer to this question is descriptive. We suggest that for some reason it takes time (about two years) to work out that emotions are determined by belief and are not a direct function of reality. We tried to substantiate this contention by showing that the same lag which occurs in understanding surprise as a function of the match between belief and reality occurs in understanding belief-based happiness.

We do not understand the reasons for this developmental lag between understanding belief and understanding its emotional impact. In fact, its existence is rather puzzling in view of 4-year-olds' great proficiency in understanding the impact of belief on action. For instance, as soon as children understand that a person believes an object is in a different place than where it really is, they also understand that the person will look for the object in that wrong place (Wimmer & Perner, 1983). There seems to be no developmental lag whatsoever (Perner *et al.*, 1987).

As it stands, the observed developmental lag between understanding belief and understanding its emotional impact is an interesting but puzzling finding. Future research into the reasons for its existence is needed. Our present study does show that children's understanding of emotions or at least their prediction of emotional reactions like 'pleased' and 'surprise' is constrained by their understanding of prerequisite mental states. Their understanding of 'pleased' ('happy') emerges very early when only the match between desire and reality has to be considered, but it emerges much later when a false belief about reality becomes relevant. Therefore children's ability to attribute surprise emerges equally late since the understanding of belief is always essential.

Acknowledgements

The authors thank Mrs C. Shane, Head of Queens Park County Primary, Mr L. Bradshaw, Head of Downs County Infant, Miss J. E. Kirkaldie, Head of Coldean County Infant, Mrs J. Brooks, Head of Patcham County Infant, Mrs H. Waddup, Head of Hangleton County Infant, Miss Lamb, Head of White House Nursery, their staff and pupils. Thanks also to the County Education Officer of East Sussex. The experimental data reported here form part of a doctoral dissertation funded by the Medical Research Council. The preparation of the manuscript was greatly helped by a Social Science Research Fellowship from the Nuffield Foundation and a Research Fellowship from the Alexander-von-Humboldt Foundation to Josef Perner.

References

Astington, J. W. (1988) Intention in the child's theory of mind. Unpublished manuscript.

Barden, R. C., Zelko, F. A., Duncan, S. W. & Masters, J. C. (1980). Children's consensual knowledge about the experiential determinants of emotion. *Journal of Personality and Social Psychology, 39*, 968–976.

Bedford, E. (1986). Emotions and statements about them. In R. Harré (Ed.), *The Social Construction of Emotions*, pp. 15–31. London: Basil Blackwell.

Bretherton, I., Fritz, J., Zahn-Waxler, C. & Ridgeway, D. (1986). Learning to talk about emotions: A functionalist perspective. *Child Development,* **57**, 529–548.

Bullock, M. & Russell, J. A. (1984). Preschool children's interpretation of facial expressions of emotion. *International Journal of Behavioural Development,* **7**, 193–214.

Bullock, M. & Russell, J. A. (1986). Concepts of emotion in developmental psychology. In C. E. Izard & P. Read (Eds), *Measuring Emotions in Infants and Children,* vol. 2., pp. 203–237. Cambridge: Cambridge University Press.

Calhoun, C. & Solomon, R. C. (1984). *What is an Emotion?* Oxford: Oxford University Press.

Churchland, P. M. (1984). *Matter and Consciousness.* Cambridge, MA: MIT/Bradford.

Cicchetti, D. & Hesse, P. (1983). Affect and intellect: Piaget's contributions to the study of infant emotional development. In R. Plutchick & H. Kellerman (Eds), *Emotion: Theory, Research and Experience.* Volume 2: *Emotions in Early Development.* London: Academic Press.

Darwin, C. (1904). *The Expressions of Emotion in Man and Animals.* London: Murray.

Dennett, D. C. (1978). Beliefs about beliefs. *The Behavioural and Brain Sciences,* **4**, 568–570.

Dennett, D. C. (1987). *The Intentional Stance.* London: MIT Press.

Dixon, W. J., Brown, M. B., Engelman, L., Frane, J. W., Hill, M. A., Jennrich, R. I. & Toporek, J. D. (1981). BMDP Statistical Software. Berkeley, CA: University of California Press.

Ekman, P. (1980). *The Face of Man.* New York: STPM.

Ekman, P., Friesen, W. V. & Ellsworth, P. (1972). *Emotion in the Human Face.* New York: Pergamon.

Fabes, R. A., Eisenberg, N., McCormick, S. E. & Wilson, M. S. (1988). Preschoolers, attributions of the situational determinants of others' naturally occurring emotions. *Developmental Psychology,* **24**, 376–385.

Gnepp, J., McKee, E. & Domanic, J. A. (1987). Children's use of situational information to infer emotion: Understanding emotionally equivocal situations. *Developmental Psychology,* **23**, 114–123.

Green, S. K. (1977). Causal attribution of emotion in kindergarten children. *Developmental Psychology,* **13**, 533–534.

Harris, P. L. (1983). Children's understanding of the link between situation and emotion. *Journal of Experimental Psychology,* **36**, 490–509.

Harris, P. L., Johnson, C. N. & Harris, P. L. (personal communication).

Harris, P. L., Johnson, C. N., Hutton, D., Andrews, G. & Cooke, T. (1989). Young children's theory of mind and emotion. *Cognition and Emotion,* **3**, 379–400.

Hogrefe, G. J., Wimmer, H. & Perner, J. (1986). Ignorance versus false belief: A developmental lag in the attribution of epistemic states. *Child Development,* **57**, 567–582.

Izard, C. E. (1971). *The Face of Emotion.* New York: Appleton Century Crofts.

Izard, C. E. (1977). *Human Emotions.* New York: Plenum.

James, W. (1884). What is an emotion? *Mind,* **9**, 188–205.

Kenny, A. (1963). *Action, Emotion and Will.* London: Routledge & Kegan Paul.

Lazarus, R. S. (1982). Thoughts on the relation between emotion and cognition. *American Psychologist,* **37**, 1019–1024.

Lazarus, R. S. (1984). On the primacy of cognition. *American Psychologist,* **39**, 124–129.

Lyons, W. (1980). *Emotion.* Cambridge: Cambridge University Press.

Michalson, L. & Lewis, M. (1985). What do children know about emotions and when do they know it. In M. Lewis & C. Saarni (Eds), *The Socialization of Emotions,* pp. 117–139. London: Plenum Press.

Ortony, A., Clore, G. L. & Collins, A. (1988). *The Cognitive Structure of Emotions.* Cambridge: Cambridge University Press.

Perner, J. (1988). Developing semantics for theories of mind: From propositional attitudes to mental representation. In J. W. Astington, D. R. Olson & P. L. Harris (Eds), *Developing Theories of Minds,* pp. 141–172. Cambridge: Cambridge University Press.

Perner, J. (in press). On representing *that*: The asymmetry in children's understanding of belief and desire. In C. Moore & D. Frye (Eds), *Childrens' Theories of Mind.* Hillsdale, NJ: Erlbaum.

Perner, J., Leekam, S. R. & Wimmer, H. (1987). Three-year-olds' difficulty with false belief: The case for a conceptual deficit. *British Journal of Developmental Psychology,* **5**, 125–137.

Roseman, I. J. (1984). Cognitive determinants of emotion. A structural theory. In P. Shaver (Ed.), *Review of Personality and Social Psychology,* vol. 5: *Emotions, Relationships and Health,* pp. 11–36. Beverly Hills: Sage.

Schacter, S. & Singer J. (1962). Cognitive, social and physiological determinants of emotional state. *Psychological Review,* **69**, 379–399.

Shatz, M., Wellman, H. M. & Silber, S. (1983). The acquisition of mental verbs: A systematic investigation of the first reference to mental state. *Cognition,* **14**, 301–321.

Stein, N. L. & Levine, L. J. (1987). Thinking about feelings: The development and organization of emotional knowledge. In R. E. Snow & M. J. Farr (Eds), *Aptitude Learning and Instruction*, vol. 3: *Conative and Affective Process Analyses*, pp. 165–197. London: Erlbaum.

Strayer, J. (1986). Children's attributions regarding the situational determinants of emotion in self and others. *Developmental Psychology,* **22**, 649–654.

Tomkins, S. S. (1962). *Affect, Imagery and Consciousness*, vol. 1, *The Positive Affects*. New York: Springer.

Wellman, H. M. & Bartsch, K. (1988). Young children's reasoning about beliefs. *Cognition,* **30**, 239–277.

Wimmer, H., Hogrefe, G.-J. & Perner, J. (1988). Children's understanding of informational access as source of knowledge. *Child Development,* **59**, 386–396.

Wimmer, H. & Perner, J. (1983). Beliefs about beliefs: Representation and constraining function of wrong beliefs in young children's understanding of deception. *Cognition,* **13**, 103–128.

Yuill, N. (1984). Young children's coordination of motive and outcome in judgements of satisfaction and morality. *British Journal of Developmental Psychology,* **2**, 73–81.

Zajonc, R. B. (1980). Feeling and thinking. Preferences need no inferences. *American Psychologist,* **35**, 151–175.

Zajonc, R. B. (1984). On the primacy of affect. *American Psychologist,* **39**, 117–123.

Received 1 August 1989

5

Theory of mind
and communication

Preface

Because no one has direct access to the thoughts and meanings of others the child must rely on communication to find out what others think, know and believe, and must rely on communication to share mental states and experiences with others. Consequently, analyses of children's natural conversations about the mind have a seminal place in research on their understanding of the mind (Bretherton & Beeghly, 1982; Piaget, 1932; Shatz, Wellman & Silber, 1983). That tradition is ably represented, and advanced, by Brown & Dunn. Surprisingly little is known about talk to young children about the mind. It is implausible that children's conceptions are untouched by information available in everyday conversation. Brown & Dunn provide a look at this missing piece of the puzzle by analysing the nature of shared conversations about thoughts, feelings and desires in a particularly important age group, namely 2- and 3-year-olds.

The research by Fox concentrates on older children and on a different form of communication, namely children's narrative writing. Fox argues that children's production of coherent stories requires them to struggle with the depiction of characters' inner mental states. Further he argues that written efforts of this sort represent 'the tip of the cognitive iceberg' requiring that children bring their understanding of mind into conscious and explicit articulation. Fox's study represents an attempt to bring together two hitherto separate but conceptually related enterprises: research on theory of mind and research on narrative. Children come to understand not only that persons have inner mental states but also how these states cause acts and experiences to unfold in meaningful sequences—that is, children come to understand character and plot. Thus mind and narrative seem intricately linked and research on these topics is inextricably interwoven as well.

The very act of communication depends on distinctions that themselves embody understandings about the mind, for example the distinction between what is said (or written) and what is meant. An understanding of mind encompasses the difference between thought and speech, messages and meanings. The next two articles deal with these important distinctions.

Mitchell & Russell tackle directly children's understanding of the distinction between what is said and what is meant. Considerable prior research seems to show that even at 5 or 6 years children are often unable to distinguish the literal message itself from the speaker's intended meaning. Mitchell & Russell exploit (here and in an earlier study) a new paradigm which shows that even 5-year-olds can judge that an object was the one intended by a speaker while at the same time acknowledging that the speaker misdescribed it. They go on to ask what do 5- and 9-year-olds think cause speakers to mis-speak their intentions (e.g. to misdescribe the intended referent). They conclude that 5-year-olds understand misdescriptions only as something like production errors (the speaker inadvertently said the wrong word) but that 9-year-olds understand that a faulty representation can cause a misdescription (the speaker misremembered the referent).

Winner & Leekam examine more subtle forms of the say–mean distinction, namely those involved in the difference between white lies and irony. In both the speaker intentionally misdescribes an occurrence, but in one case intending to deceive and in the other intending to disparage. Children's ability to understand these non-literal communications depend on their ability to construe the mind as encompassing second-order mental states or intentions (e.g. the speaker wants the listener to believe falsely).

Research on children's abilities to communicate about the mind and abilities to understand the mental underpinnings of ordinary communication, such as is represented in this section, serves substantive and methodological purposes. Consider the methods used to study children's theories of mind throughout this volume and throughout the field. Our methods are very largely verbal; we rely on our abilities to communicate to children about beliefs, desires, and feeling in order to test their understanding of these notions and we rely on their abilities to communicate their beliefs about beliefs to us in the same manner. Mind and communication go hand in hand.

References

Bretherton, I. & Beeghly, M. (1982). Talking about internal states: The acquisition of an explicit theory of mind. *Developmental Psychology,* **18**, 906–921.

Piaget, J. (1932). *The Language and Thought of the Child.* London: Routledge & Kegan Paul.

Shatz, M., Wellman, H. M. & Silber, S. (1983). The acquisition of mental verbs: A systematic investigation of the first reference to mental state. *Cognition,* **14**, 301–321.

British Journal of Developmental Psychology (1991), **9**, 237–256 *Printed in Great Britain*

'You can cry, mum': The social and developmental implications of talk about internal states

Jane R. Brown* and Judy Dunn

Dept HDFS, S-110, Henderson Building, The Pennsylvania State University, University Park, PA 16802, USA

The social processes implicated in the early development of children's talk about desires, feelings and mental states were studied by analysing the content and pragmatic context of naturally occurring conversations at home. Six second-born children were observed with their mothers and older siblings at two-month intervals from 24 to 36 months. In addition to increases in the frequency with which children referred to internal states, developmental changes were noted in the content and context of their talk. These included: more frequent references to others' inner states, increased use of inner state turns in reflective discussions and in efforts to manipulate the feelings and behaviour of others, and more frequent references to the causes and consequences of inner states. Parallel changes were noted in mothers' conversations about inner states; maternal references to the thoughts, feelings and desires of those other than the child increased, and their use of these terms in behaviour-controlling contexts decreased. Results highlight the role of social interaction in children's developing understanding of inner states.

The development of an understanding of the desires, feelings and thoughts which motivate human behaviour is an important achievement in early childhood. Children grow up in a social world in which a folk psychology of everyday experience is shared by those around them (D'Andrade, 1987; Wellman, 1988). One of the expectations of children's significant others is that they will come to understand and put to use this knowledge as well. What is remarkable is that, within a few years of birth, children do demonstrate a relatively subtle understanding of some basic tenets of this folk theory of human behaviour.

The development of very young children's understanding of inner states and the psychological causes of behaviour has received a great deal of attention in recent years. The primary focus of this research has been to clarify the nature of children's knowledge about inner states. In the study of children in the first four years of life, several lines of research stand out. In the youngest children, these include observations of the onset of intentional communication (Bates, Camaioni & Volterra, 1975; Poulin-Dubois & Shultz, 1988) and children's recognition of others' independent

---

* Requests for reprints.

agency, both of which occur in the latter half of the first year of life (Harding & Golinkoff, 1979; Wolf, 1982). In the second and third years of life, observations of children's responses to others' emotions (Radke-Yarrow, Zahn-Waxler & Chapman, 1983) are coupled with studies of natural language which document children's use of terms for desires, feelings and mental states (Bretherton, McNew & Beeghly-Smith, 1981; Ridgeway, Waters & Kuczaj, 1985; Shatz, Wellman & Silber, 1983) as well as their attributions of these states to dolls in pretend play (Wolf, Rygh & Altshuler, 1984). All point to children's increasing ability to recognize, talk about and differentiate internal states. Experimental studies have traced children's ability to make correct inferences about behaviour by first imputing desire states to the actors when they are $2\frac{1}{2}$ years old (Wellman & Wooley, in press), to the inclusion of the actor's beliefs in children's reasoning after the age of 3 (Bartsch & Wellman, 1989). After the age of 3, children also demonstrate the ability to answer questions about the emotional states of story characters (Borke, 1971; Denham, 1986), and to articulate distinctions between the mental and the physical worlds (Estes, Wellman & Wooley, 1989).

While this research illuminates both the achievements and the limitations of children's understanding, two central issues remain relatively unexplored; both relate to the connections between these developments in understanding in the preschool years and children's interactions and relationships with others. The first unexplored issue concerns the functional significance of these developments for children's social relationships. Bretherton and her colleagues (Bretherton, Fritz, Zahn-Waxler & Ridgeway, 1986) comment, in their discussion of the development of children's understanding of emotions, that the most important gap in what we know about the ability to talk about and reflect on emotions concerns the use to which these developing powers are put in children's social relationships.

In a study of children's family conversations about feeling states during the second year it was noted that, already by 24 months, children were able to use their ability to talk about feeling states for a range of social functions (Dunn, Bretherton & Munn, 1987). However, the pragmatic functions of such talk were not examined in any detail. We do not know, for instance, whether such relatively sophisticated behaviour is first shown in situations of calm, reflective discussion or if it is in the urgency of children's attempts to have their own 'needs' met that they first begin to discuss inner states. Nor do we know how the pragmatic functions of their conversations change with age, although such information might provide insight into both the nature of children's understanding and the social processes implicated in its development. In addition, although there is some evidence that children's earliest use of inner state language includes references to *others'* feelings and thoughts (Bretherton & Beeghly, 1982; Shatz *et al.*, 1983), we do not know how often, relatively, they refer to others' vs. their own inner states in daily interaction, and whether this changes with early development.

Of particular theoretical interest is the question of whether the ability to talk about emotions adds to the children's ability to control the extremes of their emotions. It has been suggested that language offers toddlers an effective means for understanding and dealing with emotions to the end of greater self-regulation (Kopp, 1989). Although there is conflicting evidence as to whether children's emotional outbursts decrease or are heightened in the third year (see for example, Goodenough, 1931, or

Church, 1966), certainly the ability to say what is upsetting them should enhance children's chances of gaining specific comfort. One simple hypothesis, therefore, might be that as children talk more about feelings, thoughts and desires we would see a concurrent decrease in their displays of intense negative affect. Alternatively, children may not use language simply to the end of greater self-control, but to influence their own and others' feelings both positively and negatively; language should facilitate the child's ability to share funny moments, tease, provoke and annoy others, as well as to gain comfort when distressed. Therefore, a second, competing, hypothesis is that children's abilities to regulate affect develop more broadly, encompassing these emotion-inducing skills as well, and that their conversations about internal states reflect this development.

It has also been argued by Stern (1985) that with the acquisition of language there is a major change in children's interpersonal relationships, made possible by their new powers of negotiating 'shared meanings'. Among these 'shared meanings' are individuals' beliefs about the psychological causes of behaviour. But do early conversations about thoughts, feelings and desires fulfil this function? Stern's argument is made in very general terms. Others, including Bretherton and her colleagues, have argued that when children and others reflect on and talk about past experiences this 'fulfils a significant regulative and clarifying function, even in young children's conduct of interpersonal relationships' (Bretherton *et al.*, 1986, p. 546). Of particular interest in this regard are discussions between children and family members about the causes and consequences of thoughts, desires and feelings, as well as conversations in which past personal experiences of inner states are reflected on. But how often do such conversations take place in the daily interactions between children and other family members? Can we find evidence that early conversations about internal states serve this hypothesized function?

The second unexplored issue is the equally notable gap in our understanding of what social processes may be implicated in the *development* of these abilities. The part that early family interactions might play in the development of children's understanding of inner states and the psychological causes of behaviour has been little studied. An examination of the contexts in which children first begin to talk about internal states might provide insights into the processes that influence the development of such social knowledge: yet such information is at present lacking.

In particular, we know very little about how mothers talk about desires, feelings and thoughts to their young children, although their discourse in emotion-charged contexts has been related to later differences in children's altruistic actions (Zahn-Waxler, Radke-Yarrow & King, 1979) and to children's ability to articulate relatively sophisticated arguments in disputes (Dunn & Munn, 1987). Our understanding of the social influences on children's developing abilities would benefit from an examination of mothers' talk about inner states as well. Do mothers tend to talk about thoughts, feelings and desires in particular conversational contexts? And are there changes across the third year which reflect a changing emphasis in the function of mothers' internal state talk?

An additional set of questions about the social influences on children's acquisition of internal state language is raised by two findings: first, that children begin to use terms for mental states last among internal state terms (Bretherton *et al.*, 1981) and, second, that before the age of 3, children tend to explain human action in terms of desires only, rather than beliefs and desires (Wellman, 1990; Wellman & Wooley, in press). Terms denoting mental states may be more difficult for children to recognize and understand than emotion or desire terms for several reasons. For example, the general lack of facial and behavioural clues associated with mental states or the unspoken consensus that people within a group share about the mundane features of their daily lives could make thoughts and beliefs less likely to be the topic of discourse.

It is also possible that certain features of conversational references to mental states make them less salient for the young child. If, for example, the *child*'s thoughts are less likely to be the subject of mothers' mental state references, or if mothers refer to beliefs in less engaging conversational contexts than desires or feelings, or if thoughts are rarely the topic of causal conversations, then children may not attend to mental state references as avidly as they do to talk about feelings and desires. Such features of conversations about mental states could contribute to the observed delay in the use of mental state references.

In this study we set out to examine the naturally occurring conversations about inner states in which children took part with other family members during their third year. Our goals were: (1) to provide a detailed description of children's and mothers' references to desires, feelings and thoughts, including the frequency with which they occurred, about whose inner states family members spoke, and the conversational context in which such references were made; (2) to examine developmental changes in these characteristics of inner state conversations over the third year; and (3) to use this description to address the following questions regarding the social functions of inner state talk and the social processes implicated in its development:

(*a*) When do children first refer to desires, feelings, and thoughts: in the context of calm, reflective discussions or in the pursuit of their own immediate 'needs'?

(*b*) Do children demonstrate both an increase in their use of feeling state language and a concurrent decrease in their displays of intense negative affect over the third year?

(*c*) Do they demonstrate greater facility to regulate their own and others' feelings by referring to feelings, thoughts and desires in emotion-provoking contexts?

(*d*) Is there evidence that children and mothers engage in reflective discussions or discussions of the causes and consequences of inner states as early as the third year?

(*e*) Is there evidence that mothers' conversations about mental states differ from their references to feelings and desires in ways which might make talk about mental states less salient to children and thus contribute to the relative 'delay' in children's use of mental state terms?

These goals were pursued in a study focusing on six children about whom pilot data concerning children's questions and their narratives about other people were reported in Dunn (1988, pp. 130, 143).

Method

Subjects

The subjects were six second-born English children observed with their mothers and their older siblings, at home, at 24, 26, 28, 30, 33 and 36 months of age. There were three girls with older sisters, one girl with an older brother, one boy with an older sister and one boy with an older brother. The social class of the families according to the Registrar-General's (1973) classification of fathers' occupation was as follows: I/II (professional/managerial) for three families, III (white-collar) for two families and IV (semi-skilled) for one family. Two mothers were working part time, and one mother was employed as a home-worker during the period of data collection. One mother had had college education. The mean age difference between the siblings was 27 months (range 18–40). In this article the second-born child will be referred to as the child and the first-born as the sibling.

Procedure

Audiotape recordings of family conversations were made when the second-born children were 24, 26, 28, 30, 33 and 36 months old. At each of these time points two observations of 1 hour each were carried out, approximately one week apart, during which tape-recordings were made with a small portable stereo audiotape recorder. One observer carried out all the observations. All recordings were made in the home, at a time when child, sibling and mother were present, although not all three were necessarily in the same room for the entire observation. The observer recorded conversation in the room in which the child was present. To reduce the intrusive effect of the observer, she made at least one visit to the family before conducting the first observation, and did not begin recording until at least 10 min after her arrival. The mothers continued to carry out their usual household routine while the observer was present. The observer emphasized that we wished to study the children in their normal daily routine, and to disrupt family interaction as little as possible. The audiotape was transcribed by the observer shortly after the observation.

Transcript coding

The transcripts were analysed for conversational turns in which references to desire, feeling or mental states were made. A conversational turn was defined as all of one speaker's utterances bounded by the utterances of another speaker. Each conversational turn was coded to reflect who the speaker was, to whom the statement was made, and to whose feeling, desire or mental state the speaker referred (the *referent*). Because the children made relatively few such utterances, all child turns in which a reference to a feeling, desire or mental state were made were included in the analyses. Only those turns directed by mothers to the child were included in the analyses of mothers' talk.

The internal state terms included in the analyses are listed in Table 1. *Desire* terms were limited to the use of the words *want*, *need* or *would like*, indicating volition, motivation or a request for an object or an action on the part of another.

Mental state references were limited to mental verbs and phrases used to denote mental states. Following Shatz *et al.* (1983), conversational uses of mental verbs such as pause fillers or tags, e.g. 'you know', or 'don't you think?' were excluded. Also excluded from the children's mental state references were simple 'don't know' or 'I don't know' phrases without expansions.

Feeling state references included utterances in which the speaker used a feeling state term, e.g. *sad* or *happy*, those in which the speaker used a phrase which connoted a feeling state, e.g. *make a fuss*, or *what's the matter?*, and those in which an expletive was used which connoted a particular feeling state, e.g. *Yuck!* (disgust). Crying, laughter and other non-verbal expressions of affect were not included in the analysis of conversational turns. The term *like* was included only when it referred to a state of enjoyment or dislike, not when it indicated desire or volition. Terms which projected feeling states as attributes into the objects that elicit them, e.g. *poor* or *scary*, were included. Internal state terms indicating intention and statements of a strictly moral or evaluative nature were not included.

The *pragmatic context* in which each conversational turn was made was determined. Pragmatic context was defined as the explicit or inferred intention of the speaker who made the utterance. Twelve

Table 1. Examples of desire, feeling state and mental state terms

---

Desire terms
Want, need, would like and like, including terms which represented requests or served a request-fulfilling function, as in 'You want an apple?'

Feeling state terms
Fatigue: sleepy, tired
Boredom: bored, be tired of, have enough of (an activity)
Disgust: dirty, pooey, smelly, yuck, ugh, yucky-poo, eeuugh
Pain and discomfort: feel sore, be or get hurt, hurt someone, get or have a pain, die, ache, ouch (temperature included only if associated with pain or comfort—to burn, freeze, be hot, be cold)
Pleasure and liking of objects: happy, enjoy oneself or something, be cheerful, be glad, cheer up, something is fun, something is someone's favourite, like something, love to do something
Surprise: surprise, surprised
Anger: cross, angry, be fed up, be a nuisance, mad, temper, bad-tempered, mean, fuss, sulk
Fear: afraid (not as figure of speech indicating apology), frightened, frighten, scared, scary
Distress: sad, unhappy, miserable, be a misery, upset, upset someone, worried, disappointed, cry, fuss, make a fuss
Indifference: not minding, not caring
Concern: what's the matter? what's wrong? what did you do?
Affection: love, like a person
Sympathy: poor (about a person, or animate replica)
Dislike, hate (persons): not like someone, not love someone, hate someone, dislike someone
Dislike (objects): not like, hate
Contempt: laugh at someone
Shyness: shy

Mental state terms
Know, think, pretend, make sense, reckon, can't tell, wonder, suppose, bet, hope

---

pragmatic context categories were defined from analysis of a subset of six transcripts. These were grouped into three broad categories each for mothers' and children's turns. The pragmatic contexts in which mothers and children used internal state references varied and the groupings reflect these differences. Examples of each pragmatic category for child and mother turns are given in Appendix 1.

Three pragmatic categories differentiated the children's utterances in several theoretically important ways. First, children's use of internal state terms simply to call attention to their own immediate needs were isolated in the category *immediate self-interest*. Such instances inferred no understanding of another's contrasting knowledge, feelings or desires and were considered the most cognitively simple, basic use of internal state terms, e.g. 'Ow! Hurt me!' Included were: soliciting comfort or assistance, attempts to alleviate distress and drawing attention to own wants and needs. In contrast, utterances were coded as *sophisticated* when the child's knowledge of another's inner state could be inferred by her or his attempt to influence that person's behaviour or feelings. Often when children manipulated others, it was in pursuit of their own interests. But this context differed from that of immediate self-interest because the child acted directly on knowledge of the other's beliefs, desires or feelings. For example, one child, hiding her sibling's toy car in a towel, challenged her to, 'Guess what's in here!' but told her watching mother, 'I don't want you to guess this'. Included were: comforting another, teasing, both friendly and provocative, deception, attempts to avoid blame, and explaining one's actions. The *commentary* category was reserved for instances when the child's immediate needs were not at stake and she or he made no effort to manipulate another. These included: reflective discussions, simple commentary, narratives, and solitary or shared pretend. Pretend was included in this category for two reasons; it did not occur frequently enough to be analysed as an independent category and, for these 2-year-olds and their mothers, pretend was more closely related to shared narratives and reflective discussions about internal states than to contexts in which conversational partners tried to satisfy their own immediate needs or act on or manipulate each other's feelings or behaviour.

Mothers' utterances were grouped into the following categories: (1) *didactic/controlling*, i.e. efforts to control the behaviour of the child, teach moral lessons, or discipline the child; (2) *non-controlling/commentary*, i.e. discussions, commentary or narratives, including simple identification of an individual's desire, feeling or mental state, and solitary or shared pretend (mothers' use of desire terms which had a request-fulfilling function, as in, 'Do you want an apple?' were coded separately, and were not included in analyses of the pragmatic contexts); (3) *other*, i.e. comforting, teasing and calling attention to her own immediate needs.

It was also noted whether the speaker referred to a causal association during the internal state turn. Turns were coded as referring to cause if an explicit causal term was mentioned, e.g. *why* or *because*, or if a reference was made to two events or states which had a conditional relationship, e.g. 'Don't jump, you'll hurt yourself' (Hood & Bloom, 1979).

Positive and negative affect

The frequency with which the child expressed positive or negative affect during the observation was recorded by the observer and entered on the transcript. The following categories of positive and negative affect were coded: (1) mild positive—smiles and brief laughter, (2) intense positive—extended or intense laughter, including screaming and jumping up and down, (3) mild negative—fuss, grizzle or whine, and (4) intense negative—sustained crying or outbursts of anger.

Reliability of the transcript coding

The transcripts were coded by two coders. Reliability was calculated from coder agreement on eight transcripts. The percentage agreement for the identification of internal state turns was as follows: feeling state turns 94 per cent, desire turns 96 per cent, mental state turns 89 per cent. Inter-coder reliability for the categorization of referents and pragmatic categories was calculated using Cohen's kappa. Kappas for these measures were as follows: the referent of the utterance, $\kappa = .75$, whether the turn referred to causality, $\kappa = .73$, and the coding of the 12 individual pragmatic contexts of feeling state turns, $\kappa = .73$. Two coders together coded the pragmatic context of the mental state utterances and any disagreements were resolved by consensus.

Analyses

Changes over time were examined with log-linear maximum likelihood modelling for ordinal interaction (Agresti, 1984). In these analyses, scores of each individual child were entered separately as one dimension of the matrix, with the six time points of the study being the other dimension. In each set of analyses, an independence model was compared with a model including an ordinal interaction term, the difference between the two models (the reduction of the chi-square between the two models) being the contribution of the linear interaction. This model differs from an ordinary log-linear model which includes an interaction term that assumes an interaction between nominal variables; our model utilized a term that specifically demanded a monotonic change along the dimension of the ordinal variable, time. We specified that the changes not accounted for by the main effects were in a specific direction (see Dunn & Shatz, 1989).

Prediction analysis was used to test for specific differences in the frequencies of pragmatic contexts, referents and references to cause made in the three categories of mothers' internal state talk: feeling, mental and desire terms. As with chi-square analysis, the computation involved in prediction analysis is based on cross-classifications of predictors with criteria and involves statistical testing of the difference between observed and expected frequencies. Unlike the standard application of chi-square testing, however, prediction analysis compares estimated with observed cell frequencies only for particular cells, specified *a priori*, rather than across all cells. These cells, termed 'hit cells' contain the events that confirm the prediction. In addition to a test of statistical significance (z test), a 'del' statistic is computed which indicates the reduction in the percentage of errors obtained by applying the prediction to the model (see Szabat, 1990; von Eye & Brandstadter, 1988).

Results

In the following analyses the patterns of change in the frequency, content and contexts of the children's and their mothers' references to internal states over the third year are examined.

Table 2. Median frequency of references to internal states per 100 conversational turns and total turns

	Children's age in months		
	24–26	28–30	33–36
1. Child–desires			
Median	5.4	6.0	9.4
Range	(3.0–9.3)	(4.0 – 9.9)	(5.5–12.9)
2. Child–feeling states			
Median	3.2	3.7	5.4
Range	(0.8–4.2)	(2.5-7.2)	(3.2–5.7)
3. Child–mental states			
Median	0	0.14	0.73
Range	(0–0)	(0–0.53)	(0.1–1.7)
4. Mother–desires			
Median	6.6	6.6	6.1
Range	(3.0–12.1)	(3.9–11.4)	(2.4–9.4)
5. Mother–feeling states			
Median	6.3	5.9	6.6
Range	(2.8–8.4)	(2.4–8.6)	(3.8–7.2)
6. Mother–mental states			
Median	2.0	1.9	3.8
Range	(1.6–4.3)	(1.1–3.2)	(2.9–6.2)
7. Total turns–child[a]			
Median	420	338	321
Range	(194–573)	(192–496)	(201–493)
8. Total turns–mother to child[a]			
Median	351	190	205
Range	(149–472)	(108–430)	(66–388)

[a] Per two hours' observation.

Frequency of talk about internal states and affective displays

The first issue addressed concerned the frequency with which children and their mothers referred to desires, feelings or mental states during the third year. Table 2 reports the median frequency, for 100 conversational turns, of these references and the total child and total mother-to-child turns for each two hours' observation, at the beginning, middle and end of the year. For the sake of clarity, the frequencies have been grouped across two time points in this table, e.g. 22–24 months. The analyses were, however, carried out on the frequencies at each of the six times of measurement for each child. All of the children referred to feeling states and desires at the earliest measurement, while not one of the six children made reference to mental states until 28 months (Table 2, rows 1, 2, 3).

We tested whether there were significant changes in the frequency with which mothers and children referred to internal states over the third year. Table 3 reports the results of the maximum likelihood analyses which test for linear changes in the frequencies of internal state references over time. The analyses confirmed that the children made more references to both desires and feeling states as the year progressed (Table 3, rows 1 and 2). The apparent increase in children's references to mental states was not, however, significant (Table 3, row 3). Because the chi-square analysis is sensitive to the cumulative frequency of all cells in the matrix, we attributed this non-significant result to the overall low frequency and multiple empty cells in this particular matrix. It is clear from the raw data, however, that while none of the children used terms to refer to mental states at the beginning of the third year, all had used them by the end of the third year.

Table 3. Log-linear analyses of changes over time in frequency of conversational turns: Changes in maximum likelihood chi-square values

Measure	Model without interaction chi-square (d.f. = 25)	Model with interaction chi-square (d.f. = 20)	$\Delta\chi^2$ (d.f. = 5)	Direction of change
Child				
1. References to wants and needs	216.92	174.94	41.98*	increase
2. References to feeling states	116.54	97.41	19.13*	increase
3. References to mental states	6.41	3.02	3.38	n.s.
Mother				
4. References to wants and needs	113.90	106.57	7.33	n.s.
5. References to feeling states	139.88	130.36	9.52	n.s.
6. References to mental states	78.26	63.39	15.87*	increase

* $p < .05$.

In contrast to the children, their mothers did not refer to either desires or feeling states with increasing frequency over the third year (Table 3, rows 4 and 5). Only the frequency of their references to mental states showed a significant increase over time (Table 3, row 6).

Children's expression of positive and negative affect

No evidence was found that the children exerted greater control over their expressed emotions during the year; the children expressed intense negative affect as frequently at the end as they had at the beginning of the year (median number of episodes in which intense negative affect was expressed; 3 per two hours of observation at 24–26 months and 2.5 episodes per two hours' observation at 33–36 months; reduction in chi-square with ordinal model = 3.42, n.s.). They did, however, demonstrate a significant increase in the frequency with which they expressed positive affect generally; the median number of episodes of either mild or intense positive affect was 19 per two hours of observation at 24–26 months and 26 at 33–36 months (reduction in chi-square with ordinal model = 21.47, $p < .05$).

In summary, the children made more references to both feelings and desires over the third year, and each child began to use terms to refer to mental states by mid-year. These results are comparable with the findings from other research on children's acquisition of internal state language (Bretherton *et al.*, 1981; Shatz *et al.*, 1983). Mothers, on the other hand, only demonstrated significant increases in their references to mental states over the third year: that is to say, in the case of feelings and desires, where children's use of expressions to denote the internal states had already

Table 4. Proportion of internal state turns by referent and conversational context (median with range in parentheses)

	Children's age in months		
	24–26	28–30	33–36
Referent			
1. Others–child	.04 (.02–.14)	.18 (.10–.37)	.25 (1.80–.42)
2. Others–mother	.35 (.23–.54)	.36 (.19–.64)	.54 (.24–.66)
Context–child turns			
3. Immediate self-interest	.59 (.42–.86)	.48 (.26–.63)	.39 (.28–.46)
4. Sophisticated	.14 (.03–.36)	.16 (.06–.31)	.21 (.15–.33)
5. Commentary	.15 (.04–.30)	.30 (.24–.46)	.38 (.23–.42)
6. Causal references	.10 (.03–.22)	.10 (.05–.24)	.17 (.14–.22)
Context–mother turns			
7. Controlling child's behaviour	.32 (.18–.51)	.31 (.17–.50)	.19 (.12–.46)
8. Non-controlling/ commentary	.32 (.19–.51)	.34 (.18–.50)	.44 (.35–.65)
9. Other	.12 (.06–.18)	.12 (.02–.20)	.20 (.12–.22)
10. Causal	.28 (.21–.35)	.28 (.16–.45)	.31 (.24–.42)

been established by 24 months, no increase in the frequency with which mothers referred to them was noted after 24 months. However, the increased frequency with which mothers referred to mental states coincided with the onset of children's use of such references mid-year. These findings extend Beeghly, Bretherton & Mervis' (1986) laboratory observations of mothers of children at 13, 20 and 28 months; they found the mothers rarely referred to mental states until the 28-month measurement. The increased frequency with which the six children in this study used words to denote feelings and other internal states was not accompanied by a decrease in children's expressions of intense negative affect.

Changes in referent, context and references to cause over the third year

In order to examine the social functions of children's and mothers' inner state talk, we next explored whether these references varied either in content or in the conversational context in which they were made over the third year. Because we were interested in general patterns of change in these conversations, turns referring to mental states, feeling states and desires were grouped for these analyses. Median values and ranges for the proportion of the child and mother internal state turns in each of these categories at the beginning, middle and end of the year are reported in Table 4. The results of the log-linear analyses for these measures are reported in Table 5.

Table 5. Log-linear analyses of changes over time in referents and conversational context: Changes in maximum likelihood chi-square values

Measure	Model without interaction chi-square (d.f. = 25)	Model with interaction chi-square (d.f. = 20)	$\Delta\chi^2$ (d.f. = 5)	Direction of change
Referent				
1. Others–child	165.68	132.64	33.04*	increase
2. Others–mother	140.98	108.07	32.92*	increase
Context–child turns				
3. Immediate self-interest	136.61	122.09	14.52*	decrease
4. Sophisticated	194.11	142.22	51.89*	increase
5. Commentary	109.11	83.67	25.44*	increase
6. Causal turns	123.88	95.43	28.45*	increase
Context–mother turns				
7. Didactic/controlling	102.87	80.63	22.22*	decrease
8. Non-controlling/ commentary	64.56	62.48	4.06	n.s.
9. Other	181.43	152.38	29.05*	increase
10. Causal turns	85.90	76.78	9.12	n.s.

*$p < .05$.

Referents of child talk.   First, we considered whose feelings, thoughts and desires were the topic of conversational turns. Consistent with the findings of earlier research (Bretherton & Beeghly, 1982), the children tested here referred most often to their own internal states throughout the year. There was, however, a large increase in the frequency of their references to others as the year progressed. The proportion of child turns in which they referred to the internal states of someone other than themselves was very small at 24–26 months (median 4 per cent), but by 34–36 months the children referred to others in a quarter of their turns (median 25 per cent) (Table 4, row 1). The log-linear analyses confirmed that there was a significant increase in the overall proportion of these turns over time (Table 5, row 1). It is important to note that the absolute frequency with which the children referred to their own feelings, thoughts and desires did not decrease substantially over the third year. Rather, the increasing proportion of references to others is related to the overall increase in the frequency of their internal state references.

Referents of maternal talk.   Although throughout the year mothers also referred to the child in the majority of their conversational turns concerned with internal states (median 60 per cent), their references to the feelings, thoughts and desires of those other than the child also increased as the year progressed (Table 4, row 2). Log-linear analyses of this increase showed it to be statistically significant (Table 5, row 2).

Conversational context of children's talk.   We next examined the context in which the turns were made. The pragmatic category of children's talk labelled immediate self-interest included primarily simple demands for objects, assistance or comfort, and children made most of their references to internal states in this context (median 52 per cent of turns throughout the year). In 16 per cent of child turns, the child referred to an internal state in order to manipulate the feelings or behaviour of another (sophisticated category). The pragmatic category commentary included simple comments or more elaborate discussions of inner states as well as occasions when internal states were the topic of pretend play; these accounted for 28 per cent of all child turns. Table 4 (rows 3, 4 and 5) shows the proportion of child turns in each conversational context category at the beginning, middle and end of the year. It is apparent from the results in Table 4 that, over the year, the proportion of internal state turns children made in the context of immediate self-interest decreased while the proportion of both the sophisticated and commentary turns increased. The log-linear analyses of the changes in the proportions of child turns in these contexts were significant (Table 5, rows 3, 4 and 5).

Child reference to cause.   Next we examined the frequency with which children made reference to either the causes or consequences of their own or others' inner states. The children made these references with greater frequency as the year progressed (Table 4, row 6) and the increase was found to be significant (Table 5, row 6).

Conversational context, reference to cause in maternal talk.   Our examination of the pragmatic contexts in which mothers referred to internal states revealed fewer changes over the year than in the children's talk (Table 4, rows 7–10). The log-linear analyses confirmed that mothers spoke less often in efforts to control the children's behaviour as the year progressed (Table 5, row 7), and they spoke significantly more often about internal states when drawing attention to their own needs, or in playful or provocative contexts ('other', Table 5, row 9). The modest increase in mothers' non-controlling/commentary turns was not significant (Table 5, row 8), and no changes were noted in the proportion of mothers' turns in which they referred to causal relationships (Table 5, row 10).

Comparison between maternal references to mental states and their references to desires and feelings

The final set of analyses concerned the issue of whether maternal references to mental states differed from their use of feeling state and desire terms in such a way as might render mental states less salient a topic of children's everyday discourse. Using prediction analysis we tested the following hypotheses: (1) that non-controlling/ commentary rather than didactic/controlling discussions would predominate in mothers' use of mental verbs, (2) that the child's thoughts would be referred to less often than those of other people, and (3) that the causes and consequences of mental states would be discussed less frequently than those of desires.

Table 6 displays the results of these analyses. For each hypothesis the cross-classification of predictor variables (type of internal state term) is displayed against

Table 6. Mother's desire, feeling and mental state turns: Comparisons of the frequency of turns for context, referent and causal reference

	Frequencies			
	Observed	Expected	Observed	Expected
Context	Didactic/controlling		Non-controlling/commentary	
Desires	137[a]	108.2	108	136.8
Feelings	200[a]	170.5	186	215.5
Mental states	42	100.3	185[a]	126.7
	$z = 7.97$	$p < .001$	del $= .26$	
Referent	Child		Other	
Desires	408[a]	311.3	102	198.7
Feelings	292[a]	307.6	212	196.4
Mental states	69	150.1	177[a]	95.9
	$z = 9.23$	$p < .001$	del $= .30$	
Causal reference	Causal		Non-causal	
Desires	148[a]	116.0	149	181.0
Mental states	64	96.0	82[a]	150.0
	$z = 5.50$	$p < .001$	del $= .23$	

[a] Hit cells.

the estimated and observed frequencies for each of the criterion variables (conversational context, referent, causal reference). In each case statistically significant support was found for the hypothesized differences between mothers' use of mental state terms and their references to feelings or desires. That is to say: (1) mothers spoke about desires and feelings more often in the didactic/controlling context and mental states in the non-controlling/commentary context; (2) the referent of mothers' turns concerned with desires and feelings was most often the child, while they referred most often to the thoughts of someone other than the child; (3) mothers made more causal references in conversations about desires while non-causal turns predominated when mothers referred to mental states.

Discussion

At 24 months, the children in this study had already begun to use terms to denote feelings and desires, although they as yet had not made any references to mental states. They were preoccupied almost exclusively with their own desires and feelings, and referred to them most often in the urgency of their own immediate needs for comfort or assistance. By 36 months, all six children had begun to use terms to denote mental states and showed much more interest in the feelings and desires of others. They also referred to feelings, desires and thoughts in a widening variety of contexts, ranging from narratives about past events, to explaining their actions based on another's feelings. The patterns of maternal discourse across this year reflected reciprocal changes as the mothers increasingly directed the children's attention to the thoughts, feelings and wants of others, and their references to inner states were less frequently made in efforts to control the children's behaviour.

Two general issues were raised in relation to these data: first, what functions do these conversations serve and how do they change with development? Second, what social processes are implicated in the development and use of these abilities?

With regard to the first issue, it has been suggested that the ability to articulate feelings is central to children's developing ability to control the extremes of their emotions during the third year (Kopp, 1989). One simple conclusion which might be drawn from this hypothesis is that we should see fewer displays of negative affect as the children became more articulate about their feelings. This was not the case, however. Instead, our data suggest that a broader interpretation of the concept of affect regulation may better describe children's developing abilities in the third year. The children did use language to solicit comfort and relieve distress, but they also put language to use to humour themselves and to influence others' emotions, both positively and negatively. Instances when the children teased or comforted other family members increased in frequency over the third year. The significant increase in these occurrences highlights the children's increasing ability to influence their own and others' feelings. And the ability to *talk* about inner states adds considerably to the children's effectiveness as teasers, as comforters and deceivers, and as excusers of their own and others' actions when in trouble. Thus the ability to refer to inner states in an increasingly differentiated way—until now seen mainly as significant as a reflection of new cognitive abilities—has profound importance for children's social relationships.

With regard to the second issue, it is notable that desires, feelings and thoughts were discussed by mothers and children in a variety of contexts. It was apparent that for the children the salience of their own concerns most often precipitated this relatively sophisticated use of language. As has been revealed in studies of siblings' quarrels, very young children often show relatively advanced behaviour—in the sense of the use of justification and deceit—when their self-interests are at stake (Dunn & Munn, 1987). As the year progressed, however, so too did the children's ability to discuss inner states in more reflective contexts, including joint narratives and pretend play. These interactions provided children and mothers with opportunities to share and 'negotiate' interpretations of the meaning of events and their respective understanding of the psychological causes of behaviour. The evidence in this study suggests that some discussions between young children and their mothers about previously occurring events did fulfil the function of clarifying individuals' feelings, desires and the role of inner states in motivating their behaviour. Not only mothers, but the children as well, contributed clarifying information in such discussions, as when one child told her mother, 'I did want to put that carrot in', in response to her mother's comment that she (the child) had become very upset when they were baking together earlier in the day.

These discussions included narratives and scenarios acted out in shared pretend play. Pretend is a particularly potent setting in which children can reflect on internal experiences. Not only does pretend play provide children with a non-threatening setting in which to act out fears and negative experiences, but the argument has also been made that the imagining of another's feelings plays a central role in the development of social understanding in young children (Harris, 1989). Even for these very young children the desires and feelings of pretend characters provided the subject matter for their hypothetical stories. In summary, although the children most often used this relatively sophisticated language in the urgency of meeting their own immediate needs, the occasions on which they talked about thoughts, feelings and desires in more reflective settings gained greater prominence as the year progressed.

Two further points should be noted. The first concerns the relative 'delay' in the appearance of children's references to mental states as compared with their references to desires and feeling states. The analyses indicated that mothers, too, used a 'desire psychology' (Wellman, 1990) in everyday interaction, engaging in significantly fewer discussions of the causes and consequences of mental states than desires. Mothers also referred less often to the children's as opposed to others' mental states, and their references to mental states were more frequently made in relatively 'abstract' non-controlling/commentary turns than in the context of attempts to control behaviour. Each of these features of discourse about mental states may have made those references less salient to children than talk about feelings and desires; thus, they may play a contributory role in the 'delay'.

The final point concerns the developmental implications of the changes in mothers' talk about inner states. These changes presumably reflect a response to the children's developing abilities. However, this response may itself have developmental significance. It is important to note that the changes in content and context of mothers' talk provided the children with new challenges to their developing understanding. Towards the end of the third year the mothers placed new demands and expectations on their children through their own more elaborate use of reference to inner states. New research within a Vygotskian framework has made a powerful case for the developmental significance of such aspects of the social context for cognitive development (e.g. Wood, 1988), for language development (e.g. Shatz, 1987) and for socialization (Miller & Sperry, 1987). It is paradoxical that in the matter of children's understanding of their own and other people's thoughts, desires and feelings the role of social interaction in development has to date been little studied. This small-scale study represents a first step. Its findings clearly need to be replicated before we can generalize with confidence to larger populations.

In this regard, several important issues and areas for further study are suggested by our findings. First, although the results focused on normative developmental changes, large individual differences in the use of inner state language by both mothers and children were noted with even this small sample. This raises questions about the extent of individual differences in the onset and use of inner state language at this age, as well as the importance of these differences as antecedents and consequences of children's social understanding. One study has shown that variability in family talk about feelings in the toddler period is related to individual differences in children's affective perspective-taking ability in middle childhood (Dunn, Brown & Beardsall, in press), yet the implications of children's understanding of others' minds have been considered so far only in terms of normative development. It should also be noted that all of these children were second-born; whether the same pattern of inner state language would be found with a group of first-born children is not known. Perhaps more important than birth order *per se*, an essential area to be explored is the contribution of child–child interaction, seen by Piaget (1932) and Sullivan (1953) as especially important in the development of children's understanding of others. Finally, two conversational contexts included in our analyses of maternal–child talk about inner states—pretend and deception—deserve further investigation with a larger body of naturalistic data. Both pretend and deception figure prominently in the current debate on the nature of very young children's understanding of others' minds (Chandler, Fritz & Hala, 1989; Leslie, 1988), and this debate would be well served by a systematic study of children's spontaneous references to inner states in these two contexts.

This study highlights the importance of looking further at children's understanding of inner states within real-life social contexts; the striking developments of the third year have important implications for children's social relationships, and children's social interactions may contribute to these developments, which have until now been examined solely in terms of cognitive change. No account of the development of children's conception of inner states will be complete without an understanding of the social processes affected by and affecting that development.

Acknowledgements

This research was supported by the Medical Research Council, and by a grant to the second author from the National Institute for Child Health and Human Development (HD 23158–02).

We are very grateful to Penny Munn who collected the data, Mike Rovine for his assistance with the statistical analyses, and especially to the families who participated in the study.

References

Agresti, A. (1984). *Analysis of Ordinal Categorical Data*. New York: Wiley.

Bartsch, K. & Wellman, H. (1989). Young children's attribution of action to beliefs and desires. *Child Development*, **60**, 946–964.

Bates, E., Camaioni, L. & Volterra, V. (1975). The acquisition of performatives prior to speech. *Merrill–Palmer Quarterly*, **21**, 205–226.

Beeghly, M., Bretherton, I. & Mervis, C. (1986). Mothers' internal state language to toddlers: The socialization of psychological understanding. *British Journal of Developmental Psychology*, **4**, 247–260.

Borke, H. (1971). Interpersonal perception of young children: Egocentrism or empathy? *Developmental Psychology*, **5**, 263–269.

Bretherton, I. & Beeghly, M. (1982). Talking about internal states: The acquisition of an explicit theory of mind. *Developmental Psychology*, **18**, 906–921.

Bretherton, I., Fritz, J., Zahn-Waxler, C. & Ridgeway, D. (1986). Learning to talk about emotions: A functionalist perspective. *Child Development*, **57**, 529–548.

Bretherton, I., McNew, S. & Beeghly-Smith, M. (1981). Early person knowledge as expressed in gestural and verbal communication: When do infants acquire a 'theory of mind'? In M. Lamb & L. Sherrod (Eds), *Infant Social Cognition*. Hillsdale, NJ: Erlbaum.

Chandler, M., Fritz, A. & Hala, S. (1989). Small-scale deceit: Deception as a marker of two-, three-, and four-year-olds' early theories of mind. *Child Development*, **60**, 1263–1277.

Church, J. (1966). *Three Babies: Biographies of Cognitive Development*. New York: Vintage Books.

D'Andrade, R. (1987). A folk model of the mind. In D. Holland & N. Quinn (Eds), *Cultural Models in Language and Thought*. Cambridge: Cambridge University Press.

Denham, S. (1986). Social cognition, prosocial behavior, and emotion in preschoolers: Contextual validation. *Child Development*, **57**, 194–201.

Dunn, J. (1988). *The Beginnings of Social Understanding*. Cambridge, MA: Harvard University Press.

Dunn, J., Bretherton, I. & Munn, P. (1987). Conversations about feeling states between mothers and their young children. *Developmental Psychology*, **23**, 132–139.

Dunn, J., Brown, J. & Beardsall, L. (in press). Family talk about feeling states, and children's later understanding of others' emotions. *Developmental Psychology*.

Dunn, J. & Munn, P. (1987). Development of justification in disputes with mother and sibling. *Developmental Psychology*, **23**, 791–798.

Dunn, J. & Shatz, M. (1989). Becoming a conversationalist despite (or because of) having an older sibling. *Child Development*, **60**, 399–410.

Estes, D., Wellman, H. M. & Wooley, J. (1989). Children's understanding of mental phenomena. In H. Reese (Ed.), *Advances in Child Development and Behavior*. New York: Academic Press.

Goodenough, F. (1931). *Anger in Young Children*. Minneapolis, MN: University of Minnesota Press.

Harding, C. G. & Golinkoff, R. M. (1979). The origins of intentional vocalizations in pre-linguistic infants. *Child Development*, **50**, 33–40.

Harris, P. (1989). *Children and Emotion*. Oxford: Blackwell.

Hood, L. & Bloom, L. (1979). What, when, and how about why?: A longitudinal study of early expressions of causality. *Monographs of the Society for Research in Child Development*, **44**, 1–47.

Kopp, C. B. (1989). Regulation of distress and negative emotions: A developmental view. *Developmental Psychology*, **25**, 343–354.

Leslie, A. (1988). Some implications of pretense for mechanisms underlying the child's theory of mind. In J. Astington, P. Harris & D. Olson (Eds), *Developing Theories of Mind*, pp. 19–46. Cambridge: Cambridge University Press.

Miller, P. J. & Sperry, L. (1987). The socialization of anger and aggression. *Merrill–Palmer Quarterly*, **33**, 1–31.

Piaget, J. (1932). *The Moral Judgement of the Child*. New York: Free Press, 1965.

Poulin-Dubois, D. & Shultz, T. R. (1988). The development of the understanding of human behaviour: From agency to intentionality. In J. Astington, P. Harris & D. Olson (Eds), *Developing Theories of Mind*, pp. 109–125. Cambridge: Cambridge University Press.

Radke-Yarrow, M., Zahn-Waxler, C. & Chapman, M. (1983). Children's prosocial dispositions and behavior. In P. H. Mussen (Ed.), *Handbook of Child Psychology*, vol. 4, *Socialization, Personality, and Social Development*. New York: Wiley.

Registrar-General (1973). *Great Britain Summary Tables, Census 1971*. London: HMSO.

Ridgeway, D., Waters, E. & Kuczaj, S. (1985). Acquisition of emotion-descriptive language: Receptive and productive vocabulary norms for ages 18 months to 6 years. *Developmental Psychology*, **21**, 901–908.

Shatz, M. (1987). Bootstrapping operations in child language. In K. Nelson & A. Van Kleeck (Eds), *Children's Language*, vol. 6, pp. 1–22. Hillsdale, NJ: Erlbaum.

Shatz, M., Wellman, H. & Silber, S. (1983). The acquisition of mental verbs: A systematic investigation of first references to mental states. *Cognition*, **14**, 301–321.

Stern, D. (1985). *The Interpersonal World of the Infant*. New York: Basic Books.

Sullivan, H. S. (1953). *The Interpersonal Theory of Psychiatry*. New York: Norton.

Szabat, K. A. (1990). Prediction analysis. In A. von Eye (Ed.), *Statistical Methods in Longitudinal Research*, vol. 2. New York: Academic Press.

Von Eye, A. & Brandtstadter, J. (1988). Application of prediction analysis to cross-classification of ordinal data. *Biometric Journal*, **30**, 651–665.

Wellman, H. (1988). First steps in the child's theorizing about the mind. In J. W. Astington, P. Harris & D. Olson (Eds), *Developing Theories of Mind*, pp. 64–92. Cambridge: Cambridge University Press.

Wellman, H. (1990). *The Child's Theory of Mind*. Cambridge, MA:MIT/Bradford Books.

Wellman, H. & Wooley, J. (in press). From simple desires to ordinary beliefs: The early development of everyday psychology. *Cognition*.

Wolf, D. (1982). Understanding others: A longitudinal case study of the concept of independent agency. In G. Forman (Ed.), *Action and Thought*, pp. 297–370. New York: Academic Press.

Wolf, D., Rygh, J. & Altshuler, J. (1984). Agency and experience: Actions and states in play narratives. In I. Bretherton (Ed.), *Symbolic Play: The Development of Social Understanding*, pp. 195–215, New York: Academic Press.

Wood, D. (1988). *How Children Think and Learn*. Oxford: Blackwell.

Zahn-Waxler, C., Radke-Yarrow, M. & King, R. (1979). Child rearing and children's prosocial initiations toward victims of distress. *Child Development*, **50**, 319–330.

Received 5 March 1990; revised version received 9 July 1990

Appendix A

Examples from the transcripts

Pragmatic categories–child turns

Immediate self-interest: soliciting comfort or assistance, attempts to alleviate distress, drawing attention to own wants and needs

1. [Mother makes toy frog jump at child]
   C: Don't.
       No. You fright me.
   M: [laughs]
       It's only a toy, look.
2. [Sib is drinking out of shared cup]
   C: Don't you get all that.
       I want some.

Sophisticated: comforting another, teasing, both friendly and provocative, deception, attempts to avoid blame, and explaining one's actions

1. [Child wrapping Sib's toy car in towel]
   C to S: *Guess what's in here?*
               Guess what's in here?
   [car falls out]
   M to C: What are you doing?
   C to M: I don't want you to guess this.
2. [Child and Sib are having a pretend party with dolls. Child sits one of the dolls on toy potty.]
   S: They should've went before they started the party.
       Shouldn't they of, Heidi?
   C: *They all want to go to the toilet!*
       [Child takes out more dolls, squeals with laughter, puts all the dolls on pot together.]

Commentary: reflective discussion, simple comments, narratives, and solitary or shared pretend

1. [Child puts doll in drawer, talks to mother]
   C: *He want go in here.*
2. [Child plays with two pieces of Lego, makes on 'hold' the other, talks to self]
   C: *Him crying.*
       Him crying.
       Cuddle him crying.

Pragmatic categories–mother turns

Didactic/controlling: efforts to control the behaviour of the child, teach moral lessons, or discipline the child

1. [Child is on mother's lap, is wearing special bead necklace]
   M: Come on, down you go.
       [Child fusses]
       Stop it. Stop it.
       Do you want your beads off?
2. [Child sitting near the stove, points at burner]
   C: Hot.
   M: *You know you don't touch that, don't you?*

Non-controlling/commentary: reflective discussion, simple comments, narratives, simple identification of an individual's desire, feeling or mental state, solitary or shared pretend

1. [Child is looking for doll clothes]
   C: Are they in this bag?
   M: *I don't know where they are.*
2. [Mother and child playing pretend game, getting ready to go shopping, C holds up shopping list]
   C: Me write my name.
   M: You write your name? Why?
        So if you lose it then they'll know whose it is?
   C: Yeah.

Other: comforting, teasing and calling attention to her own immediate needs

1. [Child pats mother's face]
   M: *Owwwwww! I'll cry!*
   C: Dadoway. [hugs mother]
   M: Hm?
   C: You can cry, mum.
   M: *I can cry if I want? Thank you.* [pretends to cry]
   C: Ahhh.
2. [Mother and child are reading nursery rhymes together]
   C: Humpty Dumpty sat on a pole. Can't read it.
   M: *Nor can I. I don't know how it goes.*
   C: Says 'Humpty Dumpty'. That one is Humpty Dumpty anyway.
   M: I know it is.
   C: You sing it then.
   M: *I don't know how it goes.*
   C: You do!
   M: *I don't. I've forgotten.*

Note. Turns coded as occurring in specified context are shown in italics.
Sib of S = sibling; M = mother; C = child.

British Journal of Developmental Psychology (1991), **9**, 257–270   *Printed in Great Britain*

257

Distinguishing irony from deception: Understanding the speaker's second-order intention

Ellen Winner*

Boston College and Harvard Project Zero

Sue Leekam

La Trobe University, Victoria, Australia

This study investigated how children detect the attitude behind irony and distinguish it from the attitude conveyed by a white lie. Two hypotheses were tested: (1) the ability to distinguish the second-order intentions of the liar vs. ironist (i.e. what each wants the listener to know) should be a prerequisite for the ability to distinguish ironic from deceptive attitude; (2) the presence of distinctive intonations (sarcastic vs. sincere) should facilitate the distinction between ironic and deceptive attitude. Five- to 7-year-olds heard two stories which ended in either a deceptive or an ironic statement. Children distinguished between the stories in two ways: (*a*) in terms of whether the speaker wanted the listener to believe him or not (second-order intention judgement); (*b*) in terms of whether the speaker was being mean or nice (attitude judgement). In one condition, the final utterances were distinguished by intonation (sarcastic for the irony, sincere for the lie); in the other condition, the utterances were spoken identically, without intonation, in the form of an indirect quote. Results supported the first but not the second hypothesis. Almost all children who failed to make correct second-order judgements also failed to distinguish which speaker was being mean (ironist) and which was being nice (white liar). However, those who succeeded on the second-order question but failed the attitude question were equally distributed across the intonation and no-intonation conditions. Thus, for children of this age, intonation failed to facilitate the ability to distinguish the negative attitude conveyed by irony from the positive attitude conveyed by a white lie.

Imagine a situation in which a mother asks her two sons to clean up their messy rooms. The older son complies, but the younger one does a sloppy, half-hearted job and then quits. After a while, the mother and older son peek into the younger boy's still messy room. The older boy turns to the mother standing in the doorway and remarks, in mocking intonation, 'Peter did a *great* job cleaning up'.

This is an example of simple verbal irony. The older brother does not say what he means; nor does he mean what he says. Instead, he has said something positive about

* Requests for reprints should be sent to Ellen Winner, Psychology Department, Boston College, Chestnut Hill, MA 02167, USA.

a state of affairs (he did a great job) to indicate something negative about the situation (he did a bad job). This form of irony is typically spoken in a negative, mocking, sarcastic tone of voice. However, it may also be uttered in a deadpan or exaggeratedly sincere tone. Finally, intonation may be entirely absent, as when irony is encountered in written form or when a speaker reports on what someone has said by indirect quote (e.g. He said that Peter did a great job).

Ironic statements are not the only kinds of utterance in which a speaker says something good about a bad situation. 'White lies' are also utterances which are false, and which claim something to be positive when the speaker knows the situation to be negative. Irony and white lies can be distinguished from each other on at least two related but distinct levels. To begin with, they differ in what the speaker wants the listener to know as a result of the utterance (referred to hereafter as the speaker's *second-order intention*). In the above example, the brother wants the mother to know that the little brother has not done his job (and also that the big brother knows this). Had the utterance been a white lie, the brother would *not* have wanted the mother to know that the job was poorly done. A similar analysis for the distinction between jokes and lies has been proposed by Leekam (1988, 1990), who argues that lies can only be distinguished from other intentional falsehoods on the basis of the speaker's intention about the listener's belief.

Irony and white lies also differ in terms of the kind of *attitude* that the speaker intends to convey. The ironic speaker intends to convey a negative attitude of some sort; the speaker who utters a white lie intends to convey a positive attitude, one of praise.

Two theories of irony have recently been proposed, both of which grant a central role to the speaker's attitude. According to the pretence theory of irony (Clark & Gerrig, 1984), the older brother in the above example would be pretending to be the kind of person who would think that the room is clean, in order to mock anyone naive enough to make such a judgement. And according to mention theory (Sperber, 1984), the big brother would be mentioning rather than asserting the statement about the room in order to mock the proposition that the room was clean, and thus mock whoever would assert such a proposition. According to both theories, therefore, the big brother would be seen as wishing to convey a hostile attitude towards the little brother. The big brother mocks the little brother by implying that the little brother thinks that the room is clean.

Verbal irony of this sort is very common, and adults in our culture seem effortlessly to understand its usage (Gibbs, 1986; Rosenblatt & Winner, 1987). In contrast, children under 6 to 8 years consistently fail to understand verbal irony (Ackerman, 1981; Demorest, Silberstein, Gardner & Winner, 1983; Demorest, Meyer, Phelps, Gardner & Winner, 1984; Winner, 1988; Winner, Windmueller, Rosenblatt, Bosco & Best, 1987). Demorest *et al.* (1984), for example, asked children to make sense of false statements such as, 'Your haircut looks terrific', in contexts in which the utterance was intended as a white lie (the speaker adopts a friendly intonation and expression) or as irony (the speaker adopts a mocking intonation and expression). Six-year-olds mistook deceptive utterances for sincere–true ones almost half the time. This age group had even more trouble with irony. About one-third of the time, 6-year-olds interpreted the ironic utterances as sincere–true or mistaken utterances. And about half the time they took the ironic utterances as white lies.

Thus, children found it relatively easy to recognize the falsehood in an ironic statement, and hence to distinguish irony from literal truth. Similarly, they found it relatively easy to recognize the deliberateness of the falsehood, and hence to distinguish irony from a mistake. Where they faltered was in the ability to distinguish a falsehood intended to mislead (deception) from a falsehood intended to be recognized as false (irony).

Previous studies of children's irony comprehension have for the most part assessed understanding by assessing understanding of the speaker's intentions about the listener's belief. Researchers have assessed the ability to distinguish between irony and deception by testing children's ability to determine that the ironic speaker wants the listener to disbelieve the statement, whereas the liar wants the listener to believe just what is said (e.g. Demorest *et al.*, 1984). In other words, what has been assessed is children's ability to make judgements about *what the speaker wants the listener to believe*. We refer to this as a second-order intention judgement because it is a judgement of the speaker's intention to affect another person's belief state. We consider a second-order intention to be structurally similar to a second-order belief, i.e. a belief about another person's belief state (cf. Perner & Wimmer, 1985; Yuill & Perner, 1987). Both second-order intentions and second-order beliefs involve one person's mental state (either an intention or a belief) about another person's belief state. And both are central components of a full theory of mind.

It is known that children understand first-order beliefs (beliefs about something other than a mental state) by at least 4 years of age (Wimmer, Gruber & Perner, 1984; Wimmer & Perner, 1983; Wellman, 1990). However, they do not understand second-order beliefs until between the ages of 6 and 8 (Perner & Wimmer, 1985). This finding is consistent with research on irony comprehension showing that children are not able to assess what it is that the speaker wants the listener to believe until after the age of 6 (Demorest *et al.*, 1984).

Recall the opening example of the ironic utterance about the clean room. Suppose the little brother failed to realize that his big brother wanted the mother to believe that the room was still a mess. In this case, we would not credit the little brother with an understanding of his older sibling's irony. Thus, grasping what the speaker wants the listener to believe is an essential component of irony comprehension.

While this level of comprehension seems necessary, it is surely not enough. To credit the little brother with full understanding, one would also need evidence that he recognized that his brother was mocking him. That is, one would need evidence that he recognized the negative attitude that his brother was trying to convey to him and his mother.

The existing research on irony comprehension does not reveal when children can distinguish the ironist's attitude from that of the liar. Nor does it indicate which factors lead to a recognition of the ironist's attitude. The purpose of this study was to investigate when children recognize the ironist's negative, mocking attitude. In addition, the study was designed to test the role of two factors in the recognition of ironic attitude: (1) the ability to detect the second-order intention of the ironic speaker and distinguish this from the second-order intention of the white liar; and (2) the presentation of the irony in sarcastic intonation. We presented children with two similar stories about a boy who did not clean up his room. One story ended in an ironic utterance by the older brother about how clean the room was, and one ended in a deceptive utterance. The two utterances were identical, but given their preceding contexts, one was interpretable as ironic, and the other as a white lie. We asked children to compare the two stories to distinguish between (1) the second-order intention of the ironist vs. the liar, and (2) the attitude intended to be conveyed by the ironist vs. the liar. We presented the ironic utterance either with sarcastic intonation or without. This design enabled us to test the following two hypotheses.

Hypothesis 1: Detecting second-order intentions facilitates attitude detection

According to hypothesis 1, the ability to distinguish between the two speakers' second-order intentions is a prerequisite for the detection of speaker attitude. Thus, children should not recognize the ironist's attitude unless they also recognize the speaker's second-order intentions (i.e. that the speaker does not want the listener to believe the statement).

Hypothesis 2: The presence of sarcastic intonation facilitates attitude detection

According to hypothesis 2, the detection of speaker attitude should be facilitated by the presence of sarcastic intonation. The most likely possibility is that once children grasp second-order intention, they are assisted in their detection of ironic attitude by the presence of intonation. Those children who grasp second-order intention would be more likely to go on to recognize that a speaker is being 'mean' when her statement is uttered with sarcastic intonation than when it is not. Another possibility, however, is that the facilitating effect of intonation might prove independent of the ability to distinguish second-order intentions. Thus, children might be able to detect the negative attitude behind irony without grasping second-order intentions if the irony is spoken in sarcastic intonation. In this case, hypothesis 1 would be disconfirmed.

In summary, the study was designed to answer two questions. First, is the ability to distinguish between the second-order intentions behind irony vs. lie a prerequisite for the detection of the attitudes intended to be conveyed by the two speakers? Second, how far does intonation further faciliate the detection of attitude? Does it enhance comprehension once the child has already grasped second-order intention? Or does it allow direct detection of attitude, independent of understanding second-order intention?

Method

Subjects

A total of 63 children were tested. The ages ranged from 5:0 to 7:0, and the mean age was 5:5. There were 36 girls (18 between 5:0 and 5:11, and 18 between 6:0 and 7:0) and 27 boys (11 were between 5:0 and 5:11, 16 between 6:0 and 7:0). The children were recruited from three schools in the Boston area, one public and two private, serving middle- and upper-middle class populations. Children were seen individually at their schools, in a small quiet room, by one or two experimenters, for one 20-minute session.

Materials and procedure

Two versions of a story (the messy room story) were created and taperecorded. Each version contained seven sentences and a final utterance that was intended either as deceptive or ironic, depending on the prior story context (see Table 1). After both stories were presented, the two final pictures accompanying each story were placed in front of the child and two questions were asked (in counterbalanced order): the second-order intention question, and the attitude question.

Table 1. Irony and deception version of messy room story

Irony version (Little brother = Peter)	Lie version (Little brother = Sam)
Peter (Sam) wants to go out and play ball with his big brother. The mother says they must first clean their messy rooms. Peter's (Sam's) big brother quickly cleans up his room and goes outside. Peter (Sam) forgets all about cleaning up and reads his new comic books.	

First Picture

Picture of Peter (Sam) in messy room reading a comic.

Fact Probe

Is Peter's (Sam's) room clean or messy?

First-order Belief Probe-1

This is the mother down here. Does the mother know the room is still messy?

Now Peter (Sam) wants to go out and play. The mother does not know whether Peter's (Sam's) room is clean now. (So she goes with the brother to check Peter's room.) (So she sends Sam's brother to check Sam's room.)

Final Picture

Picture of brother and mother looking into messy room.	Picture of brother looking into messy room, mother downstairs.

First-order Belief Probe-2

This is the mother and this is the brother. They're both looking into the room. Does the mother know the room is still messy?	This is the mother down here. Does the mother know the room is still messy?

Test utterance, no-intonation condition

Peter's brother tells the mother that Peter did a great job cleaning up.	Sam's brother goes downstairs and tells the mother that Sam did a great job cleaning up.

Test utterance, intonation condition

Peter's brother tells the mother, 'Peter did a great job cleaning up'.	Sam's brother goes downstairs and tells the mother, 'Sam did a great job cleaning up'.

Second-order intention question. In one of these stories, the big brother (wants) (does not want) the mother to know how messy the room really is. Was that in this story (experimenter points to one of the two final pictures) or in this story (experimenter points to other final picture)? (Order of pointing was varied.)

Attitude question. In one of these stories, the big brother is being (mean) (nice) to his little brother. Was that in this story (experimenter points to one of the two final pictures) or in this story (experimenter points to other final picture)? (Order of pointing was varied.)

The second-order intention question was asked to determine whether the child could recognize the second-order intention pattern distinguishing irony from deception. The attitude question assessed whether the child detected the two different kinds of attitude conveyed by irony vs. deception.

As is shown in Table 1, each story was interrupted by three probe questions posed to the child directly by the experimenter while the tape was stopped. Only if the child answered each probe correctly did the tape resume. If the child did not answer correctly, the tape was played again until the probe question was repeated. All children answered the probes correctly on either the first or second try. The purpose of the probes was to ensure that the child understood the facts of the situation (the room was messy) and the mother's first-order beliefs (she either knew it was messy or she did not) both before and after the little brother went to his room, apparently to clean it up. While the inclusion of these probes interrupts the natural flow of the stories, such probes are essential in order to ascertain the child's comprehension of the critical elements distinguishing the deceptive from the ironic story version. Such probes have been successfully used in earlier studies of children's understanding of first- and second-order beliefs (Perner & Wimmer, 1985).

As a memory check, after children heard the final utterance they were asked to repeat it. We stopped the tape and asked, 'What did the big brother say to the mother?' Verbatim responses as well as para-phrases were accepted as evidence of accurate recall. If a child could not recall the final utterance, the utterance was replayed and the child was again asked to tell the experimenter what the brother had said. Most subjects recalled the utterance correctly on the first trial; no subject needed more than two trials.

Four $8\frac{1}{2} \times 11$ in coloured pictures were used, two for each story (Figs 1*a–d*). The pictures were used to engage the children's interest and to help children attend to the critical facts distinguishing the two stories: in the lie story the mother does not know that the room is still messy; in the irony story the mother does know. As can be seen in Fig. 1*c*, the final picture accompanying the irony story, the mother is upstairs with the older brother and both see the messy room together. In Fig. 1*d*, the final picture accompanying the lie story, the mother is downstairs and cannot see the messy room that the brother sees. The pictures were laid out in front of the child as each story progressed. The pictures for the first story were removed when the second story was played.

Approximately half of the subjects ($N = 35$) heard the stories in a no-intonation condition, in which the irony was conveyed as an indirect quote (e.g. Peter's brother tells the mother that . . .) so that the irony could be stated without sarcastic intonation and yet not sound odd. The remaining subjects ($N = 28$) received the stories in an intonation condition. In this condition, the ironic final utterance was spoken with moderately sarcastic intonation, and the deceptive utterance was spoken in pleasant, sincere intonation. The two utterances differed most markedly in the way that the term 'great' was spoken: in the ironic utterance, this term was stressed and was said in a somewhat nasal, flat tone, while in the deceptive utterance this term was said in a positive, pleasant tone. Five adults who knew nothing about the topic of the study listened to the two stories and then judged the attitude conveyed by each of the two speakers. All five adults judged that the brother in the ironic story sounded either sarcastic ($N = 3$) or angry ($N = 2$). They judged that the brother in the deceptive story sounded nice ($N = 1$), charitable ($N = 1$), serious ($N = 1$), sincere ($N = 1$), and deceptive ($N = 1$).

Four tapes were constructed, each containing the two versions of the messy room story. On tapes 1 and 2, the lie version came first; on tapes 3 and 4, the irony version came first. On tapes 1 and 3, the irony was spoken in a sarcastic intonation. On tapes 2 and 4, no intonation was present. Thus, the order of the versions was crossed with presence/absence of intonation.

Story order, question order, and question wording were counterbalanced and nested within condition, yielding eight different formats within each condition. [Twice as many subjects were inadvertently given the 'Mean, does not want' wording than the alternate version ($N = 41$ vs. $N = 22$).] Children were randomly assigned to a format and a condition.

The forced-choice measure was adapted from Leekam (1988). Such a measure, in which subjects

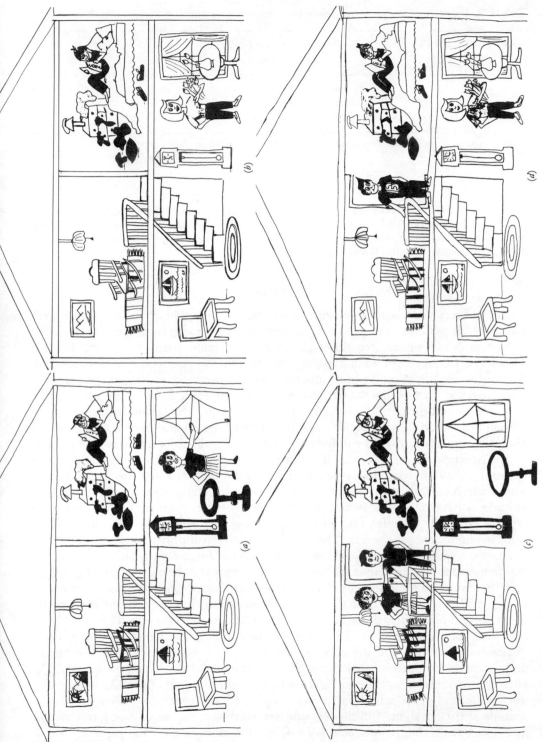

Figure 1. Story illustrations. (*a*) First irony picture; (*b*) first lie picture; (*c*) final irony picture; (*d*) final lie picture.

Table 2. Pattern of correct and incorrect responses summed across conditions

		Second-order question	
		+	−
Attitude question	+	28	4ₐ
	−	14_b	17

Note. + = correct; − = incorrect; cells a and b differ at $p < .05$, one-tailed binomial sign test.
$\chi^2 (1) = 11.3$, $p < .001$.

respond by choosing *between* two versions of a story, was designed to make the task easier. That is, the contrast between the two stories (in terms of the speaker's knowledge of what the mother knows, and, in the intonation condition, in terms of the speaker's intonation) serves to highlight the critical elements distinguishing irony from deception.

Results

Each child received a score of correct or incorrect for the two questions. There were four possible patterns of response: both correct; both wrong; second-order intention correct, attitude wrong; second-order intention wrong, attitude correct. Table 2 shows the frequency of each type of response in the two conditions combined. Responses to the second-order intention and attitude questions were strongly associated ($\chi^2 (1) = 11.3$, $p < .001$). As can be seen in Table 2, 18 of the subjects got only one question right (29 per cent). Of those, 14 got the second-order intention correct but attitude wrong, while only four showed the reverse pattern. A one-tailed binomial sign test showed the difference between 14 and 4 to be significant at $p < .05$.

The sign test result shows that if children are only going to succeed on one of our questions, they are more likely to succeed on second-order intention than attitude. This pattern of responses shows that children were rarely able to distinguish the attitude conveyed by the ironist vs. the liar when they failed to carry out the representationally complex task of distinguishing between the second-order intentions of the ironist vs. the liar. This result then gives support to hypothesis 1.

Since the questions were posed in a forced-choice format with only two choices, children responding at chance would be expected to make the correct response about half the time. Table 2 reveals that children responded correctly to the attitude question 32 times, and incorrectly 31 times. In contrast, children responded correctly to the second-order intention question 42 times, and incorrectly only 21 times. Given this, one might argue that children were responding at chance to the attitude question throughout, and thus that we can make no conclusions about whether an understanding of second-order intentions facilitates the detection of attitude. However, that this is *not* the case can be seen from the fact that of the 42 subjects who got the second-order intention question right, 67 per cent ($N = 28$) also got the attitude question right. Of the 21 subjects who got the second-order intention question wrong, only 19 per cent ($N = 4$) got the attitude question right.

Table 3. Pattern of correct and incorrect responses by condition

	Condition			
	Intonation		No intonation	
Question	Second-order		Second-order	
Attitude	+	−	+	−
+	14	1	14	3
−	7	6	7	11

Note. + = correct; − = incorrect; For the no-intonation condition: χ^2 (1) = 5.19, $p < .05$.
For the intonation condition, $x^2(1) = 3.876$, $p < .05$.

The fact that 28 out of 42 (67 per cent) of those who got second-order intention right also got attitude right (but not the reverse) suggests that understanding second-order intentions is necessary for understanding speaker attitude. However, the finding that 14 subjects succeeded on second-order but failed on attitude suggests that there is a lag between understanding the speaker's second-order intentions and grasping the speaker's attitude.

Were the 14 subjects who passed second-order intention but failed the attitude question the ones who were in the no-intonation condition? If so, this would support the second hypothesis which predicted that intonation would further facilitate the effect of second-order intention. Table 3 shows that this is not the case. Of the 14 subjects across conditions who passed the second-order but failed the attitude question, seven were in the intonation and seven in the no-intonation condition. Neither did intonation *directly* facilitate attitude comprehension: out of 15 subjects in the intonation condition who passed the attitude question, only one suceeded independently of the second-order intention question. In the no-intonation condition, of the 17 who passed the attitude question, only three did so independently of the second-order intention question.

Instead of independence between the two questions, responses to the two questions in the no-intonation condition were strongly associated, as shown by a significant chi-square test (χ^2 (1) = 5.19, $p < .05$). Responses to the two questions were also strongly associated in the intonation condition (χ^2 (1) = 3.876, $p < .05$).

The presence of intonation also had no effect on response to either question considered separately. Table 4 shows the pattern of correct and incorrect responses to each question separately by condition. Chi-square tests proved non-significant, revealing no relation between the presence of intonation and a correct response for either question.

Age also proved unrelated to performance. Table 5 shows responses to each question by age. A chi-square test proved non-significant. In addition, age was unrelated to the likelihood of subjects' showing a lag between grasping second-order intentions and speaker attitudes. Of the subjects between 5:0 and 5:11 years of age, 24 per cent showed such a lag; of those between 6:0 and 7:0 years, 18 per cent showed

Table 4. Pattern of correct and incorrect responses for each question by condition

| | Question | | | |
| | Second-order | | Attitude | |
Condition	No intonation	Intonation	No intonation	Intonation
Correct	21	21	17	15
Incorrect	14	7	18	13

Note. For the second-order question, χ^2 (1) = 0.97, n.s. For the attitude question, χ^2 (1) = 0.019, n.s.

Table 5. Pattern of correct and incorrect responses for each question by age

| | Question | | | |
| | Second-order | | Attitude | |
	Age: 5:0–5:11	6:0–7:0	5:0–5:11	6:0–7:0
Correct	21	21	17	16
Incorrect	8	13	12	18

Note. For the second-order question, χ^2 (1) = 0.39, n.s. For the attitude question, χ^2 (1) = 0.439, n.s.

Table 6. Number of subjects at each age showing a lag between understanding second-order intention and speaker attitude

| | Age | |
	5:0–5:11	6:0–7:0
Lag	7	6
No lag	22	28

Note. Lag = correct on second-order, incorrect on attitude; no lag = all other combinations of response.

the lag. This difference was not significant, as shown by a chi-square test on the number of children at each age who did and did not show a lag (see Table 6).

Both questions were affected by their wording. For the attitude question, children found the 'being nice' wording easier than the 'being mean' wording: 73 per cent responded correctly to the former vs. 31 per cent to the latter wording. In other words, when children were asked which brother was being nice, they were able to select the white liar 73 per cent of the time. But when they were asked which brother

Table 7. Pattern of correct and incorrect responses by question wording

		Wording			
		Mean, does not want		Nice, wants	
Question		Second-order			
Attitude		+	−	+	−
	+	13	3	15	1
	−	10	15	4	2

was being mean, they only selected the ironic brother 31 per cent of the time. This may have been due to what Kohlberg (1969) has termed the 'good boy' mentality, in which school-age children are reluctant to attribute bad motivations to others. If so, children should be reluctant to attribute negative motivations to speakers who utter self-serving lies rather than white lies.

For the second-order intention question, children found the 'wants to know' version easier than the 'does not want to know' (86 vs. 56 per cent correct, respectively). In other words, when children were asked which brother wants the mother to know, they correctly selected the liar 86 per cent of the time; when asked which brother did not want the mother to know, they correctly selected the ironist only 56 per cent of the time. The latter difference may have been due to the fact that negative questions are more difficult than positive questions to process (Clark & Chase, 1972). In addition, it suggests that the second-order intention behind a lie is easier to detect than that behind irony. That is, it is easier to represent 'X wants Y to know what I know' than to represent 'X does not want Y to know what I know'.

It should be stressed, however, that when the responses to each of the two kinds of wordings were separated into 2×2 contingency tables, the pattern was identical: in both, more children understood second-order intention but not attitude than the reverse pattern (see Table 7).

Discussion

The results suggest that children are for the most part unable to detect the critical attitude behind irony (and distinguish it from the attitude that the liar intends to convey) unless they are also able to make the distinction between the second-order intentions of the ironist vs. the liar. This appears to be the case even when irony is presented in an explicitly negative intonation. Even with mocking intonation, children did not recognize that the ironic speaker was trying to do something nasty unless they could also represent what the speaker wanted the listener to believe about the room as a result of the utterance.

Thus we suggest that the ability to detect the attitude behind irony and white lies is made possible by the ability to represent the speaker's second-order intentions. The inference that the speaker is being nasty, mean, or mocking (in the case of irony), or nice (in the case of a white lie) seems to be made only once one realizes that the speaker does or does not want the listener to believe the (positive) content of the utterance.

The recognition of the speaker's second-order intention appears to play just as important a role when the irony is distinguished from the white lie by sarcastic intonation. Such intonation does not further facilitate detection of attitude, nor does it provide a direct route to attitude detection. In short, the presence of intonation does not enable children to grasp the speaker's attitude if they have not grasped the speaker's second-order intention.

One possible explanation for the fact that the presence of sarcastic intonation did not alter the pattern of responses is that children did not perceive a difference in intonation between the irony and the deception in the intonation condition. A more likely possibility, however, is that the children detected the ironic intonation as different from ordinary intonation, but did not interpret it as signalling negative meaning. This explanation is consistent with other studies which have shown that children of this age do not find the presence of sarcastic intonation to be a determining factor in interpreting a statement as ironic (Ackerman, 1983; Winner *et al.*, 1987).

The generality of the findings is now being tested in a follow-up study in which children respond to another pair of stories. In addition, Perner & Wimmer's (1985) measure of comprehension of second-order mental states is being administered. If it is only those who succeed on both measures (ours and Wimmer & Perner's) of second-order mental state comprehension who also succeed on our measures of speaker attitude, convergent evidence for the present findings will be provided.

Some children who understood the ironic speaker's second-order intention still failed to detect the speaker's attitude. Understanding the attitude behind irony may require a recognition of a third-order mental state as well as a second-order one. In addition to the recognition that the 'speaker does not want the listener to believe the truth value of what is said', irony comprehension may also require the third-order judgement that 'the speaker wants (first-order) the listener to believe (second-order) that the speaker has a particular attitude (third-order)'. If so, it is not surprising that those children who can make the appropriate second-order judgement cannot necessarily distinguish the attitude of the ironist from that of the white liar. This may await the ability to understand the third-order intention above. This explanation could be tested by determining the relationship between irony comprehension and correctly inferring a third-order mental state.

To be sure, our results are correlational and we have not *proved* that understanding the attitude behind irony is facilitated by an attribution of second-order intention. It is of course possible that an understanding of the attitude behind irony and the ability to represent the second-order intentions of speakers develop independently. However, not only are our data consistent with the hypothesis of a relationship, but there are other reasons to expect such a link. According to our conceptual analysis of the kind of reasoning required to recognize the ironic speaker's attitude and distinguish it from that of the liar, understanding second-order intentions would appear to be a requirement. In addition, children's typical error of confusing irony with deception found in previous studies (Demorest *et al.*, 1983, 1984) suggests a specific failure to understand the ironic speaker's second-order intention. However, any definitive proof of causally related skills would require further, experimental intervention. One possibility, for example, would be to demonstrate that training in tasks that require the attribution of second-order intentions speeds up the ability to distinguish irony from deception in terms of speaker attitude.

The ability to represent second-order intentions is an essential component of a theory of mind. Children who are unable to represent second-order intentions, or to distinguish between two kinds of second-order intentions, appear to have a communication deficit which impedes their ability to determine whether speakers mean what they say when what they say is false. This in turn may limit children's ability to determine the speaker's attitude, at least in the case of irony vs. white lies. It would be important to determine the generality of this deficit, and to determine whether these children's problems extend to other forms of literally false utterances as well, such as idioms, indirect speech acts, and metaphors.

Acknowledgements

Portions of this paper were presented at the meetings of the Society for Research in Child Development, Kansas City, April 1989. We thank Karan Merry, Headmistress, and Wendy Borosavage, Director of the Lower School, Chestnut Hill School, Chestnut Hill, Massachusetts; Joyce Morrill, Director of the Montessori Educare School, Newton, Massachusetts; and Thomas Cavanagh, Principal of the Baker School, Brookline, Massachusetts, for allowing this research to be conducted at their respective schools.

References

Ackerman, B. (1981). Young children's understanding of a speaker's intentional use of a false utterance. *Developmental Psychology*, **17**, 472–480.

Ackerman, B. (1983). Form and function in children's understanding of ironic utterances. *Journal of Experimental Child Psychology*, **35**, 487–508.

Clark, H. & Chase, W. (1972). On the process of comparing sentences against pictures. *Cognitive Psychology*, **3**, 472–517.

Clark, H. & Gerrig, R. (1984). On the pretense theory of irony. *Journal of Experimental Psychology: General*, **113**, 121–126.

Demorest, A., Silberstein, L., Gardner, H. & Winner, E. (1983). Telling it as it isn't: Children's understanding of figurative language. *British Journal of Developmental Psychology*, **1**, 121–134.

Demorest, A., Meyer, C., Phelps, E., Gardner, H. & Winner, E. (1984). Words speak louder than actions: Understanding deliberately false remarks. *Child Development*, **55**, 1527–1534.

Gibbs, R. (1986). On the psycholinguistics of sarcasm. *Journal of Experimental Psychology: General*, **115**, 3–15.

Kohlberg, L. (1969). Stage and sequence: The cognitive–developmental approach to socialization. In D. A. Goslin (Ed.), *Handbook of Socialization Theory and Research*. New York: Rand McNally.

Leekam, S. (1990). Jokes and lies: Children's understanding of intentional falsehood. In A. Whiten (Ed.), *Natural Theories of Mind: Evolution, Development and Simulation of Everyday Mindreading*. Oxford: Basil Blackwell.

Perner, J. & Wimmer, H. (1985). John thinks that Mary thinks that: Attribution of second-order beliefs by 5- to 10-year-old children. *Journal of Experimental Child Psychology*, **39**, 437–471.

Rosenblatt, E. & Winner, E. (1987). Direct comprehension of metaphor and irony. Unpublished raw data.

Sperber, D. (1984). Verbal irony: Pretense or echoic mention. *Journal of Experimental Psychology: General*, **113**, 130–136.

Wellman, H. (1990). *The Child's Theory of Mind*. Cambridge, MA:MIT/Bradford Books.

Wimmer, H., Gruber, S. & Perner, J. (1984). Young children's conception of lying: Lexical realism–moral subjectivism. *Journal of Experimental Child Psychology*, **37**, 1–30.

Wimmer, H. & Perner, J. (1983). Beliefs about beliefs: Representation and constraining function of wrong beliefs in young children's understanding of deception. *Cognition*, **13**, 103–128.

Winner, E. (1988). *The Point of Words: Children's Understanding of Metaphor and Irony*. Cambridge, MA: Harvard University Press.

Winner, E., Windmueller, E., Rosenblatt, E., Bosco, L. & Best, E. (1987). Making sense of literal and nonliteral falsehood. *Metaphor and Symbolic Processes*, **2**, 13–32.

Yuill, N. & Perner, J. (1987). Exceptions to mutual trust: Children's use of second-order beliefs in responsibility attribution. *International Journal of Behavioural Development*, **10** (2), 207–223.

Received 5 March 1990; revised version received 9 November 1990

British Journal of Developmental Psychology (1991), **9**, 271–279 *Printed in Great Britain*
© 1991 The British Psychological Society

Children's judgements of whether slightly and grossly discrepant objects were intended by a speaker

Peter Mitchell*

Department of Psychology, University College of Swansea, Singleton Park, Swansea SA2 8PP, UK

James Russell

University of Cambridge

Five- and 9-year-olds heard stories in which a speaker described an object s/he wanted a listener to fetch. The listener found an object which was either slightly or grossly discrepant in relation to the description. Children of both ages sometimes judged positively that the discrepant object was the one the speaker intended, but only 9-year-olds judged positively more frequently when the discrepancy was small rather than gross. Therefore, children in both age groups seemed to acknowledge misdescription, but only older children utilized size of discrepancy as a clue to misdescription. We discuss the possibility that although 5-year-olds know about misdescription, unlike 9-year-olds they are weak at utilizing situational clues in judging whether misdescription has or has not occurred.

Our primary aim was to investigate further what children know about the distinction between what is said and what is meant. In particular we intended to investigate children's ability to utilize a contextual clue in conjunction with the message in judging whether a say–mean discrepancy had or had not occurred.

Most studies investigating young children's understanding of the say–mean distinction have been ones in which ambiguous messages were presented, and it seems the distinction in relation to such messages is not made until age 5 or 6 (e.g. Beal & Flavell, 1984; Robinson, Goelman & Olson, 1983). Beal & Flavell discovered that some children who had correctly judged ambiguous messages to be inadequate no longer did so when the experimenter pointed to the object which the speaker was attempting to describe. Robinson *et al.* discovered that children very often 'recognized' a disambiguated sentence as being the ambiguous one which had been uttered earlier. In both studies the conclusion was that when intended meaning and utterance meaning do not match, young children find it hard to evaluate message meaning independently of intended meaning. Other studies show that sometimes young

*Requests for reprints.

children make inappropriate non-literal interpretations, as in the examples reported by Donaldson (1978), and at other times prefer interpretations which are too literal, as in their interpretations of sarcastic remarks (e.g. Ackerman, 1981, 1982, 1983; Demorest, Meyer, Phelps, Gardner & Winner, 1984). Therefore, although children seem able to focus exclusively on the literal or the non-literal, the studies by Beal & Flavell and Robinson *et al.* suggest that they have great difficulty in attending to both simultaneously.

Mitchell & Russell (1989) tried to identify whether there were any circumstances in which young children would demonstrate awareness of mismatch between message meaning and intended meaning, and also began to investigate children's understanding of conditions which can give rise to discrepancies between what is said and what is meant. Using a technique devised by Ackerman (1979), Mitchell & Russell found that 5-year-olds did judge sometimes that an object found by a listener protagonist, which only approximated in its appearance to a description given by a speaker protagonist, was the object the speaker had intended. In judging that the approximate found object was the one intended, children apparently acknowledged that the speaker had misdescribed the object s/he intended, and thus exhibited an understanding that what is said is not always what is meant.

Moreover, we can argue that a judgement that the found object is the one intended implies a belief that the speaker has an incorrect representation of the intended object. A judgement that the found object is not the one intended implies a belief that the speaker probably does have a correct representation of the intended object (this seems a useful assumption in the absence of evidence to the contrary), but the intended object has not yet been found. Therefore, it seems 5-year-olds may have inferred discrepant speaker representation from discrepant found object.

However, 5-year-olds, unlike older children, were not influenced by information provided about the accuracy of the speaker's memory for the intended object. Under the 'bad' speaker memory condition, children were informed that the speaker could not quite remember how the object looked, but were not told explicitly what the speaker's false belief was. Children had to infer this from later information that the listener had found an object slightly discrepant with the description. Nine-year-olds judged more frequently that the approximate found object was the one intended when the speaker's memory was depicted as 'bad' than when it was depicted as 'good'. As such, they seemed to have a better grasp of the link between inaccurate representation and misdescription. This was not the case for the 5-year-olds. They judged equally often that the approximate found object was (was not) the one intended by the speaker, whether speaker memory for the referent was depicted as good or bad.

It seems, then, that when a discrepant object is found, young children are weak at utilizing available clues in judging whether this is or is not the one intended. Another way of expressing this is that although young children understand that people sometimes say other than they mean, they may be poor at recognizing the signs indicating whether a say–mean discrepancy has or has not occurred. In the Mitchell & Russell (1989) study, young children failed to utilize information concerning speaker memory quality as a sign of say–mean discrepancy. In the present study, we sought to examine children's ability to utilize another sign, namely, whether the object identified by the listener closely approximated the speaker's description, or whether it was grossly discrepant.

Would children judge that a slightly discrepant object is the one intended more frequently than they judge that a grossly discrepant object is the one intended? If they did, this would show that they can utilize magnitude of discrepancy in making a judgement relevant to (i) the speaker's representational state, and (ii) whether or not a say–mean discrepancy had occurred.

Magnitude of discrepancy between description and found object is a more ecologically valid clue to speaker representation than is narrative information about the speaker's memory quality, as presented by Mitchell & Russell (1989). In real life, no omniscient presence is available to provide a commentary on an actor's mental state. If children are to make inferences about mental states, they have to do it by focusing on clues available to them in the context, such as to what extent an object they find matches a speaker's description. Because the magnitude of discrepancy manipulation is more ecologically valid, we would expect, if children are at all capable of utilizing clues to inaccurate representations in speakers, that ability would be manifest in the following study.

Method

Subjects

We tested 128 children (68 boys and 60 girls), forming two age groups of equal number. The younger group had a mean age of 5:10 years (range = 5:5 to 6:4). The older group had a mean age of 9:9 years (range = 9:5 to 10:4). The children attended a school in Southport, UK, which had a mainly middle-class intake.

Materials

We adapted eight stories used by Mitchell & Russell (1989), which were based on the following example:

Andy and Tim were playing together. Andy asked Tim to get a box out of the toy cupboard in the dining-room. Andy asked what the box looks like. Tim replied:

'It's a blue box of crayons with the picture of an aeroplane on the lid'.

Andy went to the toy cupboard in the dining room and found only one box in there. It was a blue box of crayons (green box of Lego) with the picture of a boat on the lid.

In these stories, the speaker specified details of the location, and the listener found only one object in that location which was in the described category (e.g. only one box in the toy cupboard). Under one condition ('small discrepancy'), the found object was useful in the same way that the described object would be useful (crayons for art work), but it differed in a trivial way in one out of three attributes listed by the speaker. For example, the found box was of the correct colour and contents, but the picture of the item on the lid differed. This attribute, although different, was related to that described (e.g. *boat* and *aeroplane* are both items of transport). Under the other condition ('gross discrepancy'), the found object differed on all three attributes, with the consequence that the found object was not even useful in precisely the way that the described object would be useful (e.g. Lego could not be used for drawing pictures). With this formula, we went some way towards quantifying the discrepancy between described and found objects (there was a discrepancy on either one or three attributes).

Two memory questions and a test question followed each story. These were presented in the sequence given below:

M1   What was the ... (e.g. picture) on the ... (e.g. box) which ... (e.g. Andy) found?

M2   What did ... (e.g. Tim) say the ... (e.g. picture) was on the ... (e.g. box)?

T   Is the ... (e.g. box) ... (e.g. Andy) found really the ... (e.g. box) ... (e.g. Tim) tried [meant] to talk about?

The first two questions were about the attribute described by the speaker and the corresponding attribute of the found object, which was common to both discrepancy conditions. It was possible that under the gross discrepancy condition, children could have given the same answer to both memory questions, yet recognize that there was a discrepancy between description and found object by detecting a discrepancy on an attribute they were not questioned about. Therefore, children's answers to the memory questions might have been an *underestimate* of their awareness that there was a discrepancy under the gross discrepancy condition. An alternative procedure would have been one in which we asked extra memory questions under the gross discrepancy condition, a pair of questions for each attribute (one in each pair about the description and one about the found object). This would have given a more accurate indication of children's awareness of the discrepancy under the gross discrepancy condition, but a disadvantage would have been that discrepancy conditions would have been confounded with the number of memory questions asked. It was possible that this covarying factor would have given rise to a difference between conditions in answers to test questions, which would have been artifactual. Therefore, we avoided this problem by holding the memory question constant across the two discrepancy conditions, and accepted that their answers to memory questions under the gross discrepancy condition would have to suffice as a rough indication of children's awareness of the discrepancy.

The third (test) question was to assess whether children believed that the found object was the referent. The *tried* version of this test question was identical to the one used by Mitchell & Russell (1989), which provoked a substantial frequency of positive judgements from 5-year-olds when there was only a small discrepancy between description and found object. In the interest of variety and generality, we substituted *meant* for *tried* for half the subjects.

Design and procedure

Children heard all eight stories. In four of these, the discrepancy between described and found objects was small, and in the rest it was gross. In order to ensure that individual stories were not confounded with particular levels of described–found object discrepancy, half the children heard stories 1 to 4 under the small discrepancy condition and 5 to 8 under the gross discrepancy condition. The rest of the children heard 1 to 4 under the gross discrepancy condition and 5 to 8 under the small discrepancy condition. We arranged the stories in a random sequence, and then systematically varied the order of this sequence in a Latin square configuration. Thus, for half of the children, the first story had a small discrepancy, whereas the remainder of the children heard a gross discrepancy story first. For half the children, the test question always contained the word *tried,* and for the remainder the word was *meant*. All factors were completely crossed with each other in a balanced and complete design. We assigned subjects to conditions at random.

Children listened to stories individually in a quiet room within the school. The experimenter began by asking the child about his/her favourite stories in an attempt to set him/her at ease, and then explained that he was going to read some stories and was going to ask the child questions about them at the end of each. The experimenter stressed that it was important for the child to listen carefully for this reason. Children received no feedback concerning the correctness of answers they gave.

Results

Each time a child judged that the found object was the one that the speaker tried (meant) to talk about, we recorded a score of 1. We computed separate analyses of variance for each age group independently, of the design 2 (kind of test question) × 2 (discrepancy between description and found object), the last factor being a repeated measure. It was useful to perform separate analyses for each age, since a priority was to establish whether children in the youngest group were influenced by the discrepancy between the description and the found object. We would not be able to ascertain this clearly from an analysis performed on the data overall, whatever the outcome. Table 1 shows the mean scores.

Table 1. The mean percentage of judgements that the found object was the one that the speaker had tried (meant) to talk about under two conditions according to the extent of discrepancy between description and found object ('small' and 'gross').

Discrepancy	5 years		9 years	
	Tried	Meant	Tried	Meant
Small	46.1 (78.9)	31.3 (79.7)	43.0 (99.2)	25.8 (96.9)
Gross	46.9 (78.1)	28.1 (84.4)	22.7 (98.4)	14.8 (97.7)

Note. The figures in parentheses are the mean percentage acknowledgement of the described–found object discrepancy, indicated by children's answers to the memory questions.

In the case of the 5-year-olds, none of the effects was significant, and the F value arising from the *discrepancy* variable was small ($F < 1$). In the case of 9-year-olds, the only significant effect was associated with the discrepancy variable, which arose because children judged that the found object was the one the speaker tried (meant) to talk about more frequently when the discrepancy was small ($F(1, 62) = 18.29$, $p < .001$).

Apart from a difference between age groups according to presence or absence of effect associated with the discrepancy variable, another obvious difference between age groups was in the frequency of correct answers to the memory questions. We defined correct answers as being occasions on which children gave different answers to the two memory questions. If children exchanged described attribute for the corresponding attribute of the found object in their answers, we recorded 'correct memory', because children acknowledged that there was a discrepancy, even if they were confused about details in the message as distinct from details about the appearance of the found object.

Table 1 shows that whilst 9-year-olds nearly always gave correct answers to memory questions, 5-year-olds were less likely to do so, even though they were deemed to be correct on a good majority of occasions. This was confirmed by an analysis of variance performed on memory data, of the design 2 (age) × 2 (discrepancy between description and found object), the last factor being a repeated measure. Data were collapsed over wording of the test question, since this was irrelevant to children's answers to the memory questions. Nine-year-olds answered memory questions correctly more often than 5-year-olds ($F(1, 126) = 25.16$, $p < .001$), and all other Fs were < 1. In no way do 5-year-olds' memory errors account for all the occasions on which they answered 'yes' to the test question. It is clear from Table 1 that these 'yes' responses were more common than was the tendency to give the same answer to the two memory questions.

The occurrence of memory errors in the sample of 5-year-olds might have weakened any effect associated with the discrepancy variable in their answers to the test question. If children thought the description perfectly matched the appearance of the found object, then presumably children would judge that the found object was the one the speaker tried (meant) to talk about. Since 5-year-olds committed memory errors on about 20 per cent of occasions, the effect of this memory error would be comparable to reducing a sample of subjects who committed no errors of memory by 20 per cent. It is interesting to note that if we reduce the sample of older children by this amount, by excluding at random 13 of the 64 9-year-olds, this makes no difference to the significance of the effect of the discrepancy variable on their judgements as to whether the found object was the one the speaker tried (meant) to talk about ($t(50) = 4.12$, $p < .001$). Therefore, it seems that although 5-year-olds committed more memory errors than did 9-year-olds, this did not account for the difference between age groups in the effect associated with the discrepancy variable on children's answers to the test question.

Perhaps *some* 5-year-olds believed that a found object which closely approximated the speaker's description was the one the speaker tried (meant) to talk about, and believed a found object which grossly departed from the description was not the one the speaker meant. It seems this was not the case. Only nine out of 64 5-year-olds judged that the found object was the one the speaker tried (meant) to talk about more often when the discrepancy was small than when it was great. In all nine cases, the difference between discrepancy conditions in judgements that the found object was the one the speaker tried (meant) to talk about was only 1. Fifty of the children judged equally often under both conditions that the found object was the one the speaker tried (meant) to talk about. The surprising thing about the response pattern of individual subjects is the large number of children who made the same number of particular judgements under both conditions.

This finding raises another possibility, which is that 5-year-olds might have been sensitive to the size of discrepancy in judging whether the found object was the one the speaker tried (meant) to talk about, but based all judgements on the discrepancy condition in the first story because all stories were superficially similar, and as a consequence children might have repeated a set response to the test question on successive stories. If so, within-subject comparisons would be non-significant, though we might find that subjects for whom the first story had a small discrepancy made more judgements in total that the found object was the one the speaker tried (meant) to talk about than children for whom the first story had a gross discrepancy. However, this turned out not to be the case. The total number of particular kinds of judgement made by 5-year-olds was not influenced by the discrepancy condition of the first story ($t(31) = 0.79$, n.s.).

Though not evident in the preliminary analyses, Table 1 suggests that, generally, children in both age groups were more likely to judge that the found object was the one the speaker *tried* to talk about than they were to judge that it was the one the speaker *meant* to talk about. This was confirmed by t tests performed on data collapsed over age, but collected from the small discrepancy ($t(122) = 2.286$, $p < .05$) and gross discrepancy ($t(122) = 2.012$, $p < .05$) conditions independently.

Discussion

The main finding is that 9-year-olds judged more often that the found object was the one the speaker tried (meant) to talk about when the discrepancy between described and found objects was small than when it was gross. Five-year-olds also judged that the found object was the one the speaker tried (meant) to talk about on some occasions, but their judgements were not influenced by the size of discrepancy between described and found objects.

The finding that older children were influenced by the discrepancy variable is consistent with the possibility that they used the size of discrepancy as a clue to whether or not the speaker had an accurate representation of the intended object. Judgements that the found object was the one intended might have implied a belief that the speaker had an incorrect representation of the intended object. Judgements that the found object was not the one intended might have implied a belief that the speaker had a correct representation of the intended object, but the intended object had not yet been found. Insofar as this was the case, older children, but apparently not 5-year-olds, were attuned to the relationship between description and found object in making judgements about the representational state of the speaker.

In what way did 9-year-olds utilize the discrepancy information? It is possible that they utilized it in a pragmatic strategy. The child's task, on behalf of the listener, was to determine whether the found object was the one that the speaker wanted. If the found object differed from the description in only one attribute, it was likely to be the correct one, since the probability of finding a second object which was identical in all respects but one would be very low. In contrast, if the found object differed from the description in many ways, the probability of another substantially different object matching the description would be higher. The older children may have differed from the younger ones in their ability to assess the likelihood of the existence of the second object. By using this strategy, they would be better equipped to judge the representational state of the speaker, and in particular whether a say–mean discrepancy has occurred.

We can assume that children's judgements were of a mentalistic rather than purely pragmatic nature, however. Mitchell & Russell (1989) asked 5-year-olds if a listener would return with a discrepant object, and they often judged positively. When asked if the object was the one the speaker had been thinking about, they nearly always answered negatively. Subsequent investigations showed that children of this age answered the 'think' question in the same way as they answered a 'tried' question, as used in the present study. Mitchell & Russell interpreted the different responses produced by these question wordings to reflect a corresponding difference in pragmatic versus a mentalistic judgement made by the children: children accepted the discrepant object as a substitute for the one the speaker really wanted (a pragmatic judgement), but recognized this was not actually the object the speaker had meant (a mentalistic judgement). We can assume that in the present study children answered the test question in this mentalistic way, given that they did so in the previous study: that is, they may have made a mentalistic judgement via a pragmatic route.

Although 5-year-olds did not utilize magnitude of discrepancy between description and found object, it is possible that they did understand that a speaker might mean other than s/he says. Sometimes they judged that the discrepant object was what the speaker intended, just as in the Mitchell & Russell (1989) study. However, to show that children really do have such understanding, we need to demonstrate their competence in terms of different judgements across relevant contrast conditions. This we have succeeded in doing in a recent study, described below (Robinson & Mitchell, 1990).

The children were aged 3:11 to 4:9. We told them a story about Jane and her Mum. Mum was tidying the house, and put away bag A of multicoloured material in a red drawer, and bag B of different multicoloured material in an adjacent blue drawer. Mum left the scene and shortly after Jane got out the bags and played with them. Crucially, she then returned them to the same drawers (no change) or swapped them and put bag A in the blue drawer and B in the red drawer (change). Mum subsequently stated that she wanted the bag in the red drawer (it was appropriate to refer to it by location since the material was difficult to describe), and children were asked to specify which bag Mum really wanted.

A highly significant majority of these young children judged that Mum really wanted the bag in the blue drawer under the change condition (contrary to what she said), but that she wanted the bag in the red drawer under the no change condition (consistent with what she said). As demonstrated by this contrast effect, the children must have recognized that if Mum had not witnessed the change in location of the bags, then her message referred to a location which maintained in her outdated representation, but no longer in the real world. In giving the correct answer that Mum really wanted the bag in the blue drawer, they must have traced the bag in the red drawer of Mum's false belief to that in the blue drawer in the present state of the world. This shows that young children are able to understand that what a speaker means can be distinct from what s/he says.

Given this, it seems reasonable to suppose that when 5-year-olds in the present study judged that a discrepant object was the one the speaker intended, they believed that a say–mean discrepancy had occurred. The appropriate conclusion, then, seems to be that although young children understand about say–mean discrepancy, they are weak at utilizing available clues, such as the magnitude of discrepancy between description and found object, in making judgements as to whether a say–mean discrepancy has or has not occurred. This conclusion indicates that we should be cautious in extrapolating from competence to performance: although the child might know something about mind states, this knowledge will be of limited value if the child is unable to utilize clues available in situations in arriving at mind state judgements.

Future research should seek to assess this conclusion with alternative methodology. In particular, two issues seem pertinent. First, would young children explain the discovery of the discrepant object by reference to the speaker's inaccurate representation? If so, this would show directly in the context of the stories used that they understood inaccurate representation was responsible for incorrect description. Second, given that ecologically valid clues to say–mean discrepancy are of interest, it would be useful to devise a test that could investigate this in a naturalistic context in which there would be a wealth of clues relevant to the distinction between what is said and what is meant.

Finally, we consider the finding that the *tried* version of the test question provoked more positive judgements in general than did the *meant* version. The effect was a fairly small one, since it only emerged as significant when data were collapsed over age. Apparently, the effect associated with the test question variable was not specific to one age group and it did not interact with the discrepancy variable, so it seems that the finding has no relevance to the theoretical point we have made in relation to the difference between age groups in terms of effect associated with the discrepancy variable. There are many possible explanations of the test question effect, and it would not be useful to list these here.

Acknowledgements

The study was conducted by the first author in partial fulfilment of the requirements for the degree of PhD at the University of Liverpool. We are very grateful to E. J. Robinson for the comments she made on an earlier draft.

References

Ackerman, B. P. (1979). Children's understanding of definite descriptions: Pragmatic inferences to a speaker's intent. *Journal of Experimental Child Psychology*, **28**, 1–15.

Ackerman, B. P. (1981). Young children's understanding of a speaker's intentional use of a false utterance. *Developmental Psychology*, **17**, 472–482.

Ackerman, B. P. (1982). Contextual integration and utterance interpretation: The ability of children and adults to interpret sarcastic utterances. *Child Development*, **53**, 1075–1083.

Ackerman, B. P. (1983). Form and function in children's understanding of ironic utterances. *Journal of Experimental Child Psychology*, **35**, 487–508.

Beal, C. R. & Flavell, J. H. (1984). Development of the ability to distinguish between communicative intention and literal message meaning. *Child Development*, **55**, 920–928.

Demorest, A., Meyer, C., Phelps, E., Gardner, H. & Winner, E. (1984). Words speak louder than actions: Understanding deliberately false words. *Child Development*, **55**, 1527–1534.

Donaldson, M. (1978). *Children's Minds*. Glasgow: Collins.

Mitchell, P. & Russell, J. (1989). Young children's understanding of the say–mean distinction in referential speech. *Journal of Experimental Child Psychology*, **47**, 467–490.

Robinson, E. J., Goelman, H. & Olson, D. R. (1983). Children's understanding of the relation between expressions (what was said) and intentions (what was meant). *British Journal of Developmental Psychology*, **1**, 75–86.

Robinson, E. J. & Mitchell, P. (1990). How do children interpret messages from a speaker with a false belief? Poster presented at the IVth European Conference on Developmental Psychology, University of Stirling, August.

Received 28 November 1989; revised version received 7 December 1990

British Journal of Developmental Psychology (1991), **9**, 281–298   *Printed in Great Britain*
© 1991 The British Psychological Society

Developing awareness of mind reflected in children's narrative writing

Richard Fox*

School of Education, University of Exeter, Heavitree Road, Exeter EX1 2LU, UK

An investigation of narratives written by 135 children aged 9, 11 and 13 years reveals the steady development during middle childhood of children's ability to realize their understanding of mental events within the tradition of story writing. These developments are examined in relation to the representation of the inner world of characters, of expressive behaviour and of inferences about others. Narrative writing is seen as both a source of data for understanding the emergence into awareness of children's developing theories of mind and as a possible means for the development of such awareness.

In speaking of children's 'developing theories of mind' we may be referring to the implicit knowledge or presuppositions on which social interaction and communication are based from the earliest months of life or to the knowledge that children can make explicit, both to themselves and to others (Astington, Harris & Olson, 1988). Thus, a child may be able to project into the mind of someone else and thus predict their emotional or cognitive state, but be unable to give an account of the process of doing so. This distinction is very similar to that made by philosophers between 'knowing how' and 'knowing that', and has been reconceptualized by some psychologists as the distinction between procedural and declarative knowledge (Mandler, 1983). Recent research on children's developing theories of mind has established an intriguing mixture of early competence but also a continuing vulnerability to vagueness, error and uncertainty which lasts well into middle childhood. It seems clear that children 'know more than they can tell' and that cognitive development consists partly of developments in the differentiation and integration of knowledge itself and partly of the increasing ability to represent knowledge to the self and to others (Estes, Wellman & Woolley, 1989). This paper explores children's developing ability to make their knowledge about the outer social world, and the inner psychological world, explicit in a particular domain, that of narrative writing.

Recent research has transformed our view of the age at which children are able to begin to think and talk about their own and other people's minds (Astington *et al.*, 1988; Bretherton, 1984; Chandler, Fritz & Hala, 1989; Miller & Aloise, 1989; Palermo, 1989; Wellman, 1985; Wimmer & Perner, 1983). The striking early abilities

* Requests for reprints.

of 2–3-year-old children to use mental terms appropriately in conversation (Bretherton, 1984), their ability to distinguish early on between the physical and the mental world (Estes *et al.*, 1989; Wellman, 1985) and their ability to engage in deceptive manoeuvres which take account of the information held by others (Chandler *et al.*, 1989) leave little doubt that from the age of about 2 years children are beginning to operate with the common-sense theory of mind and intentional human action which is deeply embedded in Western industrialized culture.

An unresolved problem, and one which may be virtually impossible to resolve empirically, is the extent to which children's knowledge of mind is the product of spontaneous action and reflection, being as it were 'homemade', and the extent to which it is a product of socialization, that is the learning to use a set of culturally encoded and shared ideas about the mind and human behaviour (Vygotsky, 1962). Introspection may result from individual and largely private efforts to make sense of experience and from gradual induction into a form of discourse which encodes a culture's current beliefs about the mind and psychological functioning. Vygotsky argued that these two sources of thinking developed to some extent independently but eventually inter-penetrated one another, so that spontaneous concepts become organized within, and assimilated to, a culture's shared body of theories, whilst non-spontaneous (socially encoded) concepts were revitalized through coming to be understood in terms of the individual's personal experience.

The extent to which children need to make their knowledge in this area explicit will depend on the opportunities and challenges that face them socially. For much of the time social interaction can be carried on without any explicit reference to inner mental states and it may be hypothesized that children's interest in social interaction is initially mainly directed towards the realm of action, rather than reflection (Miller & Aloise, 1989). It is argued here, however, that an important dimension of cognitive development in middle and late childhood is developing a more refined conception of what it is to be a person (Damon & Hart, 1982; Pring, 1984; Selman, 1980) and hence of social cognition (Harter, 1983; Shantz, 1983; Sherman, Judd & Park, 1989). This involves children reflecting upon themselves, upon others and upon social relationships. Although direct evidence is difficult to obtain, it is reasonable to speculate that it is a process which may be influenced by, amongst other factors, developing literacy.

In literate cultures one of the most potent forms of representation of the mental world is provided by literature. (Moreover, preliterate cultures have a cognate tradition of oral narrative and myth.) A culture's ways of understanding and interpreting human actions, and the mental events assumed to underlie them, are made plain, albeit in an unsystematic fashion, in the culture's stories (Bruner, 1986). Indeed before the advent of psychology it would have been in the contexts of religious and literary discourse that mental phenomena were probably mostly discussed and communicated. Contemporary children in most countries are still introduced to narrative accounts of human behaviour from an early age, and narrative operates for them as one of the primary means of organizing experience (Hardy, 1977; Mandler, 1983; Wells, 1986; Wilkinson, Barnsley, Hanna & Swan, 1980). Such narratives introduce children to explicit accounts of purposeful human behaviour, typical human motives and feelings and many other mental phenomena.

As soon as they are initiated into the tradition of narrative writing, typically between the ages of 5 and 7 years in Britain, they begin to construct for themselves fictional worlds which inevitably include representations of their intuitive accounts of mind in action.

Much of the research into children's understanding and use of mental concepts has involved either oral interviews (e.g. Peevers & Secord, 1973; Johnson & Wellman, 1982), or experiments (e.g. Johnson & Wellman, 1980; Wimmer & Perner, 1983). An alternative is to look at children's writing, as a product of thinking, which offers particular insights and particular difficulties of interpretation (Fox, 1987). Some investigators (e.g. Livesley & Bromley, 1973) have asked children for written responses to direct questions about, for example, knowledge of other persons. Others have studied children's understanding and use of story structure in the context either of investigating story schemas (Applebee, 1978; Mandler, 1983; Mandler & Johnson, 1977; Peterson & McCabe, 1983; Stein & Glenn, 1979) or attempts to improve composition (Bereiter & Scardamalia, 1982, 1984; Fitzgerald & Teasley, 1986; Harris & Wilkinson, 1986). It has been rarer to examine children's narrative writing than their oral story telling (Fitzgerald, 1989), but a notable exception is provided by the research into developing narrative writing of Wilkinson and his colleagues (Wilkinson *et al.,* 1980; Wilkinson, 1986). The present work reports data from a study of children's writing which has similarities to Wilkinson's analysis of developing meaning in children's narrative writing but explores a different model of story structure, centred specifically on characterization, and thus focusing on social cognition. The data are thus primarily descriptive, plotting the gradual emergence into awareness of children's understanding of the social world.

Method

1. The broader context of the data reported

The findings reported here form part of a broader investigation into the representation of social cognition in children's narrative writing (Fox, 1987, 1990). In this broader study, children from seven school classes in five different schools wrote two specially commissioned narratives. The children were aged 7, 9, 11 and 13. The children also wrote a third piece of non-narrative writing. A further cross-sectional sample of 46 children were compared in terms of their depictions of persons in oral interviews and in their narrative writing. The development of characterization, and the representation of the social world, was further examined in longitudinal samples of the writing of seven children. The stories thus collected and commissioned were in each case subjected to a content analysis of the representation of characterization which had been developed and piloted for this purpose. Full details of the procedures and coding rules for the transcription and content analysis are provided in Fox (1987). A summary of the developmental levels of characterization is given in Fox (1990).

2. The model of narrative used

De Beaugrande (1980) argues that narratives are made up of four primary concepts, namely objects (characters and other specified items), situations (essentially the environment, in terms of place, time and circumstances), events and actions. The model of narrative on which the present study was based prefers to distinguish between characters, which are seen as a category in their own right, and other objects, which are categorized as part of the 'environment'. Since both events and actions are actually defined by the author or by one or more characters, being interpretations of the general flow of experience, they are related, in the present model, to the 'predicament' facing the characters, and to its resolution. Thus the model used in the present study defines the narrative form as an account of agents, actions and events structured in time. In its canonical form, a narrative is seen as an account of agents and their actions, or reactions, in the light of a predicament. An agent is defined as any intentional being who acts purposefully, the more general term 'agent' being rendered as 'character' in the context of narrative. Thus a written narrative, or story, can be viewed as consisting of one or more characters, in an environment, who take action in the light of their predicament. The predicament is, in the canonical form, resolved in some fashion.

Such a model may be seen as complementary to other models of story structure, which, while assuming the existence of intentional characters, have placed rather more emphasis on the elements and structure of the plot and on the goals, goal attempts and outcomes of the characters or on the evaluative point of the story (Fitzgerald, 1989; Labov & Waletzky, 1967; Mandler, 1983; Wilkinson, 1986). The present model allows a more detailed analysis to be made of the representation of the characters, their attributes, their relationships, their views of the predicament and their inner mental life. It accords well with Bruner's definition of narrative as centrally concerned with 'the vicissitudes of human intentions' (Bruner, 1986, p. 16).

In the present paper, the results reported are those relevant to children's ability to represent aspects of the inner psychological worlds of characters, a dimension of narrative writing which develops dramatically in middle childhood.

3. Subjects

The composition of the main cross-sectional sample is summarized in Table 1. For each age given the children were within six months of that birthday. Two further classes of children (20 more children aged 11 and 21 children aged from 7:0 to 7:6) completed only one of the two narrative tasks. The data from these two extra classes cannot be included in the main empirical analysis, as they did not complete both narrative tasks, but will be reported in the subsequent analysis where relevant.

Table 1. Composition of cross-sectional samples

Type of school	Class	No. of pupils	Mean age (years, months)
First	B	29	9:4
Primary (1)	C	26	9:4
Middle (1)	E	29	11:2
Middle (2)	F	24	13:0
Middle (1)	G	27	13:1
		$\Sigma = 135$	
Extra classes: Story 1 only			
Primary (1)	A	21	7:5
Primary (2)	D	20	10:6

The children for each age group in the main cross-sectional sample were drawn from more than one school and school class, with the exception of the 11-year-olds who are represented by only a single class. The subjects were all white British children, with English as their first language. They attended state schools in the southwest of England and came from a broad cross-section of socio-economic backgrounds.

4. Tasks and context of writing

All classes were recruited via their teachers, who agreed to take part in the project. The researcher visited each class and obtained the consent of the children to participate in a study which was explained in terms of 'finding out what kinds of stories children write at different ages'. All the writing was carried out in normal classroom conditions except that: (i) teachers were briefed so as to introduce each task in a standardized manner and to give no help with composition; (ii) no discussion between teacher and children, or between children themselves, was allowed in advance of, or during, the writing; (iii) teachers were encouraged to respond only to requests for help with transcription issues (spelling, punctuation and handwriting). The writing was done on loose-leaf paper and the children added their names and dates of birth to the title. Dates of birth were checked by school registers. The titles of the two narratives were: 1. 'The visitor' and 2. 'The day I ran away from home'. These titles were chosen in collaboration with the teachers in an attempt to ensure that children of all the ages studied would understand and respond to the tasks and in order to stimulate both imaginative fictional writing about a character and more personal actual, or fictionalized, reminiscences with the family as setting.

5. Content analysis

The content analysis written specifically for this study, and developed in coding previous samples of children's narratives, divides characterization into 10 'aspects', as summarized in Table 2. It is named 'CACH' (content analysis of characterization).

Table 2. Aspects of characterization in 'CACH'

A. Contextual information and needs of the reader
B. Intentions and predicaments
C. Levels of social interaction
D. Description and evaluation of characters
E. Inner world of characters
F. Expressive behaviour and inferences about others
G. Verbal communication
H. Authority relations and reciprocity
I. Cooperation and conflict
J. Resolutions and outcomes

Each story was coded in terms of a global rating for each of the 10 aspects, provided that they were represented in a story at all. (There are further rules for differentiating between non-appearance of an aspect and lack of representation at level 1.) Each rating corresponds to one of five levels of development and stories were coded for the highest level at which an aspect was represented in the narrative. The five levels of development were defined in terms of detailed coding rules for each of the 10 aspects of characterization. It is important to understand that these 'levels' are not conceptualized as residing 'within the child' but are levels of observable attainment in the developing representation of characterization. As such, they represent a level of performance, reflecting the child's competence as a writer, in a given context, and in interaction with a particular cultural tradition, namely that of narrative writing (cf. Feldman, 1980). The core descriptions of each of the five levels are summarized in Table 3. The detailed rules for coding aspects E (inner world) and F (expressive behaviour and inferences about others) are provided in the Appendix. The content analysis (CACH) thus rates each story in terms of 10 out of 50 possible categories (10 aspects × 5 levels).

Table 3. Summary of CACH: Core conceptions of character at five levels of developing attainment

---

LEVEL 1.   A single character pursues simple goals. Thought and action are not clearly differentiated.

LEVEL 2.   Characters interact physically. A single inner world. Thinking about action.

LEVEL 3.   Thinking characters exchange information. And/or a self-reflective protagonist. Thinking about thinking.

LEVEL 4.   Characters realized as individuals with feelings and attitudes. Thinking about the thinker.

LEVEL 5.   Characters in roles and relationships at a generalized level. Thinking about social issues and about the social world.

---

6. Measures and reliability estimates

In comparing the maturity of characterization of stories, ratings were analysed in terms of mean and median scores for all 10 aspects and also in terms of a more conservative system which examined the median for only the first five aspects (A to E) on the grounds that they were independent, whereas there is some overlap between the full set of 10 aspects. Median scores were used for the most part in order to avoid assumptions of more than ordinal scaling. In the case of results for individual aspects, reported below, simple frequencies can be used.

   The coding of stories using CACH requires some training and practice if consistent results are to be attained. Inter-judge reliability of coding was estimated by having three judges who had received about three hours of training carry out independent codings of a subsample of 12 stories. This subsample was selected from the main sample with randomized procedures, so as to represent age groups and sexes evenly. Each of the stories was then typed out with spelling and punctuation corrected. Names and ages were removed and the anonymous transcribed stories were then coded independently. Agreement in terms of detailed codings reached 76 per cent of the judgements made, in the absence of discussion. Disagreements were almost all in terms of codes one level apart and if discussion was allowed, which usually led to the pointing out of an instance of an aspect at a higher level than one of the judges had noticed, then agreement on codes rose to 94 per cent. In a further check on judges' agreement on the relative maturity of characterization in the 12 stories, the mean scores for all 10 aspects for each story were used to rank the order of maturity of the stories for each judge. Kendall's coefficient of concordance for this ordering of the stories came to .91. In summary, it is claimed that, although the coding task requires a measure of judgement in interpreting stories, judges are able to agree on detailed codings of aspects in about three-quarters of cases. Disagreements tend to consist of codings one level apart and most of these are removed if mutual discussion is allowed. Thus a moderately satisfactory level of reliability of inter-judge coding can be claimed for CACH. In coding the main sample, the ages of the subjects and other identifying information were removed from the scripts.

7. The representation of the mental world of characters

The results which follow refer only to the two aspects of CACH presently under consideration, namely aspects E and F. These two aspects of CACH are particularly concerned with the psychological experiences of characters: aspect E (inner world) is used to code any representation of mental faculties, attributes or experiences of characters, and aspect F (expressive behaviour and inferences about others) covers a number of related areas which have to do with 'reading' the psychological significance of the behaviour of other characters. These are: (*a*) the direct expression of emotion in observable terms (e.g. laughter, tears, shaking with fear), (*b*) non-verbal communication (including intonation, gesture and facial expression), (*c*) projections and inferences made by one character about the mental states of others, and (*d*) adverbials, that is to say, the use of adverbs, adverb clauses and adverb phrases to represent the manner of a character's behaviour and thus to reveal something about underlying intentions or feelings.

The whole coding system for CACH was worked out in a series of trials using children's stories *other* than those considered here. The detailed rules for coding aspects E and F at the five levels of development are given in the Appendix. They may be more briefly summarized as follows:

Aspect E: Inner world of characters. Level 1: Either no inner world is represented at all or a single character has an inner world only represented in terms of items from a restricted set of simple terms such as 'see', 'know', 'want', 'be hungry', etc. Level 2: The protagonist has an expanded inner world, mainly in terms of the representation of cognition, but with some simple labelling of affective states. Level 3: Any or all characters may have the range of faculties listed for the protagonist at level 2, and/or a self-reflective protagonist is represented, reflecting on current thoughts and feelings. In addition, a limited range of common attitudes and feelings may be expressed. Level 4: More complex mental states and attitudes are represented; and/or a self-reflective protagonist conducts a form of self-appraisal, going beyond a simple representation of current state of mind; and/or a character is represented both in terms of an outward 'persona' and in terms of (different) underlying intentions. Level 5: A character reflects on self in generalized terms, involving some form of evaluation or judgement with explicit criteria. Personal ideals, goals or principles may be made explicit.

Aspect F: Expressive behaviour and inferences about others. Level 1: No such expressive behaviour or inferences are mentioned. Level 2: Direct expression of simple inner states of surprise, excitement or fear (e.g. laughing, crying, shouting ...); and/or use of the verbs 'run' or close associates to imply underlying intention. Level 3: More complex signs of emotional expression; and/or type of speech used to indicate character's nature; and/or simple projection by one character into the current state of mind of another; and/or adverbs (or adverbials or verb forms) used to make clearer the intentions of a protagonist. Level 4: Feelings or attitudes of others are inferred from non-verbal cues; and/or complex, or reciprocal projection in which character *x* imagines character *y*'s view of *x*'s state of mind; and/or adverbs, adverbials and verb forms used to make clearer the intentions of characters other than the protagonist. Level 5: One character projects or empathizes with another character's thoughts and feelings about changing relationships, values or general circumstances.

Results

Results are reported for the codes (from 1 to 5) assigned to the stories for aspects E and F. A one-between and one-within subjects ANOVA was used to test for differences in terms of the variables of age (between subjects: three groups aged 9, 11 and 13) and story task (within subjects: tasks 1 and 2) for each of the two aspects E and F. In the case of aspect E (inner world) this showed a main effect for age ($F(2, 132) = 33.9$, $p < .01$), with more mature levels attained by older children, and non-significant effects for differences across the two story tasks ($F(1, 132) = 0$, n.s.) and for the interaction of age × story ($F(2, 132) = 0.68$, n.s.). In the case of aspect F (expressive behaviour and inferences about others) there was also a main effect for age ($F(2, 132) = 30.15$, $p < .01$), with older children attaining generally higher levels, and non-significant findings for differences across the two stories ($F(1, 132) = 3.7$, n.s.) and for the interaction of age × story ($F(2, 132) = 0$, n.s.).

Table 4 shows the mean scores for age groups, for aspects E and F, for each of the two stories. The differences in mean scores for the three age groups are mostly at borderline levels of significance. Thus the differences between mean scores for the 9- and 11-year-olds were found to be significant for aspect E, story 1 ($t(132) = 1.96$, $p < .05$) and aspect F, story 1 ($t(132) = 2.0$, $p < .05$), but not for story 2. The differences between mean scores for the 11- and 13-year-olds were also found to be significant for aspect E, story 1 ($t(132) = 1.76$, $p < .05$) and aspect F, story 1

(t(132) = 1.84, $p < .05$), but not for story 2. Although the differences in results between the two stories are relatively small, it seems that story task 2 ('The day I ran away from home') did not produce quite such differentiated results as task 1 ('The visitor'), in terms of age group differences.

Table 4. Mean scores by age groups, aspects E and F

	Aspect E		Aspect F	
Age group	Story 1	Story 2	Story 1	Story 2
9 years	2.56	2.65	2.18	2.43
11 years	3.03	3.03	2.66	2.66
13 years	3.47	3.43	3.12	2.96

Table 5 shows the absolute frequencies for aspect E, story 1, with which given levels of CACH were obtained by different age groups. Since both the extra class of 11-year-olds and the extra class of 7-year-olds completed this story, their frequencies are included in this table. It will be clear from inspection that CACH levels are distributed quite widely within age groups as well as between them. Table 6 shows the same data for aspect F, story 1. Again data from the two additional classes are included, to provide a clearer picture of the general distribution of levels in the sample. (NB. Because frequencies from the two extra classes are included in Tables 5 and 6 the means for the 11-year-olds are not quite the same for story 1 as in Table 4.)

Table 5. Inner world of characters. Aspect E: (Story 1) frequencies with which given levels of CACH were obtained by different age groups

	CACH level						
Age group	1	2	3	4	5	Total subjects	Group mean
7 years	11	5	5	—	—	21	1.71
9 years	—	28	23	4	—	55	2.56
11 years	—	8	27	13	1	49	2.94
13 years	—	3	24	21	3	51	3.47
						$\Sigma = 176$	

A more general analysis of all 10 aspects of CACH made use of median scores for each story and non-parametric statistics, for which assumptions of interval scaling do not need to be made. A Kruskal–Wallis one-way analysis of variance found significant differences between age groups for both story 1 (H(3) = 78.6, $p < .001$) and story 2 (H(2) = 55, $p < .001$). In addition there was evidence of significant effects in terms of membership of different school classes at the same age and in terms of

Table 6. Expressive behaviour and inferences about others. Aspect F: (Story 1) frequencies with which given levels of CACH were obtained by different age groups

Age group	CACH level					Total subjects	Group mean
	1	2	3	4	5		
7 years	—	20	1	—	—	21	2.05
9 years	—	47	6	2	—	55	2.18
11 years	—	29	11	9	—	49	2.59
13 years	—	15	17	17	2	51	3.12
						$\Sigma = 176$	

gender, in that girls scored more highly than boys overall (see Fox, 1987, for details). The children's performance was compared across the two stories written and Spearman's rank order correlation for the median scores for all 10 aspects was found to be $+.73$. In general terms, therefore, maturity of characterization, as measured by the five ordinal levels of CACH, increased with age and varied, to some extent, according to school class and the gender of subjects. The children showed a moderately high degree of consistency of performance across two pieces of writing. Returning more specifically to aspects E and F, the trends in the data are similar, but only story 1 provided clear evidence of statistically significant age group differences.

General discussion

In the following discussion, a distinction needs to be made between findings for which there is clear empirical support and findings which are more speculative. Significant main effects for differences between the age groups 9, 11 and 13 have been shown for both aspects E and F in both stories 1 and 2. These echo the more general age group differences found in the analysis of median scores for all 10 aspects of CACH. Results for 7-year-olds fit the same general pattern but cannot be supported so firmly in terms of the present data. Given the complex nature of the coding, and the variability in children's representation of different aspects of narrative from one writing task to another, it is not surprising that differences between age group means for aspects E and F just reach statistical significance for one story and just miss it for another. The difficulties of arriving at unambiguous quantitative analyses of written stories need to be acknowledged. The likelihood that some stories will produce writing which is more differentiated by age and maturity than others needs to be appreciated. Nevertheless, the trends in the data and the principal findings remain clear and warrant further inquiry. With these provisos, some of the main qualitative trends in the data will be described, using results for story 1 as the main reference point.

The small sample of 7-year-olds, who completed story 1, could either represent in their writing only the very simplest states of knowledge, perception and motivation in a single character (level E.1) or had developed the use of terms from a much wider range, centred on cognition, but which for many children was used in connection with just one main protagonist (level E.2). A minority at this age (5/20) had begun to extend this richer inner world to several characters. It appears that when children begin to construct written stories they focus principally on the observable actions of characters and introduce mental states only when they bear directly on the purposes and wants of a single active protagonist. In keeping with this depiction of a world of action, with some planning and decision making by a single protagonist, the nature of the predicaments facing characters at levels 1 and 2 are generally related either to the passage of simple everyday events (called chronicles by Wilkinson, 1986), or to physical safety, material welfare, comfort or stability. Resolutions and outcomes are heavily weighted towards the completion of the normal 'script' of a day, the restoration of a normal *status quo* or to physical rewards and punishments.

In terms of inferences about others, all but one of the 7-year-olds restricted their representation of the outer expression of inner states and feelings to level F.2, at which behaviour expresses a mental state in observable physical terms, as in a cry of fear. With one exception, they did not represent either projection by one character into the mental state of another or such indirect signs of inner emotion or disposition as facial expression or tone of voice. Nor did they use adverbs or verbs which are expressive of underlying intentions (with the exception of 'run' and 'run away').

The 9-year-olds in the sample could be split roughly in half, with half remaining at level 2 for aspect E and the other half reaching E.3 or, in four instances, E.4. Level 2 stories, as already indicated above, restrict the depiction of mental states to a single character. Such stories are thus generally 'subjective' and the inner world is represented in general only in order to clarify actions by indicating motivating states, plans or decisions. The focus of the writer is on the observable world of actions and their consequences. The writer tends to depict this from a single psychological point of view, or else represents plans or decisions as shared between two characters in an unproblematic way (e.g. 'we escaped together'). Other characters in such stories are either mere 'ciphers', who exist but appear not to have intentions of their own, or are represented solely in terms of their behaviour. Although simple dialogue may be used at level 2, it is assimilated to a kind of monologue, with 'asking and telling' but no true exchange of information.

The (roughly) half of the 9-year-olds who reached level E.3 were displaying an ability either to provide several characters with the richer inner world of thought, perception and decision making defined for E.2, or were representing a single character involved at some point in self-reflective thought. Such a character reflects on current thoughts or feelings, generally either to clarify them or as a part of planning and decision making. In either case, the 'psychic landscape' of character is beginning to make its way into the narrative. Dialogue becomes more frequent and more complex in such stories, with genuine exchanges of information. Reasoning, discussion and planning between characters, though generally at a simple level, is fairly common. The world of the mind has thus been extended from a single subjective point of view to become the means of coordinating intentions.

A limited range of attitudes seem to be represented at this level of writing, including being bored, anxious, lonely, tired, relieved, surprised or worried. Perhaps what members of such a set have in common is a clear connection with subsequent actions, or reactions, which will carry the story's plot onwards. In addition, such stories sometimes depict characters who go insane, enter trances, or engage in one of a variety of creative activities, such as composing a song. A few 9-year-olds only had reached E.4, at which more complex and differentiated attitudes are common. A large majority of 9-year-olds in this sample were still restricted to level F.2. Eight of them (15 per cent) had moved to F.3, at which adverbials are used to modify actions, but only of the protagonist, and characters may project into the mental state of another.

As children get older, the distribution of their attainments in narrative writing becomes more scattered. Thus, the 11-year-olds in the present study were spread across four of the five levels of CACH in their representation of aspect E (inner world); 16 per cent of them were still restricted to the simple subjective world of E.2 in their response to task 1. The majority (55 per cent were at level E.3, including in their story a self-reflective protagonist or several characters depicted as capable of thought and feeling. A minority (27 per cent) had developed the inner world of characters to level E.4, and one had reached E.5. At level 4 the focus of the writer's interest has shifted noticeably towards a greater concentration on the landscape of consciousness, as opposed to the landscape of action, to use Bruner's terms (Bruner, 1986). The feelings and attitudes of characters are now moving to centre stage and some characters are represented as more rounded and consistent personalities, with some past history of experience and engaged in social relationships. The writer can thus not only depict mind, or the inner world, of any number of characters, but is as much interested in realizing that world as in depicting actions and physical consequences. Thus the predicament of characters at level 4 (and at level 5) is generally seen as centred on the psychological welfare of characters rather than on their physical safety and comfort.

At E.4 moods, feelings and temperament become a focus for the interpretation of behaviour and characters may be depicted both in terms of an outer social 'persona' and the 'real' inner intentions and feelings that underlie it. Whereas cognition still tends to dominate at level E.3, the range of attitudes and mental states is much more varied at level E.4, so that the emotional weight or significance of actions and words is finally explicitly represented by the writer. The limitation of E.4 is chiefly that 'mind' is still particularized in terms of both temporal state and individual character, whereas at level E.5 it becomes generalized across time and embedded in a broader view of human nature or of society. A further feature of E.4 is that the self-reflecting character may go beyond reflection on a present state of mind to consider the self's conduct and role in events in a more detached evaluative manner. Thus not only has the writer managed to depict the inner world of thought and feeling but is she/he beginning to deliberate on past conduct and alternative courses of action.

At 11 a proportion of the writers (41 per cent) had reached level F.3 and F.4 in story 1. These included examples of simple projection into the mental state of another, signs of character signalled via cues such as facial expression and tone of voice, and adverbials relating to the protagonist alone. A majority (59 per cent) were still operating at level F.2, however, where only direct behavioural expressions of simple states of excitement are depicted.

In the sample of 13-year-olds, once again a wide range of attainments was displayed. A small minority of the children (3 out of 51, or 6 per cent) remained 'stuck' at level E.2 with its minimal acknowledgement of the inner mental world and subjective point of view. An equally small minority produced writing with examples at level E.5. The remainder were almost equally split between levels E.3 and E.4. This majority (88 per cent) were thus all able to depict a world of characters in which any, or all, were represented as psychological centres of intentional action, capable of thought and feeling. Some 41 per cent were beyond the transitional ground of E.3 and were beginning to centre the interest of their stories on the psychological experiences, in terms of motives, attitudes, thoughts and feelings, of their characters (E.4). At level E.5, which was attained by only a very few children, aspect E must be extended to 'critical self-appraisal'. This is defined as consisting of a character reflecting on self in general terms, which involved evaluation or judgement with explicit criteria. Personal ideals, general rules or principles are made explicit in some form or other. There is in some instances an awareness shown of a gap between the 'ideal self' and the 'actual self'. Personal goals or future developments in conduct or relationships may become part of such inner monologues. The writer is thus now able to represent a character who shows concern over what kind of person he or she is, or is to become.

In the case of aspect F, for story 1, the 13-year-olds were almost evenly divided across levels F.2, F.3 and F.4, with just two reaching F.5. Level 4 for aspect F extends the typical level 4 emphasis on attitude and feeling to inferences about the feelings of others as they are 'read' via non-verbal cues, or described by the author in terms of adverbials. Thus adverbs, adverb phrases and adverb clauses may be used to qualify or describe further the manner of the actions of any character, not merely the protagonist. Tone of voice and facial expression are by far the commonest cues used. A further feature of F.4 concerns examples of 'complex projection'. Here character x not only considers character y's probable state of mind but also considers y's likely view of x's state of mind. About one-third of the 13-year-olds in this sample were found to represent one or more of these features of F.4 which, once again, suggests that they are moving towards a greater interest in the landscape of consciousness as much as, or more than, the landscape of action. Two children reached level F.5, at which one character's projection into the mind of another includes some level 5 'issue', such as values, ideals or developing relationships.

Having summarized some of the apparent developments in the representation of the psychological world by this group of children, it should be emphasized that such data illuminate the 'upper reaches' of cognitive development in that they sample thinking and understanding in the context of one of the most difficult and independent tasks, namely narrative writing, which children are ever asked to undertake. Whereas much psychological research is focused on the zone of proximal development (Vygotsky, 1962) and on behaviour in contexts of maximal support, this study considers a realm in which thinking about the mind has to be made conscious, explicit and appropriate to a particular context, namely the narrative form. Intuitive thought, or inner speech, has to be rendered into the conventions of print and results must depend on the child's grasp of narrative structure and on his or her ability to manage simultaneously all the levels of decision making and skill involved in transcription and composition.

The group of children whose writing has been examined here exhibited, not surprisingly, a wide range of attainments in this task. Moreover, since attainments in writing are partly a function of the child's particular experiences of education, the absolute ages at which different features of development are attained are of less interest in the present context than the nature of the ordinal course of that development. This reveals a striking similarity to the general course of interpersonal understanding described in the work of Selman (1980) and Damon & Hart (1982), though it comes from written, as opposed to interview, data. There are also similarities between the developmental pathway summarized in CACH and Wilkinson's model of 'storying' (Wilkinson, 1986). CACH, however, may be said to have its own distinctive emphases. Greater emphasis is given, in CACH, to the development of communicative understanding and to the representation of the inner world of thought and feeling than in Selman's scheme, perhaps precisely because narratives place an emphasis on just these sorts of interpretations of actions. In comparison with Wilkinson's model, CACH provides a somewhat different view of the affective realm, leading to a greater emphasis on social cognition and hence on the development of characterization. Nevertheless, despite such differences of detail and emphasis, the present study is largely complementary in its findings to those of Selman and Wilkinson.

The world of traditional folk tale, fairy story or legend has much in common with the early narrative writing of children. The world in such stories is often depicted in simple and stereotyped terms with characters who personify aspects of good and evil, knowledge and innocence. Characters are instruments of the plot and the writer's or teller's emphasis is on the physical action, the words, the deeds and the outcomes of the protagonists, who either live out exemplary social scripts of normality or clash in seemingly inevitable conflicts. Egan's (1979) depiction of children's thinking as moving from the 'mythic' to the 'romantic' draws attention to similar parallels between the mental preoccupations of the child and the myths of preliterate cultures. In both, moral values tend to be portrayed as absolute and people, or animals, often function as personifications of those values. Simple emotions of love and hate, hope and fear, happiness and suffering are made explicit but otherwise the thought and feeling, the psychological significance of the actions portrayed, remain implicit or unstated. The characters in such stories think and act purposefully and feel emotion but the preponderance of the writer's attention is fixed on the outer world of physical appearance, of actions and of consequences. Conflict is realized only on the plane of physical confrontation and violence, or else by way of magic. Indeed magic, and supernatural powers in general, at times seem to operate in both folk tales and in children's stories, as substitutes for, or pointers towards, a yet not understood psychological power. As the child as writer becomes able to represent the inner landscape of the mind explicitly, so the reliance on magical effects recedes.

The more successful writers at 11, and even more at 13, have dramatically altered their view of what is appropriate to the narrative form. As with Western literature in general, the world of action is either accompanied by the inner world of psychological experience, which gives it its evaluative meaning, or else the outer world is largely a pretext for the exploration of the inner world of mind. Writers turn from arbitrary crimes, accidents and simple deceptions to plots and themes which centre on the writer's own social world, on plausible events and on general features of society and human relationships. Narrative writing has thus made possible, at least for some children, an arena for working out a developing theory of mind, and of the social world, within a context of imagined experience. Narrative, Bruner (1986) argues, has as its chief aim to work out 'how to endow experience with meaning'. In such a way the common-sense attempts we make to understand ourselves and others as people may draw on this interpretative tradition of plausible narrative 'readings' of people more than on logical and rational tests of explicit hypotheses. Though the present study does not attempt to go beyond the description of a common developmental pathway in this domain, it may be suggested that children's own explorations of the narrative mode in writing provide them with a tradition and a means within which to generate and criticize their own developing theories of mind.

References

Applebee, A. N. (1978). *The Child's Concept of Story*. Chicago: University of Chicago Press.

Astington, J. W., Harris, P. L. & Olson, D. R. (Eds) (1988). *Developing Theories of Mind*. Cambridge: Cambridge University Press.

Bereiter, C. & Scardamalia, M. (1982). From conversation to composition: The role of instruction in a developmental process. In R. Glaser (Ed.), *Advances in Instructional Psychology*, vol 2. London: Erlbaum.

Bretherton, I. (1984). Social referencing and the interfacing of minds. *Merrill-Palmer Quarterly*, **30**, 419–427.

Bruner, J. (1986). *Actual Minds, Possible Worlds*. Cambridge MA: Harvard University Press.

Chandler, M., Fritz, A. & Hala, S. (1989). Small-scale deceit: Deception as marker of 2-, 3- and 4-year-olds' early theories of mind. *Child Development*, **60**, 1263–1277.

Damon, W. & Hart, D. (1982). The development of self-understanding from infancy through adolescence. *Child Development*, **53**, 841–864.

de Beaugrande, R. (1980). *Text, Discourse and Process*. London: Longman.

Egan, K. (1979). *Educational Development*. New York: Oxford University Press.

Estes, D., Wellman, H. M. & Woolley, J. D. (1989). Children's understanding of mental phenomena. *Advances in Child Development and Behavior*, **22**, 41–87.

Feldman, D. (1980). *Beyond Universals in Cognitive Development*. Norwood, NJ: Ablex.

Fitzgerald, J. (1989). Research on stories: Implications for teachers. In K. D. Muth (Ed.), *Children's Comprehension of Text*. Newark, DE: International Reading Association.

Fitzgerald, J. & Teasley, A. (1986). Effects of instruction in narrative structure on children's writing. *Journal of Educational Psychology*, **78**, 424–433.

Fox, R. M. H. (1987). The development of characterization in children's narrative writing between the ages of 7 and 13. PhD thesis, University of Exeter.

Fox, R. M. H. (1990). From character to person. In D. Wray (Ed.), *Emerging Partners: Current Research in Literacy*. Clevedon: Multi-Lingual Matters.

Hardy, B. (1977). Towards a poetics of fiction: An approach through narrative. In M. Meek (Ed.), *The Cool Web*. London: Bodley Head.

Harris, J. & Wilkinson, J. (Eds) (1986). *Reading Children's Writing*. London: Allen & Unwin.

Harter, S. (1983). Developing perspectives on the self-system. In P. Mussen (Ed.), *Handbook of Child Psychology*, 4th ed., vol. 4. New York: Wiley.

Johnson, C. & Wellman, H. M. (1980). Children's developing understanding of mental verbs: Remember, know and guess. *Child Development*, **51**, 1095–1102.

Johnson, C. & Wellman, H. M. (1982). Children's developing conceptions of mind and brain. *Child Development*, **53**, 222–234.

Labov, W. & Waletzhy, J. (1967). Narrative analysis: Oral versions of personal experience. In J. Helm (Ed.), *Essays on the Verbal and Visual Arts*. Seattle: University of Washington Press.

Livesley, W. & Bromley, D. (1973). *Person Perception in Childhood and Adolescence*. Chichester: Wiley.

Mandler, J. (1983). Representation. In P. Mussen (Ed.), *Handbook of Child Psychology*, 4th ed., vol. 3. New York: Wiley.

Mandler, J. & Johnson, N. S. (1977). Remembrance of things parsed: Story structure and recall. *Cognitive Psychology*, **9**, 111–115.

Miller, P. & Aloise, P. A. (1989). Young children's understanding of the psychological causes of behavior: A review. *Child Development*, **60**, 257–285.

Palermo, D. (1989). Knowledge and the child's developing theory of the world. *Advances in Child Development and Behavior*, **21**, 269–295.

Peevers, H. & Secord, P. F. (1973). Developmental change in attribution of descriptive concepts to persons. *Journal of Personality and Social Psychology*, **26**, 120–128.

Peterson, C. & McCabe, A. (1983). *Developmental Psycholinguistics: Three Ways of Looking at a Child's Narratives*. New York: Plenum Press.

Pring, R. (1984). *Personal and Social Education in the Curriculum*. London: Hodder & Stoughton.

Selman, R. (1980). *The Growth of Interpersonal Understanding*. New York: Academic Press.

Shantz, C. (1983). Social cognition. In P. Mussen (Ed.), *Handbook of Child Psychology*, 4th ed., vol. 3. New York: Wiley.

Sherman, S., Judd, C. & Park, B. (1989). Social cognition. *Annual Review of Psychology*, **40**, 281–326.

Stein, N. L. & Glenn, C. (1979). An analysis of story comprehension in elementary school children. In R. O. Freedle (Ed.), *New Directions in Discourse Processing*, vol. 2. Norwood, NJ: Ablex.

Vygotsky, L. (1962). *Thought and Language*. New York: Wiley.

Wellman, H. (1985). The origins of metacognition. In D. L. Forrest-Pressley, G. E. Mackinnon & T. G. Walker (Eds), *Metacognition, Cognition and Human Performance*, vol. 1. Orlando FL: Academic Press.

Wells, G. (1986). *The Meaning Makers*. London: Hodder & Stoughton.

Wilkinson, A., Barnsley, G., Hanna, P. & Swan, M. (1980). *Assessing Language Development*. Oxford: Oxford University Press.

Wilkinson, A. (1986). *The Quality of Writing*. Oxford: Oxford University Press.

Wimmer, H. & Perner, J. (1983). Beliefs about beliefs: Representation and constraining function of wrong beliefs in young children's understanding of deception. *Cognition*, **13**, 103–128.

Received 26 February 1990; revised version received 7 December 1990

Appendix

E Inner World

Hopefully this title is self-explanatory. Any mental faculties or attributes (as opposed to observable behaviour or speech) are included. Often a glance through the verbs in a story will identify examples of this aspect. The inner world of characters may be directly reported by the author or revealed indirectly, e.g. via dialogue.

Inferences made by characters about the inner worlds of other characters are coded under aspect F.

E. 1 *Restricted inner world*

Either no inner world or mental faculties are mentioned at all or a single agent or character has any of a restricted set, as follows:

(i) simple perception: see, look, hear;

(ii) simple cognition: know;

(iii) simple motivating states: wants, states or drives, i.e. hunger, thirst, cold, heat, waking up or going to sleep, wanting, dreaming.

E.1–E.2 Any but the restricted set given for E.1 should be coded at E.2. If any 'other' characters have an inner world at all then code at E.2 (or above).

E.2 Rich inner world for protagonist; Others restricted

(*a*) Protagonist's inner world: this is considerably expanded, especially in terms of cognition, but also in terms of simple affect or emotion:
(i) perception (beyond seeing or hearing): touching, watching, looking for, listening, etc.;
(ii) cognition (beyond knowing): believing, choosing, deciding, discovering, doubting, expecting, planning, pretending, realizing, thinking, wondering;
(iii) sensation: especially states of pain or fatigue (feeling tired, etc.);
(iv) conation: concentrating, making an effort, trying. Expressions of determination or frustration (but not explicit descriptions of these attitudes as such);
(v) motivation and emotion: the protagonist at this level may have the following limited range of feelings and attitudes: afraid, angry, cross, happy, (unhappy), having fun, liking, (disliking), loving, (hating), sad, scared.
(*b*) 'Other' characters' inner worlds: other characters only have the restricted set of faculties listed under E.1. Their mental faculties may, however, be implied by their behaviour or speech as in: purposeful actions; speech as at G.2; asking simple questions, having likes or dislikes.

E.2–E.3 At E.2 only the protagonist has an expanded inner world. At E.3 an equivalent inner world of thought, emotion, etc. extends to any number of characters. At E.3 a self-reflective protagonist may be portrayed.

E.3 Rich inner world for all; Self-reflective protagonist

(*a*) Any or all characters may have the range of mental faculties listed for the protagonist at E.2. These may be reported directly or only implied via dialogue or behaviour. At this level such implied faculties include: reasoning, planning or discussing.
(*b*) A 'self-reflective protagonist' is one who is described as reflecting on his/her own current thoughts or feelings. Such a character may think about what to do next, make plans or consult own feelings or motives. Writing in the form of a 'stream of consciousness' starts at this level. Thinking itself is an explicit activity.
(*c*) Some attitudes, feelings and states; a limited range of attitudes and feelings may be expressed as follows: anxious, bored, disappointed, excited, feeling friendly, frightened, frustrated, lonely, sorry for, terrified, tired, relieved, surprised, worried. Characters may also be affected by mental stress, go insane or go into trances. They may also engage in creative mental activities, e.g. make up a song.

E.3–E.4 The rich inner world of E.3 is still predominantly cognitive, or concerned with a limited range of common feelings and emotions. More complex or rarer attitudes, emotions or mental faculties, not listed at E.3, should be coded at E.4. Self-reflection at E.3 develops into 'self-appraisal' at E.4.

E.4 More complex individual states, attitudes; Self-appraisal

(*a*) Attitudes and feelings are very common at level 4 and any which are not listed in the limited range under E.3 can be coded at E.4, as also can rarer mental events or states.
(*b*) 'Self-appraisal': this involves a self-reflective protagonist who goes beyond the reflection on a present state of mind typical of E.3 to consider the self's part in events, in a more detached way. It may involve evaluation of past conduct, deliberation on more than one possible course of action or attitude towards coming events.
(*c*) 'Persona': the deliberate presentation of a 'persona' is commented on, in the light of the character's real underlying intentions. The self is thus presented deliberately in some social role.

E.4–E.5   The 'self-appraisal' of E.4 develops into a full 'critical self-appraisal' at E.5.

E.5   *Critical self-appraisal*

A character reflects on self in general terms involving evaluation or judgement with explicit criteria. Personal ideals, general rules or principles may be made explicit. There may be some awareness of a gap between 'ideal self' and 'actual self'. Personal goals or future development may be involved in such inner monologue. The character is concerned about what sort of person to become or about what sort of person he or she is.

F   Expressive behaviour and inferences about others

This aspect covers four related areas:
(i) The direct expression of emotion or psychological state in behaviour (e.g. laughter and tears).
(ii) Non-verbal communication (including tone of voice, facial expression, gesture, etc.).
(iii) Projection by one character into the mental state of another.
(iv) 'Adverbials', that is to say adverbs, adverb phrases and adverb clauses which tell the reader about the manner of actions or behaviour, and hence about underlying intentions and feelings.

F.1   *None*

A simple case of none. However, if aspects B and C are coded at level 2 or above then aspect F may be omitted.

F.1–F.2   Any examples of emotional expression, non-verbal communication, projection or 'adverbials' should be coded at F.2 or above. *If* there are no instances relating to aspect F, then consider aspects B and C. If both B and C are coded at level 2 or above then F may be omitted. If either B or C are coded at level 1 then F is coded at F.1.

F.2   *Emotional expression*

This includes a variety of behaviours expressing inner states as follows:
(*a*) vocal expressions of surprise, excitement, pain or fear (Yippee, Ow! Oh! etc.).
(*b*) physical expression of emotion: laughter, tears, shouting or shaking with fear.
(*c*) use of the verbs 'run', 'run away' or 'rush' to imply the intention behind a response.

F.2–F.3   The direct expression of simple inner states of excitement and fear are coded at F.2. More complex examples of emotional expression and inferences about the mental states of others are coded at F.3, or above.

F.3   *Simple projection and inferences; Adverbials relating to self*

(*a*) 'More complex emotional expression'. Physical appearance or behaviour may indicate or signal the nature of character, emotion or disposition. Such may include 'a ripple of excitement', 'a tear trickling down a cheek' or 'a shiver running down a spine', etc.
(*b*) 'Signs of character'. Tone of voice or the content of speech may be a direct indication of a stereotyped character (thus an 'evil' character may speak or behave in an 'evil' way). But see also F.4 (*a*). (It may also be acknowledged that such stereotypes may mislead. In general F.3 inferences from appearance will link up with D.3 global evaluations.)
(*c*) 'Simple projection'. Characters at level 3 may project into the mental states of others, or in other words imagine what they are thinking or feeling. Normally at F.3 this involves character *x* considering

the general motive state of character *y*. Simple projection is here defined as one character projecting into the general state of mind of another. It does not include appraisal by *x* of *y*'s view of *x* (see F.4).

(*d*) 'Adverbials relating to self'. Adverbs or adverb phrases or clauses are used to qualify the actions of the protagonist, to imply intention or to suggest the manner in which they are carried out. Verbs may also be selected to illustrate the manner of an action or its purpose (e.g. 'he crept down stairs . . .', 'she threw herself to the ground . . .', 'reluctantly he opened the door . . .', 'she drove as fast as she could . . .').

F.3–F.4   At F.3 there are emotional expression, signs of character, simple projection and adverbials relating to self. At F.4 these develop to become inferences from non-verbal cues, complex projection and adverbials relating to others.

F.4   *Feelings and attitudes inferred*

(*a*) Non-verbal cues: The emphasis at this level is often on the intentions and feelings which lie behind, and provide the key to interpreting or understanding, behaviour. (Direct reports of thoughts, attitudes and feelings are coded under E, however.) Inferences made by one character of another from behaviour or non-verbal cues are coded here, apart from the limited range listed at F.3. Tone of voice and facial expression are the commonest cues used. Except when used to 'signal' a stereotyped character (as at F3) code at F.4. Such cues are usually specific to the current situation. Rarer cues include posture, gait, gesture, and rhythm or timing of speech.

(*b*) 'Complex projection'. Here fully reciprocal projection allows *x* not only to project into *y*'s state of mind or general point of view but also to consider *y*'s probable view of *x*'s state of mind etc. In the same way *y* may consider *x*'s view of *y*, or of *z*. Such complex projection may involve attitudes and feelings of all kinds.

(*c*) 'Adverbials relating to others'. Selected verbs, adverbs or adverbial phrases or clauses may be used to qualify or illustrate the manner of actions of characters besides the protagonist.

F.4–F.5   Most general inferences about thoughts and feelings are dealt with under F.3 and F.4. F.5 is reserved for cases in which a character projects or empathizes with another character's thoughts and feelings about changing relationships, general values and change (as in B.5 and D.5).

F.5   *Relationships, values and change in projection and empathy*

One character considers another character's thoughts or feelings concerning some typical level 5 issue such as changing or developing relationships, ideals, general issues of value or major changes in life circumstances.

6
Autism: Failure to acquire a theory of mind

Preface

Part of the interest in the development of theory of mind lies in the availability of a neuropsychological model. Baron-Cohen, Leslie & Frith (1985) found that autistic children, but not mental age-matched Down's syndrome children, showed a markedly poorer performance on a standard false belief task than would be expected from their general intellectual level. This discovery suggested that specific psychological processes underlying the development of theory of mind could be *factored out* from among the tangled mass of processes, skills and knowledge that comprise normal development. The autistic child's difficulty with false belief had been predicted theoretically by applying ideas about normal development to the triad of impairments (Wing & Gould, 1979) that constitute the core symptoms of autism. These ideas (in an early formulation in Leslie, 1983, and later in Leslie, 1987) could link the autistic child's difficulties with pretence to the other two features of the triad (social and communicative impairment) via the notion of a single processing system which is selectively damaged in autism. This postulated processing system was characterized in terms of the particular representations, dubbed *metarepresentations*, that it handled. The metarepresentational theory of autism comprises a set of ideas which is still very much under development (for recent reviews see Baron-Cohen, 1990; Leslie & Frith, 1990) and still controversial. The four papers in this section illustrate a number of questions that concern workers in this area.

Simon Baron-Cohen takes up the question of just how *specific* the impairment is in the autistic child's theory of mind. Does the autistic child have a general difficulty with the social world? Does the autistic child have a general problem with constructing just any kind of 'theoretical' knowledge? Baron-Cohen's latest results add new evidence that autistic children have some quite adequate social and biological notions. Establishing the pattern of spared abilities is just as important as the pattern impairments.

Roth & Leslie note that on many theory of mind tasks autistic adolescents perform as normal 3-year-old children do. Does this mean that the autistic person fails for precisely the same reasons 3-year-olds do? They investigate this in a modified standard task and show that while normal 3- and 5-year-olds differ from one another, autistic adolescents show a third pattern of performance that is different from both the normal groups. These patterns are explained in terms of the metarepresentational theory.

Russell, Mauthner, Sharpe & Tidswell compare a deceptive pointing task with a standard false belief task, using groups of normal, Down's syndrome and autistic children. They replicate previous results that normal 4-year-olds and Down's syndrome children perform alike on these tasks (passing), while normal 3-year-old and autistic children perform alike (failing). They then point out an interesting similarity in the way the latter groups fail the pointing task. This leads them to suggest a common reason for their failure, namely, a difficulty in suppressing the 'salience' of a present reality.

Our final paper, by Eisenmajer & Prior, returns to the metarepresentational theory and asks what is the correlation between autistic performance on a standard theory of mind task and various psychometric tests. They find an association between false belief passing and pragmatic ability in autism, and also between passing and skill at 'abstract reasoning' and conclude that, on the whole, the metarepresentational theory is supported by these results but argue that allowance must be made for different degrees of impairment. Their work also raises the challenge of reconciling psychometric concepts with the information-processing notions which form the framework for the metarepresentational theory.

All four papers bring out, in their different ways, the point that the study of normal and handicapped development is a two-way street with implications and controversies moving in both directions.

References

Baron-Cohen, S. (1990). Autism: A specific cognitive disorder of 'mind-blindness'. *International Review of Psychiatry*, **2**, 79–88.

Baron-Cohen, S., Leslie, A. M. & Frith, U. (1985). Does the autistic child have a 'theory of mind'? *Cognition*, **21**, 37–46.

Leslie, A. M. (1983). Pretend play and representation in the second year of life. BPS Developmental Section Conference, Oxford University, September 1983.

Leslie, A. M. (1987). Pretense and representation: The origins of 'theory of mind'. *Psychological Review*, **94**, 412–426.

Leslie, A. M. & Frith, U. (1990). Prospects for a cognitive neuropsychology of autism: Hobson's choice. *Psychological Review*, **97**, 122–131.

Wing, L. & Gould, J. (1979). Severe impairments of social interaction and associated abnormalities in children: Epidemiology and classification. *Journal of Autism and Developmental Disorders*, **9**, 11–29.

British Journal of Developmental Psychology (1991), **9**, 301–314 *Printed in Great Britain*

The theory of mind deficit in autism: How specific is it?*

Simon Baron-Cohen†

Departments of Psychology and Child Psychiatry, Institute of Psychiatry, University of London, De Crespigny Park, London SE5 8AF, UK

Abnormalities in the social and communicative development of children with autism have recently been related to an impairment in their ability to attribute mental states to others, that is, in the development of their 'theory of mind'. The present paper investigates if this deficit is *specific* to understanding mental states, or if it extends to domains of social cognition in autism which do not involve a theory of mind. This is tested in three areas: (1) relationship recognition, (2) interpersonal reciprocity, and (3) understanding the animate–inanimate distinction. Results from experiments in these three areas show that subjects with autism are unimpaired in all three domains, relative to non-autistic mentally handicapped or normal control groups. This suggests that the deficits in their theory of mind may well be highly specific.

Recent studies of social cognition in autism suggest that the ability to attribute propositional mental states (such as beliefs and knowledge) to other people is severely impaired, even relative to control groups of a lower mental age (Baron-Cohen, 1989*a,b*, 1991*a*; Baron-Cohen, Leslie & Frith, 1985, 1986; Dawson & Fernald, 1987; Harris & Muncer, 1988; Leekam & Perner, in press; Leslie & Frith, 1988; Mitchell, 1989; Perner, Frith, Leslie & Leekam, 1989; Reed & Patterson, in press; Russell, Sharpe, Mauthner & Tidswell, 1991; Shaw, 1989; Sodian & Frith, 1990; Swettenham, 1990). This finding appears to be highly robust, in that despite wide variations in techniques used to assess it, comparable results are still obtained. Thus, studies to test if children with autism understand false beliefs have used a range of stimuli that include dolls (Baron-Cohen *et al.*, 1985; Leekam & Perner, in press; Mitchell, 1990; Reed & Patterson, in press), picture stories (Baron-Cohen *et al.*, 1986), people (Leslie & Frith, 1988; Perner *et al.*, 1989; Russell *et al.*, in press), and even computer-graphic images of people (Swettenham, 1990). In addition, although most of these experiments have been administered by psychologists, similar results are still obtained if the tests are administered by the child's mother (Shaw, 1989).

Three questions arise concerning the *specificity* of this deficit. First, is it confined to people with autism? To date, the only other clinical groups that have been tested are

* Parts of this paper were presented at invited seminars to the MRC Cognitive Development Unit, London, June 1989, to the 2nd National Congress on Autism in Denmark, 1990 and to the Zangwill Club, Cambridge University, 1990.

† Requests for reprints should be addressed to the author at the Department of Psychology.

subjects with Down's syndrome (Baron-Cohen, 1989*a*; Baron-Cohen *et al.*, 1985, 1986), specific language impairments (Leslie & Frith, 1988; Perner *et al.*, 1989), deafness (Leslie & Sellars, forthcoming), and mental handicap of mixed aetiology (Baron-Cohen, 1989*b*) all of whom perform normally on the tests. Whilst this does not exhaust the set of clinical populations that need to be tested using such techniques, the deficit so far does seem to be specific to autism.

Secondly, is the deficit in autism confined to understanding propositional mental states, or does it apply generally to their understanding of all mental states? Evidence so far suggests that understanding the propositional mental states believe (Baron-Cohen *et al.*, 1985, 1986), know (Leslie & Frith, 1988), think and dream (Baron-Cohen, 1989*b*) are all impaired in people with autism, whilst their understanding of non-propositional mental states such as 'simple' emotions (e.g. happiness and sadness as outcomes of situations) is unimpaired* (Baron-Cohen, in press; Harris, 1991). Thus, the deficit may well be confined to (or at least most severe in) their understanding of propositional mental states.

Finally, is the deficit in autism confined to understanding mental states (propositional or otherwise), or does it extend to other domains of their social cognition? The term social cognition is used here to refer to those aspects of the cognitive system that are used in understanding the social world. The evidence to date shows that people with autism are relatively 'intact' in a number of domains of social cognition. These include person permanence (Sigman & Mundy, 1989), visual perspective taking (Baron-Cohen, 1989*c*; Hobson, 1984), mirror self-recognition (Baron-Cohen, 1985; Dawson & McKissick, 1984; Ferrari & Matthews, 1983; Flannery, 1976; Neumann & Hill, 1978; Spiker & Ricks, 1984) and gender recognition (Abelson, 1981; Weeks & Hobson, 1987). Similarly, children with autism pass tests of face recognition, although they may use unusual strategies (Goode, 1985; Hobson, Ouston & Lee, 1988; Langdell, 1978; Volkmar, Sparrow, Rende & Cohen, 1989).

However, there are many other domains within social cognition which do not involve a theory of mind and which have not yet been systematically investigated in autism. The possibility remains, therefore, that there may well be a 'lower level' social cognitive deficit in autism. This article attempts to fill a gap in our knowledge by reporting on three areas of social cognition which do not involve a theory of mind and which have not been previously tested in autism. These abilities are relationship recognition, interpersonal reciprocity and understanding the animate–inanimate distinction. The rationale for testing each of these is outlined below.

Three hypotheses

One possibility is that the social difficulties in autism stem from an inability to recognize social relationships, that is, an inability to perceive how people are related to each other, *independent* of the mental states people possess. A failure to recognize social relationships would, one imagines, leave a person seriously confused by the

---

* Hobson and his colleagues (see Hobson, 1989, for a review) have found emotion recognition for people with autism is impaired relative to recognition of non-emotion stimuli, when compared to matched controls. How such recognition skills relate to comprehension remains to be investigated (see also Ozonoff, Pennington & Rogers, 1990).

social world. Some evidence that this occurs was reported by Dewey & Everard (1984) who noted that social relationships such as social class might go unrecognized by people with autism, since they often fail to modify their language according to their listener's social status.

Social relationships are, at the simplest level, defined by the physical characteristics of the particular individuals. For example, a mother–child relationship is defined by a relative age gap and by the gender of the adult, although the absolute age or physical appearance of that mother or her child, and the absolute gender of her child, are irrelevant to the definition. Naturally, relationships can be defined on more subtle levels, such as in terms of the ways in which the two people behave ('relate') towards each other. Thus, in the case of a mother–child relationship, nurturing behaviour might be thought of as important to the definition of the relationship. In the first of our experiments, however, we investigated judgements about relationships simply in terms of the physical attributes of the relative age difference between the adult and child, plus the adult's female gender.

The capacity for relationship recognition, also known as non-egocentric discrimination of kin association,* has been demonstrated in the higher primates (Dasser, 1988). This ability has not, as far as I know, been tested in normal children. It is conservatively estimated here that normal children of 3.5 years old would possess such an ability, using Premack's (1988, p. 173) rule of thumb that 'capacities that do not appear in the 3.5-year-old child will not be found in the ape'. Can people with autism also identify such relationships? Experiment 1 tested this question.

A second possibility is that the social difficulties in autism arise from a general inability to understand anything about interpersonal reciprocity (Rutter, 1983), that is, that relationships have a symmetry, again independent of the mental states people possess. Again, such a deficit could be expected to have a profoundly disruptive effect on their attempts at social interaction, leaving them oddly one-sided and 'egocentric'. In Expt 2 we tested this in two ways, by asking (*a*) Do people with autism appreciate that, if we are sitting opposite each other, their left and right is my right and left?† (*b*) Can they demonstrate simple reciprocity in a turn-taking ball game, such that their turn alternates with mine, and mine with theirs?

These are tests of interpersonal reciprocity to the extent that they involve people in symmetrical relationships. But this type of simple reciprocity is unlikely to involve a theory of mind. For example, left–right reciprocity could be solved simply by 180° mental rotation of one's own left and right, whilst the ball-rolling reciprocity could be solved by employing a simple schema in which direction and repetition of movement are specified. In this sense, these tasks could be solved without any awareness of people with their own mental states.

The third and final hypothesis is that the social difficulties in autism might arise from an early incapacity to distinguish between animate and inanimate objects, again

---

* Dasser (1988, p. 91) makes the point that non-egocentric discrimination of kin association is different to simple kin recognition. The latter involves differentiating if an individual is a genetically close relation to oneself or not, and this ability is widespread in animals. The discrimination of kin-associations between others can be thought of as *non-egocentric* when it entails judging the relationship between any two individuals, even if they are completely unrelated to oneself.

† I am grateful to Cathy Peng for suggesting this non-mentalistic control task.

independent of whether those objects possess mental states. Imagine a human being who was 'blind' to such a distinction. Such a person would not only find the world confusing, but might attempt to communicate with entirely the wrong class of objects. Indeed, Kanner, the psychiatrist who first described autism in 1943, suggested such a deficit might exist:

> He never looked up at people's faces. When he had any dealings with persons at all, he treated them, or rather parts of them, as if they were objects. He would use a hand to lead him. He would, in playing, butt his head against his mother as at other times he did against a pillow. He allowed his boarding mother's hand to dress him, paying not the slightest attention to *her* ... People, so long as they left the child alone, figured in about the same manner as did the desk, the bookshelf, or the filing cabinet. (Kanner, 1943, reprinted in 1973, pp. 15, 38).

Although Piaget (1929) believed young normal children were confused about the distinction between animate and inanimate objects, recent work shows he considerably underestimated young children in this regard (Carey, 1985). In Expt 3, we tested if children with autism had the ability to distinguish animate and inanimate objects.

Experiment 1: Recognizing social relationships

Subjects

The experiments were administered in random order, and all subjects took part in all three experiments. Each subject was tested in a quiet room in his or her school, alone with the experimenter. There were 17 subjects with autism, all of whom had been diagnosed according to established criteria (DSM III–R, 1987) and were attending a special school for autism. In addition, there were 16 subjects with mental handicap, to control for mental age (MA) and chronological age (CA), and 19 clinically normal children, included to provide some normative data for the abilities tested. The sex ratio in the normal group and the group with mental handicap was approximately 1:1, whilst in the group with autism it was 3:1 (M:F). Details of the subjects are summarized in Table 1.

Table 1. Subject variables: Means, SDs and ranges of chronological age (CA) and mental age (MA)

Diagnostic groups	N	CA	Non-verbal MA	Verbal MA
Autism	17			
Mean		13.78	8.48	6.91
SD		2.8	1.81	1.77
Range		9.7–19.8	5.6–11.2	4.0–9.9
Mental handicap	16			
Mean		15.44	6.03	6.47
SD		2.13	1.0	1.5
Range		9.3–18.3	5.0–8.5	4.0–10.0
Normal	19			
Mean		5.3	—	
SD		0.87	—	—
Range		4.1–6.8	—	—

Note. Non-verbal MA measured by Raven's Matrices; verbal MA by the BPVS.

The inclusion criterion for the clinical subjects was a verbal MA of at least 4 years old, representing the age at which normal children comfortably passed our pilot tests. Non-verbal MA was higher than verbal MA for both clinical groups, markedly so in the case of the subjects with autism, reflecting typical discrepancies in the IQ profile (De Myer, 1976). Using a minimum verbal MA as an inclusion criterion was therefore a conservative precaution against the risk that the clinical groups might be developmentally disadvantaged in comparison with the normal control group. Our normal control group had a mean CA of 5.3 years, ranging from 4.1 to 6.8. We assumed that, for the normal group, MA would roughly correspond to CA. Verbal MA was assessed using the British Picture Vocabulary Scale (BPVS, Dunn, Dunn, Whetton & Pintilie, 1982). Non-verbal MA was assessed using the Raven's Coloured Progressive Matrices (Raven, 1956).

Procedure

Four sample pictures were put on the table in front of the subject. Each picture was taken from one of the four categories of relationship tested, namely (*a*) mother–child, (*b*) father–child, (*c*) peer, and (*d*) husband–wife. These categories were selected on the basis that subjects in all three groups would have had direct or indirect experience of all four types of relationship. The experimenter first named the four sample pictures for the subject ('Here is a picture of a mother and a child', etc.). The subject was then given 20 further pictures, in random order, containing five further examples from each category, and was asked to place each one next to one of the four sample pictures. With each picture the subject was reminded 'Look at these [sample pictures]' and was then asked 'Where does this one go?'*. All subjects seemed to grasp the nature of the matching to sample task without any warm-up, training or additional explanation being necessary.

Materials. The 24 pictures were colour photographs taken from popular magazines, mounted on card measuring 3 x 3 in. In each category, care was taken to ensure that the models differed in terms of age, and in categories *a*, *b* and *c*, the child's sex was in some instances male, others female. Schematic examples of the sample picture in each of the four categories and a randomly selected token of each category are shown in Fig. 1.

Scoring. After the subject had sorted the 20 pictures, incorrect classifications were noted, and these were then deducted from a possible total score of 20. The probability of correctly sorting any one picture by chance alone was assumed to be .25, since there were four piles of pictures. Therefore, using the binomial test at $p < .05$, an overall score of 9 or more was taken as above chance performance.

Results and discussion

The results of Expt 1 are shown in Table 2. As can be seen, all three groups performed clearly above chance. A one-way analysis of variance revealed that the groups differed significantly ($F = 4.894$, $p < .01$), and a Scheffé *post hoc* test showed that this difference was due to the group with autism scoring significantly higher than the group with mental handicap (Scheffé test, $p < .05$). The same Scheffé test showed that the group with autism and the normal group did not differ from one another on this task ($p > .05$).

The relatively poorer performance of the subjects with mental handicap was not predicted prior to the experiment, but one possible reason for this may have been their tendency to be more impulsive than the other groups. They frequently put a picture down on to one of the four piles without any delay. It seems likely that, in

---

* A pilot version of this task required the child to place the pictures *over* the targets. This was considered less satisfactory than the present procedure because it introduced unnecessary memory factors. In the final form of this experiment, the target pictures were therefore visible at all times, eliminating additional memory factors from the task.

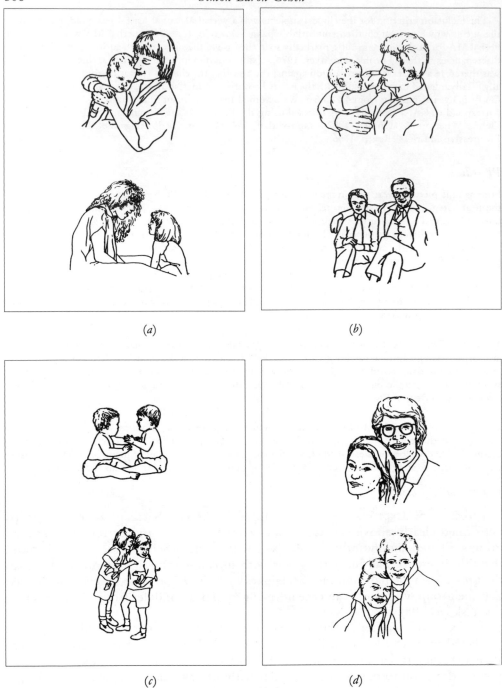

(a)

(b)

(c)

(d)

Figure 1. Schematic examples of the sample illustration in the four categories of relationship, and a schematic token of a match for each. Category names: (*a*) mother–child; (*b*) father–child; (*c*) peer; (*d*) husband–wife.

These drawings are by Cathy Clench, St Bartholomew's Hospital Medical Illustration Department, London.

Table 2. Results on the relationships test

Diagnostic group	N	Score (max. = 20)	
		M	SD
Autism	17	17.7	2.25
Mental handicap	16	14.5*	3.85
Normal	19	17.0	3.02

* $p < .05$.

their case alone, some pre-training might have improved their score. In contrast, the subjects with autism and the normal subjects were virtually at ceiling on this task.

These results suggest that the detection of mother–child, father–child, husband–wife, and peer relationships in unfamiliar and unrelated individuals poses no special difficulty for subjects with autism. This kind of social perception can be carried out purely in terms of relative age and gender cues, without necessarily involving attribution of mental states. Naturally, more subtle aspects of relationship perception, not tested here, may entail mental state attribution, but the present data are consistent with the notion that the social-cognitive deficit in autism is specific to the development of a theory of mind. This was tested further in Expt 2.

Experiment 2: Demonstrating 'reciprocity'

Procedure

We used two tests of reciprocity: (i) distinguishing own left–right from other left–right, when sitting opposite another person, and (ii) maintaining a ball-rolling game. These two tests were administered in random order. The instructions for the left–right test were as follows. The experimenter said 'Which is your left hand? And which is your right hand? OK, now, which is my left hand? And which is my right hand?' The order of hands and of self–other in the questions was randomized. Then, after the experimenter and the subject had switched sides of the table, this was repeated in order to control for position effects. Correct performance was credited if the subject passed on both trials of own left–right and other left–right.

The instructions for the ball game were as follows. The experimenter said 'Look! Here's a little ball. Would you like to play ball with me? OK, let's roll the ball to each other'. The experimenter then rolled the ball to the subject, and waited to see if the subject rolled it back. If the subject did not, the experimenter said, 'Now it's your turn. Can you roll it back to me?' This was the only time a prompt was given. If the subject did roll it back, the experimenter silently rolled it back to the subject, and then counted to establish if the subject could maintain the alternate turn taking for five to-and-fro turns.

Results and discussion

The results of this experiment are shown in Table 3. Taking the left–right test first, it is evident that the majority of subjects in all three groups passed this without any difficulty. Furthermore, statistically the three groups did not differ from each other (autism × mental handicap, and mental handicap × normal, both $\chi^2(1) = .25$; $p < .62$). And again, on the ball-rolling task, all three groups functioned at a similar

Table 3. Results from the reciprocity tasks

Diagnostic group	N	Left–right test		Ball-rolling test	
		Pass	Fail	Pass	Fail
Autism	17	14 (82)	3	15 (88)	2
Mental handicap	16	11 (69)	5	13 (81)	3
Normal	19	11 (59)	8	18 (95)	1

Note. Numbers in parentheses indicate percentage of whole group passing each test.

level, close to ceiling (autism × mental handicap, $\chi^2(1) = .01$, $p < .94$; autism × normal, $\chi^2(1) = .01$, $p > .91$).

Thus, the majority of our subjects with autism showed no deficit in their ability to demonstrate reciprocity at this simple level, revealing their awareness of the basic symmetrical structure of reciprocal social relationships. As with Expt 1, this result is also consistent with the impaired theory of mind model of autism, as reciprocity at this level does not necessarily entail attribution of mental states. Of course, more complex forms of social reciprocity (e.g. sharing, helping) are likely to entail mental state attribution, and these would be expected to be impaired in autism. Such complex forms were not tested here. We shall return to this point in the General Discussion section. Before this, the final experiment is described, which tested understanding of the animate–inanimate distinction in autism.

Experiment 3: Understanding the animate–inanimate distinction

Method

The experimenter said, 'I've got some more pictures to show you. Would you like to see them? OK, now can you tell me what this is? Good. Is this alive or not alive?' The experimenter then proceeded to ask the same two questions (naming and alive questions) for the subsequent 29 pictures (total = 30). The pictures are described below. With each response, the experimenter put the picture into the pile identified by the subject as alive or not alive. At the end of the task, the experimenter spread out the pictures on the table in front of the subject, retaining the two piles the subject had made, and said, 'OK. Now let's look at all of these' (here, he indicated all the pictures the subject had classified as alive). He then said, 'Why are all these alive?' (the Why question).

Materials.   The pictures comprised colour photographs obtained from popular magazines, each picture containing one object. The objects fell into six categories (three animate and three inanimate), and the five examples of each are listed here:

(*a*) animals (bird, cat, fox, dog, otter)
(*b*) plants (four types of flower and a tree)
(*c*) people (boy, baby, man, girl, woman)
(*d*) domestic objects (table, cup and saucer, camera, television, hammer)
(*e*) mobile objects (tricycle, wheel-barrow, car, lawn-mower, vacuum cleaner)
(*f*) toy creatures (a furry duck, a furry Mickey Mouse, a teddy bear, a soft clown, a plastic female doll).

These categories were chosen in order to facilitate investigation of the kinds of errors that subjects might make, based on the criteria they might use to define being alive. Thus, if they used the criterion of movement, category (*e*) would be wrongly sorted as alive whilst category (*b*) might be wrongly sorted as not alive. In contrast, if they used the criterion of having eyes, again category (*b*) would be wrongly sorted as not alive, but this time category (*f*) would be wrongly sorted as alive. Or, to give a final example, if they used the criterion of being able to talk, categories (*b*) and (*c*) would both be wrongly sorted as not alive.

Scoring. There were 15 pictures that could be categorized correctly as alive [namely the five pictures in each of categories (*a*), (*b*) and (*c*)] and 15 that could be categorized correctly as not being alive [namely the five pictures in each of categories (*d*), (*e*) and (*f*)]. Each subject was therefore allocated an animate score out of 15, depending on how many of (*a*), (*b*) and (*c*) had been classified as alive, and an inanimate score out of 15, depending on how many of (*d*), (*e*) and (*f*) had been classified as not being alive. Subsequently, errors were classified by type and criteria used in response to the why question. Since the probability of correctly classifying any one picture by chance alone was .5, an animate or inanimate score of equal to or more than 9 out of 15 was considered to be non-random responding (binomial test, $p < .05$).

Results

The correct animate and inanimate scores for each group are shown in Table 4. The group with autism scored well above chance on both, whilst the group with mental handicap and the normal group, although well above chance on their inanimate scores, were only just above chance on their animate scores. However, a one-way ANOVA showed that the correct animate score did not differ significantly between groups ($F = 2.26$, $p > .11$). A similar ANOVA of the correct inanimate scores also showed that the groups did not differ ($F = 1.53$, $p > .22$). However, when the group with autism and the normal group were compared by a further *t* test, the difference in performance approached significance ($t(34) = 1.91$, $p = .06$). This suggests that the normal group tended to find it *more* difficult to define correctly what was not alive compared to the group with autism.

Table 4. Correct classification of animate objects (and number of errors) on the animate–inanimate test

Diagnostic groups	N	Correct animate score[a]		Correct inanimate score[a]	
		M	*SD*	*M*	*SD*
Autism	17	11.4	2.96	13.41	2.67
Mental handicap	16	9.6	3.3	12.06	3.68
Normal	19	9.1	3.46	11.2	4.02

[a] Max. score = 15.

An examination of the types of error made (shown in Table 5) revealed first that when errors occurred, they tended to be consistent within a discrete category (e.g. if a subject excluded any plants, then he or she excluded all examples of plants, not just one or two examples of them). This meant that errors tended to occur in groups of five points, corresponding to the category wrongly classified. Secondly, although fewer subjects with autism showed random errors (guessing) than the other two groups, and although more normal children excluded animals from the alive category than the other two groups, neither these nor any other differences in Table 5 were

Table 5. Number of subjects in each group making different error types in the animate–inanimate distinction

Error type	Diagnostic groups Autism	Mental handicap	Normal
Animate			
Plants excluded	10	9	12
Animals excluded	0	1	4
People excluded	0	0	1
Inanimate			
Mobile objs excluded	1	0	2
Toy creatures excluded	2	2	2
Domestic objects excluded	0	0	0
Random errors	2	4	4
No errors	5	3	2

statistically significant (Fisher's exact test, $p > .05$). The most common error for all three groups was excluding plants as being alive, and the least common errors for all groups were excluding people, or including domestic objects, as being alive.

There were also a number of similarities between the three groups in the criteria they used to define being alive (see Table 6). First, for all three groups the most commonly used criteria were movement, followed by reference to a biological function (eating, growing, or dying), followed by sight. Two subjects in the normal group used an additional criterion of familiarity (any object seen or owned) which no subjects in the other two groups used. This strengthens the statistically non-significant trend that the normal subjects seemed the most unclear about the animate–inanimate distinction. Indeed, it was the normal group which contained the highest number of bizarre criteria (e.g. familiarity). This contrast with the group with autism replicates an earlier unpublished study (Donald Cohen, personal communication).

Table 6. Number of subjects in each group using the various criteria in the animate–inanimate distinction

Criteria used	Diagnostic groups Autism	Mental handicap	Normal
Moves	6	5	6
Biological function[a]	5	6	4
Sight (has eyes)	2	2	4
Familiarity[b]	0	0	2
'Don't know'	4	4	3

[a](Grows, can die, or eats).
[b](Seen or has one).

Indeed, the only subject with autism who produced a really bizarre response in his sorting was a bright, teenage boy who said that things that are alive can 'swallow'. He explained that it was on this basis that he had classified the picture of the vacuum cleaner and the lawn-mower as alive. In our coding this subject's criterion was scored as biological (eats). But apart from him, the surprising level of development of this distinction in autism demonstrates yet another intact area of their social cognition, and underlines the real possibility of the specificity of their deficit in understanding mental states.

Influence of MA and CA on performance in all three experiments

It is worth noting briefly that although few significant differences emerged between groups in any of the experiments, there was nevertheless a trend within groups for performance to be related to both CA and MA, that is, the older and higher functioning subjects in both clinical groups tended to make fewer errors on any of the tasks, relative to both younger and lower functioning subjects. The same was true for the normal group with respect to CA. (MA was not assessed in the normal group.) Thus, correct performance steadily increased with age for the normal children, on all three tasks.

General discussion

The question behind the three experiments described here is whether the previously reported deficit in the development of a theory of mind in people with autism is *specific* to that aspect of their social cognition, or whether there is a lower level deficit in other domains of their social cognition that do not involve a theory of mind. The results of these three experiments produced a clear answer to this question, in relation to three such social cognitive abilities. Subjects with autism are neither impaired in their ability to recognize simple relationships, nor in their ability to show simple reciprocity, nor in their understanding of the animate–inanimate distinction, relative to normal subjects and subjects with mental handicap. I argued at the outset of this article that none of these skills, at this basic level, require mental state attribution. On this assumption, the present results are therefore consistent with the hypothesis that the deficit in the development of a theory of mind in autism is highly specific.

However, although good performance was observed in all three areas, the tests used here were of such a simple level that deficits in each of these areas might still exist at higher levels. Nevertheless, both I and others (Baron-Cohen, 1988, 1990, in press; Baron-Cohen *et al.*, 1985, 1986; Leslie & Frith, 1990) have made the claim that the complexity such higher-level tests would require is likely to be of a kind which entailed using a theory of mind. For example, some evidence suggests that people with autism are unaware or only dimly aware of certain complex types of relationship, such as deception (Russell *et al.*, in press; Sodian & Frith, 1990), or embarrassment. Similarly, there are certain kinds of reciprocity which people with autism are incapable of demonstrating, such as pragmatic competence in language (Baltaxe, 1977; Baron-Cohen, 1988; Perner *et al.*, 1989) or complex social games. Given the role of mental state attribution in the normal functioning of these skills

(Dennett, 1978; Grice, 1975), failure at all of these levels may well be related to deficits in their use of a theory of mind.

The exception to this qualification may be in the understanding that people with autism have of the animate–inanimate distinction, which the present results suggest is highly advanced, and which may even be free of deficits at higher levels. For example, on questioning those subjects who produced biological explanations for the distinction, I found their understanding of biology was no weaker than that of either of the control groups. Thus, some referred to growth, or to the existence of bones and blood, to the need to eat, and to the inevitability of death. In another study (Baron-Cohen, 1989*b*), I found a surprisingly normal understanding of the location and function of the heart and the brain, relative to control groups. However, consistent with the theory of mind deficit in autism, many subjects with autism believed the brain's main function was solely in generating and controlling *movement*, whilst most normal subjects, as well as those with mental handicap and with the same MA believed its main function was to generate and control *thought*.

In conclusion, social cognition that is independent of a theory of mind seems to be spared of any damage in autism. In contrast, as more replications of their deficits in theory of mind are attempted, the specificity of this deficit becomes all the clearer. One clinical implication of this is that, if social skills that do not involve a theory of mind are taught in schools for autism, these are likely to be successfully acquired, without necessarily affecting the crucial deficits in the person's theory of mind. It will be important for future studies of the theory of mind deficit in autism to establish further the respective roles played by emotion (Hobson, 1990) and cognition (Leslie & Frith, 1990), as well as investigating whether this highly specific deficit is amenable to treatment.

Acknowledgements

I am indebted to the staff and children at the following London schools: St Luke's, and Rosemary Schools, Islington, and the Sybil Elgar School, Ealing. Finally, I would like to thank Paul Harris, Deborah Zaitchik, Helen Tager-Flusberg and Susan Carey for valuable comments on this work.

References

Abelson, A. G. (1981). The development of gender identity in the autistic child. *Child: Care, Health, and Development*, **7**, 347–356.

Baltaxe, C. (1977). Pragmatic deficits in the language of autistic adolescents. *Journal of Paediatric Psychology*, **2**, 176–180.

Baron-Cohen, S. (1985). Social cognition and pretend play in autism. Unpublished PhD thesis, University College, University of London.

Baron-Cohen, S. (1988). Social and pragmatic deficits in autism: Cognitive or affective? *Journal of Autism and Developmental Disorders*, **18**, 379–402.

Baron-Cohen, S. (1989a). The autistic child's theory of mind: A case of specific developmental delay. *Journal of Child Psychology and Psychiatry*, **30**, 285–298.

Baron-Cohen, S. (1989b). Are autistic children behaviourists? An examination of their mental–physical and appearance–reality distinctions. *Journal of Autism and Developmental Disorders*, **19**, 579–600.

Baron-Cohen, S. (1989c). Perceptual role taking and protodeclarative pointing in autism. *British Journal of Developmental Psychology*, **7**, 113–127.

Baron-Cohen, S. (1990). Autism: A specific cognitive disorder of 'mind-blindness'. *International Review of Psychiatry*, **2**, 79–88.

Baron-Cohen, S. (1991*a*). The development of a theory of mind in autism: Deviance and delay? *Psychiatric Clinics of North America*.

Baron-Cohen, S. (1991*b*). Precursors to a theory of mind: Understanding attention in others. In A. Whiten (Ed.), *Natural Theories of Mind*. Oxford: Blackwell.

Baron-Cohen, S. (in press). Autistic children's understanding of some causes of emotions. *Child Development*.

Baron-Cohen, S., Leslie, A. M. & Frith, U. (1985). Does the autistic child have a 'theory of mind'? *Cognition*, **21**, 37–46.

Baron-Cohen, S., Leslie, A. M. & Frith, U. (1986). Mechanical, behavioural and intentional understanding of picture stories in autistic children. *British Journal of Developmental Psychology*, **4**, 113–125.

Carey, S. (1985). *Conceptual Change in Childhood*. Cambridge, MA: MIT Press/Bradford.

Dasser, V. (1988). Mapping social concepts in monkeys. In R. Byrne & A. Whiten (Eds), *Machiavellian Intelligence: Social Expertise and the Evolution of Intellect in Monkeys, Apes and Humans*. Oxford: Oxford University Press.

Dawson, G. & Fernald, M. (1987). Perspective-taking ability and its relationship to the social behaviour of autistic children. *Journal of Autism and Developmental Disorders*, **17**, 487–498.

Dawson, G. & McKissick, F. C. (1984). Self-recognition in autistic children. *Journal of Autism and Developmental Disorders*. **14**. 383–394.

De Myer, M. K. (1976). Motor, perceptual–motor and intellectual disabilities of autistic children. In L. Wing (Ed.), *Early Childhood Autism*. Oxford: Pergamon.

Dennett, D. (1978). *Brainstorms: Philosophical Essays on Mind and Psychology*. Hemel Hempstead: Harvester Press.

Dewey, M. & Everard, P. (1984). The near normal autistic adolescent. *Journal of Autism and Developmental Disorders*, **4**, 348–356.

DSM III–R (1987). *Diagnostic and Statistical Manual of Mental Disorders*, rev. 3rd ed. Washington, DC: American Psychiatric Association.

Dunn, L., Dunn, L., Whetton, C. & Pintilie, D. (1982). *British Picture Vocabulary Scale*. Windsor, Berks: NFER–NELSON.

Ferrari, M. & Matthews, W. S. (1983). Self-recognition deficits in autism: Syndrome-specific or general developmental delay? *Journal of Autism and Developmental Disorders*, **13**, 317–324.

Flannery, C. N. (1976). Self-recognition and stimulus complexity preference in autistic children. Unpublished Masters thesis, University of Orleans.

Goode, S. (1985). Recognition accuracy for faces presented in the photographic negative: A study with autistic adults. Unpublished MPhil thesis, Institute of Psychiatry, University of London.

Grice, H. P. (1975). Logic and conversation. In R. Cole & J. Morgan (Eds), *Syntax and Semantics: Speech Acts*. New York: Academic Press. (Originally published in 1967.)

Harris, P. (1991). Reasoning in and about possible worlds. In A. Whiten (Ed.), *Natural Theories of Mind*. Oxford: Blackwell.

Harris, P. & Muncer, A. (1988). The autistic child's understanding of beliefs and desires. Paper presented at the BPS Developmental Psychology Conference, Harlech, September.

Hobson, R. P. (1984). Early childhood autism and the question of egocentrism. *Journal of Autism and Developmental Disorders*, **14**, 85–104.

Hobson, R. P. (1989). Beyond cognition: A theory of autism. In G. Dawson (Ed.), *Autism: Nature, Diagnosis, and Treatment*. New York: Guilford Press.

Hobson, R. P. (1990). On acquiring knowledge about people, and the capacity to pretend: A response to Leslie. *Psychological Review*, **97**, 114–121.

Hobson, R. P., Ouston, J. & Lee, A. (1988). What's in a face? The case of autism. *British Journal of Psychology*, **79**, 441–453.

Kanner, L. (1943). Autistic disturbance of affective contact. *Nervous Child*, **2**, 217–250. Reprinted in L. Kanner (1973), *Childhood Psychosis: Initial Studies and New Insights*. New York: Wiley.

Langdell, T. (1978). Recognition of faces: An approach to the study of autism. *Journal of Child Psychology and Psychiatry*, **19**, 225–238.

Leekam, S. & Perner, J. (in press). Does the autistic child have a metarepresentational deficit? *Cognition*.

Leslie, A. M. & Frith, U. (1988). Autistic children's understanding of seeing, knowing, and believing. *British Journal of Developmental Psychology*, **6**, 315–324.

Leslie, A. M. & Frith, U. (1990). Prospects for a cognitive neuropsychology of autism: Hobson's choice. *Psychological Review*, **97**, 122–131.

Leslie, A. M. & Sellars, C. (forthcoming). The deaf child's theory of mind. Unpublished MS, MRC Cognitive Development Unit, 17 Gordon St, London, WC1.

Mitchell, S. (1989). Exploring the autistic child's impaired theory of mind. Unpublished manuscript, Department of Experimental Psychology, University of Oxford.

Ozonoff, S., Pennington, B. & Rogers, B. (1990). Are there emotion perception deficits in young autistic children? *Journal of Child Psychology and Psychiatry*, **31**, 343–363.

Neuman, C. J. & Hill, S. D. (1978). Self-recognition and stimulus preference in autistic children. *Developmental Psychobiology*, **11**, 571–578.

Perner, J., Frith, U., Leslie, A. M. & Leekam, S. (1989). Exploration of the autistic child's theory of mind: Knowledge, belief, and communication. *Child Development*, **60**, 689–700.

Piaget, J. (1929). *The Child's Conception of the World*. London: Routledge & Kegan Paul.

Premack, D. (1988). 'Does the chimpanzee have a theory of mind?' revisited. In R. Byrne & A. Whiten (Eds), *Machiavellian Intelligence: Social Expertise and the Evolution of Intellect in Monkeys, Apes, and Humans*. Oxford: Oxford University Press.

Raven, J. C. (1956). *Coloured Progressive Matrices*. London: H. K. Lewis.

Reed, T. & Patterson, C. (in press). A comparative study of autistic subjects' performance at two levels of visual and cognitive perspective taking. *Journal of Autism and Developmental Disorders*.

Russell, J., Sharpe, S., Mauthner, N. & Tidswell, T. (1991). The 'windows task' as a measure of strategic deception in preschoolers and autistic subjects. *British Journal of Developmental Psychology*, **9**, 331–349.

Rutter, M. (1983). Cognitive deficits in the pathogenesis of autism. *Journal of Child Psychology and Psychiatry*, **24**, 513–531.

Sigman, M. & Mundy, P. (1989). Social attachments in autistic children. *Journal of the American Academy of Child and Adolescent Psychiatry*, **28**, 74–81.

Sodian, B. & Frith, U. (1990). Can autistic children lie? Paper presented at the European Conference of Developmental Psychology, Stirling University, August.

Spiker, D. & Ricks, M. (1984). Visual self-recognition in autistic children: Developmental relationships. *Child Development*, **55**, 214–225.

Swettenham, J. (1990). The autistic child's theory of mind: A computer-based investigation. Unpublished PhD thesis, Psychology Department, University of York.

Volkmar, F. R., Sparrow, S., Rende, R. D. & Cohen, D. J. (1989). Facial perception in autism. *Journal of Child Psychology and Psychiatry*, **30**, 591–598.

Weeks, S. J. & Hobson, R. P. (1987). The salience of facial expression for autistic children. *Journal of Child Psychology and Psychiatry*, **28**, 137–152.

Wellman, H. (1990). *Children's Theories of Mind*. Cambridge, MA: Bradford/MIT Press.

Received 1 December 1989; revised version received 9 August 1990

British Journal of Developmental Psychology (1991), **9**, 315–330   *Printed in Great Britain*

The recognition of attitude conveyed by utterance: A study of preschool and autistic children

Daniel Roth*

Department of Psychology, Tel Aviv University, Tel Aviv, Israel

Alan M. Leslie

MRC Cognitive Development Unit, University of London

A growing body of work shows that autistic children and adolescents have very limited understanding of propositional attitudes. One aspect of this is their typical failure to employ a concept of *belief*. In normal children the concept of *belief* seems to undergo an important development around age 4 years. The question naturally arises whether autistic impairment comprises simply a 3-year-old level of conceptual competence or whether their similarity to 3-year-olds in performance on certain theory of mind tasks masks underlying differences at the level of cognitive mechanism. We present data which show that in following a conversational interaction, normal 5-year-olds display a sophisticated understanding of the beliefs of the protagonists. Three-year-olds showed a much more limited comprehension but were able to attribute propositional attitudes. Our autistic adolescents did not display even this limited understanding of the conversational situation. We interpret our findings in terms of the metarepresentational theory of autism and point out the theoretical importance of a comparative approach to understanding normal cognitive development.

Recent research has shown that autistic adolescents perform poorly on a range of 'theory of mind' tasks which are passed by normal 4-year-old children (see Baron-Cohen, 1990; Frith, 1989*a,b*; Leslie & Frith, 1990 for reviews). On tasks testing comprehension of *false beliefs*, for example, autistic adolescents with verbal mental ages (MA) in excess of 8 years often perform like normal 3-year-olds. Does this surface behavioural similarity between autistic adolescents and normal 3-year-olds reflect an underlying cognitive similarity or are the deeper processes of development different in the two cases? To put it crudely, does the autistic person simply get 'stuck' at the 3-year-old level in theory of mind or is his/her development in this domain abnormal all along?

Our main objective is to show that the behavioural similarity between very young normal and older autistic children is misleading, and that the 3-year-old child, in

* Requests for reprints.

some respects, knows more about the mind than the typical able autistic adolescent. We present evidence that at certain 'theory of mind' tasks young normal children and autistic adolescents will perform differently.

Leslie's (1987, 1988; Leslie & Frith, 1990; see also Baron-Cohen, 1988) metarepresentational theory postulates that young normal and autistic children differ in their underlying representational capacities. We explore this assumption in the context of verbal communication. We tested the ability to conceive false utterances as expressing the speaker's and affecting the hearer's intentions and beliefs. As predicted, 3-year-old children and able autistic adolescents demonstrated different patterns of performance, supporting the metarepresentational conjecture.

Leslie's metarepresentational theory

Leslie (1987) hypothesized that the normal development of 'theory of mind' depends upon an innately specified mechanism which emerges during the second year of life. Because of factors at a biological level, this mind/brain mechanism fails to emerge in autistic children leading to an abnormal pattern of development at the cognitive level.

Leslie distinguished between types of mental representations, including a system of 'primary' representations, which are typically the product of perceptual and inferential processes involved in a literal understanding of the world, and higher order representations which he dubbed *metarepresentation*.* In this theory, the term 'metarepresentation' is applied to certain internal symbolic structures constructed by the operation of a special representational mechanism (called variously the 'decoupler' [Leslie, 1987] or 'theory of mind module' [Leslie, 1991]). This representational structure revolves around an element called an 'informational relation'. This element encodes particular propositional attitudes, e.g. *believes* or *pretends*, and, as defined by Leslie (1987), is a function with three arguments, namely: an agent, an aspect of reality described by means of primary representation, and an imaginary or counterfactual situation described by means of a 'decoupled' representation. For example: **Father** BELIEVES/PRETENDS **the marble 'it is in the box'**. The mechanism underlying the capacity to acquire a 'theory of mind', then, specifies a basic set of attitude concepts (e.g. *pretends, believes, wants*) and employs them for the construction of metarepresentations. Such a mechanism is therefore considered to be the core and the initial state of the young child's rudimentary 'theory of mind'.

Following his analysis of the ability to pretend, which revealed similarities between types of pretence and the semantic properties of belief statements (e.g. referential opacity) and which highlighted the importance of the related ability to understand pretence in others, Leslie suggested that the capacity for pretence is linked, via metarepresentational mechanisms, to the ability to construe belief statements (see Leslie, 1987, 1988 for detailed discussion). The conclusion that follows from Leslie's analysis and from the early appearance of pretence is that young children have the basic representational resources for belief attribution from about 2 years onwards.

* The term *metarepresentation* has recently been used in different senses (e.g. Forguson & Gopnik, 1988; Perner, 1988, in press). We refer to it in the sense originally proposed by Leslie (1987; see also Leslie, 1983 and Baron-Cohen, Leslie & Frith, 1985).

Young children might fail to demonstrate mature belief attribution, however, for a number of reasons. For example, their concept of *believing* might be available only in limited contexts. Or they may fail when the inferential requirements of the task are too demanding. In this view, metarepresentations are constructed as the conclusions of inferential processes. For example, from the rule, *iff X saw that p then X believes that p*, together with the fact that a certain person (say, Sally) saw only the previous situation and not its transformation, the conclusion that *Sally believes that p is still true* should follow. It is possible that 3-year-old children fail to employ or to see the relevance of such inferences when presented with standard false belief scenarios.

By contrast to normal children, autistic children are assumed to suffer a different and more profound limitation. These children are impaired in the representation system underlying 'theory of mind' and therefore fail to form and/or process metarepresentations.

An intriguing contrast, then, emerges from the theory. On the one hand, young normal children are assumed to have the capacity to form and process metarepresentations and to employ a (limited) variety of basic attitude concepts. Autistic children, on the other hand, are hypothesized to lack that normal capacity, and consequently, to develop abnormally. This contrast, however, will be empirically demonstrable only in those cases where the young children are able to draw the required inferences and thus to reveal their competence.

Communication and beliefs

One way of testing the conjecture suggested above is by using a situation which involves verbal communication. Normal children spontaneously engage in intentional communication from very early on (e.g. Shatz, 1983), whereas autistic children show a serious and enduring impairment (e.g. Baron-Cohen, 1988; Frith, 1989*b*; Perner, Frith, Leslie & Leekam, 1989; Rutter, 1978). In light of the metarepresentational theory, this deficit is hardly surprising (Leslie & Happé, 1989) since communication depends upon continuing recognition of intentions and attitudes (Grice, 1957; Levinson, 1983; Sperber & Wilson, 1986).

Communication theorists (e.g. Grice, 1957; Searle, 1969; Sperber & Wilson, 1986), draw a distinction between the content of an utterance and its function as an expression of the speaker's intention and attitude. The content consists of certain relevant information that the speaker intends to convey by the interpretation of his utterance as a proposition. In pragmatics theory, this is often called the speaker's 'informative intention'. Thus the speaker's intention to inform is normally fulfilled when the hearer decodes the linguistic meaning of the message. As to their function, utterances are frequently employed to convey evidence about the speaker's state of mind or attitude. Some of the evidence is quite straightforward: For example, when the attitudes are conveyed by the mood of the sentence (e.g. indicative mood as an expression of *belief*). Other sorts of evidence are less direct (Bach & Harnish, 1979; Sperber & Wilson, 1986).

The above distinction between types of information conveyed by utterances corresponds roughly to the types of mental representation postulated earlier. Thus, the informative content may portray a situation and therefore be processed as a primary representation, while the recognition of the speaker's mental attitude requires metarepresentation.

In light of the metarepresentational theory of autism, we expected verbal autistic children to decode the linguistic meaning of utterances and to consider the information they portray, but to fail to conceive of them as expressing the attitudes of the speakers. By contrast, we assumed that normal children would be able to consider both aspects: the informative content, as well as the speaker's attitude towards it.

To explore this conjecture we constructed a story in which a speaker is asked for information and in response produces an assertion which the observer (i.e. the subjects) should recognize as false. Normally, assertions express the speaker's belief about a situation. We assumed that the processing system of the autistic child, lacking metarepresentation, will construe the linguistic meaning of the false utterance, compare it with other representations of the same situation (i.e. his knowledge about reality), and consequently, reject it as false and uninformative. The normal 3-year-old, in contrast, who is able to metarepresent, should also reject the utterance as a source of information about reality, but at the same time he/she should be able to conceive it, under certain circumstances (e.g. when it is emphasized or made explicitly relevant), as an expression of the speaker's mistaken belief.

The ability to metarepresent, then, could enable the very young child to conceive an utterance as expressing a speaker's mistaken belief and to separate it from her/his own representation of reality. This 3-year-old ability, however, is still rudimentary and allows only a limited understanding of communication processes. More complex communication acts, such as for example deception and lying, would be beyond such a capacity. We assume that recognition of a speech act as a lie requires an ability to discern the speaker's intention to deceive and, minimally, to understand that the speaker believes his utterance to be false (Coleman & Kay, 1981). Recent studies have shown that the ability to recognize higher order intentions to deceive develops only around 5–6 years of age (Leekam, 1991). Other studies showed that the ability to deceive an opponent also emerges around the same age (Russell, Sharp & Mauthner, 1989; Sodian, 1991). We expected to find the same developmental pattern in our task which requires recognition of an utterance as a lie.

To investigate the above assumption, we compared 3-year-olds with a group of 5-year-olds. We also manipulated whether or not the speaker's motivation to produce the lie was made explicit. We predicted that the manipulation would affect only older normal children who already have the notion of a lie. Such children might do better in the explicit motivation condition than in the implicit motivation condition. The limited number of autistic subjects available to us did not allow large enough subgroups for this comparison. In any case, from the existing literature, we did not expect the autistic subjects to understand deception. Therefore, only a subgroup of the normal subjects received the explicit motivation condition.

To summarize, three groups of subjects, older and younger normal children and autistic adolescents, were presented with an acted-out story in which a protagonist first hid an object in one location, and then, when asked about the object's location by another character, produced a misleading assertion. The question–answer exchange was dramatized by a conversation between the story characters. Following presentation of the story, the subjects were asked about the speaker's and the listener's beliefs as well as about their own knowledge. We expected the 5-year-old children to discern the false belief of the listener and the lie of the speaker, and thus, to point to two different locations when asked about the characters' beliefs. The 3-year-old children were expected, on the one hand, to conceive of utterances as expressing or influencing attitudes and thus to demonstrate their ability to metarepresent, but, on the other hand, to fail to recognize the speaker's lie (i.e. that the speaker believes his own utterance to be false). Consequently, we expected them to provide utterance-based answers to the two belief questions (i.e. to ignore the deceiver's belief that his/her utterance is false) but to refer to the true location when asked about their own knowledge. Finally, the autistic subjects, we predicted, would fail to conceive the utterances as expressing or influencing attitudes and would consider them only as a source of information (true or false) about reality. We expected them then to produce a series of reality-driven answers to both belief and own-knowledge questions.

Experiment 1

Before the testing session, subjects were given a screening task which was modelled on the test situation. It was introduced to filter out subjects who were unable to cope with the linguistic demands of the task. Both the screening and the experimental tasks consisted of a conversation of the form:

Speaker 1: 'where is X?'
Speaker 2: 'X is in *a*!'

with similarly phrased test and control questions.

In the screening task, subjects had no other information available besides that expressed in the utterances, while in the main task they knew where the object was placed prior to the conversation and thus had independent information about reality. The screening task, then, provided a test for the subjects' ability to comprehend the conversation and the test questions. It also contrasted with the main task in the information needed for successful performance. In the screening task, subjects could answer questions correctly by considering only the informative content of the utterances. In the main task, the falsehood of the critical utterance was evident, and therefore, a distinction had to be made between reality and the utterance as an expression of a mistaken belief.

Method

Subjects.   Two groups of normal children, 34 3–4-year-olds (mean 3:4, range 2:9–4:0) and 28 5–6-year-olds (mean 5:5, range 5–5:11) were drawn from kindergarten and nursery schools in the Tel Aviv area. Fifteen young autistic adults and adolescents (mean age 18:5 years, range 13–28 years) came from a special school and a hostel specialized for autism in Tel Aviv, having been diagnosed according to established criteria (Rutter, 1978). Most of them were relatively old and appeared fairly verbal. Since the experimental task was based on verbal communication, we needed a comparative measure of the subjects' verbal capabilities. However, given that standardized verbal mental age (MA) tests are not available in Hebrew, we considered success on the screening task, which was modelled exactly on the linguistic demands of the main task, as an inclusion criterion. Such a task should be at least as relevant as a picture-vocabulary test in establishing a minimum verbal ability across the 3-year-old and autistic groups, though it does not guarantee equality.

Materials.   The protagonists were dramatized by two linen dolls about 30 cm high, one was dressed as a boy and the other as a girl. In the screening task, a bed was represented by a $80 \times 20 \times 15$ cm wooden shelf covered by a sheet. The main task used a $30 \times 30 \times 45$ cm cardboard model house. A $15 \times 15 \times 20$ cm kennel made of the same material was placed beside the house. Opposite stood a model of a tree with a wooden box beside it.

Procedure.   Each subject was tested individually in a quiet room. The display was placed on a large table facing the subject. The experimenter sat opposite the child and manipulated the dolls. The story and the conversations were presented by tape-recorder.

In the initial phase the experimenter produced two linen dolls, introduced them by their names and made sure that the child was familiar with them. The screening task's display was then set up and the testing immediately followed.

Following are English translations of the experimental protocols which were presented in Hebrew.

Screening task.   [two dolls are sitting on model bed]
'Rina and Yosi are sitting on Yosi's bed. It's a nice day and Yosi wants to play with the ball. So, he says:
         Yosi: Let's go to play with the ball.
         Rina: OK, I agree.
      [experimenter to the subject: 'now listen carefully']
         Yosi: where is my ball?
         Rina: It's under the bed!
[Belief question:] 'where does Yosi/Rina think the ball is?'
[Reality question:] 'where is the ball?' [answer: under the bed]
   The testing phase was immediately presented to the subjects who passed the screening task.

Main task.   [On scene there is a display representing a playground in front of the protagonists' house]
'Yosi and Rina are going to play outdoors. Yosi has some chocolates in his hand. He leaves them on the ground until they finish the game. Now they are playing.'
      [Yosi and Rina are seen playing with the ball]
'suddenly, the ball is thrown behind the house. Yosi runs to bring it back'
      [Yosi is placed behind the house and the experimenter ensures that the subject understands that he cannot see what Rina is doing]
'In the meanwhile, Rina hides the chocolate in the box beside the tree'
      [in the + motivation condition Rina said to the subject: 'I love chocolate, I want to eat them all by myself'
      in the − motivation condition Rina's motive was left implicit]
'then Yosi returns, he looks around for his chocolates and says:
         Yosi: 'who took my chocolate?'
         Rina: 'the dog took it'
      [experimenter to the subject: 'Listen now!']
         Yosi: 'where are my chocolates now?'
         Rina (pointing): 'they're over there, in the kennel!'
Then the following questions were presented:
[Memory question:] 'Yosi asked where his chocolates are, what did Rina answer?'
[Listener's belief question] 'where does Yosi think his chocolate is?'
[Speaker's belief question] 'where does Rina think the chocolate is?'
[Reality question:] 'where do *you* think the chocolate is?'
The order of the speaker/listener belief questions was counterbalanced, while the order of the control questions was constant.

Results

Four autistic subjects failed to understand either the conversation or the critical questions of the screening task. Four 3-year-old subjects also failed the screening task. All were excluded from further testing. Furthermore, as an inclusion criterion for the analysis of the data, subjects had to answer the two control questions correctly. Therefore, five of the younger children who failed either one or both of these questions were eliminated from the final analysis. The final sample consisted of 29 3-year-olds, 28 5-year-olds and 11 autistic adolescents who passed both the screening task and the control questions.

We were interested in different patterns of responding across the three groups and not just pass/fail. We therefore looked at responses to the two test questions (listener's and speaker's belief) together. This error analysis is more informative than examining responses separately, since, for example, a 'correct' answer to speaker's belief question could be given spuriously on the basis of reality. Table 1 thus shows the four possible patterns of answers.

Table 1. Categories of responses to the belief questions of Expt 1

Response pattern		
Listener's belief	Speaker's belief	Categorized as:
Kennel	Box	'Fully correct'
Kennel	Kennel	'Attitude based': *Listener deceived/speaker utt. based*
Box	Kennel	'Attitude based': *Listener reality/speaker utt. based*
Box	Box	'Reality based'

The children whose answers were 'fully correct' demonstrated an adult-like understanding of both the listener's mistake and the speaker's lie (speaker believes what is true, not what he says). Those who produced 'attitude-based' answers of the *listener deceived/speaker utterance-based* type attributed correctly the mistaken belief to the listener, but failed to recognize the speaker's disbelief in what he says. The subjects who provided the *listener reality-based/speaker utterance-based* type of answers showed substantially less understanding but, like the last category, at least attributed to the speaker a belief that diverges from reality. The significance of these three patterns of answers is that they show an ability to divorce the counterfactual expression from reality and to relate at least one of the characters to the alternative situation. The fourth category, 'reality based', which covers responses on the basis of reality for *both* the speaker and the listener, is thus qualitatively different and does not require (meta)representing an agent's attitude to a counterfactual situation.

Table 2 shows percentages of children responding in these four categories. It can readily be seen that a majority of the 5-year-olds gave 'fully correct' answers, apparently aware of the speaker's deceptive utterance. In this, the 5-year-olds stand out from the other two groups. However, it would be misleading to suppose that the

Table 2. The patterns of answers to the two test questions of Expt 1 (in percentages)[a]

Group	(N)	Fully correct %	Attitude based		Reality based %
			Listener deceived/speaker utterance based %	Listener reality/speaker utterance based %	
5-year-old	(28)	64	29	4	4
3-year-old	(29)	10	62	24	4
Autistic	(11)	18	18	0	64

[a] Figures may not sum to 100 because of rounding.

3-year-olds and autistic adolescents were equatable simply because of similar proportions in this category. A breakdown of their errors shown in Table 2 reveals different patterns across the groups. Thus, a majority of the 3-year-olds were apparently not aware of the speaker's deception, and instead attributed to the speaker a mistaken belief. These 3-year-olds correctly recognized that this mistaken belief would be imparted to the listener.* In contrast, a clear majority of the autistic adolescents (64 per cent) simply made reality-based responses. Only 3.5 per cent of the normal children fell in this category.

We analysed the above results in the following way. The number of autistic adolescents who passed the screening task meant that an overall χ^2 test did not meet requirements for expected frequencies (Siegel, 1956). However, we were able to demonstrate two crucial patterns in the data. First, that the number of normal 5- and 3-year-olds giving 'fully correct' vs. 'attitude-based' answers (collapsing across the two 'attitude-based' subcategories) is different: 18 older children were 'fully correct' and nine 'attitude based', while only three younger children were 'fully correct' and 25 were 'attitude based' (χ^2 (1) = 15.94, $p < .001$). This confirms the prediction that only the older normal children would understand the speaker was lying.

Second, we found the number of 3-year-old normal children giving at least attitude-based answers was different from the autistic adolescents (collapsing across the three 'fully correct' and 'attitude-based' categories): 28 younger children were at least attitude based and only one gave a 'reality-based' response, while four autistic subjects were at least attitude based and seven gave 'reality-based' responses (Fisher's exact, $p = .0001$). This confirms the prediction that normal 3-year-olds would have a greater availability of metarepresentationally based answers than autistic adolescents.†

* In standard false belief tasks, the age of 3 years 9 months and above marks a kind of 'watershed' for passing (see e.g. Wellman, 1990). We looked, therefore, at our subjects who were 3 years 8 months or less. Their success on the listener's belief question was still evident (binomial, $N = 26$, $x = 8$, $p = .038$).

† The reliability of the autistic subjects' performance was tested by presenting the story again with slight variation about a week after the first testing session. For most autistic subjects, performance was reliable and consistent across testing sessions. Three subjects, however, changed their answers when the story was repeated: two subjects in the 'fully correct' category and one of the subjects in the first 'attitude-based' category changed their responses on retest to 'reality based'. On retest, then, 93 per cent of autistic responses were 'reality based'. The results reported above may thus slightly overestimate the competence of the autistic sample.

Table 3. Frequencies of answers to the test questions of Expt 1 according to age and motivation conditions (normal children only)

Age	Implicit motivation				Explicit motivation			
	FC^a	$AB1^b$	$AB2^c$	RB^d	FC^a	$AB1^b$	$AB2^c$	RB^d
3 years	2	10	4	0	1	8	3	1
5 years	9	6	0	0	9	2	1	1

^{a} = 'Fully correct'.
^{b} = 'Attitude based': Listener deceived/speaker utterance based.
^{c} = 'Attitude based': Listener reality/speaker utterance based.
^{d} = 'Reality based'.

Next we looked at the effect of the explicitness of the speaker's motivation to lie on the two groups of normal children. The results are shown in Table 3. As predicted, 3-year-olds were not helped by making the motivation of the speaker to lie explicit; only one child in that condition responded in the 'fully correct' category. Somewhat surprisingly, the 5-year-olds too were little affected by making motivation explicit. It seems, however, that ceiling effects have limited the scope for an improvement in 5-year-old performance by making motivation explicit. On the whole, then, it appears that 5-year-olds do not require motivation to be made explicit in the detection of deceit.

Discussion

Our predictions were broadly confirmed, particularly those concerning different bases for responding across the three groups. But first we should consider some possible objections. One objection could be that the utterance was more salient than the actual situation, and as a consequence, superseded the children's representation of reality. However, the children's correct answers to the reality (control) question rules this out. Furthermore, the results cannot be attributed to memory failures given that all subjects whose data are reported passed two control questions. Thus, for example, all the autistic subjects repeated correctly the speaker's mistaken answer, yet indicated where the object really was.

A third objection could be that normal children were merely 'parroting' the false utterance without attending to the details of the scenario. Such a possibility seems unlikely in light of the children's correct responses to the reality question, which was phrased similarly to the test questions (i.e. where do *you* think the object is?). However, one might still argue that the children understood the difference between the questions, and answered only the test questions by repeating the words of the utterances. Experiment 2 was designed to rule out such an objection.

Experiment 2

One reason for taking seriously the 'parroting' objection mentioned above is that it is compatible with the assumption that children would always reject a false utterance once they have recognized its inconsistency with reality (Perner, 1988, in press). To meet this objection, the normal children were tested again, a week later, with the story presented in the presence of a new puppet character who was placed next to the child. This puppet acted as an observer exposed to the same events as the child. Since the puppet observer saw the liar hiding the chocolate, he should have a true belief. Children who were able to refer to the true location when asked about the observer's belief, and then to point to the other location when asked about the deceived character's belief (the listener), would thus show that their answers did not result from merely 'echoing' the false utterance.

Pilot study revealed that 3-year-old children were indeed capable of distinguishing the two characters' beliefs, but that such performance required explicit indication of the differences between the character's exposure conditions. That is, when the deceived character left the scene, the experimenter emphasized that only the observer can see, and therefore know, where the object really is, as opposed to the other character who is not present. In doing that, the experimenter may be helping the subjects to draw the required inferences. However, as previous studies demonstrate (Perner & Wimmer, 1988), understanding that a person knows (or does not know) is in itself insufficient for appreciating his belief. Therefore, though the children were told that the observer can see and therefore knows what the girl (in the story) was doing and though this may help to emphasize what the listener does *not* know, they still had to infer her belief. The introduction of an observer, then, allowed us to gauge whether the 3-year-olds simply attribute the speaker's utterance to all characters in the scenario (i.e 'parroting').

To test the reliability of the results obtained in the first experiment, a randomly selected subgroup was also asked the second belief question (about the speaker's belief). The question was presented in addition to the repeated belief question (about the listener) which was presented to the entire group.

Method

Subjects. The same normal children who participated in Expt 1 were tested again for this study which was administered a week later. Three children dropped out. Therefore, 28 3-year-olds and 26 5-year-olds were tested.

Procedure. The material and procedure of Expt 1 were used again. Children heard the same stories in terms of the motivation conditions to which they were previously assigned.

Before the story was presented, the experimenter introduced a big toy monkey and told the subject that it would accompany her/him in observing the scenario. The monkey was then seated next to the child where it could 'see' the modelled playground.

Then the story was presented: The procedure described in Expt 1 was repeated up to the point where the ball is thrown behind the house. At that point the experimenter indicated that only the monkey, but not Yosi (the boy) could see and therefore knows what Rina is doing.

Then, the conversation of Expt 1 (see Procedure section) was presented. The child was then asked the control and test questions in the following order:
[Memory question:] 'Yosi asked where his chocolate is, what did Rina answer?'
[Observer belief question:] 'remember, the monkey saw everything, where does the monkey think the chocolate is?'
[Speaker/listener's belief question:] 'where does Yosi/Rina think the chocolate is?'

[Reality question:] 'Where do you think the chocolate is?'
All the children were asked the listener's belief question. The last 13 children of each age group were asked also the speaker's belief question.

Results and discussion

The percentages of children in the two age groups who answered the test questions correctly are presented in Table 4. A large majority in both age groups answered the observer's belief question correctly pointing to the real location of the chocolate (binomial test, $p < .002$). The listener's belief question was also answered correctly by a large majority of both groups, this time by pointing to the (deceptive) location specified by the speaker (binomial test, $p < .002$). The children were not then responding to the test questions by merely parroting the words of the speaker.

Table 4. Percentages of children correctly responding to the test questions of Expt 2

Group	Observer's belief (%)	Listener's belief (%)	(N)
3-year-olds	89	85	(28)
5-year-olds	84	100	(26)

Table 5 presents the concordance between the performance of the 3-year-old group on listener's belief questions across Expts 1 and 2. It will be seen that 16 3-year olds answered correctly in *both* experiments while 11 changed their answers. The numbers changing in each direction were not significantly different (McNemar Q, n.s.). The performance of the 3-year-old group overall in terms of *consistently* correct responses to listener's belief question was highly significant (χ^2 (3) = 18.0, $p < .0001$, one-tailed).

Table 5. Reliability of 3-year-olds' answers to listener's belief question across experiments

		Experiment 1	
		Pass	Fail
Experiment 2	Pass	16	7
	Fail	4	1

The above effect can be contrasted with the subgroup of 3-year-olds who were also retested on the speaker's belief question. All 13 of these children gave speaker utterance-based answers in both experiments. In the normal 3-year-old, then, belief attribution to the speaker (based on what he/she says) may be a more robust phenomenon than belief attribution to the listener (based on what he/she hears).

General discussion

Our main finding concerned the difference between autistic adolescents and normal 3-year-old children. Three-year-olds show a limited understanding of *belief* in the communication situation we tested. Specifically, they show little appreciation of the intention to deceive, and tend to attribute belief to a speaker based on what the speaker has just said rather than on what the speaker should know. Limited though this understanding may be, it still requires, we would maintain, the employment of metarepresentation in the sense outlined in the introduction. We found that even this limited 3-year-old type of understanding was largely absent from our sample of autistic adolescents who approached the main task in a highly literal way, sticking to reality and discarding the significance of the conversational interaction as expressing the speakers' attitudes.

These findings are consistent with the idea that different information processing mechanisms underlie the performance of the autistic adolescents and the normal children in this task. In particular, in line with the metarepresentation theory, we contend that the autistic children relied on primary representations, whereas the normal children, both young and old, were additionally able to entertain metarepresentations as an interpretation of the utterances. More specifically, the autistic subjects were able to interpret the meaning of the utterances both in the screening and the test tasks as conveying information about the situation they referred to. They used these interpretations to answer correctly the reality and belief questions of the screening task. They failed, however, to refer to the utterance when this interpretation contradicted their knowledge of reality.

This pattern of results can be explained on the assumption that the meaning of an utterance is entertained by an autistic person only as a primary representation.* Such representations are subjected to verification procedures and should be consistent with other representations stored in memory. Therefore, when the situation portrayed by the utterance contradicts the representation of reality, the utterance must be rejected as false. To reconcile simultaneously a model of reality and a person's counterfactual expression concerning that reality, one needs to construe a metarepresentation (e.g. speaker *believes* that 'p'). According to the metarepresentational theory, autistic subjects will fail to do this because of their specific impairment. Therefore, when faced with conflicting information about the situation, they simply reject the counterfactual and consult their model of reality. The young normal children, in contrast, are able to coordinate the contradictory representations. They explicitly represent the actual state of affairs, and refer to it in their answers to the reality question, while, at the same time, they entertain a model of the situation conveyed by the false utterance, and answer belief questions accordingly.

Did the 3-year-old children ascribe a *false belief* to the speaker? The evidence obtained in this study is still inconclusive on this point. There are other possibilities. For example, it might be that the children conceived the false utterance as a special

---

* We are disregarding here the distinction between decoupled representations and primary representations (to focus on metarepresentations). This distinction may be important, however, when considering the different weights attached to perceptual evidence and to utterances in the fixation of beliefs about a situation. Some decoupled representations, i.e. those not involved in metarepresentation, do seem to be available to autistic children (Leslie & Thaiss, submitted).

case of pretence. Another option would be that they entertained it as an act of informing (e.g. speaker *asserts* 'p'). We claim, however, that in both cases the child is entertaining a metarepresentation since it is only the construction of metarepresentation that enables the children (but not the autistic subjects) to divorce the misleading expression from reality (see Fodor, 1981 for the parallelism between verbs of saying and propositional attitudes). Further research is needed to decide between the alternatives. As regards the 3-year-olds' attributions to the listener, it seems more difficult to escape the conclusion that the majority of the children attributed something like a belief attitude.

The second prominent finding concerns the 3-year-olds' failure to conceive the true belief of the deceiver (the speaker). The findings show that though the 3-year-olds were aware of the actual situation and witnessed the speaker hiding the object, they ignored these facts and consulted only the false situation mentioned in the utterance. The 5-year-olds, by contrast, were able to discount the speaker's false utterance in attributing speaker's belief while calculating the impact of that utterance on the listener's belief. The 5-year-olds thus showed a much more expert use of metarepresentational analysis in this conversational scenario.

Why did the 3-year-old children fail to appreciate the speaker's true belief though they appreciated correctly the listener's mistaken belief? We suggest that this striking result reflects the fact that young children do not recognize deliberate false utterances as lies. This assumption is strengthened by the children's indifference to the explicitness of the speaker's motivation to lie. To understand a false utterance as a lie, one has to discern its falsehood but also to recognize that the speaker believes it to be false and that the speaker produced it with an intention to deceive (Coleman & Kay, 1981). The 3-year-old subjects were apparently able to discern the falsehood of the utterance (as indicated by their answers to the reality question), but failed to appreciate the fact that the speaker conceives it as false, and therefore, holds a different belief. This may result from a failure to consider the higher order intention to deceive (i.e. S *wants* L to *believe* that 'p'). This may be beyond the capacity of children younger than 5 (Perner, 1988). By contrast, in order to discern the listener's false belief the child needs only to appreciate a first order belief statement and to identify the content of the listener's attitude with that of the speaker's assertion. This failure to discern a lie is consistent with other recent studies finding that 3-year-old children fail to deceive an opponent in a carefully controlled situation (Russell, Mauthner, Sharpe & Tidswell, 1991; Sodian & Frith, in press).

As for the autistic subjects, our results do not allow us to rule out the possibility that they thought the speaker was lying. However, it would be surprising if they did, given that they did not recognize any impact of this lie on the listener. It is more plausible in view of this and in light of previous studies of the autistic child's ability to deceive (Russell *et al.*, in press; Sodian & Frith, in press) that our autistic subjects had little or no understanding that the speaker was lying.

We can compare the 3-year-olds' performance on the present task to the results obtained in previous studies employing 'standard' false belief scenarios (Baron-Cohen *et al.*, 1985; Wimmer & Perner, 1983). In both cases a failure to infer the character's belief on the grounds that he/she has put the target object in a certain location was revealed. However, the children's patterns of answers were different in the two tasks. In standard tasks, 3-year-old children tend to answer the belief questions by referring to reality, whereas in the present study they seem to ignore reality and to consider only the utterance as a source of information about the character's belief.

Two alternative explanations might account for this discrepancy. The first would emphasize the temporal order of the events, and the second the communicative nature of the conversation. According to the first view, the fact that in the present study the critical utterance was produced after the hiding event might have facilitated the children's ability to consider it as relevant information. The memory question, which immediately followed the conversation might also help to focus the subjects' attention on the utterance. An assumption consistent with this view would be that young children conceive of the speaker's belief as a continuously updated description of the situation, and hence, update it according to the latest available information (e.g. standard scenario: change in reality, present scenario: latest utterance). Development, then, will consist of a more sophisticated appreciation of relevant information across the unfolding sequence of events.

Alternatively, it is possible that the metarepresentation mechanism is initially employed in communicative settings, and only later in development is 'extrapolated' to conceptualize non-communicative behaviours (e.g. seeing, putting, etc.). In this view, it might be easier for the children to construe metarepresentations of *speakers'* attitudes towards counterfactual expressions. For example, in contrast to situations comprising standard scenarios which exist as independent states of affairs in the world, communicated situations exist only by virtue of being communicated. Representations of such events should therefore specify the communicator as well as the communicated situation and thus invite metarepresentation.

The evidence provided by the present study is still insufficient to decide between these alternatives. A study in progress will explore these issues further.

Finally, we would like to discuss the apparent inconsistency between the present experiment and two previous studies (Johnson & Maratsos, 1977; Perner & Wimmer, 1988). In the first of these studies (Johnson & Maratsos, 1977), children were told a story about a character who hid an object and then lied about its location. Johnson & Maratsos, however, employed an indirect report of the event and did not display a conversation. This may be an important factor as we have already indicated.

The second study (Perner & Wimmer, 1988) did employ a conversation as a means of misinforming a character about the false location, but the children were asked only about the listener. In both the above studies, the 3-year-olds pointed to the actual location when asked to predict the misinformed character's future behaviour. A major difference between these studies and the present one then concerned the test question. While in these other studies the children were asked about the character's future behaviour (i.e. where will Maxi *look* for x?), we asked directly about the character's belief. It may be that the additional inference required to predict future behaviour leads to greater difficulty for younger children. We should also recall the greater difficulty within our own task of inferring the listener's belief (see the consistency results above). It may be that focusing the 3-year-old on the speaker's belief helps them with that of the listener.

To conclude, let us consider two implications of these results. The first is that similarities of performance (i.e. behaviours) on various tasks can yet reflect very different underlying processes at the cognitive level. Such differences may only be uncovered under particular circumstances. In the case of 3-year-old children and autistic adolescents, the results we obtained support the theoretical assumption that they are indeed different in their representational capacities. The second point we would like to make concerns the theoretical importance of studying abnormal development as a frame of reference for understanding normal development (see also Leslie & Thaiss, submitted). We suggest that this constitutes an important kind of comparative psychology. Without the results from the autistic group one might have missed or dismissed the peculiar pattern of results demonstrated by the 3-year-old children. The clear contrast between normal and autistic groups in this and other studies requires a searching theoretical analysis of the underlying structures and processes which produce normal development.

Acknowledgements

We are grateful to John Morton and to two anonymous reviewers for comments on an earlier draft. The experiments reported here were carried out by the senior author in partial fulfilment of the requirements for the MA degree, Tel-Aviv University. He is grateful to his supervisors Yosef Grodzinsky and Sidney Strauss for their help and support. The experiments were supported in part by grant #89–00173 from the US–Israeli Binational Science Foundation and by the Basic Research Fund of the Israeli Academy of Science to Yosef Grodzinsky. We also wish to thank the head, staff and children of Kfar Ofarim and Yachdav school for autistic children and the staff and children of Lewinsky college kindergarten, Tel Aviv.

References

Bach, K. & Harnish, R. (1979). *Linguistic Communication and Speech Acts*. Cambridge, MA: MIT Press.

Baron-Cohen, S. (1988). Social and pragmatic deficits in autism. *Journal of Autism and Developmental Disorders*, **18**, 379–402.

Baron-Cohen, S. (1990). Autism: A specific cognitive disorder of 'mind-blindness'. *International Review of Psychiatry*, **2**, 79–88.

Baron-Cohen, S., Leslie, A. M. & Frith, U. (1985). Does the autistic child have a 'theory of mind'? *Cognition*, **21**, 37–46.

Coleman, L. & Kay, P.(1981). Prototype semantics: The English word *lie*. *Language*, **57**, 26–44.

Fodor, J. A. (1981). Propositional attitudes. In J. A. Fodor (Ed.), *Representations: Philosophical Essays on the Foundations of Cognitive Science*, pp. 177–203. Brighton: Harvester Press.

Forguson, L. & Gopnik, A. (1988). The ontogeny of common sense. In J. W. Astington, P. L. Harris & D. R. Olson (Eds), *Developing Theories of Mind*, pp. 226–243. Cambridge: Cambridge University Press.

Frith, U. (1989a). *Autism: Explaining the Enigma*. Oxford: Blackwell.

Frith, U. (1989b). A new look at language and communication in autism. *British Journal of Disorders of Communication*, **24**, 123–150.

Grice, H. P. (1957). Meaning. *Philosophical Review*, **LXVI**, 377–388.

Johnson, C. & Maratsos, M. (1977). Early comprehension of mental verbs: 'Think' and 'know'. *Child Development*, **48**, 1743–1748.

Leekam, S. (1991). Jokes and lies: Children's understanding of intentional falsehood. In A. Whiten (Ed.) *Natural Theories of Mind*, pp. 159–174. Oxford: Blackwell.

Leslie, A. M. (1983). Pretend play and representation in the second year of life. Paper presented to BPS Developmental Conference, Oxford University.

Leslie, A. M. (1987). Pretense and representation: The origins of 'theory of mind'. *Psychological Review*, **94**, 412–426.

Leslie, A. M. (1988). Some implications of pretence for mechanisms underlying the child's theory of mind. In J. Astington, P. Harris & D. Olson (Eds), *Developing Theories of Mind*, pp. 19–46. Cambridge: Cambridge University Press.

Leslie, A. M. (1991). The theory of mind impairment in autism: Evidence for a modular mechanism of development? In A. Whiten (Ed.), *Natural Theories of Mind*, pp. 63–78. Oxford: Blackwell.

Leslie, A. M. & Frith, U. (1990). Prospects for a cognitive neuropsychology of autism: Hobson's choice. *Psychological Review*, **97**, 122–131.

Leslie, A. M. & Happé, F. (1989). Autism and ostensive communication: The relevance of metarepresentation. *Development and Psychopathology*, **1**, 205–212.

Leslie, A. M. & Thaiss, L. (submitted). Domain specificity in conceptual development: Neuropsychological evidence from autism. Submitted for publication.

Levinson, S. (1983). *Pragmatics*. Cambridge: Cambridge University Press.

Perner, J. (1988). Developing semantics for theories of mind: From propositional attitudes to mental representation. In J. Astington, P. L. Harris & D. Olson (Eds), *Developing Theories of Mind*, pp. 141–172. Cambridge: Cambridge University Press.

Perner, J. (in press). *Towards Understanding Representation and Mind*. Cambridge, MA: MIT Press.

Perner, J., Frith, U., Leslie, A. M. & Leekam, S. (1989). Exploration of the autistic child's theory of mind: Knowledge, belief and communication. *Child Development*, **60**, 689–700.

Perner, J. & Wimmer, H. (1988). Misinformation and unexpected change: Testing the development of epistemic state attribution. *Psychological Research*, **50**, 191–197.

Russell, J., Mauthner, N., Sharpe, S. & Tidswell, T. (1991). The windows task as a measure of strategic deception in preschool and autistic subjects. *British Journal of Development Psychology*, **9**, 315–330.

Russell, J., Sharpe, S. & Mauthner, N. (1989). Strategic deception in a competitive game. Paper presented to the BPS Developmental Section Annual Conference, University of Surrey.

Rutter, M. (1978). Language disorder and infantile autism. In M. Rutter & E. Schopler (Eds), *Autism: A Reappraisal of Concepts and Treatment*, pp. 85–104. New York: Plenum.

Searle, J. N. (1969). *Speech Acts: An Essay in the Philosophy of Language*. Cambridge: Cambridge University Press.

Shatz, M. (1983). Communication. In J. H. Flavell & E. M. Markman (Eds), *Cognitive Development*, vol. III of P. H. Mussen (Ed.), *Handbook of Child Psychology*, pp. 841–889. New York: Wiley.

Siegel, S. (1956). *Nonparametric Statistics for the Behavioral Sciences*. New York: McGraw-Hill.

Sodian, B. (1991). The development of deception in young children. *British Journal of Developmental Psychology*, **9**, 173–188.

Sodian, B. & Frith, U. (in press). Deception and sabotage in autistic, retarded and normal children. *Journal of Child Psychology and Psychiatry*.

Sperber, D. & Wilson, D. (1986). *Relevance: Communication and Cognition*. Oxford: Blackwell.

Wellman, H. M. (1990). *The Child's Theory of Mind*. Cambridge, MA: MIT Press.

Wimmer, H. & Perner, J. (1983). Beliefs about beliefs: Representation and constraining function of wrong beliefs in young children's understanding of deception. *Cognition*, **13**, 103–128.

Received 9 November 1990; revised version received 13 February 1991

British Journal of Developmental Psychology (1991), **9**, 331–349 *Printed in Great Britain*

The 'windows task' as a measure of strategic deception in preschoolers and autistic subjects

James Russell*, **Natasha Mauthner, Sally Sharpe†** and **Tom Tidswell**

Department of Experimental Psychology, Cambridge University, Downing Street, Cambridge CB2 3EB, UK

We gave 3- and 4-year-old children and autistic subjects (plus a group of Down's syndrome children of equivalent ability) a task which measured their capacity for strategic deception. This was a competitive game played between the subject and an experimenter in which the participants tried to win chocolates. In the training phase the subjects learned that it was in their interest to tell the experimenter, by pointing, to look into an empty box for the chocolate, although subjects did not know until after the search which box *was* empty. In the testing phase, the boxes had windows facing the child so he or she could now see which was the empty box. The 4-year-olds and the Down's children, but not the 3-year-olds and the autistic subjects, generally pointed to the empty box on the first trial. Moreover, the younger children and the autistic subjects frequently continued to point to the baited box for the full 20 test trials. We also found that the ability to apply the correct strategy on the 'windows task' was associated with success on a standard 'false belief' task and argue from this that both tasks may be difficult because they require subjects to inhibit the tendency of salient knowledge about object locations to overwrite knowledge of epistemic states.

The claim that children develop a 'theory of mind' around the fourth year of life (Astington, Harris & Olson, 1988) can be taken to mean that before that time they have no explicit and accessible knowledge of how their own and others' mental states relate to the world. Specifically, they now have explicit knowledge that mental states can only be 'in the running for truth', where previously this was only implicit in their behaviour (Russell, 1987*a*). Once they know, for example, that the essence of a belief is that it can be either true or false, they may also be able to understand how people's behaviour and verbal judgements are determined by these beliefs and not by the way the world happens to be. To put it simply: they understand how *false* beliefs might determine behaviour and judgement.

The qualifying phrase 'explicit and accessible' is important here because without *some* conception of themselves and others as representers of reality 3-year-olds would not be the cognitively and socially competent creatures we know them to be. There are two main reasons for saying this. First, it is difficult to see how children could

* Requests for reprints.

† This paper is published in memory of Sally Sharpe who died in a road accident in August 1990.

converse with others without the ability to see themselves as informing another person about a fact through some symbolic means: minimally, intending that the addressee should recognize their intention to mean, say, that it is cold by words *It's cold* (Grice, 1957). Second, it is reasonable to suppose that a toddler who has a 'theory' of the external world cannot have this without some conception of himself or herself as a mental representer of the world (Russell, 1989).

Of course, neither of these conceptions requires any insight into how the fact of being misinformed can influence behaviour. To date, two main criteria have been used to assess whether young children understand the role of false beliefs in action, judgement and emotion. The more popular technique involves understanding how the state of being misinformed influences behaviour and judgements. For example, a person may be unaware that an object that she put in location A has been transferred, in her absence, to location B, but her belief 'it's at A' should nevertheless lead her to search at A. Typically, 3-year-olds and autistics with mental ages of at least 4 years say that the person will search at B (Baron-Cohen, Leslie & Frith, 1985; Wimmer & Perner, 1983). Similarly, somebody who is unaware that a matchbox actually contains chocolate and not matches should say that it contains matches. However, 3-year-olds typically say that such a person will say that it contains chocolate, despite their being aware of the person's ignorance (Hogrefe, Wimmer & Perner, 1986).

Children show the same kind of misunderstanding when it is they themselves who have been misinformed. Gopnik & Astington (1988) found that 3-year-olds fail to report past belief states, describing these beliefs in terms of the information that is currently available to them. In a variant of the matchbox task described above, they will deny that they had previously believed that the contents of the box were other than they later discovered them to be. Such 'representational change' experiments tell us that it is understanding mental representation in general that is the problem for 3-year-olds rather than imputing false beliefs to other people. We shall refer to these three kinds of task as 'ignorance tasks'.

The other criterion for whether children understand the role of false beliefs in behaviour and mental life requires an understanding of deception. We shall refer to the tests for this understanding as 'deception tasks'. Indeed, it was this criterion which led Premack (Woodruff & Premack, 1979) to coin the phrase 'theory of mind' to describe the behaviour of a chimpanzee who seemed to be deliberately misinforming, by pointing, an uncooperative keeper about the location of food. If we tell another person the opposite of what we know to be the case with the intention of making that person believe it—rather than simply because we have learnt that this is a good strategy for guiding another's behaviour—then we clearly have the conception of a false belief. The caveat about whether the deceptive behaviour *has* a mentalistic motive is important because it is certainly possible to conceive of deceptive behaviour which has evolved or has been learned simply because it happens to pay dividends (Bennett, 1988).

If the ignorance and the deception tasks are tapping the same basic ability, then we should expect children of 3 years of age to be as handicapped in their understanding of deception as they are in their understanding of the consequences of ignorance. The evidence is somewhat equivocal here. Chandler, Fritz & Hala (1989) report that children as young as 2 years remove true trails and leave false ones in order to mislead someone about where an object has been hidden. However, a replication and extension of the Chandler *et al.* task by Sodian, Taylor, Harris & Perner (in press) showed that when such behaviour does occur it is not only highly dependent on cueing from the experimenter but is unaccompanied by insight into where the 'misinformed' person will now search. Moreover, subjects below 4 years of age deployed deceptive and informative strategies indiscriminately. Therefore, what Chandler *et al.* had probably succeeded in doing was encouraging very young children to use deceptive ploys which they did not understand.

The ignorance and the deception tasks each have their own set of problems. The primary aim of the study described was to devise a deception task which would be relatively free of these attendant problems and to see how performance on that task related to performance on a standard ignorance task.

There are two related problems with the ignorance tasks. First, they are highly dependent upon linguistic skill. Because children as old as 6 years frequently interpret questions about what a protagonist is 'thinking' in terms of the physical situation rather than mentalistically (Russell, 1987*b*), it is very likely that 3-year-olds will do something similar when asked where a protagonist 'thinks' something is hidden. Additionally, although questions about where an agent will search are not directly mentalistic, they involve a significant amount of interpretation relative to context. We must be sure, in particular, that the child is not confusing where the agent can reasonably be expected to search with where he should want to search (see Wellman & Bartsch, 1989, for a discussion). We must also be sure that the child interprets the question about what another will say or think in the matchbox task as being about saying or thinking *before* the contents of the box are revealed (Lewis & Osborne, in press).

A second problem with ignorance tasks is that when it is knowledge of others' mental states that is being tested the child has to understand a narrative set aside from the normal stream of behaviour. Indeed, when dolls are used as protagonists (as in Wimmer & Perner, 1983), the child must also be able to engage in shared fantasy, something which, on the face of it, might explain why autistic children find such tasks so difficult (de Gelder, 1987). Although later studies used experimenters as protagonists rather than dolls (Leslie & Frith, 1988), the children still had to hold at bay powerful assumptions about what adults normally know and about their general competence in finding objects.

For these reasons it would appear that deception tasks might be purer tests of false belief understanding—'purer' in the sense of being less verbal and less narrative. In Woodruff & Premack's (1979) deceptive pointing task for chimpanzees there was certainly nothing of a linguistic or narrative nature which had to be understood. There was, however, a different kind of problem. Deception pays obvious dividends whether it is to obtain a natural reward, such as food or sex (Whiten & Byrne, 1988), or whether it is a strategy to win a game; so how can we be confident that the deceptive behaviour is not simply a ploy without mental content? This objection applies with a vengeance to situations, such as Woodruff & Premack's, where the behaviour was the outcome of training over a long period. As Dennett (1978) pointed out, it is the *natural* development of a theory of mind which is psychologically relevant. The ability to *learn* to deceive is interesting, but it may be psychologically closer to bears learning to ride bicycles than to children developing conceptions of the mind (cf. the above remarks about Chandler *et al.*). Dennett (1978) gives a good example of the unlearned appreciation of the consequences of ignorance and deception and presciently ascribes this understanding to 4-year-olds who:

> ... watching a Punch and Judy show squeal in anticipatory delight as Punch prepares to throw the box over the cliff. Why? Because *they know Punch thinks Judy is still in the box*. They know better: they saw Judy escape while Punch's back was turned. We take the children's excitement as overwhelmingly good evidence that they understand the situation (italics in original, p. 569).

The point about learning also applies to some of the developmental work on deception in competitive games. Shultz & Cloghesy (1981) showed that children of 5 years produce deceptive strategies in a card game and act on the expectation that the competitor will do the same. But this behaviour developed over a number of trials in which the children were being reinforced for pointing to the card they knew was *not* the target card. It is possible that they had simply acquired the strategy without attending to the competitor's mental states.

Even without the element of reinforcement, however, deceptive behaviour is difficult to assess. We can be confident, as Dennett says, that the children who squeal with delight at Mr Punch's behaviour are understanding a state of ignorance, but without comparable emotional clues (e.g. giggling before the deceptive act) it is extraordinarily difficult to say when deceptive behaviour is or is not mentalistic. In the absence of such criteria, we adopted the strategy of devising a test of deception—the 'windows task'—which had no element of reinforcement, in order to see how success on this task related to success on a more obviously mentalistic ignorance task. We need to discuss carefully the theoretical implications of comparing an apparently mentalistic task with one which may or may not *necessarily* require mental knowledge, but before doing so the task is briefly described.

The windows task involved the child in playing a game against an experimenter for chocolate. A chocolate was in one of two closed boxes on each trial. In the first phase, neither competitor knew the location of the chocolate so the child was told to point randomly to one of the two. The experimenter then had to look into the indicated box, with the result that if the chocolate was there the experimenter kept it and if the box was empty the child had the chocolate. Thus, the child saw that it was in his or her interest to make the experimenter go to the empty box. In the second phase, similar boxes were used except that they now had windows in them, which faced towards the child and away from the experimenter, so that only the child could see the location of the chocolate. Would the child now point to the box that he or she *knew* to be empty? If the predominant behaviour is to point to the empty box then we have prima facie evidence that the children are deliberately misdirecting the experimenter *despite having not previously been reinforced for doing so*. They had not been reinforced for pointing to the empty box in the first phase because it is logically true of instrumental reinforcement that it can only occur when the information about what response is required is available to the organism (Russell, 1980). In this experiment the children did not know what response was required, only, of course, what outcome was desirable.

The obvious disadvantage of a single trial task is that subjects have a 50 per cent chance of being correct. For this reason the children received a further 19 trials with the windowed boxes, making 20 in all.

The task was devised in the hope that it would either be as difficult as an ignorance task or that it would be easier. (It did not seem likely that it would be more difficult.) What implications would these two outcomes have for the general question of whether 3-year-olds understand the role of false beliefs in mental life and behaviour?

Outcome 1: the windows task is easier than a standard ignorance task. In this case, either (*a*) the windows task is a 'purer' test of understanding false beliefs because it requires little linguistic skill and no understanding of narratives, or (*b*) this is because the windows task can be done without considering another's mental states: it involves no more than learning to indicate a particular location (the empty one) to get a reward.

Outcome 2: the windows task and the ignorance task are equally difficult. In this case, either (*c*) this is clear evidence that the 3-year-olds are not failing the ignorance tasks because of difficulties with linguistic interpretation and with understanding narratives, or (*d*) we should retain (*b*): that is, we may conclude from this that the reason why ignorance tasks are difficult is *not* that they require understanding of false beliefs. Of course, whether we believe the claims in (*b*) and (*d*) depends upon details of the success and failure on the windows task, and this cannot be discussed in advance of the results.

Finally, we not only gave the task to preschool children but also to a group of autistic children and adolescents, and to a group of children with Down's syndrome. The latter group was used as a clinical comparison group for the autistic sample. A number of workers have claimed that autistic children whose mental ages are at or above 4 years perform similarly to 3-year-olds on ignorance tasks (Baron-Cohen *et al.*, 1985; Leslie & Frith, 1988). If we were to find that autistics with mental ages of 4 years or over, but not Down's children with similar mental ages, performed like 3-year-olds on the windows task, this would be further evidence that deception tasks and ignorance tasks tap the same kind of knowledge.

Method

Subjects

The preschool sample consisted of 17 3-year-olds (range 3:0—3:10) and 16 4-year-olds (range 4:0—4:10). They were attending nursery schools in Cambridge. There were 11 autistic subjects who had been diagnosed according to the criteria of Rutter (1978). They were aged between 7:5 and 17:2 and were attending special schools in Cambridge or Hertfordshire. There were 14 mentally handicapped, non-autistic children aged between 7:2 and 18:9, attending special schools in Cambridge. All but one of these children had Down's syndrome, so they will be referred to as the 'Down's children'.

Assessment of intelligence

The assessment of the intelligence of the two clinical groups was carried out by means of two subtests of the British Ability Scales (BAS) (Elliot, Murray & Pearson, 1983). Verbal intelligence was assessed by means of the Verbal Comprehension test,* because we reasoned that this would provide a more

---

* In this test the child has to carry out instructions of the following kind: (by pointing) 'Which one barks?' (easy item) and 'Before you give me the van, give me the little house' (difficult item).

sensitive measure of verbal understanding than the picture vocabulary tasks which are in standard use. The disadvantage of the task, for our purposes, is that it is designed for use with normal children up to the age of 5 years, which meant that some of the children were at ceiling. However, this was not a major problem because the purpose of the testing was to determine whether the autistics' verbal intelligence was at least equivalent to that of a normal child of 4 years of age and to ensure that the Down's children and the autistics were of comparable intelligence.

The non-verbal measure of intelligence was the Blocks Design test from the BAS. This test was chosen because all the autistic subjects had recently received matrices tests, some on two occasions, and their scores on these were not available. These children were therefore too practised at matrix tasks to yield interpretable scores. However, there is a problem with using the Blocks Design test with this population: performance on this test, it is claimed, demonstrates one of the 'islets'* of autistic ability (Frith, 1989). These scores may, therefore, be overestimating general non-verbal intelligence. This matter will be discussed when the data are reported.

The raw scores from these tests were treated in the following manner. On conversion to ability scores, the age at which such an ability score would be an average score was derived from the table. This was possible because the T scores which the BAS table presents have a mean of 50. Thus, if a child scored 24 out of a possible 27 on the Verbal Comprehension test, this was converted into an ability score of 98. For a T score of 50 on the table, 98 would be scored by a child between 4:3 and 4:5 years. Thus, the child's performance age on that task was recorded as 4:4.

Because the data are reported in a quasi-clinical fashion, we postpone detailed comparison of the autistic subjects with the Down's children to the Results section.

Procedure for windows task

One experimenter (E1) sat beside the child and the other experimenter (E2) sat facing them. E2 was the child's competitor. Two cardboard boxes, about 4 in cubed and with the same coloured pattern, were placed between the child and E2. E1 told the child that in the game there would always be a chocolate (*Cadbury's Buttons, M and Ms* or *Smarties*) in one of the two boxes, but that neither of the players would know which box contained it. The child was told that what he or she had to do was to point to one of the boxes each time 'to tell [E2] where to look'. If the competitor found the chocolate, he or she could keep it, but if the competitor went to the box which was empty, the child won the chocolate. This initial phase continued for 15 trials. Before each trial and as the boxes were put in place, E1 would remind the child that he or she could get the chocolate by making the competitor go to the empty box. This principle was also reiterated after each trial. In the second phase, the windowed boxes were introduced. These were similar boxes to the first two, except that square apertures had been cut in one face and covered with clear cellophane. The windows faced the child, so that now the chocolate was clearly visible to the child but not to the competitor. After the introduction of the windowed boxes, E1 pointed out that it would now be easier to make the competitor go to the wrong box. There were 20 trials in this phase of the task. Before each trial, E1 reminded the child that he or she had to point so that E2 did not get the chocolate. Also, E1 continually encouraged the child to prevent E2 from winning the chocolate.

In order to gauge the degree of insight which correct children had into their deceptive behaviour and to investigate why incorrect children responded as they did, E1 posed the following questions. After E2 had looked into the indicated box on the first test trial (with windows), the child was asked, 'Why did you point to that one?' They were also asked about where E2 'thought' the chocolate was. This question

---

* However, the notion of an islet of intelligence can be rather difficult to maintain when applied to performance on a visuo-spatial intelligence test (as against, for example, musical or arithmetical ability). This is because it requires the theorist to take a very hard line on whether the test recruits 'central' intellectual processes or lower level 'input' processes and to argue that it recruits, predominantly, the latter. Frith (1989, pp. 99–101) argues that, as the test requires fragmentation ability rather than a search for 'coherence', it is not primarily a test of central intelligence. However, (1) one can also view the Blocks Design task as requiring the (more or less) global ability to *synthesize* fragments, and (2) such an argument can become circular—anything at which autistics excel is an islet of ability not an index of general intelligence.

was posed during the second test trial, after a box had been indicated but before the competitor searched.

Procedure for false belief task

We modelled our procedure on that of Leslie & Frith (1988), because this presentation of the problem involved two experimenters rather than acting out a vignette with puppets. E1 and E2 took up the same positions as before and there were two tins (one blue and one green) and a £1 coin between the child and E2. The child was told that the coin belonged to E2 and that he or she was going to put it away in one of the tins. E2 put it in the green tin and left the room. *Question 1* (control): 'Where did [E2] hide the coin?' E1 then said that they were going to play a trick on E1 and moved the coin from the green tin into the blue tin. *Question 2* (control): 'Does [E2] know where the coin is now?' *Question 3* (critical question): 'Where will [E2] look for the coin when she comes back in?' *Question 4* (control): 'Where did she put the coin in the beginning?' *Question 5* (control): 'Where is the coin really?' On E2's return the child was asked *Question 6* (critical): 'Where does E2 think that the coin is now?' The control questions were so called because they involved either memory checks or a check that an inference to knowledge had been made (Question 2). We corrected the children's answers to the control questions but did not repeat the questions until the child produced the correct answer. A subject was deemed to have succeeded on the false belief task if he or she answered all six questions correctly.

Results

As will become evident, the principal result concerned performance throughout the 20 test trials. However, the first test trial responses tell a clear story. Table 1 demonstrates that the 4-year-olds generally pointed to the visibly empty box on the first trial and the 3-year-olds generally did not ($\chi^2(1) = 12.05$, $p < .001$). Similarly, the Down's children generally pointed to the empty box on the first test trial and the autistic subjects did not ($\chi^2(1) = 8.89$, $p < .01$). The distributions for the 4-year-olds vs. the Down's children and for the 3-year-olds vs. the autistic subjects were not significantly different.

However, Table 1 also shows that a substantial proportion of the 3-year-olds and autistic subjects not only pointed to the baited box on the first trial with the windowed boxes, but also *continued* to point to the baited box throughout the 20 trials. They did this despite the fact that they could see that the consequence of doing so was losing the chocolate and despite E1's continual encouragement to ensure that E2 did not win any more. The details of responding over the 20 trials for the two preschooler groups are shown in Appendix A, and it can be seen clearly from this

Table 1. Responses of all subjects on first trial with windows (number of subjects pointing to the baited box on all 20 trials in parentheses)

Group	Points to empty box	Points to baited box
3-year-olds	1	16 (11)
4-year-olds	10	6 (0)
Down's syndrome children	11	3 (0)
Autistic subjects	2	9 (7)

that perseveration with the incorrect response was what characterized the data from the younger children. Some of the 4-year-olds did point to the baited box, but in almost every case, when they were asked why they did so, they said—in effect—that it was not fair that they should be winning all the chocolates so they decided to give the competitor one or two. Only two of the 4-year-olds were not responding above chance: subjects 6 and 16. Subject 6 told us that his parents would not like him to take home too many sweets, but subject 16's behaviour was inexplicable.

In Appendix B can be found the same kind of data for the clinical groups, in addition to the subjects' performance on the Blocks Design and the Verbal Comprehension subtests of the BAS. The first point to make is that the parallels between the 3-year-olds and the autistic subjects, and between the 4-year-olds and the Down's children, are equally strong when we see performance on all 20 trials. However, before describing the data in more detail we need to consider the intelligence levels of the groups.

First, as mentioned previously, the fact that the Blocks Design scores are dramatically higher in the autistic subjects should be interpreted with some caution because this is a task on which autistics frequently excel (Frith, 1989; though see footnote on p. 336). Note that the Blocks data for the Down's children demonstrate that success on the false belief task and on the windows task can occur in children who fail to complete any of the designs successfully within the time limit (shown as 'under 5' in Appendix B).

Performance on the Verbal Comprehension test is clearly important because, although the windows task required no verbalization, the subjects had to understand E1's description of the game and of what was necessary for winning. Turning to the autistic subjects, we see that six of the 11 subjects had performance ages above 4 years of age. However, all but one of these did very poorly on the windows task (see below for criteria for 'failing'). The picture is quite different in the Down's children. Even taking the very liberal criterion of having a performance age of 3 years or above (all but one child), we see that eight out of 13 children (61 per cent) correctly pointed to the empty box on *every* trial. In short, from the Down's data at least, it would appear that children do not need a very high level of verbal comprehension—as measured on the BAS—to perform well on the windows task. The autistic subjects, however, typically failed to point to the empty box even when their scores were at ceiling on the Verbal Comprehension test.

We now turn to the degree of association between success on the windows task and success on the false belief task. As mentioned before, success on the false belief task meant answering all six questions correctly. We used both a 'liberal' criterion and a 'conservative' criterion for success on the windows task. The liberal criterion was that the subject should indicate the empty box on 17 of the 20 test trials ($p < .001$). This meant that 28 of the subjects (48 per cent) succeeded on the windows task as against 36 subjects (62 per cent) succeeding on the false belief task. Twenty-seven subjects passed both, one subject passed the windows and failed the false belief, whilst 21 failed both and nine failed the windows and passed the false belief. This produces a phi correlation coefficient of .524, which is significant ($\chi^2(1) = 15.92$, $p < .001$). On the liberal criterion, therefore, the two tasks are closely associated.

Our conservative criterion for success on the windows task was that the subject should correctly indicate the empty box on the *first* test trial and then go on to make no more than three subsequent errors ($p < .002$). In this case 20 children (34 per cent of subjects) passed the windows task. All 20 of these also passed the false belief task, whilst 22 subjects failed both and 16 subjects failed the windows and passed the false belief task. This produced a phi correlation coefficient of .180, which is not significant ($\chi^2(1)$, $p > .05$). We would argue, however, that the liberal criterion is the more appropriate because some of the errors on the first test trial could have been due to impulsive pointing at the chocolate. Appendix A shows that a number of children only made errors on the first test trial. Also, note that of the 28 children who succeeded on the windows test on the liberal criterion, 20 had pointed to the empty box on the first test trial and five never indicated the baited box again after the initial incorrect point.

The Appendices also show that the autistic subjects answered the control questions on the false belief task correctly in every case, whereas the 3-year-olds typically failed the control as well as the critical questions. Of the 13 3-year-olds who failed control questions, seven failed only the 'know' question and six failed both the 'know' and the 'memory' questions. It may be that the difficulty which young children have with knowledge questions, as opposed to the more inferential belief questions, has been underestimated. This result also conflicts with the findings of Wimmer, Hogrefe & Perner (1988) who showed that young children typically *deny* knowledge to another person, for such a denial would have produced the 'correct' answer in this case. With regard to the data from the autistic subjects, Perner, Frith, Leslie & Leekam (1989) also report that autistics find questions about another's state of knowledge easier to answer than questions about another's beliefs. Further studies are required to determine whether there is really a disjunction between the 3-year-olds and the autistic subjects in this respect.

We shall finally report the children's responses to the two questions. Recall, first, that the subjects were asked why they pointed to a particular box on the first test trial, and after the competitor had searched, in order to see whether any of the justifications included reference to the mental states of E2. We reasoned that the answers to these questions would only be informative in the case of those 20 subjects who fulfilled our conservative criteria for success on the task (i.e. who then went on to make no more than three errors). Of the 10 preschoolers who were in this category, three said nothing, two said ''Cos I wanted the other one', and the rest said: 'So [E2] would look in the empty box'; 'I saw where the *Smartie* was'; 'So I can win', 'I looked', and ''Cos I wanted to win'. Of the nine Down's children in this category, we only had two answers to the question: 'Because the sweet's in the other box' and 'So I can get the sweet'. The one autistic said, 'Hasn't got a sweetie'. There are no mentalistic answers here, but it should be noted that a small number of these children (we did not record this systematically) whispered their answers to the question or grinned conspiratorially when the new boxes were set before them.

The second question we asked was, 'Where does [E2] think the chocolate is now?' The child heard this after a box was indicated on the second test trial but before the competitor searched. Here we looked at the data for the 23 children who pointed to the empty box and did not make more than three errors in the 20 trials. Eleven of the children said that the competitor thought that the chocolate was in the empty box, four of the children said that the competitor thought it was in the baited box, and the rest did not answer. The four children who referred to the baited box were the younger normals and in three cases they had pointed to the baited box on the first test trial. It is unlikely, therefore, that interpreting this thinking question in terms of the actual location (an 'extensional' misinterpretation of the question) was a common occurrence.

Discussion

We must now reconsider the alternatives sketched in the introduction. First, we have produced evidence which is broadly consistent with Outcome 2: success in this new test of strategic deception and success on the false belief task are associated. This association depends, as we have seen, on how success on the windows task is measured; and if we make pointing to the empty box on the *first* test trial a condition of success then the association between the two tasks is weakened. In any event, there is no evidence that the windows task is easier than the false belief task (Outcome 1). This means that there is no reason to explain failures on the false belief task by citing difficulties with verbal concepts and difficulties with predicting a protagonist's behaviour in terms of certain narrative conventions.

However, interpretation (*d*) of this outcome is still possible. That is to say, we may wish to deny that subjects *do* fail the windows task because they lack mental knowledge, in which case the association between the two tasks is *not* due to the fact that both involve knowledge of how mental states relate to the world. What makes the tasks difficult may be nothing to do with understanding epistemic states.

We do not have to look hard for some feature of the subjects' behaviour which suggests that representing the mental states of their opponent is not the main impediment to success. What is striking about the failure of the younger preschoolers and the autistic subjects is their perseverance with the wrong response: the fact that they do not learn to point to the empty box over 20 trials which show them that the result of pointing to the baited box is losing the chocolate. Given this, how might the association between the two tasks be explained?

The possibility we shall discuss is that the two tasks are difficult because they both require subjects to inhibit reference to a salient object: inhibiting pointing in one case and verbal reference in another.* We might assume, furthermore, that the judgements (verbal or non-verbal) that a subject makes at any one time are a product of competition between different kinds of knowledge with different levels of salience. 'Salience' here means cognitive salience, not perceptual salience;

---

* The claim is not being made here that the younger children and the autistic subjects are simply more impulsive: that they lack self-control. In any event we know from Wimmer & Perner (1983, Expt 2) that including a condition in which the children are encouraged to stop and think before answering does not improve performance. As will become evident, the claim is a cognitive one, concerning executive control over the determination of judgements derived from different sources of knowledge.

and we intend a usage similar to that found in Flavell's discussion of children's capacity to draw the appearance–reality distinction (Flavell, Flavell & Green, 1983, p. 99).

The claim is that for 3-year-olds and for autistic children knowledge of physical reality (e.g. 'a chocolate in the left-hand box'; 'a coin in the blue tin') is more salient than knowledge of mental reality ('the competitor can be made to think it's in the empty box'; 'the experimenter should still think it's in the green tin'). Thus, in order for the subjects to play the game deceptively, or for them to answer the question about belief mentalistically, it is necessary to suppress the tendency for physical knowledge to overwrite mental knowledge. Development during the late preschool years, on this view, consists not in the acquisition of mental knowledge but in the acquisition of executive control (cf. Baddeley, 1986, ch. 10; Shallice, 1988, ch. 14) over the generation of judgements and behaviour from different knowledge states.

It is now necessary to review the evidence for and against this salience hypothesis. First, the perseveration encouraged by the windows task is easier to regard as a failure of inhibition than as the behaviour of subjects who, through inability to understand that deception is required, have abandoned all attempts at succeeding and are therefore responding stereotypically. Why should lack of comprehension have this particular effect, as opposed to random responding or to the adoption of left- or right-side perseveration?

Second, as mentioned above, the salience hypothesis is influenced by Flavell's suggestions about how children of this age come to fail appearance–reality tasks. We know that performances on ignorance and appearance–reality tasks are empirically related (Gopnik & Astington, 1988) and the conceptual relation is inherent in the salience hypothesis. In both cases the child's task is to hold two representations in mind at one time whilst accessing the representation about which he or she is being questioned (see Flavell, 1988). In the appearance–reality task the children must balance the facts that, for example, what is before them is both a real piece of rock and an apparent egg and then answer a question about what the object 'looks like'. The fact of its being a rock is more, in Flavell's terminology, 'cognitively salient', and this wins out. The empirical association between performance on ignorance and appearance–reality tasks is consistent with the salience hypothesis.

Third, some recent data from Gopnik (1989) on performance in representational change tasks is explicable in terms of the salience hypothesis. Three-year-olds perform far worse on belief change questions, in which they have to report their prior beliefs about the contents of a box before it was opened and their beliefs disconfirmed, than on pretence change experiments. In the latter, the child is initially instructed to pretend that, for example, a stick is a spoon and is later told to pretend that it is a magic wand. When questioned at Time 2 about what they had been pretending earlier, the answers of the 3-year-olds were frequently correct. On the present argument, this would be because there could be no 'magic wand' present at Time 2 to attract reference to itself.

Moreover, a study by Moses & Flavell (1990) which tested the ability to understand belief change in a protagonist is explicable in a similar way. The subjects watched acted-out vignettes in which an actor was 'surprised' that a *Bandaid* box contained a toy car and not bandaids and were then asked to say what the protagonist thought was in the box before she opened it. The 3-year-olds usually said 'a car'. On the salience hypothesis, their own knowledge that a car was in the box was determining their answer. Interestingly, the authors suggest that 'many of these children understood little about beliefs and, hence, responded with whatever seemed most salient to them at the time of the test question'. How do we distinguish between 'understanding little' and 'an understanding that is easily overwritten by physical knowledge'? We will return to this question later.

Fourth, the salience hypothesis makes the prediction that 3-year-olds should be able to describe an agent's behaviour in terms of mental state language in cases where the incorrect response does *not* consist in referring to an object's known location, or does not consist of referring to a new, unexpected object. Some recent data from Bartsch & Wellman (1989) support this prediction. Children watched a puppet search for sticking plasters with two boxes in front of it: one was a *Bandaid* box and was empty and the other was a plain box and contained bandaids. The children knew which of the two boxes contained bandaids. After they had seen the puppet look in the *Bandaid* box and find it empty, the children were asked why he had searched there. If a child did not say something like 'because he thinks there are bandaids in there' he or she was prompted about what the puppet did think, in which case the child might say 'that there are bandaids in there'. Bartsch & Wellman found that around 66 per cent of the 3-year-olds could answer appropriately.

Finally, in considering evidence in favour of the salience hypothesis, we turn to the difficulties which autistic subjects have with the windows task. The hypothesis accords quite well with some recent suggestions of Frith's (1989) about the nature of the deficit. An inability to inhibit a response to a salient object implies that the processing of information by autistic subjects has a bottom–up rather than a top–down character. This is a feature of autistic thought on which Frith focuses. Arguing from Fodor's (1983) distinction between the 'input' and the 'central' systems, Frith suggests that one of the major difficulties in autism is with central— in the sense of 'global'—processing. However, the input systems, which package perceptual inputs and deliver up mandatory representations (e.g. a sentence parse or a coding of an object as rigid), function efficiently. This is supposed to explain why autistics find embedded figures and Blocks Design tasks relatively easy: because in normals the natural tendency towards global cognition makes the kind of focusing on local detail which these tasks require so difficult (see footnote on p. 336). Frith explains autistics' over-literal, context-insensitive language in a similar way.

There are, however, other data which the salience hypothesis cannot accommodate so easily. First, children who fail the 'belief' question are also frequently able to answer the 'memory' question correctly about where the object was before its transfer. (Though recall that six of our 3-year-olds failed this question.) If there is a problem with inhibiting reference to present objects, these children should be saying that the object was originally in the place where it currently is. In answer to this, although there could be a very strong version of the salience hypothesis which would be that young children's answers to questions are always determined by their knowledge of the current state of reality, this is not the salience hypothesis stated here. The hypothesis is that in young children, and in at least some clinical populations, physical knowledge is more salient than mental knowledge so that in circumstances where the two are in competition the former wins out. A question about the previous location of the object is a question about physical knowledge and so is not relevant to the hypothesis.

Second, it may appear that in their classic paper Wimmer & Perner (1983) tested the salience hypothesis and showed it to be false. To explain: if there is *no* object present at the time of the belief question then it is possible to ask the belief question without simultaneous competition from salient physical knowledge. In their Expt 2, Wimmer & Perner tested this prediction and raised the question of 'the possible interference between mental representations', namely, the child's knowledge that the chocolate is now in the green cupboard as against the description of the protagonist's false belief that it is in the blue cupboard. They suggest that representations of the protagonist's belief 'may be easily overwritten by the dominating description of the true state of affairs' (p. 112), which is exactly what is entailed by the salience hypothesis. They attempted to discourage this overwriting by having a 'disappear' condition in which Maxi's mother put *all* of the chocolate in the cake, so that there was none left to transfer into the green cupboard. The chocolate was *in fact* 'removed from the scene and placed behind a wall' and the subjects asked about where Maxi would look for the chocolate on his return.

The result was that children of all ages were helped, at least a little, by the inclusion of the disappear condition. At age 4–5 years, for example, 70 per cent of the children gave correct answers to the question on both stories, as against 45 per cent in the standard format. In the 3–4-year-olds, however, the improvement was very slight. What is important is that all 85 per cent of the youngest children who failed to say that the protagonists in the stories would search where the object was originally 'claimed that the protagonist would search behind the scenes' (p. 115). In other words, although the object (chocolate or picture book) was taken beyond the 'stage' on which the vignettes were being acted out, the young children thought that the protagonist would search *there*. This would seem to be rather good evidence for the salience hypothesis.

One caveat needs to be inserted here, however. If the objects had literally ceased to exist (e.g. if the experimenter had eaten the chocolate), and if the youngest children then said that the protagonist would search at the original location, this would not necessarily be evidence for the salience hypothesis because this answer could be determined by their own physical knowledge of where the object had been placed. The object would need to be moved to the new location before being destroyed, so the subject would have two sets of physical knowledge and both locations would be equally salient.

The salience hypothesis and the standard account make contrasting predictions about the outcome of experiments. They can do this because the former entails that subjects who fail on ignorance tasks have an appreciation of epistemic states which is masked by the salience of their physical knowledge, whilst the latter entails that they have no understanding of epistemic states. But a great deal hinges on what 'appreciation of epistemic states' is supposed to mean. What if we take it to mean 'an appreciation of the *theoretical structure** of mental state language'? In this case, a supporter of the salience hypothesis could agree that, in a sense, such children do lack a theory of mind, because they lack the ability to direct their own minds away from their own physical knowledge in cases where mental language is being used. An increase in mental autonomy—in the sense of an increasing ability to direct thoughts towards mental states (of which such children already have an implicit and pre-theoretical understanding) and away from physical states—would therefore make possible the adoption of the theory that is implicit in our language.

Under this interpretation, the salience hypothesis and the standard view would not, strictly, be competing: because the former would contain the seeds of an explanatory cognitive theory of how the acquisition described by the 'theory of mind theory' proceeds. Clearly, the conceptual issues in this area are going to be more difficult to sort out than the empirical ones.

Acknowledgements

We are very grateful to the following Cambridge nursery schools for their help: Brunswick Road, Joint Colleges, Harvey Road and the Cambridge Day Nursery. We are also indebted to Radlett Lodge School in Hertfordshire and to the Green Hedges and Rees Thomas schools in Cambridge. Usha Goswami provided valuable comments on an earlier draft.

This work was funded, in part, by a grant from the Grindley Fund, Cambridge University, and by a grant from Pembroke College to the last author.

References

Astington, J. W., Harris, P. L. & Olson, D. R. (1988). *Developing Theories of Mind*. Cambridge: Cambridge University Press.

Baddeley, A. (1986). *Working Memory*. Oxford: Oxford University Press.

Baron-Cohen, S., Leslie, A. M. & Frith, U. (1985). Does the autistic child have a 'theory of mind'? *Cognition*, **21**, 37–46.

Bartsch, K. & Wellman, H. (1989). Young children's attribution of action to beliefs and desires. *Child Development*, **60**, 946–964.

Bennett, J. (1988). Thoughts about thoughts (Commentary on Whiten and Byrne). *Behavioral and Brain Sciences*, **11**, 246–247.

Chandler, M. J., Fritz, A. S. & Hala, S. (1989). Small-scale deceit: Deception as a marker of 2-, 3- and 4-year-olds' early theories of mind. *Child Development*, **60**, 1263–1277.

de Gelder, B. (1987). On not having a theory of mind. *Cognition*, **27**, 295–296.

Dennett, D. D. (1978). Beliefs about beliefs (Commentary on Premack and Woodruff). *Behavioral and Brain Sciences*, **4**, 568–569.

Elliot, C. D., Murray, D. J. & Pearson, L. S. (1983). *British Ability Scales*. Windsor, Berks: NFER-NELSON.

---

* By 'theoretical structure' is intended everything from the semantics of mental state language to everyday ways of talking about mental states (e.g. that they are 'in the head'). With regard to the former, children need to appreciate that, for example, the verb *to know* is factive, that the truth of what is *known* is assumed, whilst verbs like *think* and *believe* bracket off the question of truth vs. falsity. We are justified in calling these theoretical constructs for two reasons. First, reality does not impose this particular semantic system upon us, and it is easy to imagine languages with different kinds of semantics for mental states. Second, they are theoretical in the sense that they include terms (such as 'belief' itself) which entail a particular folk psychological theory about the ontology and causal powers of mental states. Some philosophers (e.g. Stich, 1983) have argued that this bit of folk psychology is wrong.

Flavell, J. H. (1988). The development of children's knowledge about the mind: From cognitive connections to mental representations. In J. Astington, P. L. Harris & D. R. Olson (Eds), *Developing Theories of Mind*. Cambridge: Cambridge University Press.

Flavell, J. H., Flavell, E. R. & Green, F. L. (1983). Development of the appearance–reality distinction. *Cognitive Psychology*, **17**, 95–120.

Fodor, J. A. (1983). *The Modality of Mind*. Boston, MA: MIT Press/Bradford Books.

Frith, U. (1989). *Autism: Explaining the Enigma*. Oxford: Blackwell.

Gopnik, A. (1989). Young children's understanding of changes in their mental states. Paper presented at the Annual Conference of The British Psychological Society, Developmental Psychology Section, University of Surrey, September.

Gopnik, A. & Astington, J. W. (1988). Children's understanding of representational change and its relation to the understanding of the appearance–reality distinction. *Child Development*, **59**, 26–37.

Grice, H. P. (1957). Meaning. *Philosophical Review*, **66**, 377–388.

Hogrefe, G.-J., Wimmer, H. & Perner, J. (1986). Ignorance versus false belief: A developmental lag in attribution of epistemic states. *Child Development*, **57**, 567–582.

Leslie, A. M. & Frith, U. (1988). Autistics' understanding of seeing, knowing, and believing. *British Journal of Developmental Psychology*, **6**, 315–324.

Lewis, C. & Osborne, A. (in press). Three-year-olds' problems with false belief: Conceptual deficit or linguistic artefact? *Child Development*.

Moses, L. J. & Flavell, J. H. (1990). Inferring false beliefs from actions and reactions. *Child Development*, **61**, 629–645.

Perner, J., Frith, U., Leslie, A. M. & Leekam, S. (1989). Exploration of the autistic child's theory of mind: Knowledge, belief and communication. *Child Development*, **60**, 689–700.

Russell, J. (1980). Action from knowledge and conditioned behavior: I. The stratification of behavior. *Behaviorism*, **8**, 87–89.

Russell, J. (1987a). Reasons for believing that there is perceptual development in childhood. In J. Russell (Ed.), *Philosophical Perspectives on Developmental Psychology*. Oxford: Blackwell.

Russell, J. (1987b). 'Can we say . . .?' Children's understanding of intensionality. *Cognition*, **25**, 289–308.

Russell, J. (1989). Cognisance and cognitive science: II. Towards an empirical psychology of cognisance. *Philosophical Psychology*, **2**, 165–201.

Rutter, M. (1978). Language disorder and infantile autism. In M. Rutter & E. Schopler (Eds), *Autism: A Reappraisal of Concepts and Treatments*. New York: Plenum.

Shallice, T. (1988). *From Neuropsychology to Mental Structure*. Cambridge: Cambridge University Press.

Shultz, T. R. & Cloghesy, K. (1981). Development of recursive awareness of intention. *Developmental Psychology*, **17**, 465–471.

Sodian, B., Taylor, C., Harris, P. L. & Perner, J. (in press). Early deception and the child's theory of mind: False trails and genuine markers. *Child Development*.

Stich, S. P. (1983). *From Folkpsychology to Cognitive Science: The Case against Belief*. Cambridge, MA: MIT Press/Bradford Books.

Wellman, H. & Bartsch, K. (1989). Young children's reasoning about beliefs. *Cognition*, **30**, 239–277.

Whiten, A. & Byrne, R. (1988). Tactical deception in primates. *Behavioral and Brain Sciences*, **11**, 233–273.

Wimmer, H. & Perner, J. (1983). Beliefs about beliefs: Representation and constraining function of wrong beliefs in young children's understanding of deception. *Cognition*, **13**, 103–128.

Wimmer, H., Hogrefe, C.-J. & Perner, J. (1988). Children's understanding of informational access as a source of knowledge. *Child Development*, **59**, 386–396.

Woodruff, G. & Premack, D. (1979). Intentional communication in the chimpanzee: The development of deception. *Cognition*, **7**, 333–363.

Received 15 January 1990; revised version received 12 April 1990

Appendix A

Preschoolers' performance on the windows and on the false belief tasks

Subject	Age	\multicolumn{20}{c}{Windows[a] — Trials}																			False belief[b] Control	Critical
		1	2	3	4	5	6	7	8	9	10	11	12	13	14	15	16	17	18	19	20		
(i) 3-year-olds																							
1	3:0	0	0	0	0	0	0	0	0	0	0	0	0	0	0	0	0	0	0	0	0	×	×
2	3:0	0	0	0	0	0	0	0	0	0	0	0	0	0	0	0	0	0	0	0	0	×	×
3	3:1	0	0	0	0	0	0	0	0	0	0	0	0	0	0	0	0	0	0	0	0	×	×
4	3:1	0	0	0	0	0	0	0	0	0	0	0	0	0	0	0	0	0	1	1	1	×	×
5	3:2	0	0	0	0	0	0	0	0	0	0	0	0	0	0	0	0	0	0	0	0	×	×
6	3:2	0	0	0	0	0	0	0	0	0	0	0	0	0	0	0	0	0	0	0	0	×	×
7	3:3	0	0	0	0	0	0	0	0	0	0	0	0	0	0	0	0	0	0	0	0	×	×
8	3:3	0	0	0	0	0	0	0	0	0	0	0	0	0	0	0	0	0	0	0	0	×	×
9	3:4	0	0	0	0	0	0	0	0	0	0	0	0	0	0	0	0	0	0	0	0	×	×
10	3:4	0	0	0	0	0	0	0	0	0	0	0	0	0	0	0	0	0	0	0	0	×	×
11	3:4	0	0	0	0	0	0	0	0	0	0	0	0	0	0	0	0	0	0	0	0	×	×
12	3:4	0	1	1	1	1	1	1	1	1	1	1	1	1	1	1	1	1	1	1	1	✓	✓
13	3:7	0	1	1	1	1	1	1	1	1	1	1	1	1	1	1	1	1	1	1	1	✓	×
14	3:7	0	0	0	0	0	0	0	1	1	0	0	0	0	0	1	0	1	0	0	0	×	×
15	3:8	0	0	0	0	0	0	0	0	0	1	0	1	0	1	0	1	1	1	1	1	×	×
16	3:9	0	1	1	1	1	1	1	1	1	1	1	1	1	1	1	1	1	1	1	1	✓	✓
17	3:10	1	1	1	1	1	1	1	1	1	1	1	1	1	1	1	1	1	1	1	1	✓	✓

(ii) *4-year-olds*

1	4:0	1	1	1	1	1	1	1	1	1	1	1	1	1	1	1	1	1		>	>
2	4:0	1	1	1	1	1	1	1	1	1	1	1	1	1	1	1	1	1		>	>
3	4:2	0	1	1	1	1	1	1	0	1	1	1	1	1	1	0	1	1		>	>
4	4:3	1	1	1	1	1	1	1	1	1	1	1	1	1	1	1	1	1		>	>
5	4:3	0	0	1	1	1	1	0	1	1	1	1	1	1	1	1	1	1		>	>
6	4:3	0	1	1	1	1	0	1	1	0	1	1	0	1	1	1	1	1		>	>
7	4:4	1	0	0	1	1	1	1	1	1	1	1	1	1	1	1	1	1		>	>
8	4:4	1	1	1	1	1	1	1	1	1	1	1	1	1	1	1	1	1		>	>
9	4:4	1	1	1	1	1	1	1	1	1	1	1	1	1	1	1	1	1		>	>
10	4:5	1	1	1	1	1	1	1	1	1	1	1	1	1	1	1	1	1		>	>
11	4:6	0	1	1	0	1	1	1	1	1	1	1	1	1	1	1	1	1		>	>
12	4:6	1	1	1	1	1	1	1	1	1	1	1	1	1	1	1	1	1		>	>
13	4:6	1	1	1	1	1	1	1	1	1	1	1	1	1	1	1	1	1		>	>
14	4:8	1	1	1	1	1	1	1	1	1	1	1	1	1	1	1	1	1		>	>
15	4:10	0	1	1	0	1	1	1	1	1	1	1	1	0	1	1	1	1		>	>
16	4:10	0	0	0	0	1	1	1	1	1	1	0	1	1	0	1	1	1		>	>

[a] 0 = points to wrong (baited) box; 1 = points to correct (empty) box.

[b] A tick indicates that the subject answered both critical questions correctly or all four control questions correctly, and a cross indicates that at least one question was answered incorrectly.

Appendix B

Performance of the clinical groups on the windows task and on the false belief task

				Windows[a] Trials																				False belief[b]	
Subject	Age	Blocks design	Verbal compreh.	1	2	3	4	5	6	7	8	9	10	11	12	13	14	15	16	17	18	19	20	Con.	Crit.
(i) *Down's group*																									
1	9:0	under 5	3:10	0	0	0	0	0	0	0	1	1	1	1	1	1	1	1	1	1	1	1	1	✓	✓
2	8:9	under 5	2:10	1	0	0	0	0	1	1	1	1	1	1	1	1	1	1	1	1	1	1	1	✓	✓
3	11:7	5:0	4:10	1	0	0	0	0	0	1	1	1	1	1	1	1	1	1	1	1	1	1	1	✓	✓
4	15:8	under 5	3:0	1	1	1	1	1	1	1	1	1	1	1	1	1	1	1	1	1	1	1	1	✓	✓
5	16:1	under 5	4:11	1	1	1	1	1	1	1	1	1	1	1	1	1	1	1	1	1	1	1	1	✓	✓
6	15:3	6:4	4:11	1	1	1	1	1	1	1	1	1	1	1	1	1	1	1	1	1	1	1	1	✓	✓
7	15:8	5:9	4:11	1	1	1	1	1	1	1	1	1	1	1	1	1	1	1	1	1	1	1	1	✓	✓
8	9:8	5:0	4:11	1	1	1	1	1	1	1	1	1	1	0	1	1	1	1	1	1	1	1	1	✓	✓
9	7:2	under 5	3:10	1	0	0	0	0	0	0	0	0	1	1	1	1	1	1	1	1	1	1	1	✓	✓
10	18:9	5:0	4:5	0	0	1	1	1	1	1	1	1	1	1	1	1	1	1	1	1	1	1	1	✓	✓
11	15:8	6:4	4:11	1	1	1	1	1	1	1	1	1	1	1	1	1	1	1	1	1	1	1	1	✓	✓
12	12:7	under 5	ceiling	1	1	1	1	1	1	1	1	1	1	1	1	1	1	1	1	1	1	1	1	✓	✓
13	8:1	5:0	ceiling	1	0	1	1	1	1	1	1	1	1	1	1	1	1	1	1	1	1	1	1	✓	✓
14	9:2	5:0	4:11	1	1	1	1	1	1	1	1	1	1	1	1	1	1	1	1	1	1	1	1	✓	✓

(ii) *Autistic group*

#																								
1	15:2	12:5	3:8	0	0	0	0	0	0	0	0	0	0	0	0	0	0	0	0	0		✓
2	15:5	6:6	ceiling	0	0	0	0	0	0	0	0	0	0	0	0	0	0	0	0	0	✓	✗
3	16:4	12:5	ceiling	0	0	0	0	0	0	0	0	0	0	0	0	0	0	0	0	0	✓	✓
4	15:9	13:6	ceiling	1	1	1	1	1	1	1	1	1	1	1	1	1	1	1	1	1	✓	✓
5	17:2	9:6	ceiling	0	0	0	0	0	0	0	0	0	0	0	0	0	0	0	1	1	✓	✗
6	7:6	5:0	3:8	1	1	1	1	1	1	1	1	1	1	1	1	1	1	1	0	0	✓	✗
7	15:7	13:7	4:6	0	1	1	1	0	1	1	1	0	0	0	0	0	0	0	0	0	✓	✗
8	9:4	11:5	2:6	0	0	0	0	0	0	0	0	0	0	0	0	0	0	0	0	0	✓	✗
9	14:5	5:9	3:5	0	0	0	0	0	0	0	0	0	0	0	0	0	0	0	0	0	✓	✗
10	7:5	under 5	4:5	0	0	0	0	0	0	0	0	1	1	1	1	1	1	1	0	0	✓	✗
11	9:10	7:5	3:5	0	0	0	0	1	1	0	0	0	0	0	0	0	0	0	1	0	✓	✗

Note. See text for explanation of how age equivalents on the Blocks Design and Verbal Comprehension tests were calculated. For explanation of symbols, see Appendix A.

British Journal of Developmental Psychology (1991), **9**, 351–364   *Printed in Great Britain*

Cognitive linguistic correlates of 'theory of mind' ability in autistic children

Richard Eisenmajer and **Margot Prior***

Department of Psychology, La Trobe University, Bundoora, Victoria 3083, Australia

A specific deficit in theory of mind has been proposed to explain the distinct pattern of social/cognitive deficits in autistic individuals (Frith, 1989). However, it is clear that a number of children are able to demonstrate knowledge of mental states in others (Prior, Dahlstrom & Squires, 1990), hence an important question is what particularly characterizes those autistic children who do show theory of mind. Baron-Cohen (1988) has argued that pragmatic language skills and theory of mind ability ought to be intimately related since they draw on similar representational abilities. We examined the cognitive linguistic correlates of this ability in 29 high functioning autistic children. The 11 children who could reliably show this ability were compared with those who could not, on CA, verbal MA, pragmatic language skills, WISC Vocabulary, Comprehension and Similarities, and were superior on all measures except Vocab and CA. A stepwise discriminant function analysis showed an 86 per cent correct classification of the two groups with pragmatic skills and abstract thinking as the best discriminators.

Procedural and instructional variables were also assessed in this study, as was reliability of theory of mind ability from one year to the next. Most children were stable in their demonstrated knowledge. The addition of the word 'first' to the false belief question (Where will Sally first look for the marble?) allowed 50 per cent of the originally failing group to answer the question correctly, suggesting the need for extreme care in the details of replication experiments of this kind. Our results support the likelihood of a developmental delay in theory of mind in autism rather than endorsing the notion that this is a specific deficit with pervasive explanatory power. However, the findings might also support the 'continuum' conceptualization of autism with more mildly autistic children able to demonstrate knowledge of mental states and to develop adequate pragmatic language competence.

Recent investigations suggest that the social and communicative dysfunctions observed in autistic individuals may be a consequence of an underlying inability to form 'meta-representations' (see Leslie, 1987). It is argued that this disability is a key aspect of the more general cognitive problems which are basic to the disorder (Baron-Cohen, 1988; Prior, 1984; Rutter, 1983). One manifestation of this proposed deficit is a lack of a 'theory of mind'; that is, an inability to attribute mental states to oneself and other people and to understand and predict their behaviour. Such a deficit could explain autistic individuals' indifference to other people, and poor

---

* Requests for reprints

knowledge of social rules, as well as certain communicative abnormalities, such as impaired pragmatic language ability (Baron-Cohen, 1988).

Several studies have found that autistic children suffer an inability to attribute mental states to other people by comparison with mental age-matched control groups (Baron-Cohen, Leslie & Frith, 1985; Baron-Cohen, 1989*a,b*; Leslie & Frith, 1988; Perner, Frith, Leslie & Leekam, 1989). Consequently, an *autism-specific* deficit in theory of mind has been proposed to explain the results (Frith, 1989). However, the generality of the conclusions about such autistic deficits is somewhat undermined by the fact that in each study a small number of children (between 18–28 per cent) has been successful in demonstrating a theory of mind. This would suggest that a lack of a theory of mind is not inevitable in autism, as clearly some children do have this capacity.

A recent Australian study conducted by Prior *et al.* (1990) also investigated mental state attributions (false belief and ignorance) in autistic children. Unlike previous studies where autistic children performed poorly on theory of mind tasks, they found that an unusually high number out of their 20 subjects (55 per cent), successfully attributed a false belief to another. In this same study a similar proportion of autistic subjects was able to show knowledge of another person's ignorance which would lead them to a wrong judgement; and in a theoretically related task, to correctly interpret emotional expression or affect. Prior *et al.* (1990) suggested that the difference in results could reflect their samples' higher verbal mental age. When their subjects were matched on verbal MA with the sample of an earlier study by Baron-Cohen *et al.* (1985) (by selecting children with a verbal MA lower than 7 years and 5 months), only four out of 12 children were seen to pass the false belief task, resembling more closely the results obtained by Baron-Cohen *et al.* (1985). Thus, it could be argued that verbal skills in some way influenced performance on the task and that children above a certain level of development do possess theory of mind.

Other studies have reported similar trends. For example, Leslie & Frith (1988) found that autistic subjects who demonstrated comprehension of false belief tended to have a higher CA and verbal MA. The subjects involved in Baron-Cohen's (1989*a,b*) study who demonstrated theory of mind, were also of a higher CA and verbal MA compared to their unsuccessful counterparts, and in terms of verbal MA, similar to the subjects in the Prior *et al.* (1990) study. These authors have suggested that language competence could be a discriminating factor for the ability to attribute mental states. One could posit that once a certain level of language competence is reached, the capacity to demonstrate a theory of mind appears. Such a proposal might suggest a developmental cognitive/linguistic delay as an explanation for the impairments, rather than an autism-specific deficit.

However, other evidence questions this proposition. The four children who were successful in the original Baron-Cohen *et al.* (1985) study did not appear to be distinguishable from their autistic counterparts in terms of CA and verbal MA; there being other children of equal and higher CA and verbal MA failing to demonstrate a theory of mind. This discrepancy was also found in some children in the study by Prior *et al.* (1990). Moreover, specific language-impaired subjects matched with autistic children on verbal MA to control for the effects of language dysfunction were unimpaired on the false belief task (Leslie & Frith, 1988).

Although it is clear that certain autistic children do possess metarepresentational ability as assessed via the reported experimental tasks, no investigation has as yet been made of the cognitive–behavioural consequences of having a theory of mind. Certain hypotheses have been offered in regard to the communicative ability of the autistic children able to demonstrate such ability. Baron-Cohen (1988) has suggested that these children will display better pragmatic language skills than autistic children unable to pass theory of mind tasks. A pragmatically competent individual is able to initiate a conversation, respond appropriately to different conversation partners, relate new information to information already possessed (Rees, 1978 cited in Cromer, 1981), and emit and respond to subtle turn-taking cues (Bernard-Opitz, 1982). It is argued that to be able to demonstrate these pragmatic skills, the speaker must continually assess and have *beliefs* regarding what the listener knows, does not know, wants to know and needs to know. Pragmatic competence would thus appear to require an appreciation of the mental states of others.

Marked deficits in the pragmatic skills of autistic children have been reported (Ball, 1978; Baltaxe, 1977; Dewey & Everard, 1974 cited in Baltaxe & Simmons, 1977; Simmons & Baltaxe, 1975 and Ackerly, 1984 both cited in Hurtig, Ensrud & Tomblin, 1982; Westby, 1980). These well-documented pragmatic deficits could be argued to be further evidence of an underlying deficit in theory of mind abilities. Theories depicting the association between communication and mental states are not new; for example, Piaget (1932, cited in Cunningham, 1968) realized that for an exchange of information to occur, the speaker is required to place him or herself at the 'point of view' of the listener. More recently, communication-intention theorists such as Grice (1975, 1968); Searle, (1969) and Strawson (1964—all cited in Leslie, 1987) have proposed that for 'intelligent' communication to occur, the speaker and listener must recognize each other's mental states. Thus it is of interest to examine the pragmatic skills of autistic children in relation to theory of mind ability.

Possession of a theory of mind would probably also allow for a better understanding of social and moral rules, and interpersonal relations. An ability to understand the consequences of one's actions in terms of other people would also require metarepresentational, or rather, theory of mind ability. Thus it is predicted that autistic children able to pass a theory of mind task will perform better on a measure of social understanding than children who fail these tasks. One exemplar test of a child's ability to understand commonly experienced social situations and to provide common-sense answers to everyday problems is provided by the Comprehension subtest of the Wechsler Intelligence Scale for Children (WISC). Success on this subtest requires an ability to understand social conventions and interpersonal relations (Sattler, 1988). Such factors are likely to require theory of mind ability. Hence this measure was included as a reliable, valid, normed test of social reasoning which is likely to require theory of mind abilities.

A further possibility which we considered is that there could be a connection between metarepresentational ability and symbolic or categorical (higher order) thinking. Those autistic children who have developed some degree of abstract reasoning ability may be able to solve theory of mind problems by virtue of this capacity to move from a concrete level of thinking to an abstract or metarepresentational level. Hence, again, from the WISC, we adopted the Similarities subtest as a measure of verbal concept formation (symbolic thinking) and logical reasoning (Sattler, 1988) which might illuminate this hypothesized relationship.

An additional measure of interest in this study was word knowledge and whether this was a discriminator between children passing or failing a theory of mind task. It is possible that the children who fail do so simply because they have a poor understanding of the meaning of words and ideas, and are generally deficient in expressive language skills. We therefore included the Vocabulary subtest of the WISC.

The aims of this study were thus to provide further investigation of theory of mind abilities in a sample of autistic children and in particular to examine the cognitive– linguistic correlates of the capacity for understanding false belief in other people. It was predicted that those children showing such understanding would be of higher verbal MA and pragmatic language skills than those who did not. The same false belief task used in previous studies (e.g. Baron-Cohen *et al.*, 1985 Prior *et al.*, 1990) was employed here.

Four language areas were thus investigated. Three subtests of the Wechsler Intelligence Scale for Children—Revised (WISC-R) (Wechsler, 1974) or the Wechsler Preschool and Primary Scale of Intelligence (WPPSI) (Wechsler, 1967) were used depending on the CA and verbal MA of the child. These tests were the Comprehension, Similarities and Vocabulary subscales. A recent study conducted by Lincoln, Courchesne, Kilman, Elmasian & Allen (1988) on autistic children's performance on the Wechsler tests found them to be a valid measure for investigating verbal intellectual abilities in autism since a remarkably similar and stable pattern of results was observed across studies considering the social, geographic and age characteristics of the populations tested, and the use of different versions of the test (WISC, WAIS-R and WISC-R). This pattern was stable over time.

Method

Subjects

Thirty-five autistic children originally took part in this study; however, six were excluded because they were unable to correctly answer essential control questions in the false belief task ('Where was the block in the beginning?', 'Where is the block really?'). This was a relatively low functioning subgroup all having verbal MAs below the age of 4 years and 11 months (range 3:9 to 4:11). The final sample consisted of 20 boys, and nine girls, with mean CA, 11 years 8 months (range 6:5 to 17:8). The mean verbal MA was 7 years 5 months (range 3:11 to 14:1) on the Peabody Picture Vocabulary Test (PPVT) (Dunn & Dunn, 1981). Concurrent performance IQs were not available for all children but for those who had been tested previously (Prior *et al.*, 1990) the average PIQ was 89.

All of the subjects had been diagnosed as autistic by established criteria (DSM III, APA, 1980). Five children appeared to be currently functioning at a mildly autistic level with less severe symptoms but had indisputably been classical cases. All but two of the subjects had at one time attended early intervention programmes at various facilities and many of the more capable children were attending mainstream schools on a regular or part-time basis. Most of these children were receiving assistance from an aide while in a classroom. It should be noted that integration of all handicapped children into regular classrooms is educational policy in Australia and does not bear any systematic relationship to the level of functioning of the child. Thirteen of the subjects were tested at their school while the rest were tested at home. Eleven subjects had participated in a previous theory of mind experiment (Prior *et al.*, 1990).

Since the focus of the study was on the cognitive correlates of theory of mind ability *within* a group of autistic children, no control group was included.

Materials

The 'false belief' task. Two dolls with sufficiently different characteristics were used. Sally had straight blond hair and was approximately 57 centimetres long. Anne was smaller in stature, had blue curly hair and was approximately 43 centimetres long. A cardboard box and a basket both with lids were also used. The dimensions of the box were $17 \times 16 \times 9$ centimetres (length $\times$ width $\times$ height) and it was green in colour. The basket was a red and brown cane sewing basket with the dimensions $17 \times 24 \times 10$ centimetres. A red block was used as the object to be hidden. A second trial of the false belief task using different hiding locations was carried out to test for the reliability of the children's answers. This condition required the experimenter to wear an item of clothing with a pocket and the use of a straw sunhat.

The Wechsler subtests. The Comprehension, Similarities and Vocabulary subtests of the WISC-R or WPPSI were used as language assessments. Subjects of verbal MA of 6 years or more (as assessed by the PPVT) and CA of 6 years 6 months or more were tested using the WISC-R. Subjects with a lower verbal MA and/or CA were tested on the WPPSI. The use of verbal MA as a criterion to determine which test was given was so that, for example, a subject of CA 14 years with a mental age of 4 was not given the WISC-R but the WPPSI. Clearly, the WISC-R would have been out of reach for children with this profile. Consequently, the (PPVT) verbal MA of each subject was used to calculate their scaled score. In the three cases where the verbal MA was actually higher than the CA, the CA was used to determine the scaled score so as not to disadvantage the subjects.

Test of Pragmatic Skills. The Test of Pragmatic Skills (Shulman, 1986) is an assessment of communicative intention designed for 3- to 9-year-old children. This test is comprised of four structured play interactions through which the subject's pragmatic ability is assessed. As the test is specifically designed for children 3 to 9 years of age, there were concerns over whether the test would be appropriate for the sample. However, the age limits of the test are only particularly important if the standardized norms are to be used, rather than a relative measure as in our case. Furthermore, the seven children with a verbal MA over 8 years 11 months participated happily and enjoyed playing 'the games'. Pragmatic language abilities were well within the test ceiling in all cases.

The test encompasses a wide range of communicative intentions, including: requesting information; requesting action; rejection/denial; naming/labelling; answering/responding; informing; reasoning; summoning; calling; greeting; and closing conversation. Four games through which probe questions were administered according to the manual, involved playing with puppets, drawings, telephones, and blocks, and proved to be the most popular test with all of the children. An audiotape recording was made of the verbal responses which were transferred to a scoring sheet after the testing session. Appropriate non-verbal responses were noted during the test. A total of 34 probes over the four tasks are given to the subject. Each response is scored depending on its level of response. Five levels are offered:

'No response' (score 0);
'Contextually inappropriate response' (score 1);
'Contextually appropriate non-verbal/gestural response only (score 2);
'Contextually appropriate one-word response without elaboration' (score 3);
'Contextually appropriate response with minimal elaboration'—two or three words (score 4, and
'Contextually appropriate response with extensive elaboration—more than three words (score 5).
Since older children tend to be more linguistically sophisticated than younger children, it was important to primarily judge the subject's response in terms of conversational context appropriateness. The subject's pragmatic score was obtained by adding the individual scores over the four tasks and dividing the total by four. Total possible individual score is 42.5.

Procedure

After an initial familiarization period, the tasks were presented in the following order: PPVT; false belief task trial 1; Vocabulary; Similarities; Comprehension; 'Test of Pragmatic Skills'; and false belief task trial 2. A third and final trial of the false belief task was given to subjects who had failed one or both of the preceding trials to determine whether the word 'first' affected performance. This was included as a procedural check since our previous study (Prior *et al.*, 1990) had asked the false belief question 'where will Sally first look for the marble' whereas in this study exactly the same wording as in Baron-Cohen *et al.* (1985) was used.

The 'false belief' task.

The box and the basket were placed on the table. The children were told, 'Now we are going to play a game with dolls'. The two dolls, Sally and Anne, were introduced to the children. The children were then required to name each doll (naming question). If the children failed to remember, they were reminded until able to do so correctly.

Sally then picked up the red block, placed it inside the box and closed the lid. The children were made aware that Anne also saw this action. Having done this, Sally then 'went away' under the table out of the children's sight. It was emphasized to the children that Sally could neither hear nor see what was happening. The children were then told and shown that Anne was taking the red block out of the box and hiding it in the basket. Then they were told that Sally was 'coming back'.

The next question depended on which condition was being used. In the study conducted by Baron-Cohen *et al.* (1985), the question asked upon Sally's return was the belief question, 'Where will Sally look for her marble?' followed by the control questions, 'Where is the marble now?' (reality question) and 'Where was the marble in the beginning?' (memory question). However, Prior *et al.* (1990) had presented the control questions before and after the belief question. To determine whether this change had any effect on performance it was necessary to create two conditions, pre- and post-belief. In the first case, the control questions were placed before the belief question, and in the latter case the control questions were placed after the belief question. As the false belief task was presented to the subjects on two occasions using different hiding locations, the order of the pre- and post-belief conditions was counterbalanced.

To ensure that the children did not unwittingly give a correct answer by favouring a position or giving an echolalic response, the order of the control questions were such that no two correct responses using the same word followed one another. Therefore, in the pre-belief case, the order of presentation would be memory, then reality and then the belief question. The subject, if correct, would reply 'box', 'basket', then 'box'. In the post-belief condition, the belief question would be first, followed by the reality question, and the memory question last of all. The subject would have to respond 'box', 'basket', then 'box'. It was felt that these conditions, although appearing elaborate and conservative, were necessary to ensure against correctly answering by chance.

The false belief task with the dolls was repeated after the Test of Pragmatic Skills using two different locations, hat and pocket, to provide replication and to eliminate any problems of position preference. The red block was moved from under a hat and hidden in the experimenter's pocket. This constituted trial 2 of the false belief task.

To determine whether the word 'first' assisted autistic children on the false belief task, a third and final presentation of the task was given to those children who had failed one or both of the earlier trials. In this case, the red block would be moved from the hat to the basket. The children were asked upon Sally's return, 'Where will Sally first look for the marble?' The memory and reality questions followed in that order.

The Wechsler subtests.   The tests were conducted in the manner outlined by the manual using probes where necessary to encourage a response consistent with true level of knowledge.

Results

Language and age variables

Inclusion criteria required all subjects to answer both control questions (Where was the block in the beginning?, Where is the block now?) correctly. To qualify for a pass on the false belief task the subjects had to answer (either by pointing or verbal response) the belief question *correctly on both trials* i.e. dolls and pocket conditions).

Eleven (38 per cent) of the 29 autistic children passed the false belief task. The means and standard deviations of the 'passers' and 'failers' of the false belief task on the language variables and verbal MA are shown in Table 1.

Table 1. Means and standard deviations of language variables for the 'passers' and 'failers' of the false belief task

Variables		'Passers'	'Failers'
CA	*M*	11:9	11:7
	SD	2:3	3:7
Verbal MA	*M*	9:0	6:6
	SD	3:4	2:1
Similarities	*M*	14.55	12.17
Scaled Score	SD	2.55	2.62
Vocabulary	*M*	13.55	11.72
Scaled Score	SD	4.03	3.21
Comprehension	*M*	13.27	9.94
Scaled Score	SD	3.88	3.10
Pragmatic	*M*	32.11	24.40
Language	SD	2.51	5.82

Note. Scaled scores are relative to mental not chronological age.

No subject below the CA of 8 years 7 months passed the false belief test. The influence of verbal MA followed a similar trend. All but one of the children who passed had a verbal MA of above 5 years 11 months. There was doubt, however, whether the PPVT score reflected the particular discrepant child's true level of functioning. This subject's performance on the WPPSI and Pragmatic Skills Test was slightly above the sample's average (except on Comprehension, when it was 1 SD lower). He tended to be inattentive and appeared quite uninterested in looking at pictures, yet was far more cooperative during tasks involving greater verbal exchanges. This interpretation was confirmed with the child's parents who reported that he had never enjoyed looking at, or talking about, pictures in books.

Significant correlations were found between performance on verbal MA and pragmatic skills ($r = .59$, $p < .001$); Comprehension and Similarities ($r = .55$, $p < .002$); Comprehension and Pragmatic skills ($r = .58$, $p < .001$); Similarities and Pragmatic skills ($r = .37, p < .05$); Similarities and Vocab. ($r = .39, p < .04$) and Vocab. and Comprehension ($r = .4, p < .03$).

A (non-parametric) Hotellings *t* test comparing the 'passers' and the 'failers' of the false belief task on the language variables, CA, and verbal MA, showed that the two groups differed significantly ($F(6,22) = 3.56, p < .013$). Follow-up univariate analyses of variance showed that the 'passers' differed significantly from the 'failers' on verbal MA ($F(1,27) = 5.52; p < .023$); Similarities ($F(1,27) = 5.76; p < .02$); Comprehension

$(F(1,27) = 6.25; p < .012)$; and Pragmatic Skills $(F(1,27) = 17.15; p < .000)$. No significant differences were found between the 'passers' and 'failers' on CA $(F(1,27) = .025;$ n.s.$)$ or the Vocabulary test $(F(1,27) = 1.81:$ n.s.$)$.

A discriminant function analysis was performed to assess the ability of these variables to correctly classify the 'passers' and the 'failers'. The percentage of subjects correctly predicted by the discriminant function is referred to as the classification rate. An overall classification rate of 86.21 per cent was obtained overall, with all of the 'passers' and 77.8 per cent of the 'failers' correctly classified. Four subjects who failed the false belief task were misclassified as 'passers'. These children all obtained high scores on the Test of Pragmatic Skills.

Table 2. The pooled-within-groups correlations between discriminating variables and the canonical discriminant function. The variables are ordered by size of correlation within the function

Variable	Canonical coefficients	Correlation with function
Pragmatic skills	0.737	.809
Comprehension	− 0.286	.499
Similarities	0.521	.469
Verbal MA	0.392	.459
Vocabulary	0.427	.263
CA	0.317	.031

Table 2 shows that pragmatic language competence was by far the best discriminator overall, followed by Comprehension, Similarities, and verbal MA; with Vocabulary and CA least associated with discrimination.

A stepwise discriminant function analysis to determine the best predictors of passing or failing the false belief task analysis did not proceed further than step 2. Two variables, Pragmatic Language skills and Similarities, were found to be the best discriminating variables of average or failure on the false belief task. Not unexpectedly the stepwise analysis discontinued after the Similarities variable was included in the function and did not proceed to Comprehension. This is because the correlation between the two variables was quite high $(r = .55, p < .002)$. This suggests that the variables share common properties making the inclusion of Comprehension in the analysis redundant.

Procedural variables

The ordering of belief and control questions was found not to have any bearing on the number of correct false belief responses from the subjects. However, half the 18 subjects who had failed, passed on a further (third) trial when the word 'first' was introduced in the belief question. (This result was a procedural check only and was not included in the analyses.) The mean CA of this group was 12 years 2 months and the mean verbal MA was 7 years 5 months. This pass rate closely resembled the results of Prior *et al.* (1990) where 11 of 20 (55 per cent) autistic children had correctly answered on the false belief task when the word 'first' was included in the question. As 11 of the subjects from the present study had also been involved in the Prior *et al.* study, other comparisons were possible. Seven of these 11 subjects responded consistently in both studies (five passed, two failed). One subject who had passed in the preceding year and failed this year, later passed when the word 'first' was introduced. The remaining three subjects had failed last year and failed this year, but passed when the word 'first' was given.

Discussion

The results show that on a task in which most normal 4- and 5-year-old children are able to attribute a false belief (e.g. Wimmer & Perner, 1983), only 38 per cent of the autistic children, all of whom were at least $8\frac{1}{2}$ years old, were able to do so. It is worth noting here that only three of the 29 children were not consistent in their responses (failing or passing on *both* trials) hence the theory of mind capacity appears very much an all-or-none affair (cf. Leslie & Frith, 1988). The percentage pass rate of the present study was lower than obtained by Prior *et al.* (1990) (55 per cent) but higher than that of Baron-Cohen *et al.* (1985) (20 per cent) and Leslie & Frith (1988) (28 per cent). The differences in pass rate between the present and previous British studies could be due to the higher functioning sample tested here. The mean verbal MA of the autistic children in Baron-Cohen *et al's.,* (1985) study was the lowest at 5 years 5 months, for Leslie & Frith (1988) it was 7 years 2 months, and in the present study, 7 years 5 months. Thus it would appear that as the verbal MA of the sample is increased, so is the likelihood of a greater pass rate on false belief tasks. As hypothesized, the children who passed the false belief task were found to significantly differ from those who failed, in terms of pragmatic competence, abstract reasoning and level of social understanding. However, the two groups did not differ on level of vocabulary knowledge. Thus it was only on certain linguistic tasks that relationships with therapy of mind ability emerged. The results also suggest that performance on the false belief task at least at this level, may perhaps be most parsimoniously explained in terms of a *cognitive* developmental delay.

The placement of control question before or after the belief question had no effect on the subjects' responses. This is in agreement with the study by Leslie & Frith (1988). However, the results of the procedural check do suggest some effect of using the word 'first' in the belief question as occurred in the study conducted by Prior *et al.* (1990). Whilst we did not use responses to this extra question in our analyses of the relationships between theory of mind ability and cognitive/linguistic capacities, it is of methodological interest to note that half of the subjects in the present study who had failed the false belief task were able to pass when 'first' was introduced in the belief question. The verbal MA (7 years 5 months) of these particular children fell in between the verbal MA of the children who clearly passed the task (9 years) and those who failed (6 years 6 months). This would suggest that as autistic children become older, they develop compensatory strategies which enable them to give appropriate responses without necessarily fully comprehending the situation. However, the results of this procedural variation highlight the fact that even minimal changes in test presentation can markedly affect the responses of autistic children and demonstrate the importance of keeping to a set script of probes and questions.

Language variables

Vocabulary skill was a poor discriminator between the 'passers' and the 'failers' on the false belief task. This may be due to the nature of the test and the nature of the sample of autistic children. The Vocabulary test comprises a series of words for which the child is asked to explain the meaning (for example, 'What is a ———, or 'What does ——— mean?'). The scoring of the test does not allow enough differentiation between a child giving an associative/automatic-type response (e.g. Q. 'What is a donkey?', A. 'eehaw') and a child whose answers demonstrate a more 'true' understanding of the word (e.g. 'a donkey is an animal'). The associative response would score 1 point, the latter answer would score 2 points; the 1 point difference is not a large reflection of the difference in the understanding of the two children. It is possible that the test of the ability to define word meanings could not provide a sufficiently discriminating test for this group, or that responses can be sufficiently 'learned' so that metarepresentational ability may play a minor role.

It is also important to note that the autistic children in the present study were an atypically high functioning group, most of whom were quite verbal and had mastered the use of many words.

The results support the proposition proffered by Baron-Cohen (1988) that those who demonstrate a theory of mind will be more pragmatically competent than those children who do not show such an ability. The four children who were misclassified via the discriminant function analysis as passing the false belief task had all obtained high scores on the Test of Pragmatic Skills. However, their answers were frequently of far more detail than was necessary, often requiring the experimenter to interrupt their rambling monologues. It could be argued that these children, although able to give appropriate responses to questions and probes, still have limited pragmatic language ability (Perner *et al.*, 1989). Their inability to assess the informational needs of the listener and hence the appropriate length of response, shows a lack of sensitivity to the listener. Unfortunately, the scoring of the test did not penalize inappropriate length of response but rather rewarded longer answers. This is a shortcoming of the test which further revisions or future studies would need to rectify. Despite the significant association between performance on this test and the ability to show theory of mind, it is important to note that all but two children were at or below the 10th percentile (with reference to their CA) on this test, i.e. were seriously deficient in pragmatic skills.

The results of the Similarities subtest show that the 'passers' of the false belief task have better abstract skills than the 'failers'. This test requires the subject to recognize the relation between two objects. For example, a two-point answer to the question, 'In what way are anger and joy alike?', is that they are both feelings. The subject must conceptually link the shared aspects of the two expressions and represent them to be related to the one concept, i.e. feelings. Leslie (1987, p. 30) notes in reference to autism that 'such children are decoupling impaired . . . for example, suffer a dysfunction in expression raising'. Failure to move from a concrete to an abstract level of thinking may be analogous to a failure in 'expression raising'. Hence by this argument a relationship between capacity for understanding false belief and abstract thinking could be expected. The children who did not demonstrate a theory of mind, while not performing as well on the Similarities test, were still able to correctly answer some questions. This, however, is a consequence of the task. Sattler (1988) argues that the former may be a conventional response, in contrast to the latter which is more likely to 'reflect a more abstract level of conceptualizing ability' (p. 149).

The 'passers' of the false belief task were more able to understand interpersonal relations, social norms and rules than the 'failers', via the comprehension subtest. Social 'awareness' is typically lacking in autistic individuals, who usually perform worse on Comprehension than on any other scale in the Wechsler tests (Ohta, 1987). Possession of a theory of mind, and a more developed understanding of social mores appear to go together in these children, a finding which may support the proposition that a lack of a theory of mind underlies the social dysfunction in autistic people. If a person is unable to conceptualize other people's mental states, he/she would not be expected to have wider understanding of the social concepts which form the basis of society.

As was the case with the other Wechsler subtests, the children who did not pass the false belief task were still capable of responding to the Comprehension test questions to some extent. This could be due to the nature of the questions in this test. For example, a response to the questions, 'What should you do when you cut your finger?', or, 'Why do you have to wash your face and hands?' may be answered from special training or simply over-learned experience of these behaviours and may not necessarily reflect social awareness. However, questions referring to reciprocal social codes (Why should you keep a promise?) or personal privacy (Why is it good to have elections by a secret ballot?) would certainly be out of reach of these children because they entail understanding of the more complex implications of the social milieu.

Evidence for a developmental cognitive deficit

Perhaps the most significant aspect of this study is that certain autistic children were able to demonstrate a theory of mind via the false belief task. This would suggest that if a deficit exists, it is certainly not chronic or inevitable. The present study is the first to show a significant difference in verbal MA between the 'passers' and 'failers' of a theory of mind task. Although many studies have shown this trend in their data, none to date have been significant. This could be due to the relatively small numbers of children passing in previous studies. In any case, it appears that once a certain level of verbal competence is reached, an autistic child is likely to be able to demonstrate a theory of mind at least at the 'first order' level tested here.

The likelihood of verbal MA being an important factor for theory of mind ability is supported by the fact that in the present study and the experiments conducted by Baron-Cohen *et al.* (1985) and Leslie & Frith (1988), the percentage of children passing the false belief task becomes larger with increasing verbal MA. Baron-Cohen *et al.* (1985) do not provide the mean verbal MA of their group of 'passers', however they do report the range to be from 2 years 9 months to 7 years. Thus, it is presumed that the mean is lower than 7 years. The mean verbal MA of the 'passers' in the Leslie & Frith (1988) study was 7 years 9 months. Finally, the 'passers' in the present study had the highest comparative verbal MA of 9 years. However, it is clear that verbal MA is not the only factor regulating demonstration of theory of mind in autistic children. In each study there have been children of relatively high verbal MA who are unable to pass the task. Future studies may wish to address this anomaly and attempt to find other factors which are preventing certain children from demonstrating a theory of mind. No significant difference was observed between 'passers' and 'failers' on CA. However, since most autistic children experience some level of intellectual handicap, CA often has little relevance to their true level of cognitive functioning. Nevertheless, it is important to note that no child below the age of 8 years 7 months was able to pass the false belief task. This is similar to other studies where there was a tendency for the 'passers' to be the older children of the sample (Baron-Cohen, 1989*a,b*; Leslie & Frith, 1988).

Each study which has investigated theory of mind abilities in autistic children has found that a small number of children have passed the tasks. If we accept that the tasks are testing what they are purporting to, these children must be accounted for in Leslie's (1987) meta-representational deficit theory. One possibility is the inclusion of a recognition of levels of severity of the disorder into the theory (see e.g. Frith, 1989). On the basis of informal evaluation, the children in this study who were able to pass the false belief task generally displayed milder autistic disturbances (although the youngest of the five 'mild' cases noted earlier did not pass). Whether these children were less handicapped as a result of a more developed theory of mind, i.e. this capacity contributed to their considerable clinical improvement, or were more able to develop a theory of mind because of the less severe 'dose' of the autistic disorder is not clear since all we have here are correlational data. However, as autism is at present a behaviourally defined syndrome and theory of mind ability appears to mainfest in certain behaviours (at least in pragmatic language skills), the former explanation seems more plausible. Future studies could investigate other observed behavioural deficits in autistic children and how they relate to theory of mind/meta-representational ability. The evidence on other measures of social competence such as interpersonal friendships and social skills and experience in the natural setting is so far equivocal (Dawson & Fernald, 1987; Prior *et al.,* 1990).

A problem which exists at present with Leslie's metarepresentational model is that it is an all-or-none affair. That is, either the proposed 'decoupler' mechanism is functional and higher-order representations are available or, it is inoperative, leaving the individual capable of only base-level representations. It is suggested that this model needs to account for 'degrees' of metarepresentational ability: from basic, first demonstrations of such an ability, e.g. joint attention behaviour, pretend play, through to quite sophisticated levels of representation required for such abilities as sarcasm, lying, or third- and fourth-order beliefs. Thus, the model must account for a *developmental* sequence of metarepresentational ability for it to be of heuristic value (Mundy & Sigman, 1989). In a more recent discussion, Leslie & Frith (1990) have elaborated the theory in a way which reduces the necessity for the 'expression-raiser' and which takes into account the possibility of differentiating between representational deficits, conceptual deficits, or processing deficits, in the pattern of cognitive disabilities in autistic children. They note the need for more data on 'general inferential abilities and conceptual-knowledge-building capacities of autistic children' (p. 129). Our findings may be seen as contributing in a small way to this endeavour although it says little about the specifics of the putative metarepresentational deficit.

Another interesting proposition is whether the children who pass theory of mind tasks are a clinically separate population from those who fail. It is well established that the severity of the autistic syndrome can be represented on a continuum (Wing, 1989). However, a disorder such as Asperger's syndrome (Wing, 1981; Tantam, 1988; Gillberg, 1989), which is similar to autism in certain respects, may have some clinical distinctiveness. Is it possible that the autistic children who display a theory of mind also deserve such a dissociation from those not demonstrating theory of mind ability? Certain advantages can be envisaged. For example, early recognition of metarepresentational abilities, such as pretend play, in children diagnosed autistic could serve as an indicator for the instigation of concentrated intervention strategies aimed at increasing development of social-communicative skills.

In summary, this study suggests that as is the case with normal young children (Baron-Cohen, 1989*b*) the development of theory of mind abilities in autistic children is related to developmental factors especially facility with language. It is not an inevitable consequence of being autistic. It has also confirmed the proposition posited by Baron-Cohen (1988) that autistic individuals capable of demonstrating a theory of mind will be more pragmatically able than those lacking a theory of mind. Furthermore, such children are shown to have a better understanding of abstract concepts and social mores. These abilities are presumed to require metarepresentational ability.

Acknowledgements

The authors thank Dr Susan Leekam and Dr Kristina Macrae, La Trobe University, for constructive comments on this research.

References

American Psychiatric Association (1980). *Diagnostic and Statistical Manual of Mental Disorders—DSM 111.*

Ball, J. (1978). A pragmatic analysis of autistic children's language with respect to aphasic and normal language development. Unpublished Honours Thesis, Melbourne University.

Baltaxe, C. A. M. (1977). Pragmatic deficits in the language of autistic adolescents. *Journal of Pediatric Psychology*, **2**, 176–180.

Baltaxe, C. A. M. & Simmons, J. Q. (1977). Bedtime soliloquies and linguistic competence in autism. *Journal of Speech and Hearing Disorders*, **42**, 376–393.

Baron-Cohen, S. (1988). Social and pragmatic deficits in autism: Cognitive or affective. *Journal of Autism and Developmental Disorders*, **18**(3), 379–402.

Baron-Cohen, S. (1989*a*). The autistic child's theory of mind: A case of specific developmental delay. *Journal of Child Psychology and Psychiatry*, **30**(2), 285–297.

Baron-Cohen, S. (1989*b*). Critical notice: Thinking about thinking: How does it develop?. *Journal of Child Psychology and Psychiatry*, **30**(6), 931–933.

Baron-Cohen, S., Leslie, A. M. & Frith, U. (1985). Does the autistic child have a 'theory of mind'? *Cognition*, **21**, 37–46.

Bernard-Opitz, V. (1982). Pragmatic analysis of the communicative behaviour of an autistic child. *Journal of Speech and Hearing Disorders*, **47**, 99–109.

Cromer, R. F. (1981). Developmental language disorders: Cognitive processes, semantics, pragmatics, phonology, and syntax. *Journal of Autism and Developmental Disorders*, **11**, 57–74.

Cunningham, M. A. (1968). A comparison of the language of psychotic and non-psychotic children who are mentally retarded. *Journal of Psychology and Psychiatry*, **9**, 229–244.

Dawson G. & Fernald D. (1987). Perspective-taking ability and its relationship to the social behavior of autistic children. *Journal of Autism and Developmental Disorders*, **17**, 487–498.

Dunn, L. M. & Dunn, L. M. (1981). *Manual for the Peabody Picture Vocabulary Test—Revised*. Circle Pines, MN: American Guidance Service.

Frith U. (1989). *Autism: Explaining The Enigma*. Oxford: Blackwell.

Gillberg, C. (1989). Asperger Syndrome in 23 Swedish children. *Developmental Medicine and Child Neurology*, **31**, 520–531.

Grice, H. P. (1975). Logic and conversation. In P. Cole & J. Morgan (Eds), *Syntax and Semantics*, vol. 3: *Speech Acts*. New York: Academic Press.

Hurtig, R., Ensrud, S. & Tomblin, J. B. (1982). The communicative function of question production in autistic children. *Journal of Autism and Developmental Disorders*, **12**(1), 57–69.

Leslie, A. M. (1987). Pretense and representation: The origins of 'theory of mind'. *Psychological Review*, **94**(4), 412–426.

Leslie, A. M. & Frith, U. (1988). Autistic children's understanding of seeing, knowing and believing. *British Journal of Developmental Psychology*, **6**, 315–324.

Leslie, A. & Frith, U. (1990). Prospects for a cognitive neuropsychology of autism: Hobson's choice. *Psychological Review*, **97**(1), 122–131.

Lincoln, A. J., Courchesne, E., Kilman, B. A., Elmasian, R. & Alen, M. (1988). A study of intellectual abilities in high-functioning people with autism. *Journal of Autism and Developmental Disorders*, **18**(4), 505–523.

Mundy, P. & Sigman, M. (1989). The theoretical implications of joint-attention deficits in autism. *Development and Psychopathology*, **1**, 173–183.

Ohta, M. (1987). Cognitive disorders of infantile autism: A study employing the WISC, spatial relationship conceptualization, and gesture imitations. *Journal of Autism and Developmental Disorders*, **17**(1), 45–62.

Perner, J., Frith, U., Leslie, A. & Leekam, S. (1989). Exploration of the autistic child's theory of mind: Knowledge, belief and communication. *Child Development*, **60**, 689–700.

Prior, M. R. (1984). Developing concepts of childhood autism: The influence of experimental cognitive research. *Journal of Consulting and Clinical Psychology*, **52**(1), 4–16.

Prior, M. R., Dahlstrom, B. & Squires, T. L. (1990). Autistic children's knowledge of thinking and feeling states in other people. *Journal of Child Psychology and Psychiatry*, **31**, 587–602.

Rutter, M. (1983). Cognitive deficits in the pathogenesis of autism. *Journal of Child Psychology and Psychiatry*, **24**(4), 513–531.

Sattler, J. M. (1988). *Assessment of Children*, 3rd ed. California: Allyn & Bacon.

Shulman, B. B. (1986). *Test of Pragmatic Skills—revised*. Tucson, AZ: Communication Skill Builders.

Tantam, D. (1989). Asperger's syndrome. Annotation. *Journal of Child Psychology and Psychiatry*, **29**, 245–255.

Wechsler, D. (1987. *Manual for the Wechsler Preschool and Primary Scales of Intelligence*. New York: Psychological Corporation.

Wechsler, D. (1974). *Manual for the Wechsler Intelligence Scale for Children—Revised*. New York: Psychological Corporation.

Westby, C. E. (1980). Understanding the cognitive abilities of autistic children. (Presentation for American Speech Hearing Language Association Annual Convention). Detroit, Michigan.

Wimmer, H. & Perner, J. (1983). Beliefs about beliefs: Representation and constraining function of wrong beliefs in young children's understanding of deception. *Cognition*, **13**, 103–128.

Wing, L. (1981). Asperger's syndrome: A clinical account. *Psychological Medicine*, **11**, 115–129.

Wing, L. (1989). The continuum of autistic characteristics. In E. Schopler & G. Mesibov (Eds), *Diagnosis and Assessment*. New York: Plenum Press.

Received 5 February 1990; revised version received 4 January 1991

Author Index

Subject Index

Subject Index